Earth, Space and Fractals

Real and Imagined Worlds

Wayne Labs

PARAMETER PUBLISHING

Doylestown, PA

ISBN: 978-1-944280-04-8

Library of Congress Control Number: 2024911489

This book is also available in standard EPUB reflowable text format as ISBN 978-1-944280-05-5 and as a Special Kindle Edition (Fixed Layout) with additional pictures not contained in the print edition as ISBN 978-1-944280-06-2

Printed in the United States of America

PARAMETER PUBLISHING

Doylestown, PA
July, 2024

About the Cover

The front cover is a combination of fractal images ("planets" and radiating sky pattern) created in Mandelbulb 3D, assembled in an image editor and combined with the starfield being added in Luminar Neo™. The text was added in with layer effects. Mandelbulb 3D is an open-source program that can be downloaded freely. Luminar Neo™ is a commercial program that allows fine adjustments of photos and can be used as a plugin in image editors such as Adobe® Photoshop® and Affinity® Photo©. The cover was designed and constructed by the author, Wayne Labs.

Edited by Nancy Labs

All folio/chapter headings: Starfield galaxy fractal created in JWildfire.

Acknowledgments

Thanks to my wife, Nancy, novelist and artist, and my son Jon, web designer and programmer, for salient comments on images and layout. They made sure that out of nearly 10,000 images, the "best" were selected for this book.

Also thanks to Steve S. and Mike Gerow for their helpful comments on the content of this book.

Earth, Space and Fractals

Real and Imagined Worlds

TABLE OF CONTENTS

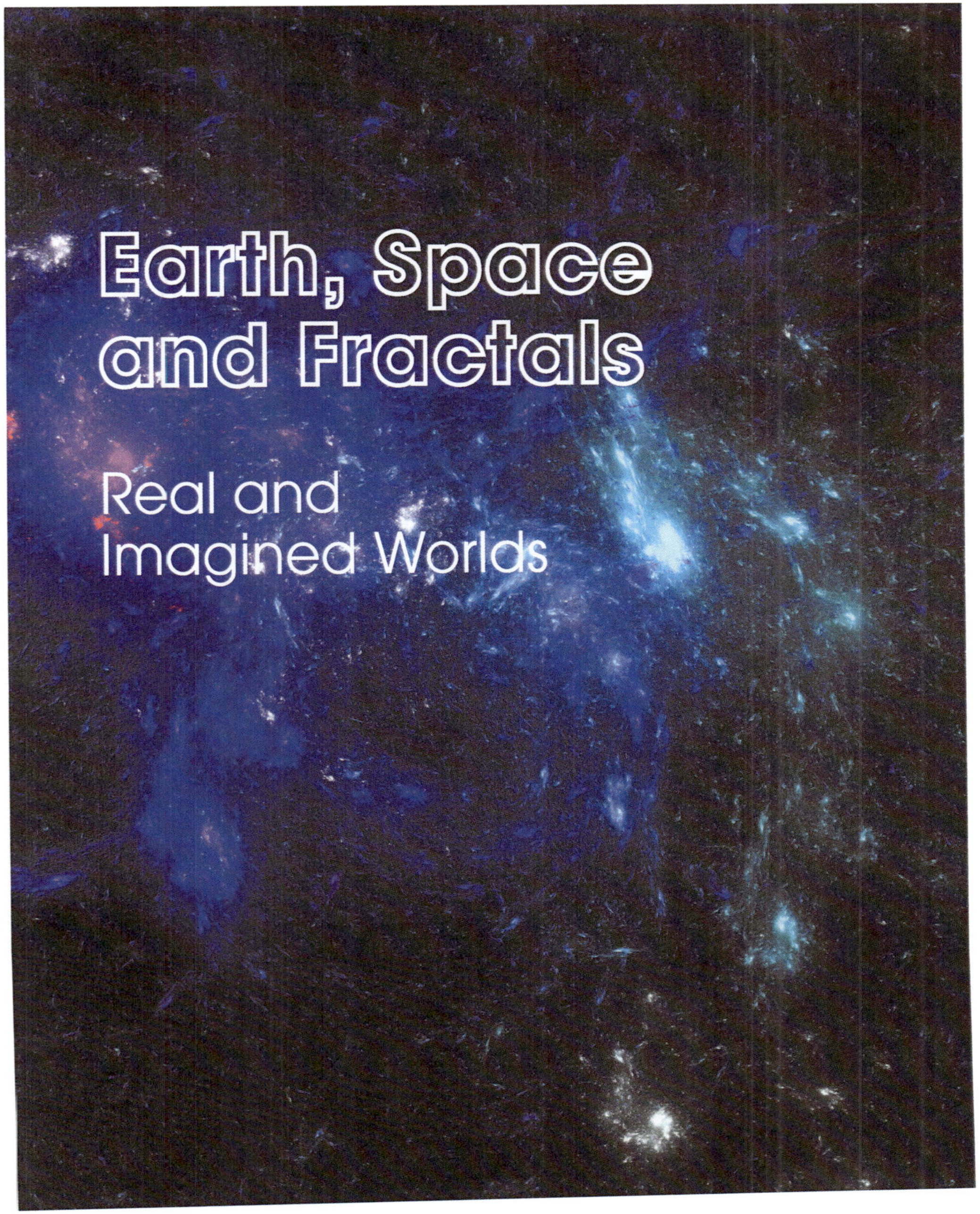

Folios:

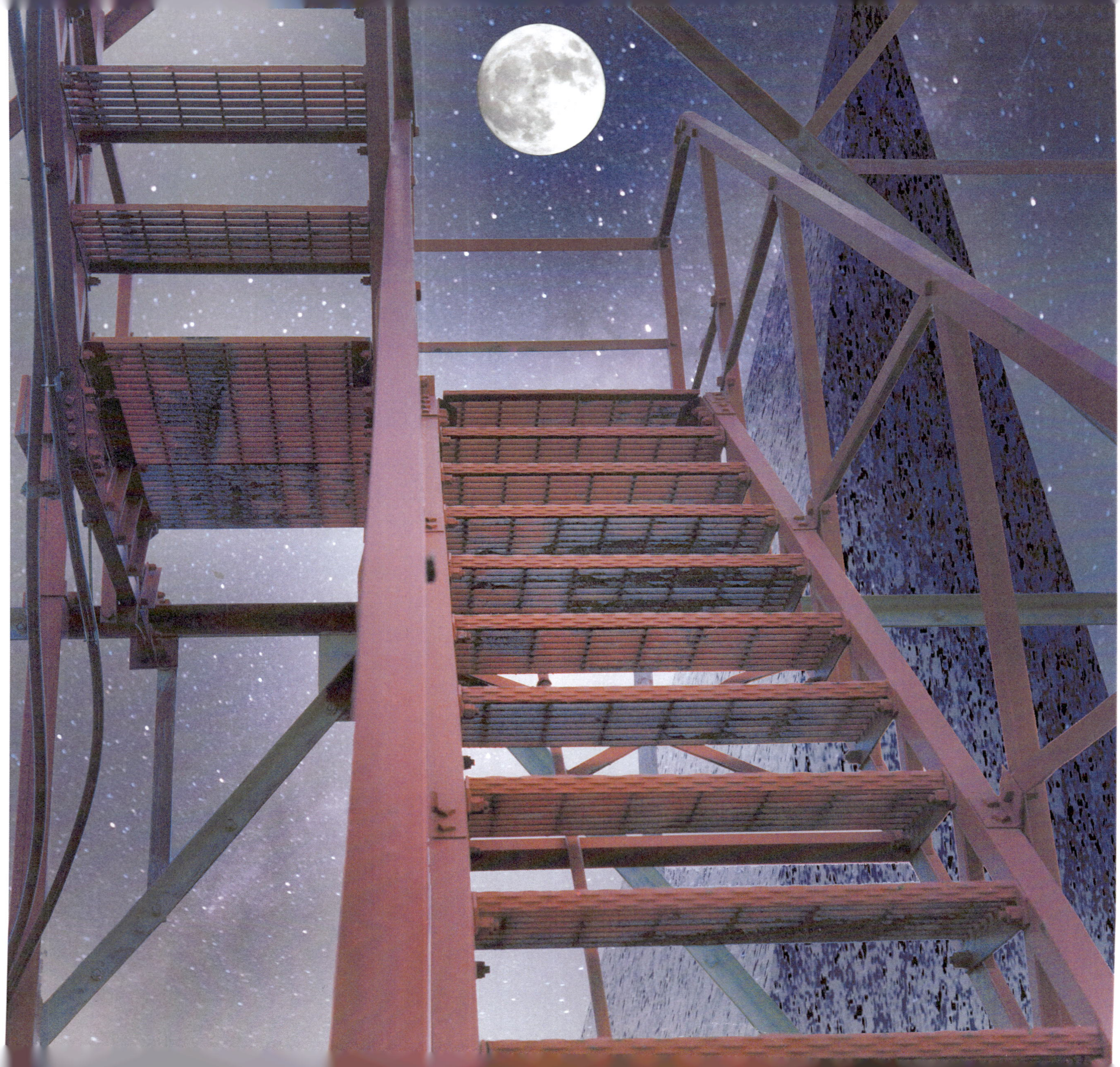

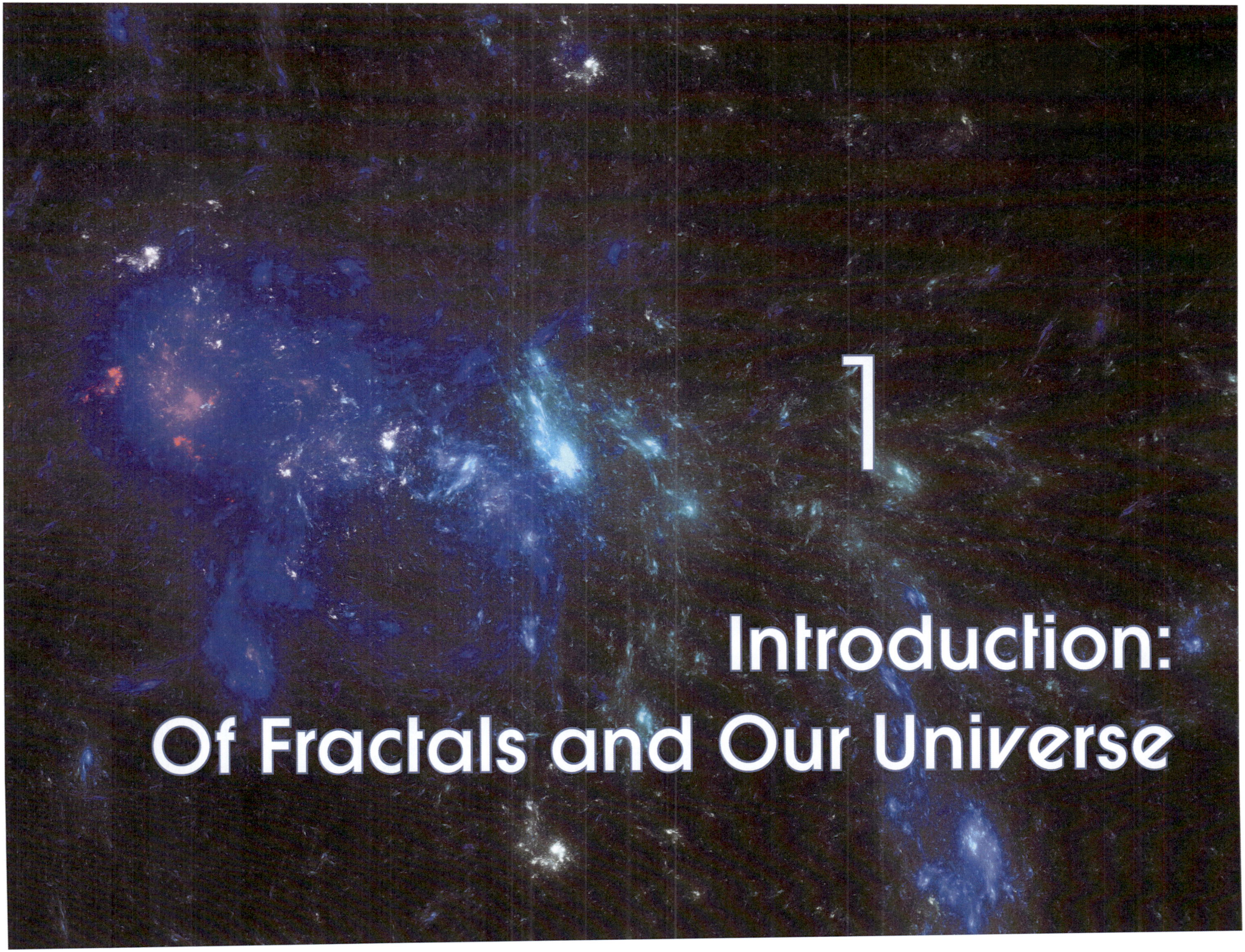

1

Introduction: Of Fractals and Our Universe

Fractals are ubiquitous in our world, but few people are able to define them. In layman's terms, a fractal is a pattern that when seen as an image, produces a picture, which when zoomed into reveals the original picture *(see inset immediately below)*. In other words, cut a large fractal into incremental parts, and those parts still resemble the fractal.

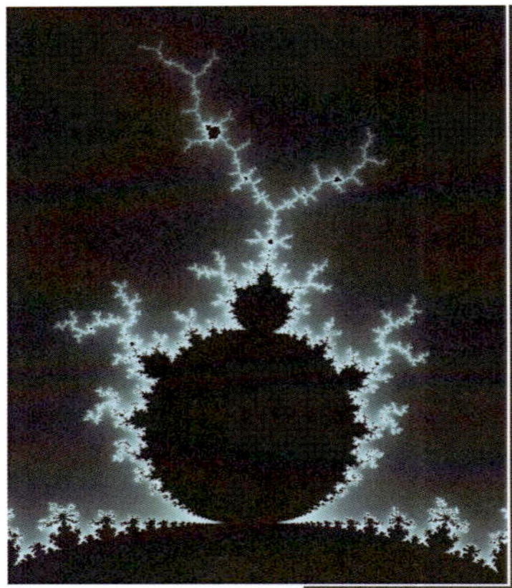

If you've seen films with fantastic topographies and landscapes, you've no doubt seen fractal modeling in action. Fractals have played a key role in creating scenery and special effects in a diverse range of films. Some examples include *Star Trek II: The Wrath of Khan, Star Wars: Return of the Jedi* (and later films), *Tron, Guardians of the Galaxy, The Abyss, Terminator 2 (remastered), Mary Poppins Returns, Apollo 13, Dante's Peak* and *Titanic.*

Creating fractal landscapes in film wasn't always an easy task. Since movies traditionally ran at 24 frames/second, rendering a single frame could take upwards of an hour on a single computer. To solve the problem studios built banks of computers to work together to create fractal motion sequences, vastly decreasing production time. Today, thanks to modern computing systems, rendering complex fractal images for use in films can be done at near or in real time.

But fractals are more than computerized special effects. Whether you are looking at plants, animals, insects, coastlines, ocean waves, flames, mountains, clouds—fractals and their inherent mathematics define the forms surrounding you.

Nowadays, you don't need to be a computer geek to create fractal images. Free, "open-source" software allows you to generate fractal images like the ones in this book. (To get you started in this exciting exploration, check out the information in Appendix A.)

Why this book?

In this book, I intend to demonstrate the similarities between fractal images and re-

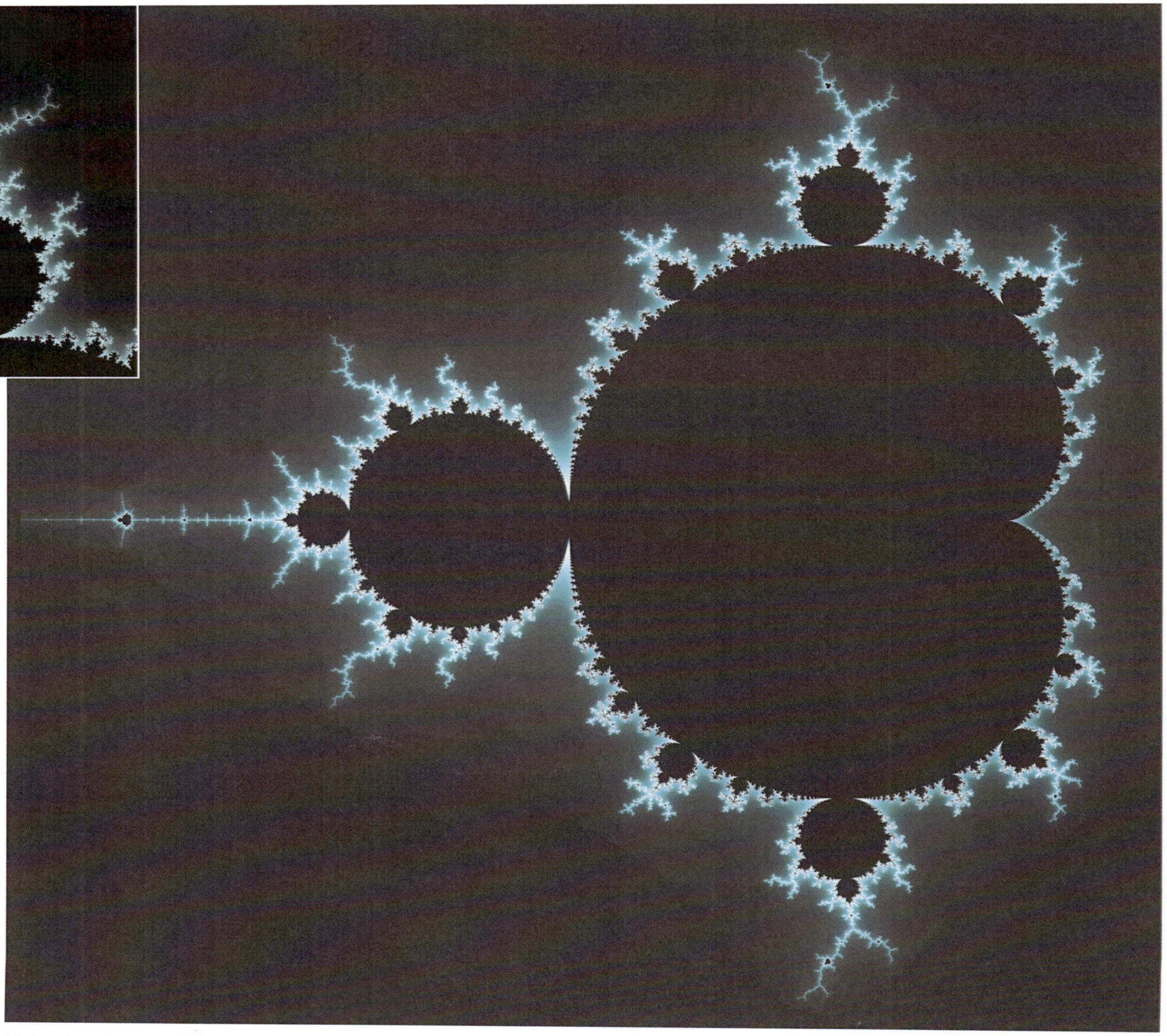

This classic Mandelbrot set, two-dimensional fractal was drawn by the fractal generator in GiMP software.

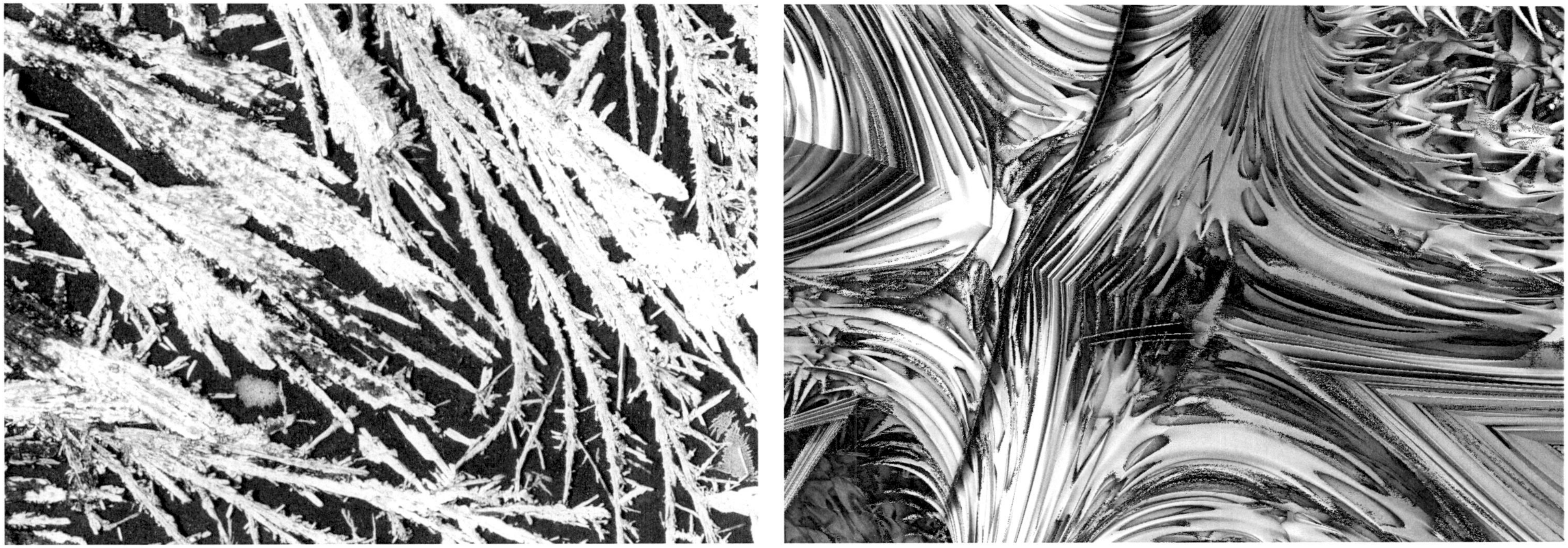

On the left, unknown crystal growth on a piece of sheet metal photographed on a 5x7-inch negative, and on the right, a Mandelbulb 3D fractal resembling crystal growth.

peated patterns that seem to pop up everywhere. As a photographer, I was determined to document these similarities, and to do so, I paired fractal images with analogous forms drawn from nature and manmade structures. But since not every fractal has an obvious analog, I included some that usher us into a dreamlike world, much like the special effects you experience in films. Since small changes in fractal parameters create new images, one quickly realizes that the range of potential images is essentially infinite.

Fractals and fractal math

In technical terms, a fractal is a curve (plot) or geometric figure produced by a mathematical formula where each part of the generated curve has the same statistical character as the whole. Unlike standard Euclidean math that, when graphed, produces lines, parabolas, logarithmic curves, sine waves, etc., fractals produce replicate patterns at progressively smaller scales without end. They can be used to describe partly random or chaotic phenomena such as the formation of our galaxy, fluid turbulence (e.g., weather patterns) and crystal growth—and are used to model structures such as mountain ranges, coastlines and snowflakes.

The math behind fractals was developed by pioneering mathematicians, the most familiar of whom is Benoit Mandelbrot, born in Warsaw, Poland on 20 November 1924. As a child he moved with his family to France and later graduated from universities in Paris and the United States where he began a 35-year career at IBM. He became an IBM Fellow while concurrently teaching at Harvard University.

In the 1970s and 80s, Mandelbrot made use of large-scale computers to graph a relatively simple, two-dimensional plot. The results became known as the Mandelbrot set, first defined and drawn in 1978 by Robert W. Brooks and Peter Matelski. When calculated and graphed, the Mandelbrot set—while described in a simple formula—produces great complexity when magnified. Rather than tediously plotting the results of iterating and re-iterating fractal algorithms—even relatively simple ones—on paper, Mandelbrot applied computer and graphics technologies to create and display the Mandelbrot set (see the images on p. 4). (For a more detailed look at the math behind fractals, see Appendix B at the back of the book.)

As previously stated, while Euclidean math defines simple curves and geometry—squares, circles, cubes and such—it is fractal math that more precisely describes our world and the marvelous designs of both non-living things and living creatures—from mountains and coastlines to plants; fungi, trees, fish, humans and DNA.

Fractal geometry and chaos theory

Fractal math or geometry grew out of chaos theory, the study of apparently random or unpredictable behavior in systems governed by deterministic laws—as in Newtonian systems. Sir Issac Newton posited that if one knew the initial conditions of any system—for example, the entire universe—one could know the past and predict the future of the universe at any point in time. But Newtonian math has a problem: the behavior of planets and stars becomes unpredictable after given a period of time and can no longer be easily defined.

In the 1950s, MIT Professor Edward Lorenz created mathematical models for calculating weather conditions. The models showed that these patterns were predictable for about a month, but after longer periods of time, weather loses all predictability. His research led to the birth of chaos theory.

Lorenz discovered that when using six decimal places to describe initial conditions, weather could be predicted up to about a month. However, when he rounded off initial condition values to three decimal places, predictions no longer tracked earlier systems using six-decimal inputs for initial conditions.

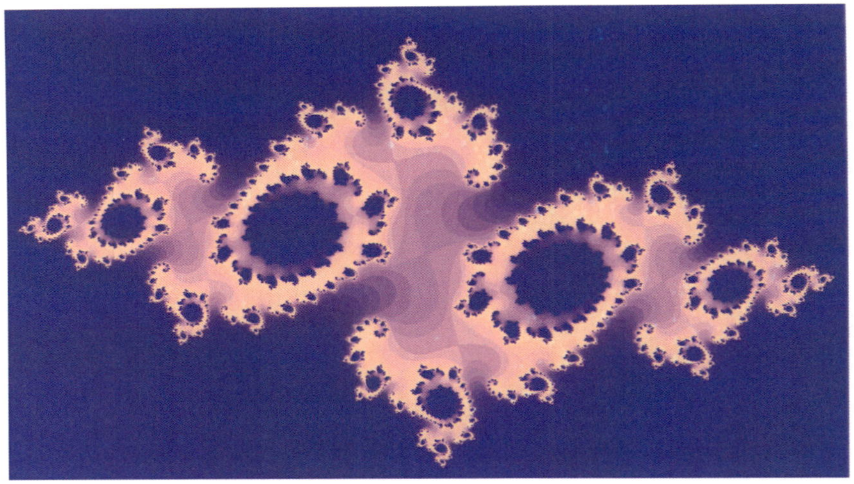

The Julia set is named after the French mathematician Gaston Julia who investigated their properties in 1915 and culminated in his famous paper in 1918: Mémoire sur L'itération des Fonctions Rationnelles. This image was created in the GiMP open-source photo editing software fractal generator.

But, even with the apparent randomness of chaotic phenomena (like the behavior of the universe or weather), there is an underlying order to such phenomena. This underlying order is called fractal geometry. (For further information, see the web article: "Chaos and Fractals," Gregory Leal, Greg School, 5 November 2017; https://www.gregschool.org/gregschool-lessons/2017/5/4/chaos-3gdk9 (accessed January, 2024).

Today, fractal geometry and chaos math are used in engineering to describe the quality and predictability of transmitting and receiving an intelligible or decodable radio signal over a noisy channel affected by atmospheric and manmade interference. The same type of mathematical system is used by engineers to describe and predict computer network data flow, thus revealing bottlenecks, and defining network traffic; by meteorologists to predict the weather; and by doctors to describe aspects of the human body, such as our circulatory, cardiac and nervous systems.

In short, the discoveries of Mandelbrot and fellow fractal/chaos mathematicians have been applied in fields as diverse as statistical physics, geomorphology, anatomy, taxonomy, information technology, cardiac arrhythmias, medicine, engineering, neurology, financial systems, forestry, weather—the list goes on and on.

For those who would like to take a deep dive into chaos math and fractal geometry, *The Great Courses®* offers an approachable,

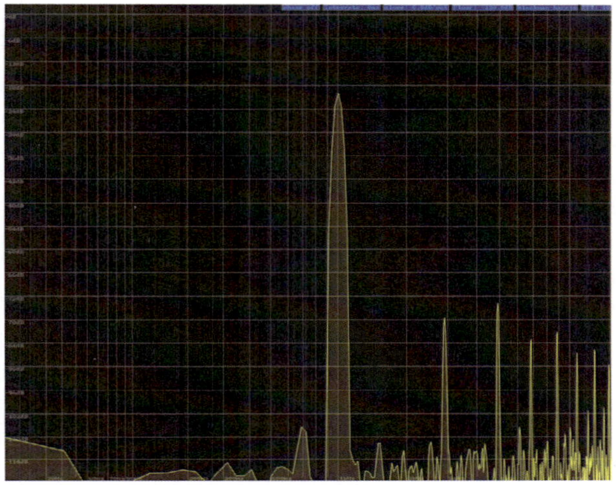

Fractal math can be used to predict the signal-to-noise ratio of a radio or audio channel as shown in this spectrum analysis. The primary signal and harmonics exceed the residual noise at the baseline.

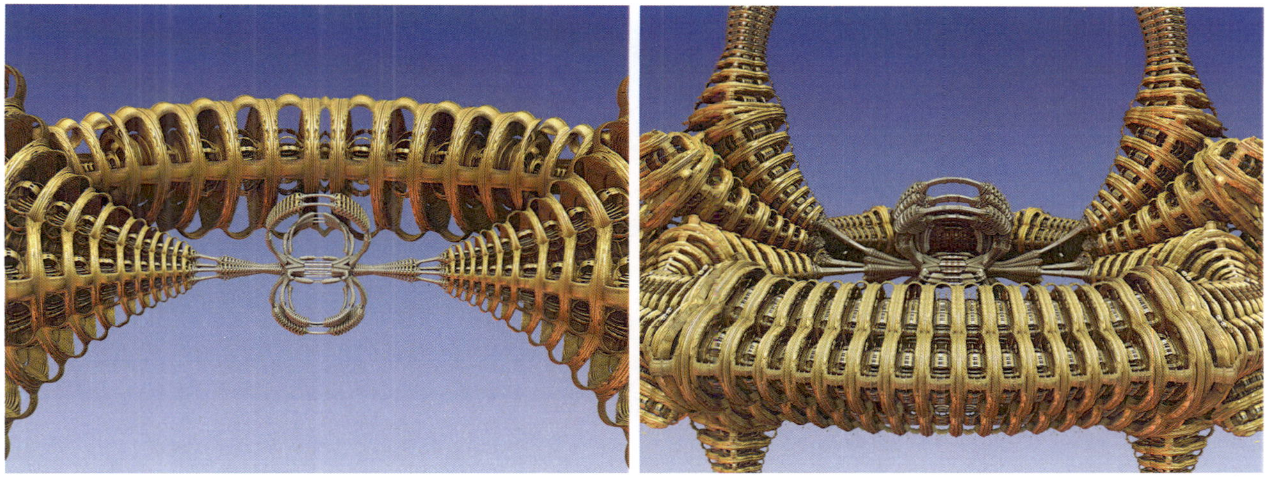

In these two fractal images, only one parameter ("folding") out of a total of 13 in three formulas was changed by a factor of 0.02, and these results were obtained. No other changes were made, for example, iterations, etc.

college-level course entitled "Chaos," presented by Professor Steven Strogatz, PhD, Cornell University. He begins by showing the differences between Euclidean and chaos math and takes you on a journey toward an understanding of chaos and fractal geometry. It can be found at www.thegreatcourses.com.

Fractals and the PC

I was introduced to the world of fractals years ago when I stumbled upon a DOS-based shareware program called FRACTINT. The program ran on pre-Windows computers and produced two-dimensional and rudimentary 3D images. Since then, things have changed dramatically Today's 3D fractal programs are able to produce stunning images, many of which resemble real-world objects or life forms.

The majority of fractal images in this book were created over the last ten years using Mandelbulb 3D fractal software. The program is available at no charge, and is known for creating 3D "bulbs" or objects in space. Some of the background images in this book were partially created in JWildfire, another free, open-source fractal generator, (For more details on the software and its application in creating this book, see Appendix C.)

Most fractals in this book are the result of pure experimentation and patience—and having a general idea what combination of fractals produces certain image types. While it's possible to know generally how a final image will appear after rendering, the end result is often a surprise as even a small parameter or coefficient change can make a relatively large change in the final image (see above pair of comparison images). The software does provide the tools to approximate the end result, but it is not until the "final image" is created at full resolution that it's possible to know the final output.

In terms of matching fractals to photographs and vice-versa, I did not set out to create fractal images to match a particular photograph. In most cases, I pulled a picture from my collection of several decades of photographs, which seemed to be an artistic match for a particular fractal after I had created it. Giving fractals file names that approximate their appearance (e.g., *tree, bark, cathedral, snake,* etc.) makes it a lot easier to locate a file in a batch of nearly 10,000 fractal images when trying to match a photo to a particular fractal.

Note: If you have any questions about this book or would like to acquire any prints of the images, please email the author at books@waynelabs.com.

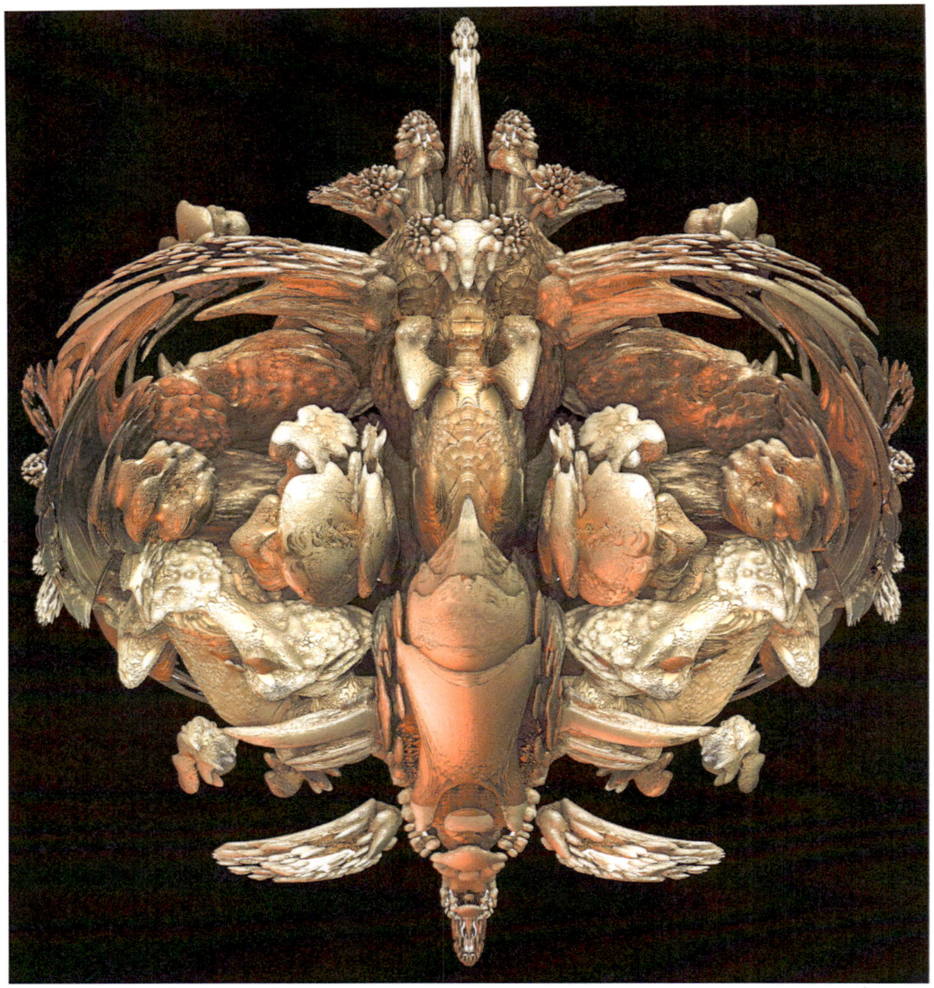

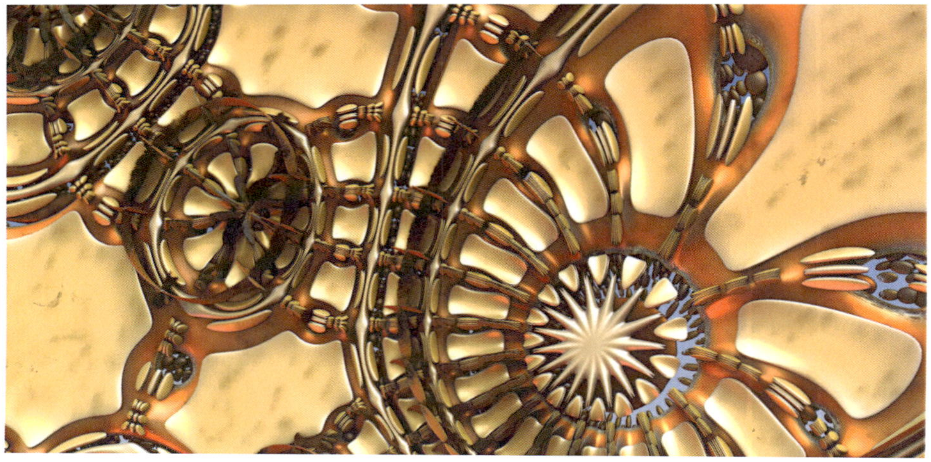

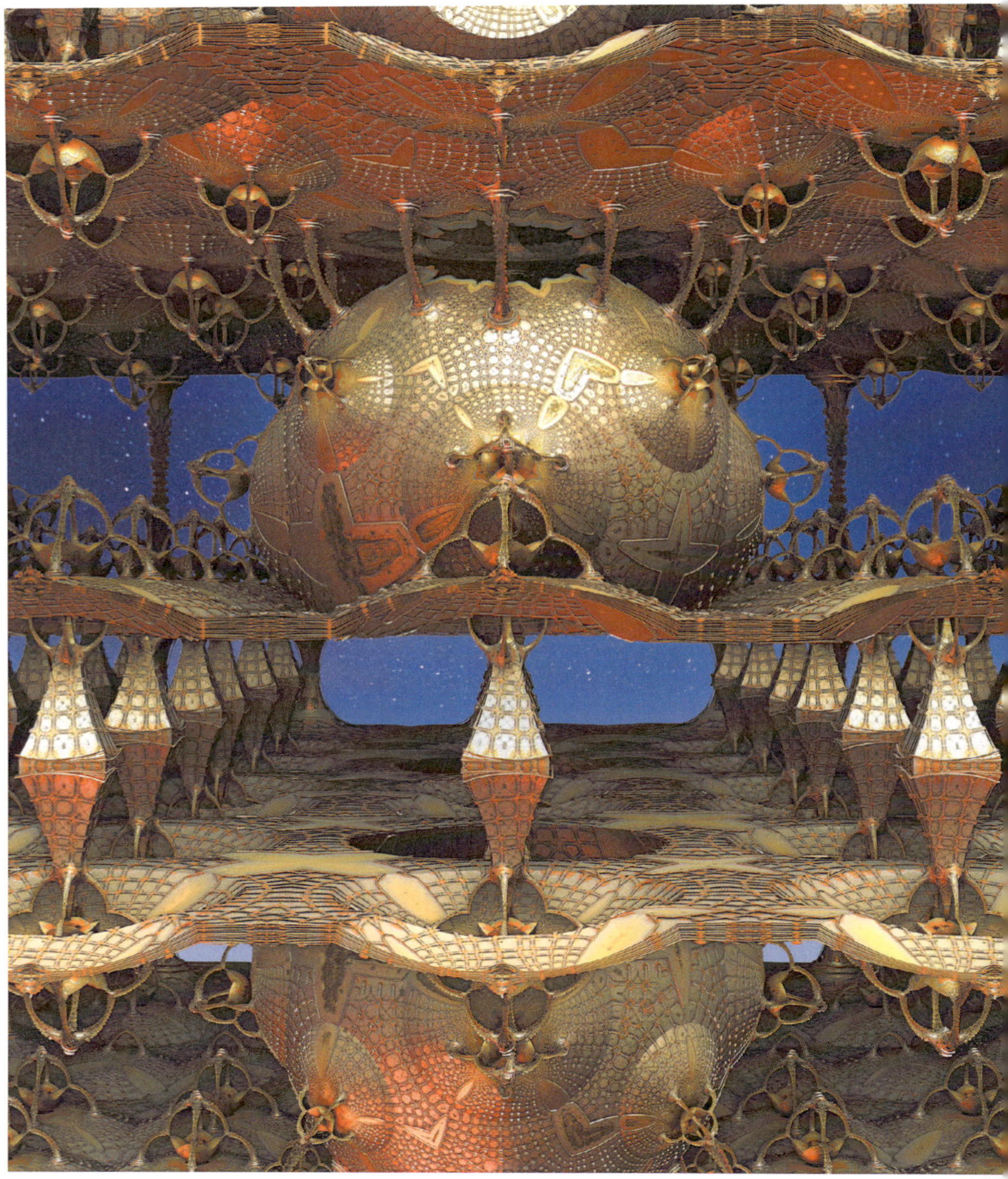

Even when fractals appear "orderly," upon close inspection, something can always seem a little out of kilter, chaotic—never quite perfect. ***This page, upper-left,*** *a "bug" or "metallic ornament;"* ***left,*** *close-up of a "decorative carving."* ***Immediately above,*** *a "structure against a night sky."* ***Opposite page, left,*** *an asymmetrical section of an "arch with columns."* ***To the far right:*** *a fractal somewhat reminiscent of brain neurons and synapses where all connect with many pathways—an analog computer so to speak. All fractals were generated in Mandelbulb 3D.*

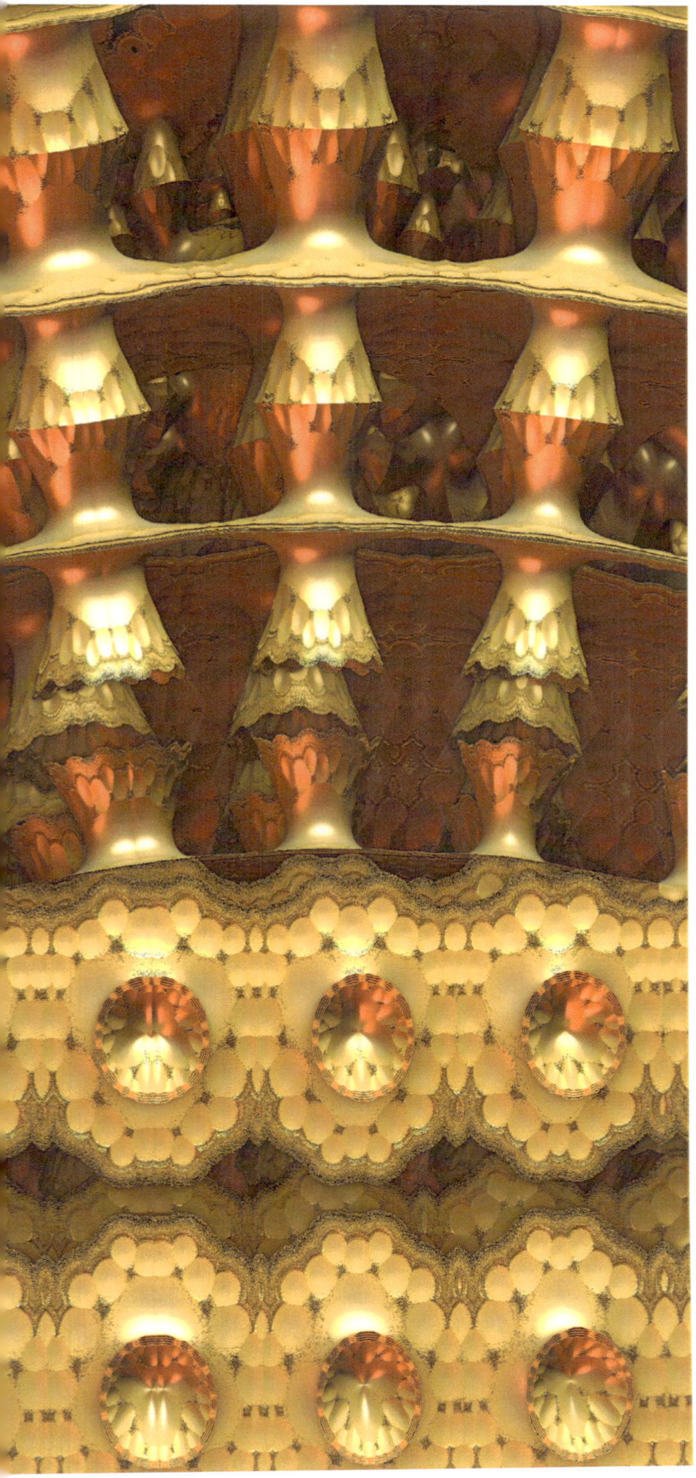

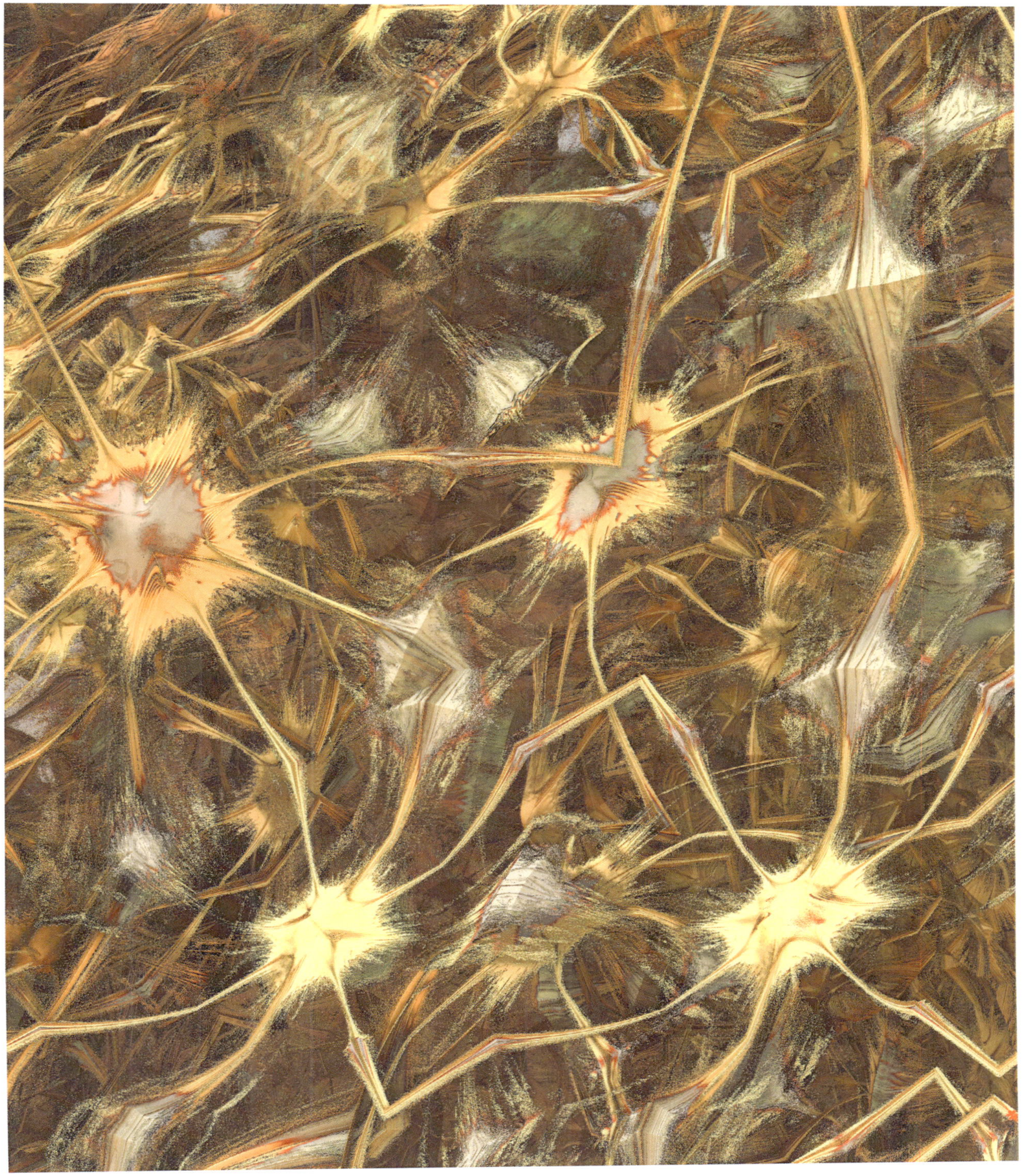

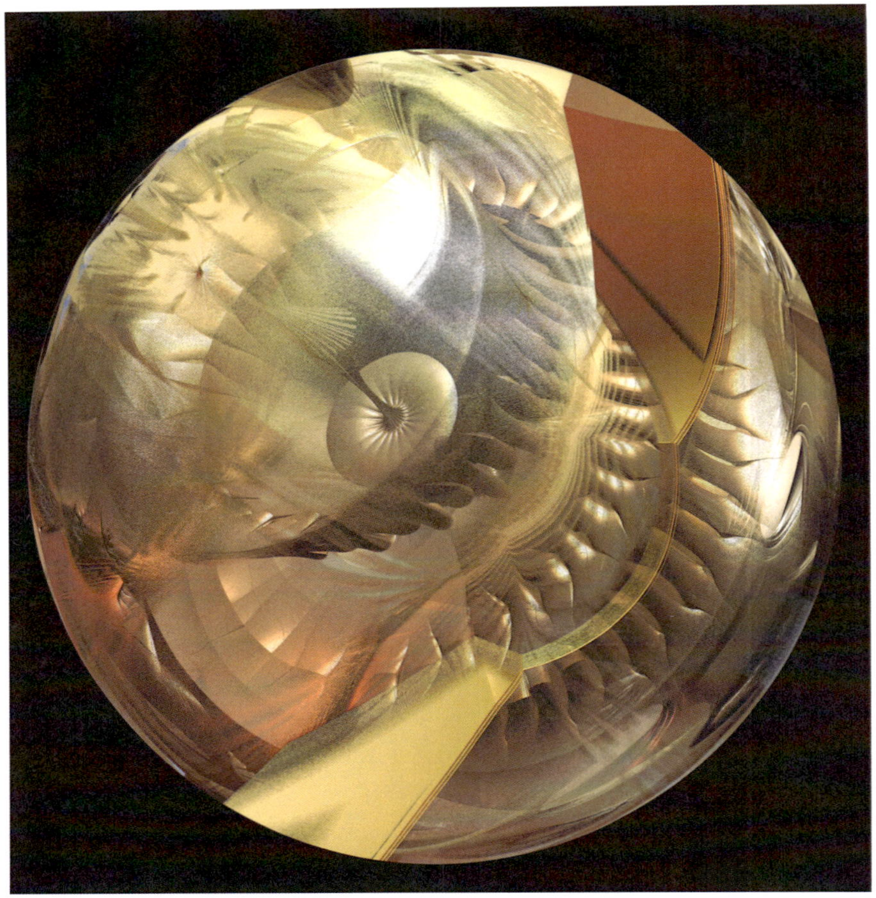

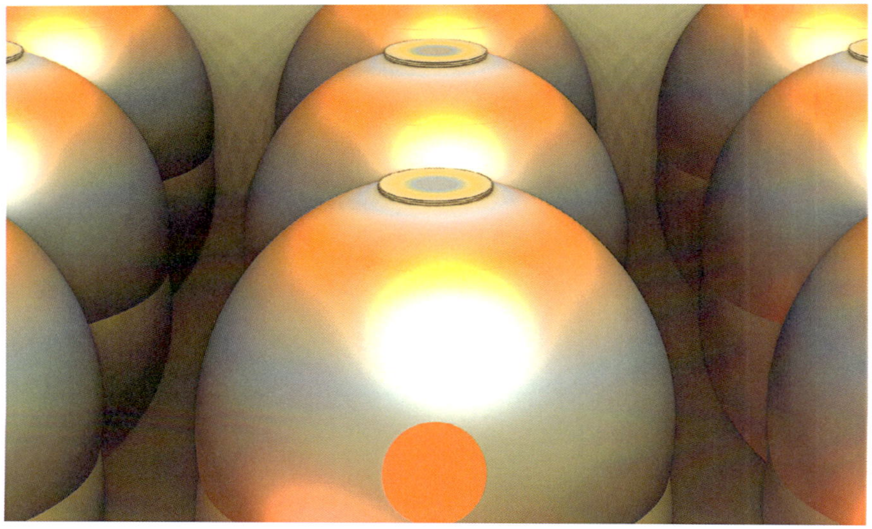

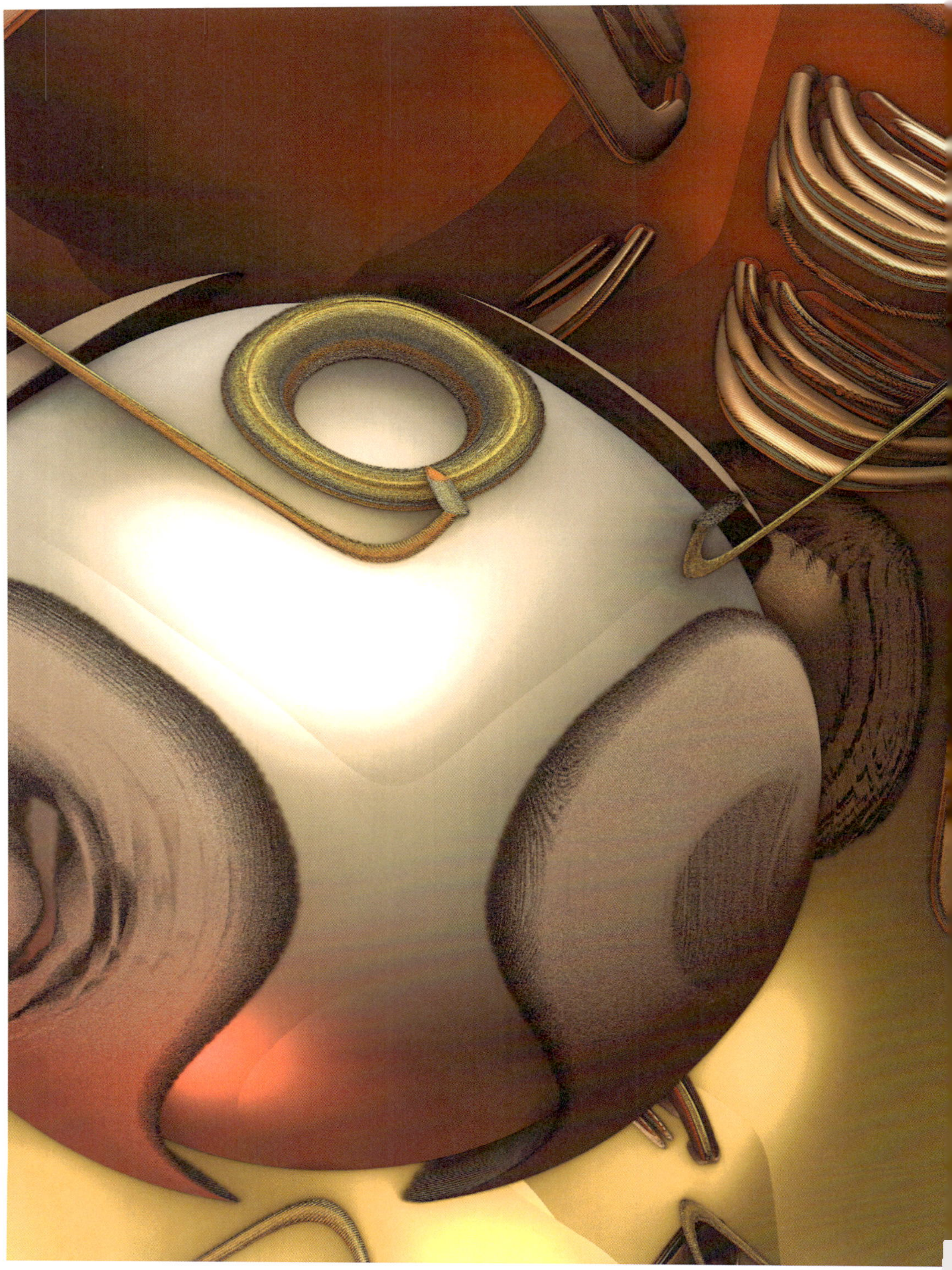

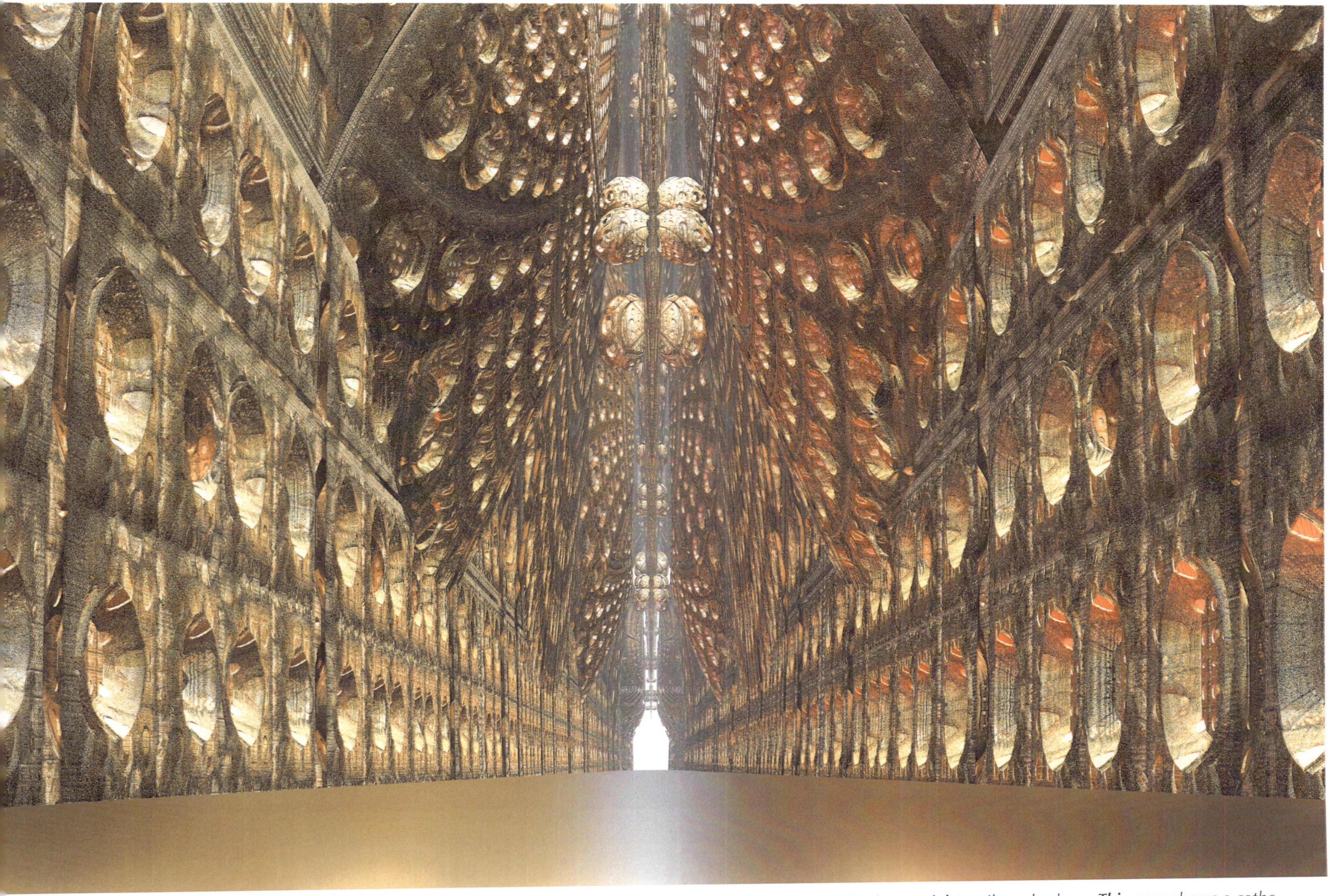

Opposite page, upper-left, *a "microwave-emitting device with focusing sphere;"* **bottom-left,** *a 3×3 matrix of spheres;* **right,** *coils and sphere.* **This page** *shows a cathedral-like structure. The cathedral "floor" was a mirror image of the top part of the fractal, but was smoothed to give the appearance of the floor. All of the fractals on these two pages were generated in Mandelbulb 3D.*

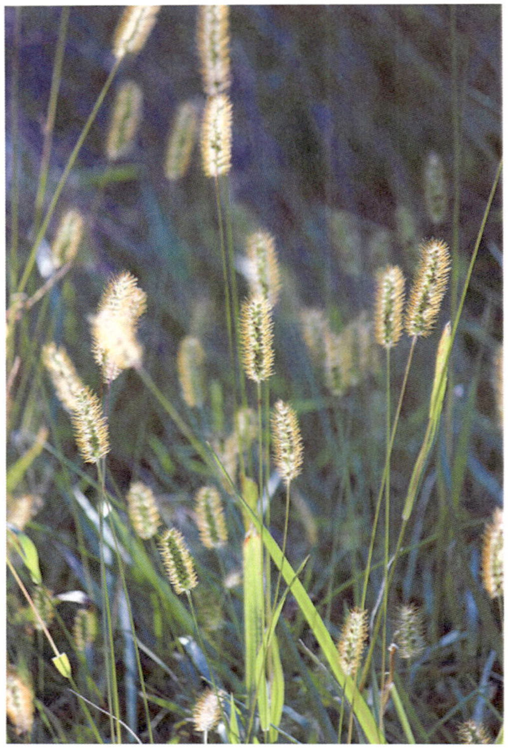

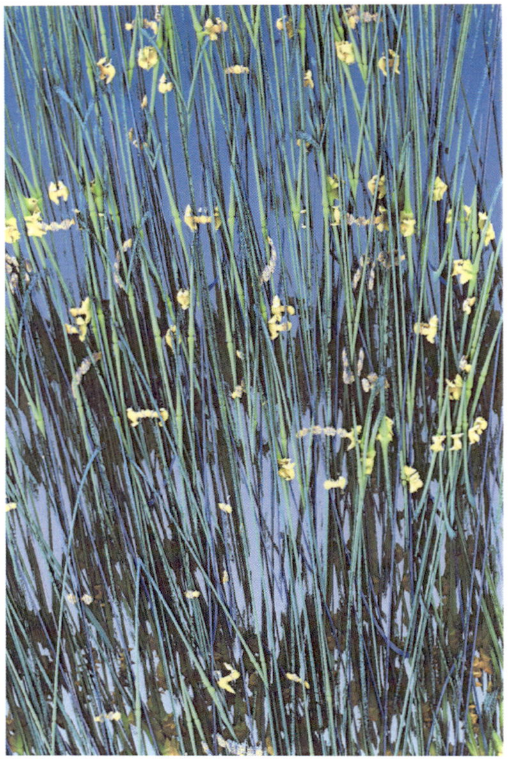

Left, photo of grass in the woods; *right*, fractal image

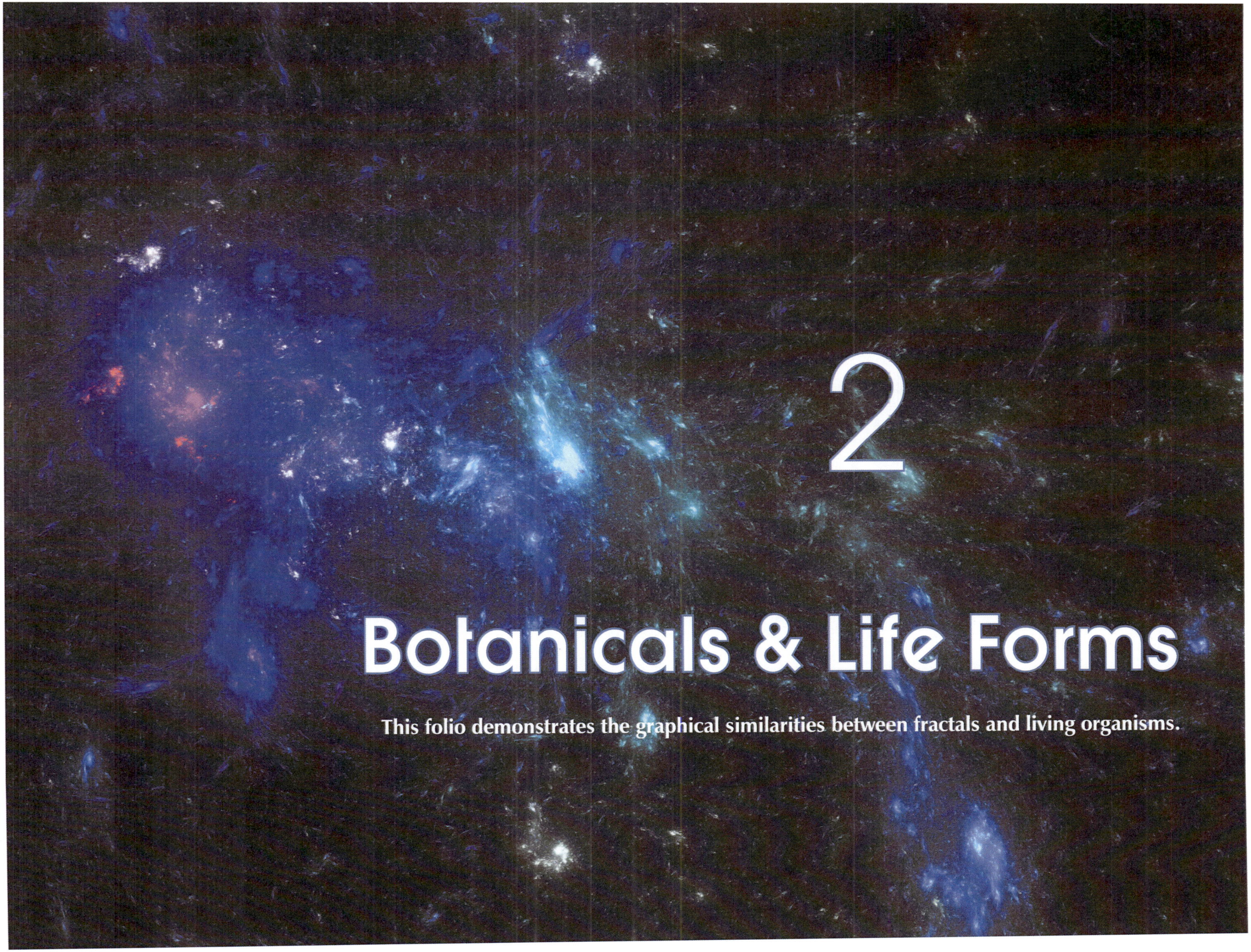

2

Botanicals & Life Forms

This folio demonstrates the graphical similarities between fractals and living organisms.

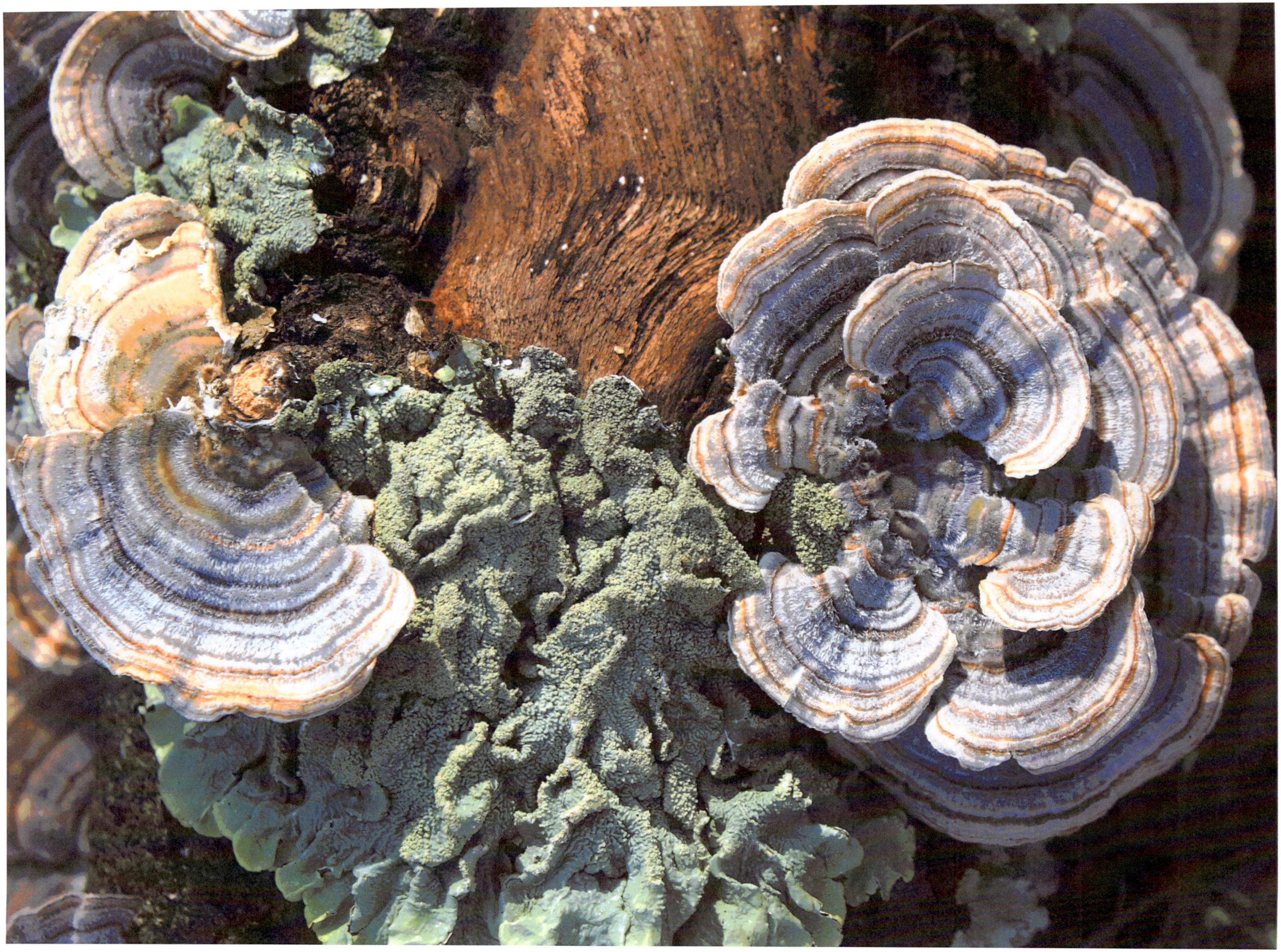

Fungus on a fallen, decaying tree stump (digital photo)

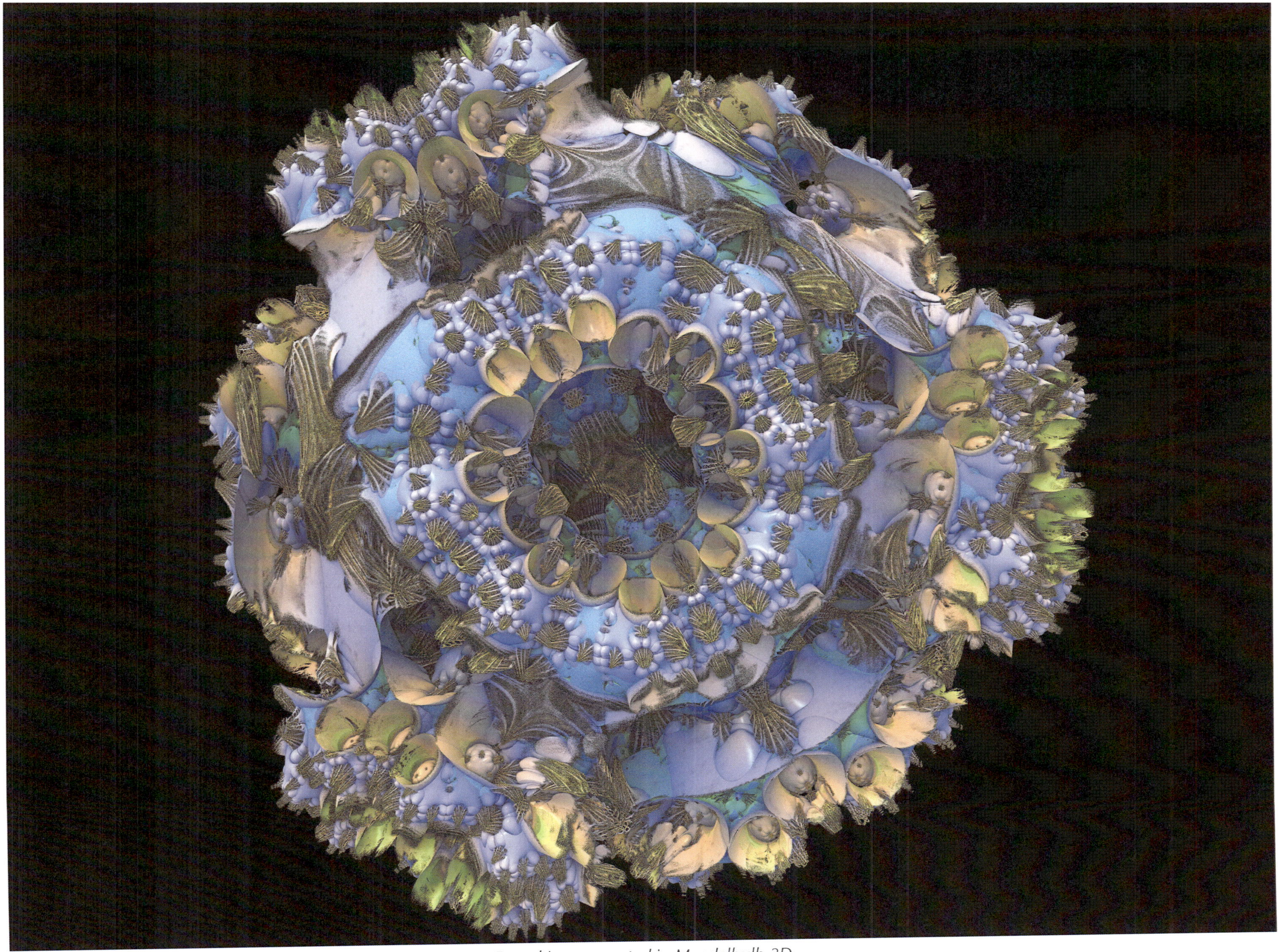

Fractal image created in Mandelbulb 3D

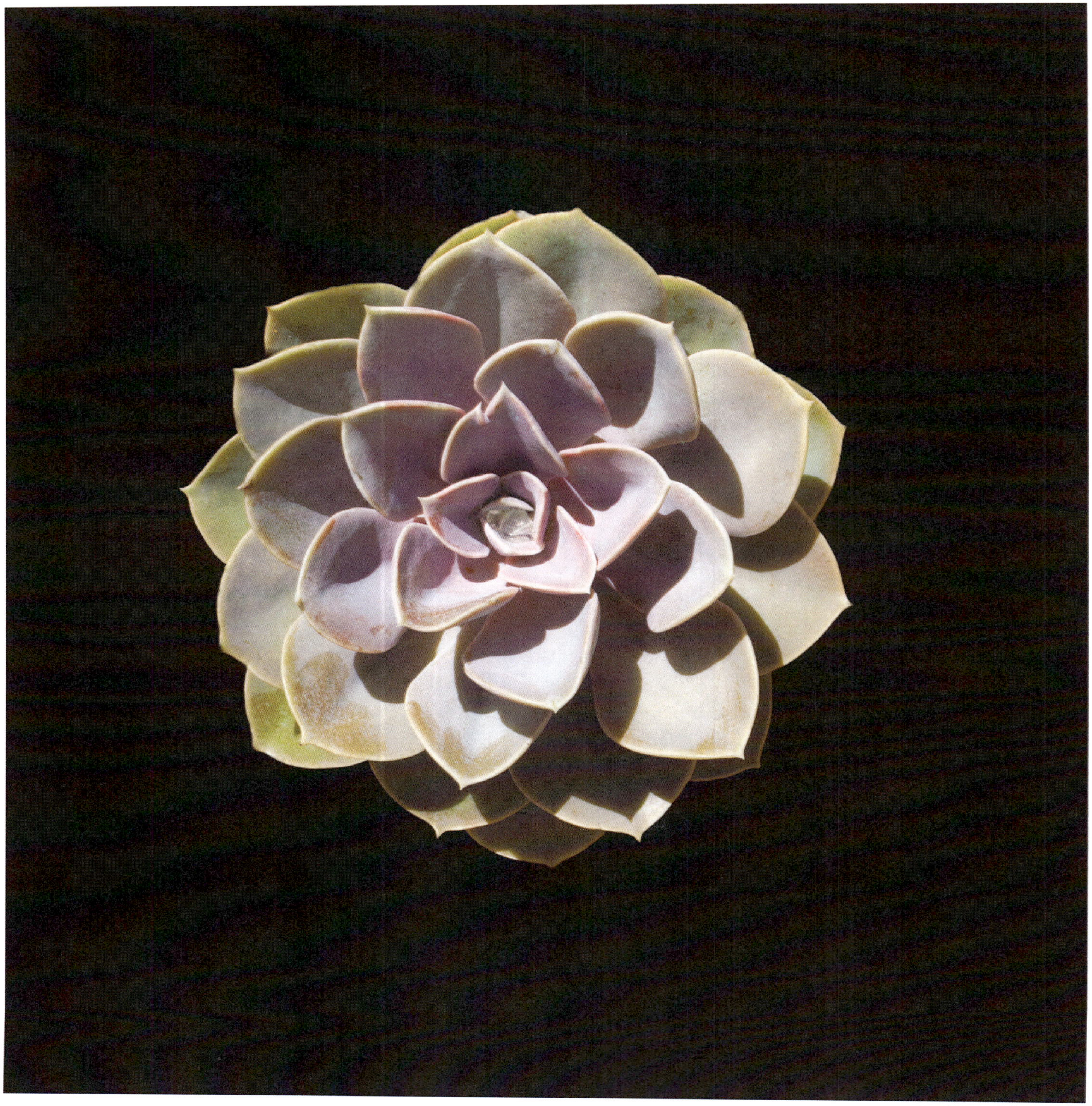

Digital photo of an Echeveria

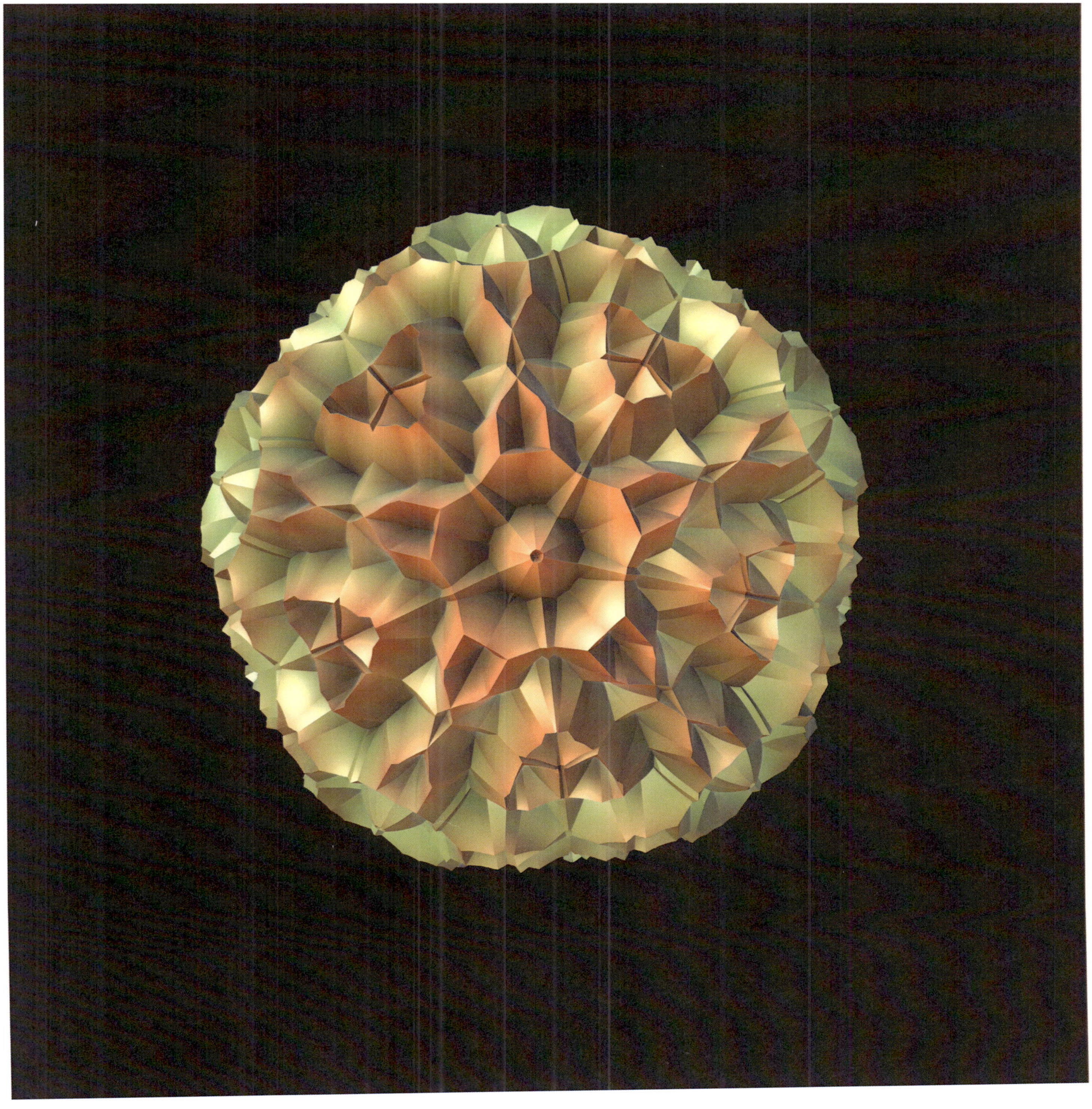

Image created in Mandelbulb 3D

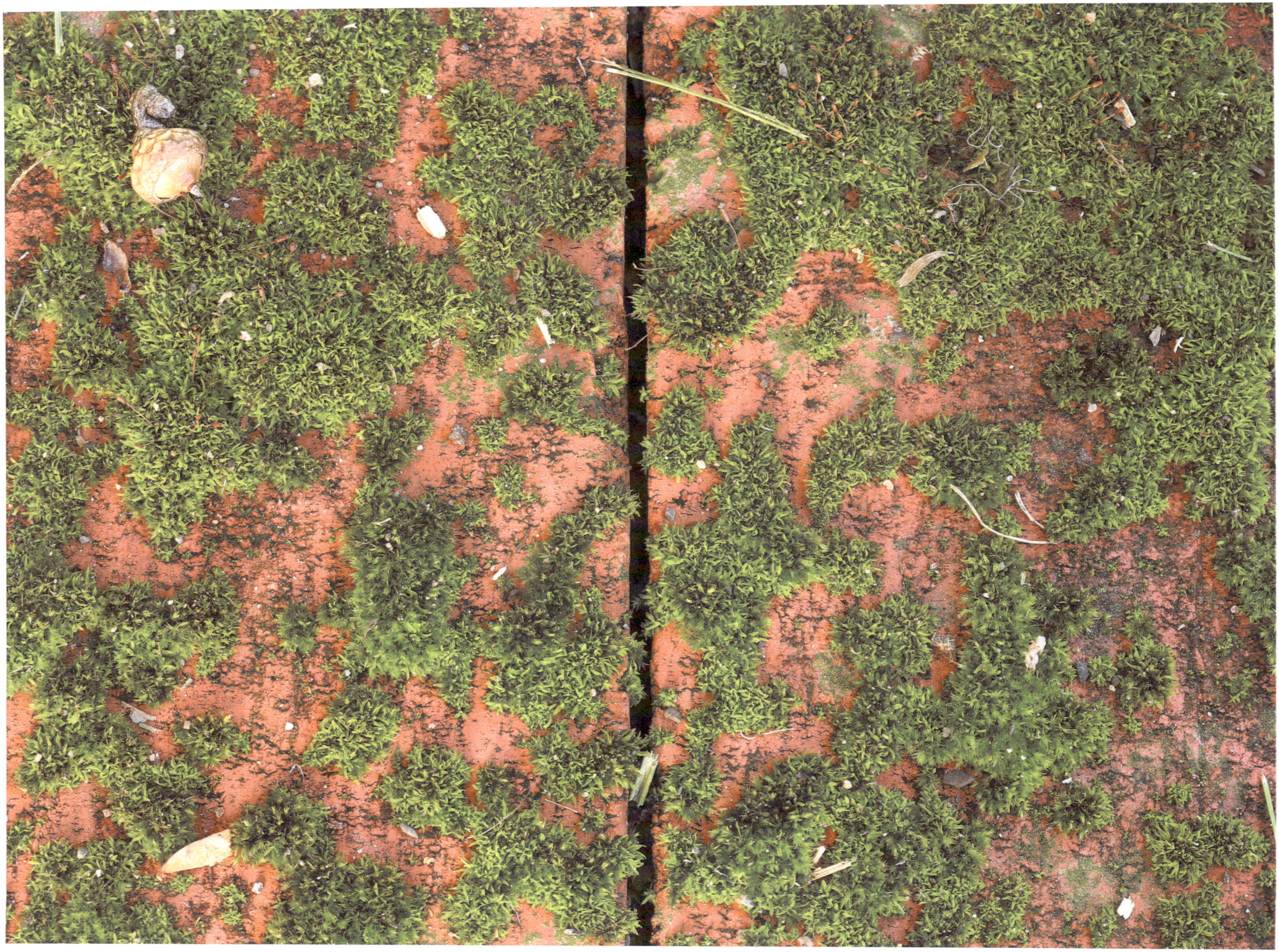

Moss growing on bricks after a few rainy days (digital photo with macro lens)

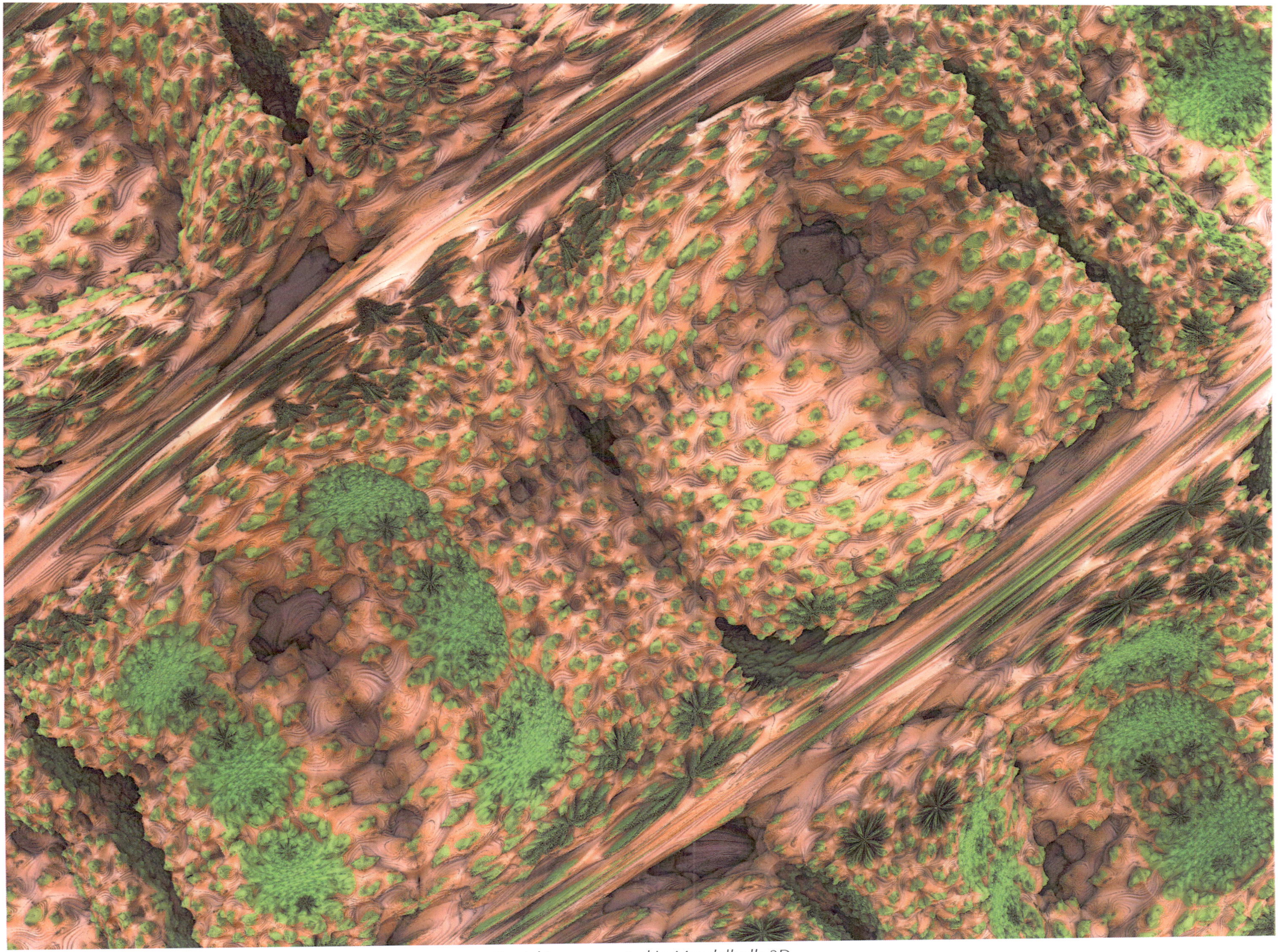

Fractal image created in Mandelbulb 3D

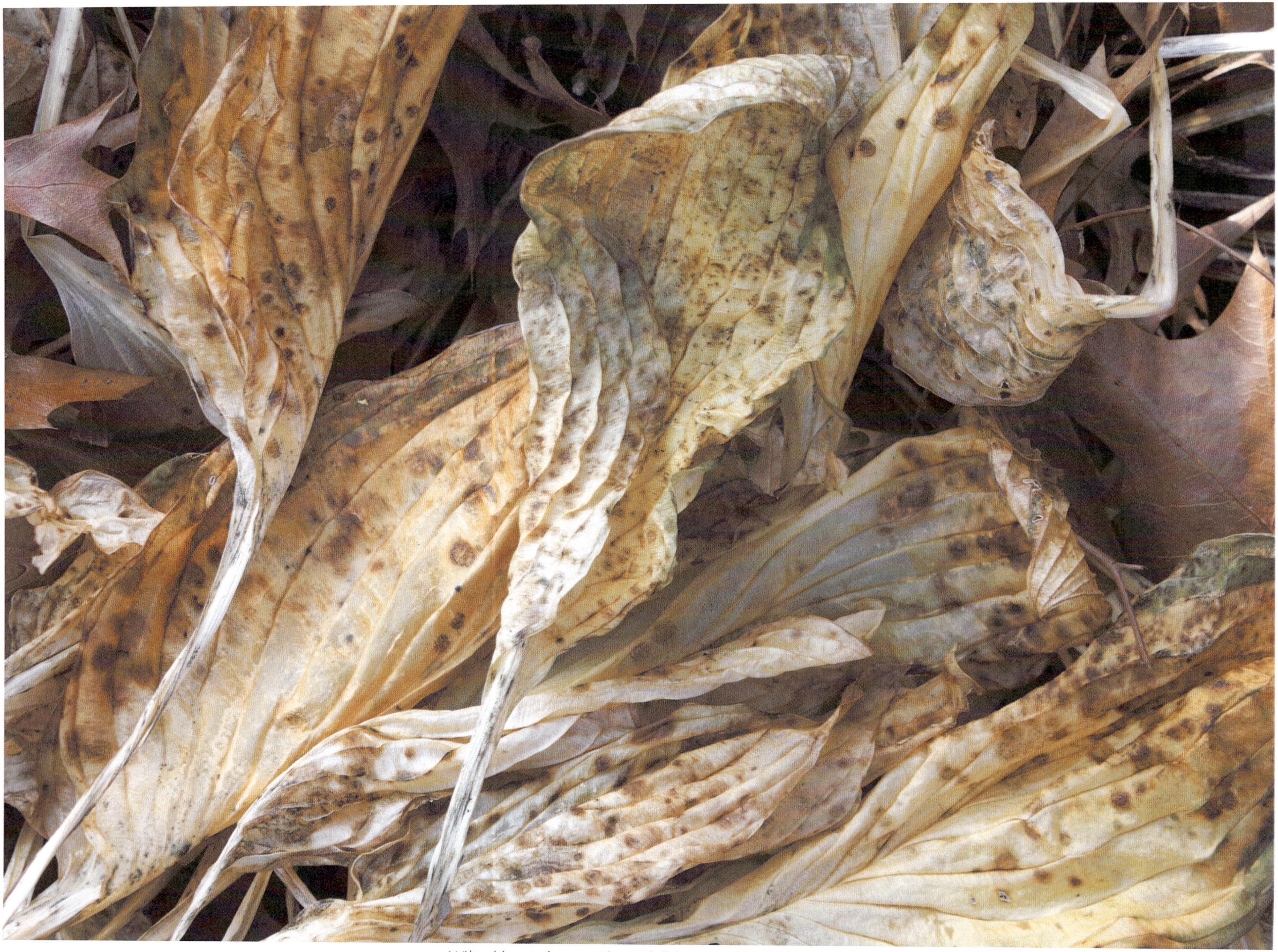

Wilted hosta leaves after a fall freeze (digital photo)

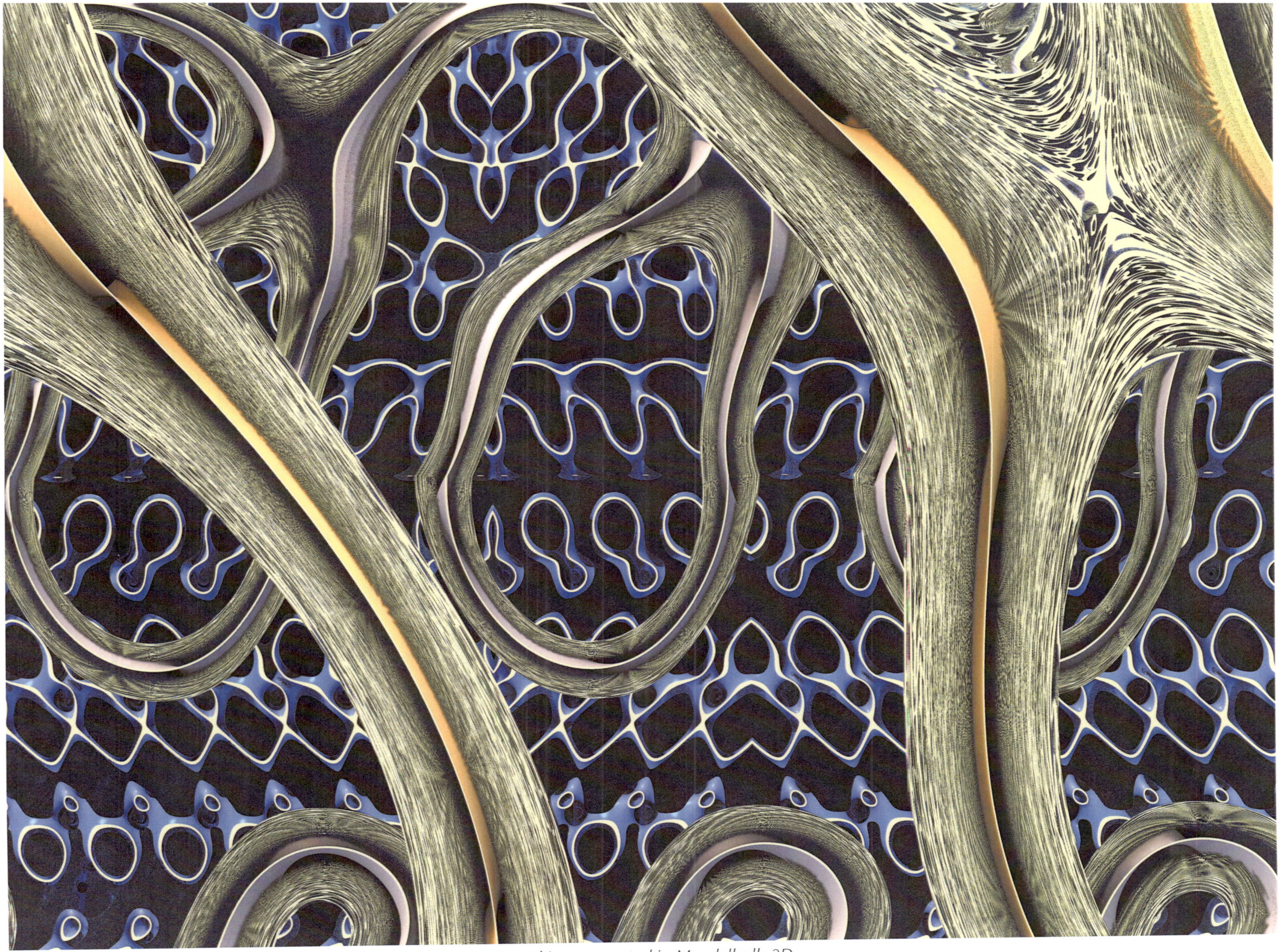

Fractal image created in Mandelbulb 3D

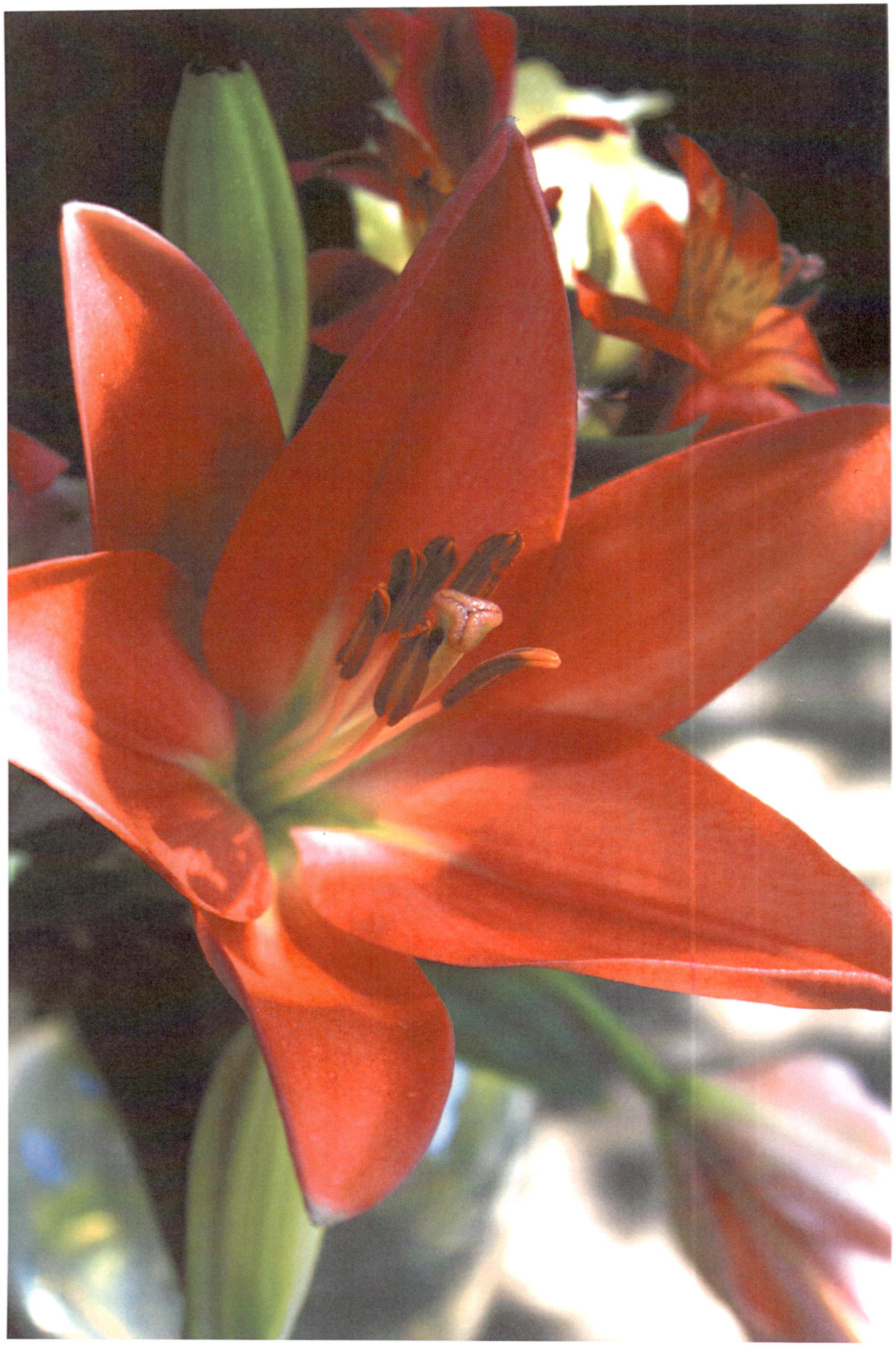

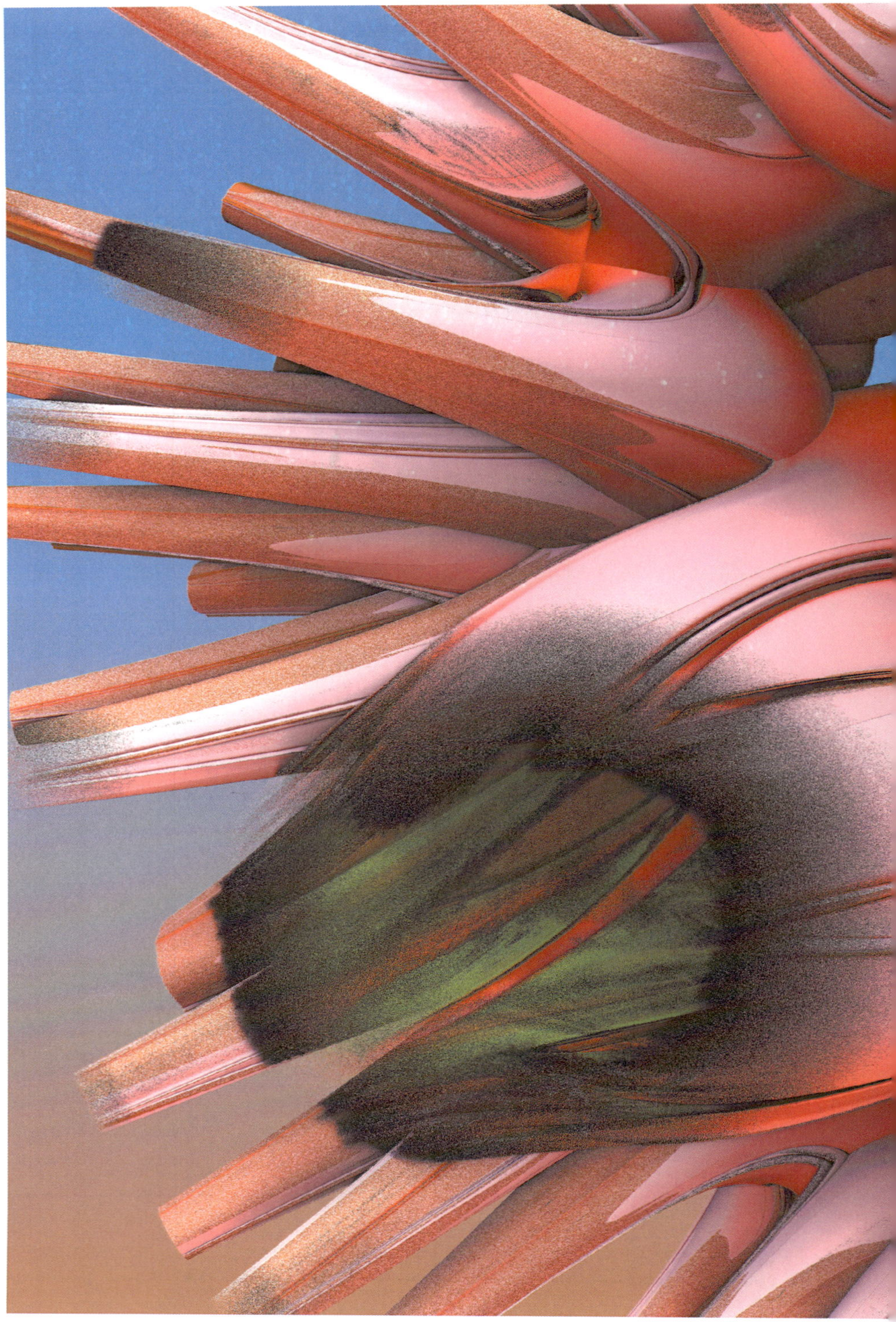

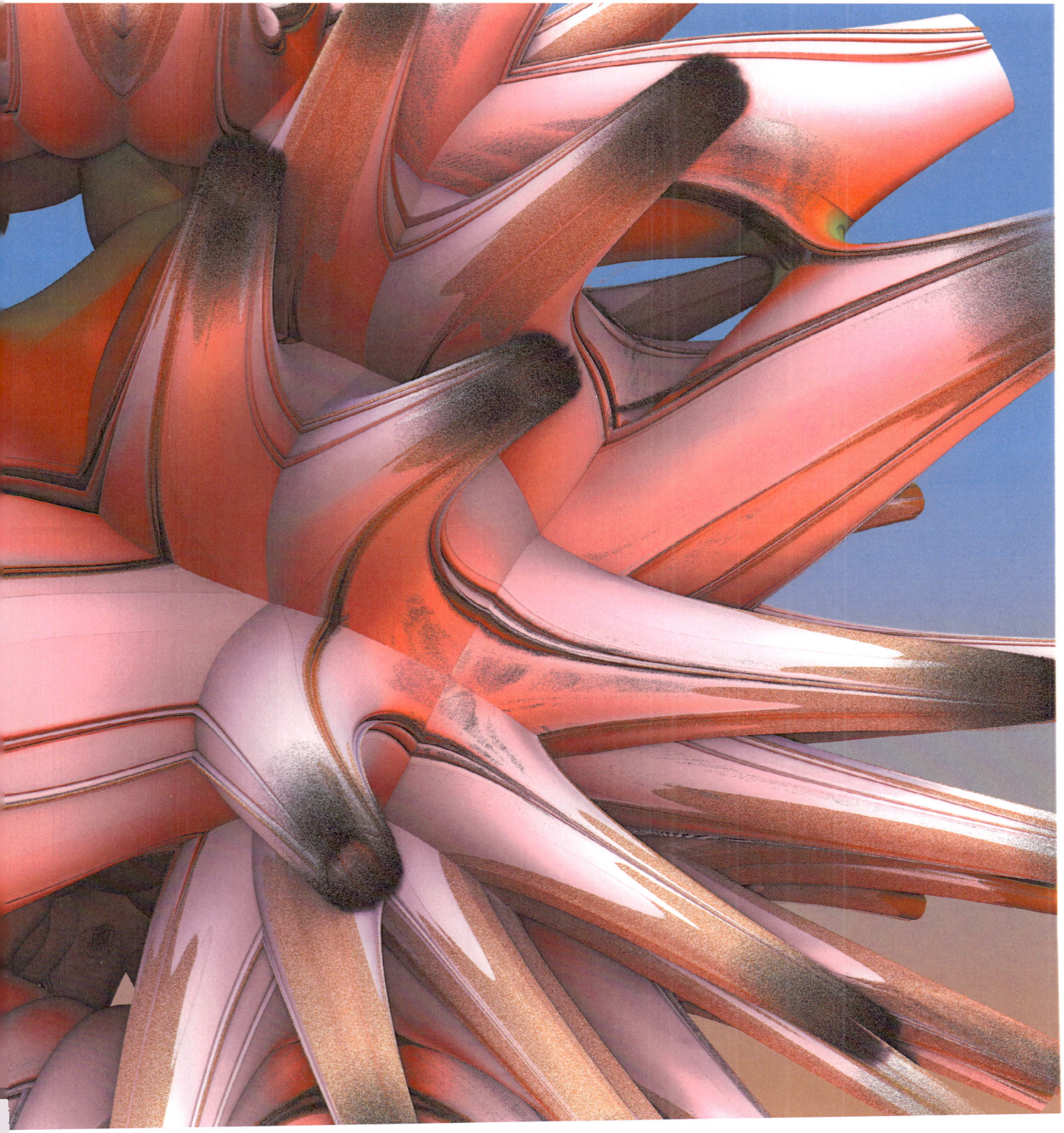

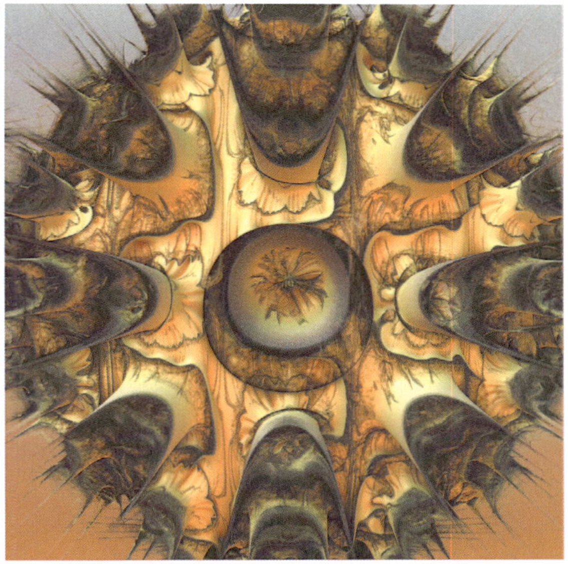

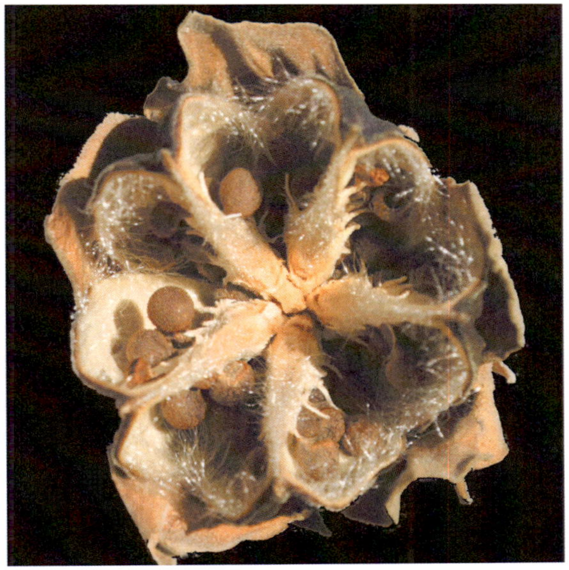

Plants and fractals often appear similar or parallel in structure. **Opposite page, far-left,** a real lily; and **center-spread,** a fractal image from Mandelbulb 3D. At the **very top of this column** is another fractal image; and **below,** a seed pod directly imaged by an Epson photo scanner.

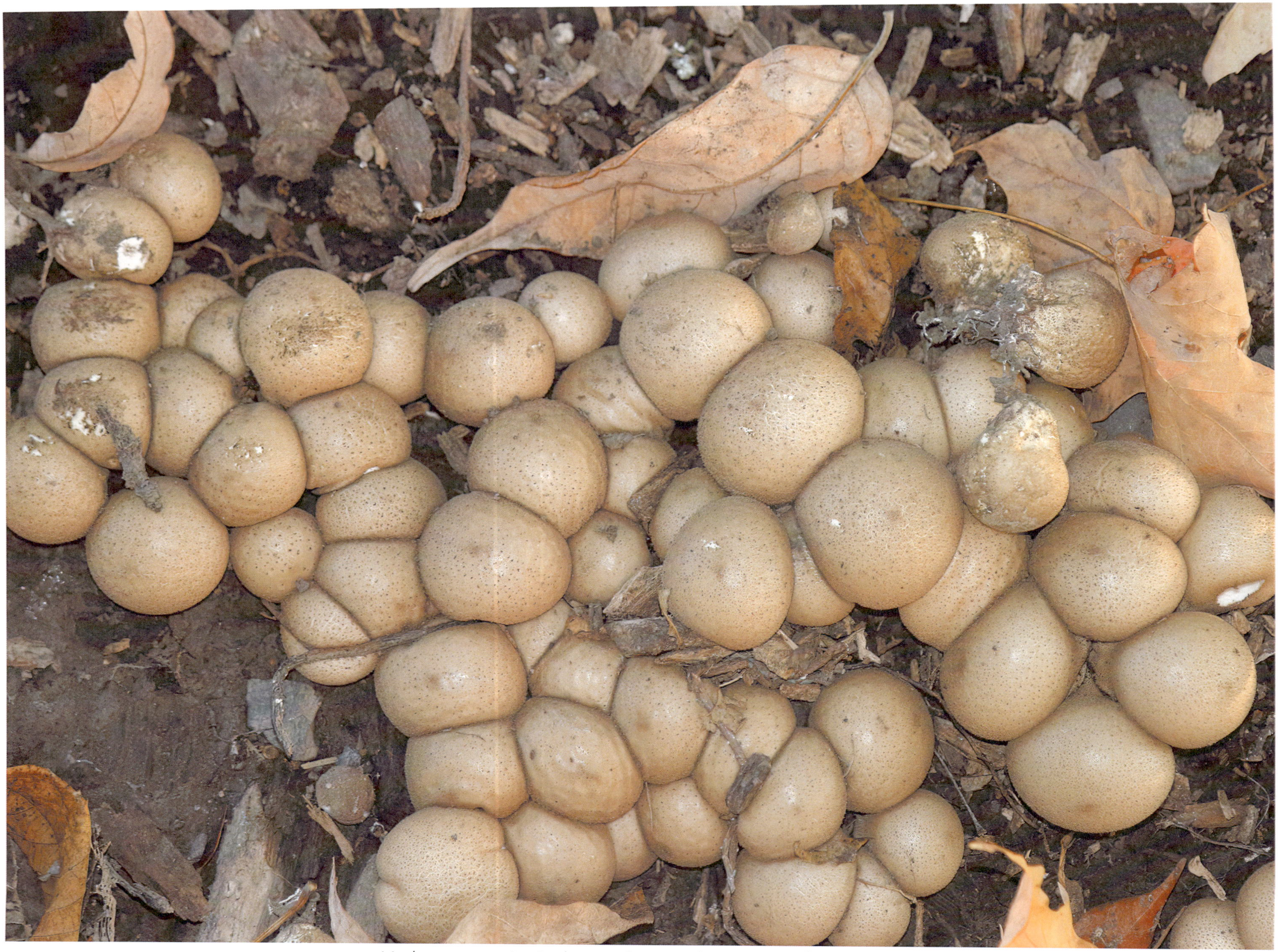

Mushrooms growing in the woods near a decaying tree (digital photo)

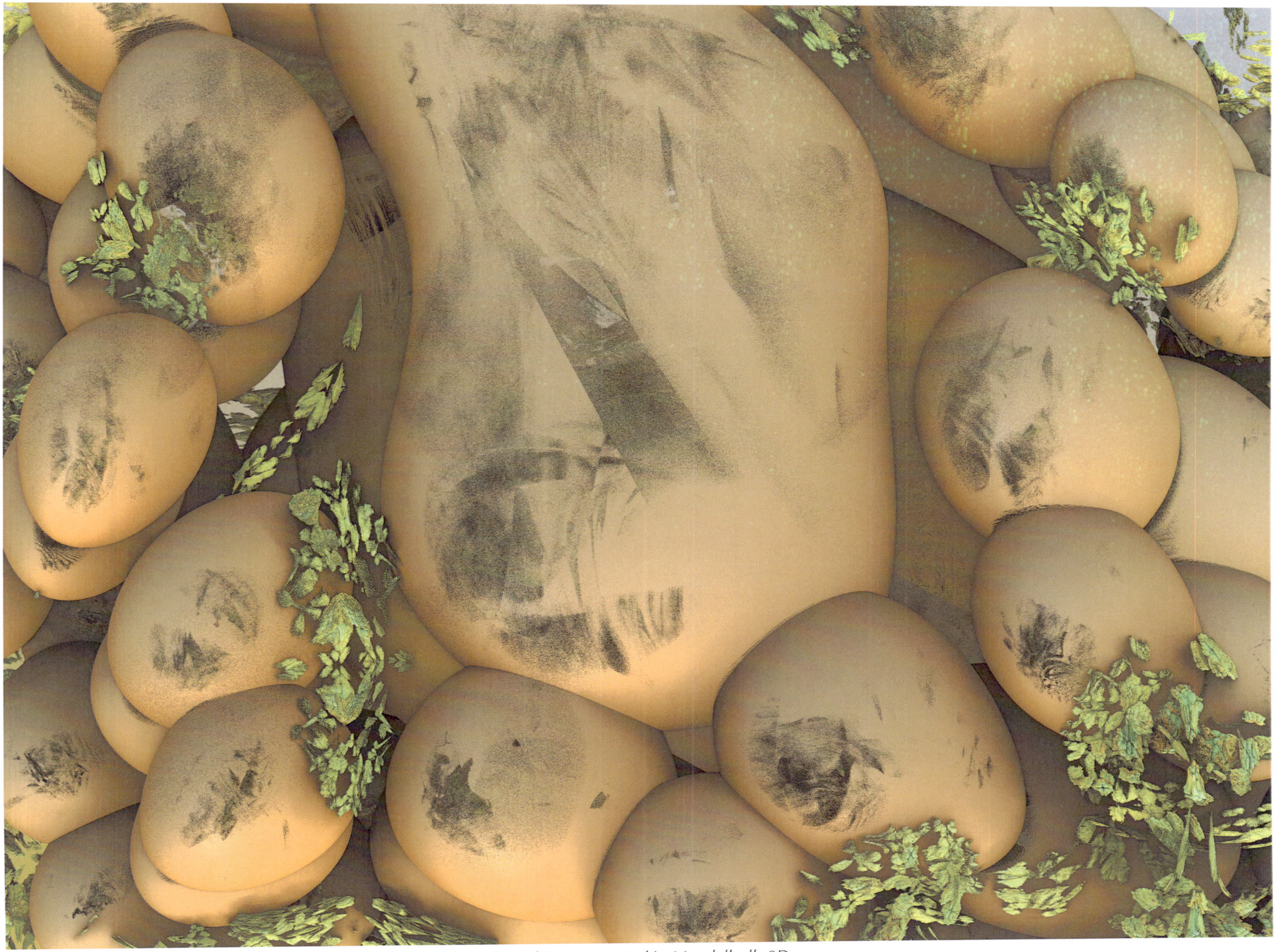

Fractal image created in Mandelbulb 3D

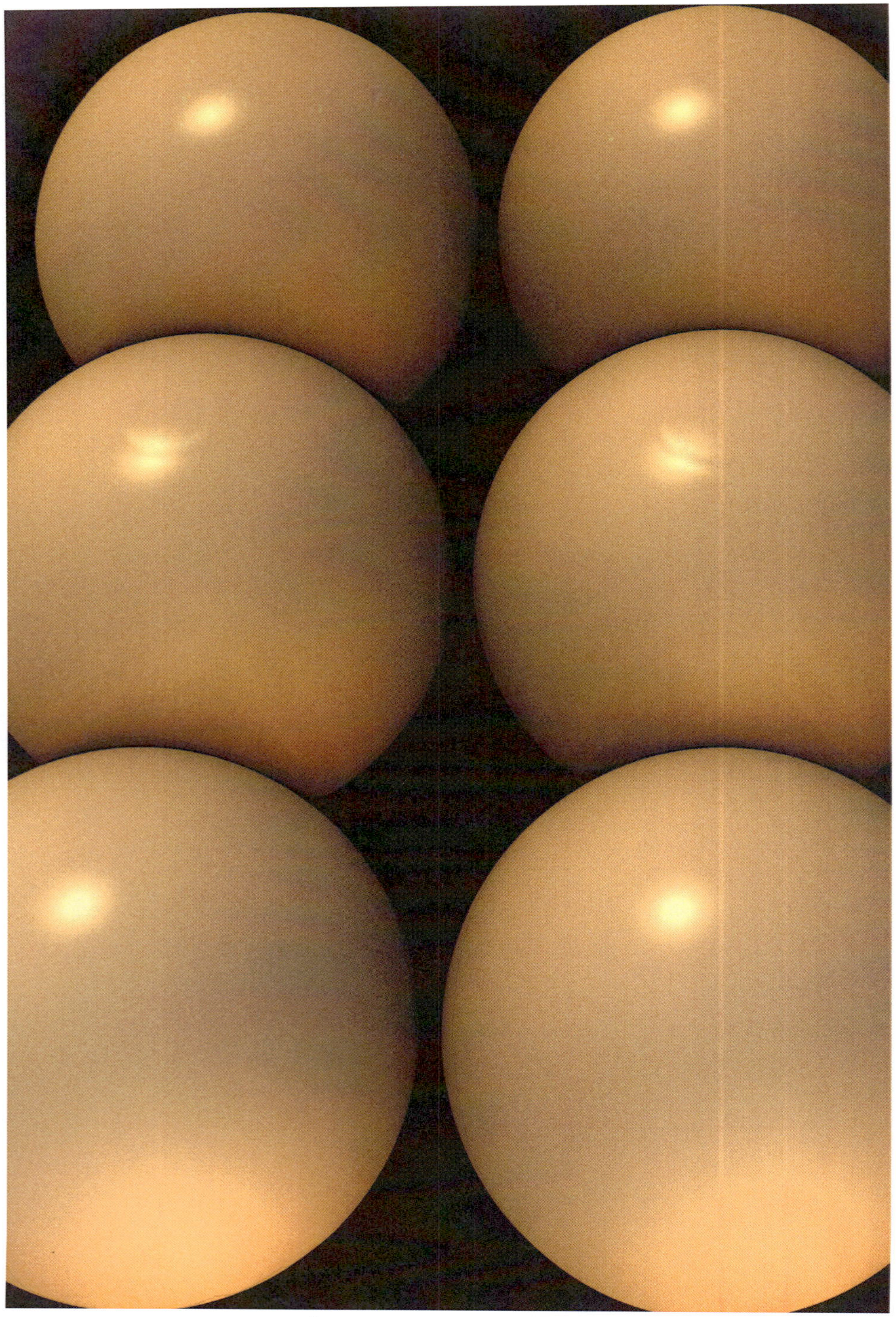

"Fractal eggs" imaged in Mandelbulb 3D

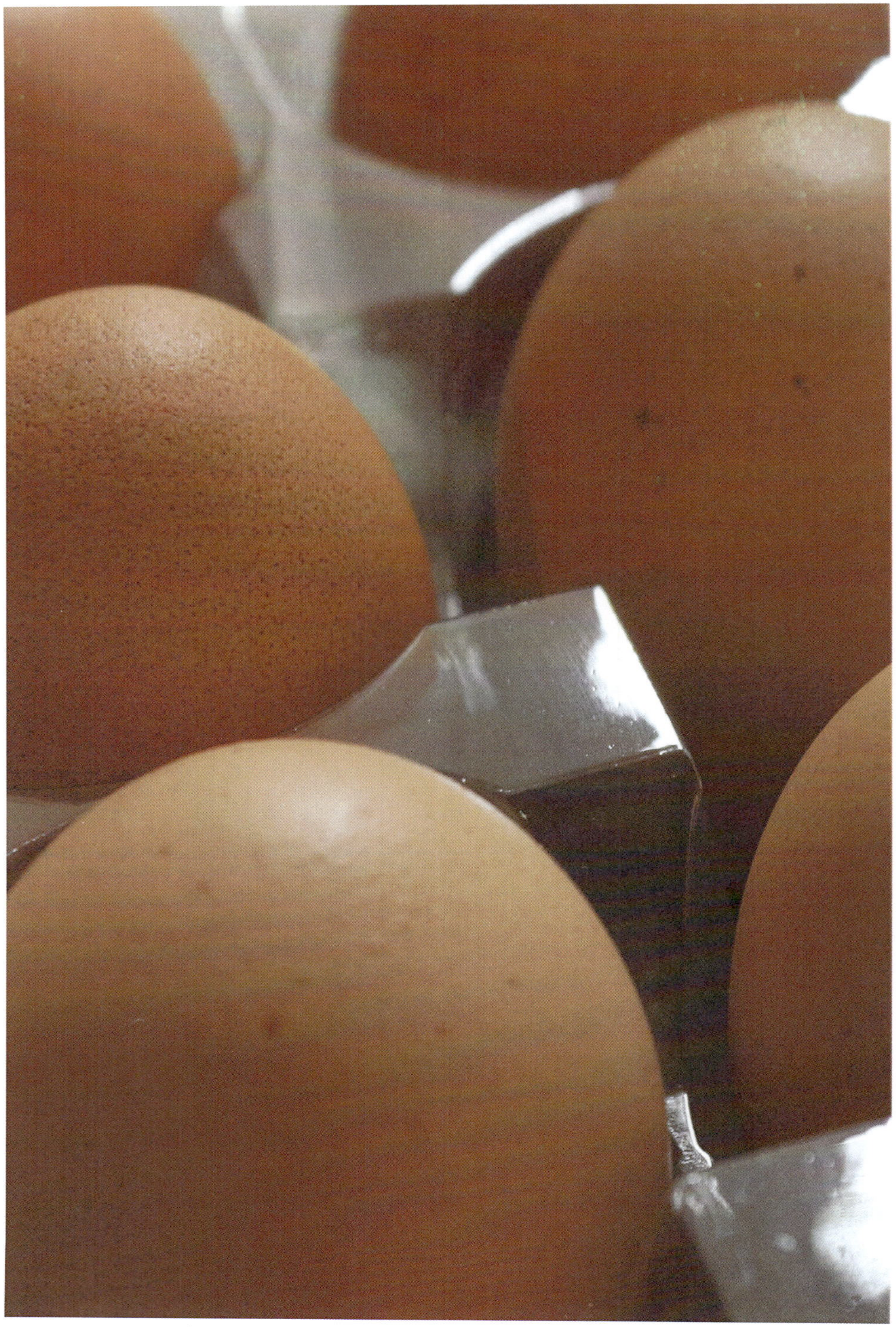

Real eggs purchased from the grocery store (digital photo)

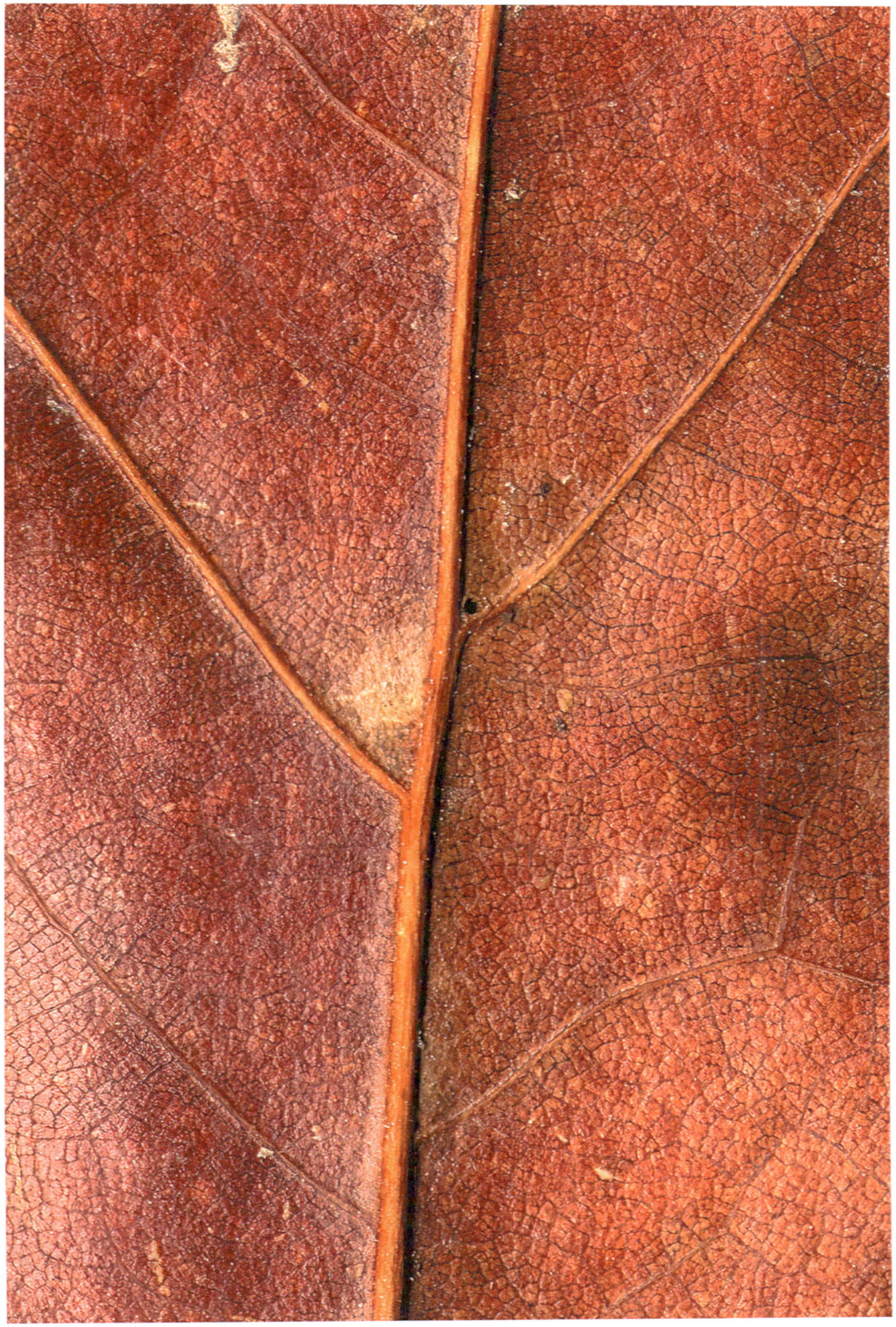

Digital scan of the underside of a pin-oak leaf in fall

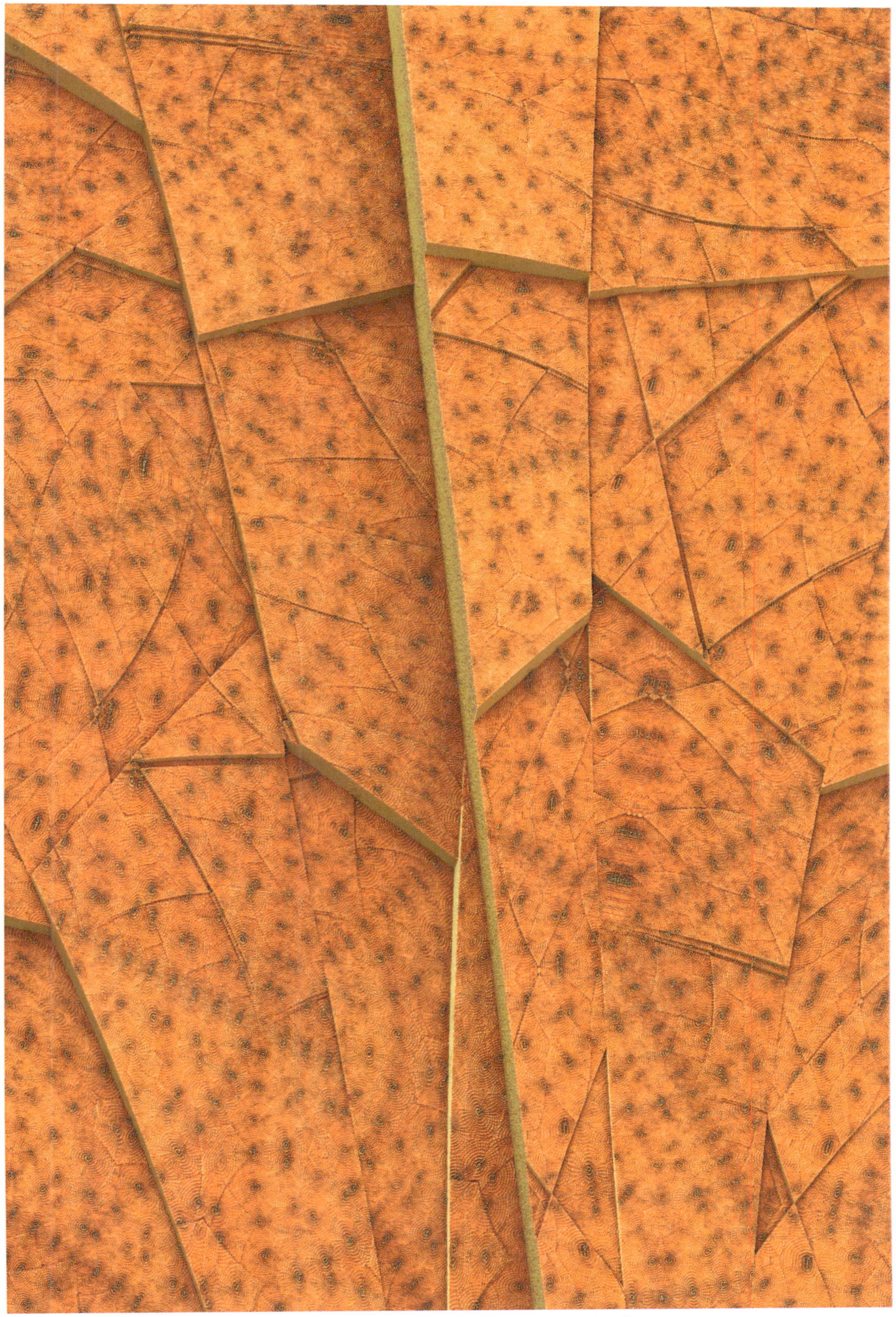

A "fractal leaf" generated in Mandelbulb 3D

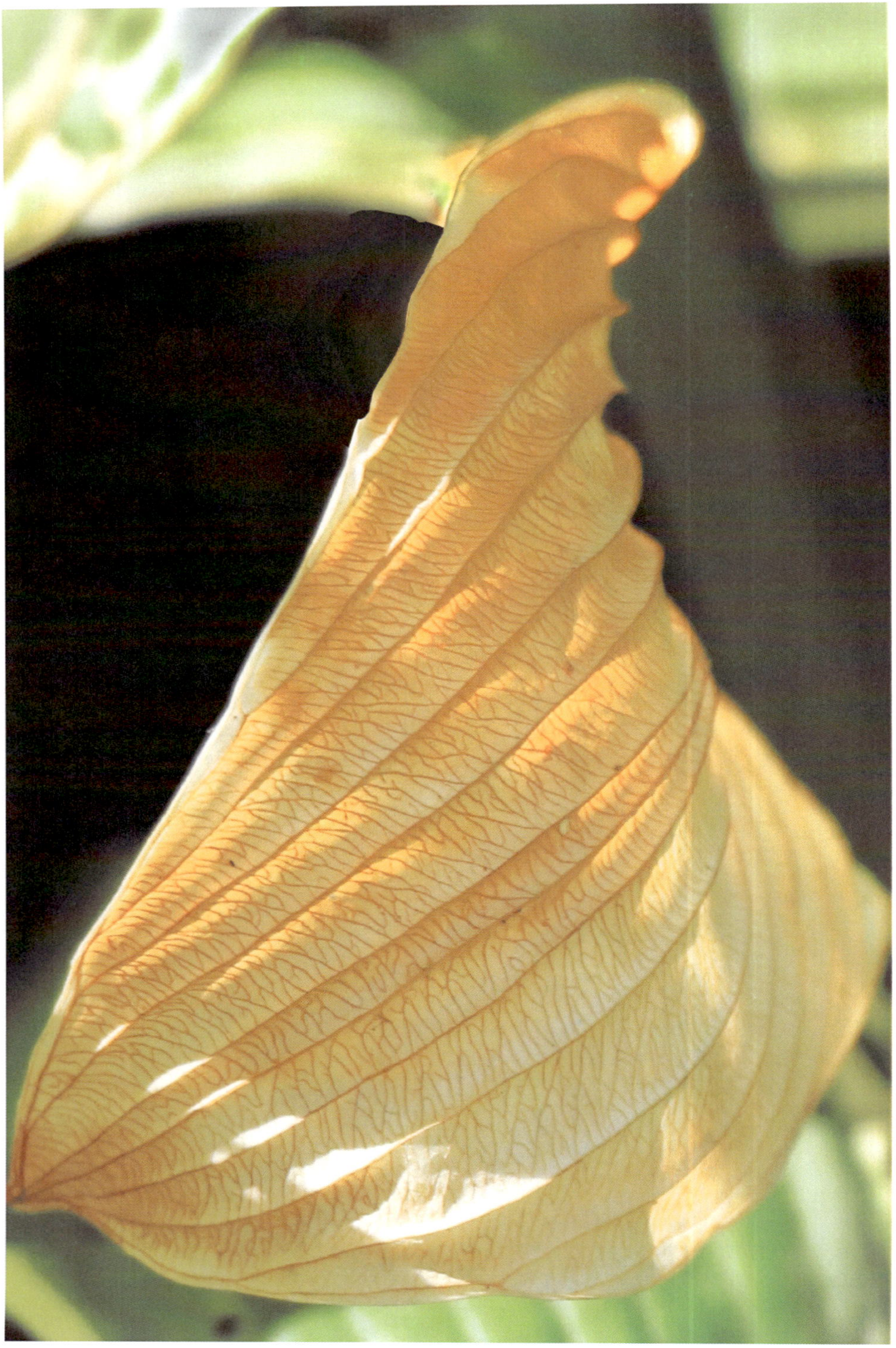

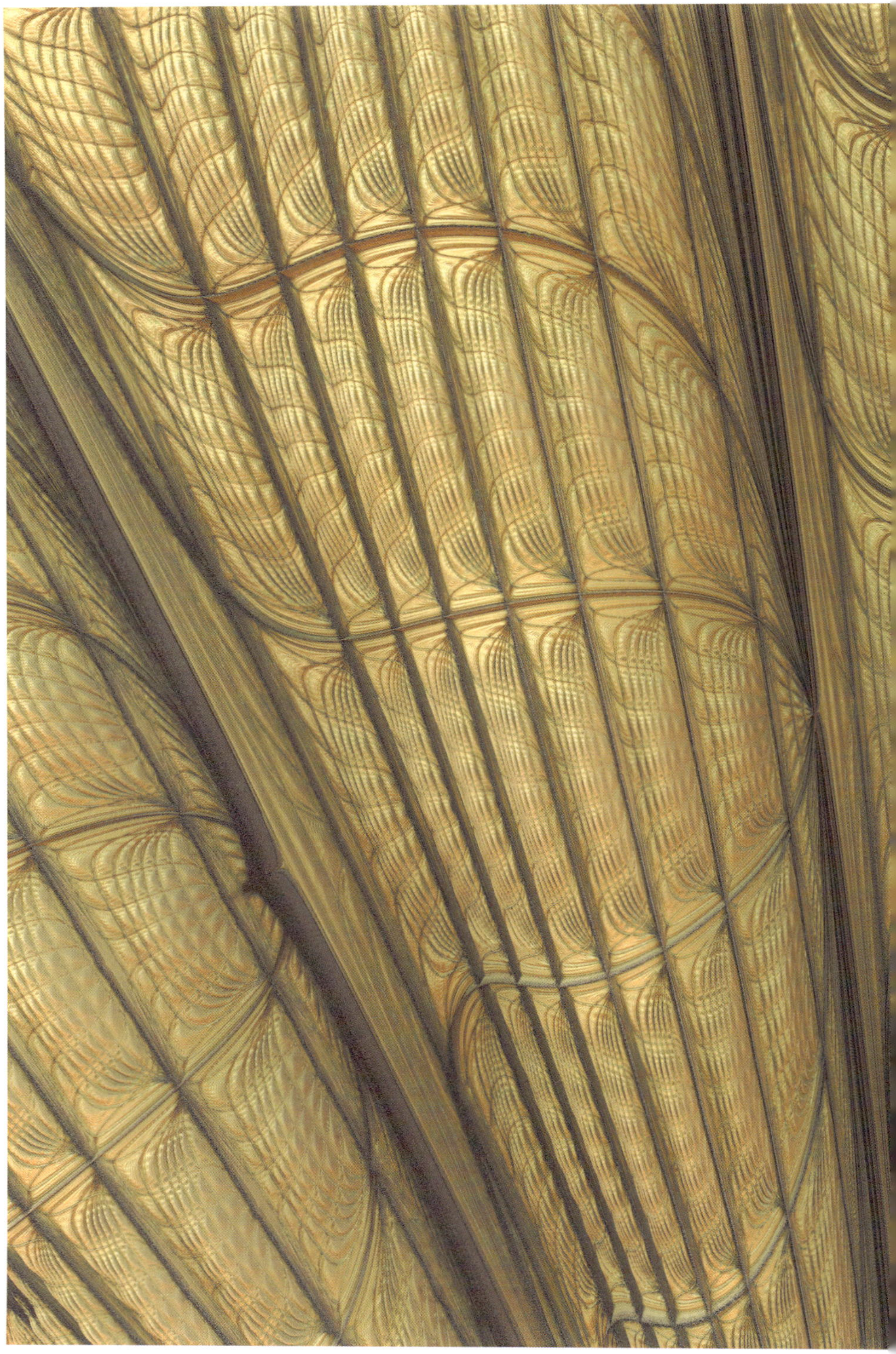

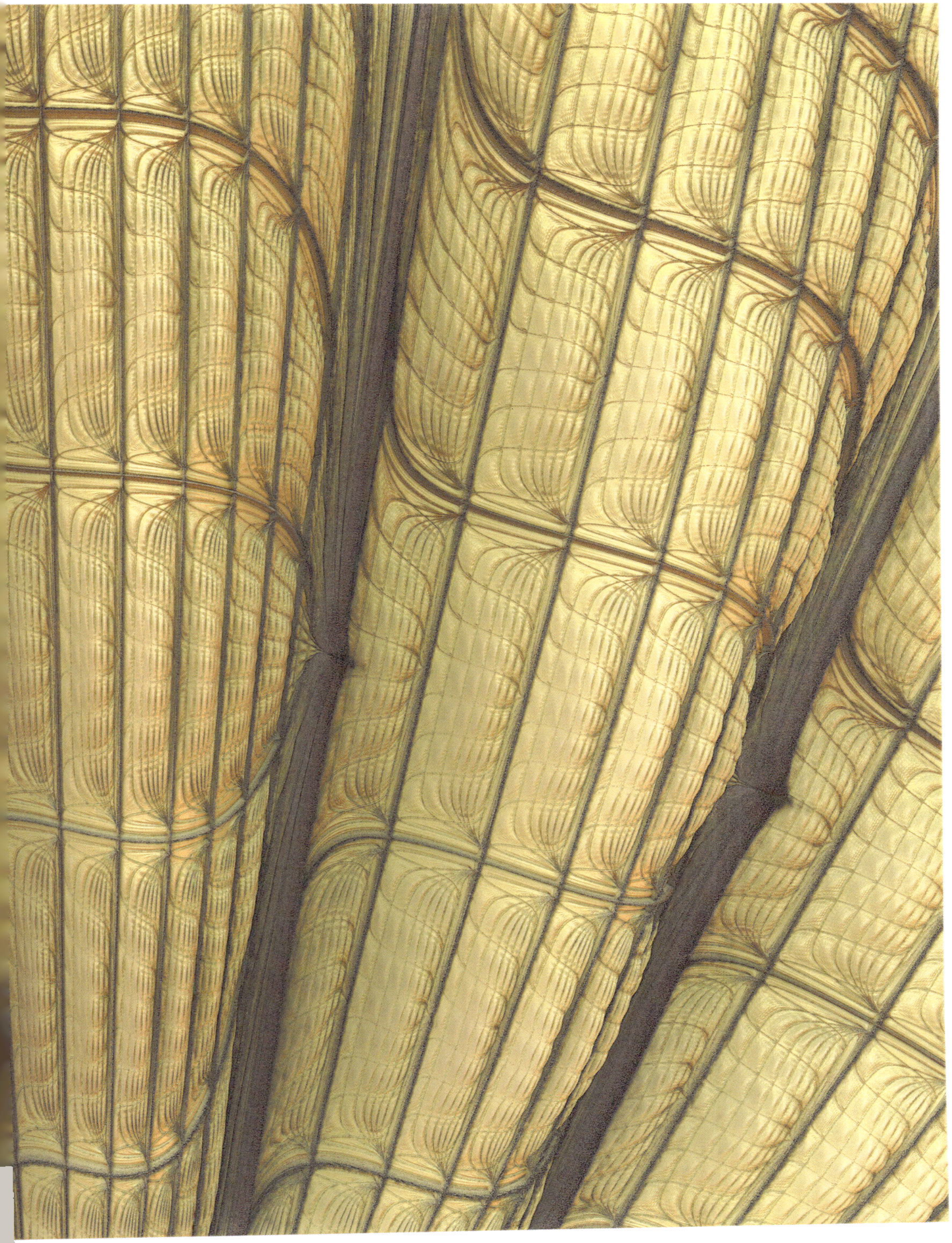

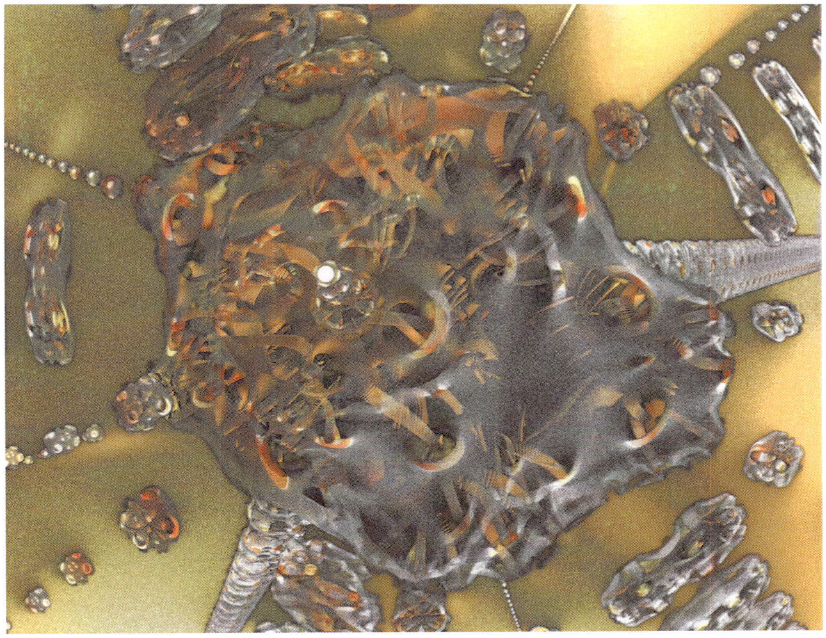

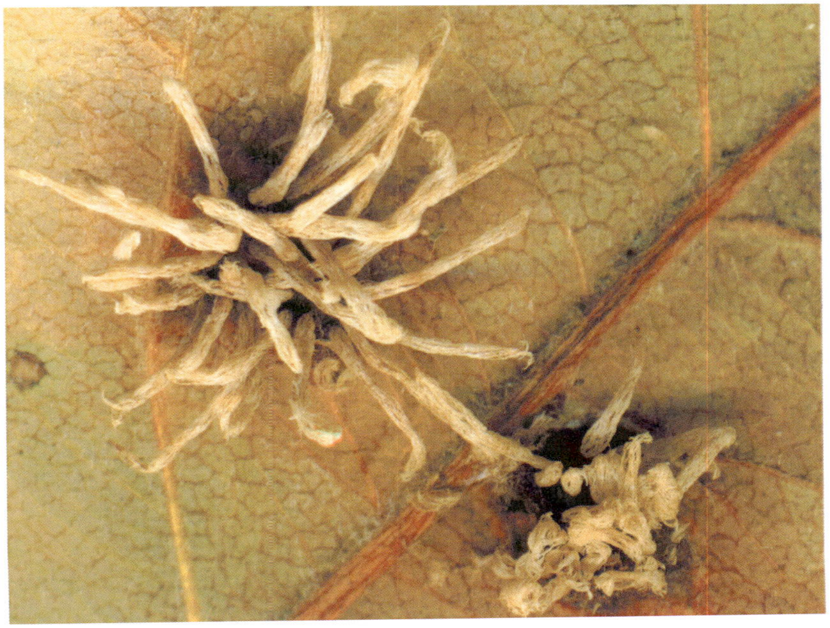

Opposite page, far-left, wilting hosta plant leaf in late summer; **center-spread**, a fractal created by Mandelbulb 3D loosely resembles the veins in the hosta leaf. **This column, top,** fractal; and **immediately above** is the underside of an oak leaf with spot fungus and mycelia (direct scan of the leaf on an Epson 4490 Photo scanner).

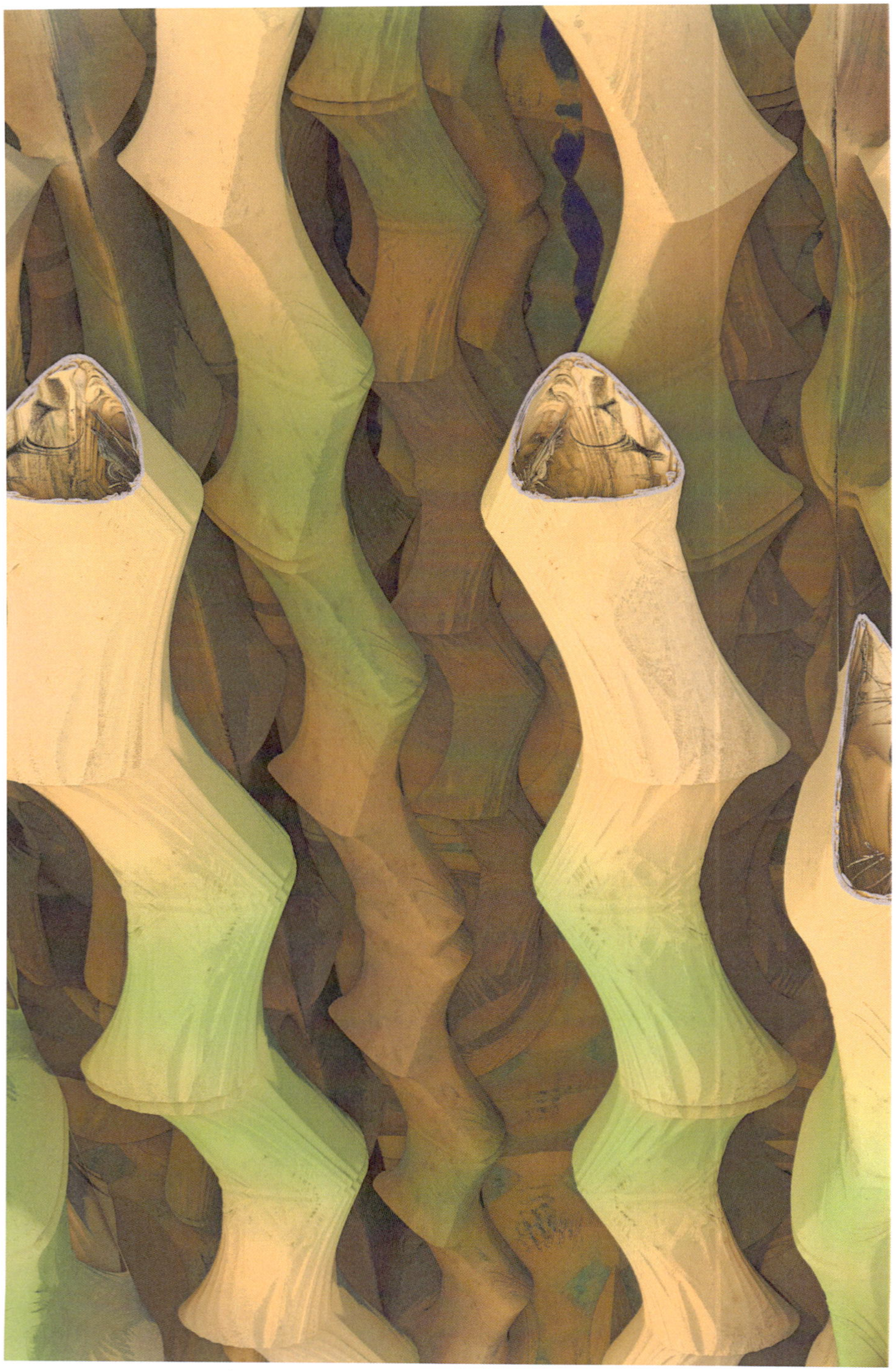

Fractal image created in Mandelbulb 3D

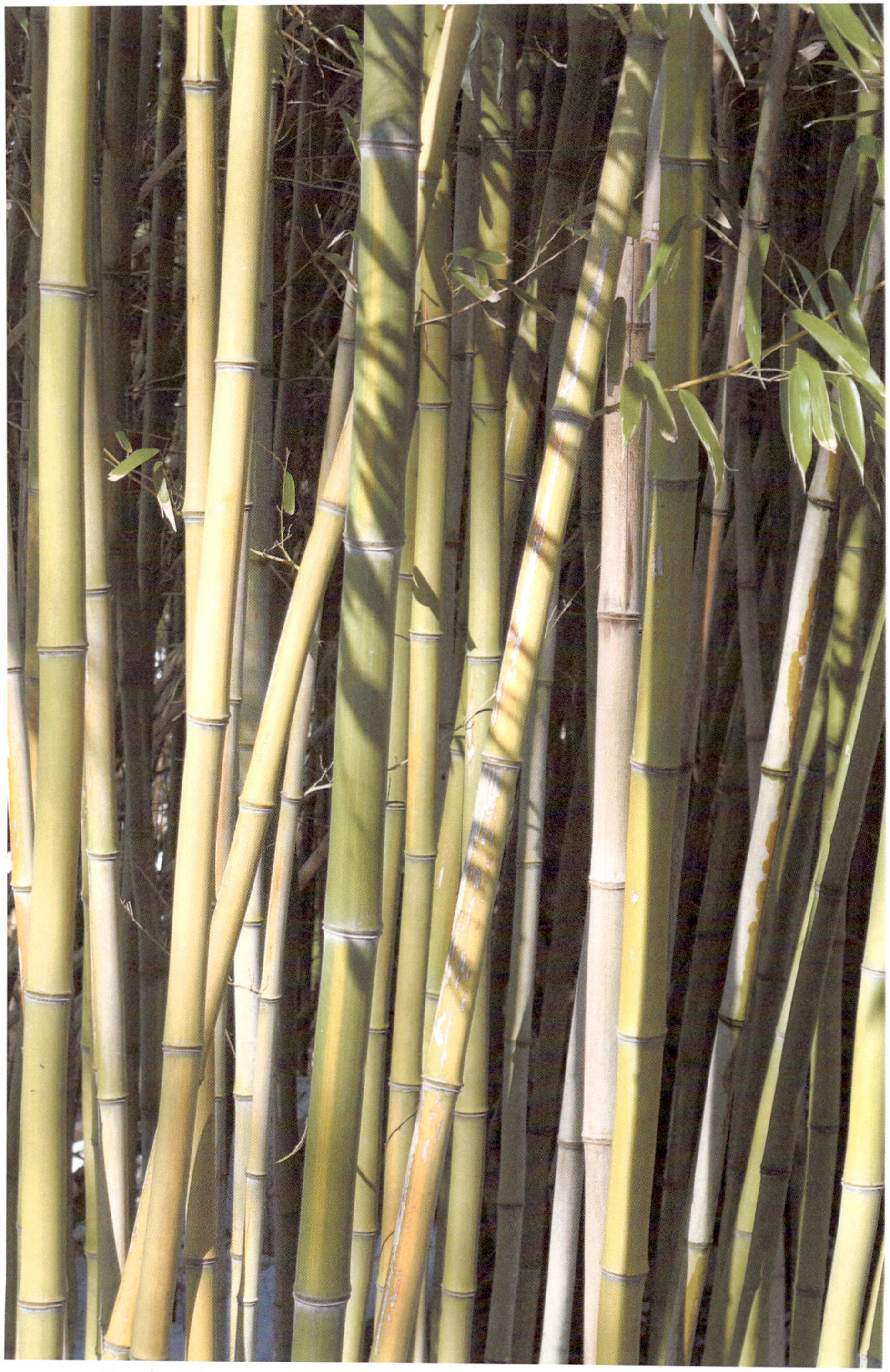

Bamboo found growing in a Southeastern, Pa. plot (digital photo)

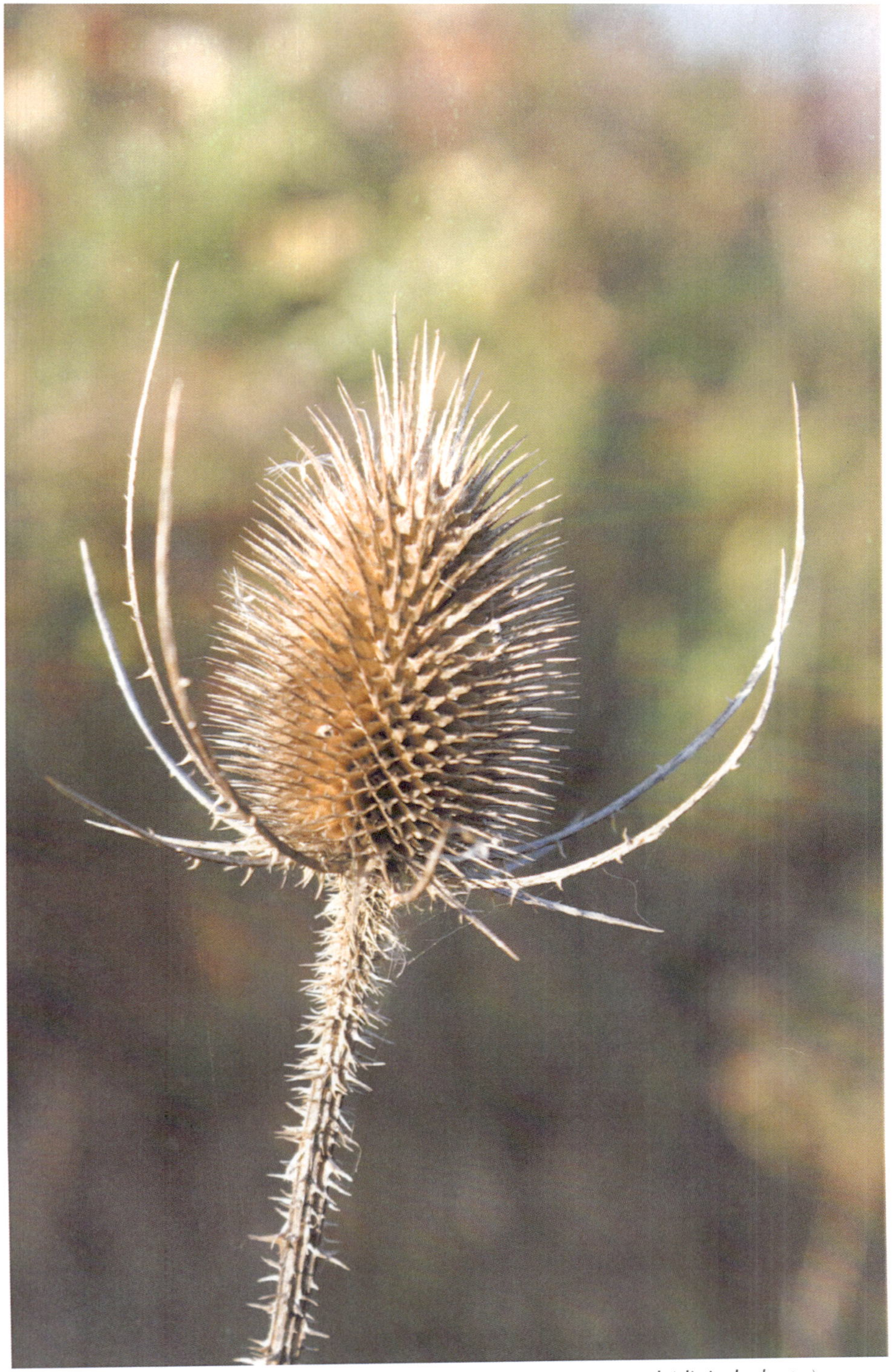

Thistle plant on the edge of the woods has gone to seed (digital photo).

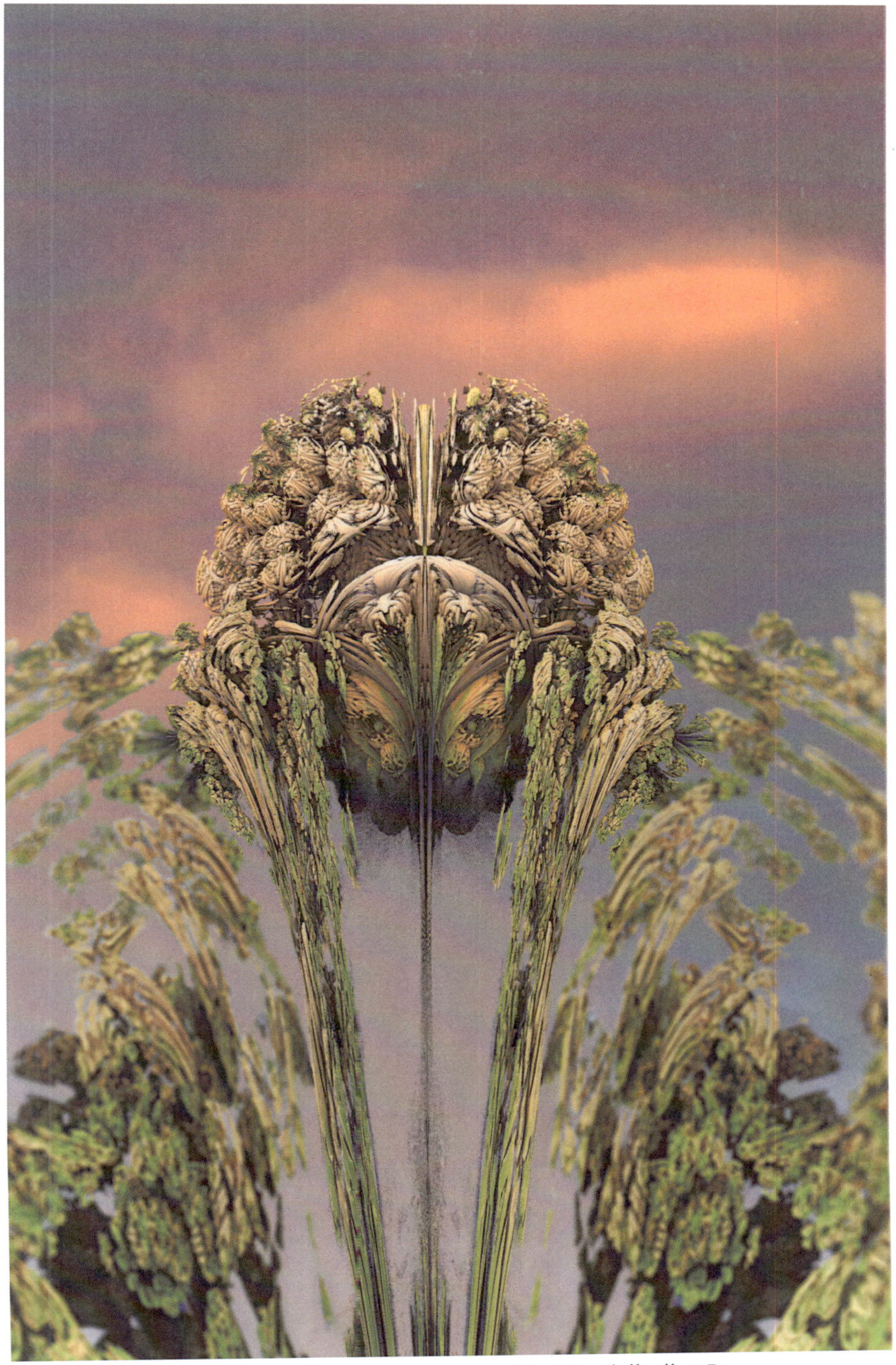

This fractal image was created in Mandelbulb 3D.

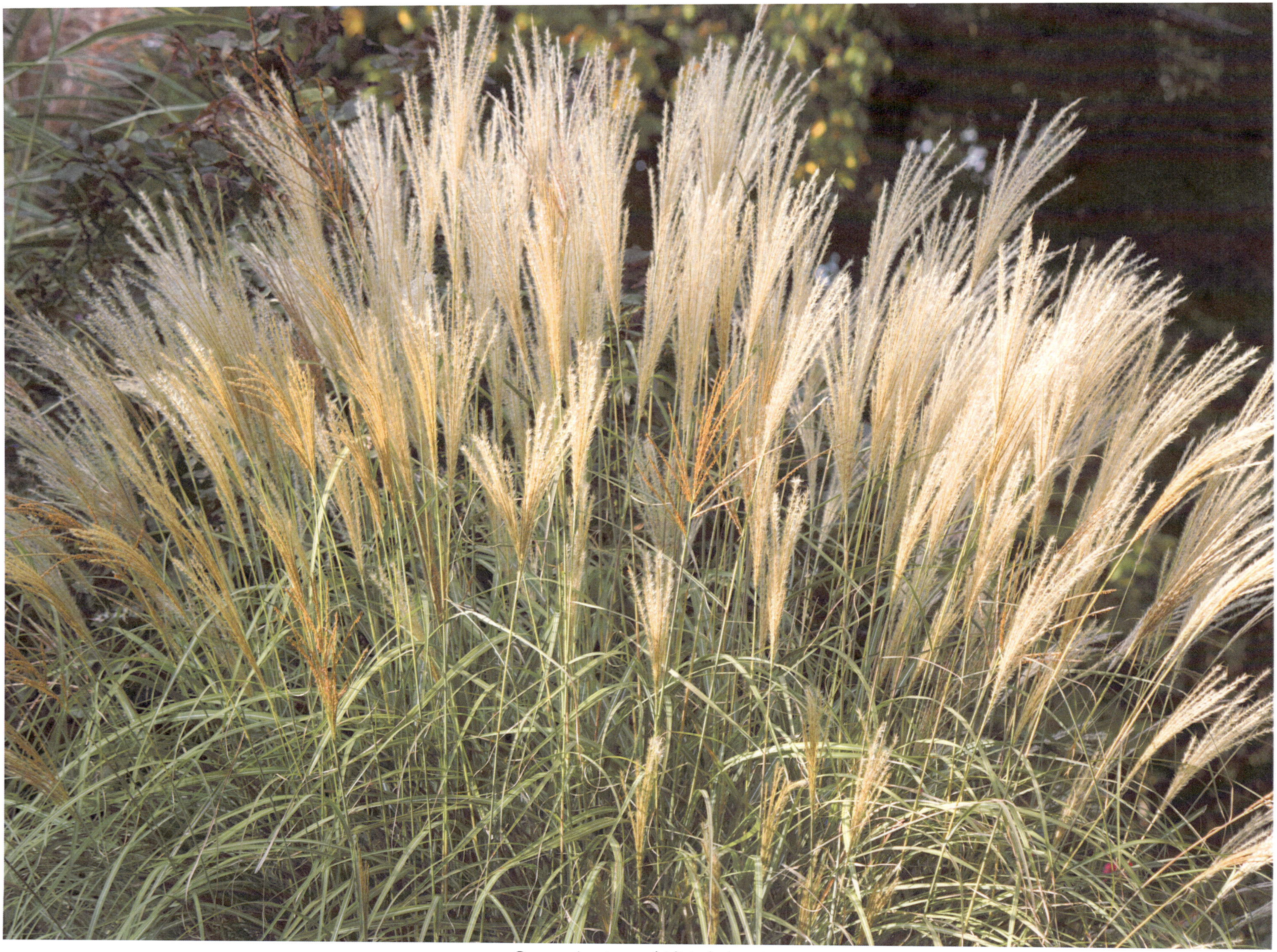

Grass going to seed (digital photo)

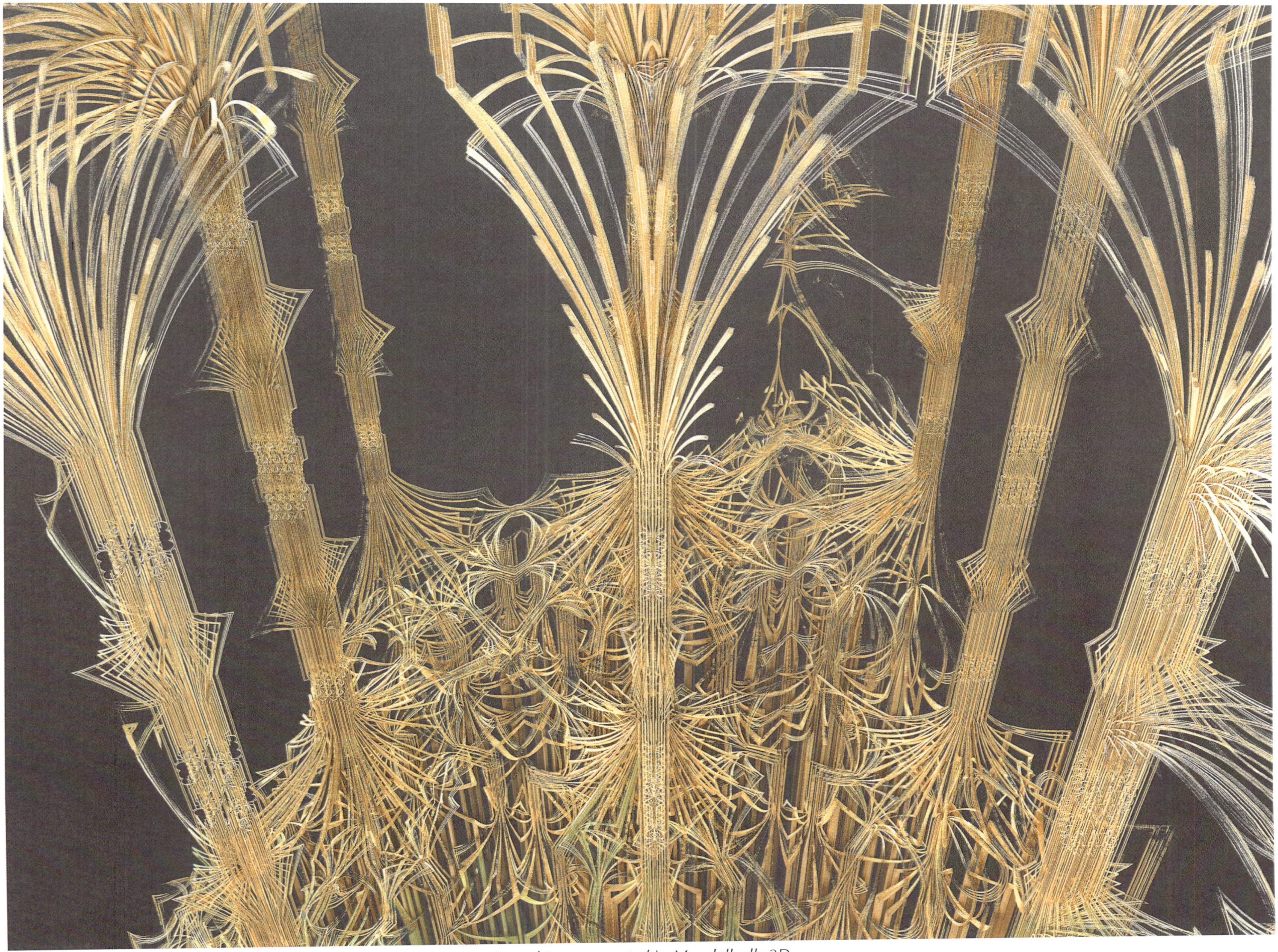

Fractal image created in Mandelbulb 3D

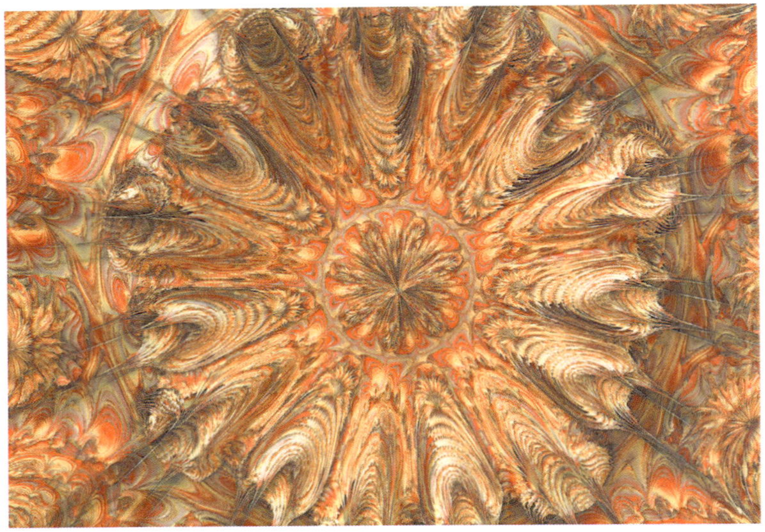

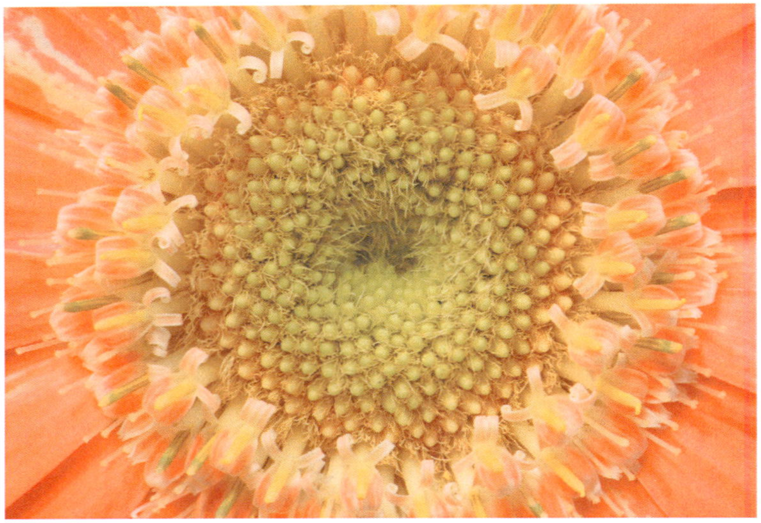

Top, Fractal image was created in Mandelbulb 3D. ***Below,*** this flower close-up was shot with a 60 mm/F2.8 Canon macro lens (APC format) and was focus-stacked using Affinity Photo on Windows. ***Right,*** this mushroom was growing in a mulch bed in Doylestown, Pa. and measured approximately eight to ten inches (20 to 25 cm) in diameter. ***Opposite page, far-right,*** this "stone mushroom" fractal was created in Mandelbulb 3D.

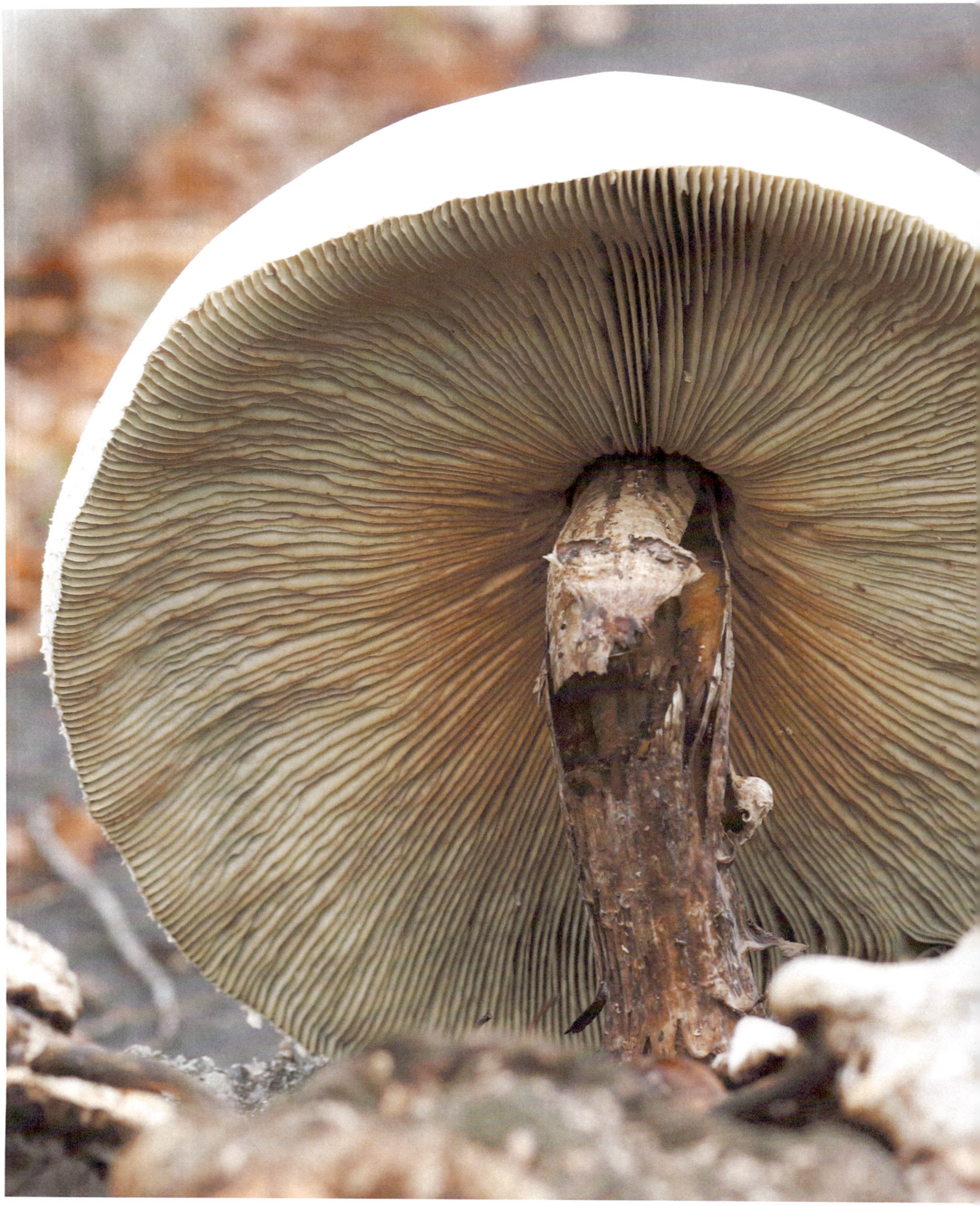

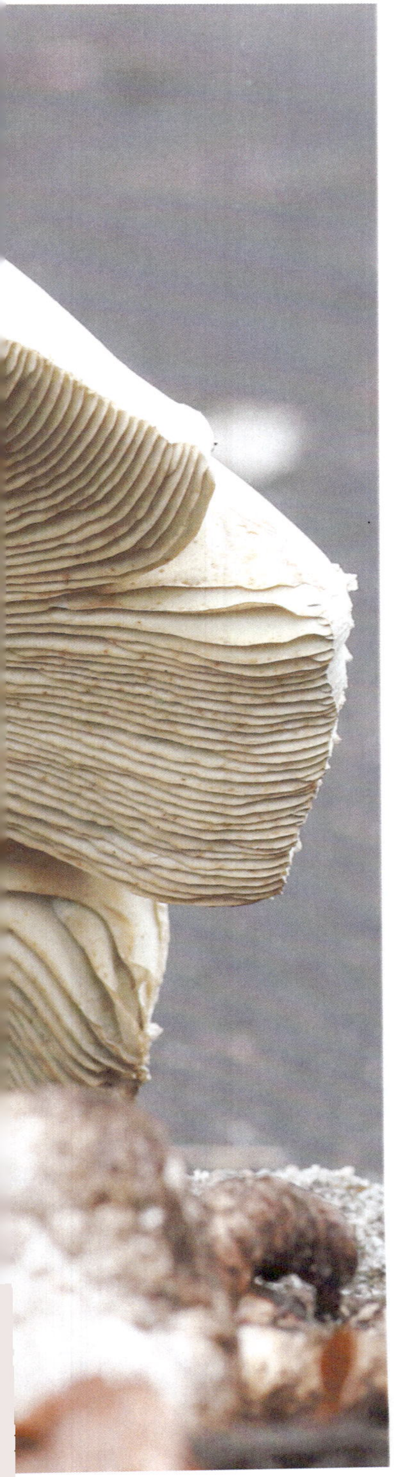

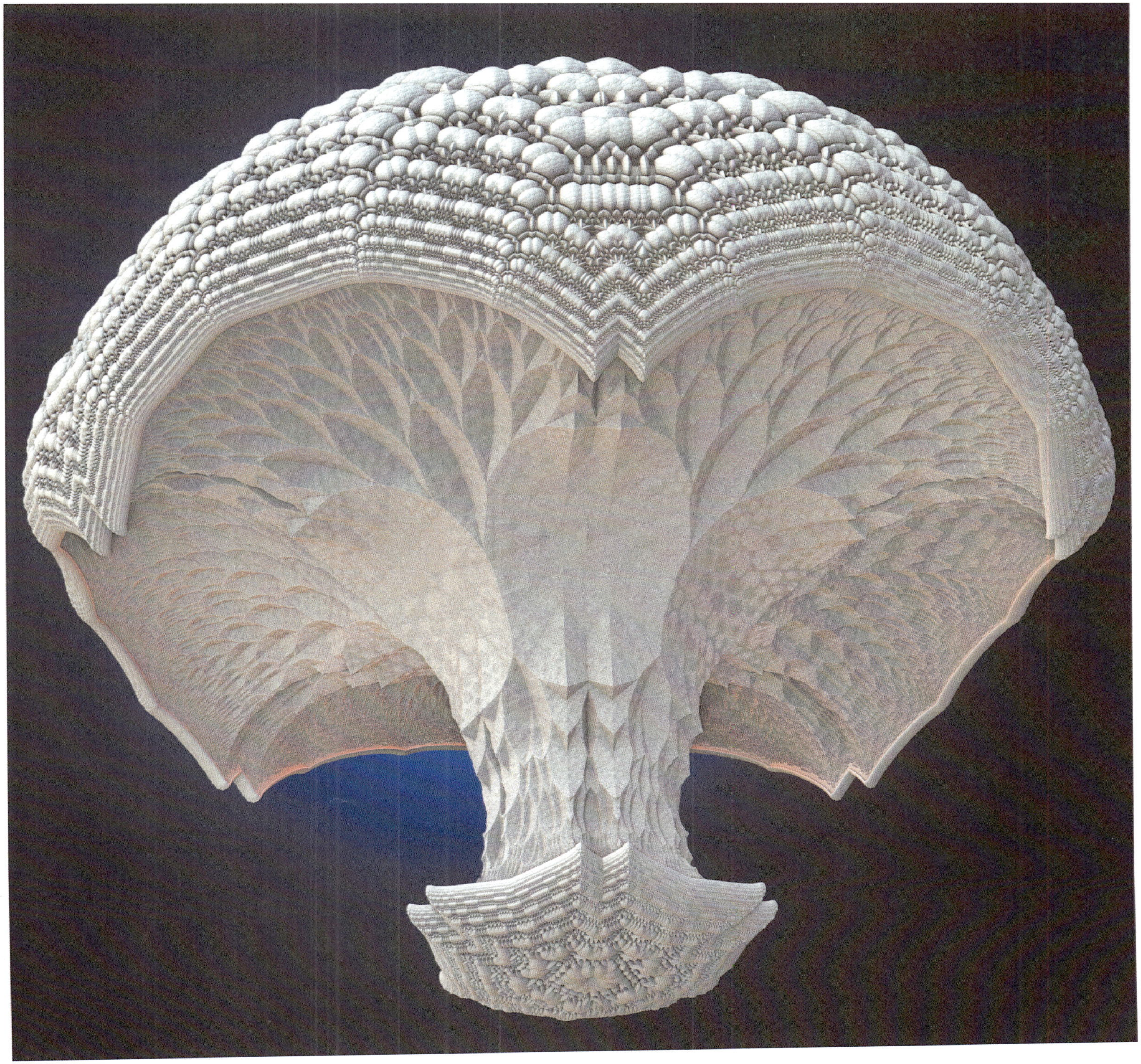

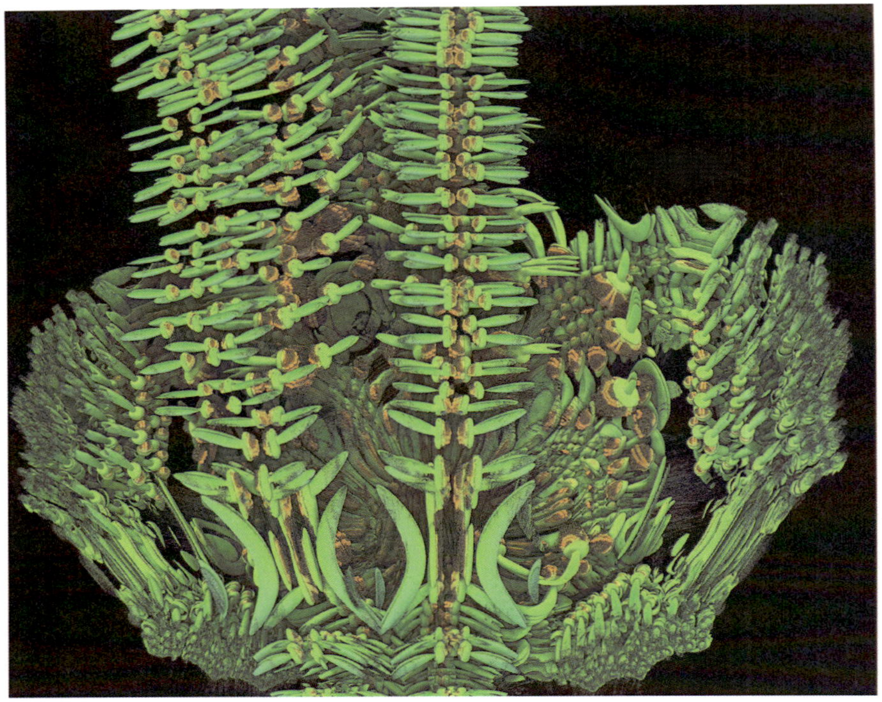

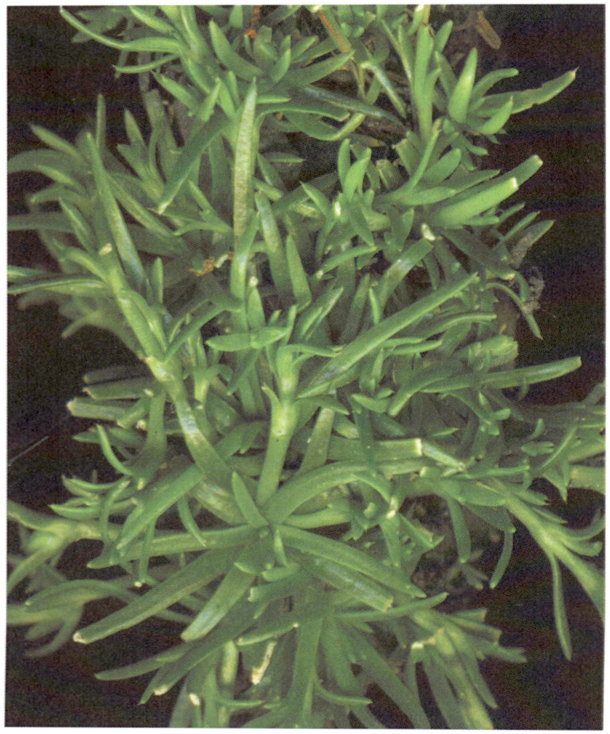

Above*, fractal created in Mandelbulb 3D*

Left*, moss found between patio stones and scanned on an Epson 4490 photo scanner at extremely high magnification (4800 ppi)*

Right*, close-up digital photo of a hosta leaf*

Opposite page*, fractal image created in Mandelbulb 3D*

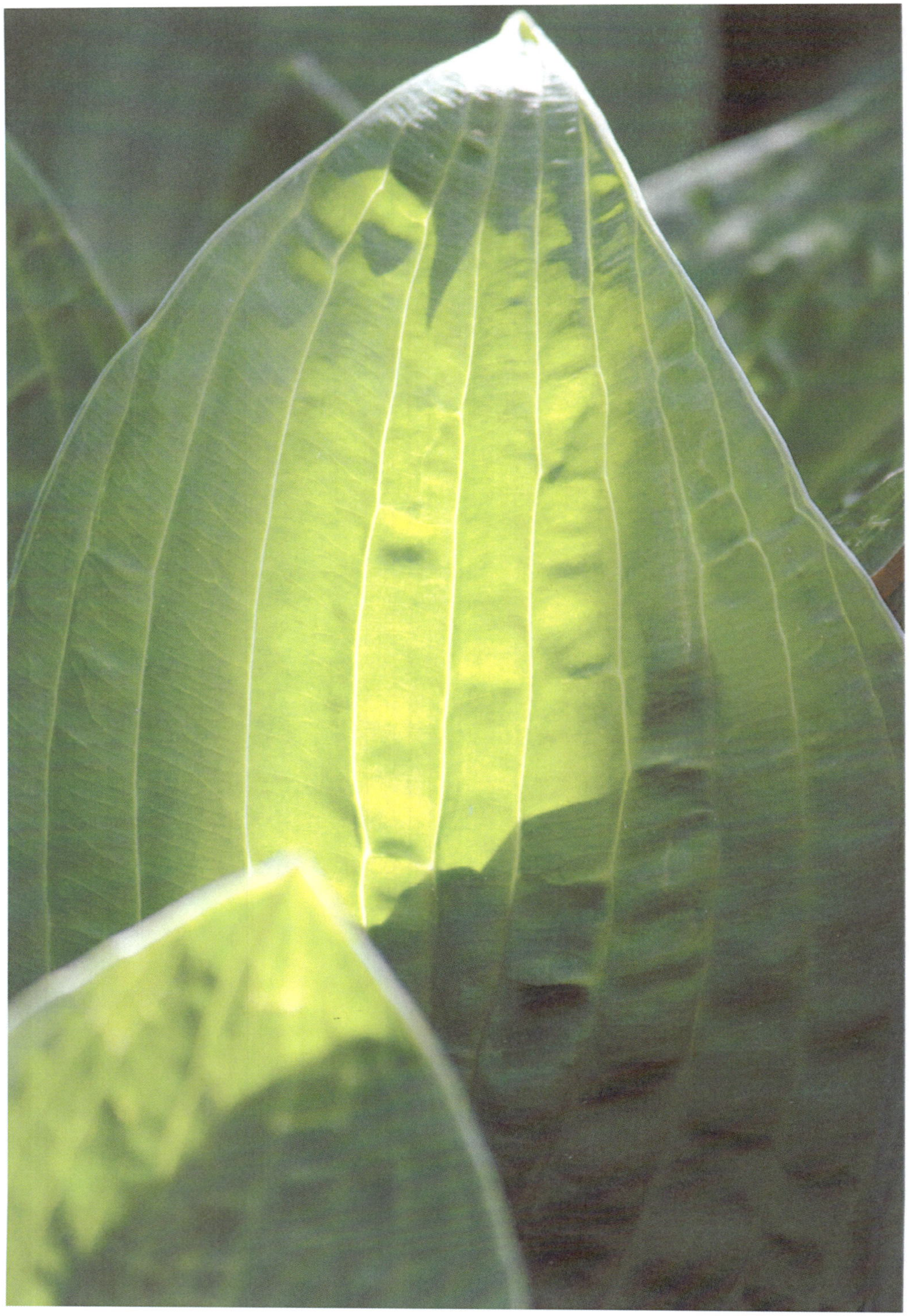

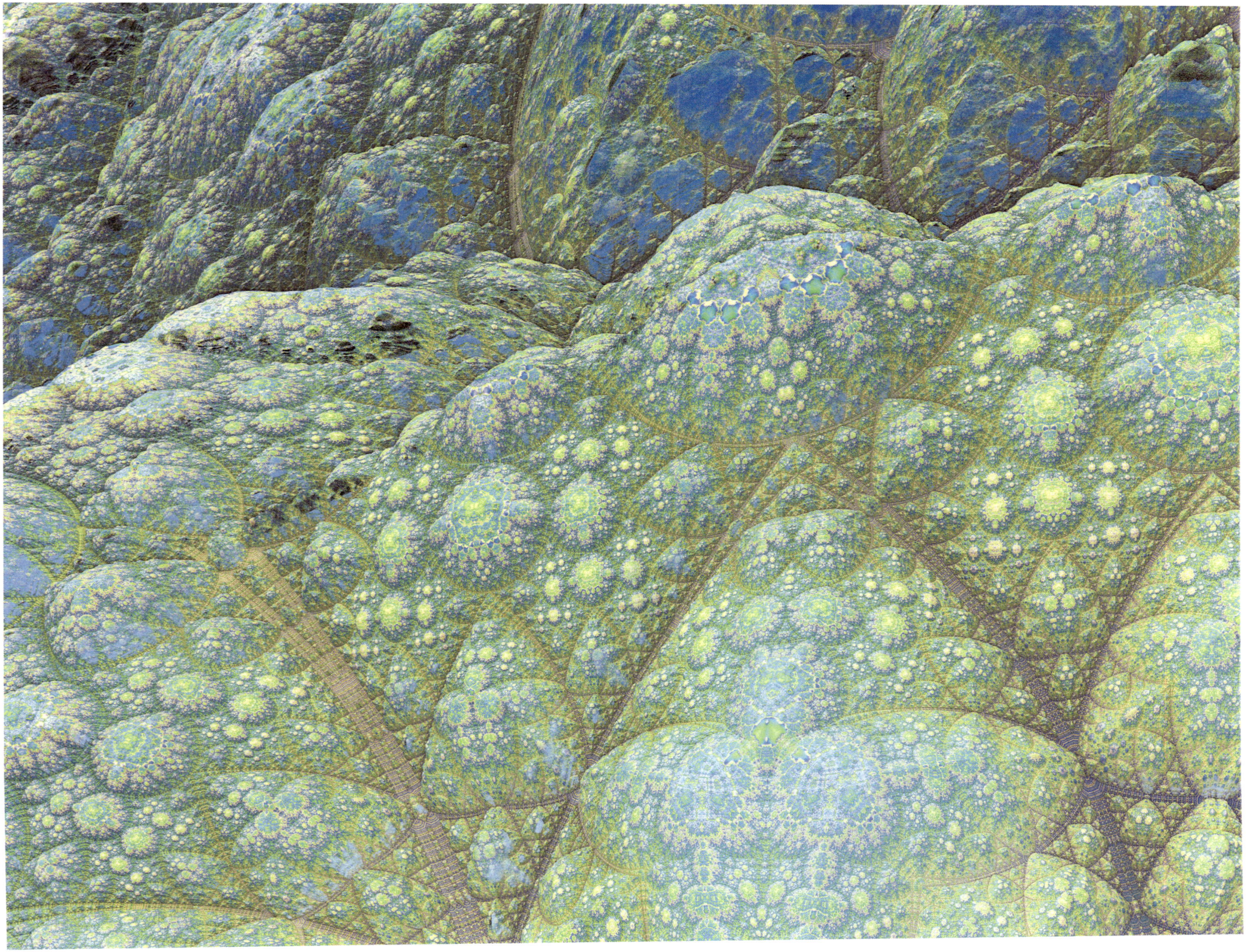

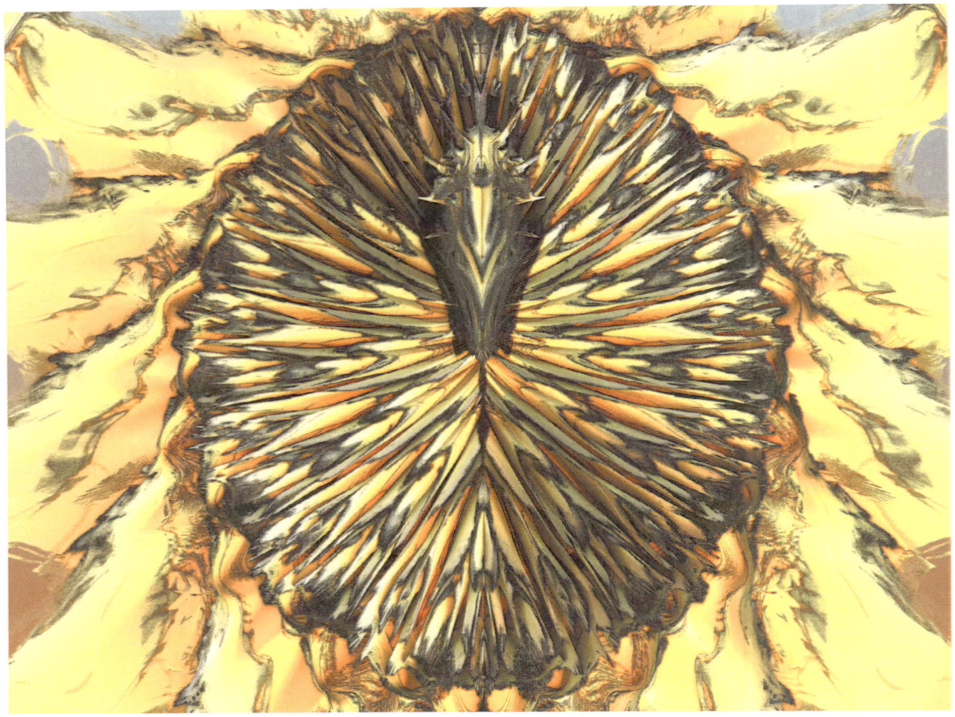
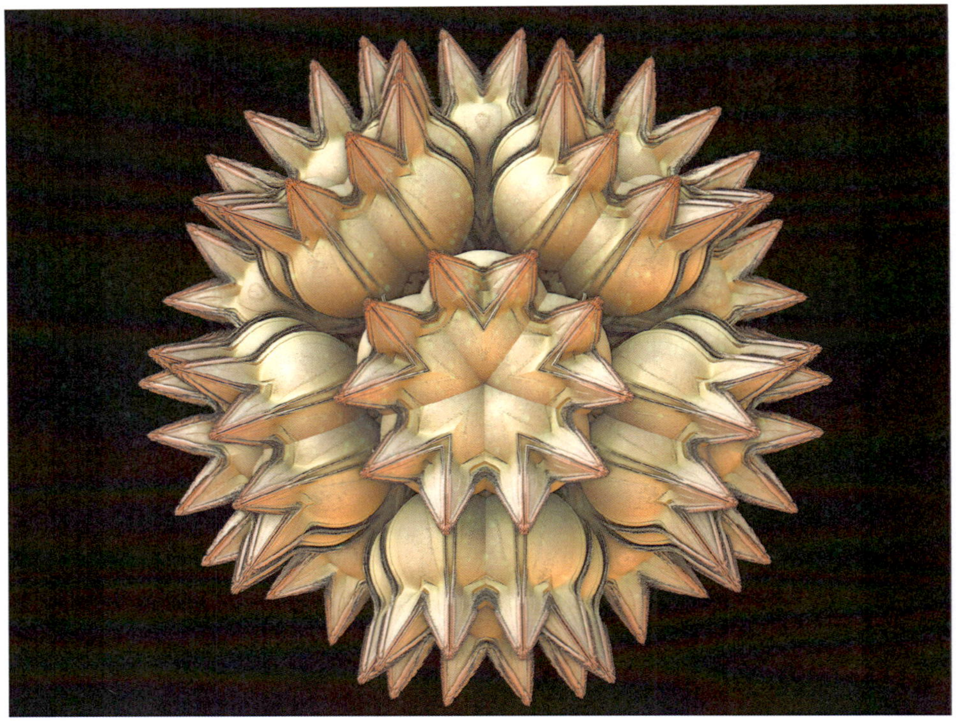
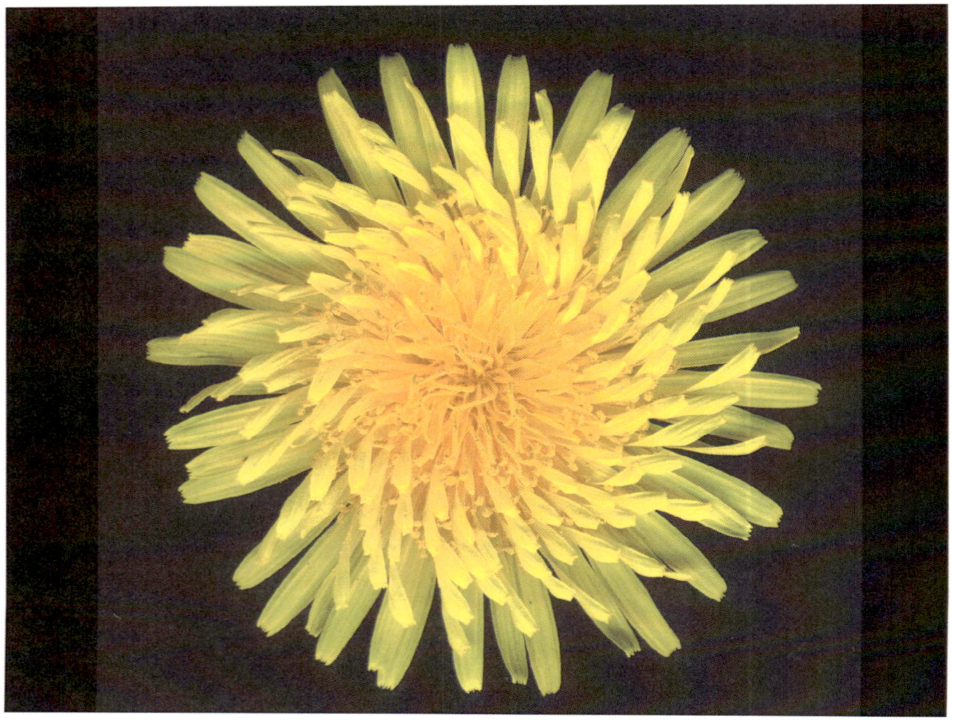
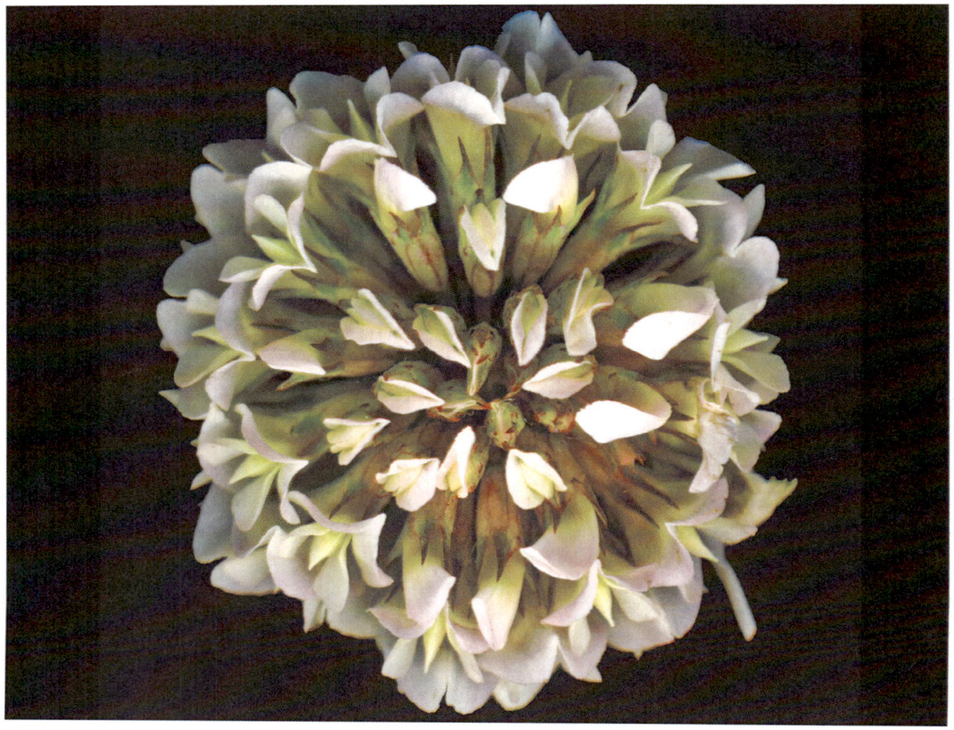

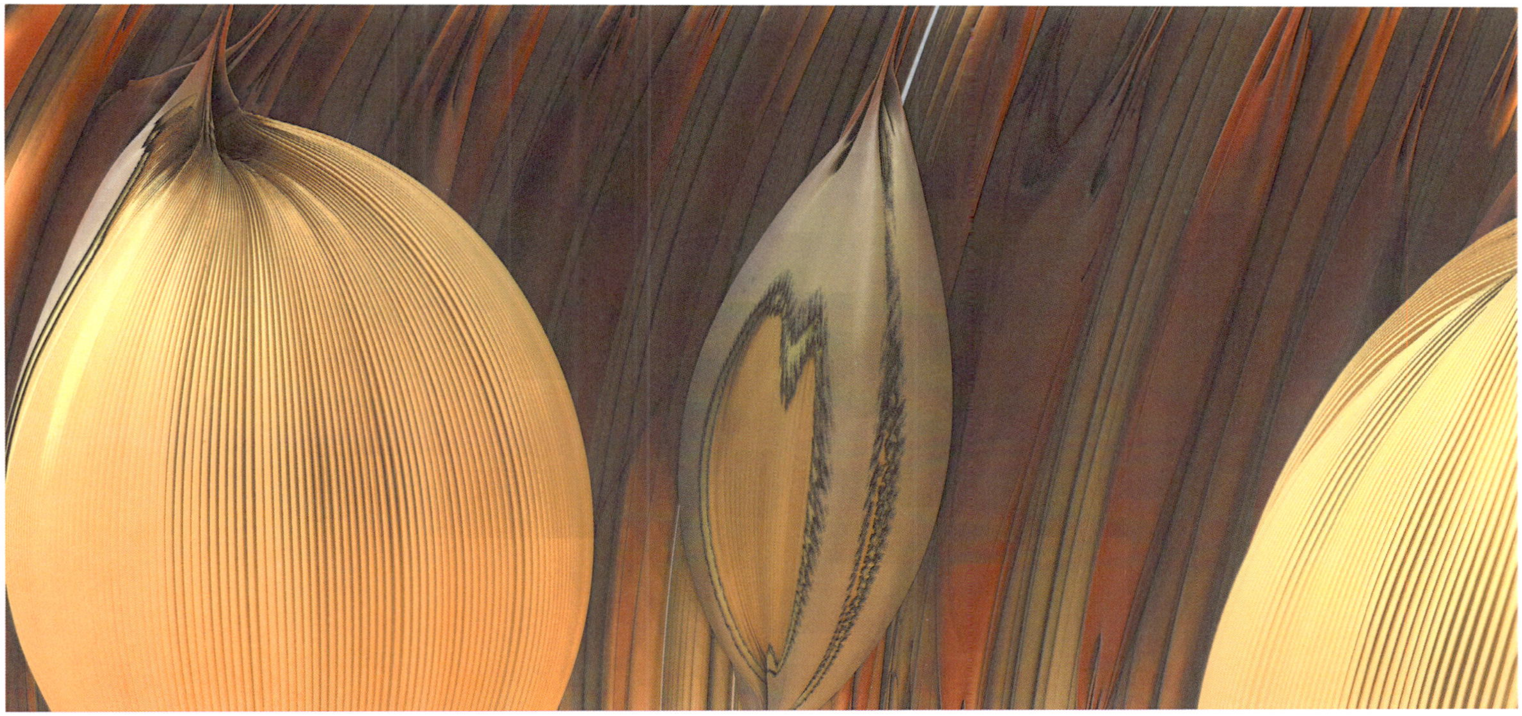

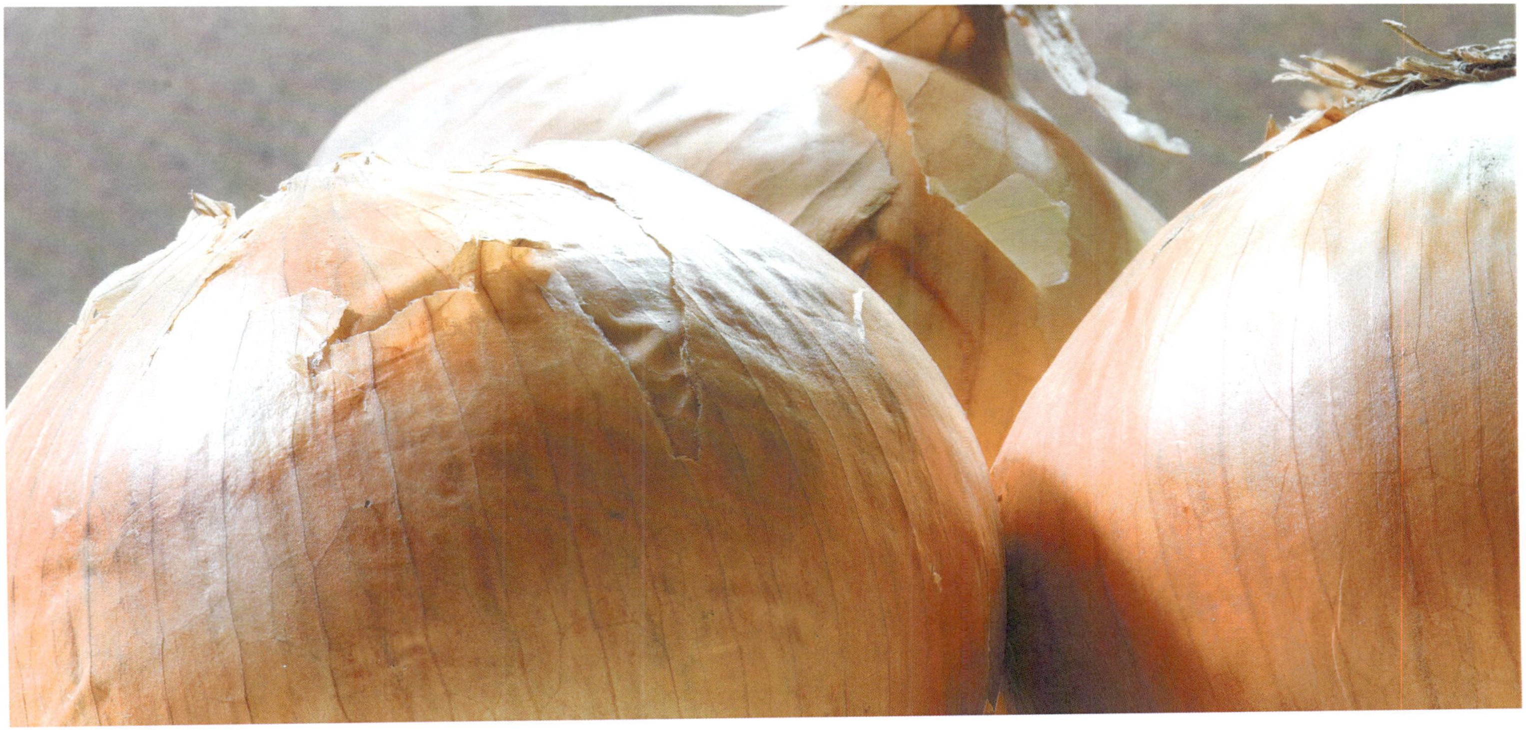

Sometimes fractal images may closely resemble real-world plants. The images ***along the top*** *of these two pages are fractals generated by Mandelbulb 3D.*

The ***bottom images*** *are* ***from left to right, beginning on the opposite page****, a dandelion flower scanned by an Epson 4490 photo scanner at 4800 ppi, a clover flower scanned by the same device, and on this page, onions photographed by a digital camera.*

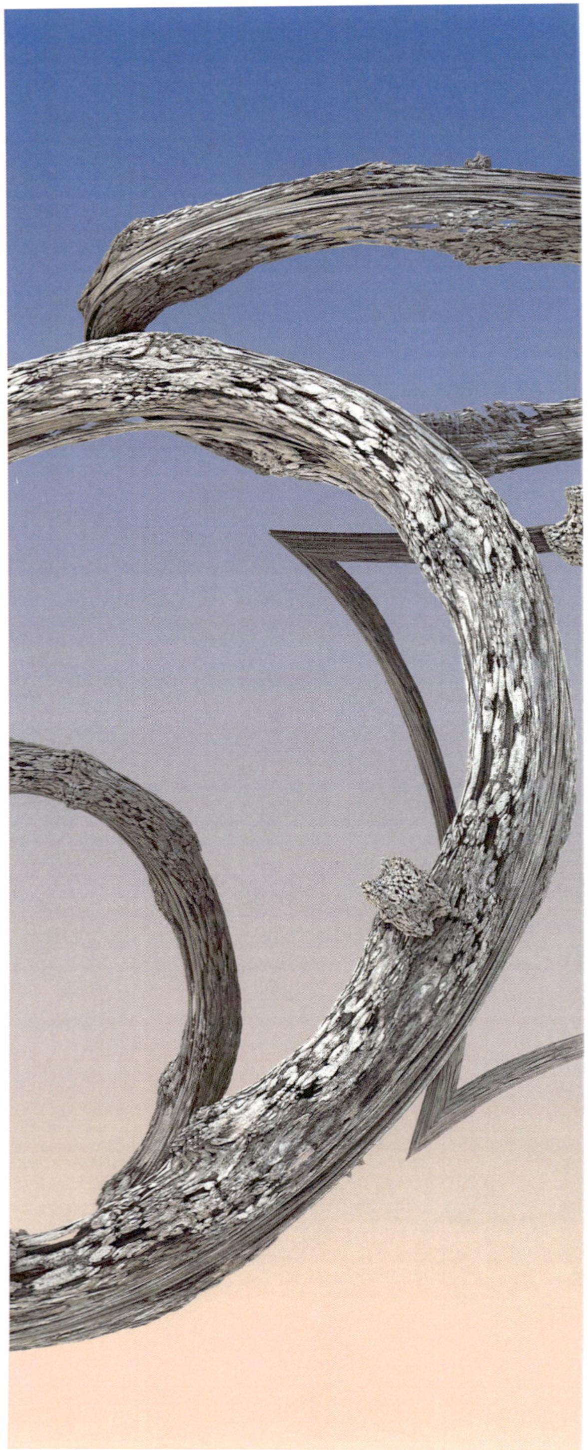
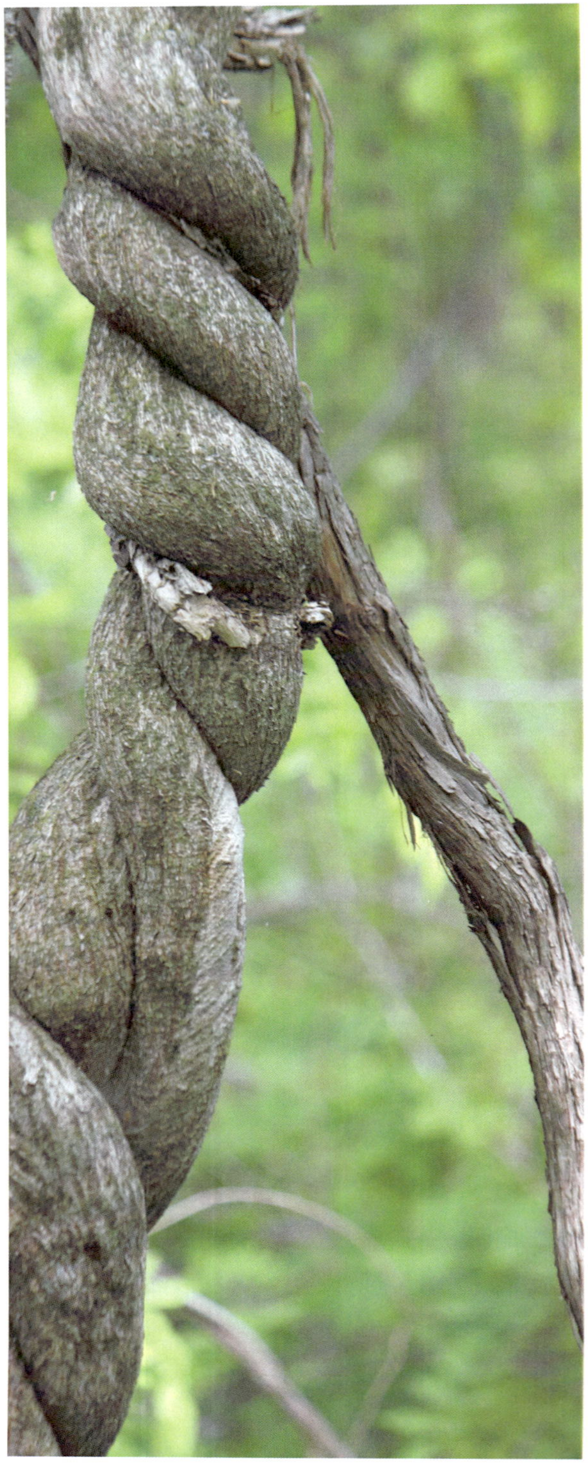
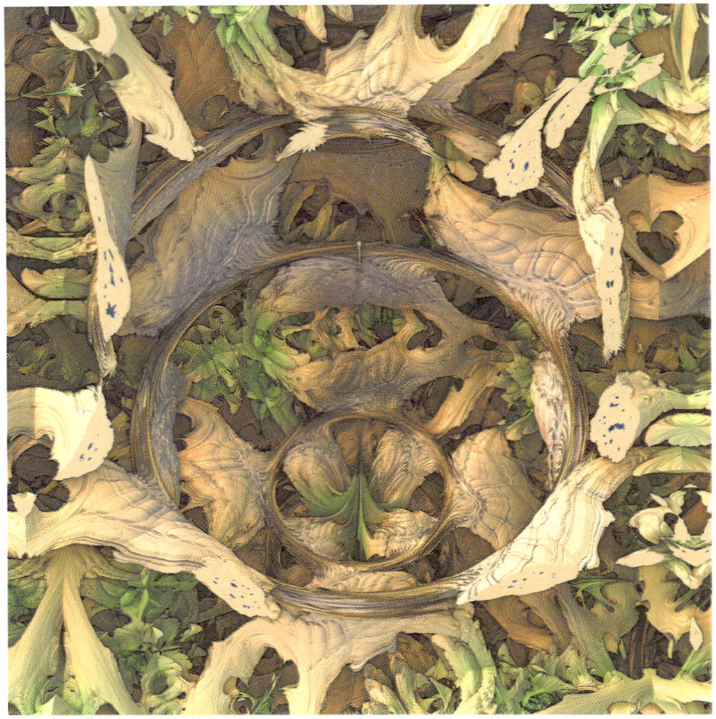
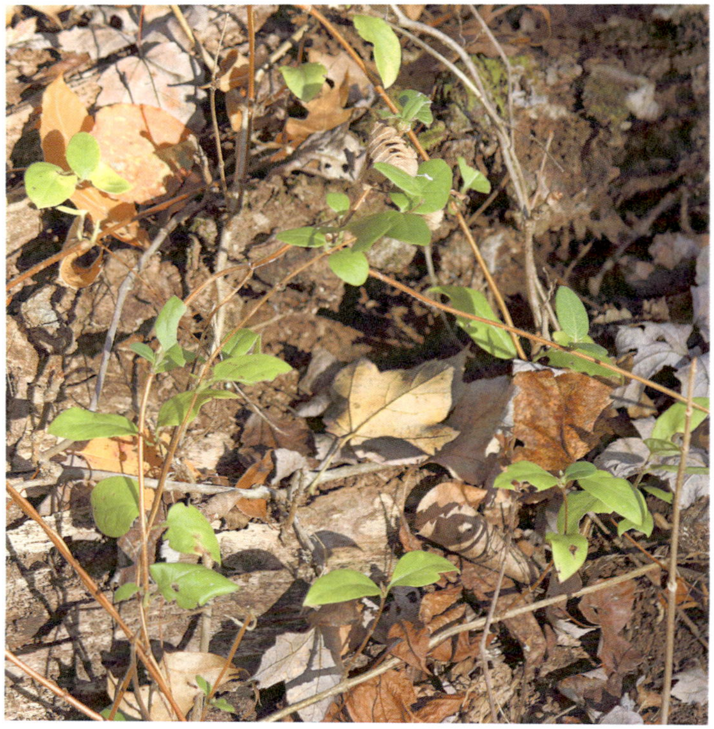

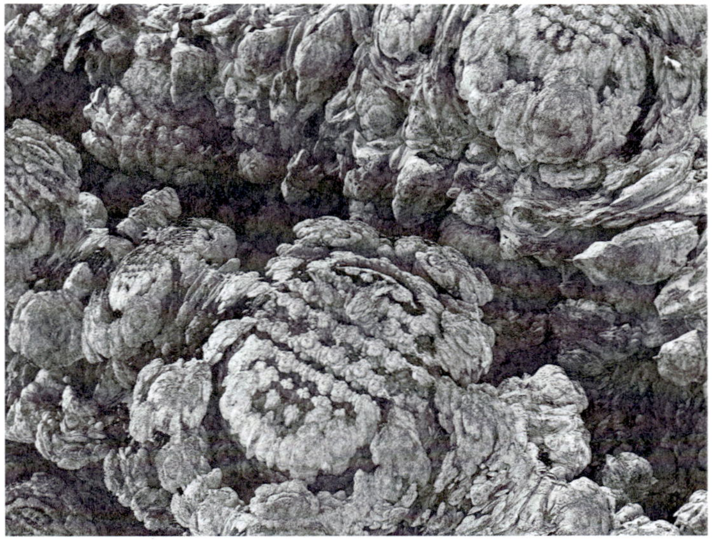

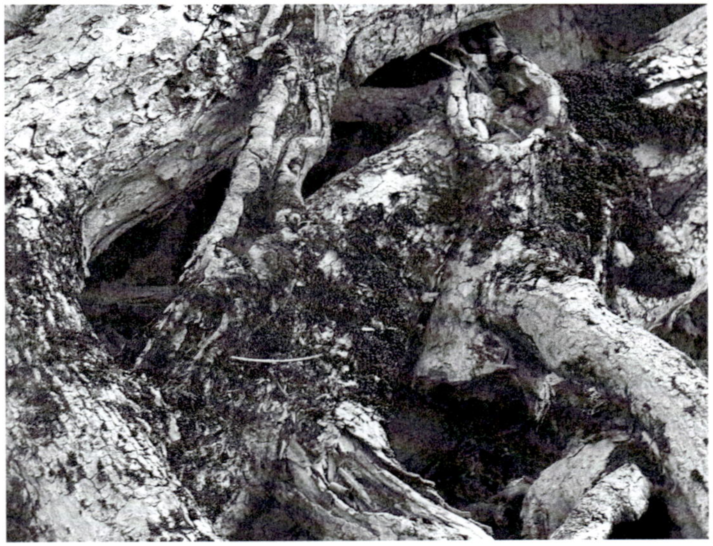

Opposite page, far-left, *fractal image;* **to the right or middle column,** *twisted vines in the woods.* **Opposite page, top-right,** *fractal image, and* **bottom-right,** *digital photo of a vine and fallen leaves in the forest.*

This page, immediate column, top, *fractal image;* **below,** *digital photo of exposed tree roots.* **Immediately to the right,** *ivy growing on a nearby building wall,* **and far-right,** *a fractal image. All fractals were imaged in Mandelbulb 3D.*

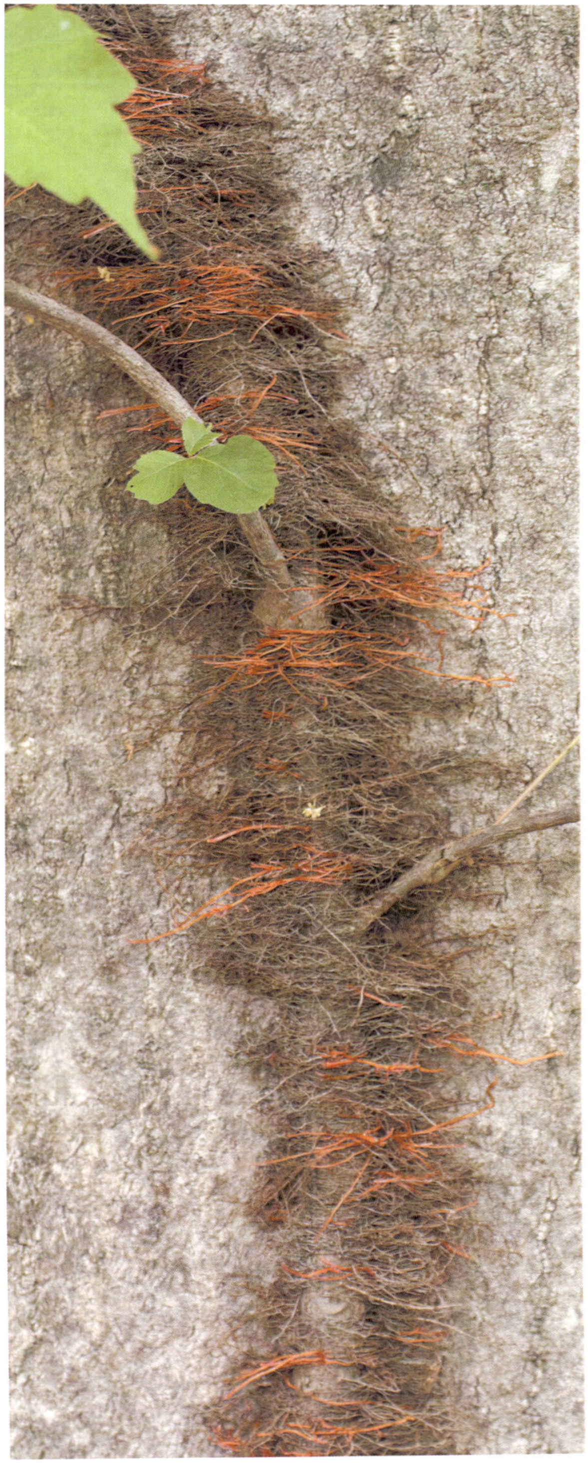

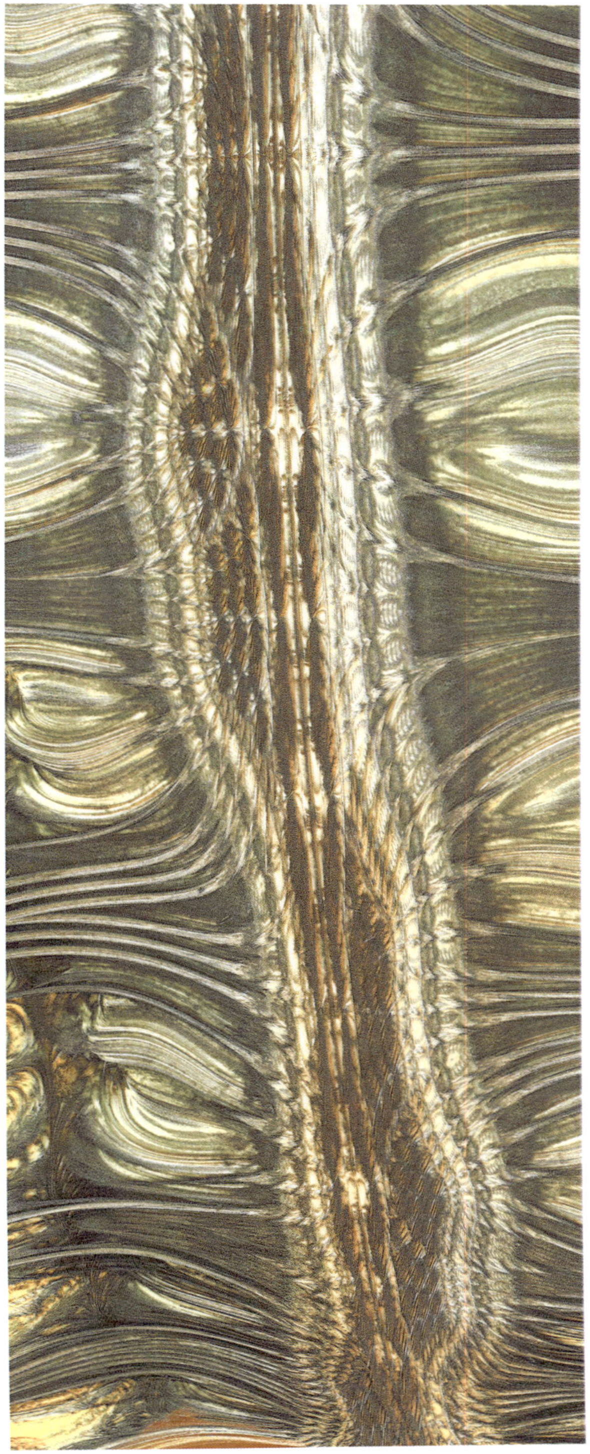

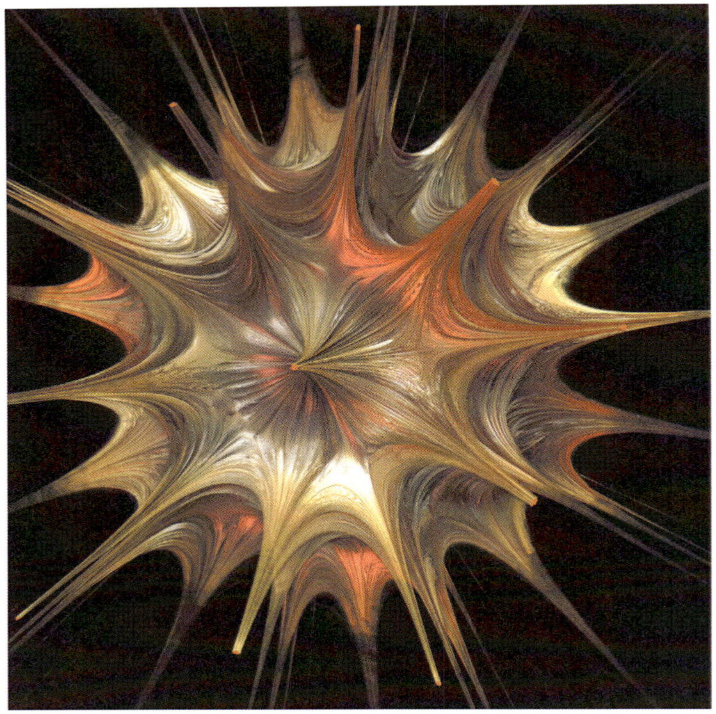

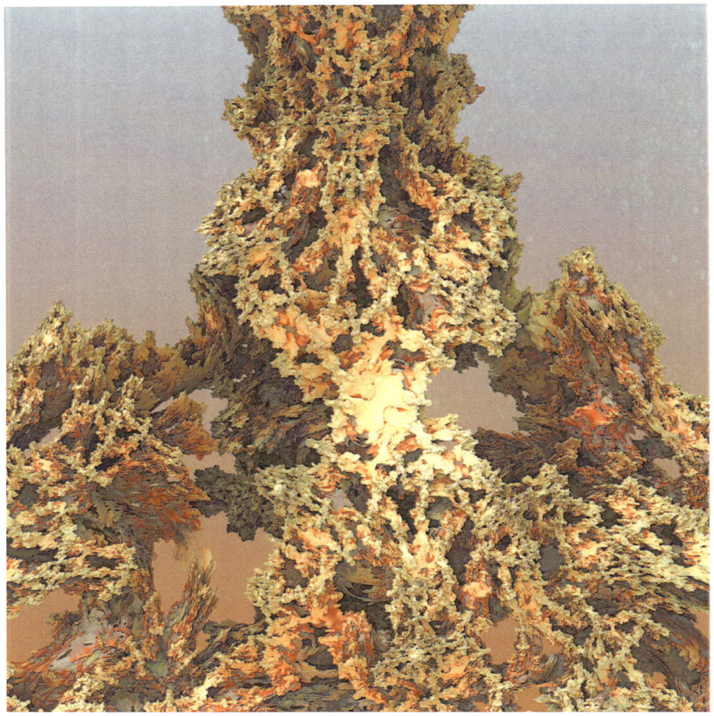

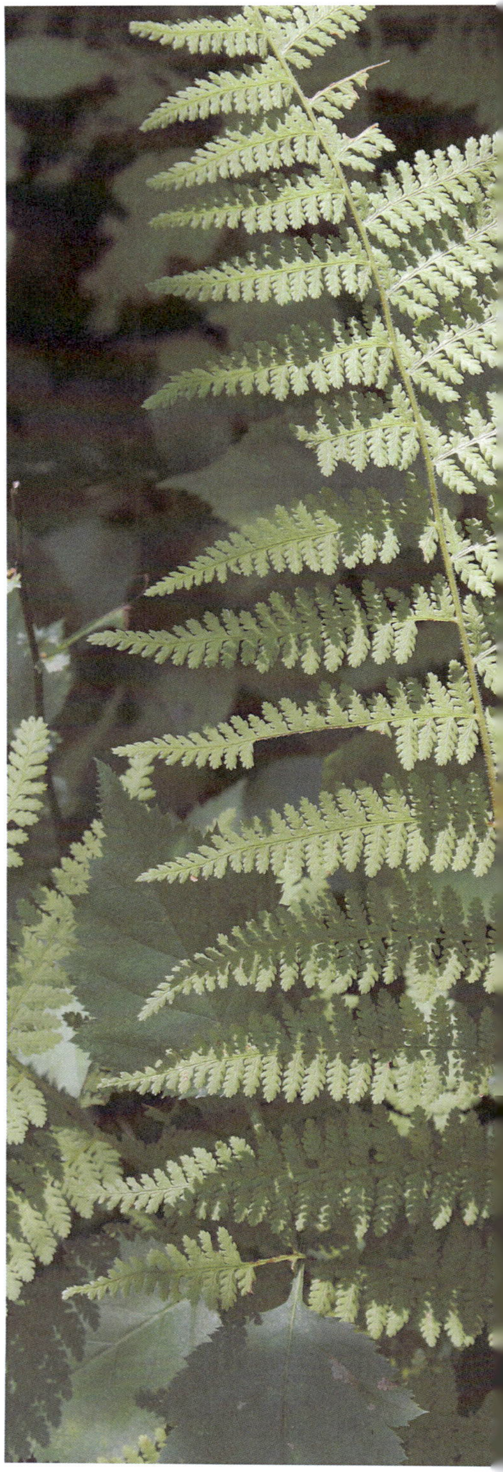

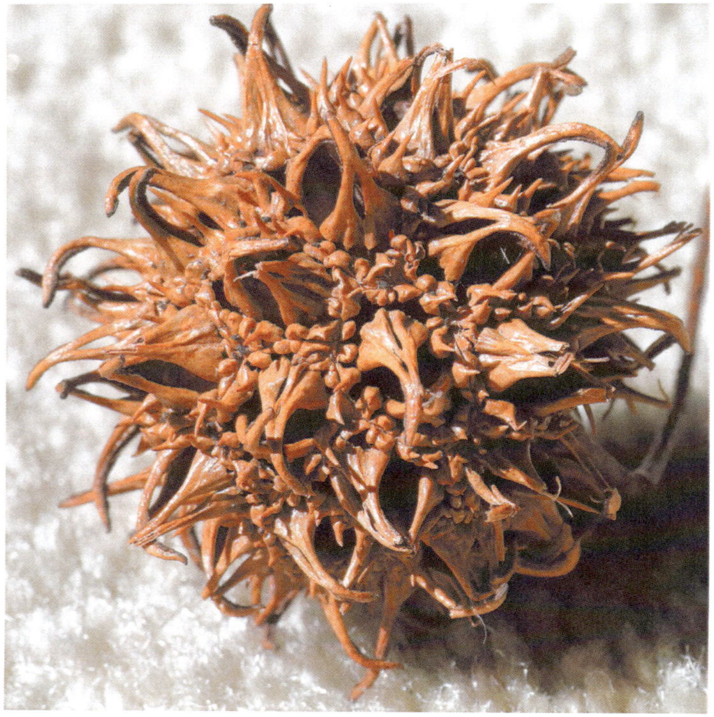

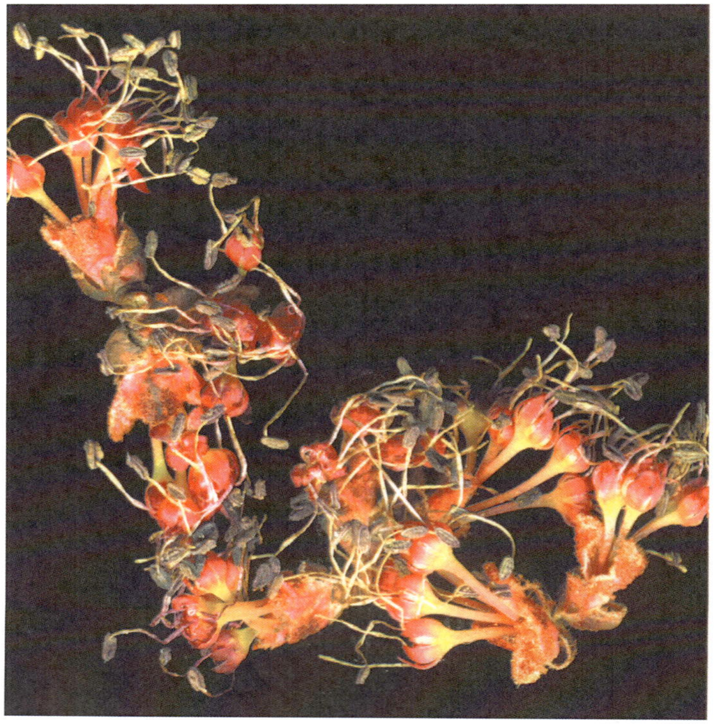

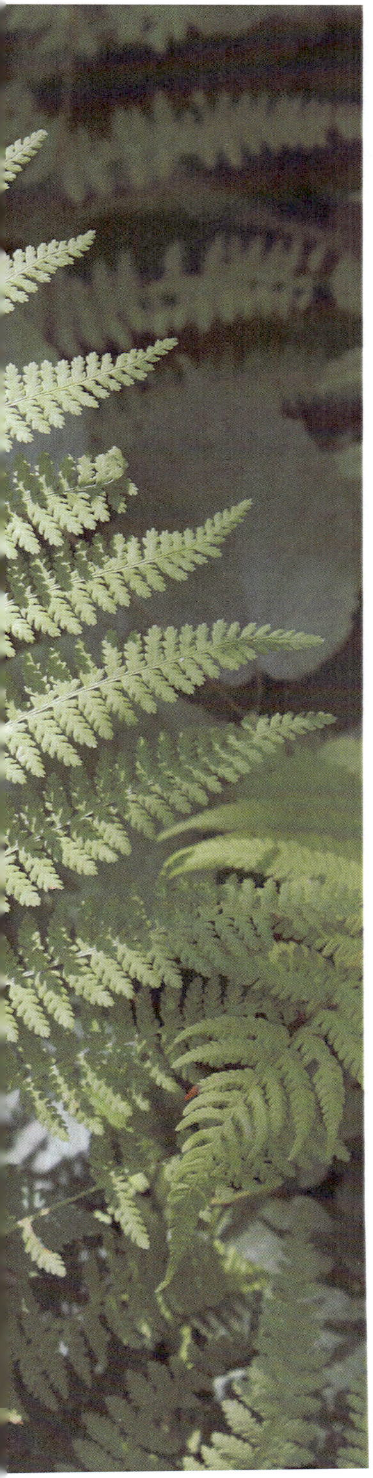

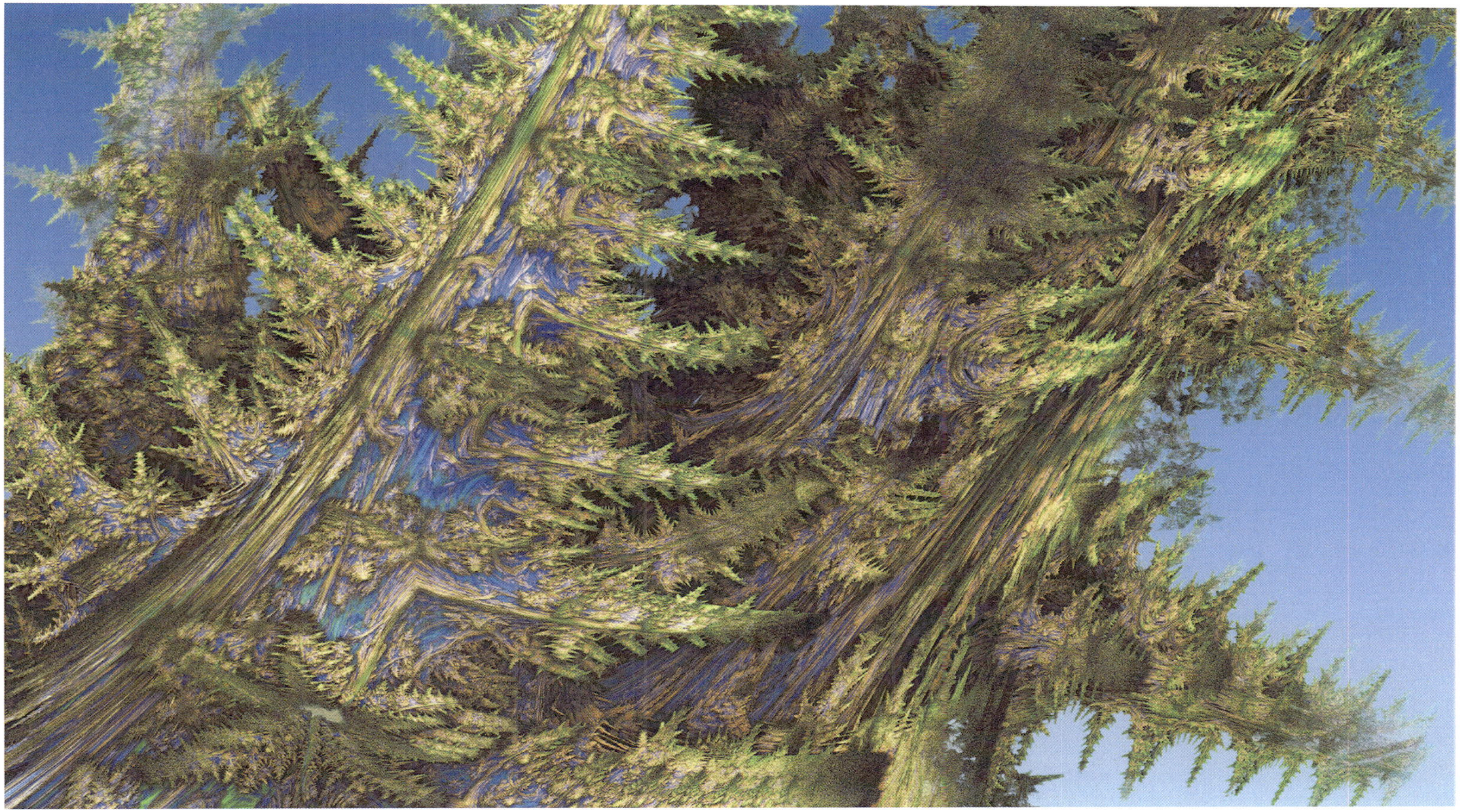

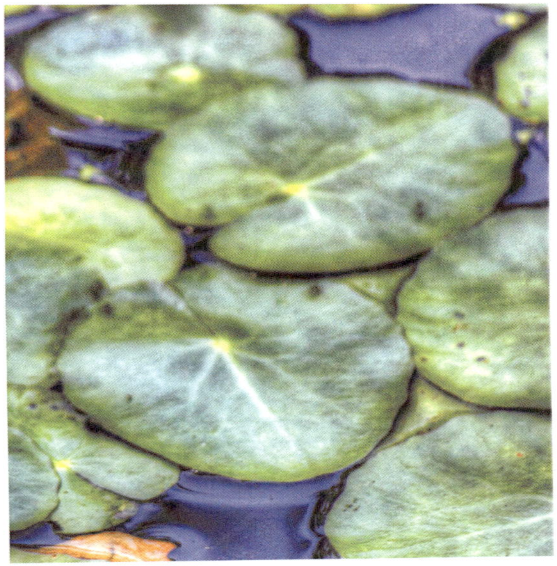

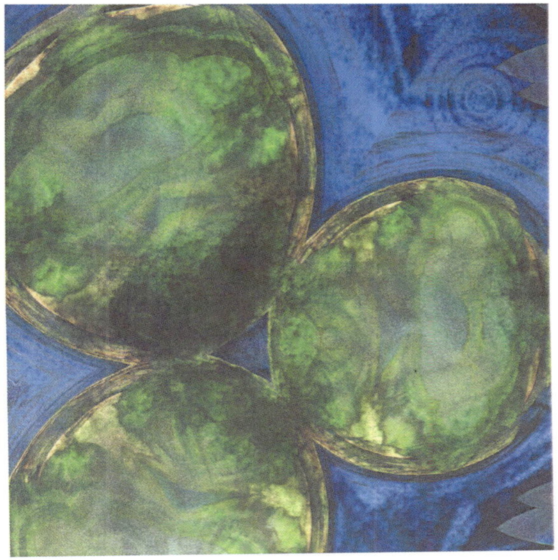

Opposite page, far-left, top, *fractal image;* **and immediately below,** *a seed pod from a tree photographed with a macro lens.* **Middle column, top,** *a fractal image, and* **immediately below,** *a pin oak tree blossom imaged on the Epson 4490 photo scanner.*

Center-spread, *a photo of a fern, and* **above-right,** *this fern-like fractal was imaged in Mandelbulb 3D.*

Immediate-left, *fractal image generated by Mandelbulb 3D,* **and to its left,** *lilies on a pond (digital photo, manipulated image).*

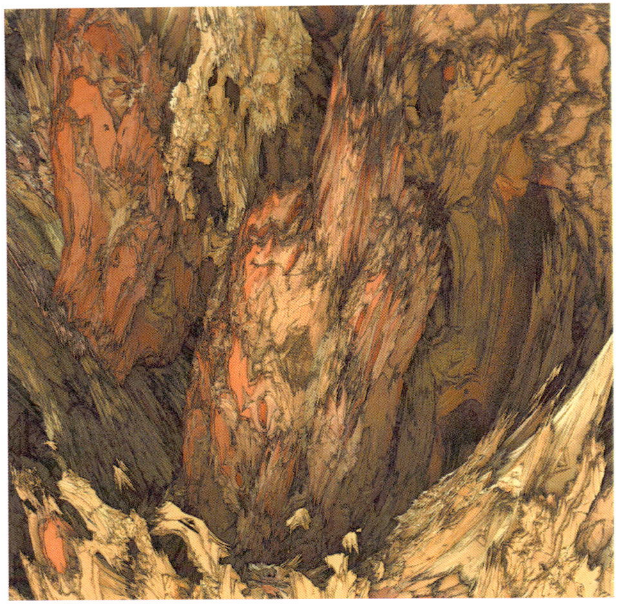
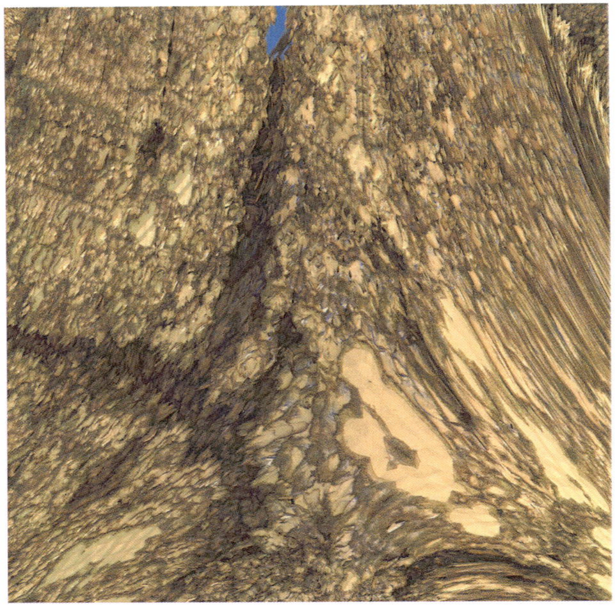
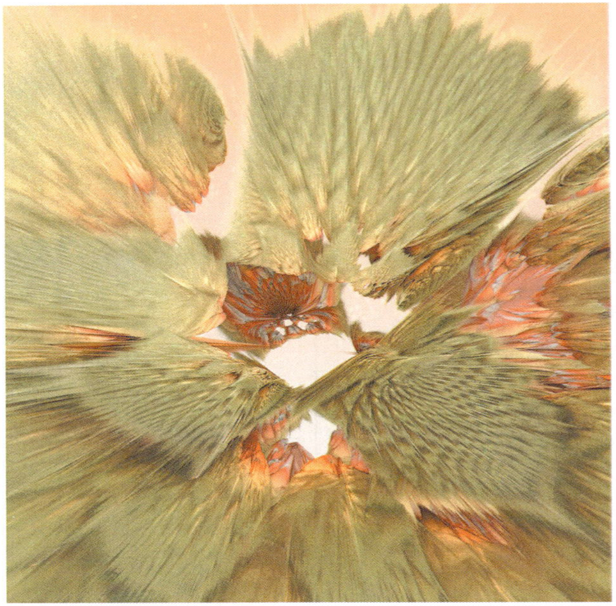
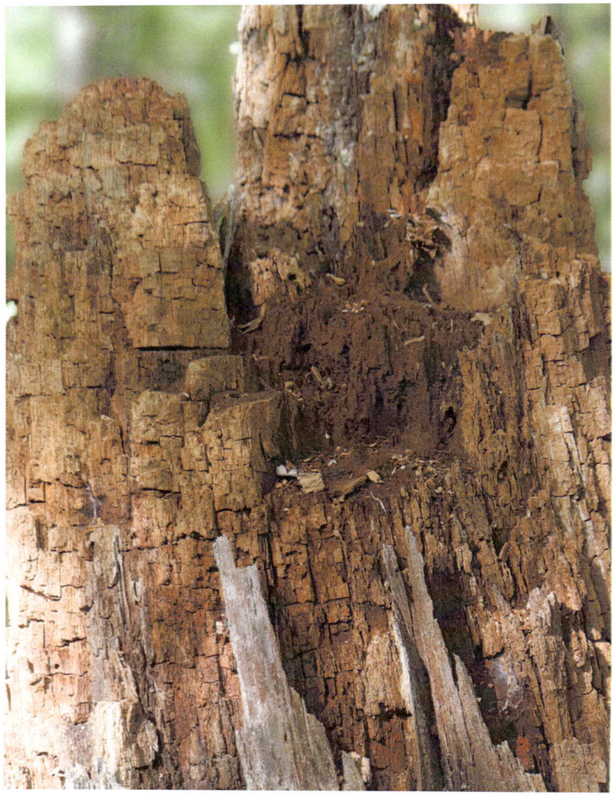
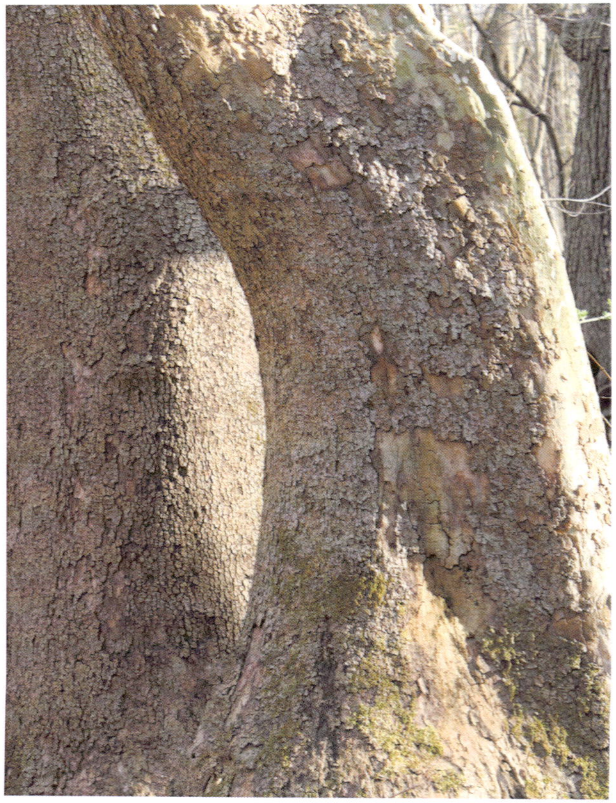
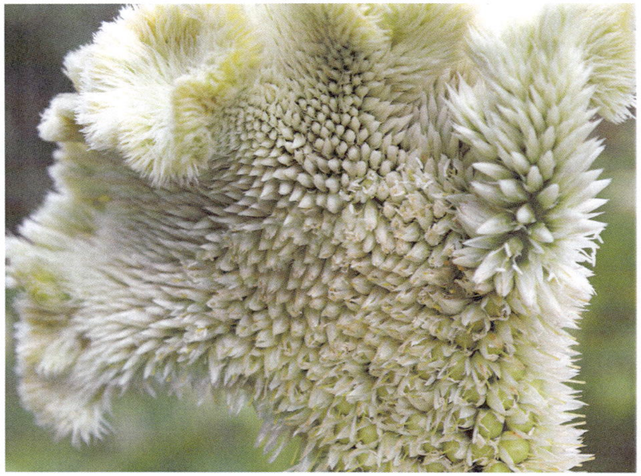

The ***top row*** *of images, generated in Mandelbulb 3D, resembles corresponding images directly below. The* ***bottom*** *digital images, from* ***left to right,*** *are a decaying tree stump in the woods, a pair of trees with patchy bark, and white cockscomb (Celosia)—or plumed cockscomb.*

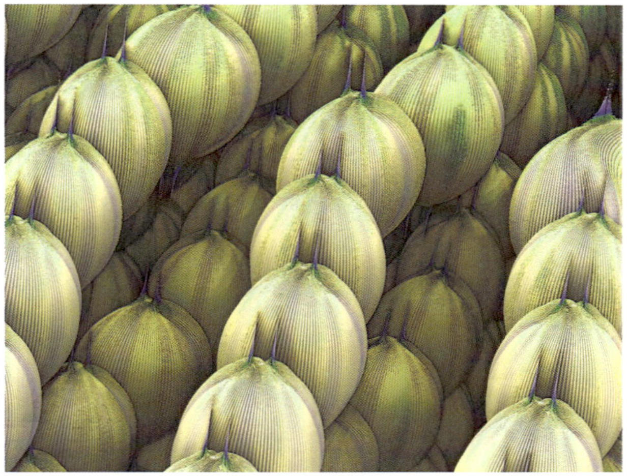

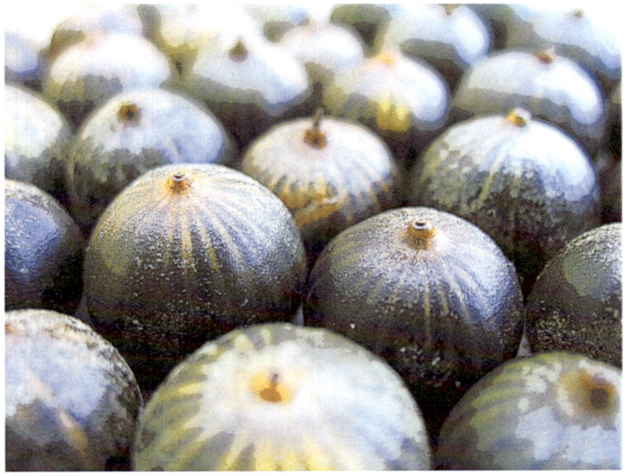

Fractals or real? In **this column the top image** *was generated by Mandelbulb 3D; the* **image below** *is a digital photo (manipulated slightly) of unripe acorns arranged in a matrix fashion.*

To the right (middle column), *a set of photographs* **(top to bottom)** *is paired with a set of analogous fractal images* **(far-right column)**. *The* **top photo** *is a snail shell in shallow creek water; the* **middle** *is a clam shell from a New Jersey beach, and the* **bottom** *is a shelf-like fungus growing on a fallen tree. All fractals in the right column were generated in Mandelbulb 3D.*

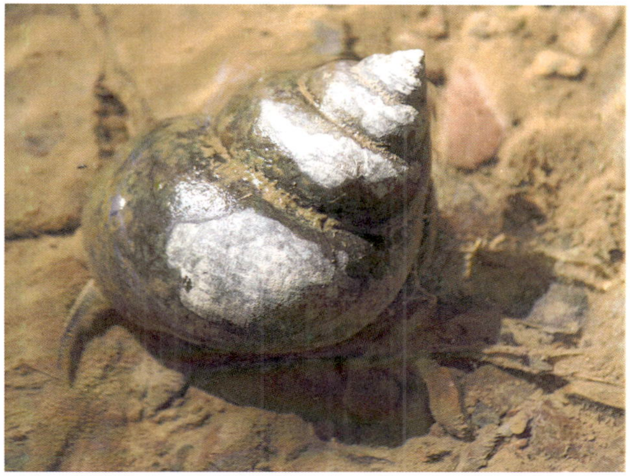

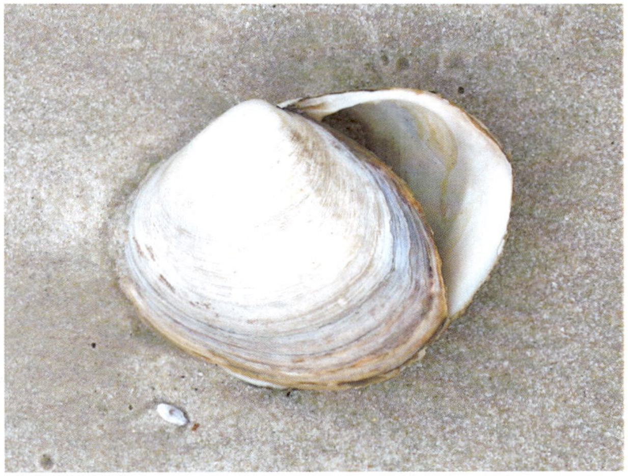

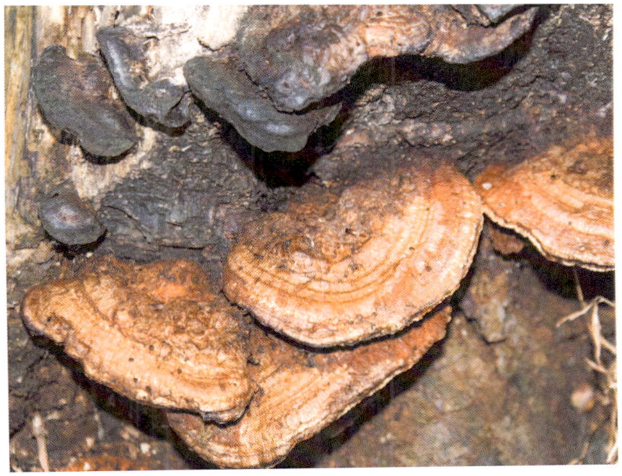

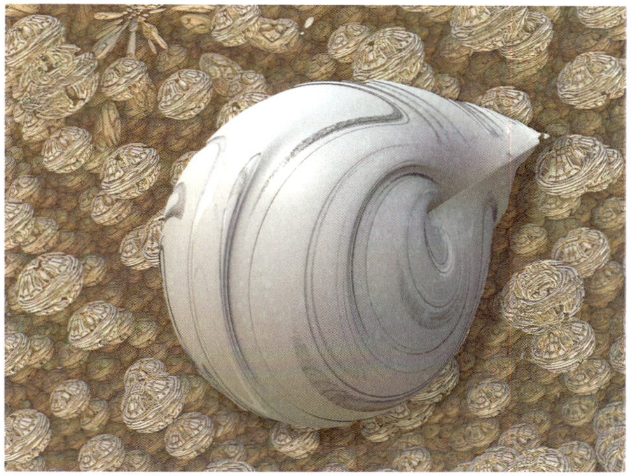

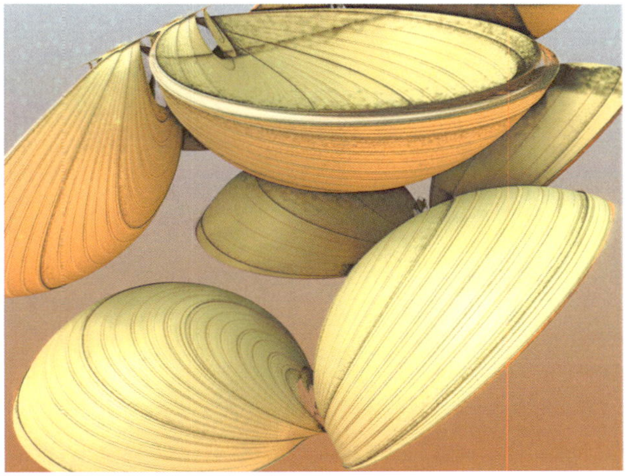

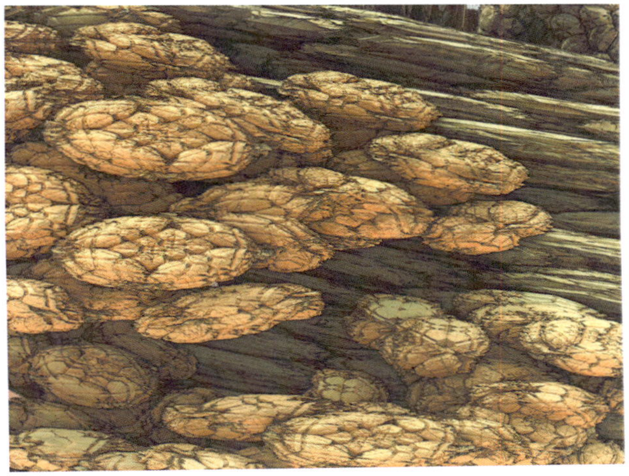

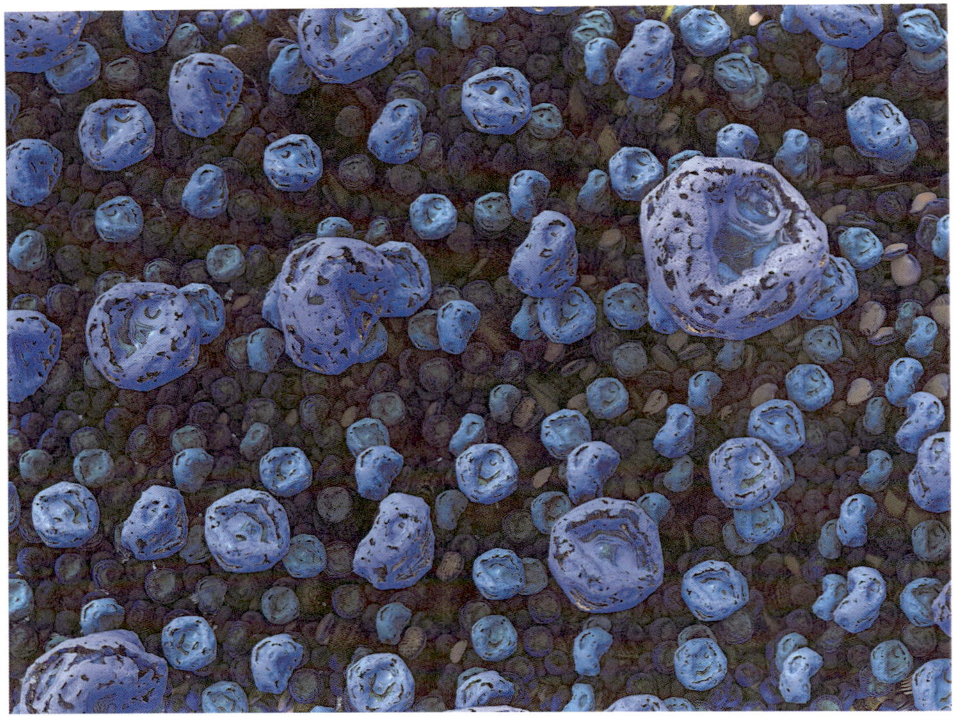
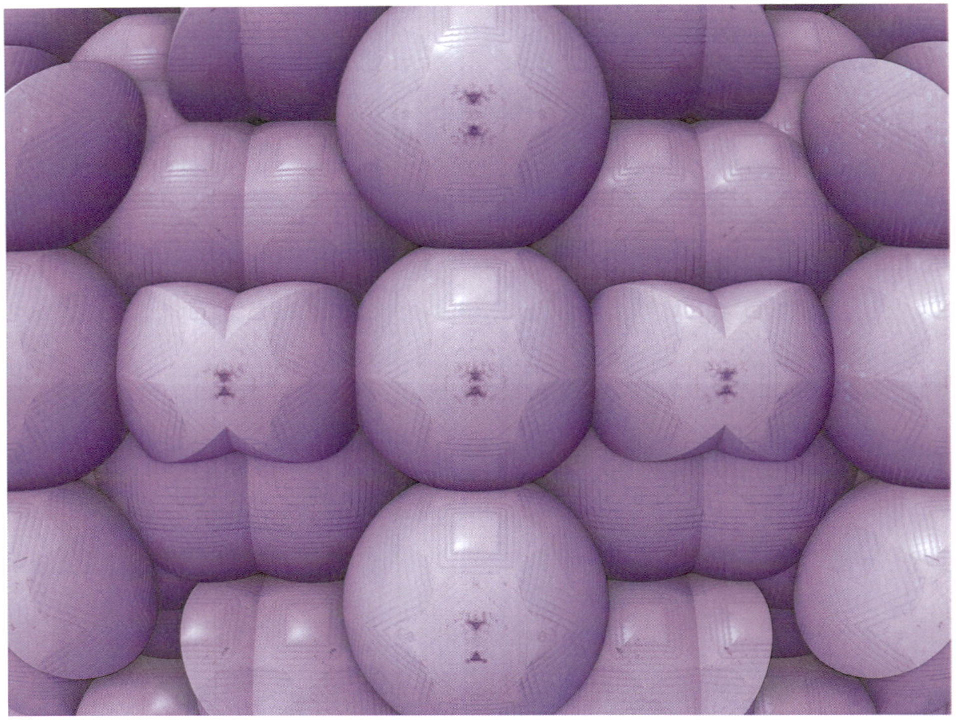
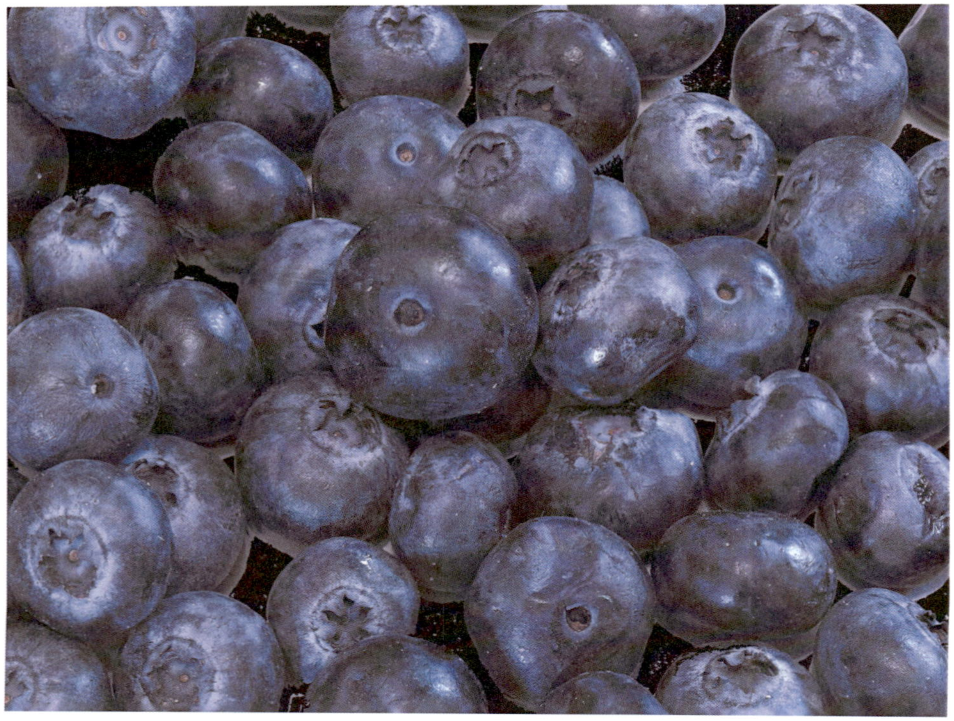
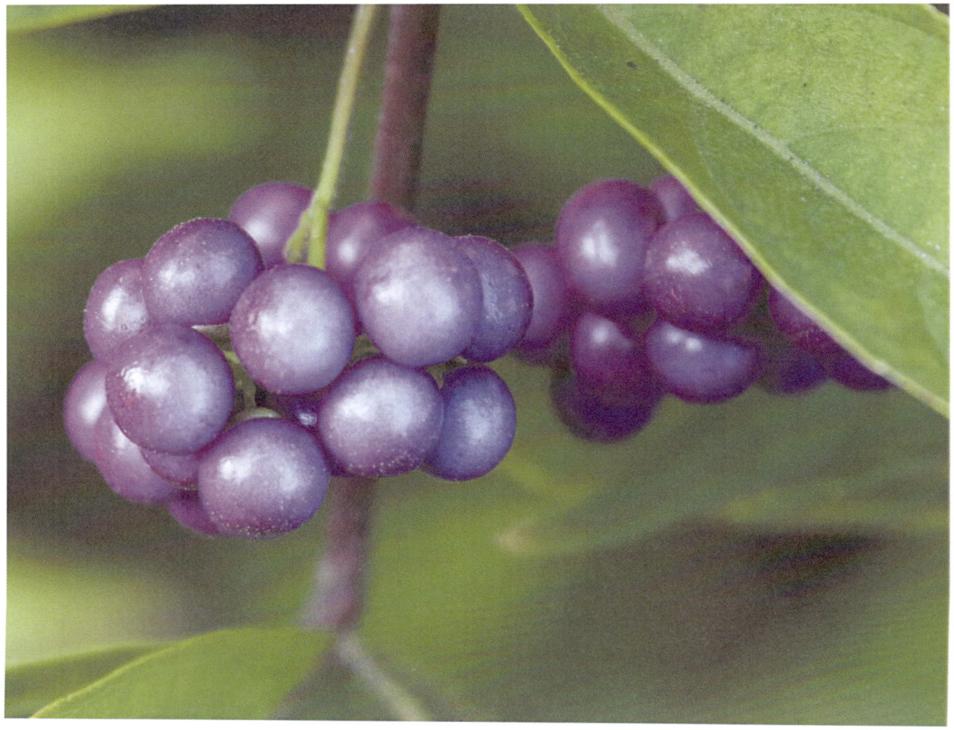

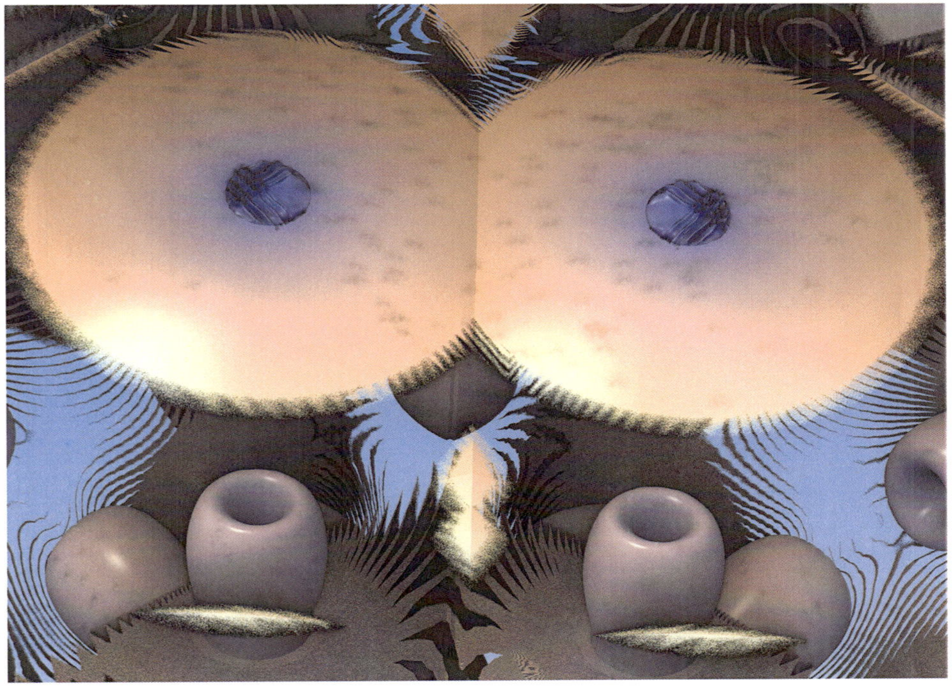

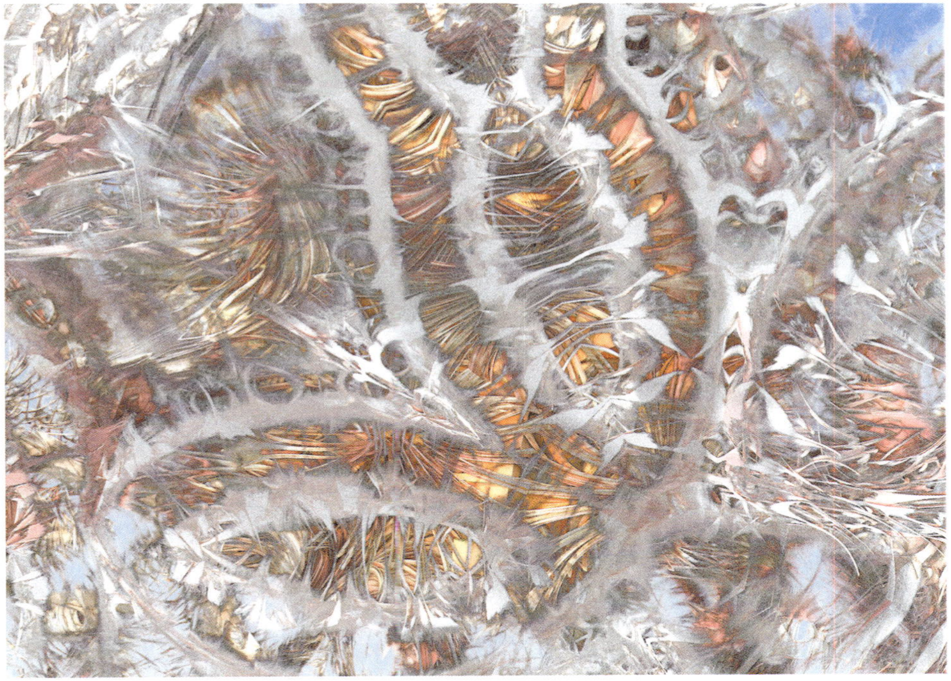

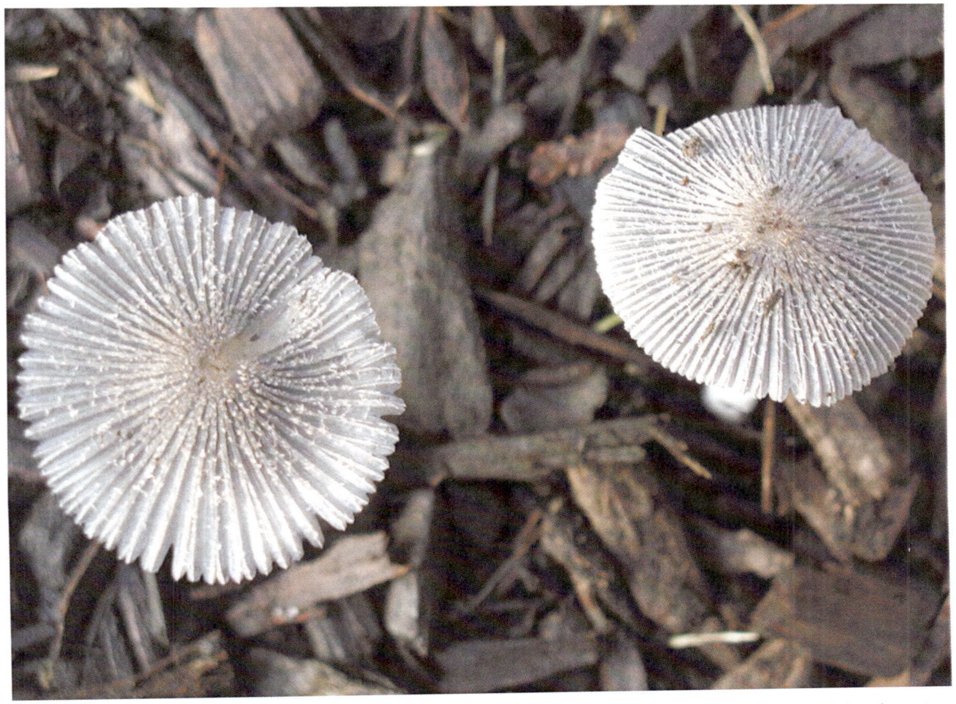

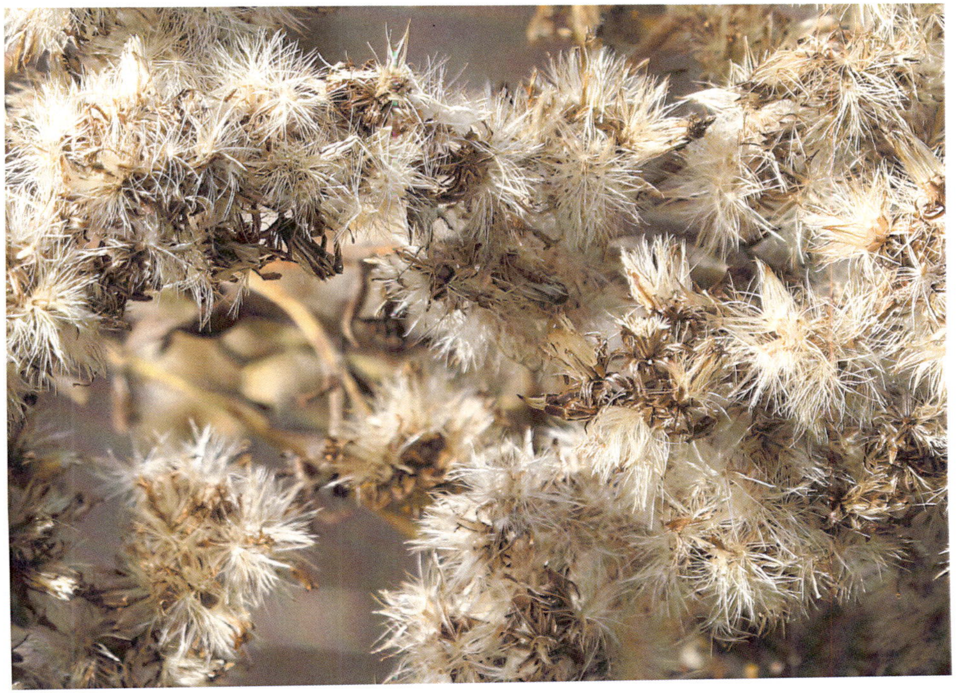

Opposite page, top-left, *fractal blueberries;* ***bottom-left,*** *digital photo of blueberries;* ***top-right,*** *fractal berries;* ***bottom-right,*** *digital image of berries from an evergreen shrub.* ***This page, top-left,*** *fractal mushrooms;* ***bottom-left,*** *fragile mushrooms (found in Pa.);* ***top-right,*** *fractal image;* ***bottom-right,*** *thistles going to seed (digital photo).*

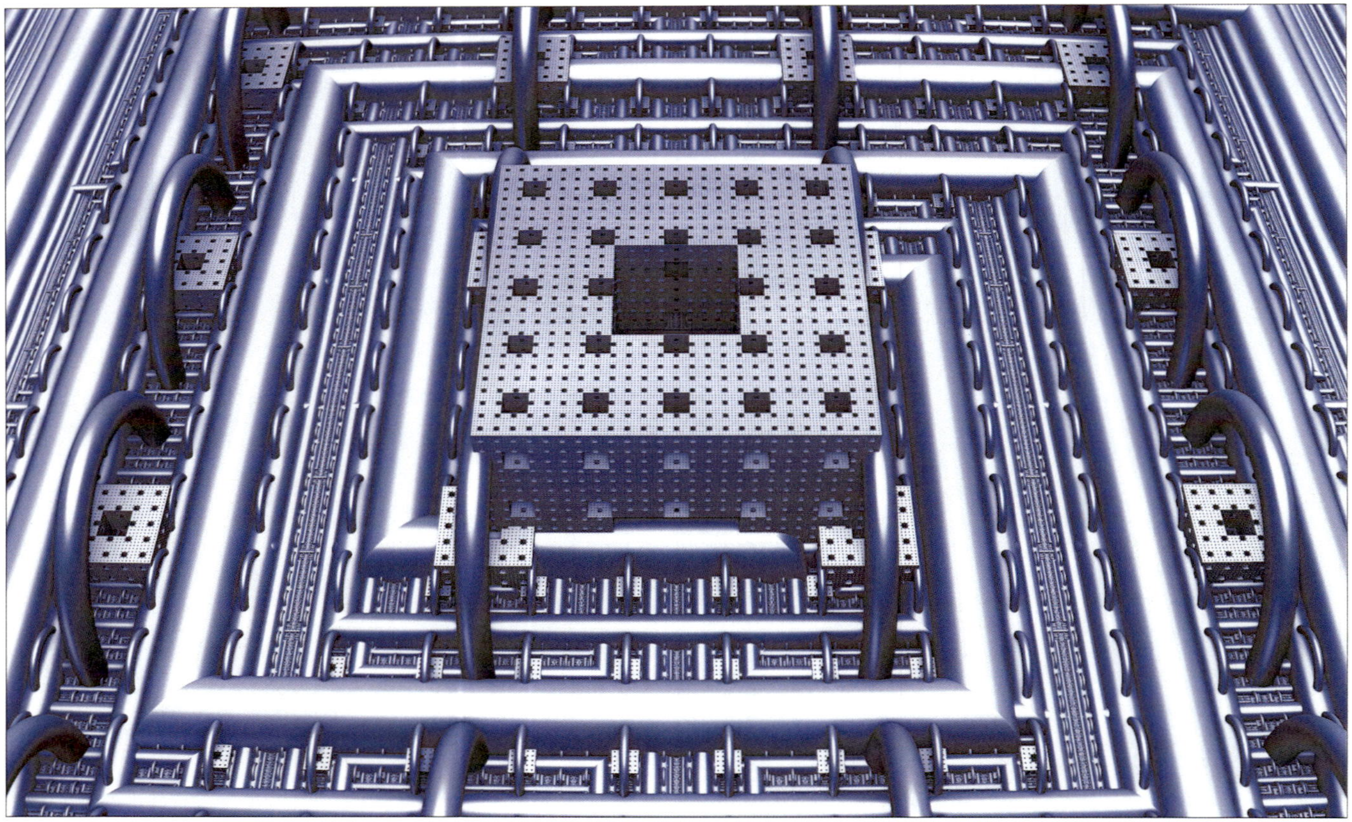

Fractal image created in Mandelbulb 3D

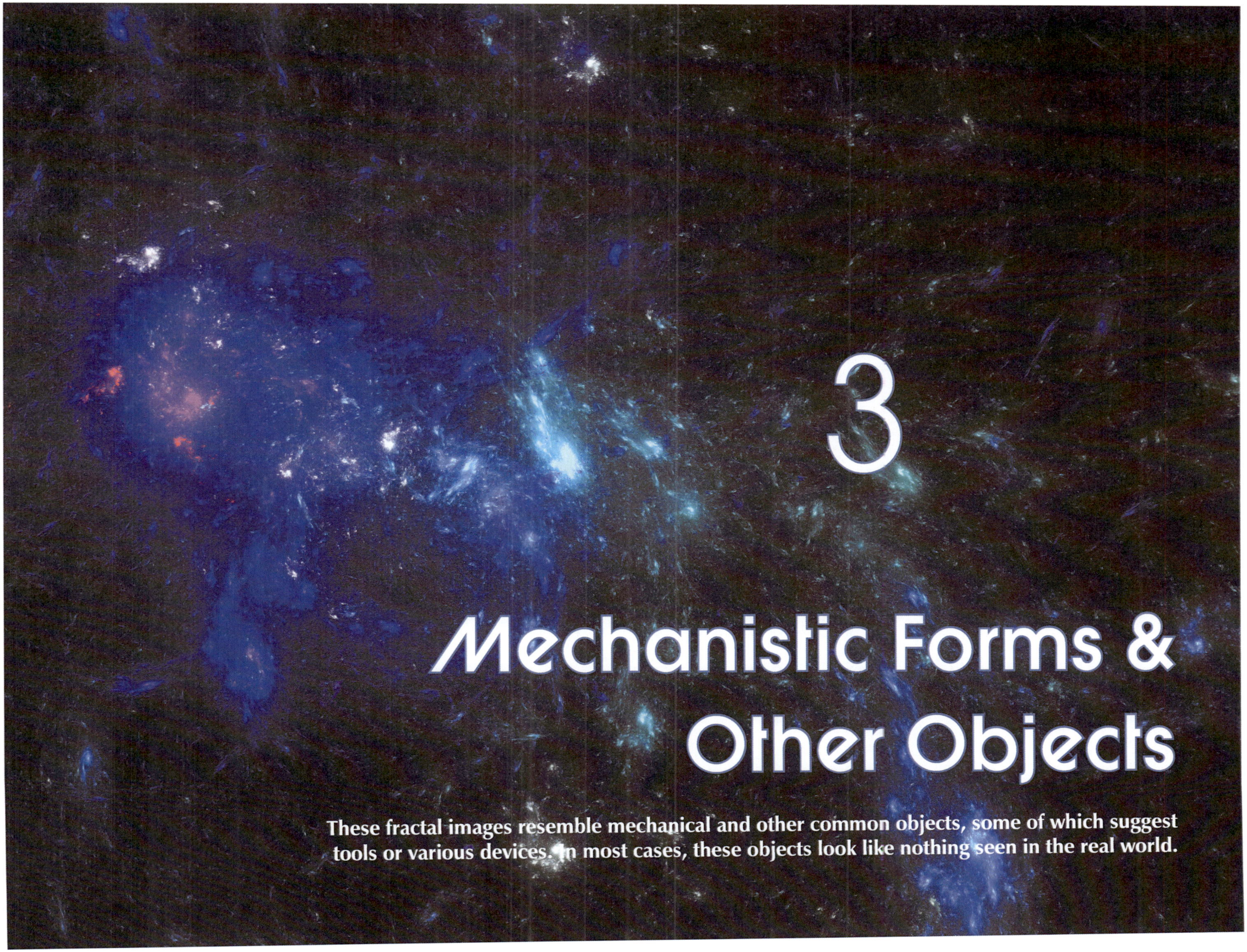

3

Mechanistic Forms & Other Objects

These fractal images resemble mechanical and other common objects, some of which suggest tools or various devices. In most cases, these objects look like nothing seen in the real world.

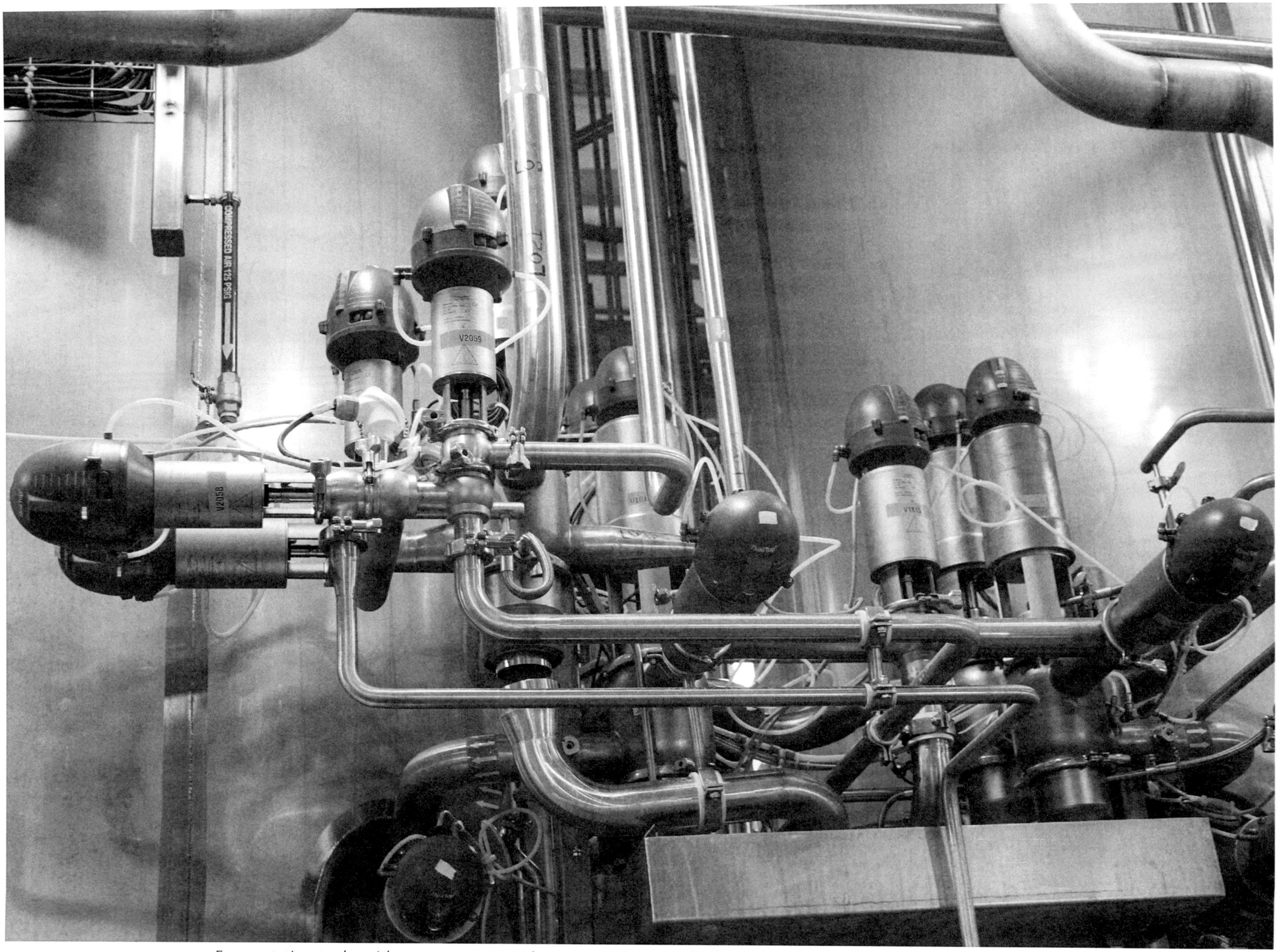

Fermentation tanks with smart sensors and actuators photographed at a dairy food processing plant (digital photo)

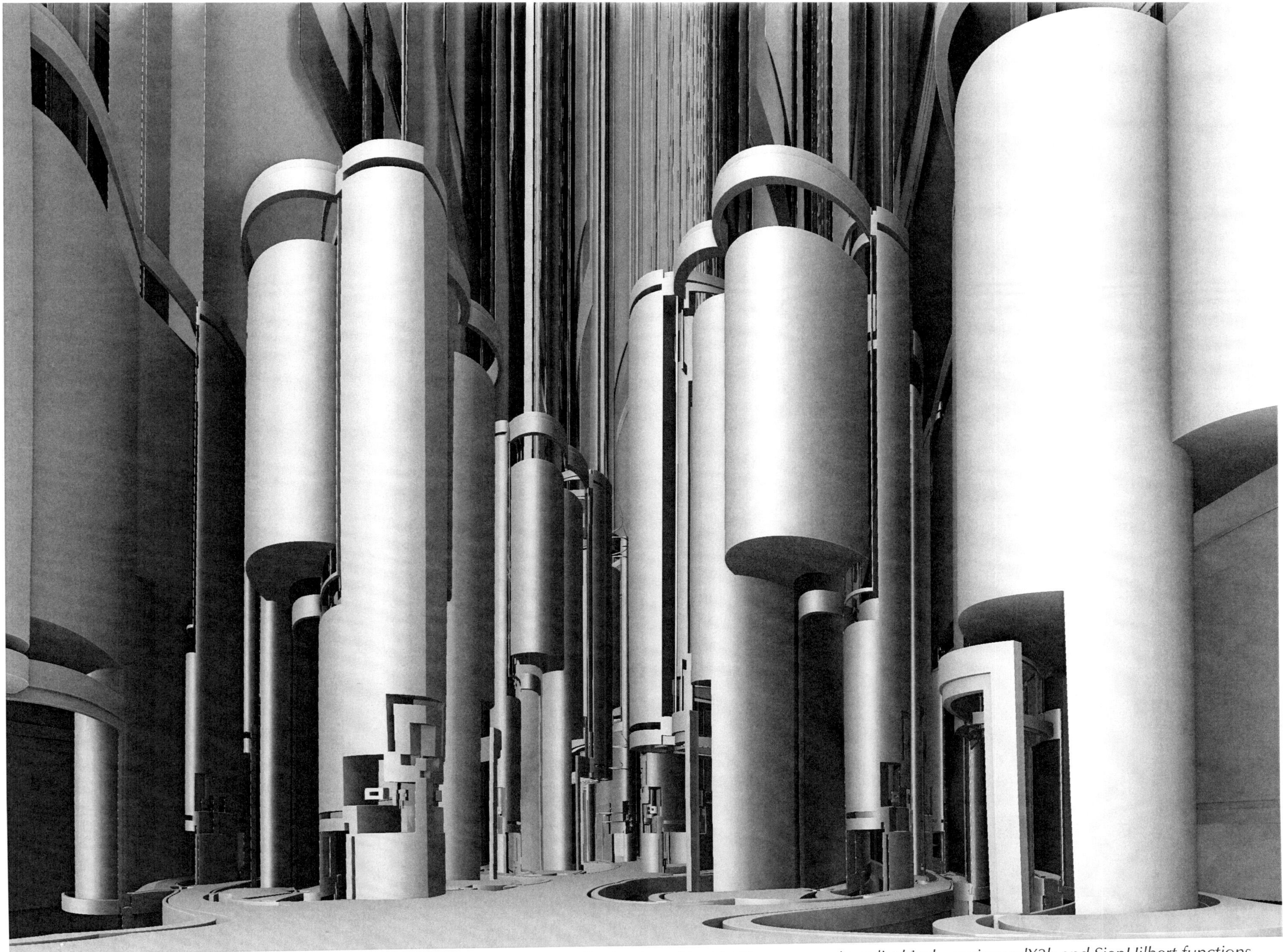

Fractal image, created in Mandelbulb 3D with a modified formula originally developed by Hal Tenny, uses _invcylindrical, _reciprocalX3b and SiepHilbert functions.

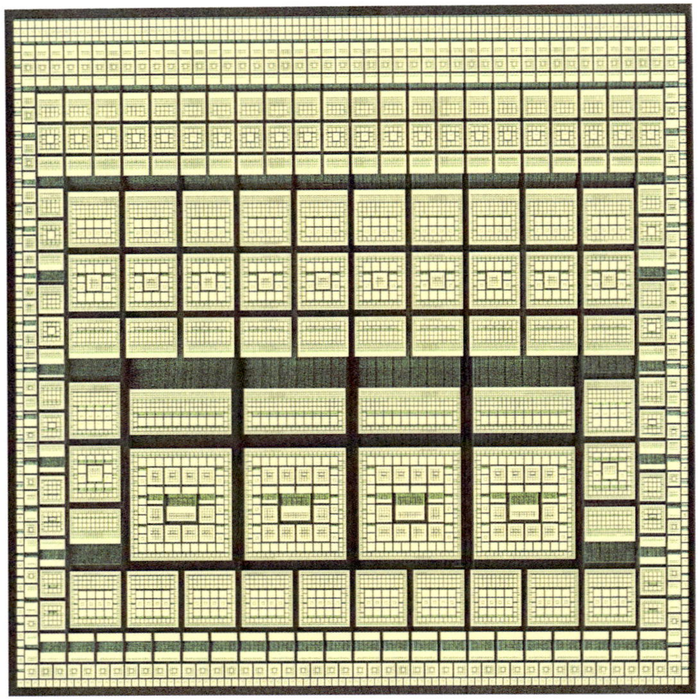

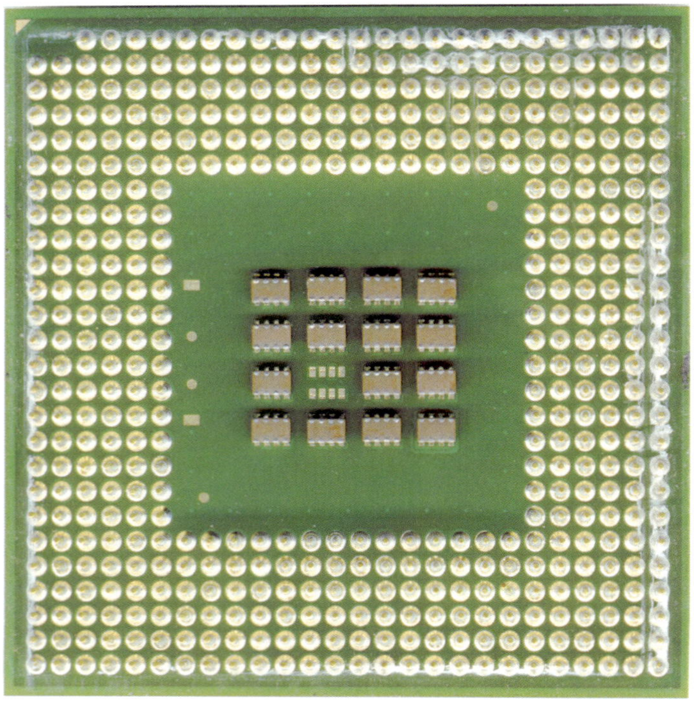

Top, fractal image; *above*, modern CPU scanned from below.

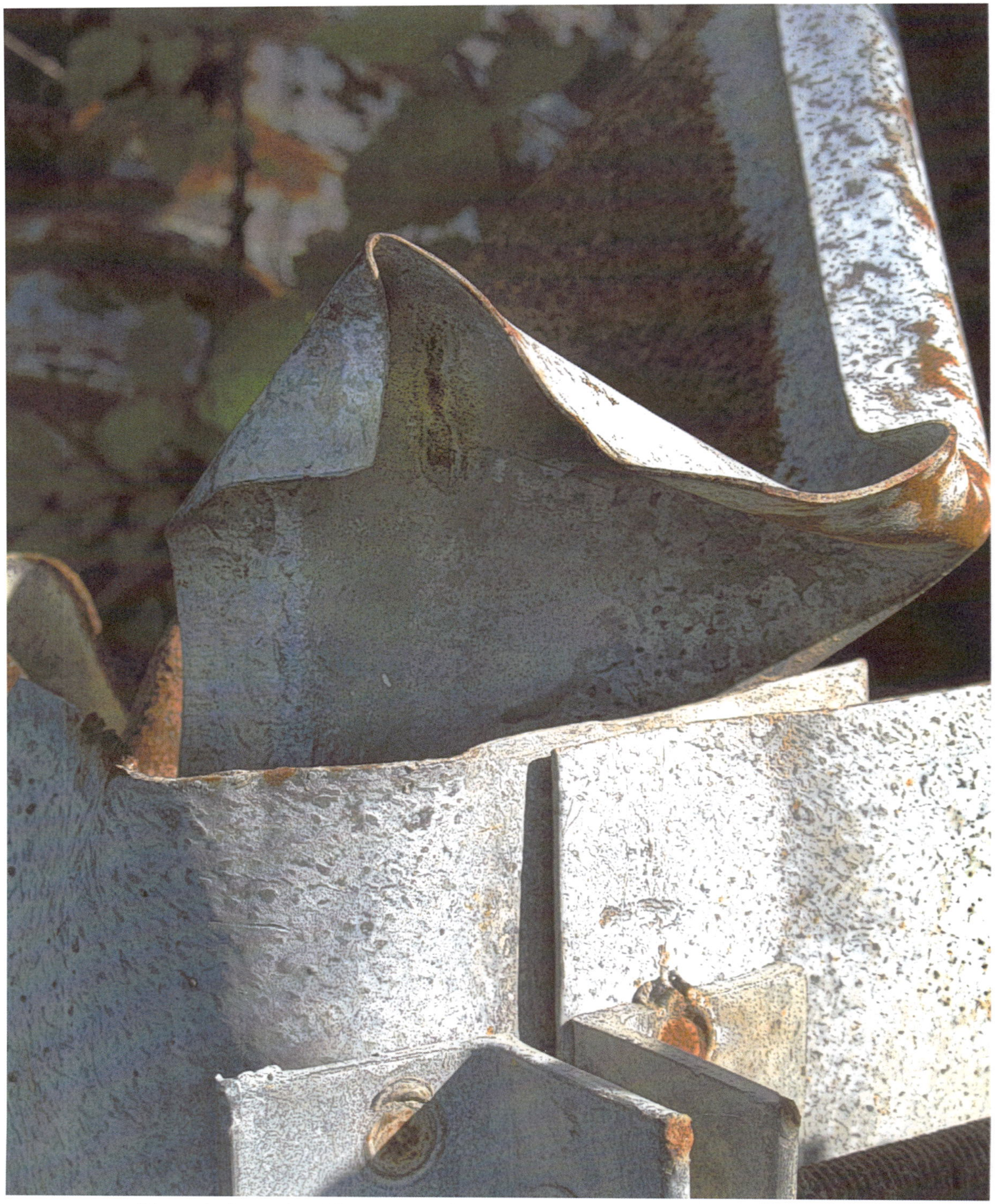

Discarded guard-rail fence in Bucks County, Pa. (digital image)

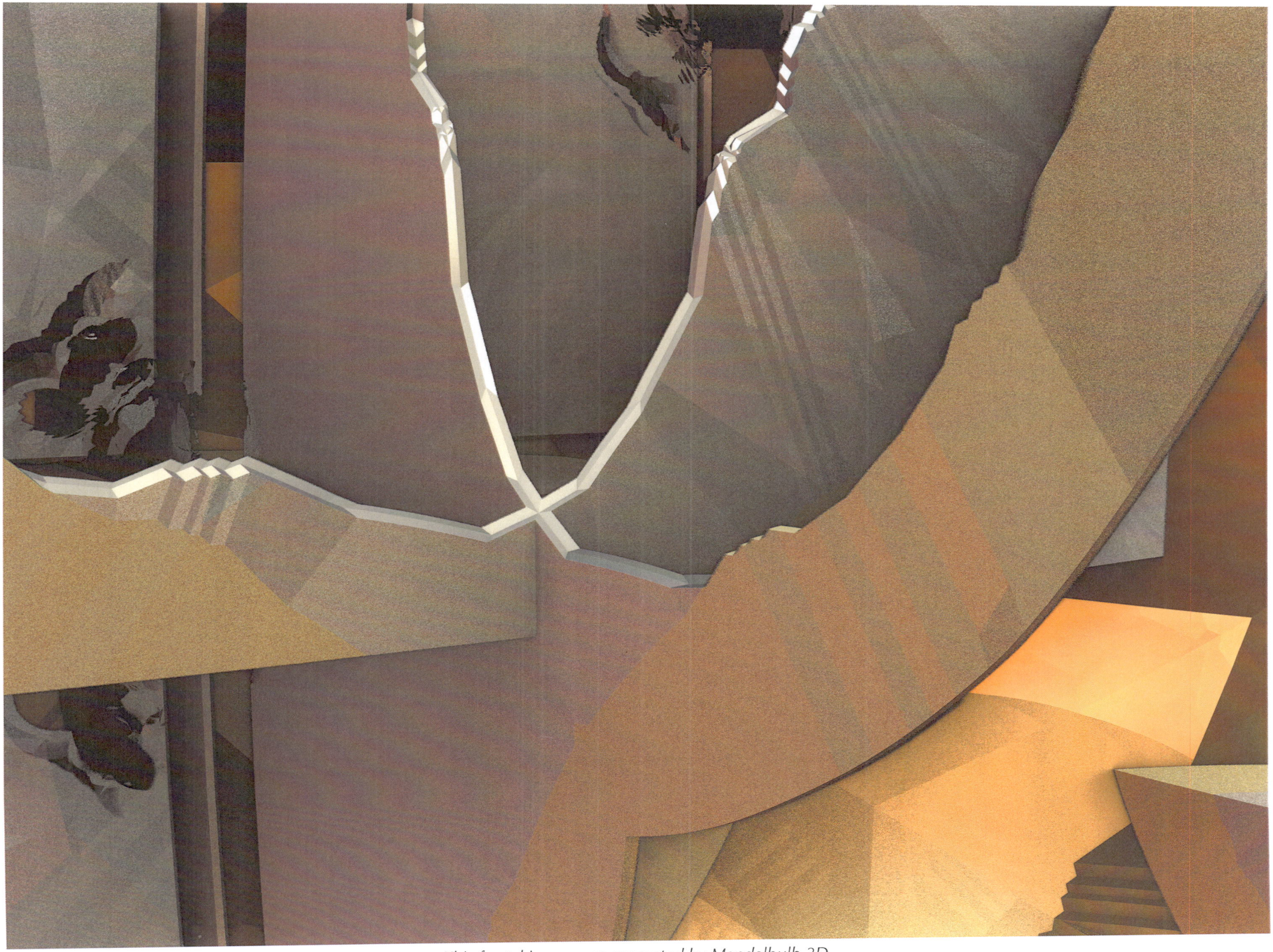

This fractal image was generated by Mandelbulb 3D.

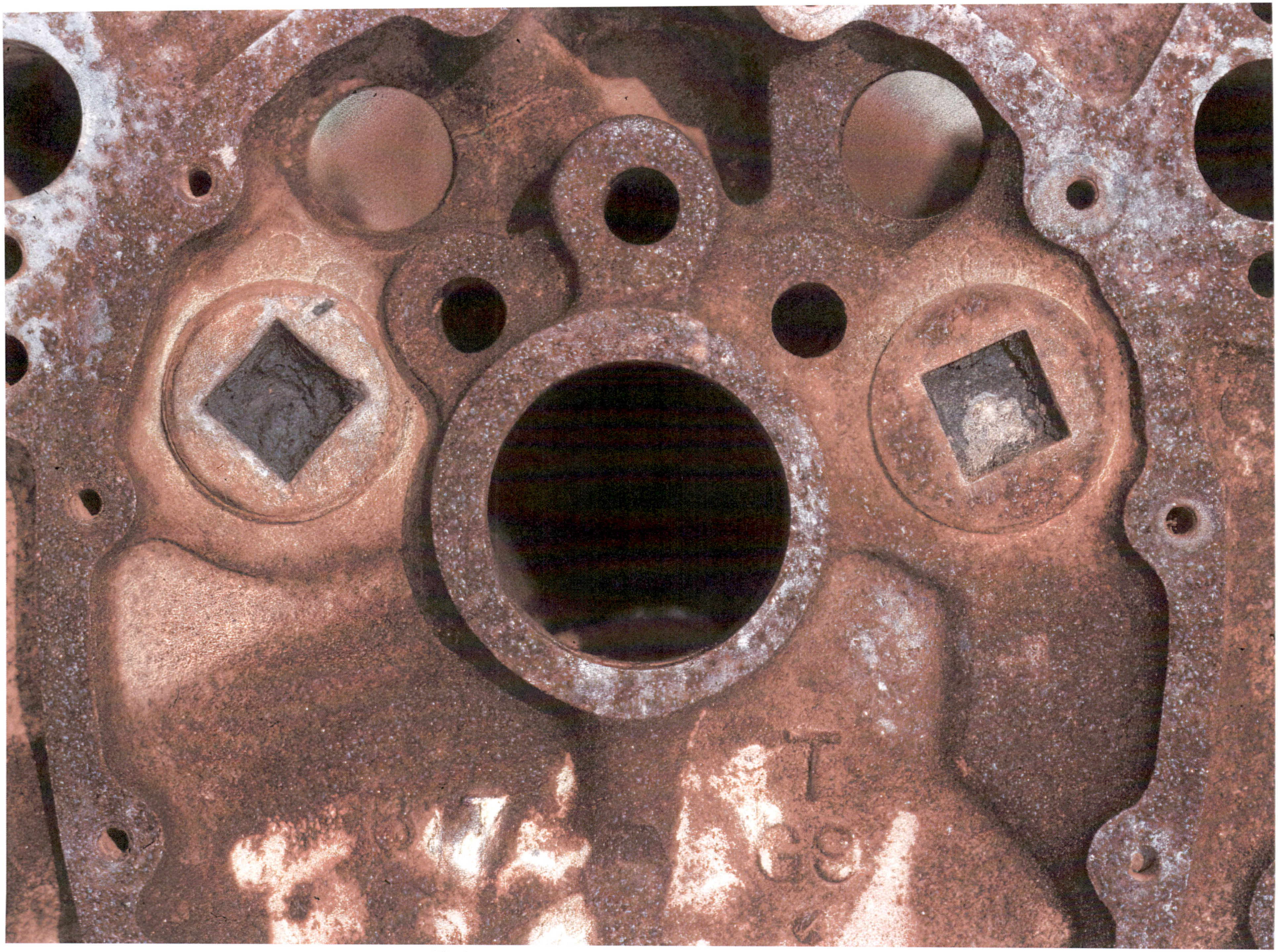

Engine block image scanned from a 35-mm Kodachrome transparency

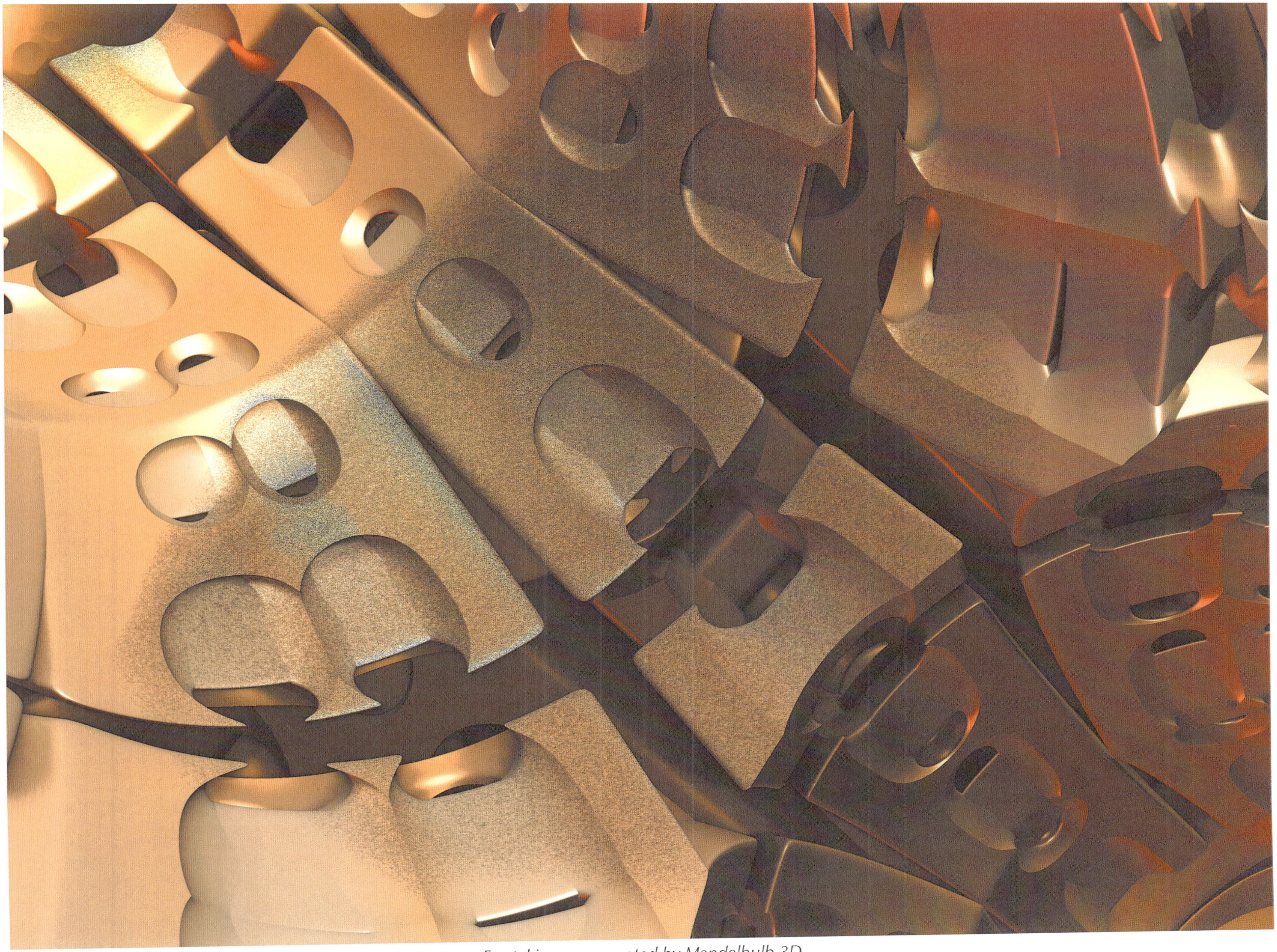

Fractal image generated by Mandelbulb 3D

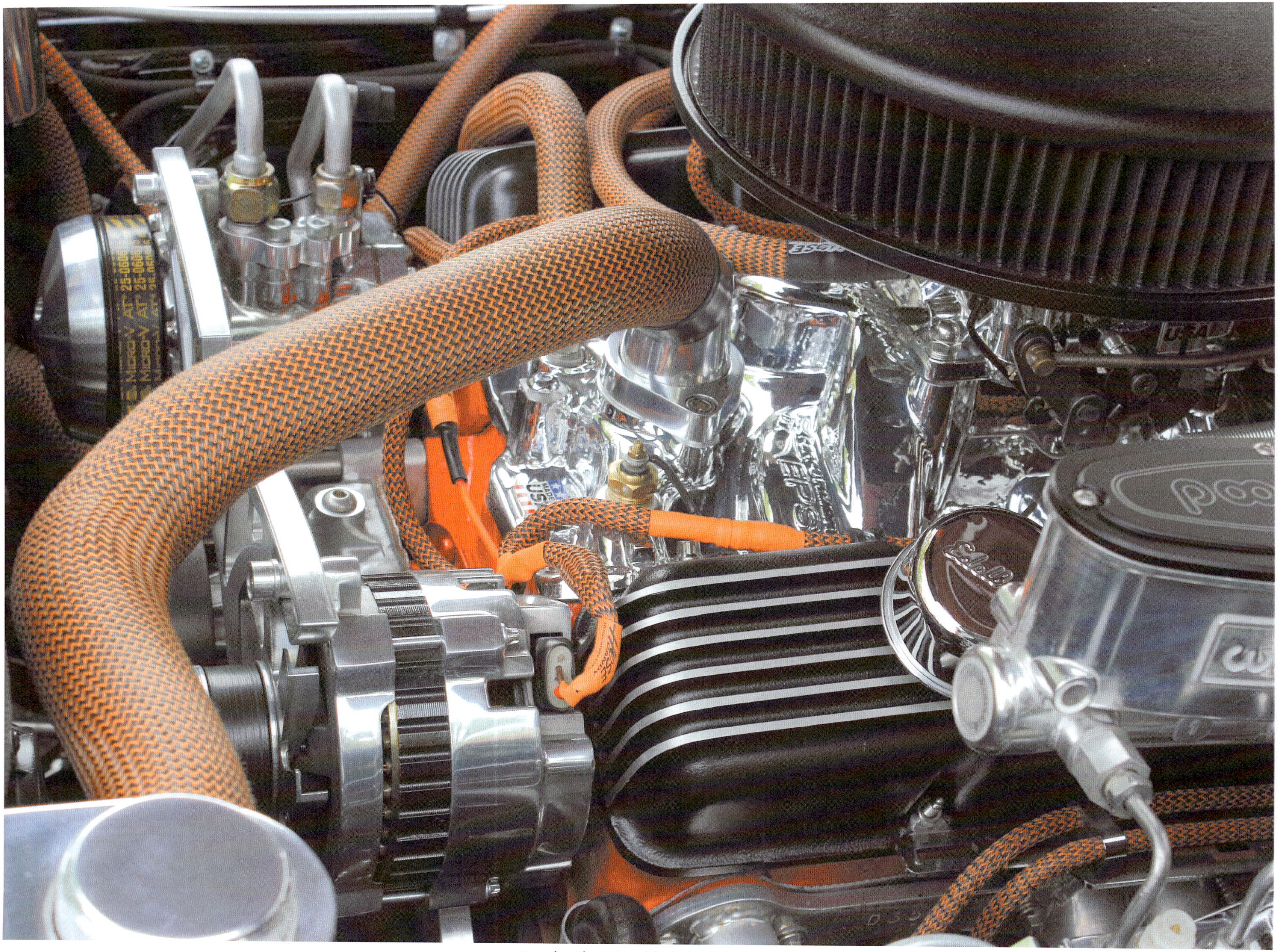

"Under the Hood," digital photo

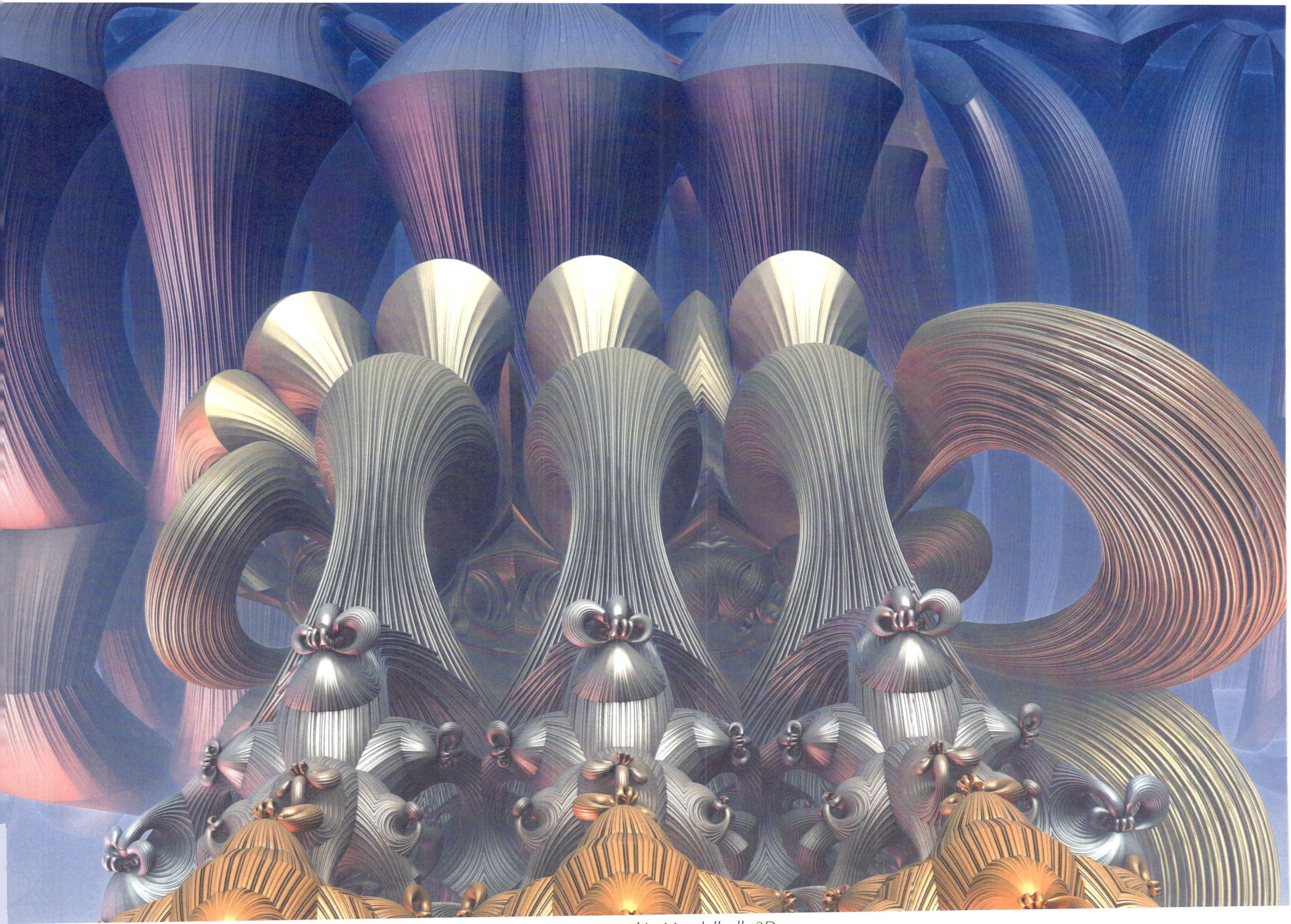

Image created in Mandelbulb 3D

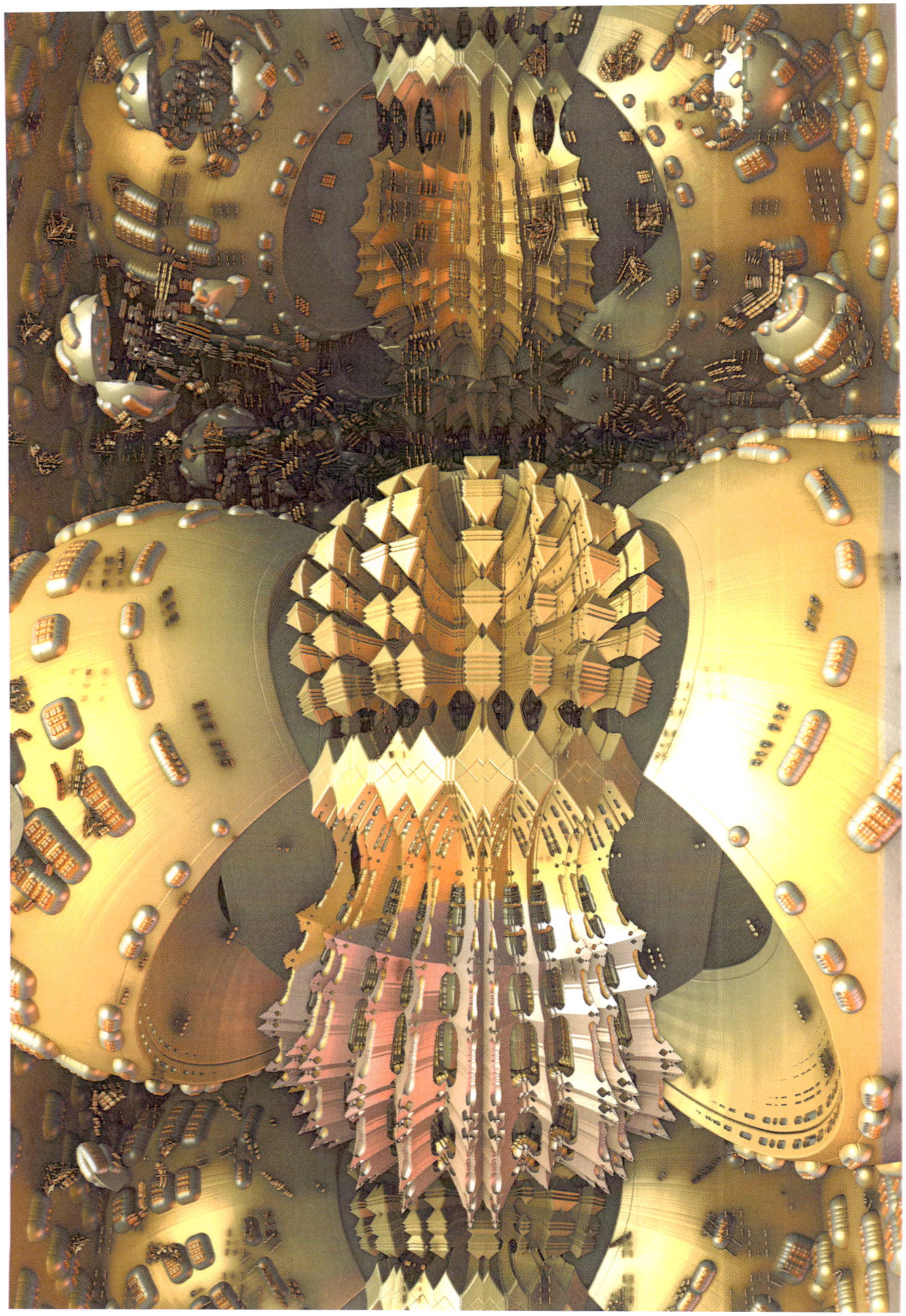

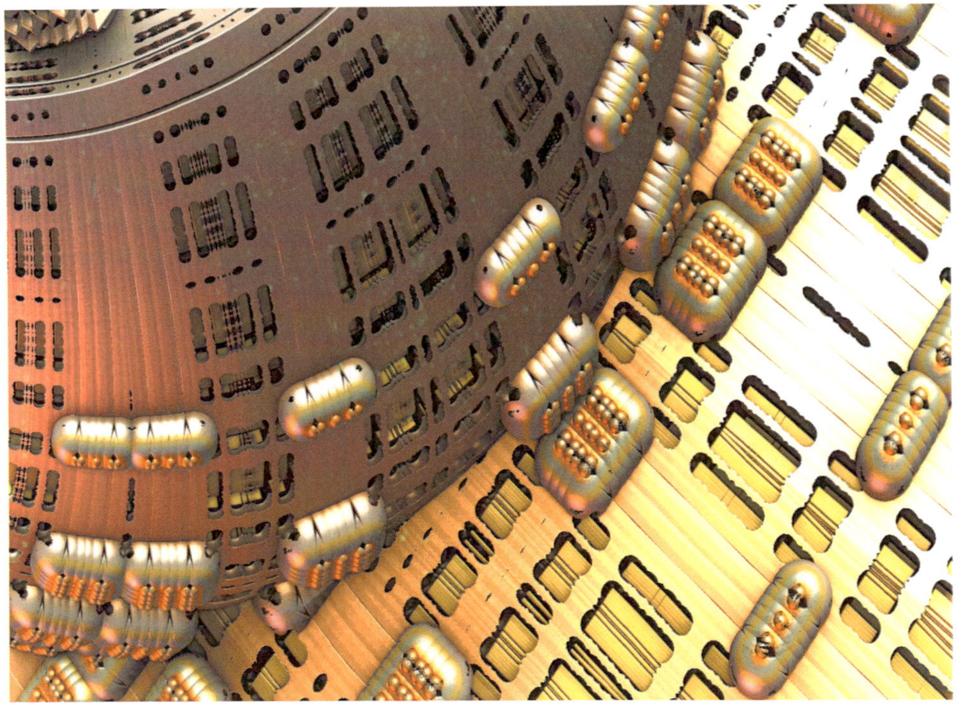

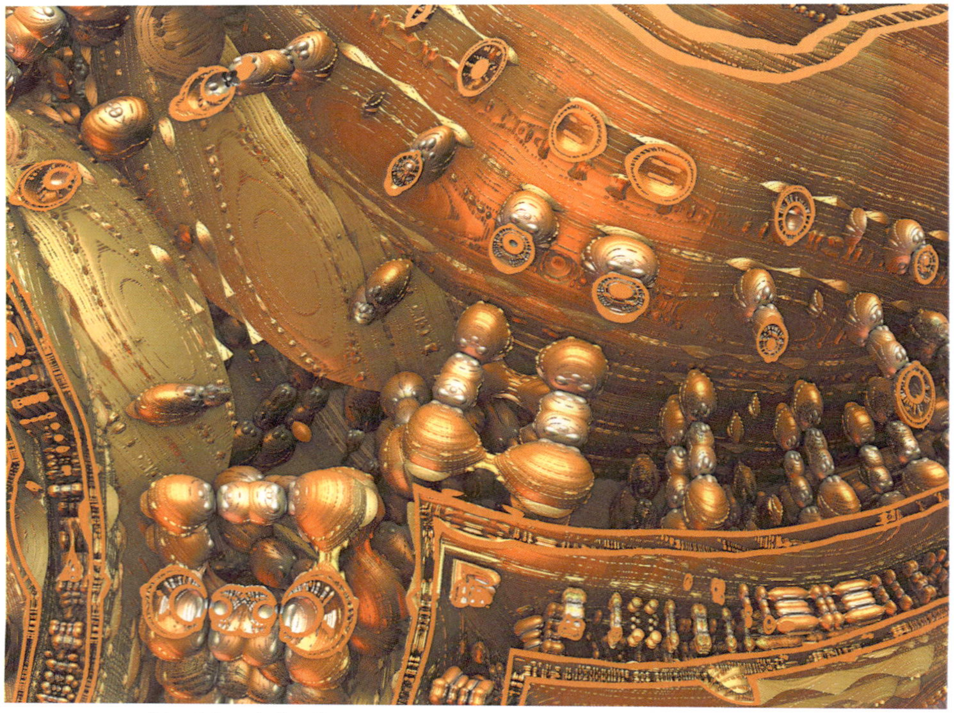

Various "machine parts" (fractal images generated by Mandelbulb 3D)

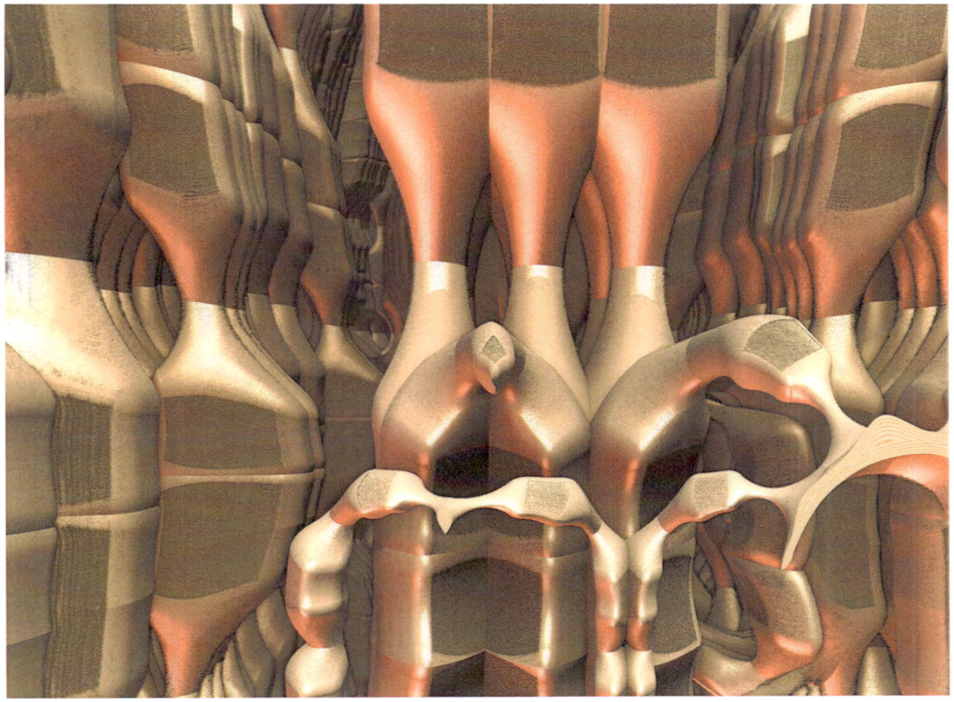

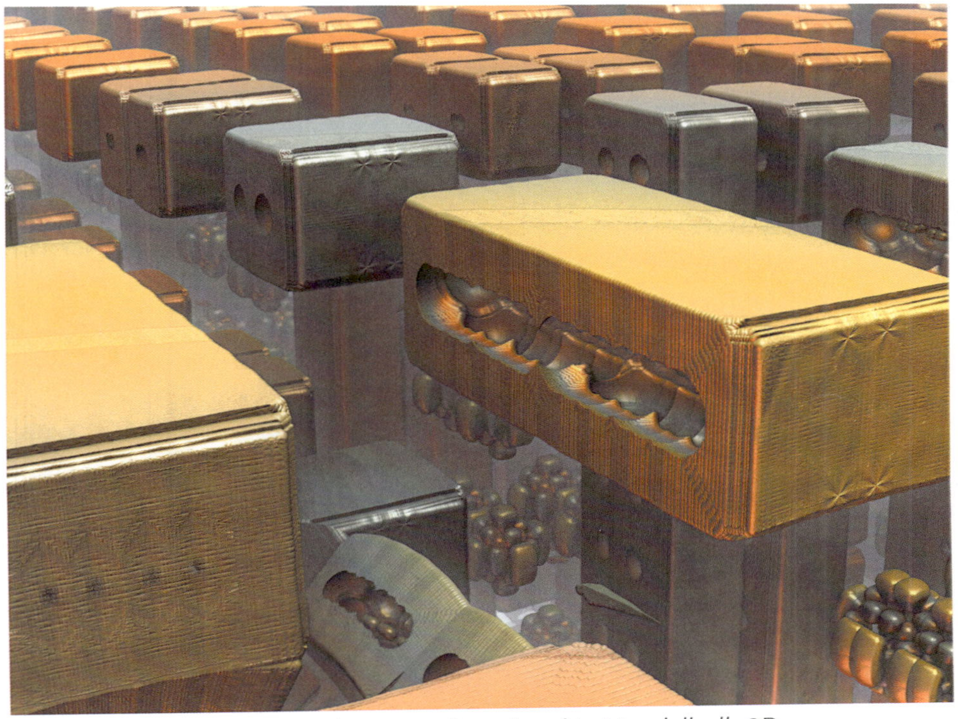

Various "machine parts" rendered in Mandelbulb 3D

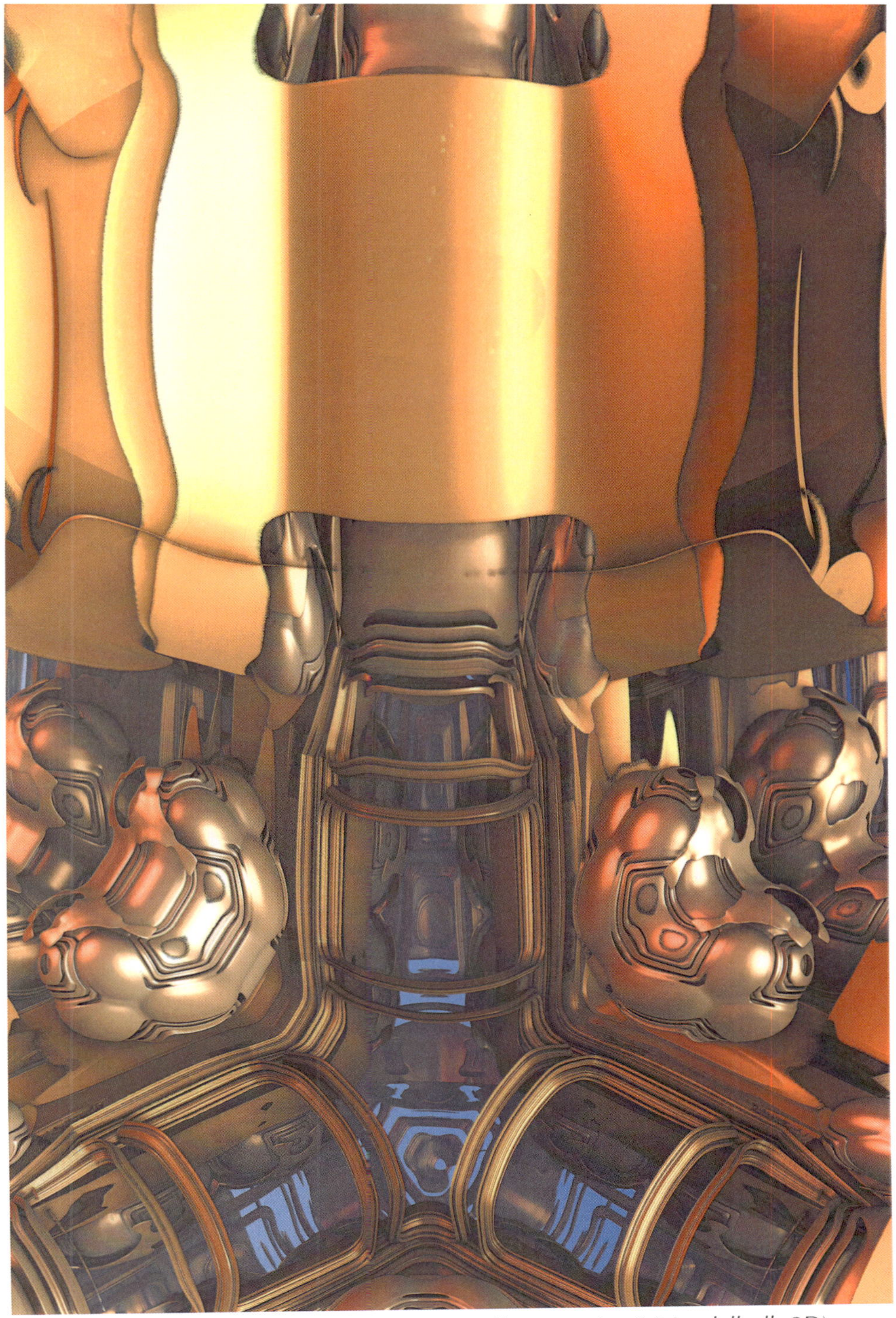

"Three-phase, fusion-powered magnetic flux capacitor" (Mandelbulb 3D)

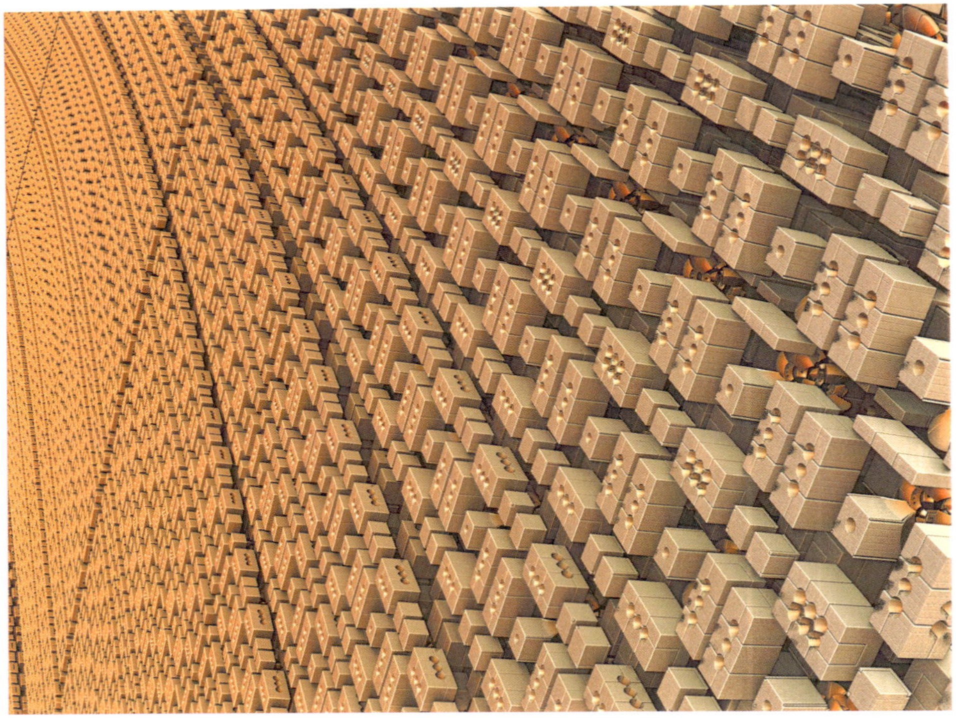
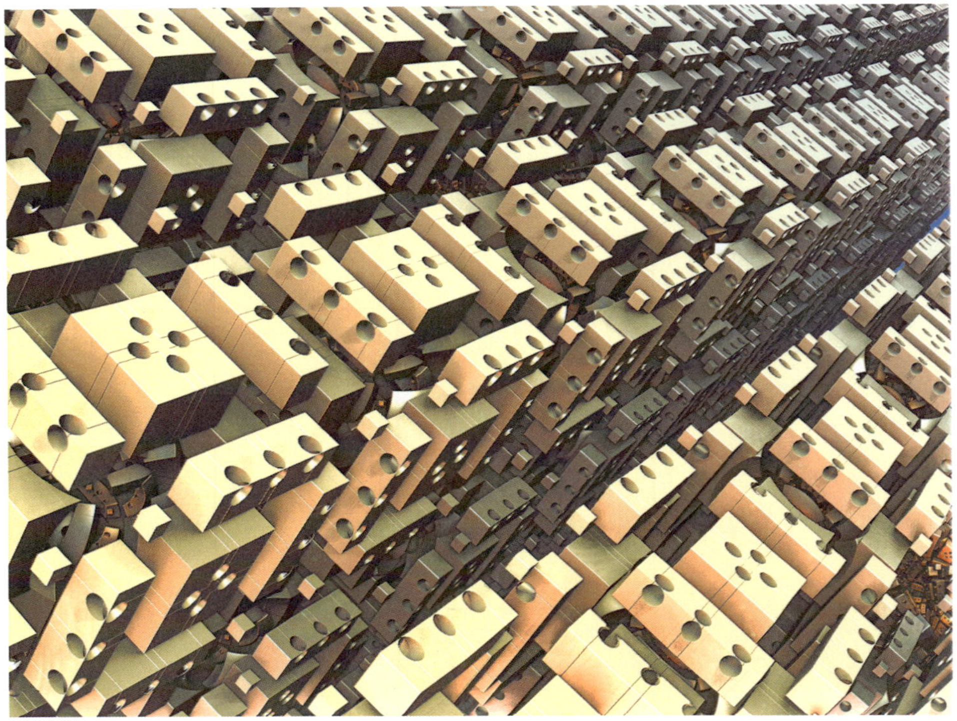
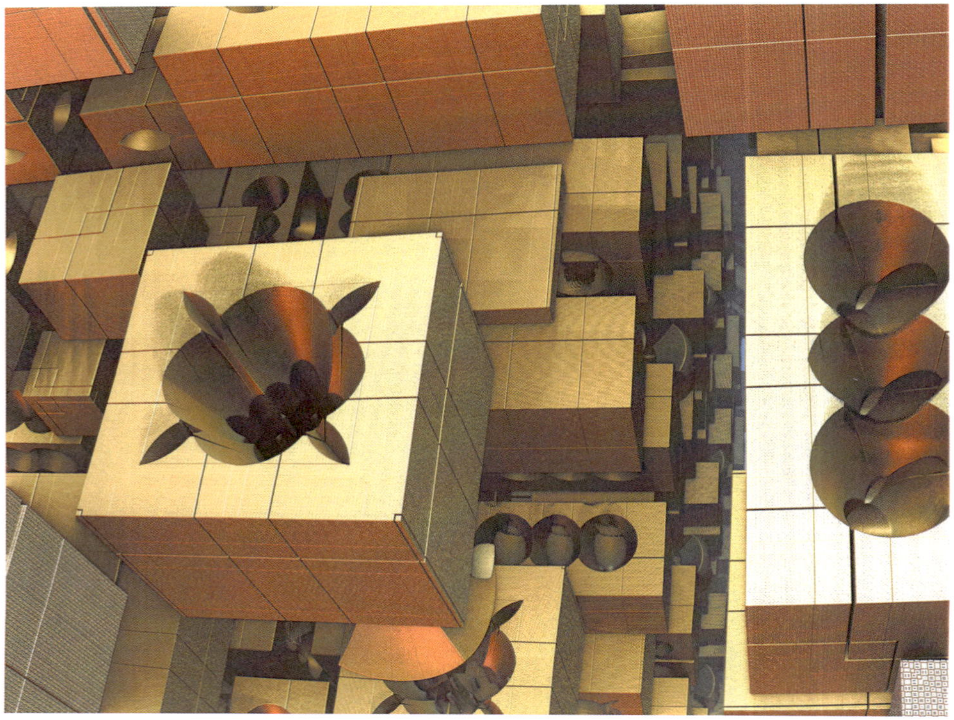
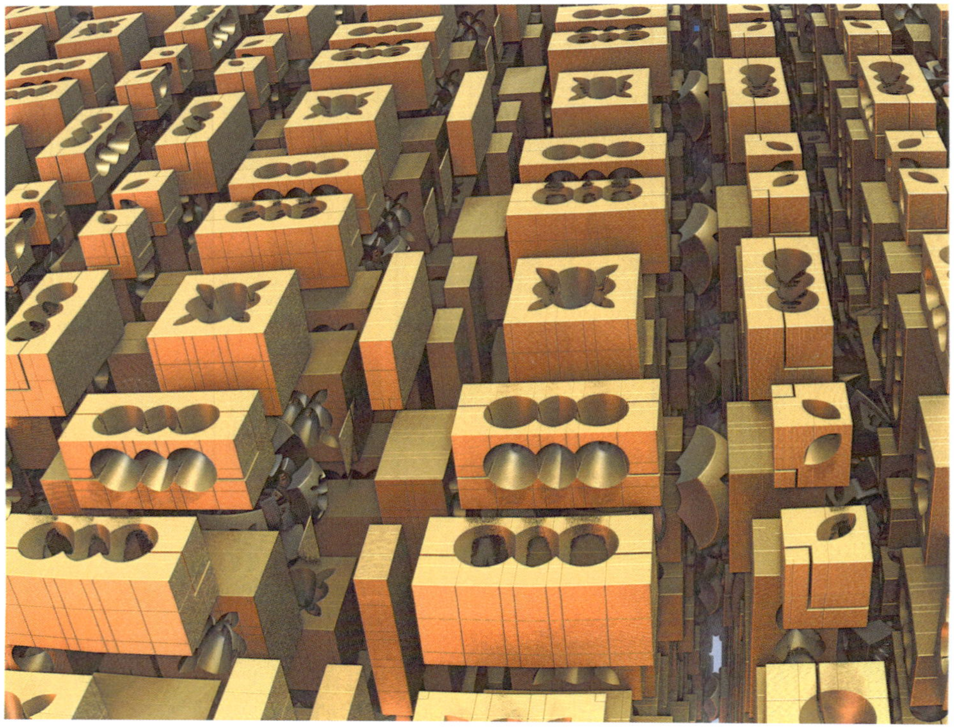

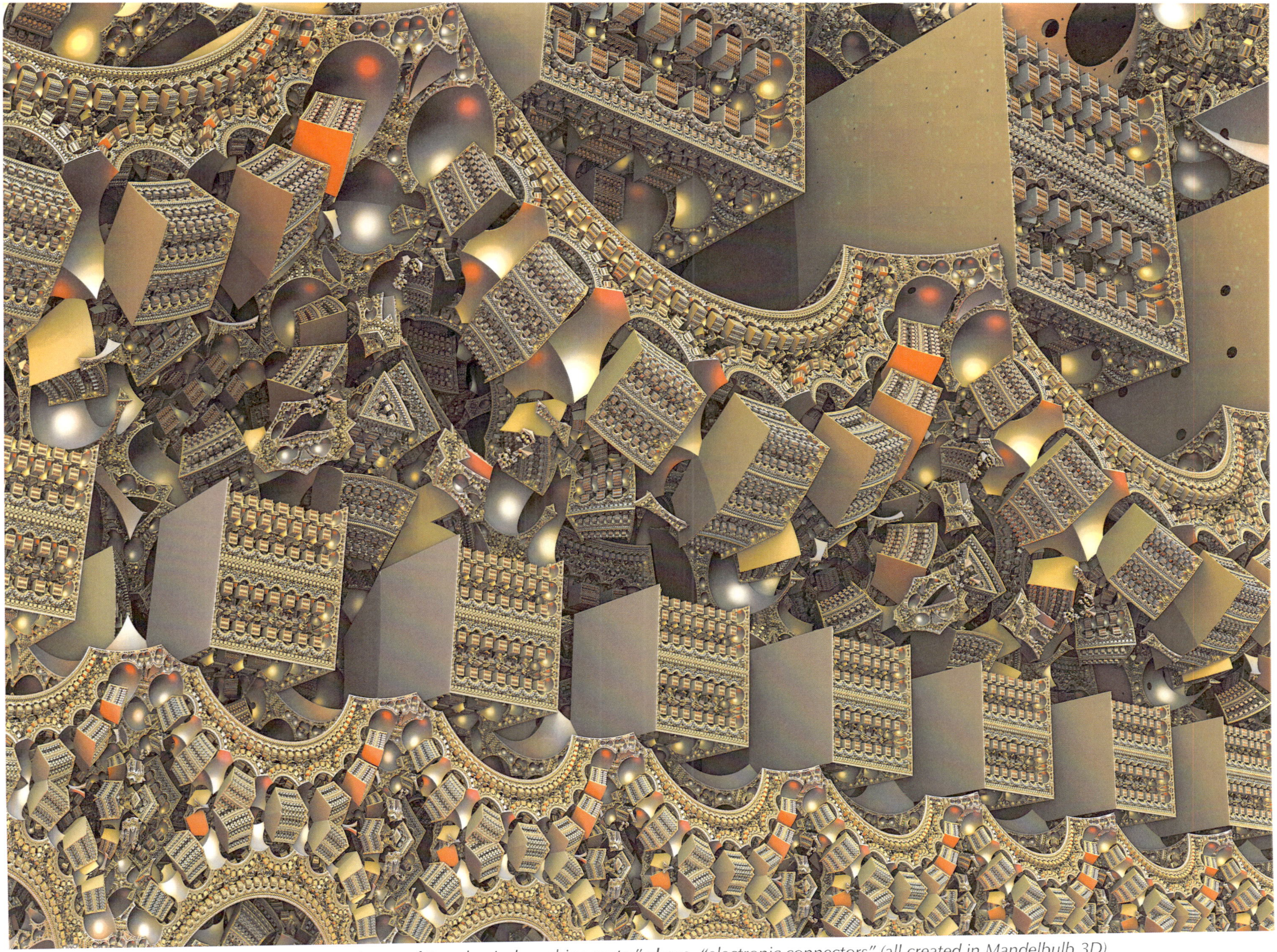

***Opposite page**, rows and rows of "mechanical machine parts;" **above**, "electronic connectors" (all created in Mandelbulb 3D)*

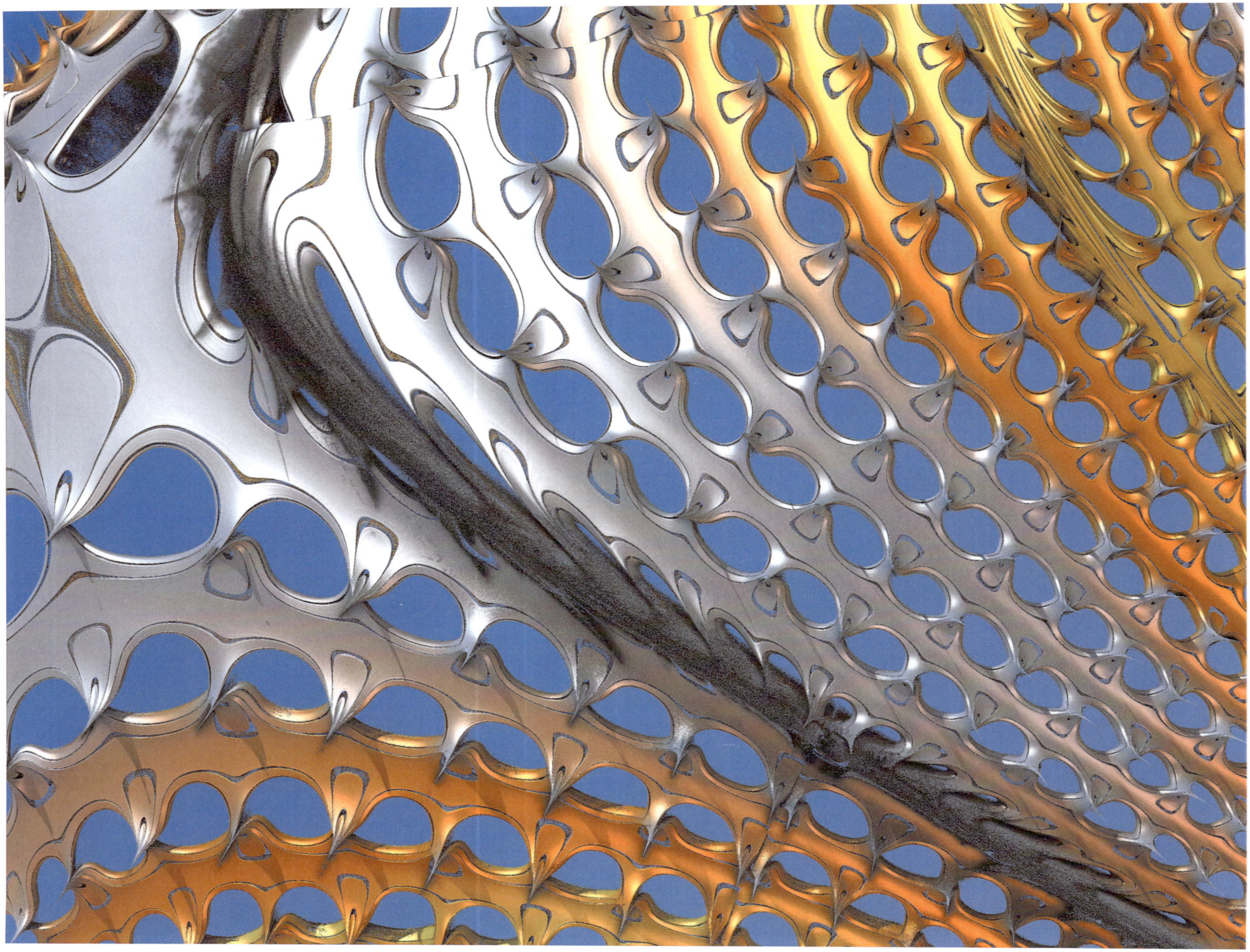

Fractal image generated by Mandelbulb 3D

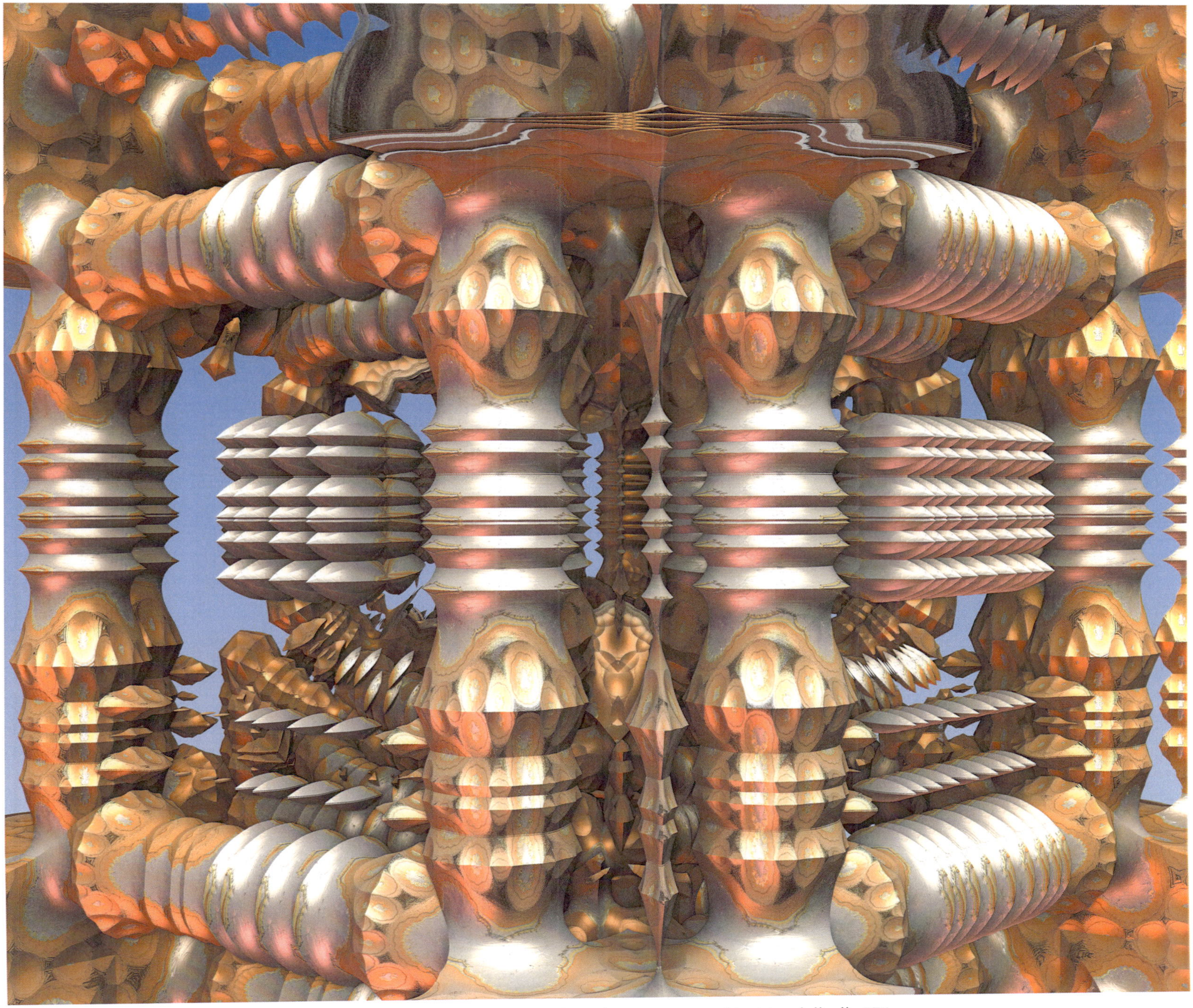

"Process machinery system" (fractal image created in Mandelbulb 3D)

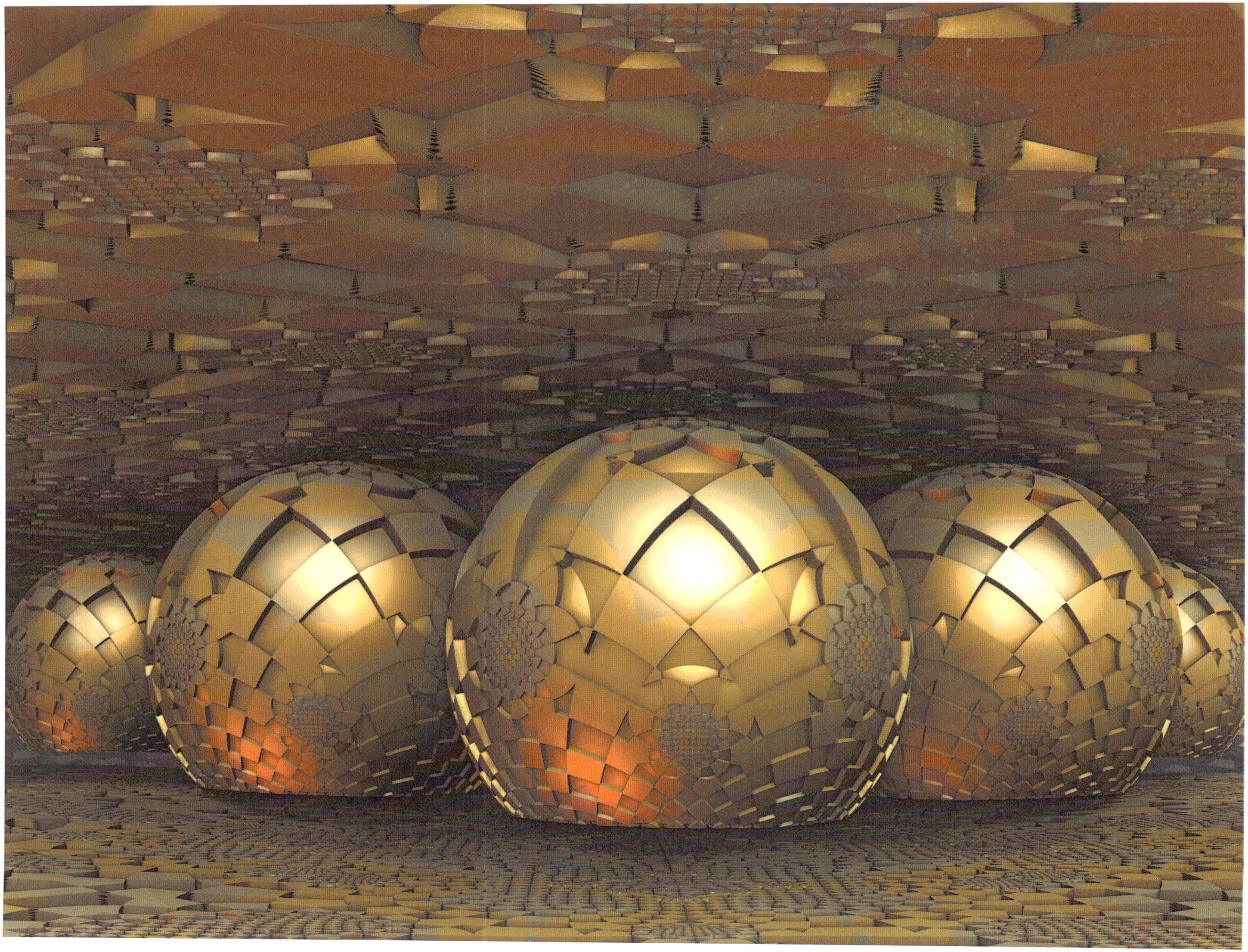

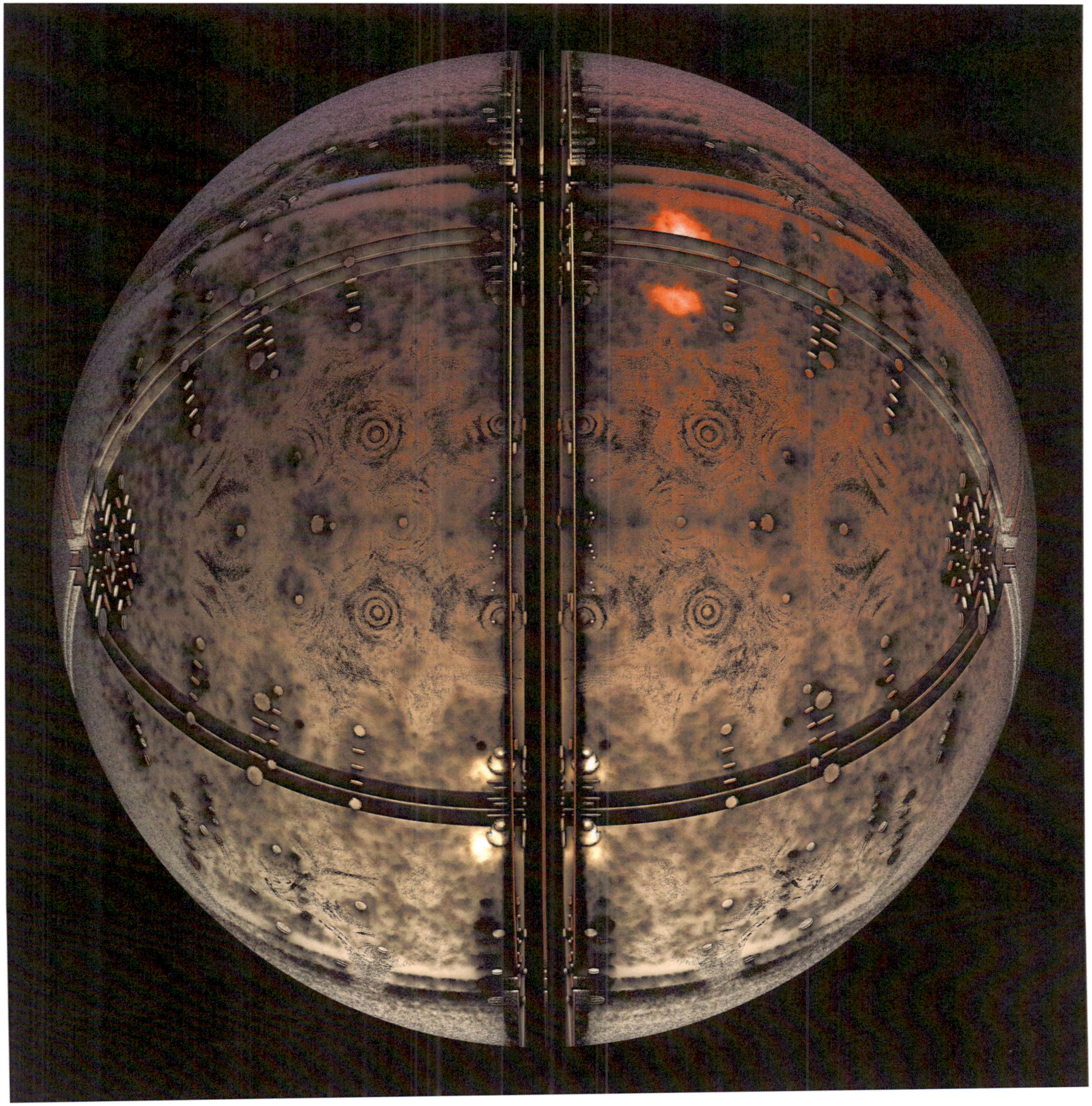

Opposite page, *a collection of partial spheres;* **this page,** *a metallic sphere. Both images were created in Mandelbulb 3D.*

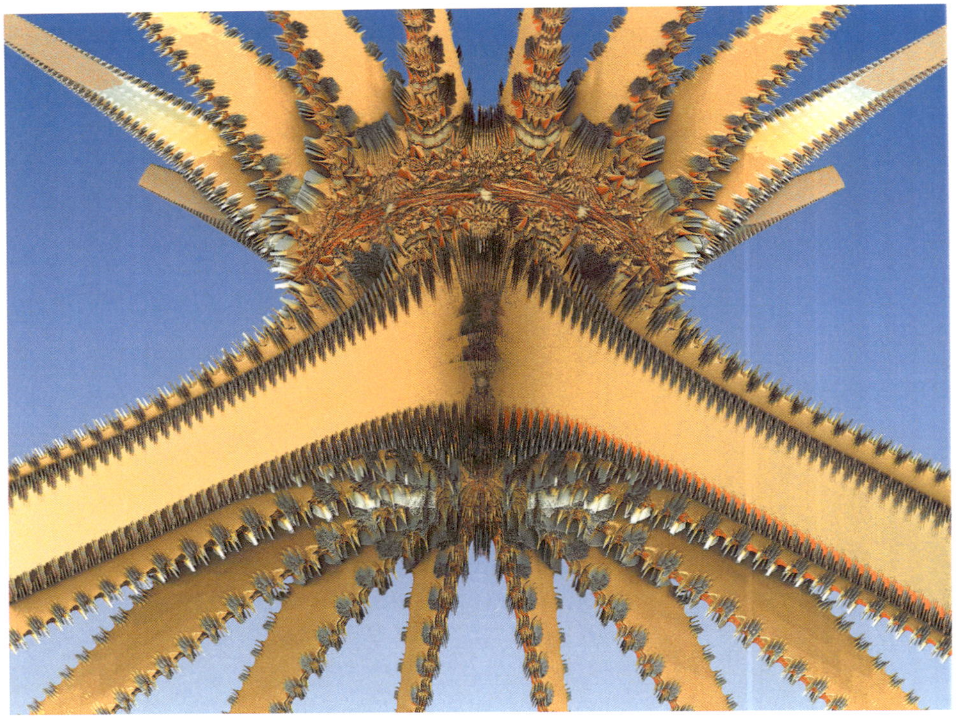
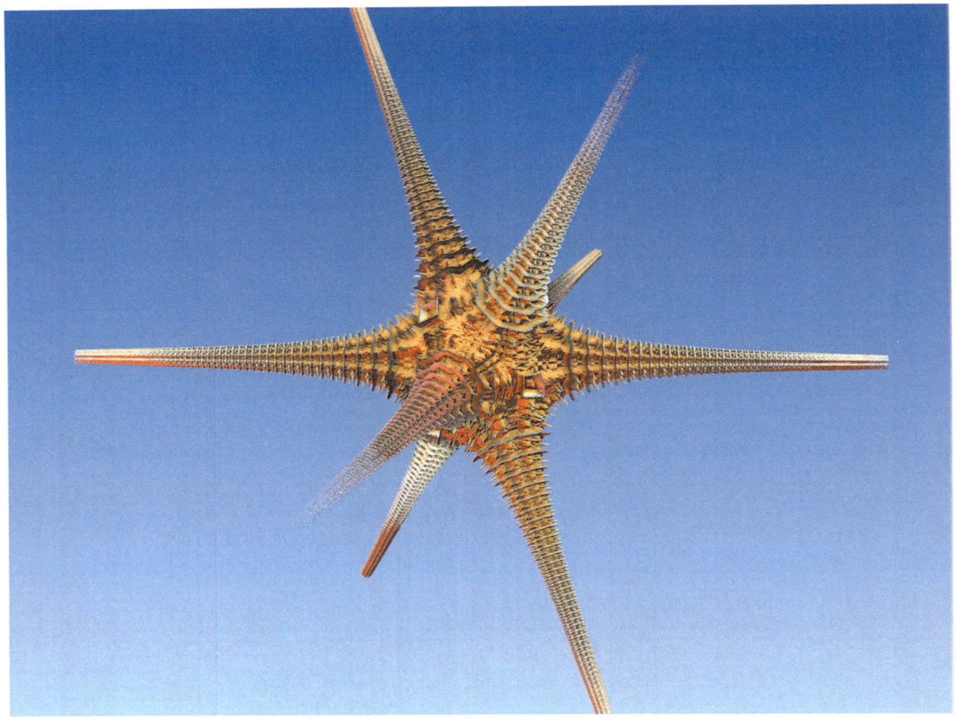
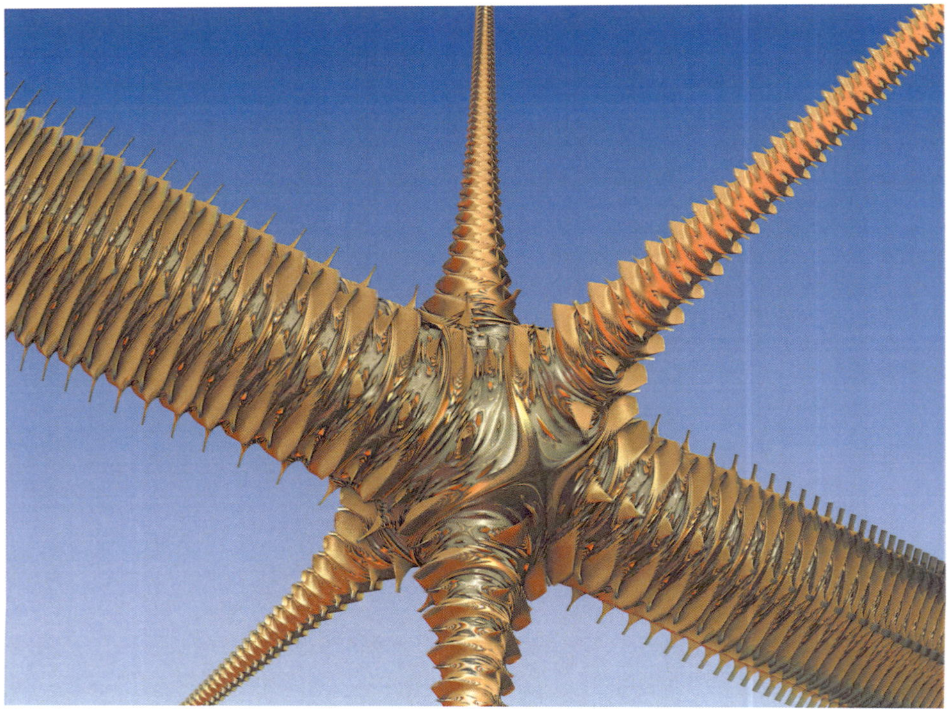
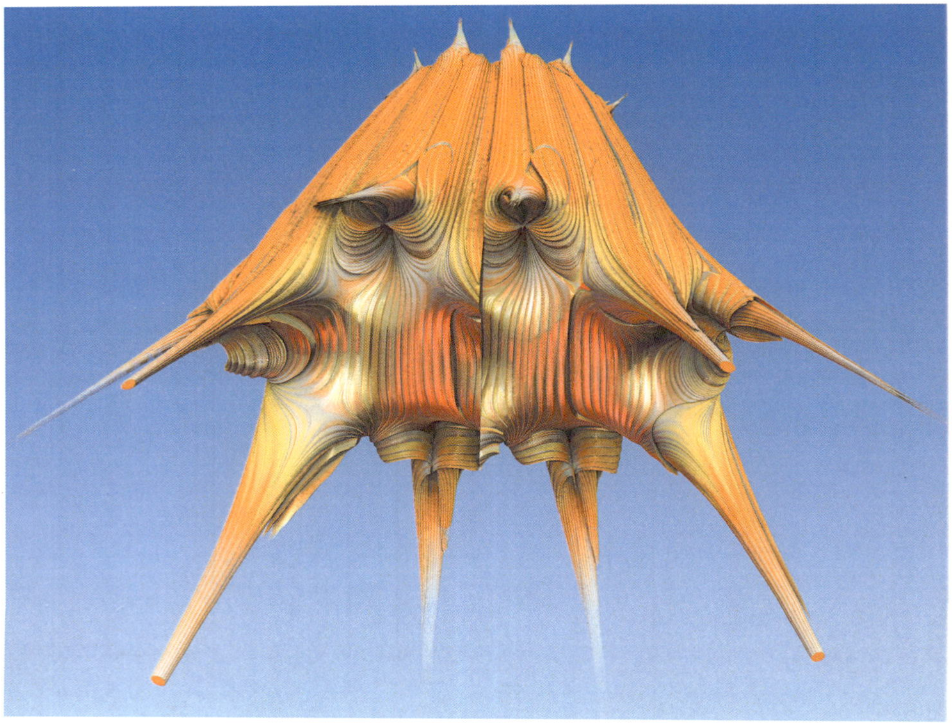

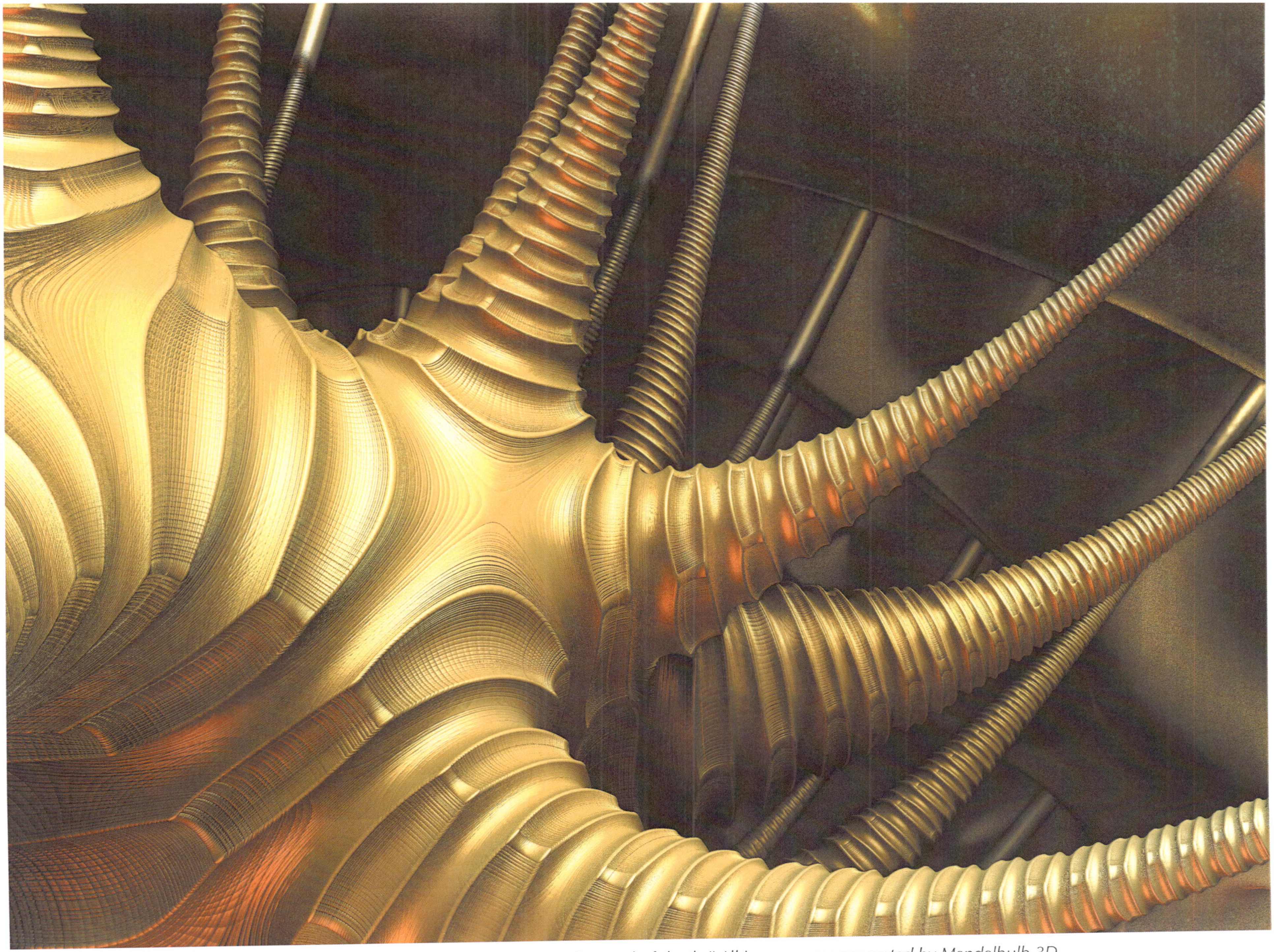

Opposite page, *"alien torture tools;"* **above,** *"alien tool of death." All images were generated by Mandelbulb 3D.*

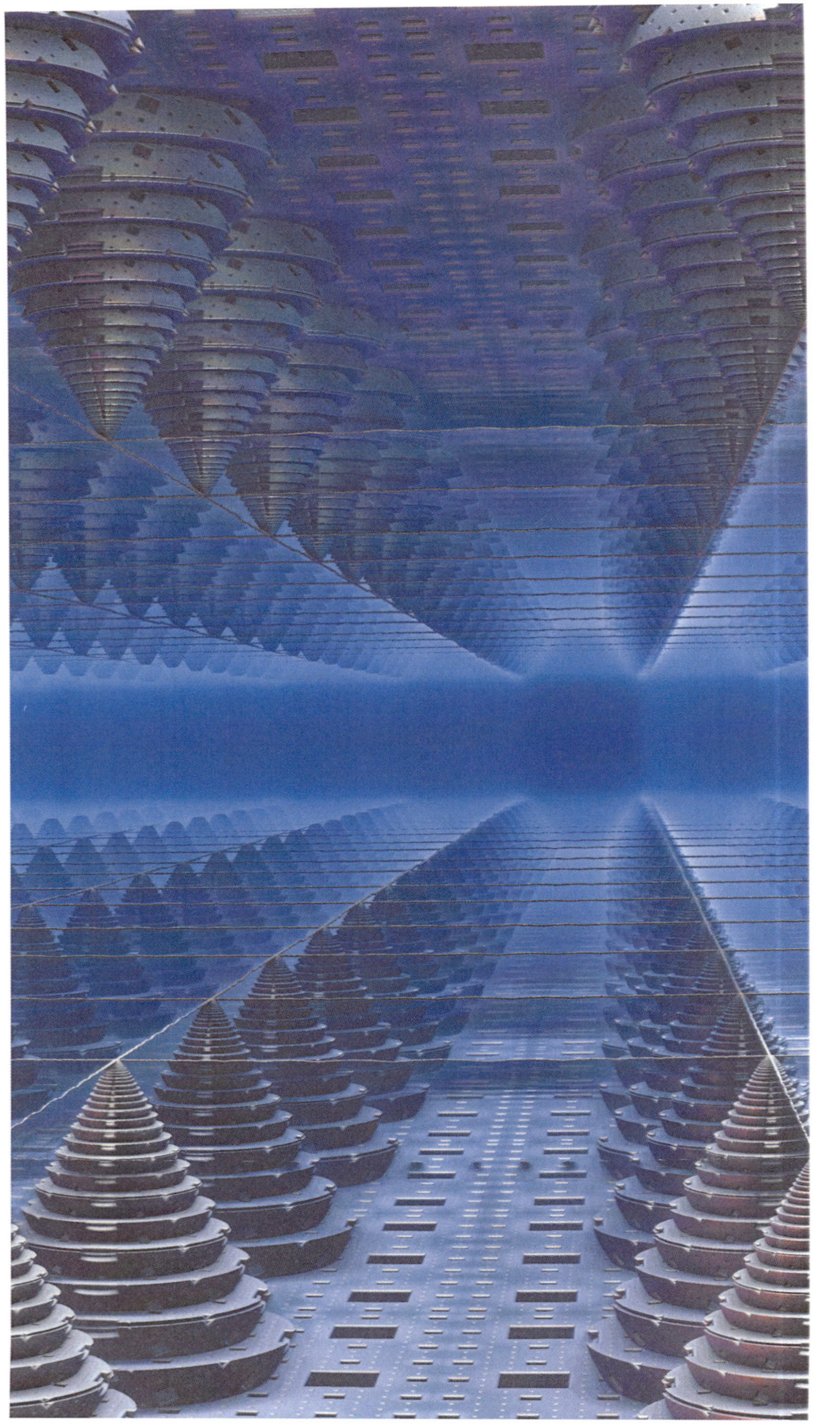

"High-voltage space with insulators" imaged by Mandelbulb 3D

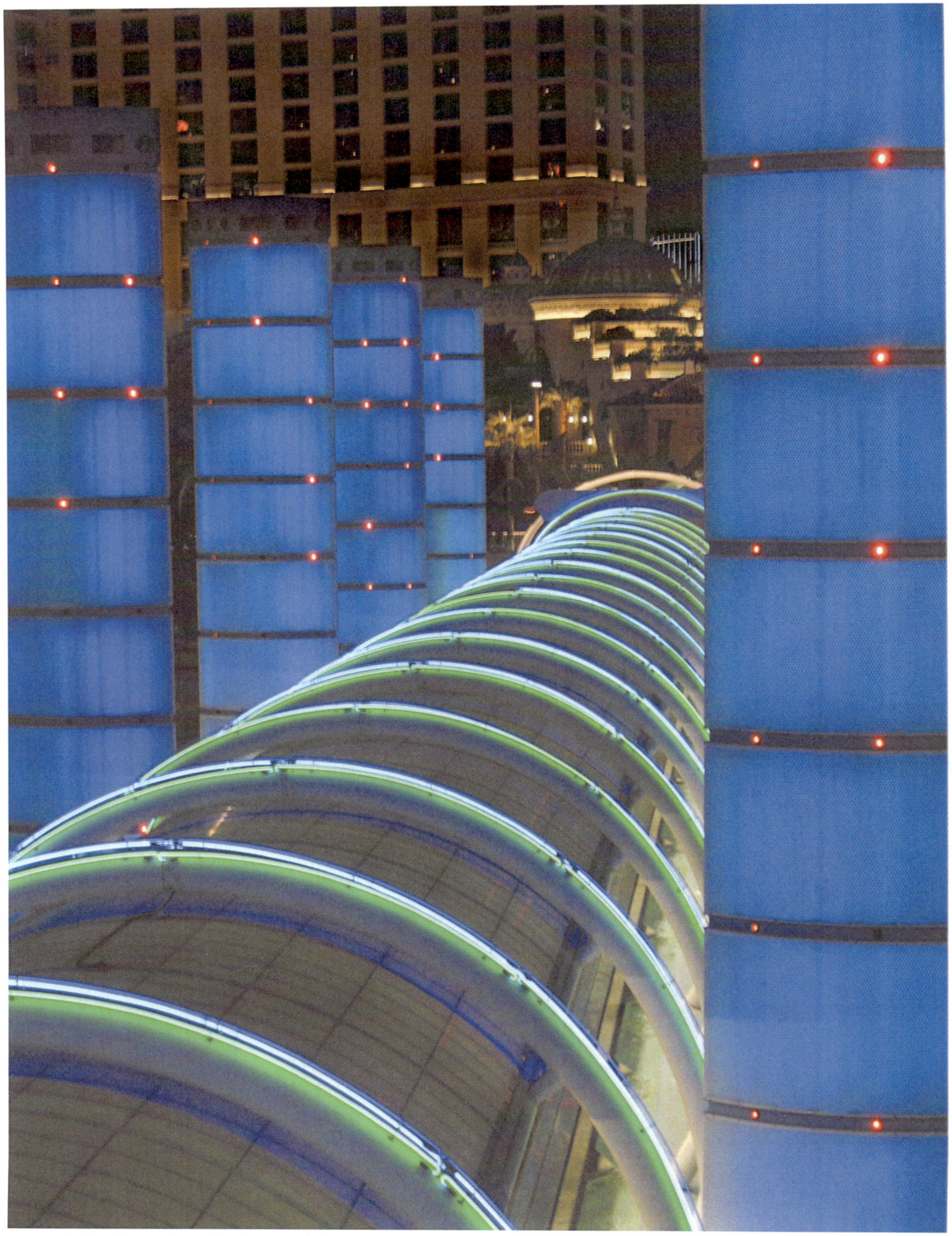

Night-time digital photo of the People Mover station near the Venetian Hotel in Las Vegas

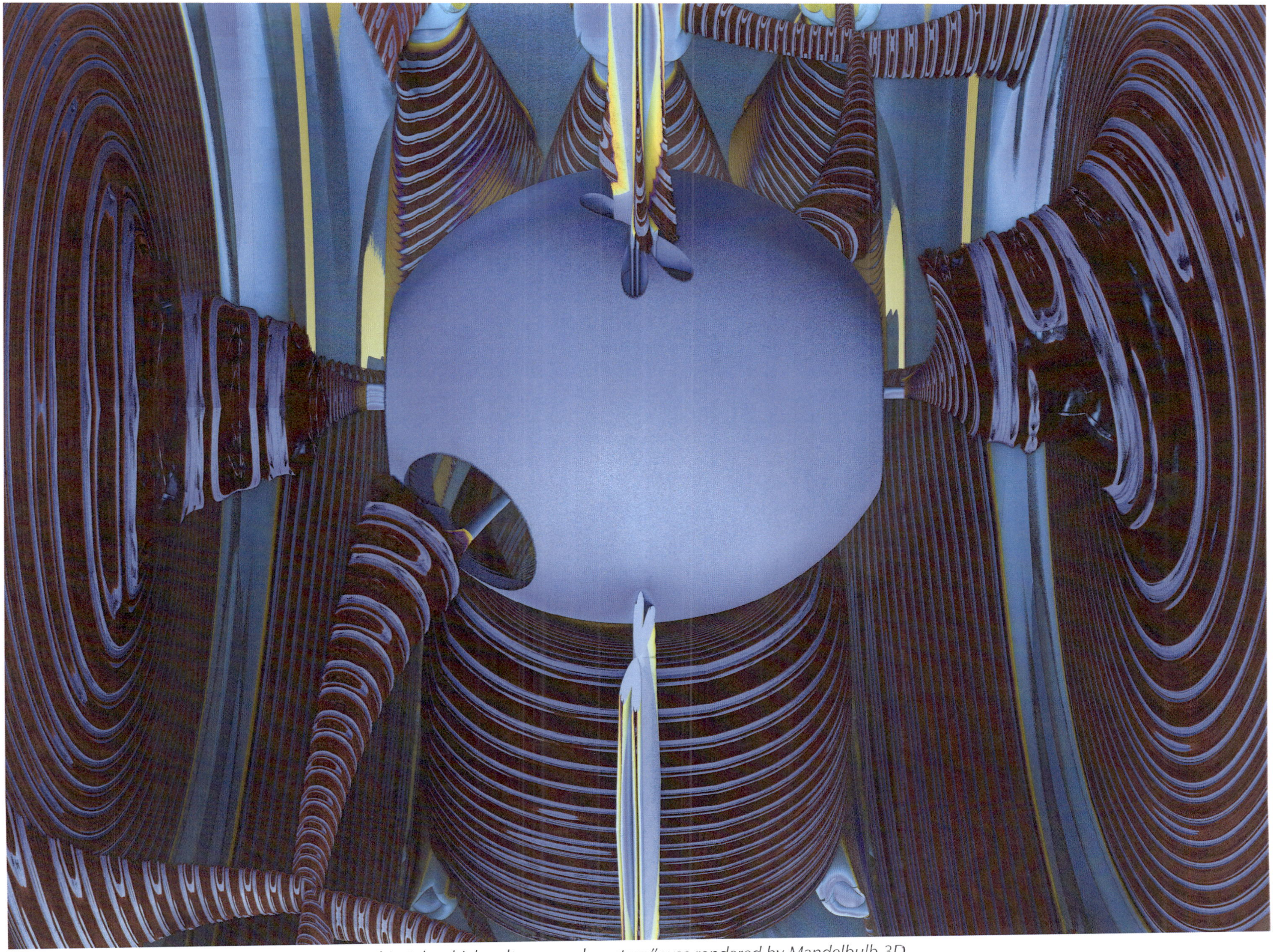

This "ultra-high voltage supply system" was rendered by Mandelbulb 3D.

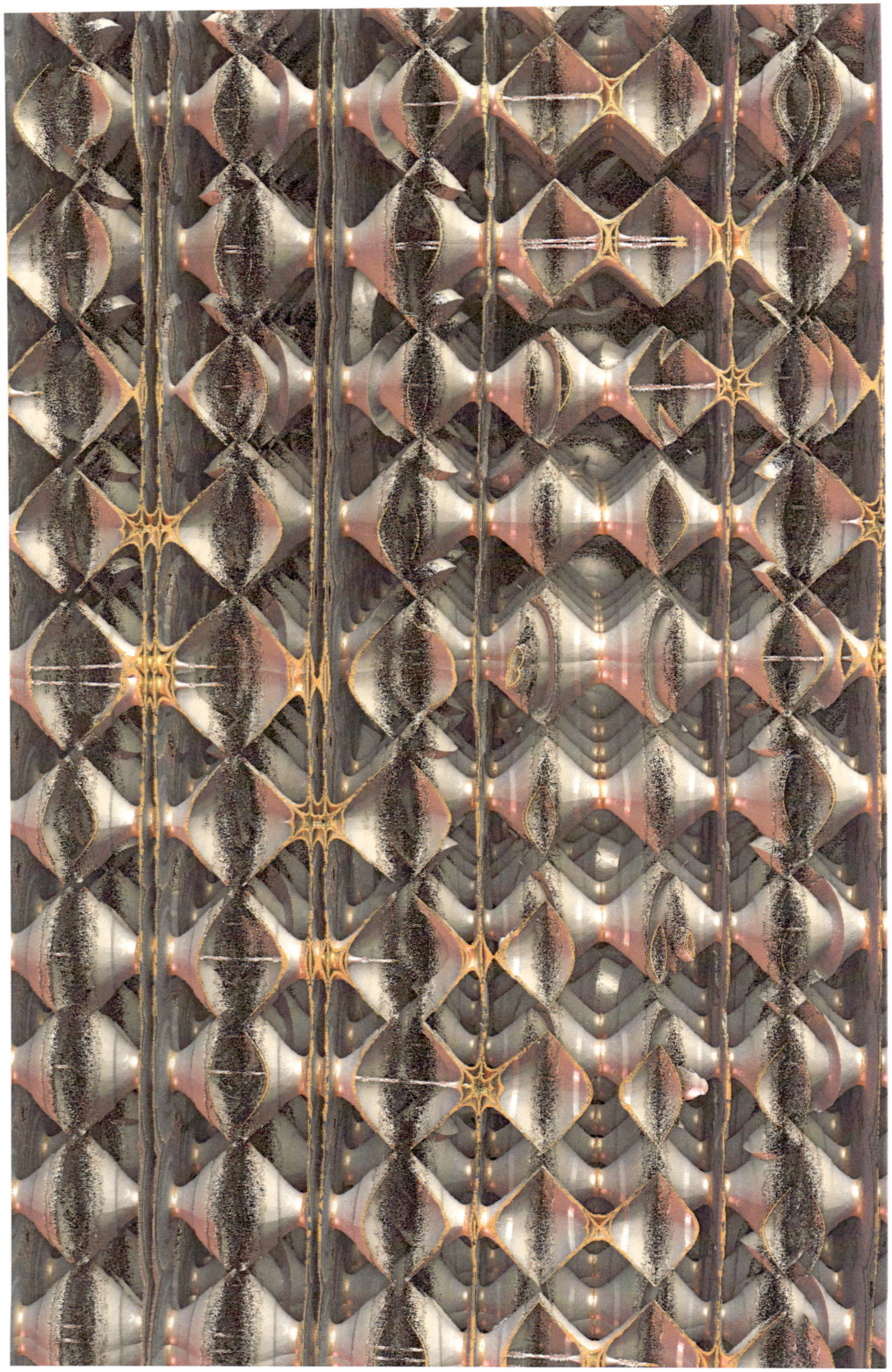

Fractal image from Mandelbulb 3D

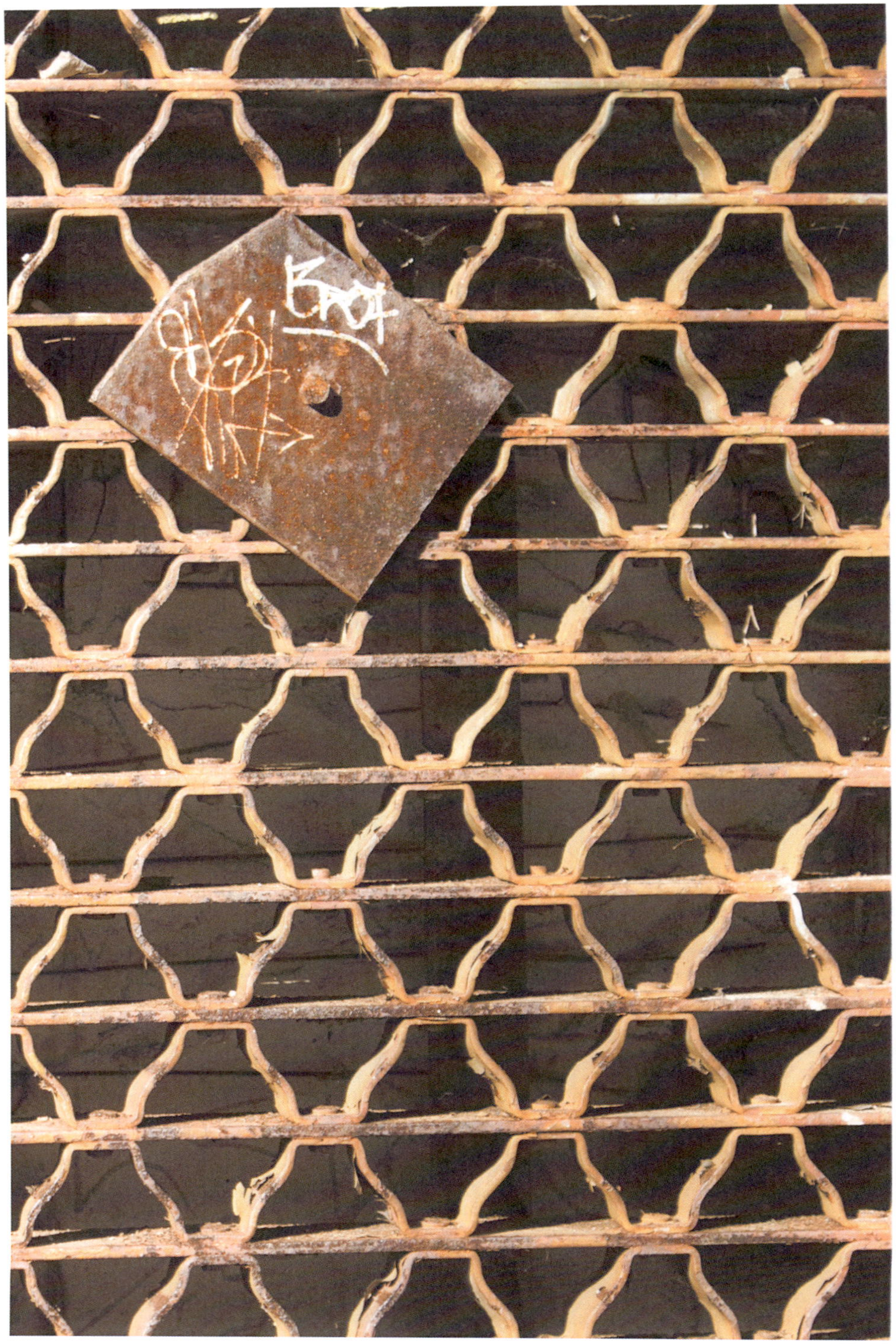

Digital photo of a metal grate placed over a window to keep trespassers out

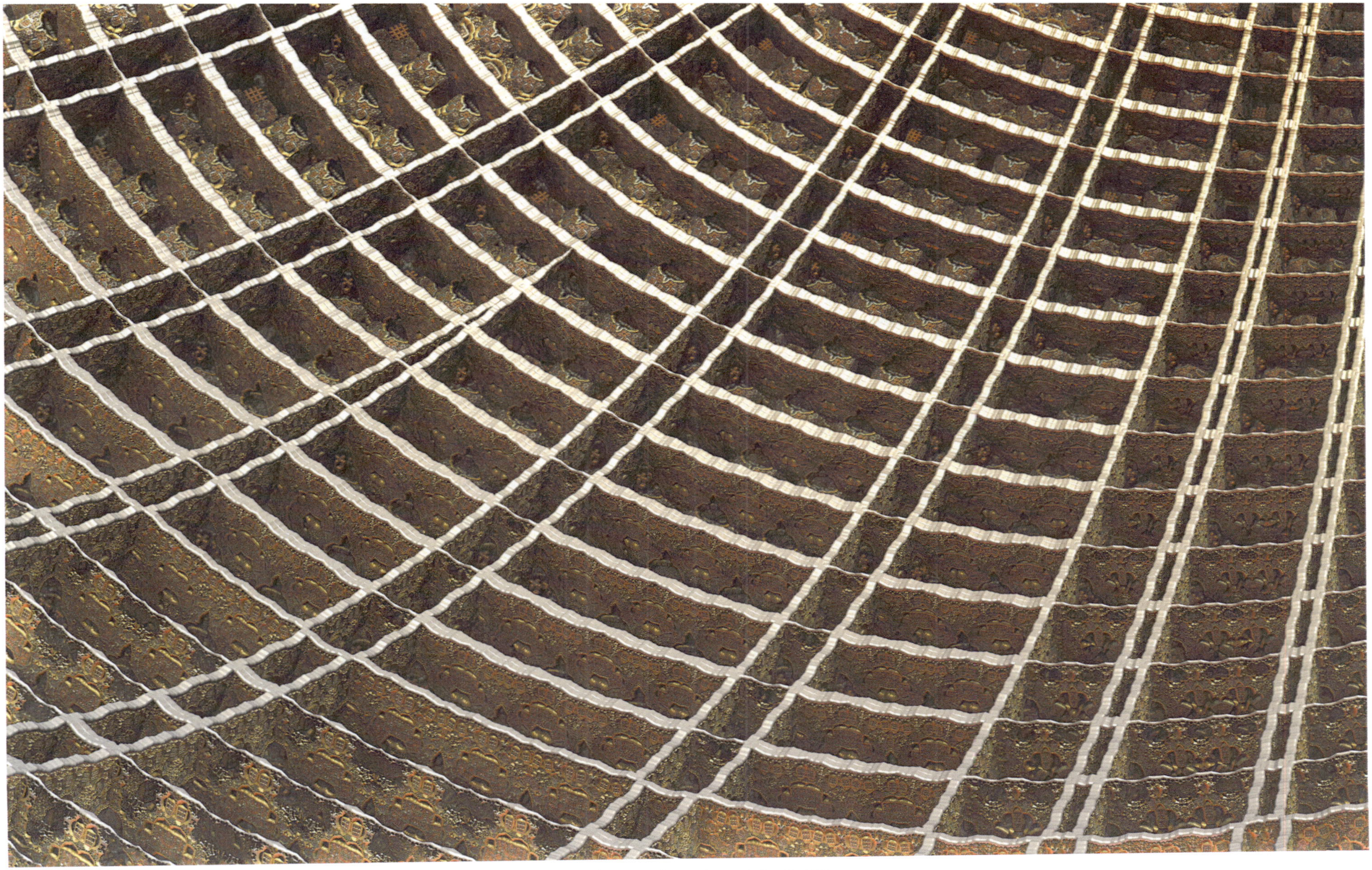

Fractal image from Mandelbulb 3D

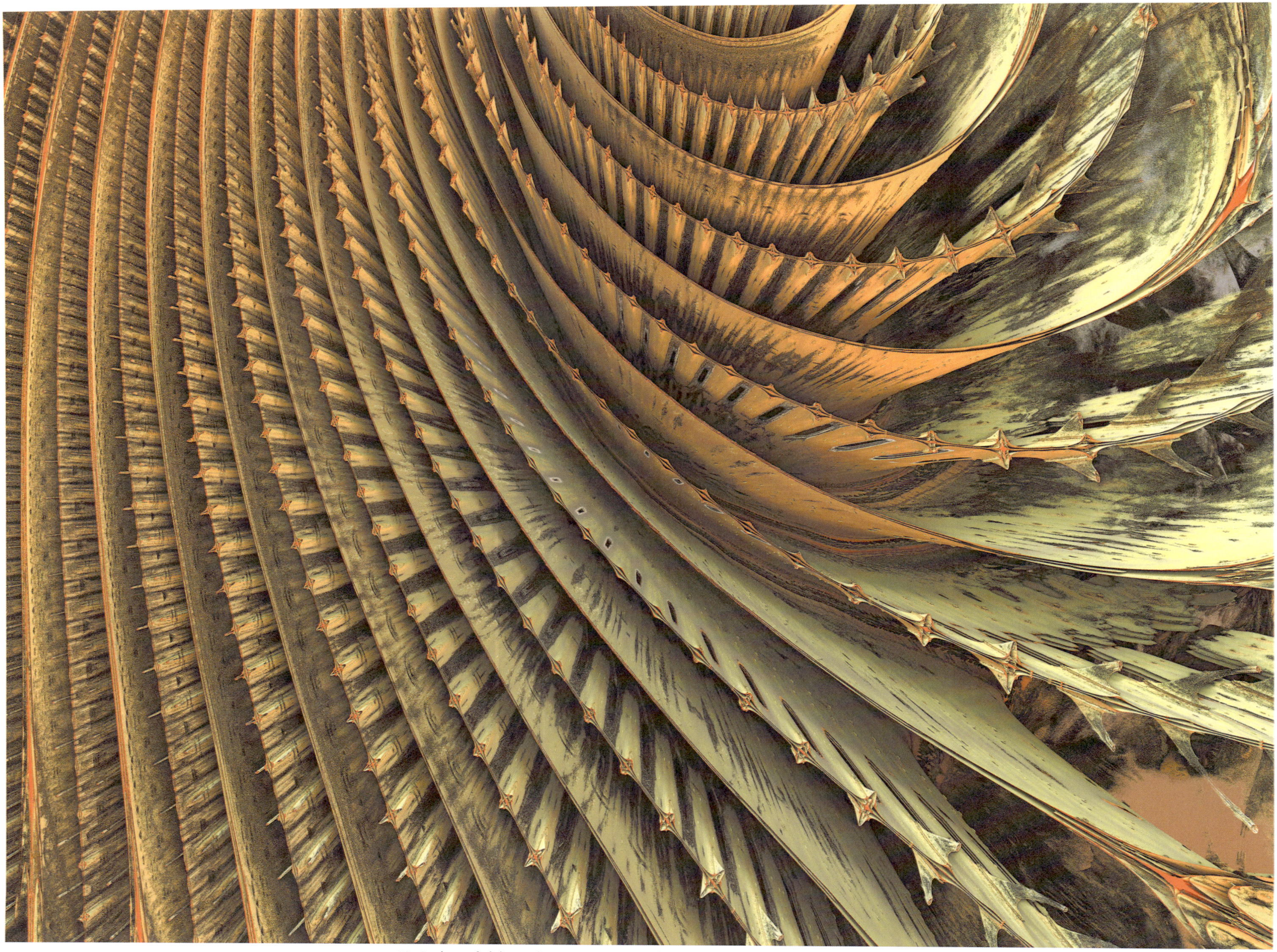

"Spiral, unfolding sheet cutting tool," image from Mandelbulb 3D

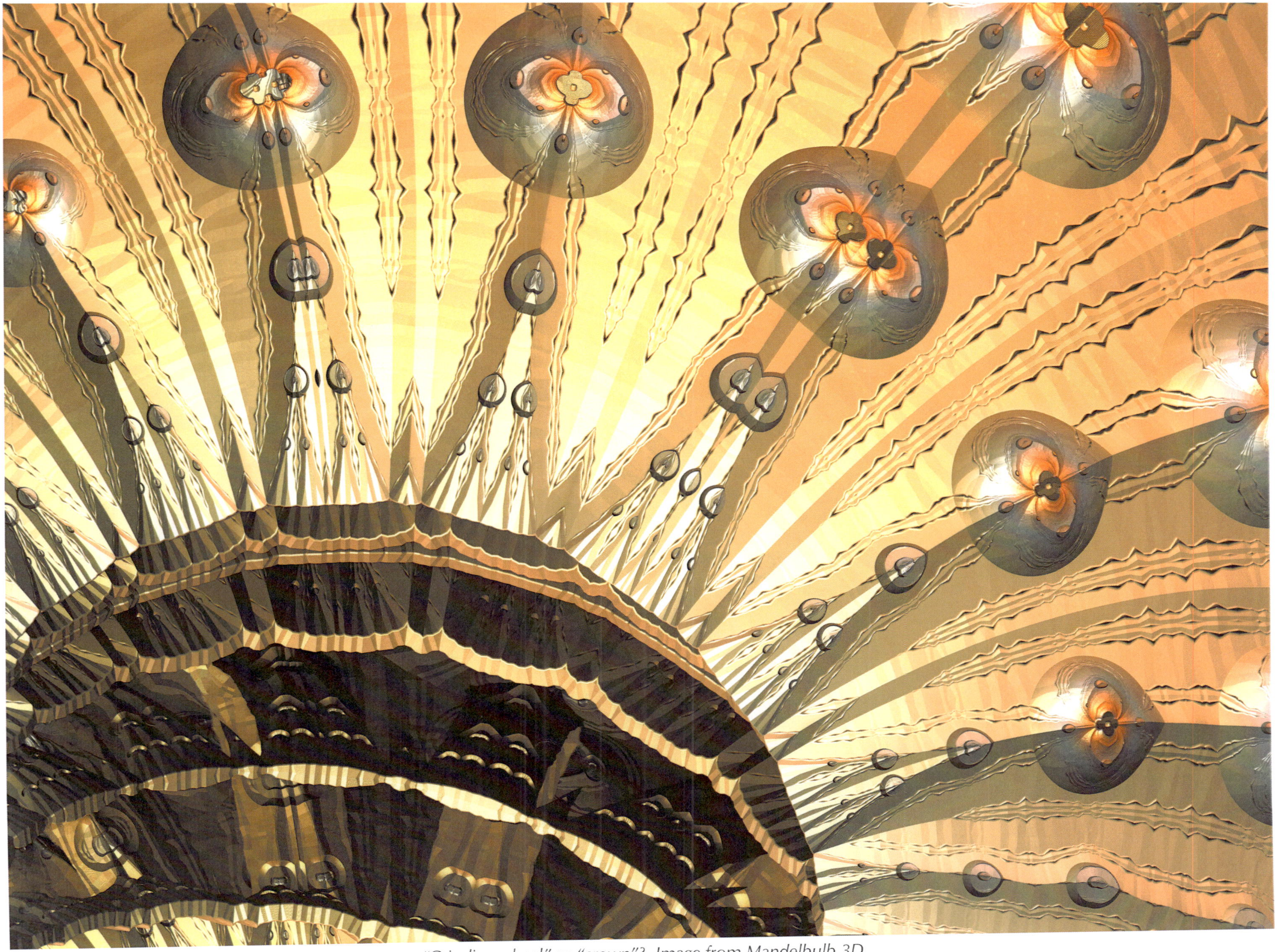

"Grinding wheel" or "crown"? Image from Mandelbulb 3D

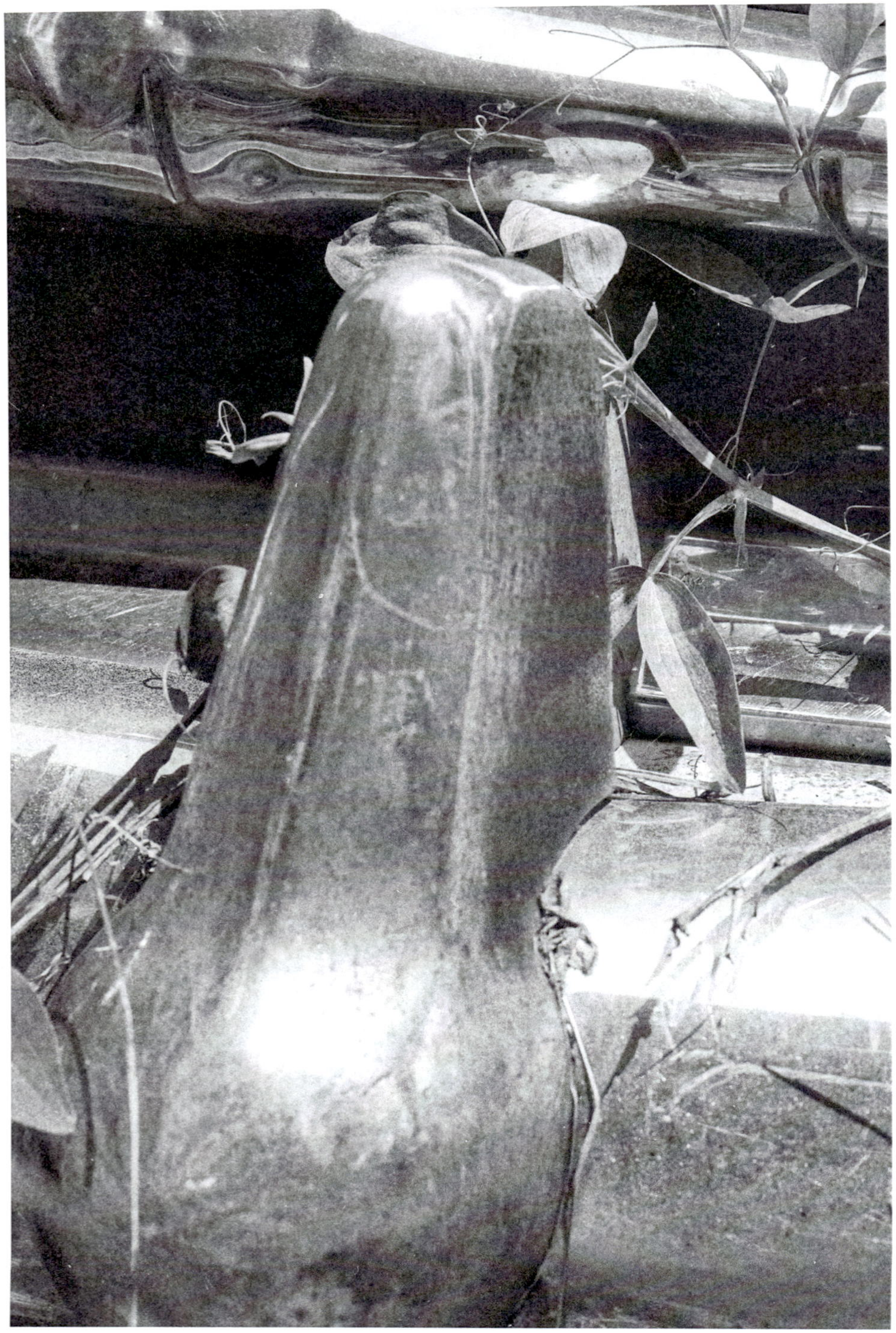

Bumper of junked car photographed on 6×6 cm B&W negative film

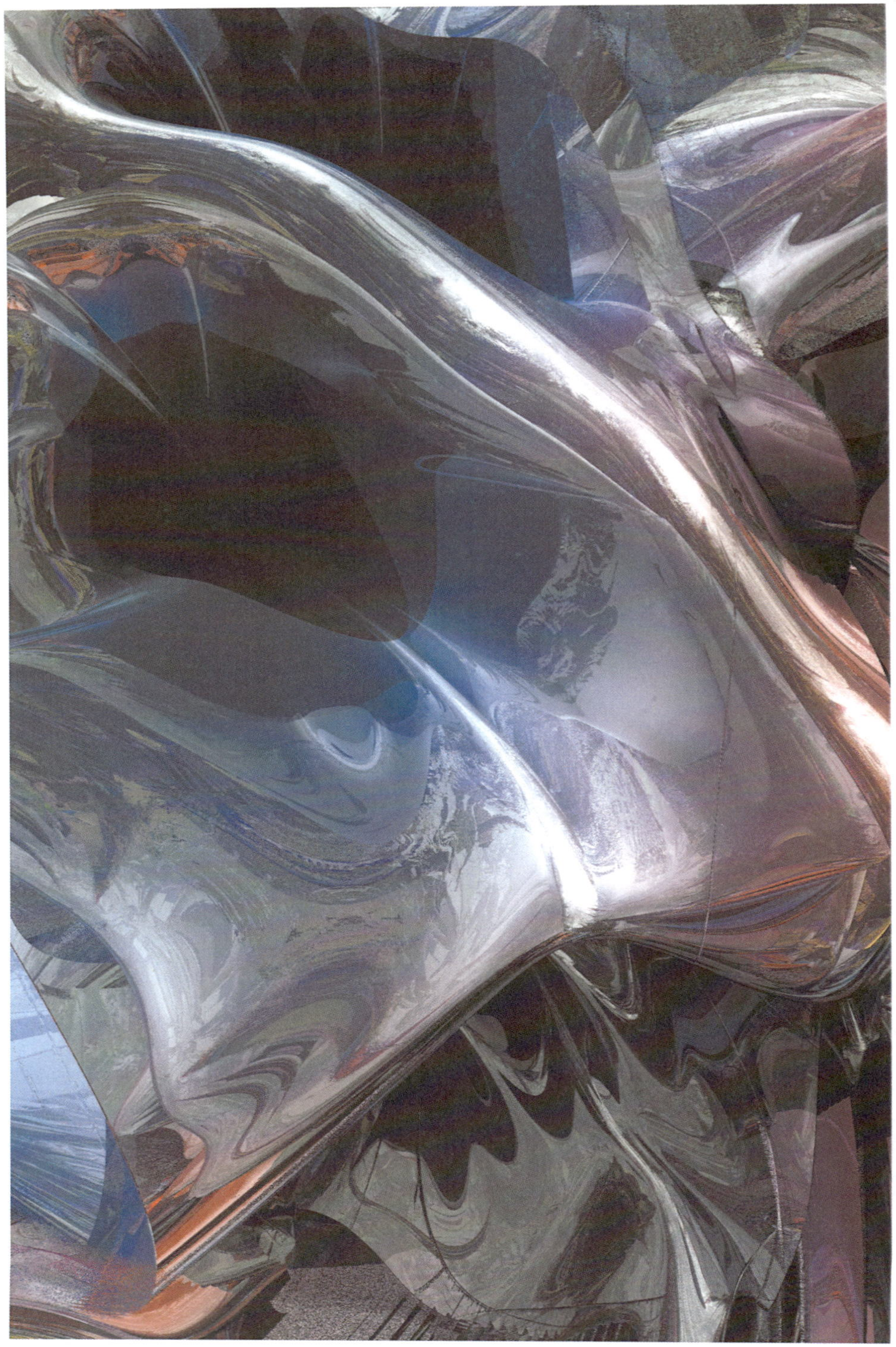

Mandelbulb 3D image resembling twisted metal

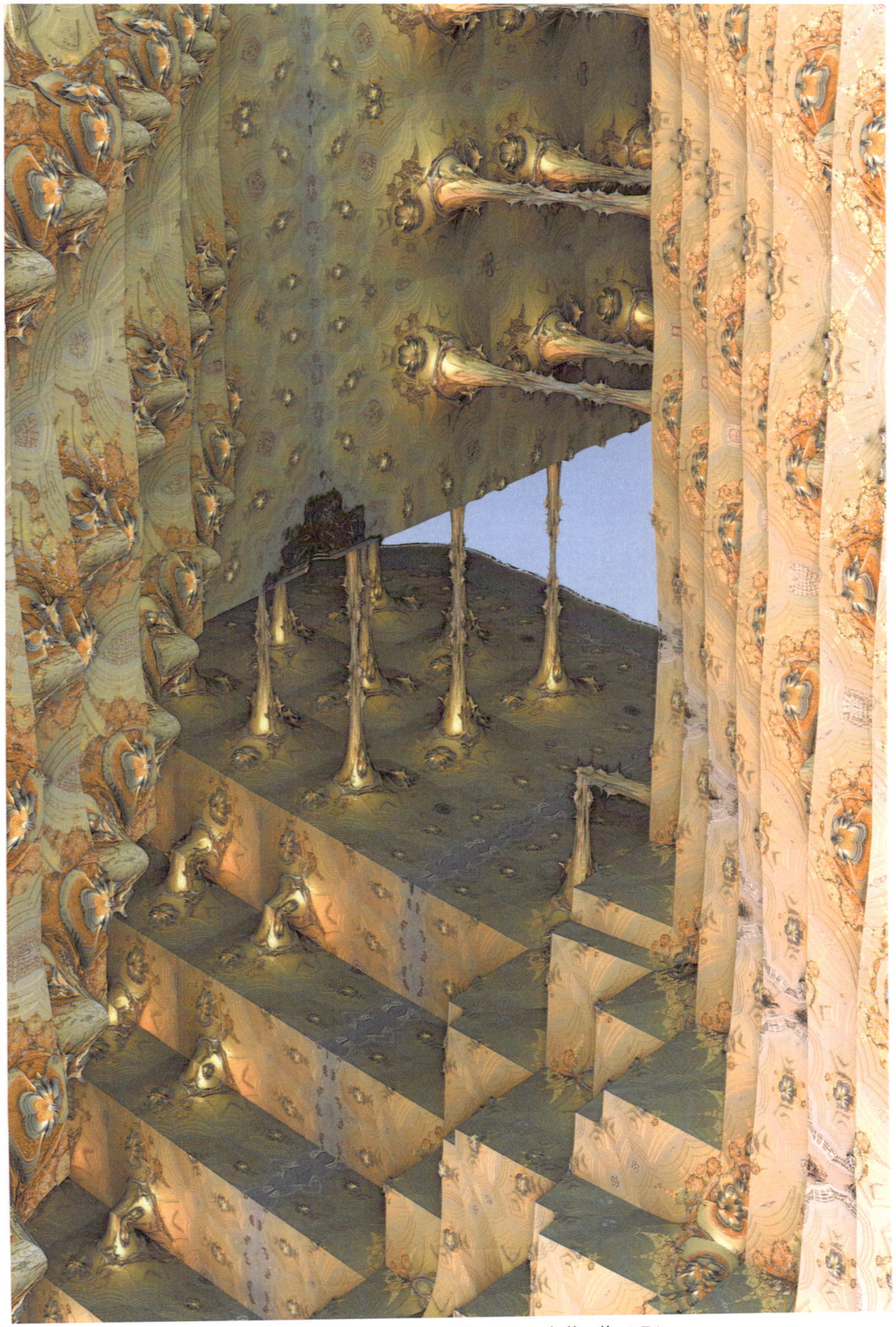

"Stairway" (image created by Mandelbulb 3D)

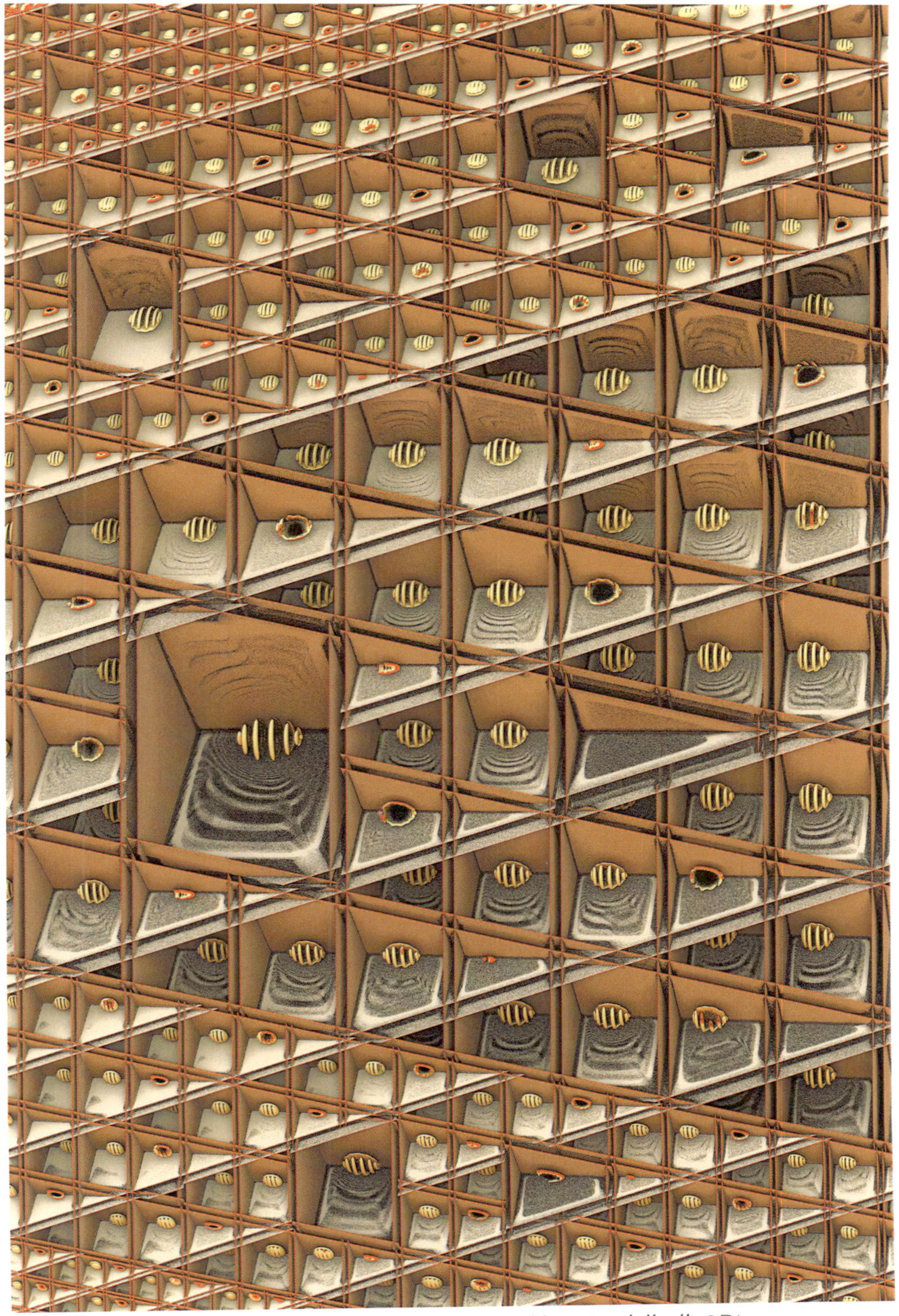

"Little boxes" (image created by Mandelbulb 3D)

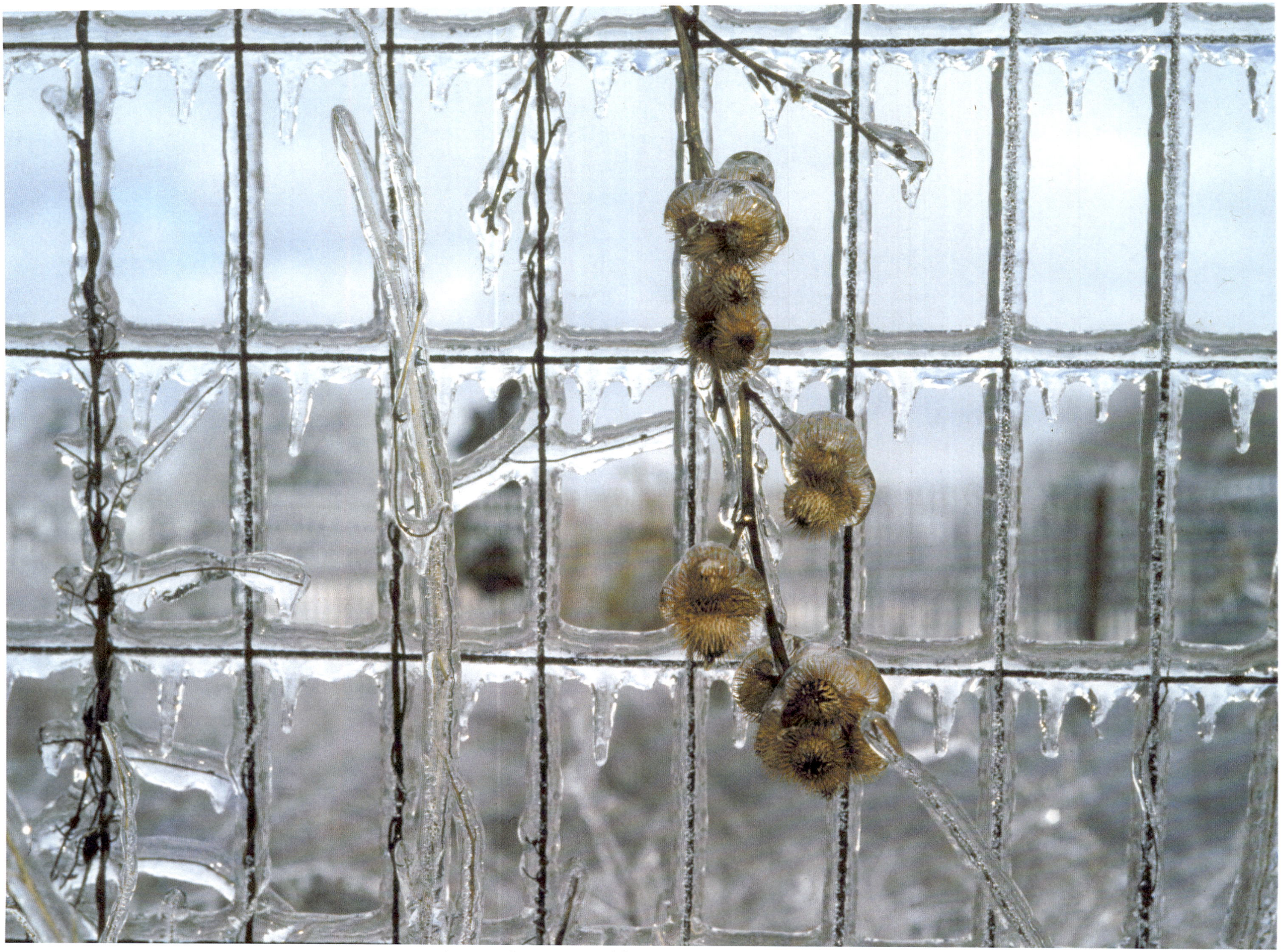

Ice on a fence scanned from a 6x6 cm color negative

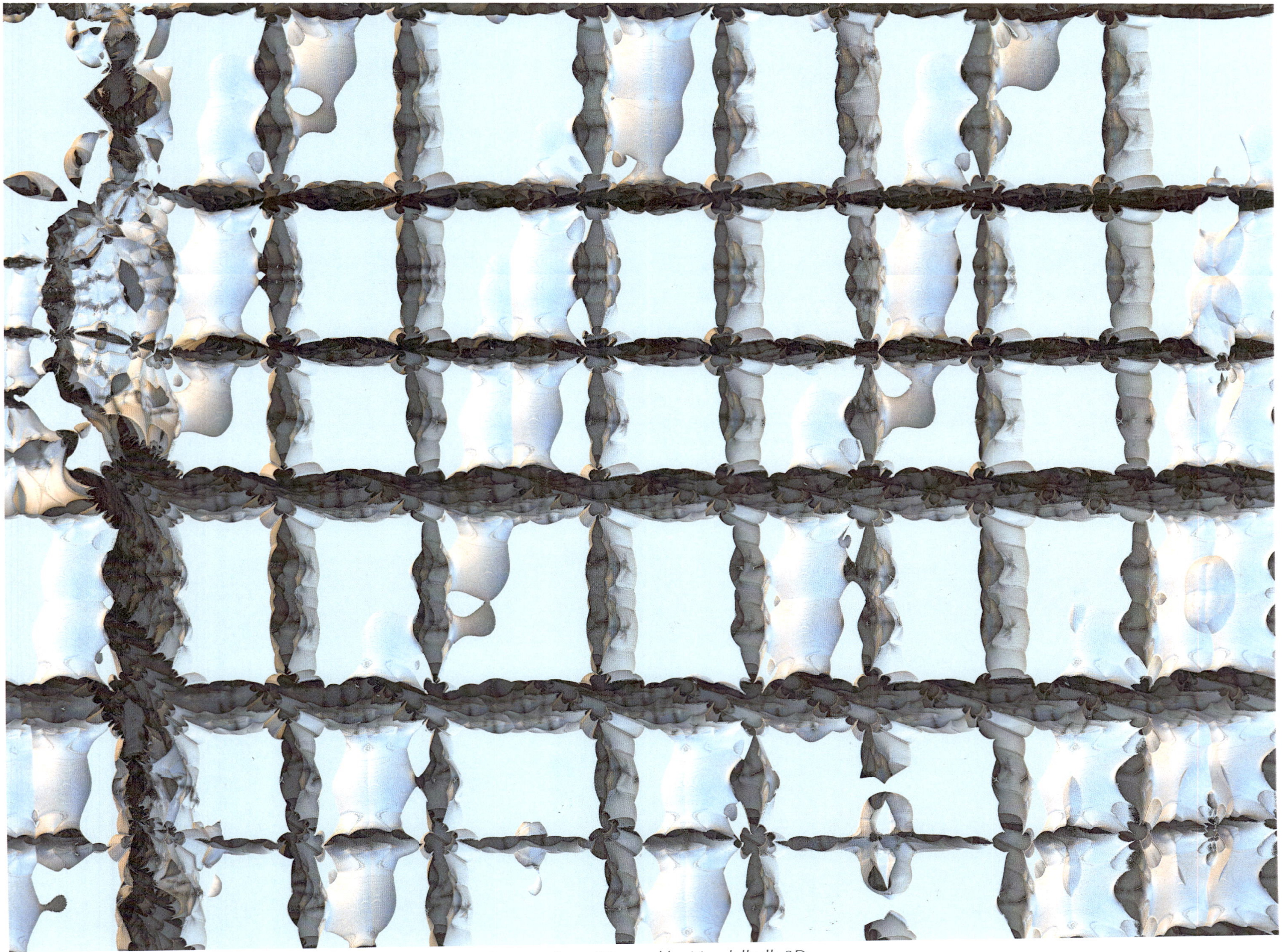

"Ice on a fence" imaged by Mandelbulb 3D

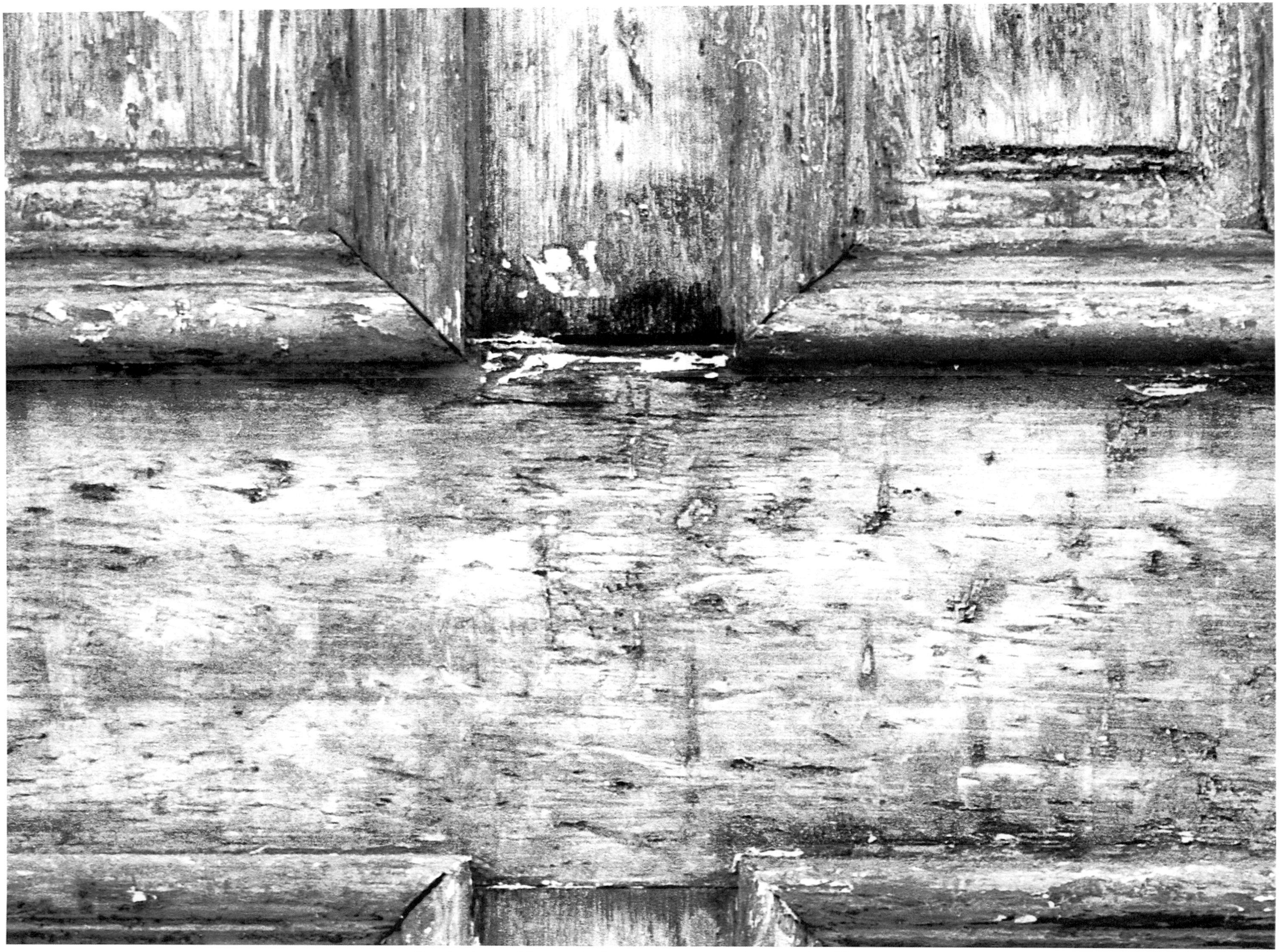

Rustic door with panels shot on 6×6 cm color negative film.

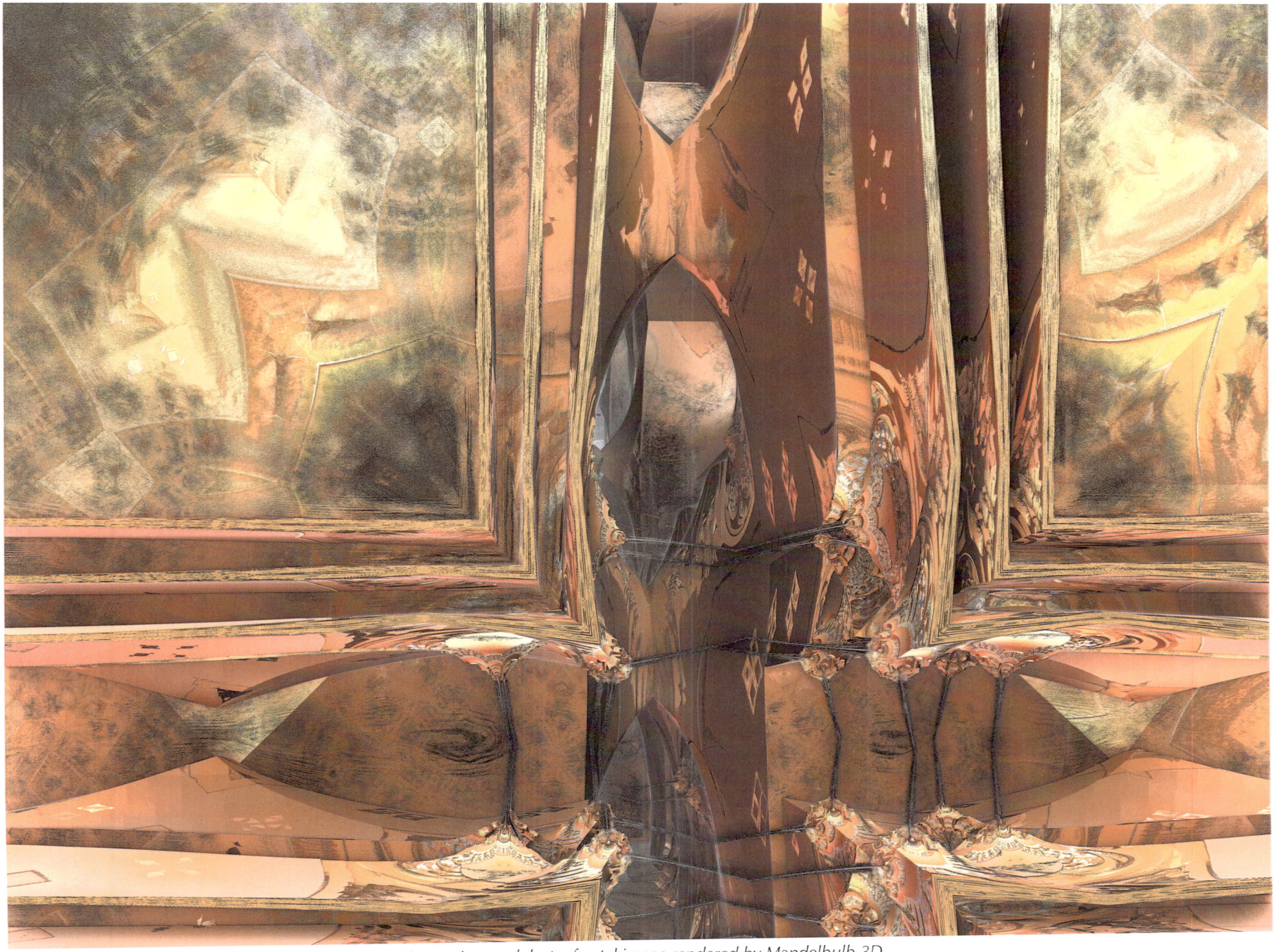

Not rustic wood, but a fractal image rendered by Mandelbulb 3D

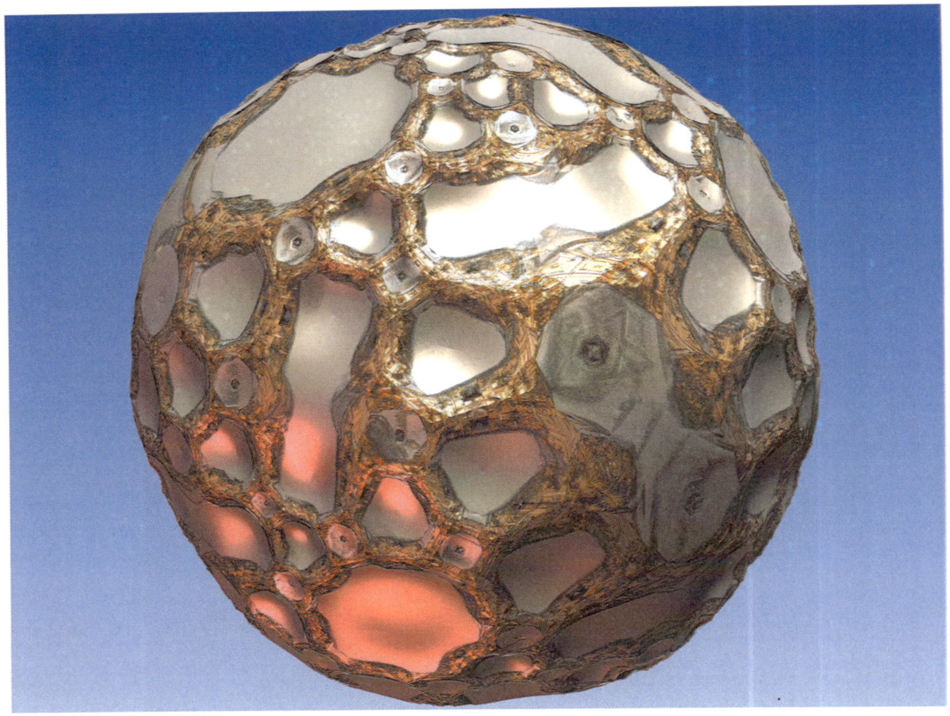
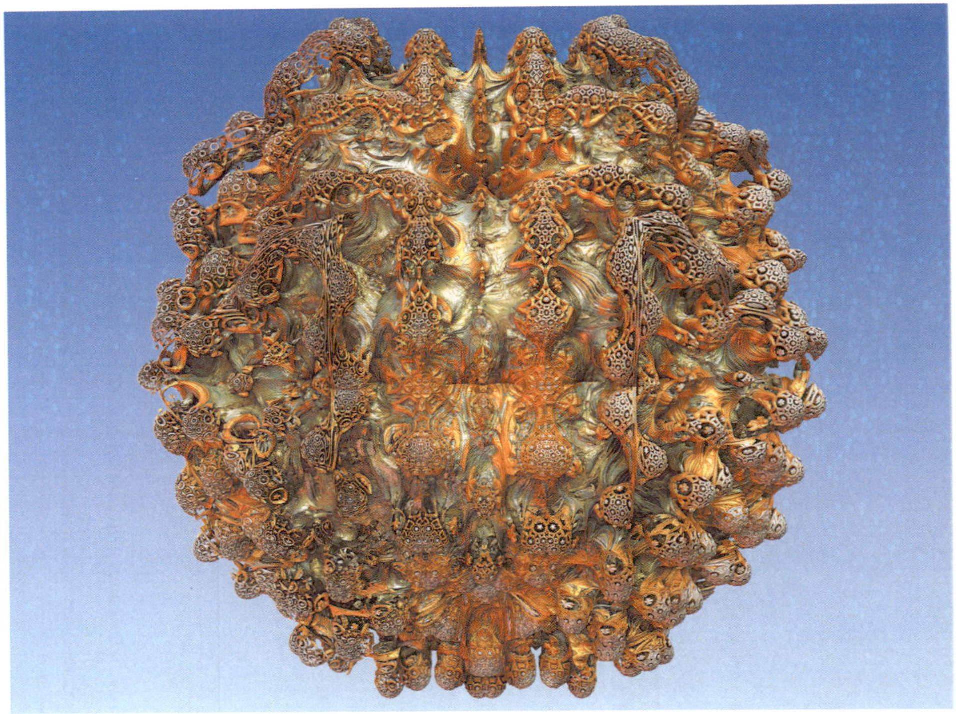
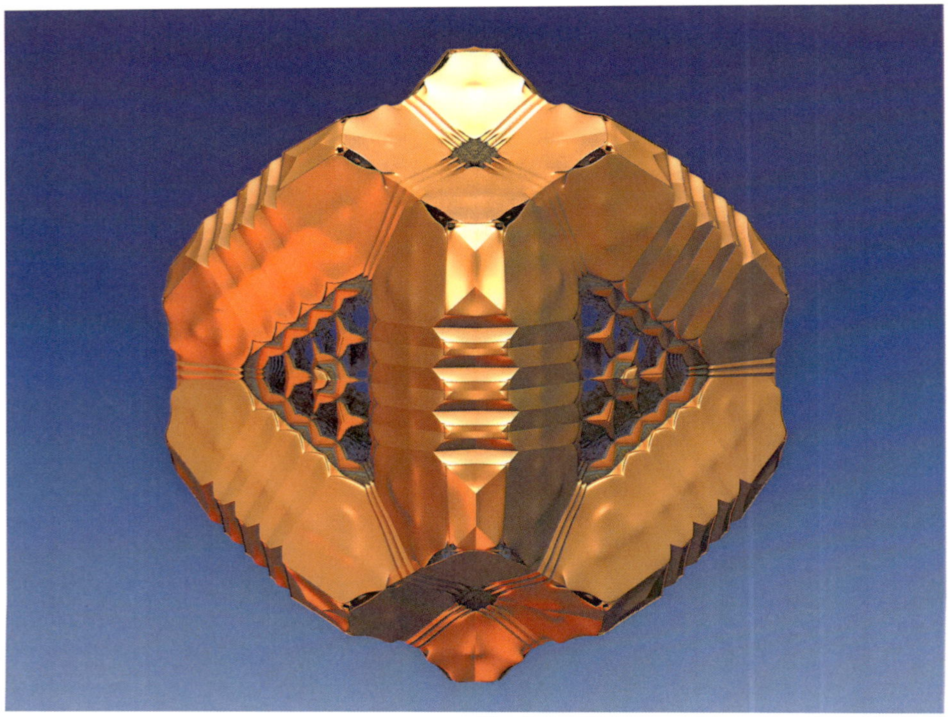
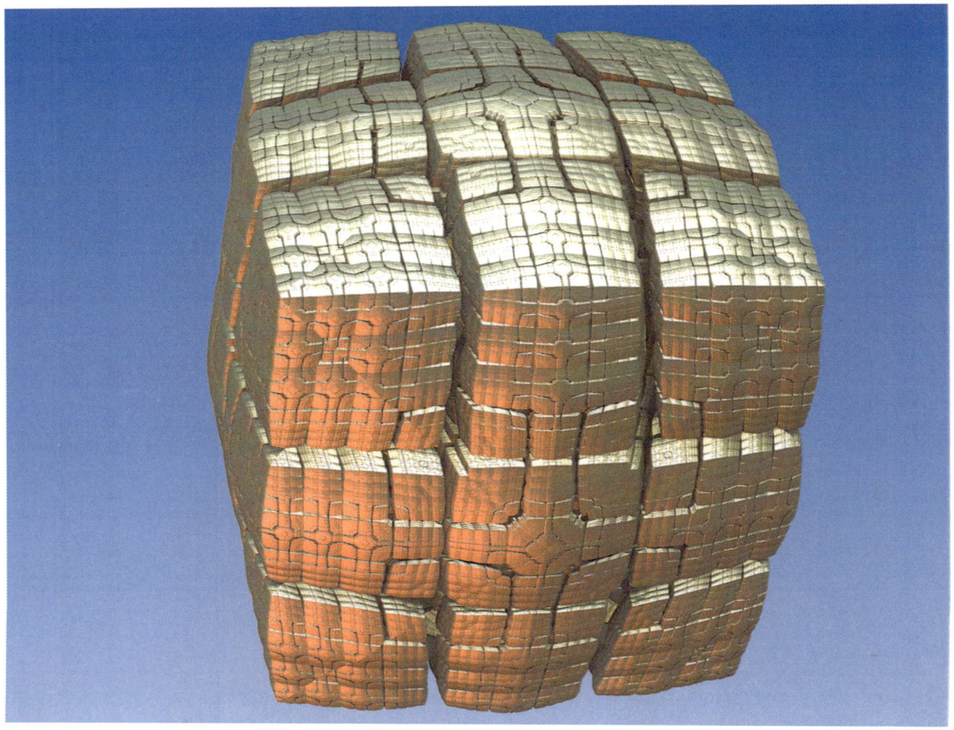

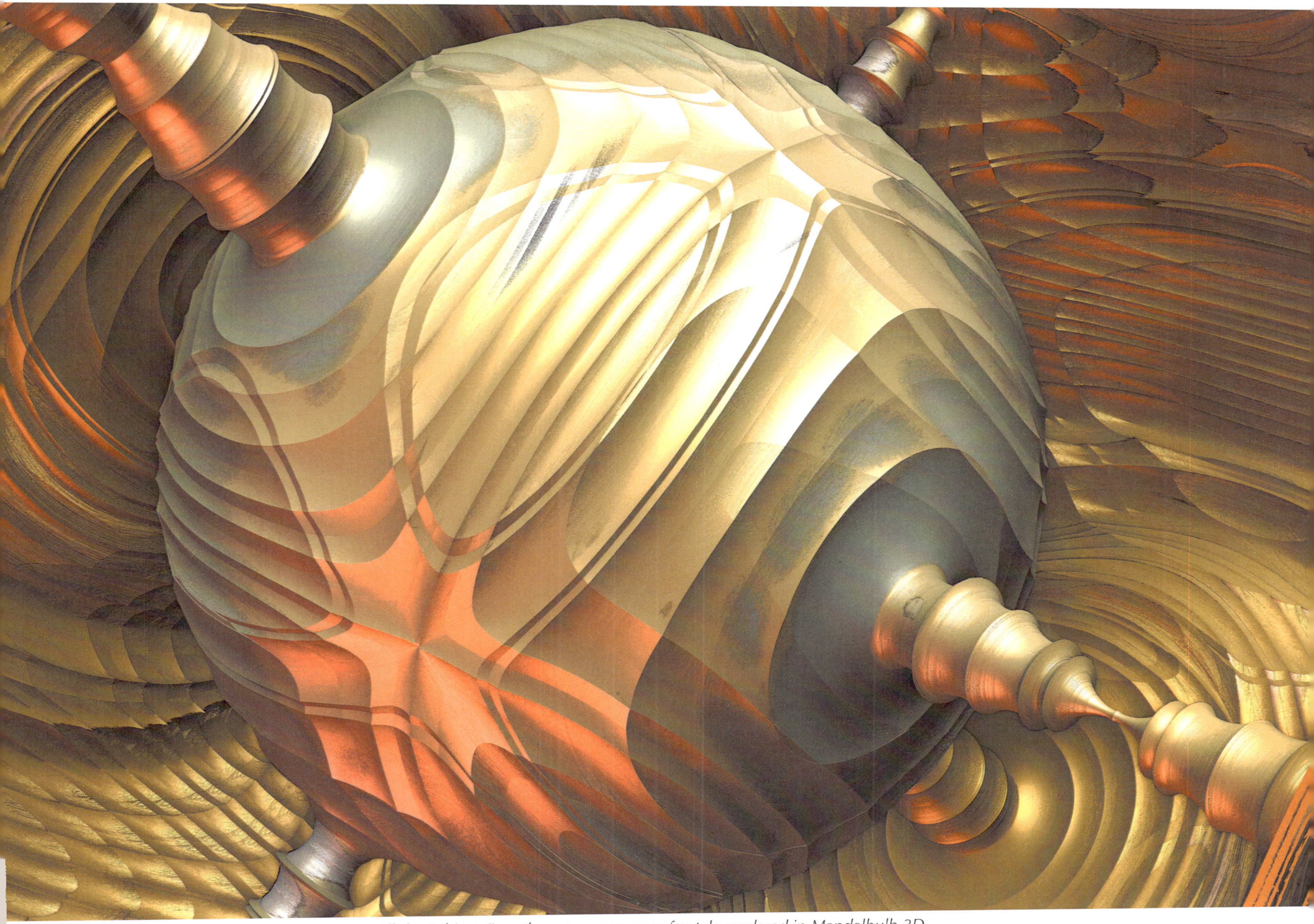

All the "objects" on these two pages are fractals rendered in Mandelbulb 3D.

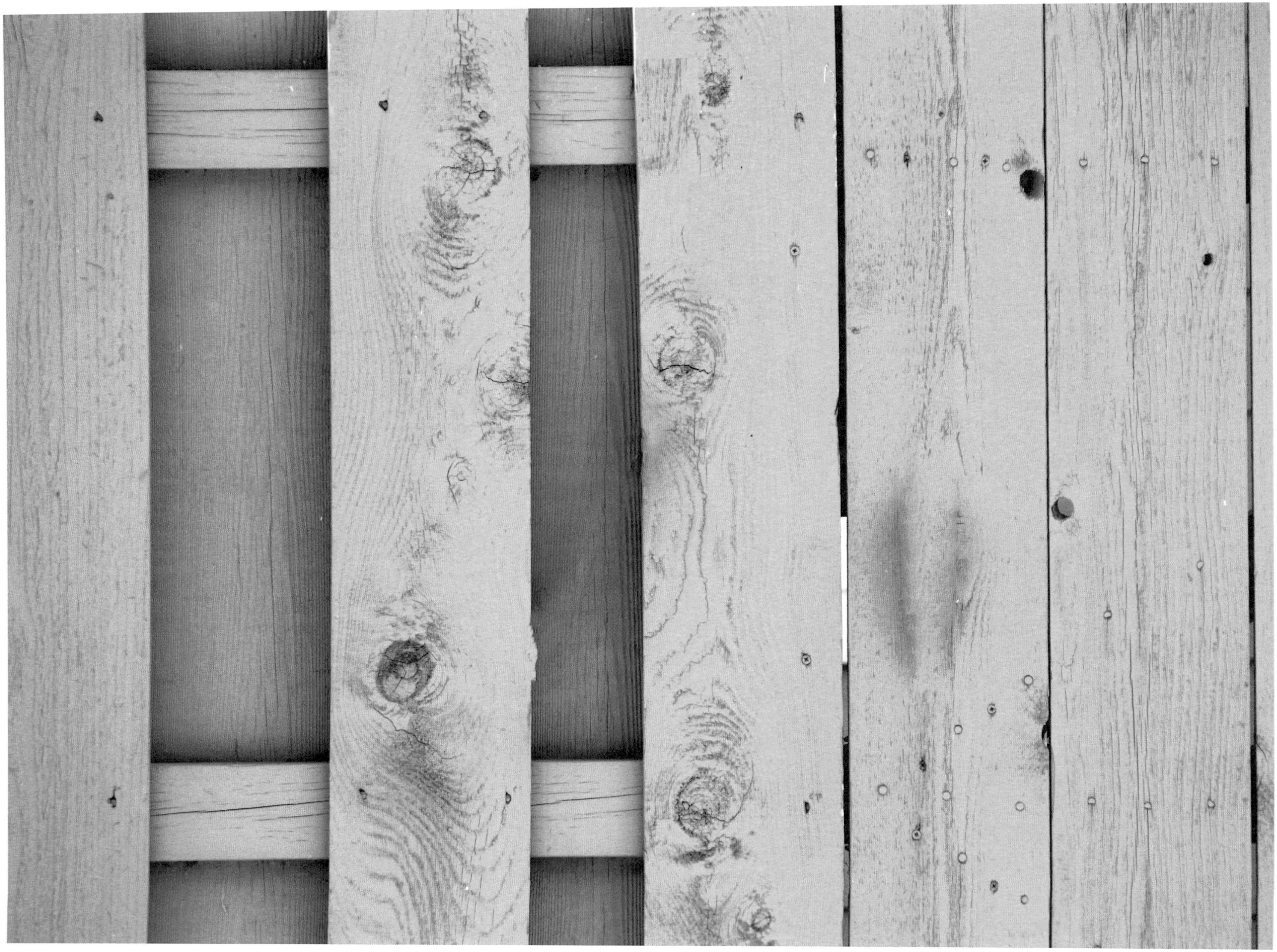

Opposite page,** backyard fence in a digital photo;* ***above, *"peeling paint on the wall" fractal from Mandelbulb 3D*

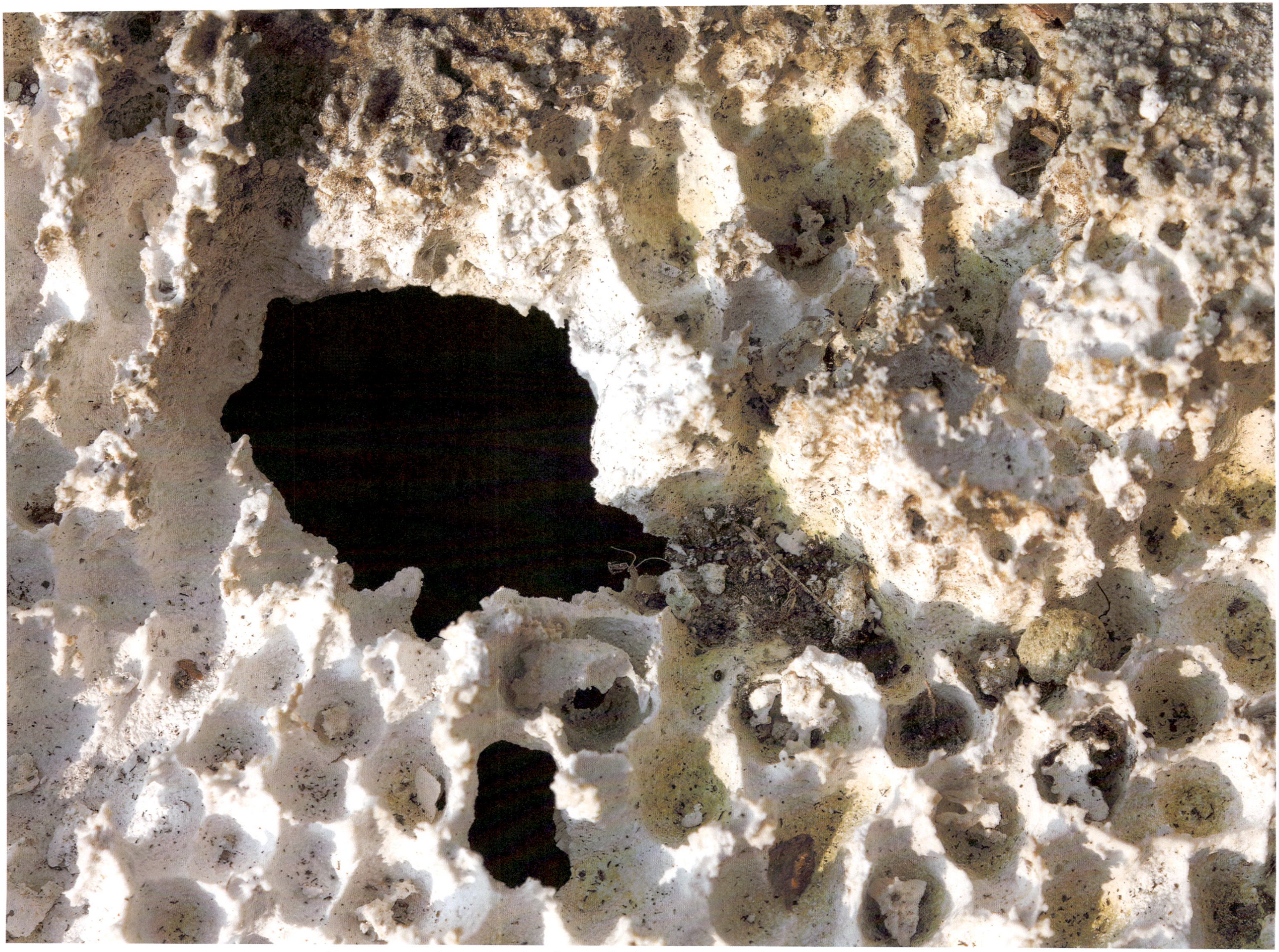

Limestone garden pedestal surface etched away over time by acid rain (digital photo)

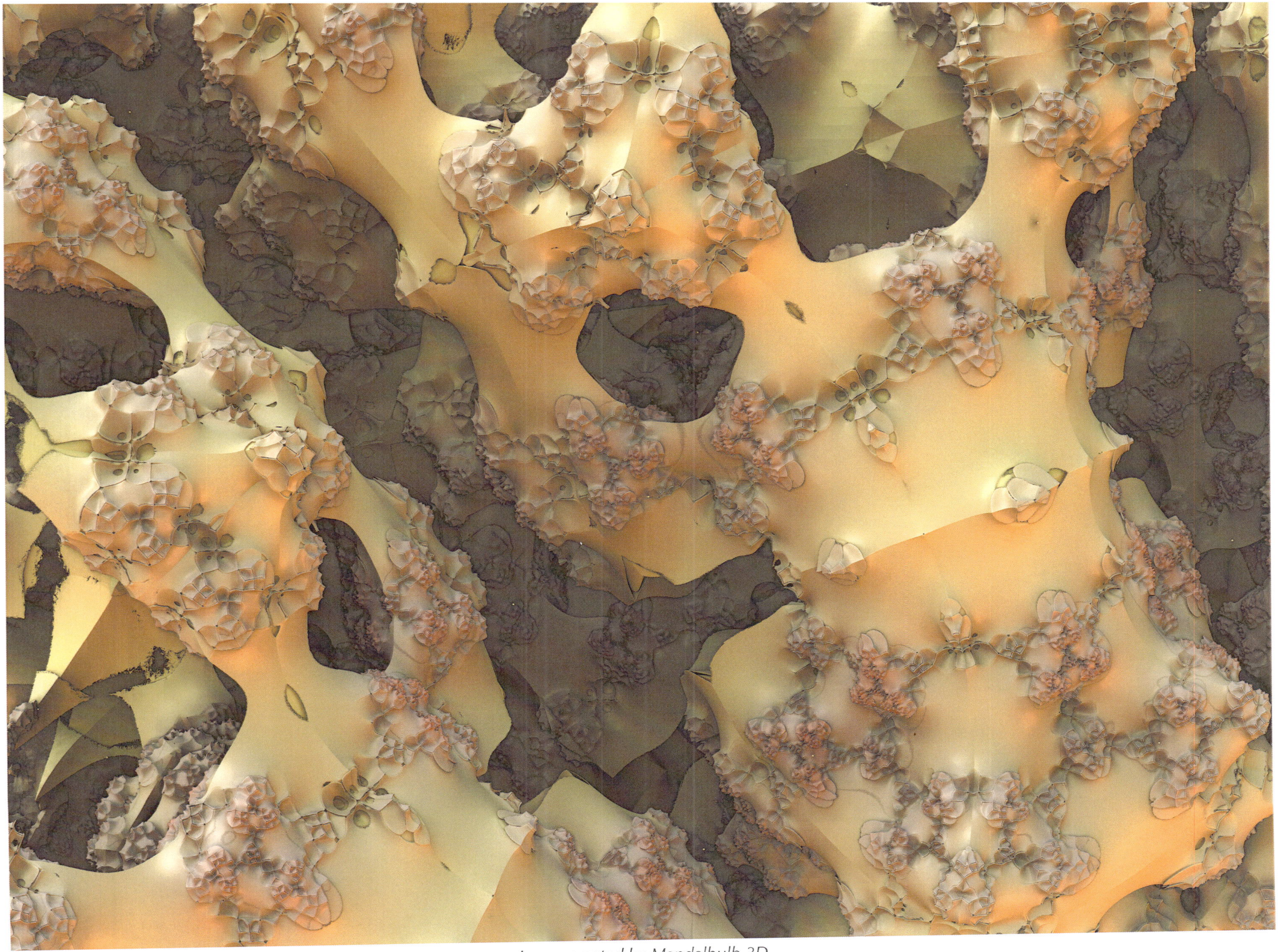

Image created by Mandelbulb 3D

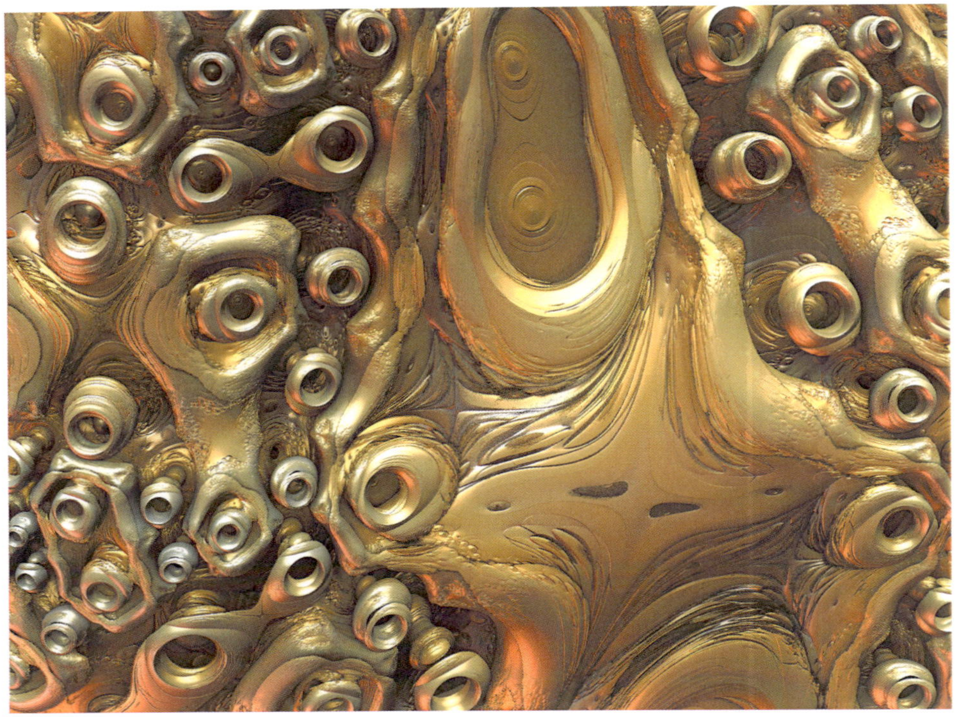
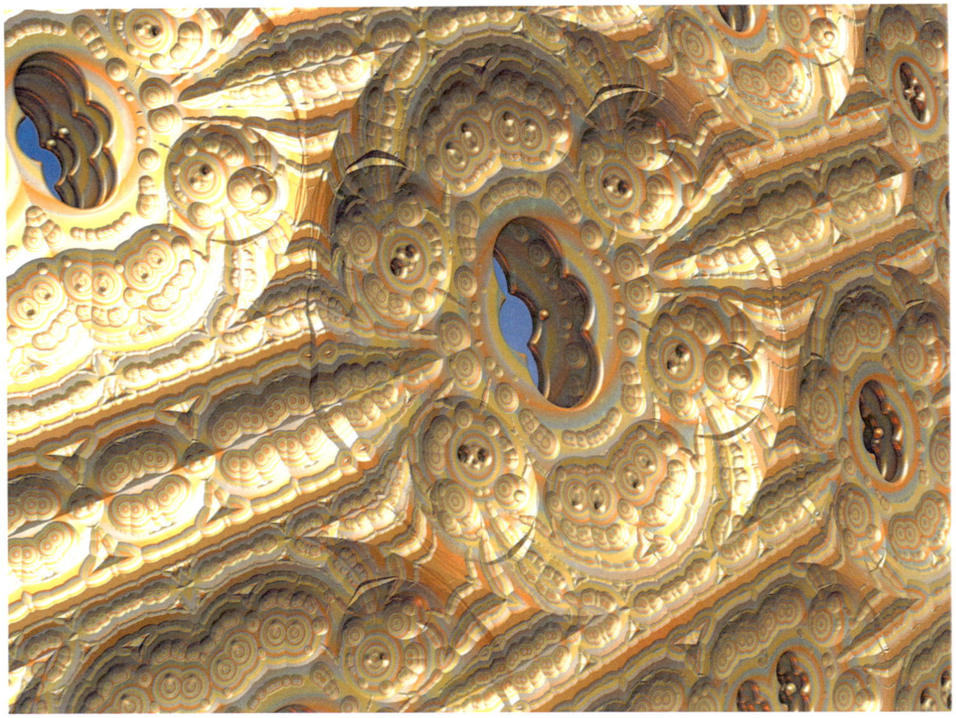
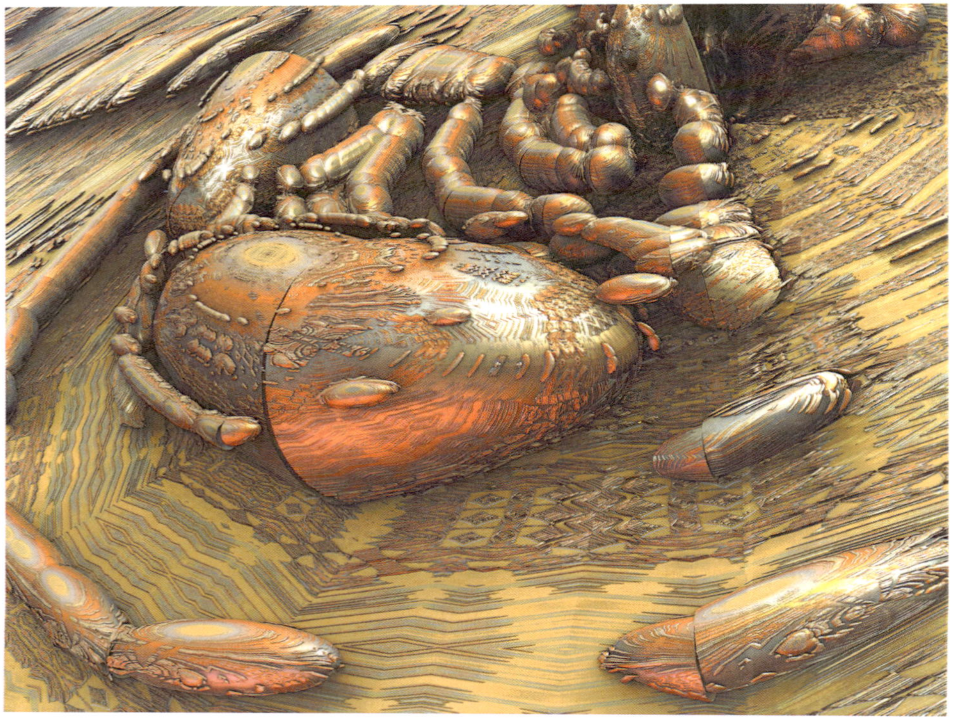
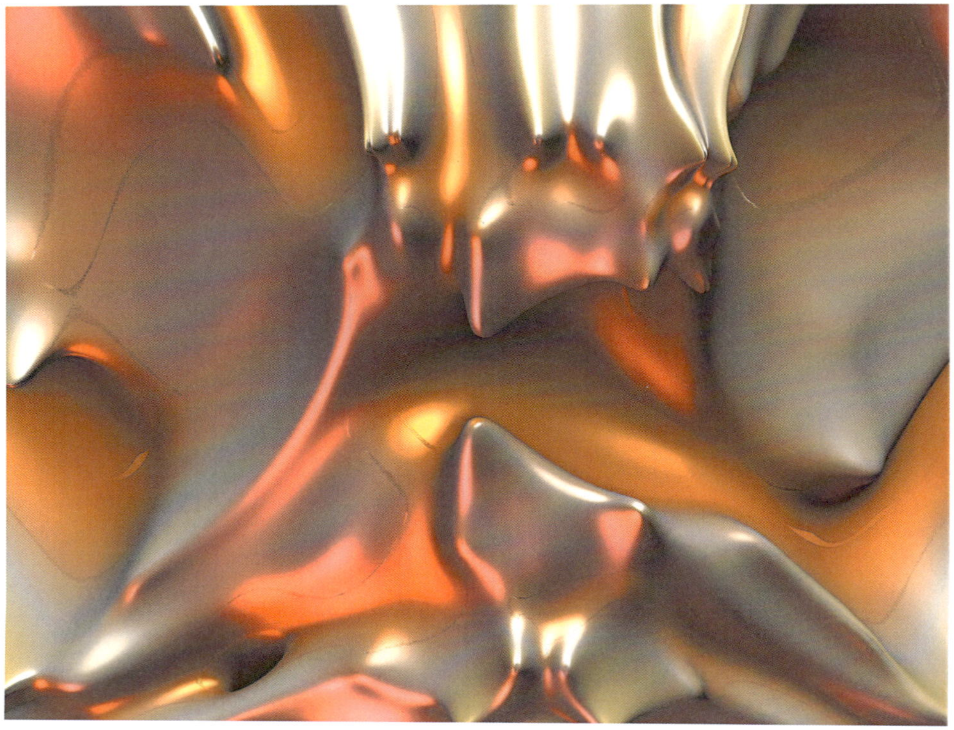

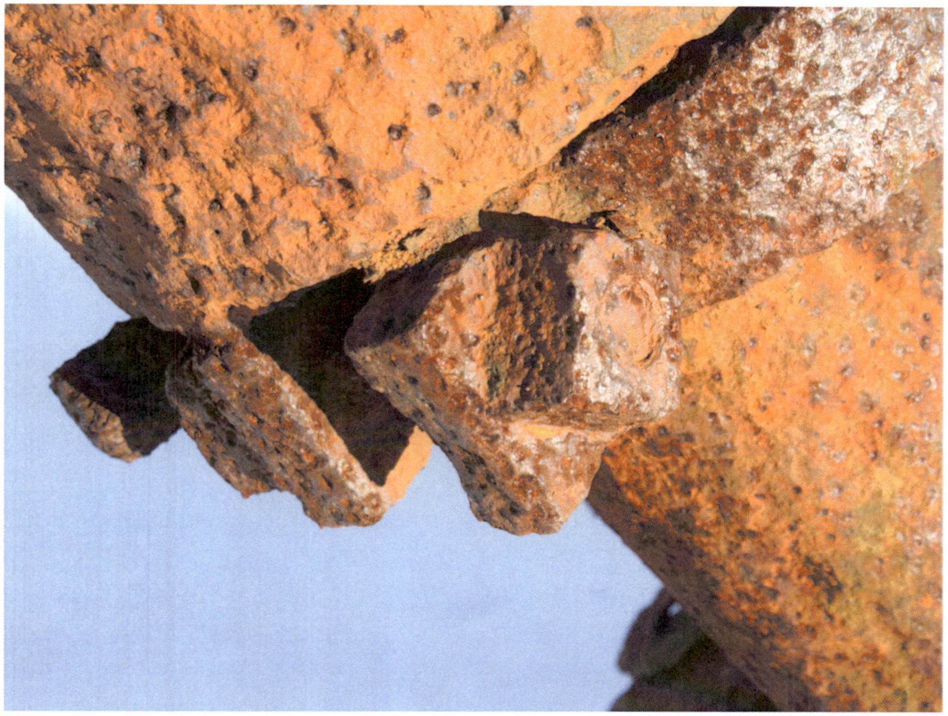

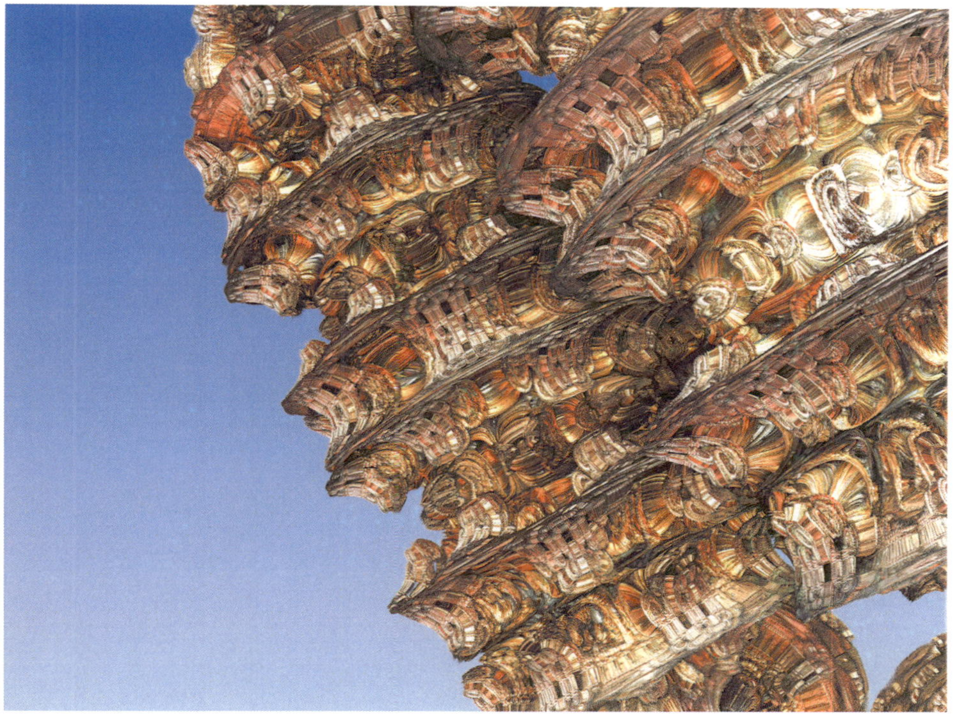

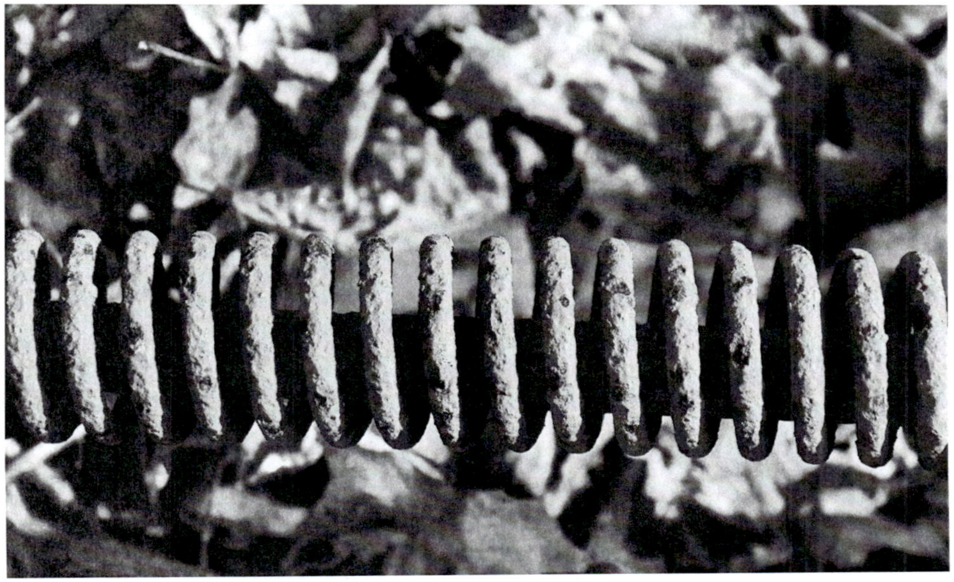

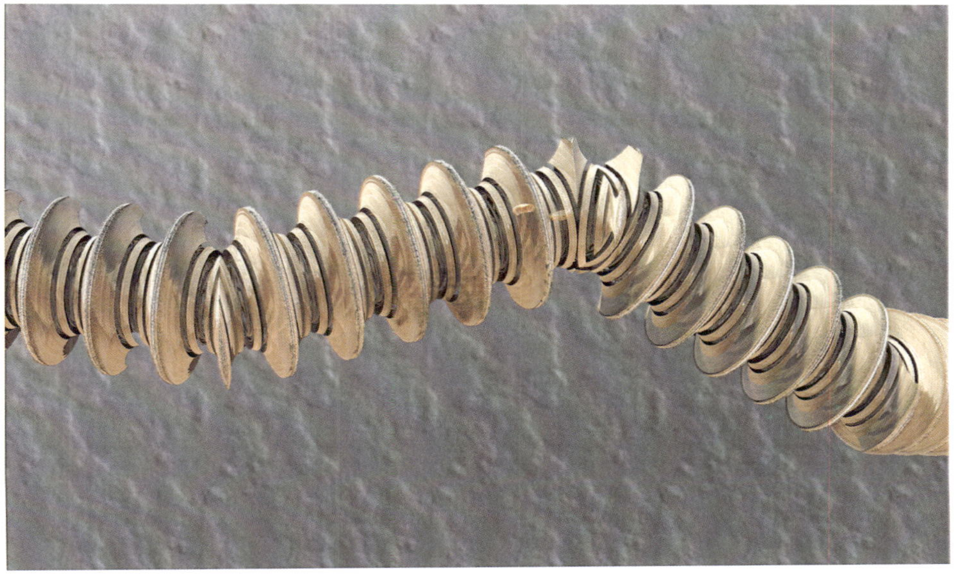

Opposite page, *all metal-like images were created by Mandelbulb 3D.* ***This page, top-left,*** *digital photo of a metal gear-shaft from an old water-wheel powered grist mill in Bucks County, Pennsylvania.* ***Bottom-left,*** *digital photo shows a rusting spring from a piece of abandoned farm equipment in a Bucks County forest. At the* ***right, top and bottom,*** *both images were rendered by Mandelbulb 3D.*

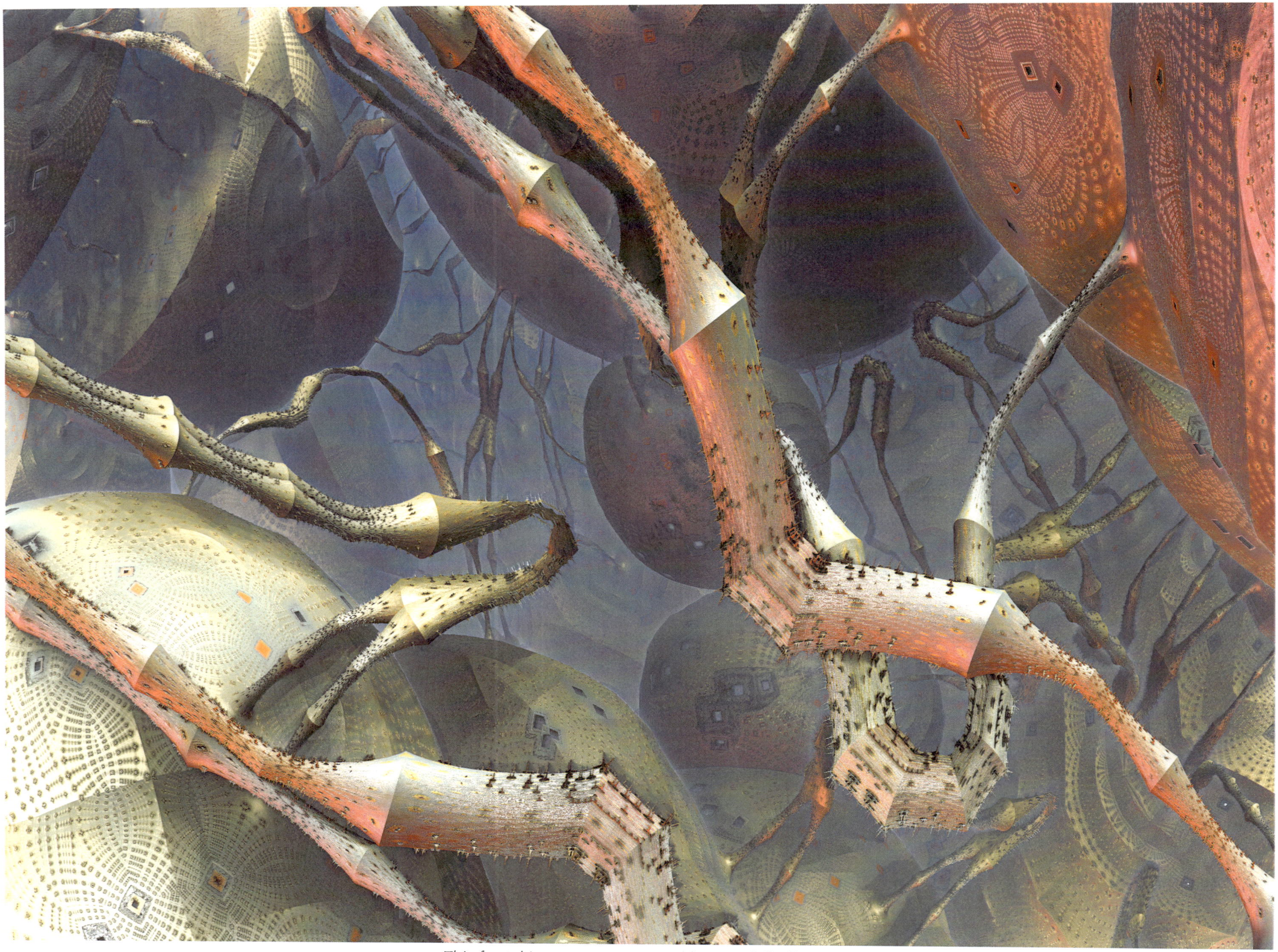

This fractal image was generated by Mandelbulb 3D.

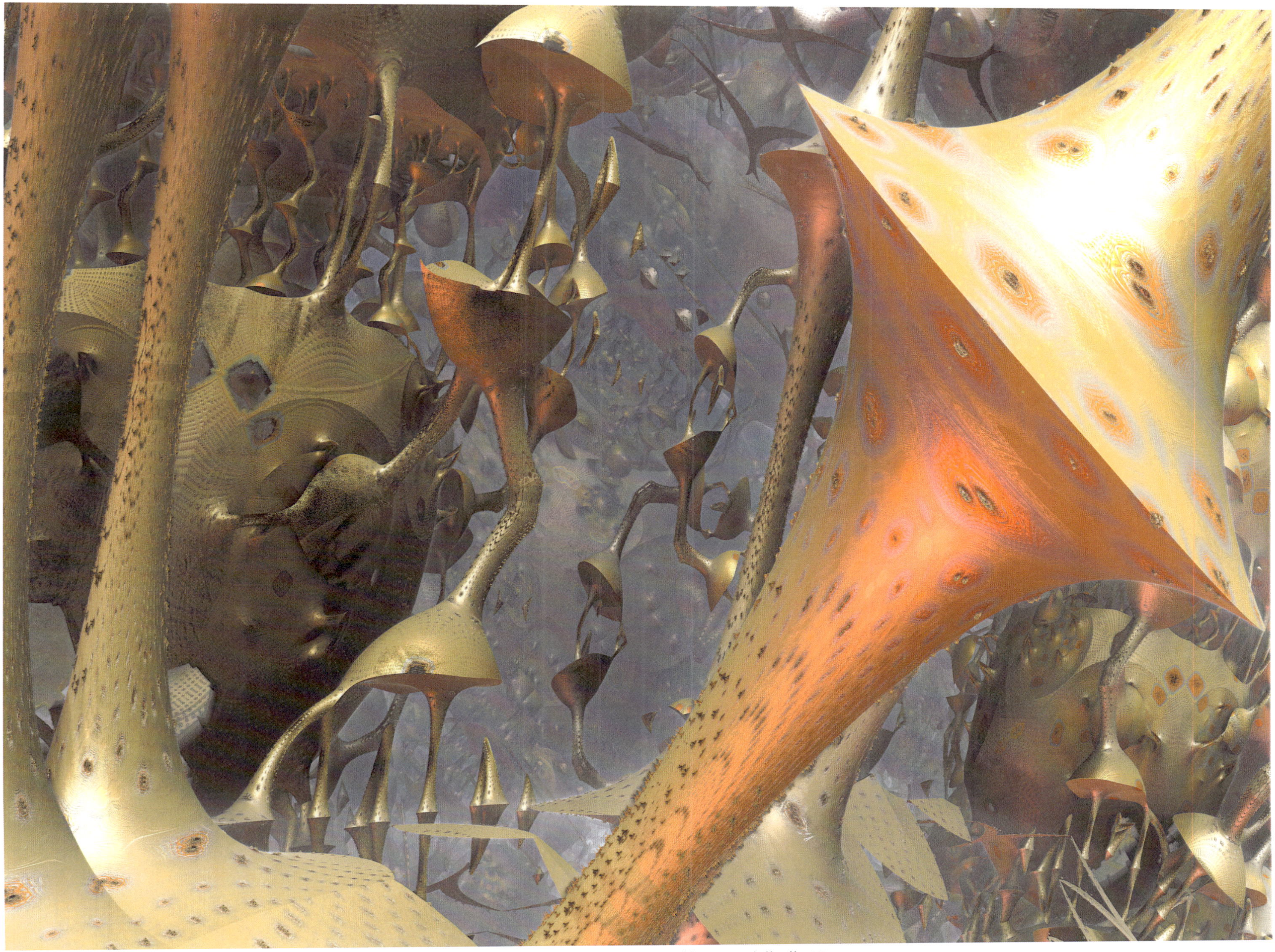

This fractal image was generated by Mandelbulb 3D.

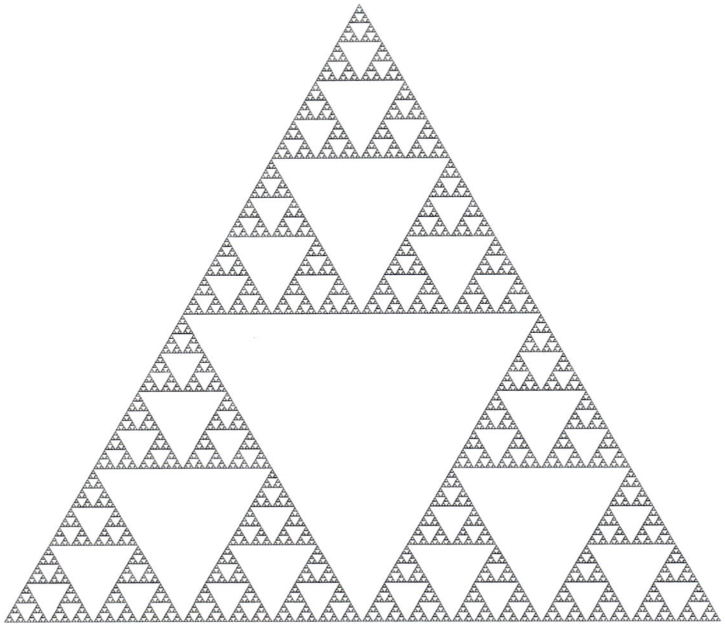

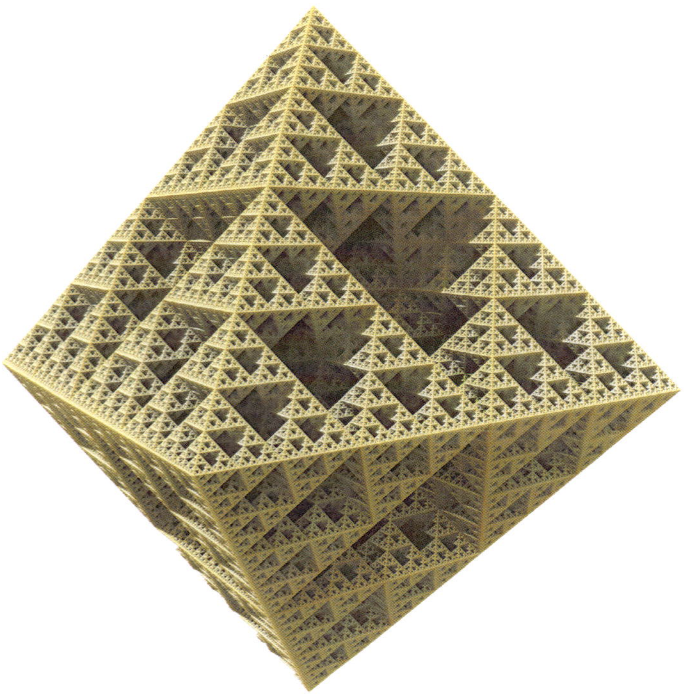

3D rendering of the Sierpinski triangle (above)

Sierpinski Triangle & Menger Sponge: Architectural Building Blocks

The Sierpinski triangle (left), also called the Sierpinski gasket or Sierpinski sieve, is a fractal attractive, fixed-set with the overall shape of an equilateral triangle, subdivided recursively into smaller equilateral triangles. Originally constructed as a curve, this is one of the basic examples of *self-similar sets*—that is, it is a mathematically generated pattern that is reproducible at any magnification or reduction. It is named after the Polish mathematician Wacław Sierpinski, but appeared as a decorative pattern many centuries before the work of Sierpinski.

Directly below is the Menger sponge (also known as the Menger cube, Menger universal curve, Sierpinski cube, or Sierpinski sponge), which is a three-dimensional generalization of the one-dimensional Cantor set and two-dimensional Sierpinski carpet. It was first described by Karl Menger in 1926, in his studies of the concept of topological dimension.

—*Text from Wikipedia*

For more detailed information, see the Wikipedia section entitled "Fractal" located at https://en.wikipedia.org/wiki/Fractal

Note: All three images on this page were generated in Mandelbulb 3D using the most basic parameters.

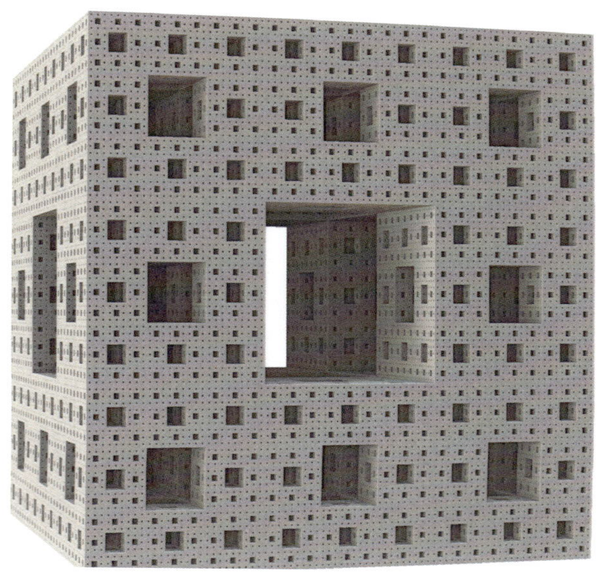

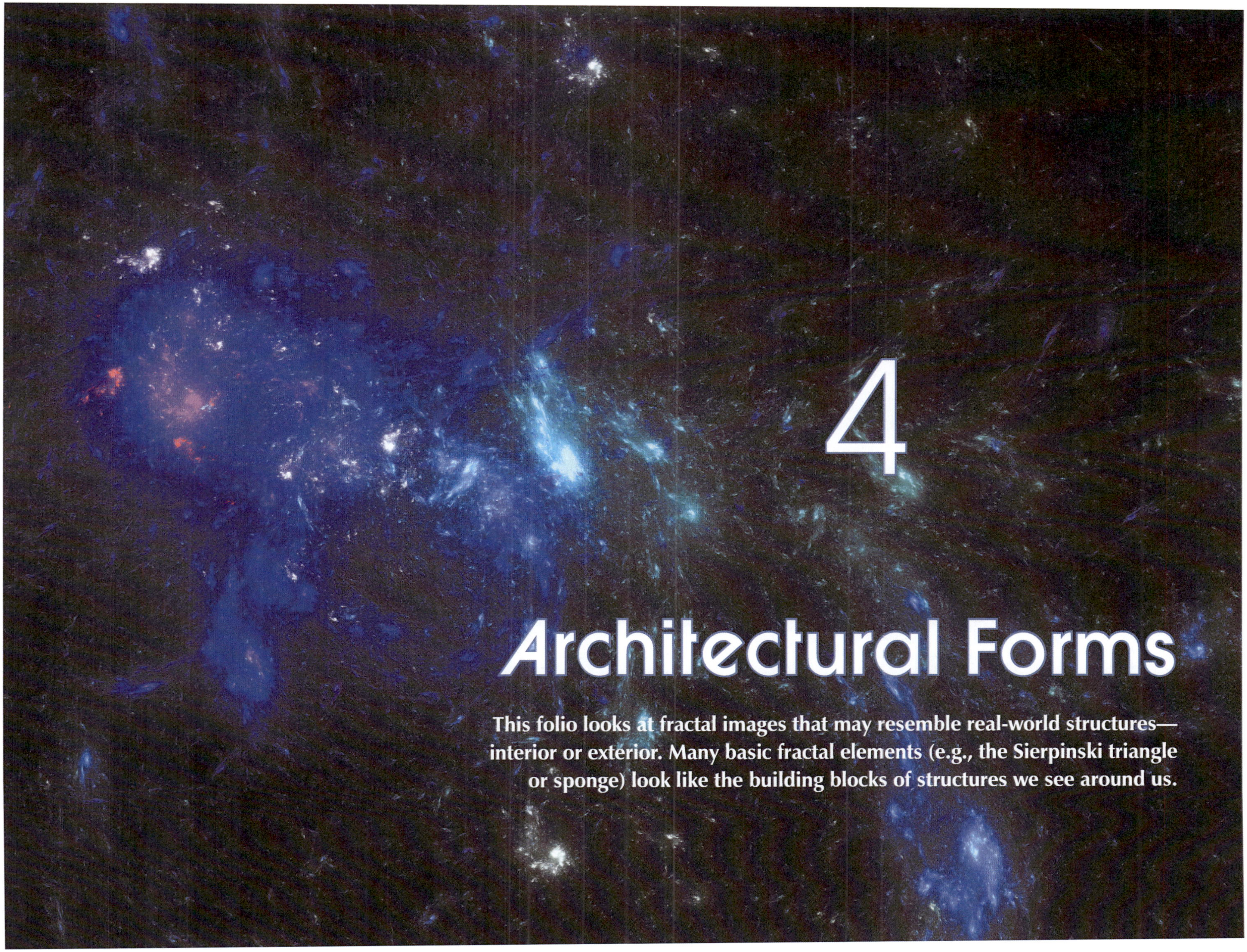

4

Architectural Forms

This folio looks at fractal images that may resemble real-world structures—interior or exterior. Many basic fractal elements (e.g., the Sierpinski triangle or sponge) look like the building blocks of structures we see around us.

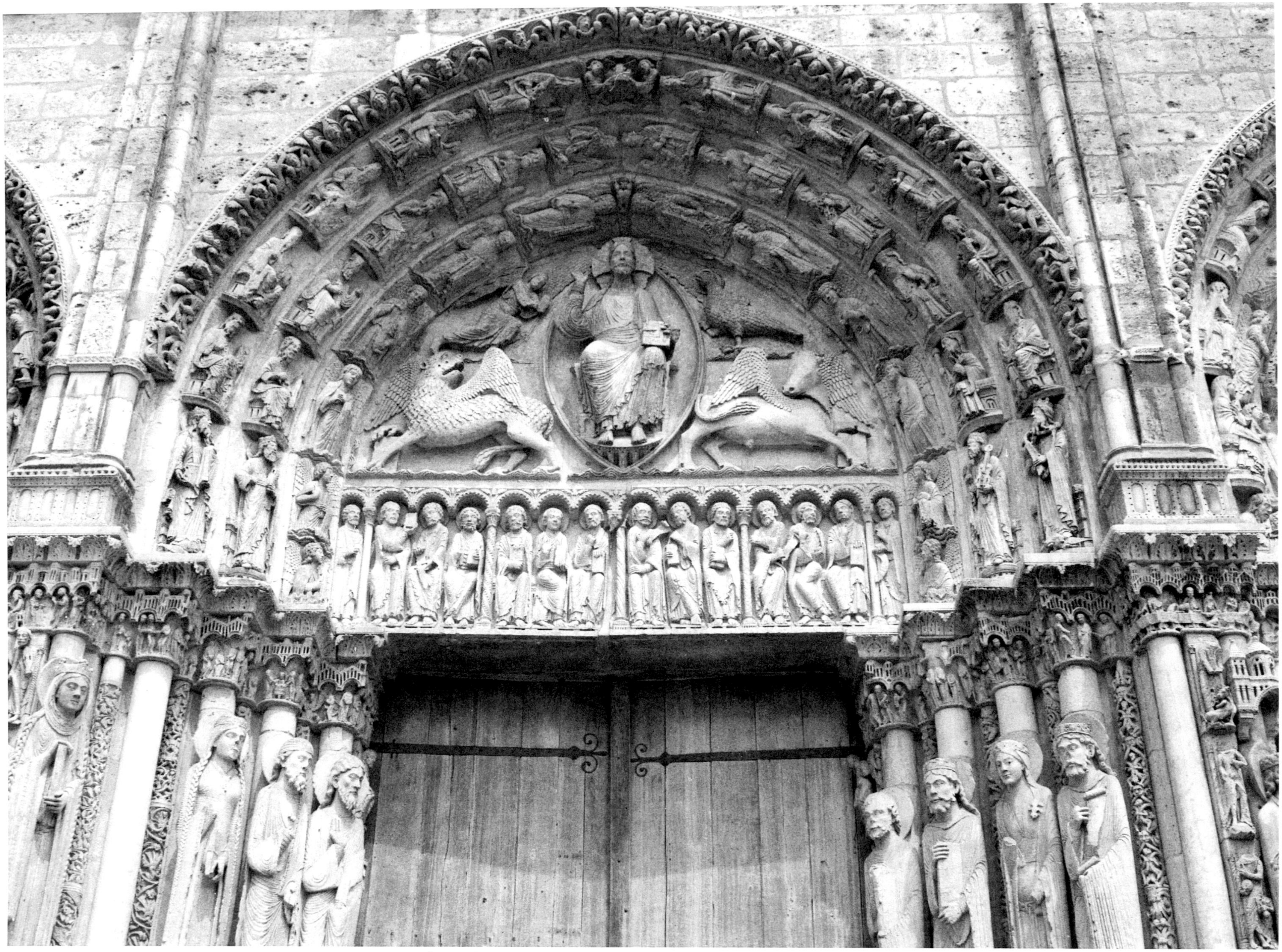

Main portal (north) of Chartres Cathedral, (France, 1984, 6x6 cm B&W negative)

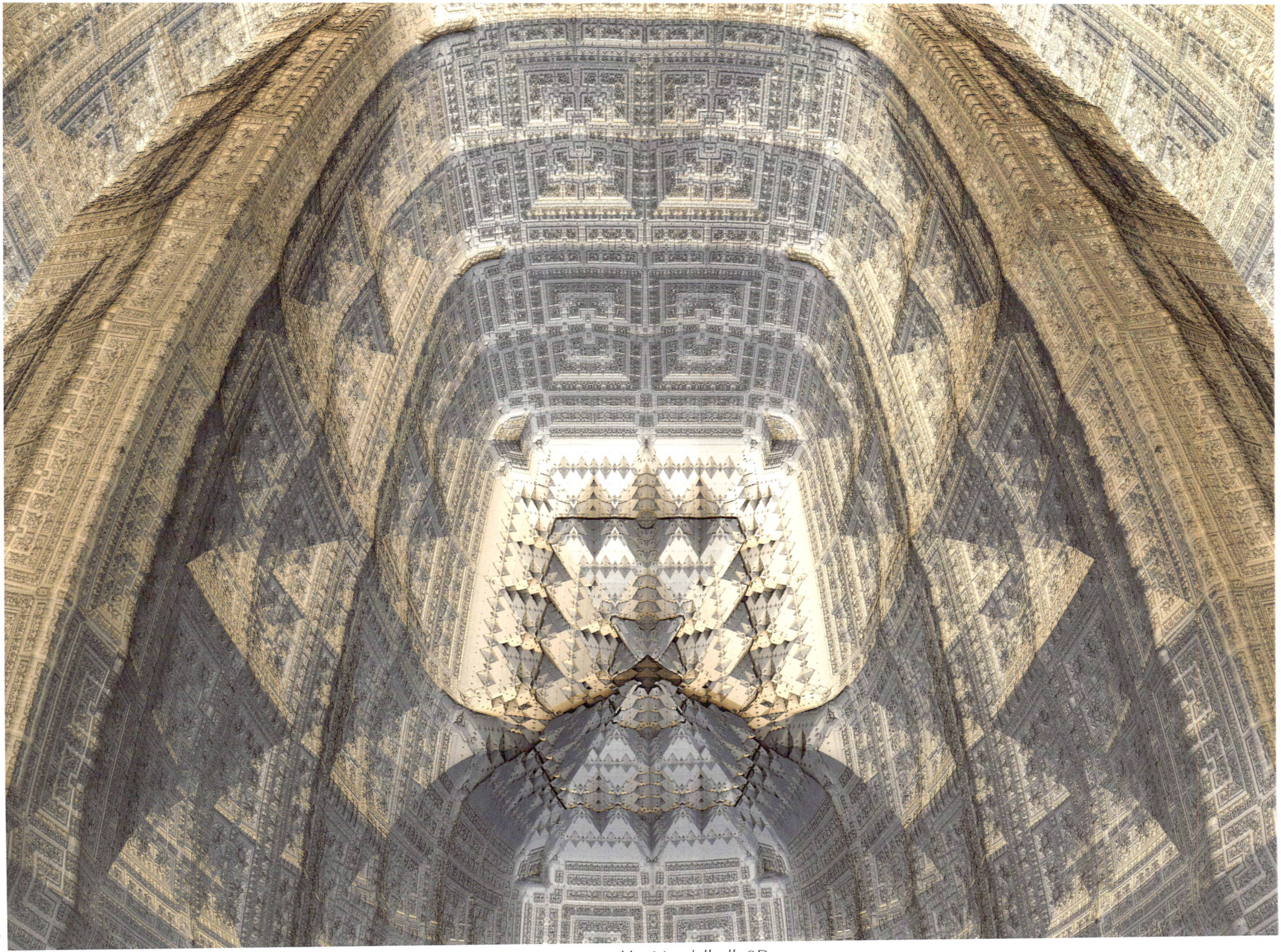

Image created by Mandelbulb 3D

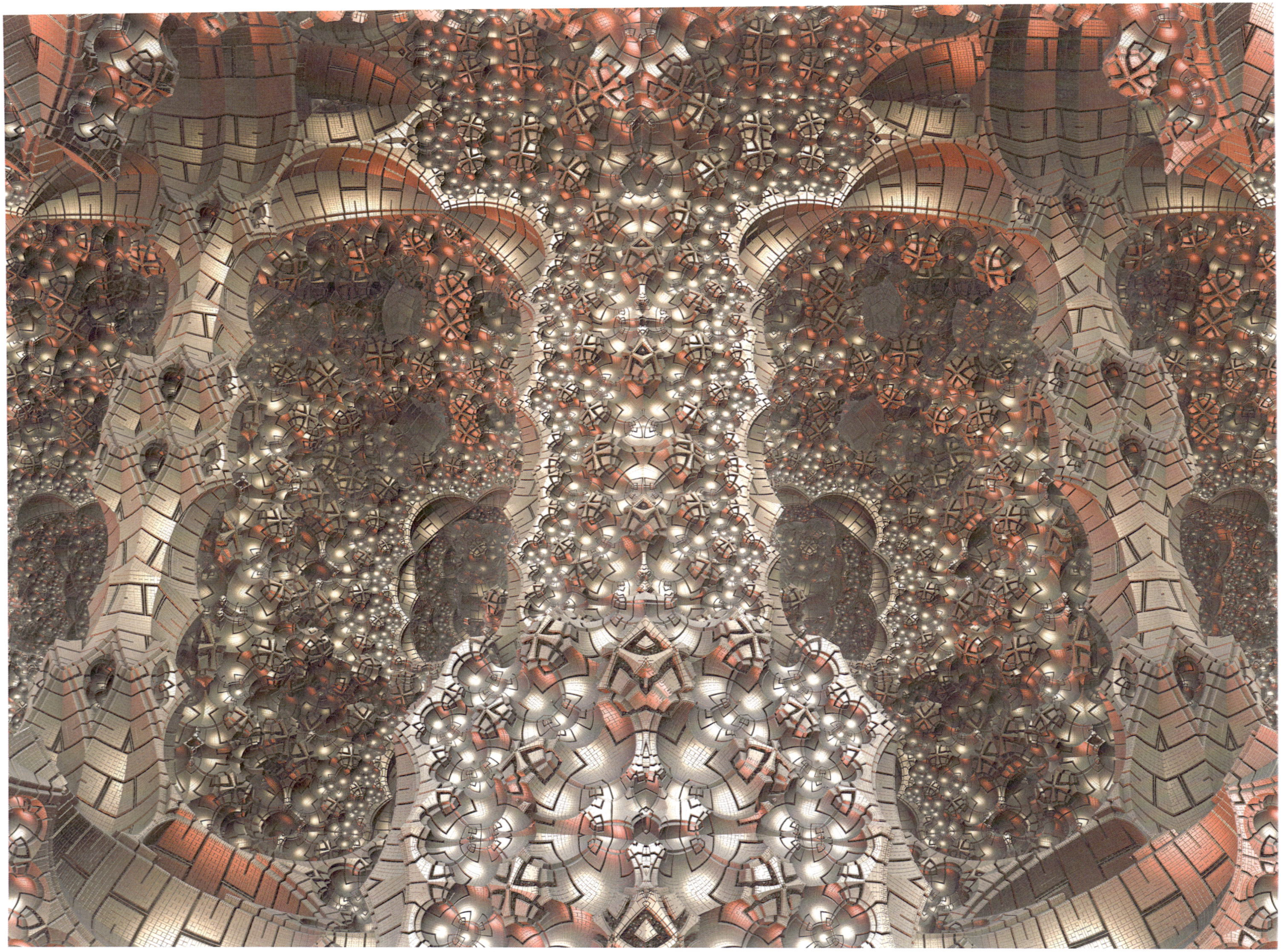

"Jeweled rococo altar" (image created by Mandelbulb 3D)

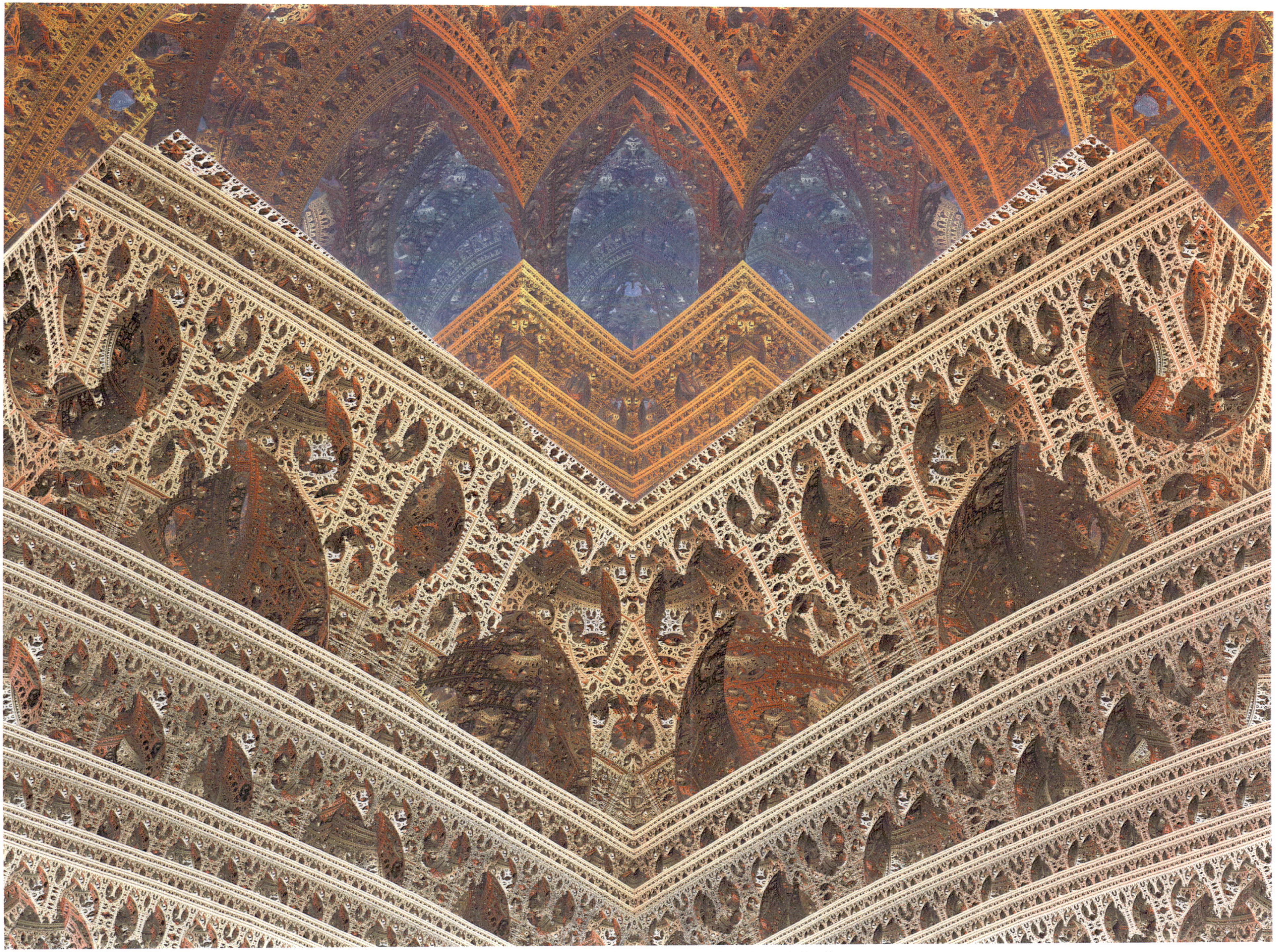

"Interior, gothic cathedral" (image created by Mandelbulb 3D)

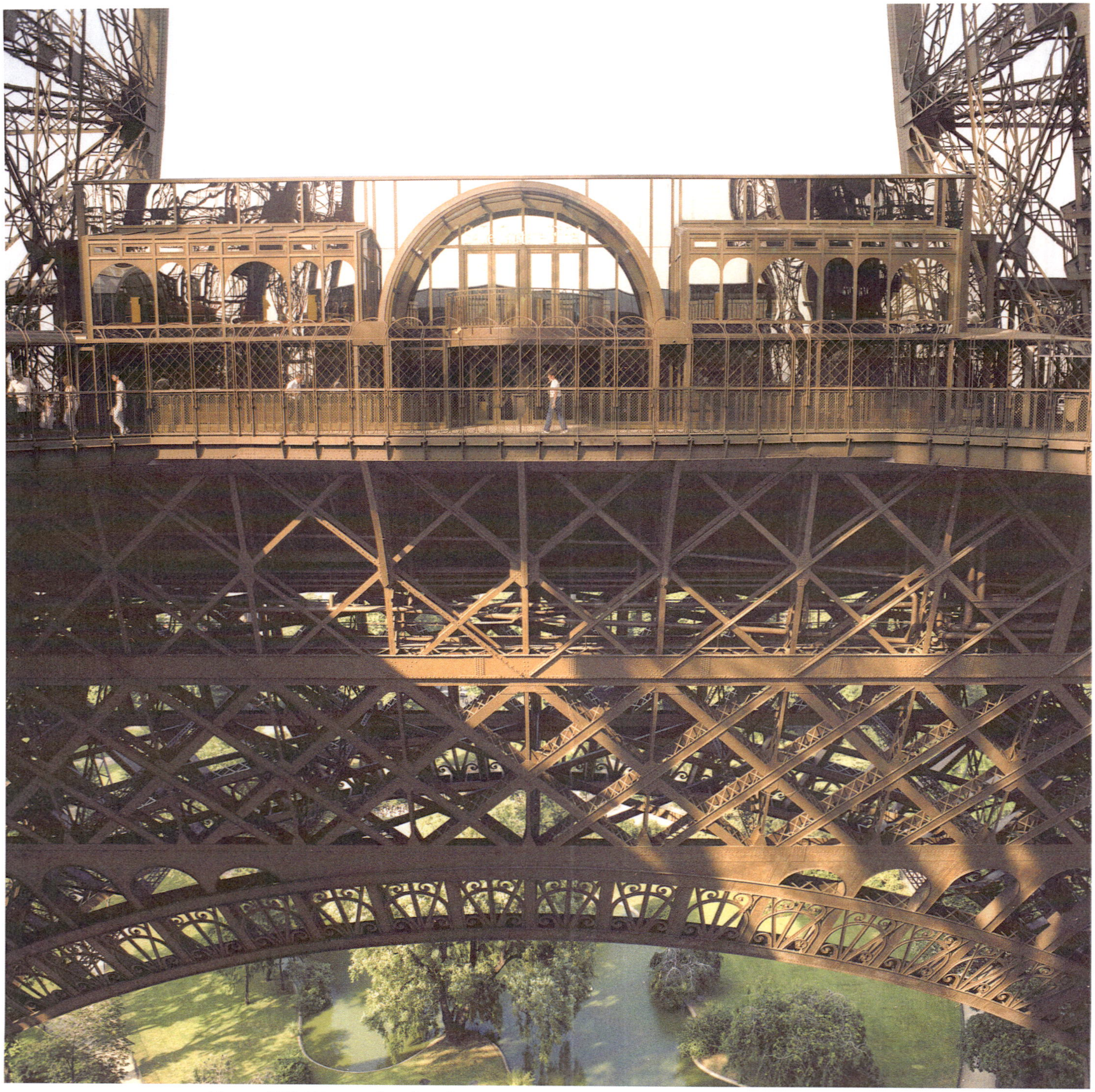

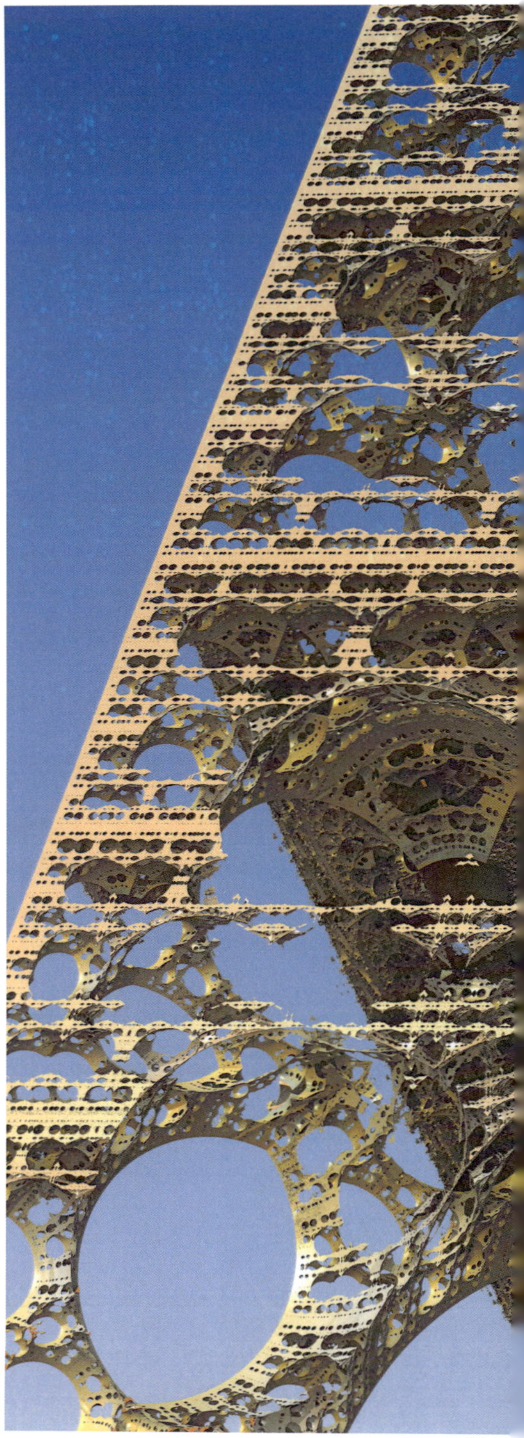

***Above**, Eiffel Tower, first level, Paris, France (1984, 6×6 cm color negative); **right**, fractal image generated by Mandelbulb 3D*

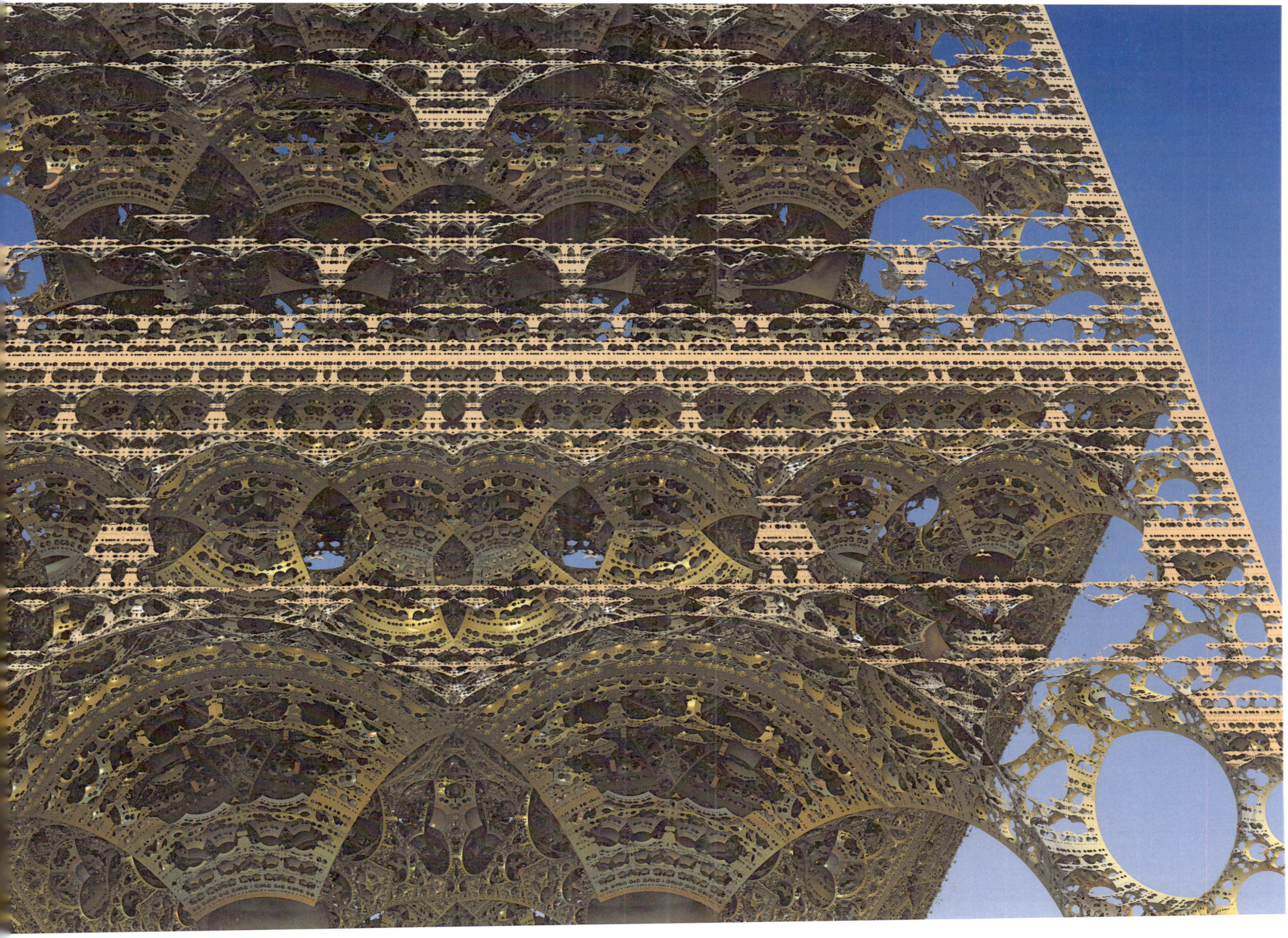

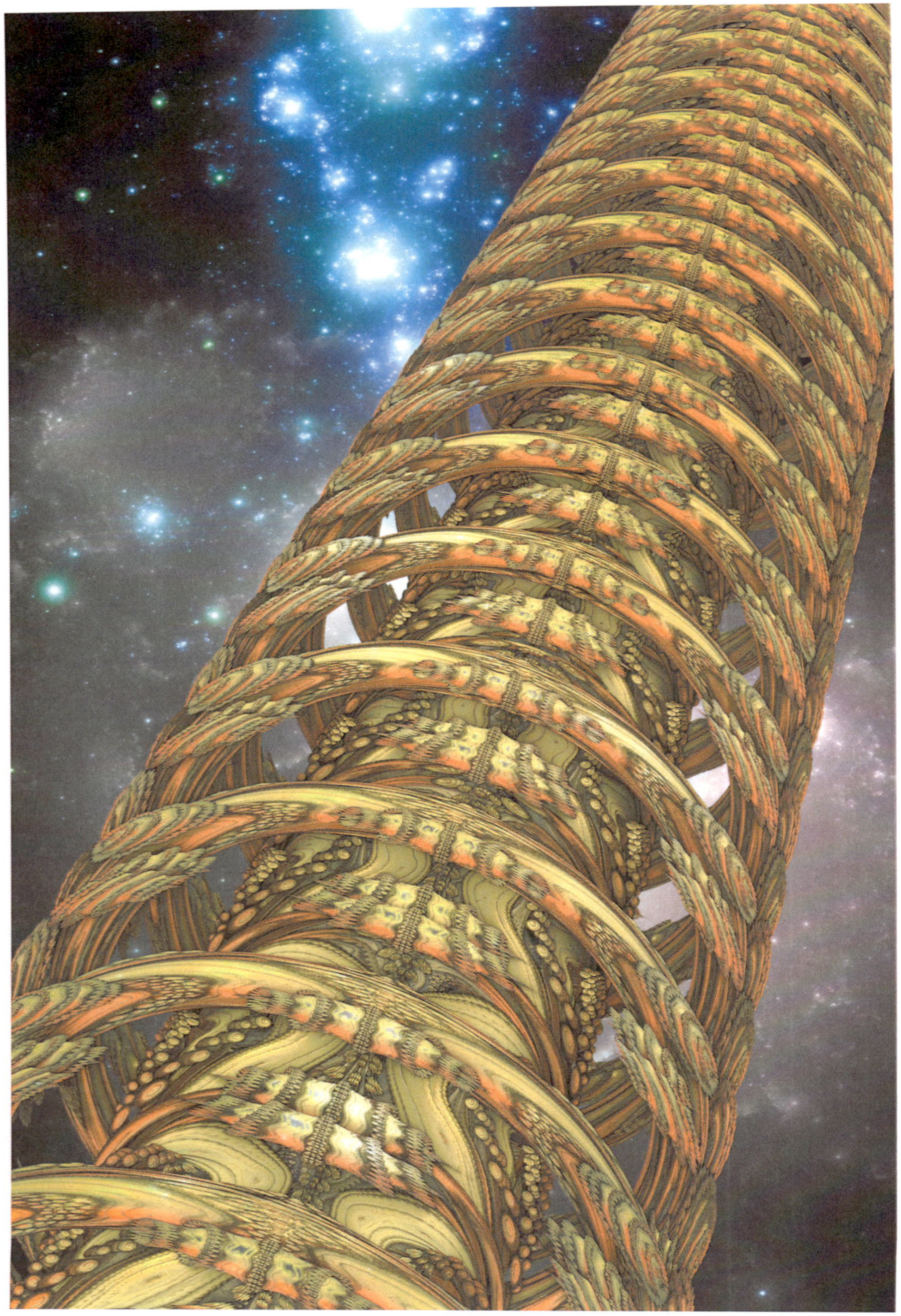

Image created by Mandelbulb 3D, and background by JWildfire

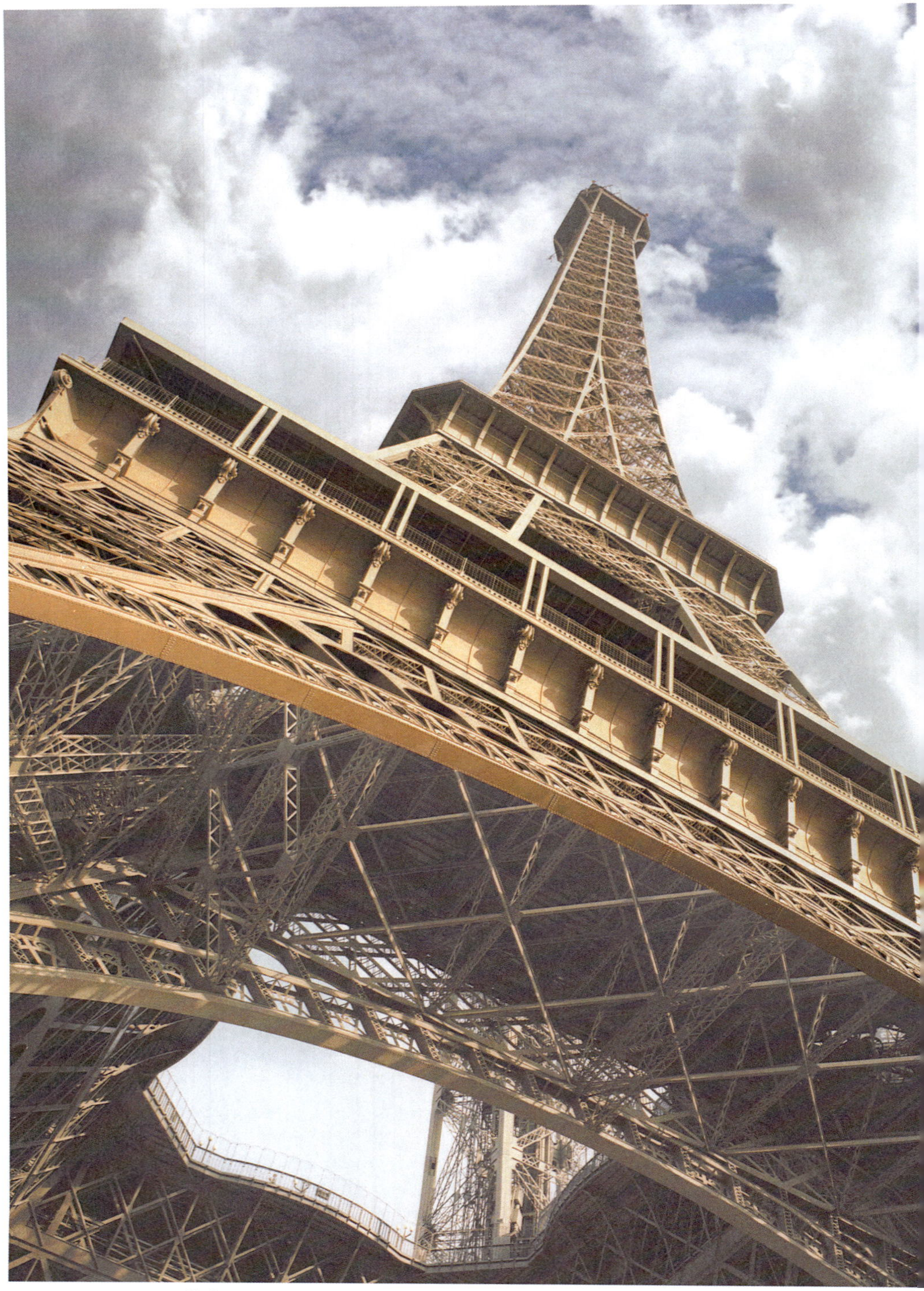

Eiffel Tower, Paris, France (1984, 6×6 cm color negative)

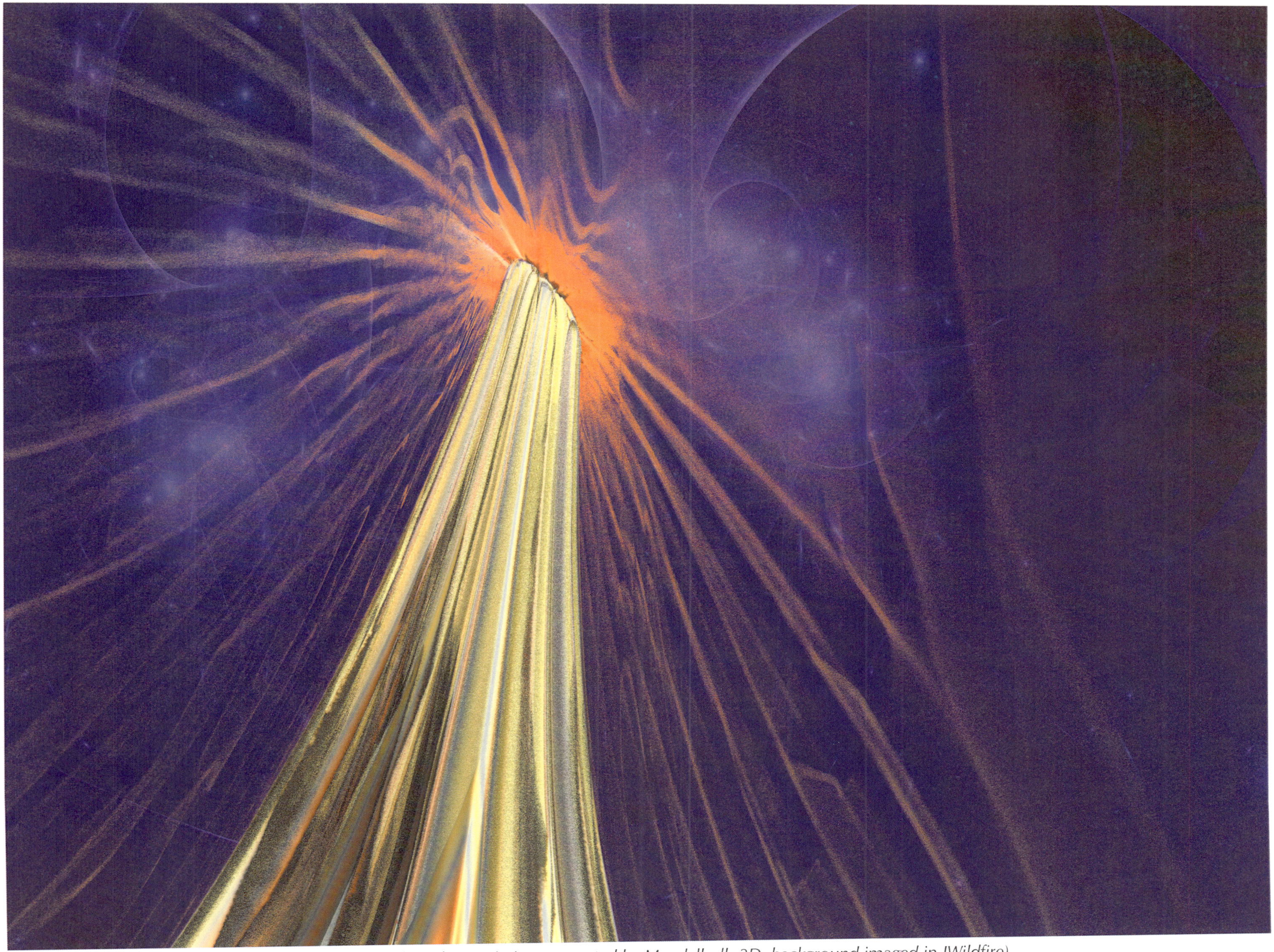

"Homage to Nikola Tesla" (main image created by Mandelbulb 3D, background imaged in JWildfire)

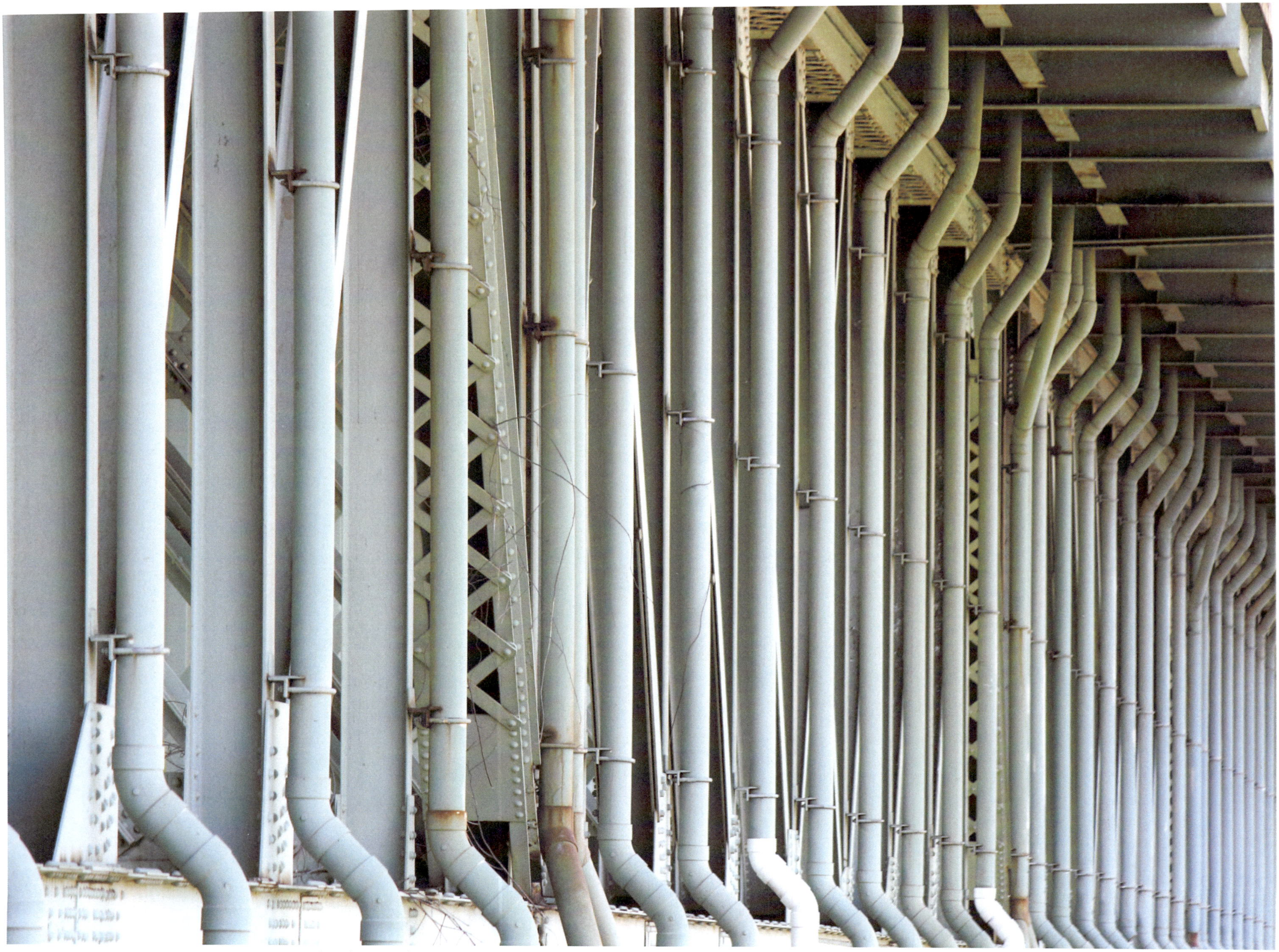

Receding lines—drainage pipes under I-78 near Easton, Pennsylvania (digital image, telephoto lens)

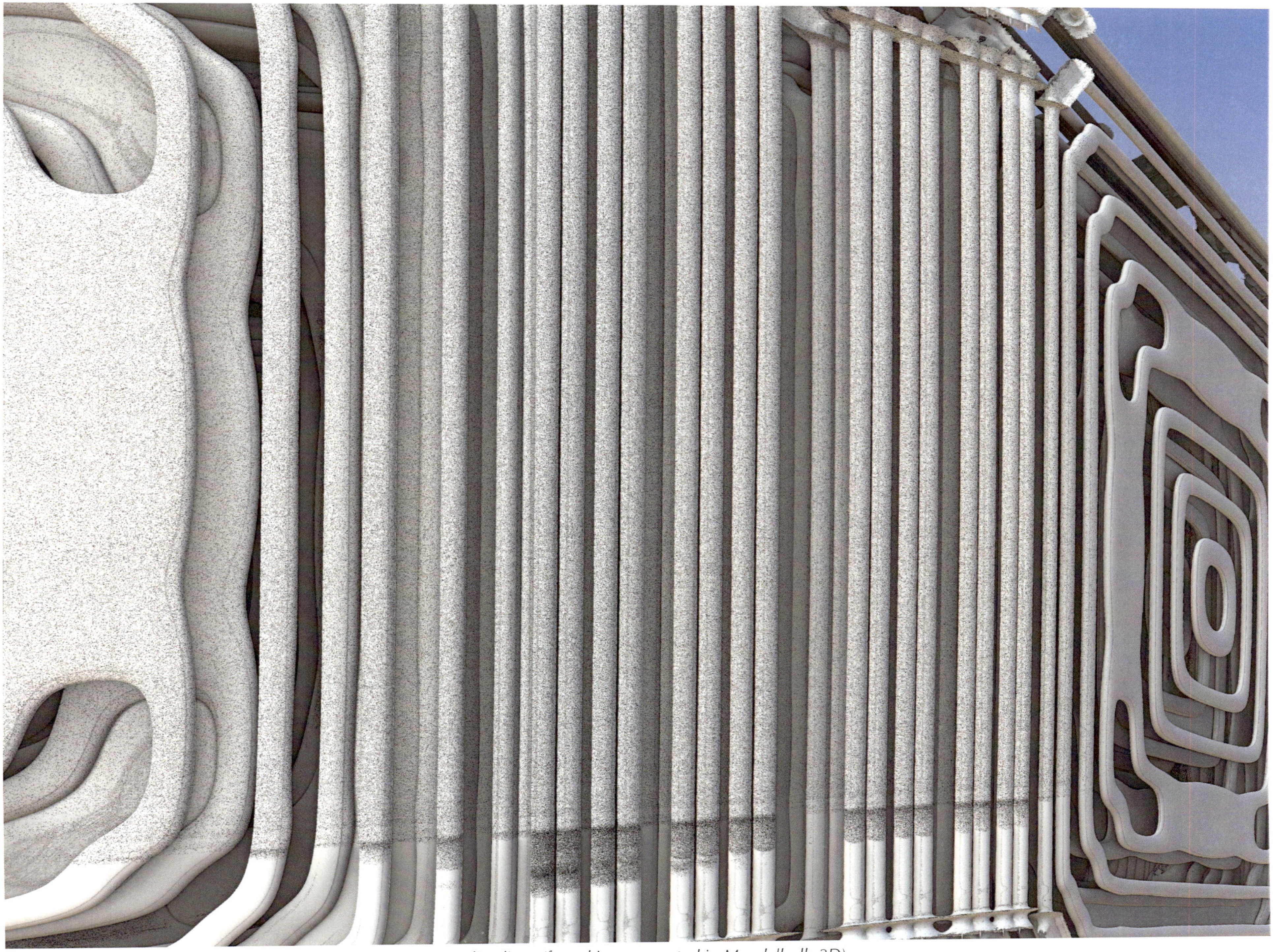

Receding lines (fractal image created in Mandelbulb 3D)

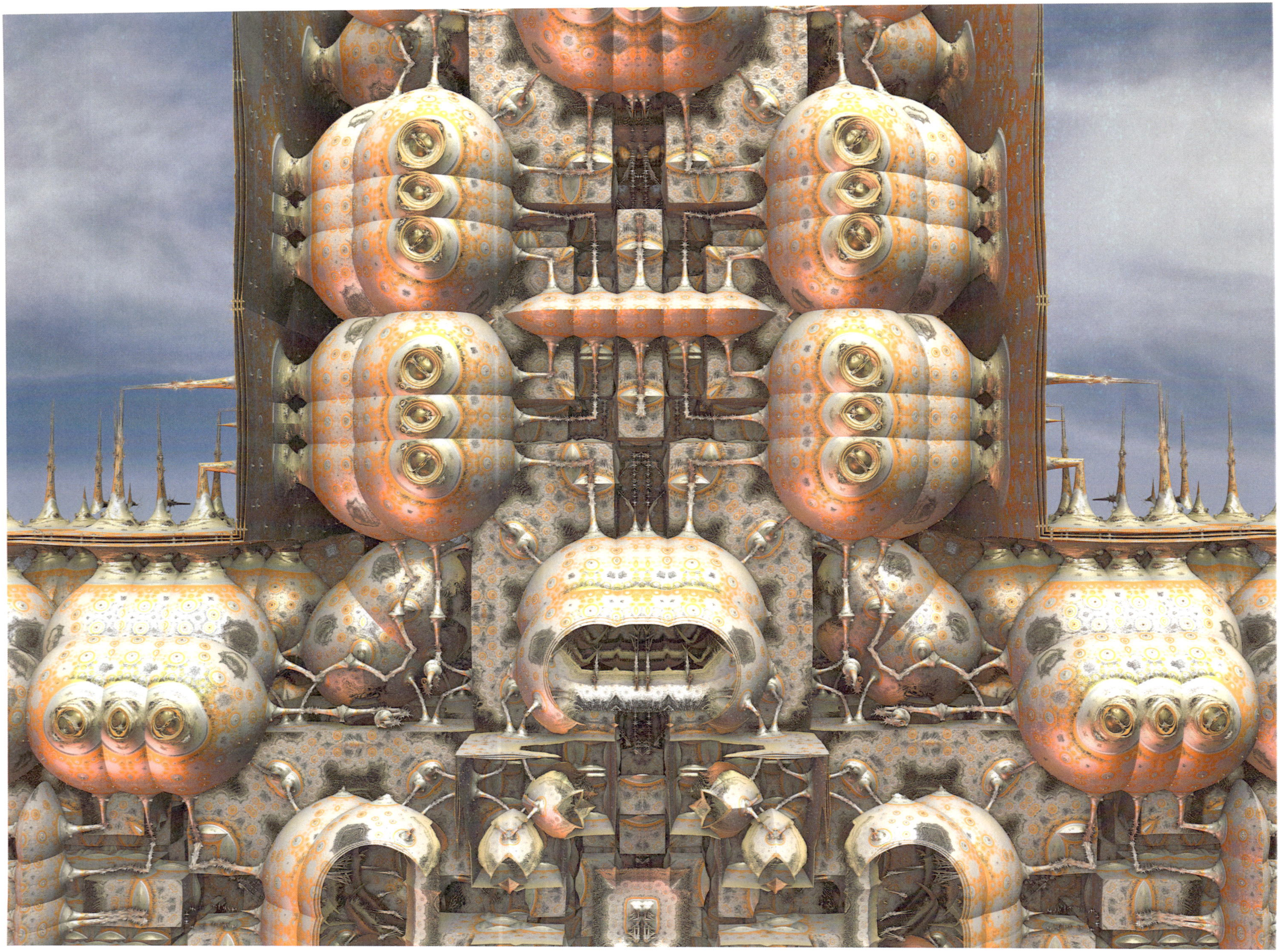

"Factory of the Future" (image from Mandelbulb 3D)

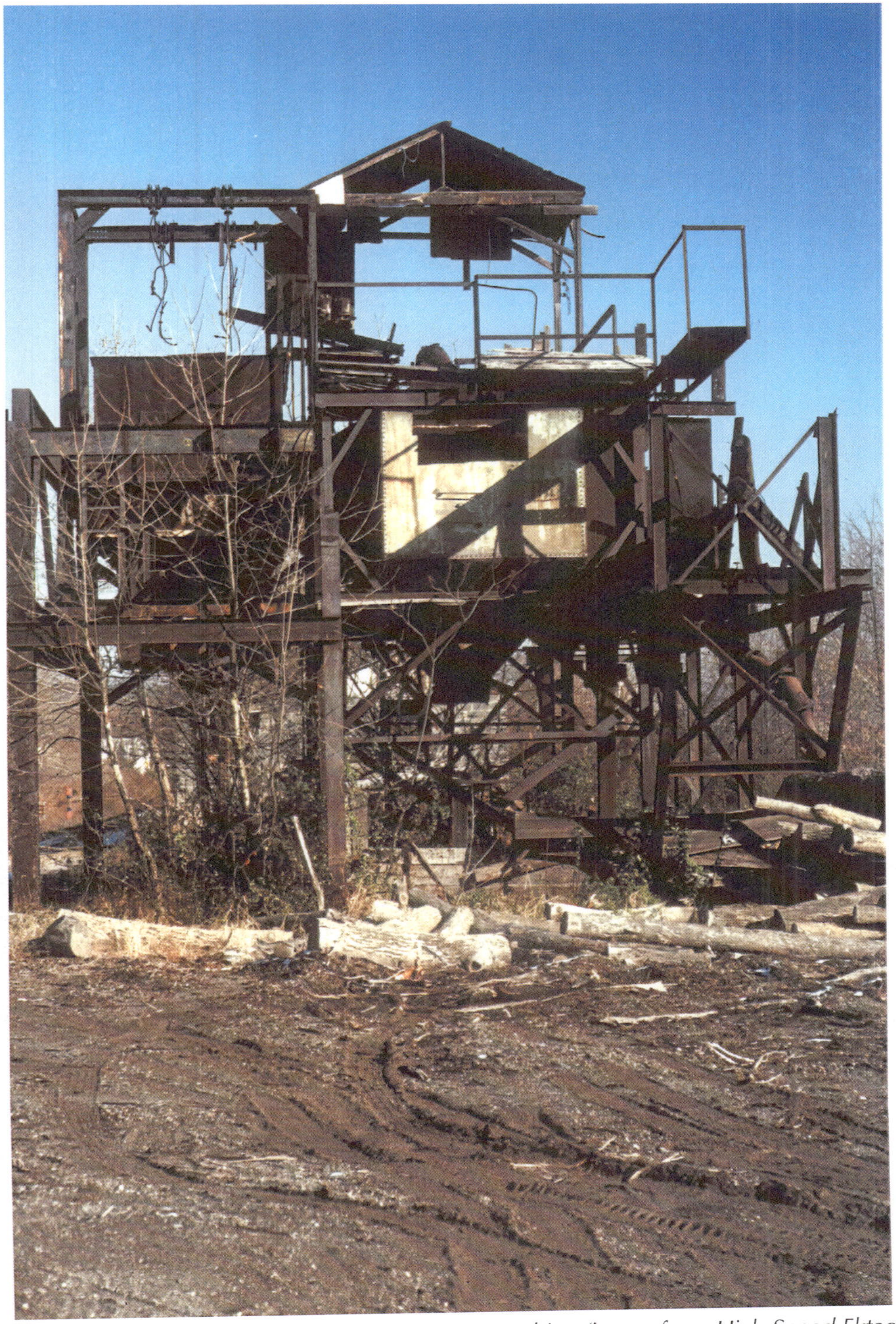

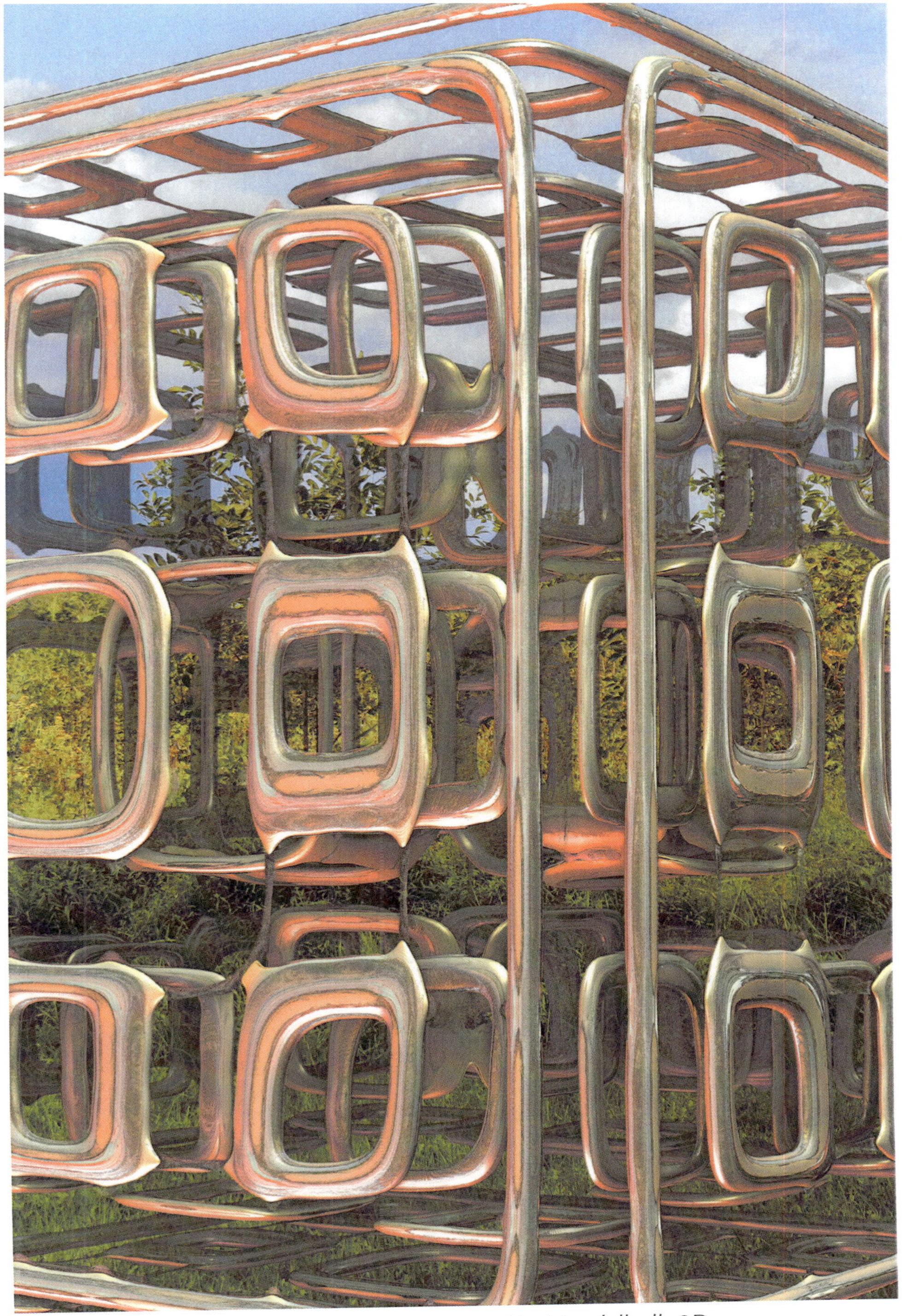

***Left**, dilapidated quarry machine (image from High-Speed Ektachrome 35 mm, circa 1973); **right**, structure created in Mandelbulb 3D*

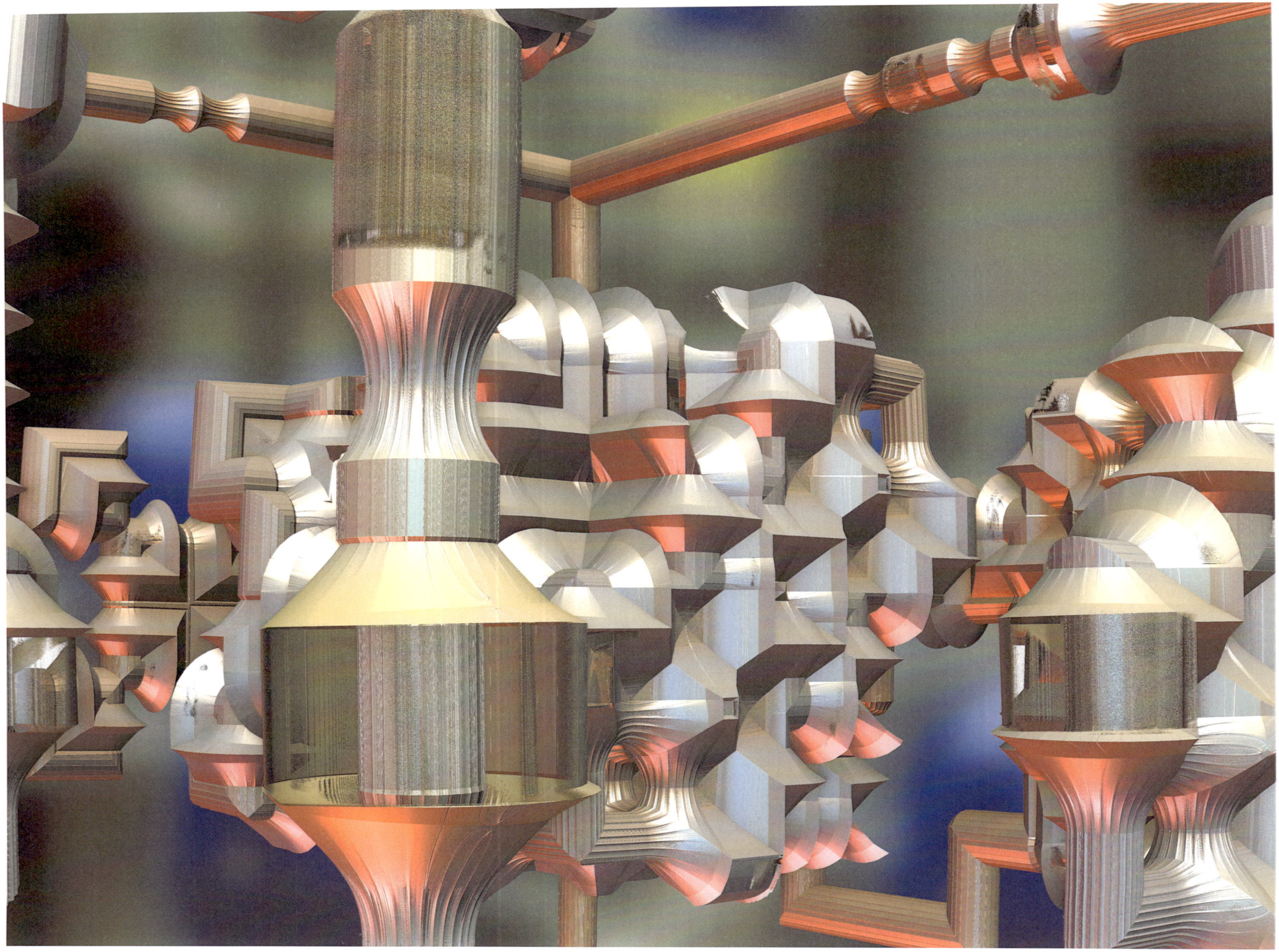

"Interior Process Machinery" created in Mandelbulb 3D; background, interior process equipment (digital photo)

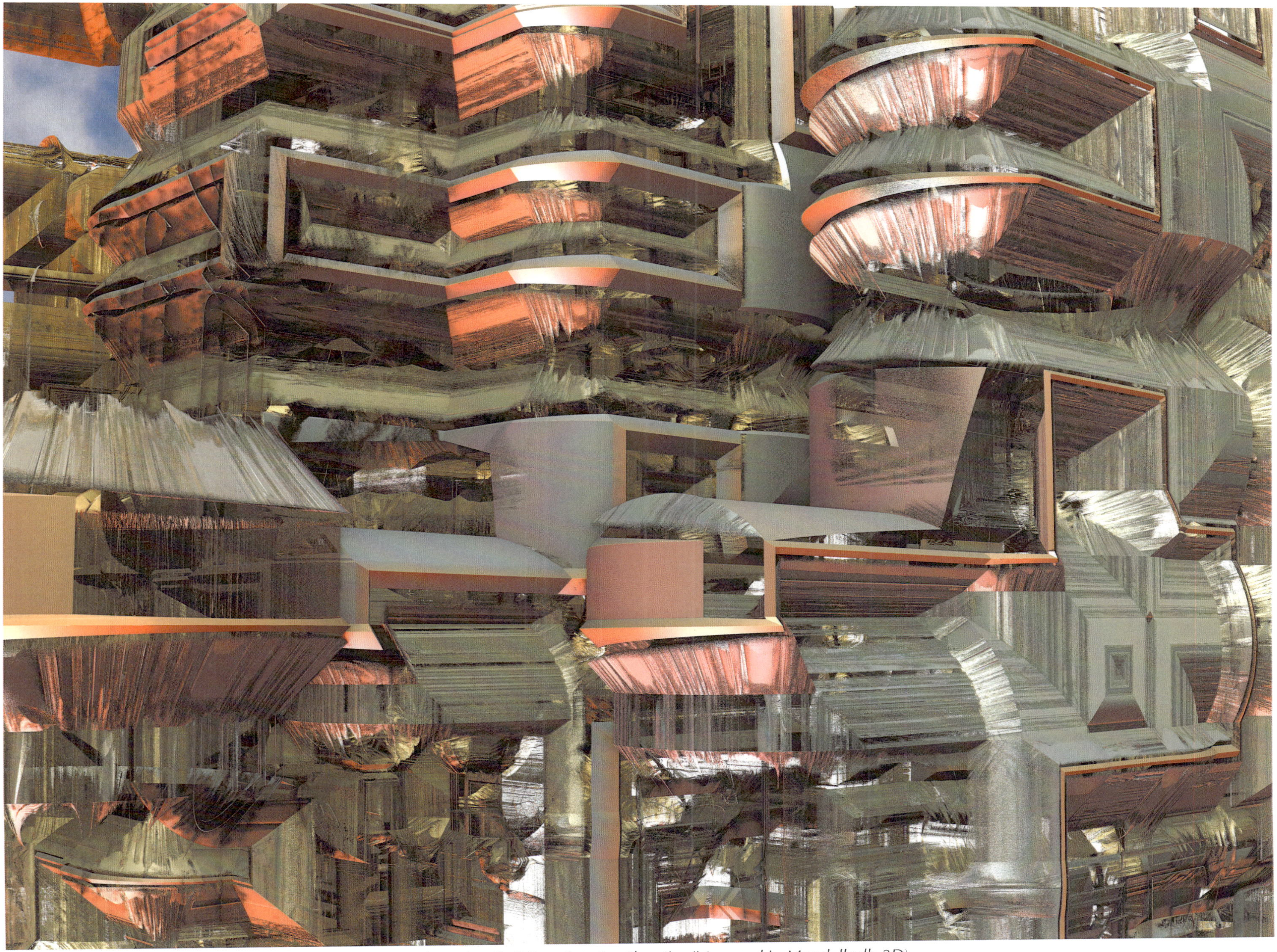
"Manufacturing Building, Exterior Elevation" (created in Mandelbulb 3D)

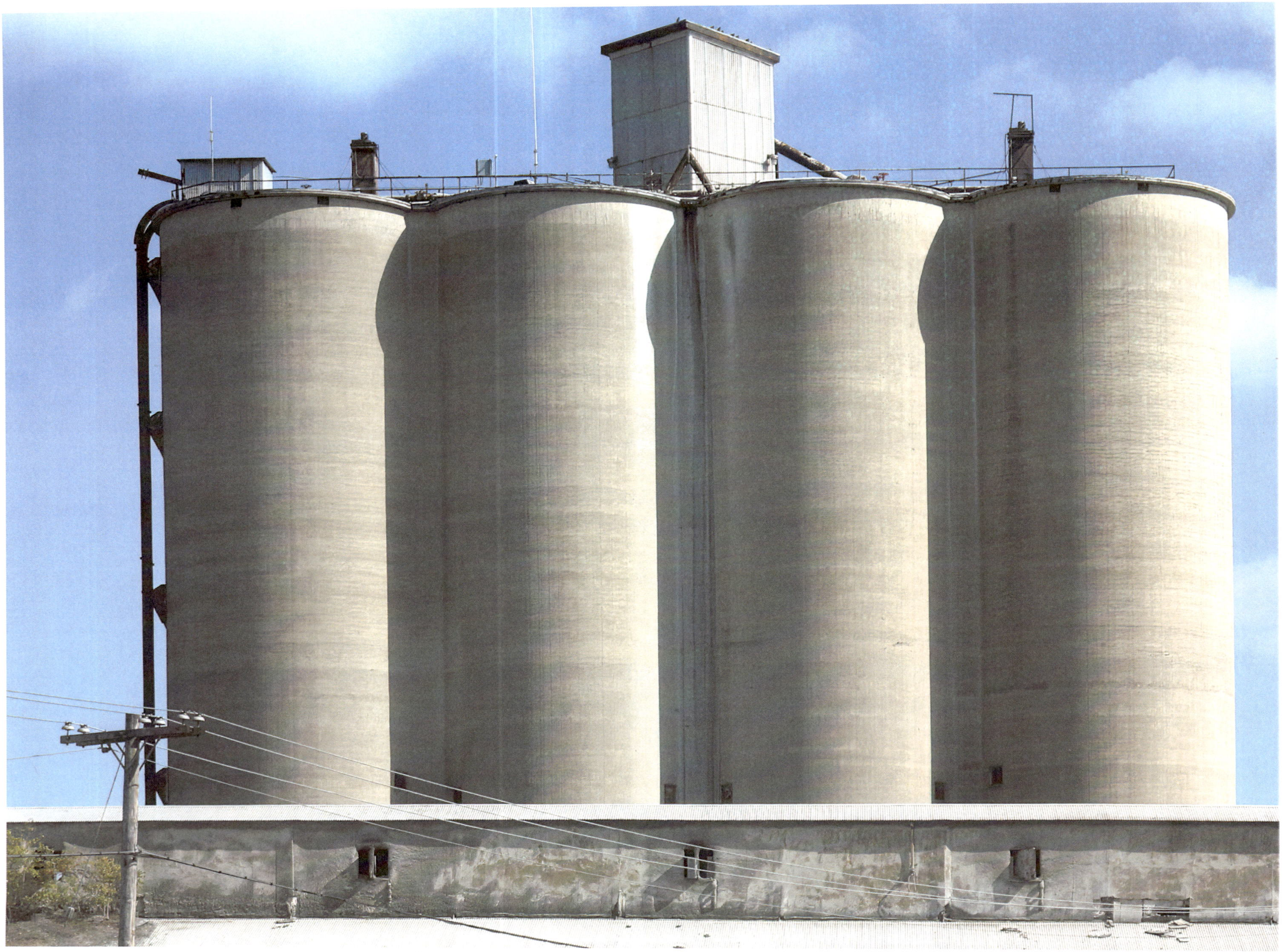

Silos at cement processing facility in Pennsylvania (digital photo)

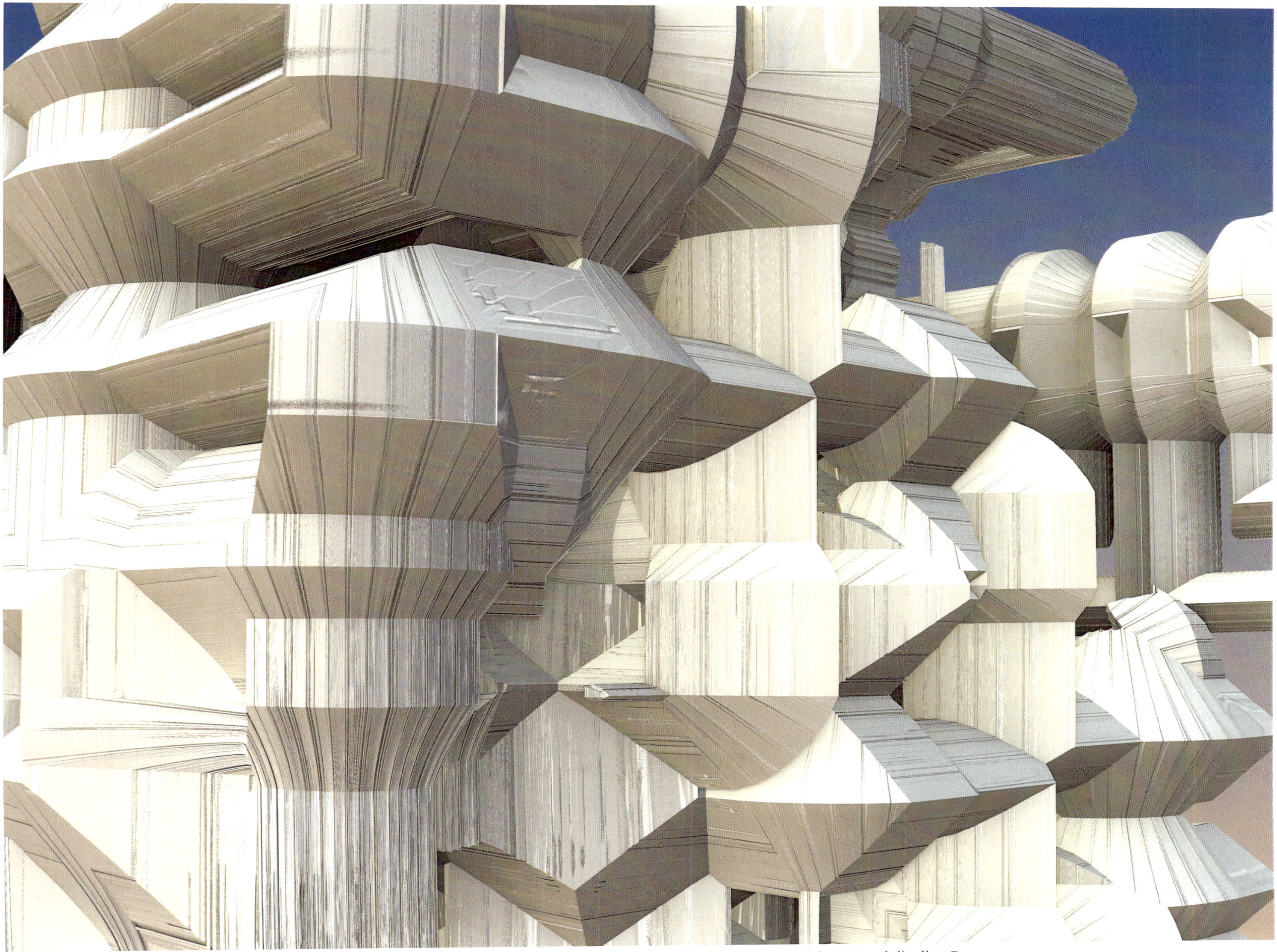

Exterior, "Powder Processing Operation"—not really; image created in Mandelbulb 3D

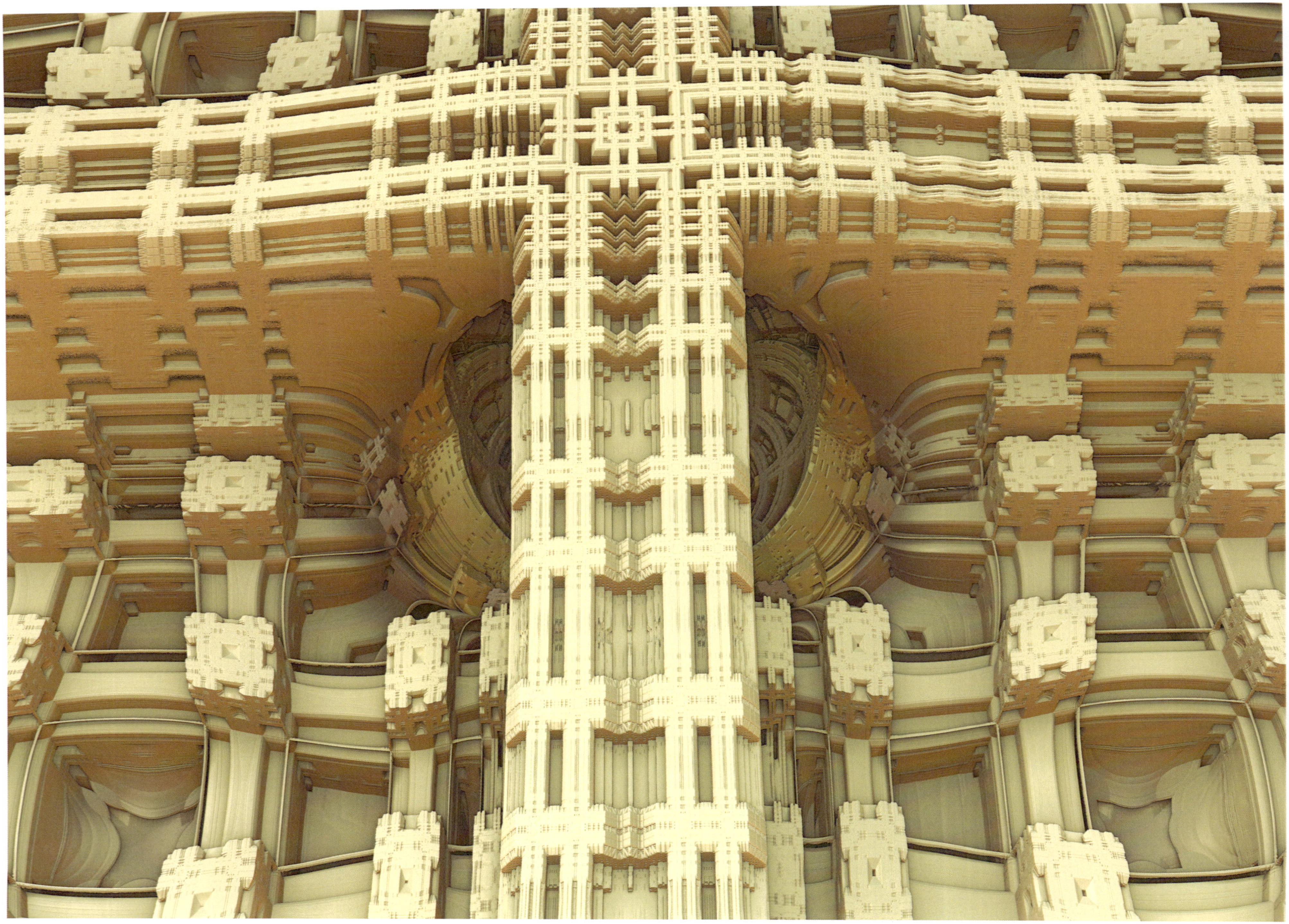

Image generated by Mandelbulb 3D is reminiscent of Gaudi architecture in Barcelona, Spain.

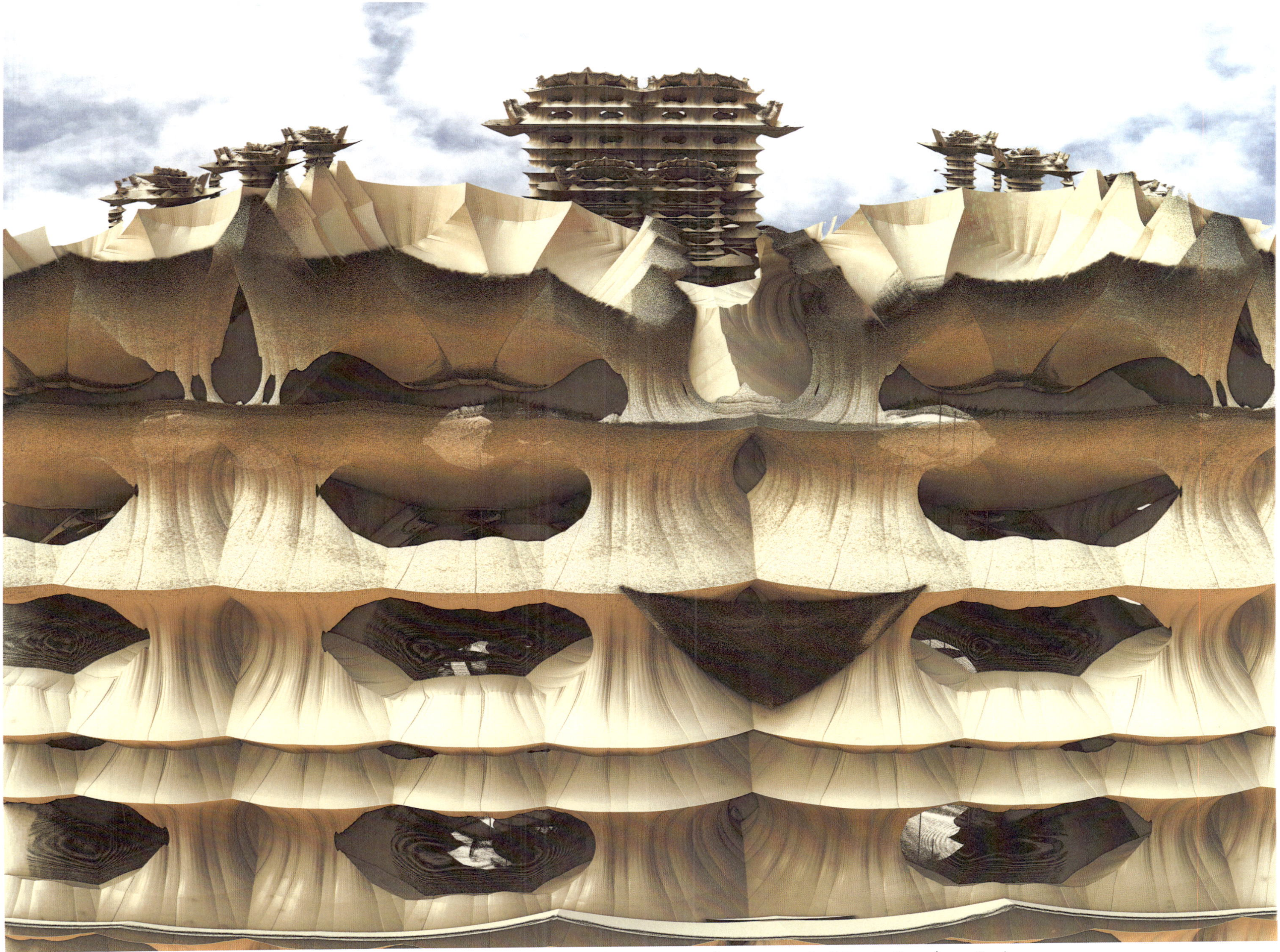

Image created by Mandelbulb 3D has similar lines to a Gaudi apartment building in Barcelona, Spain.

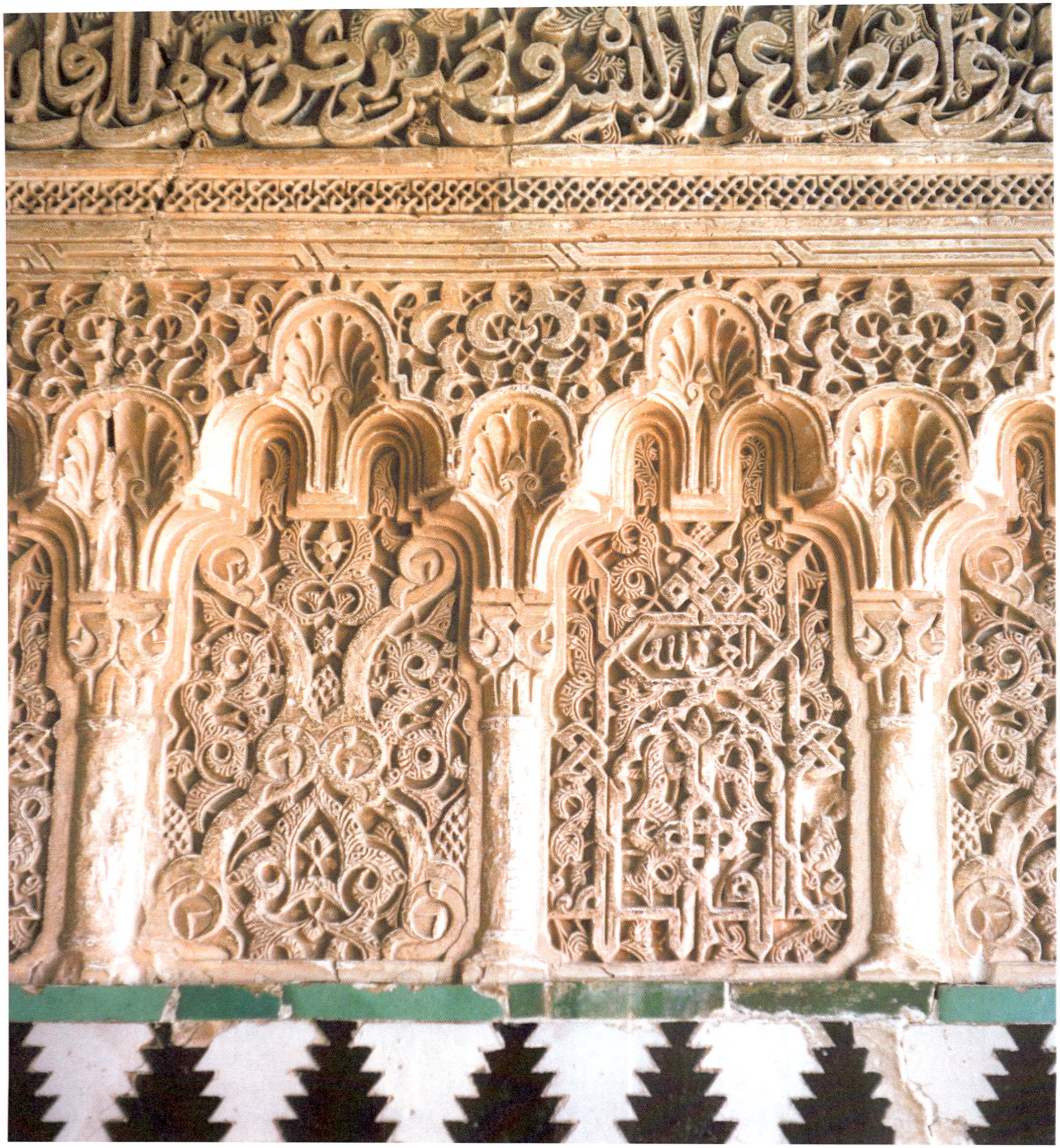

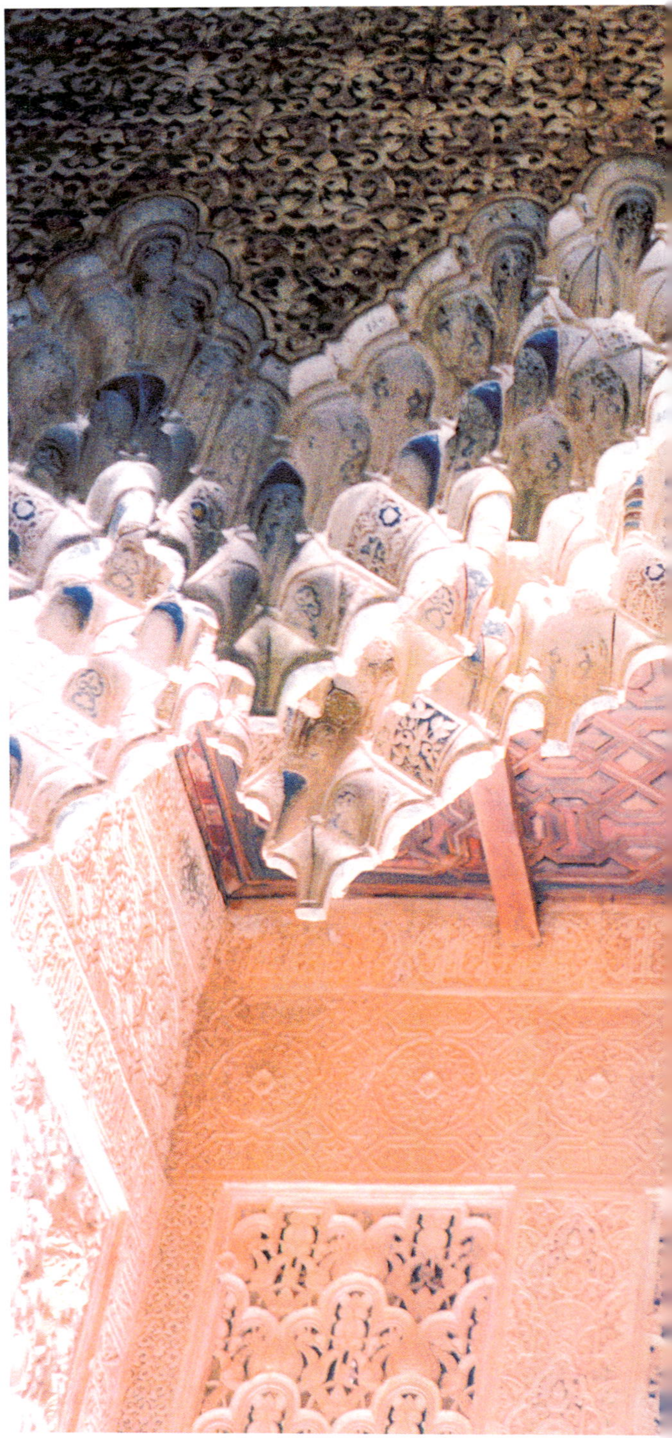

Left, *wall detail, Alhambra, Granada, Spain;* ***center spread,*** *ceiling detail, Alhambra. Photos, 6×6 cm color negative film.)*

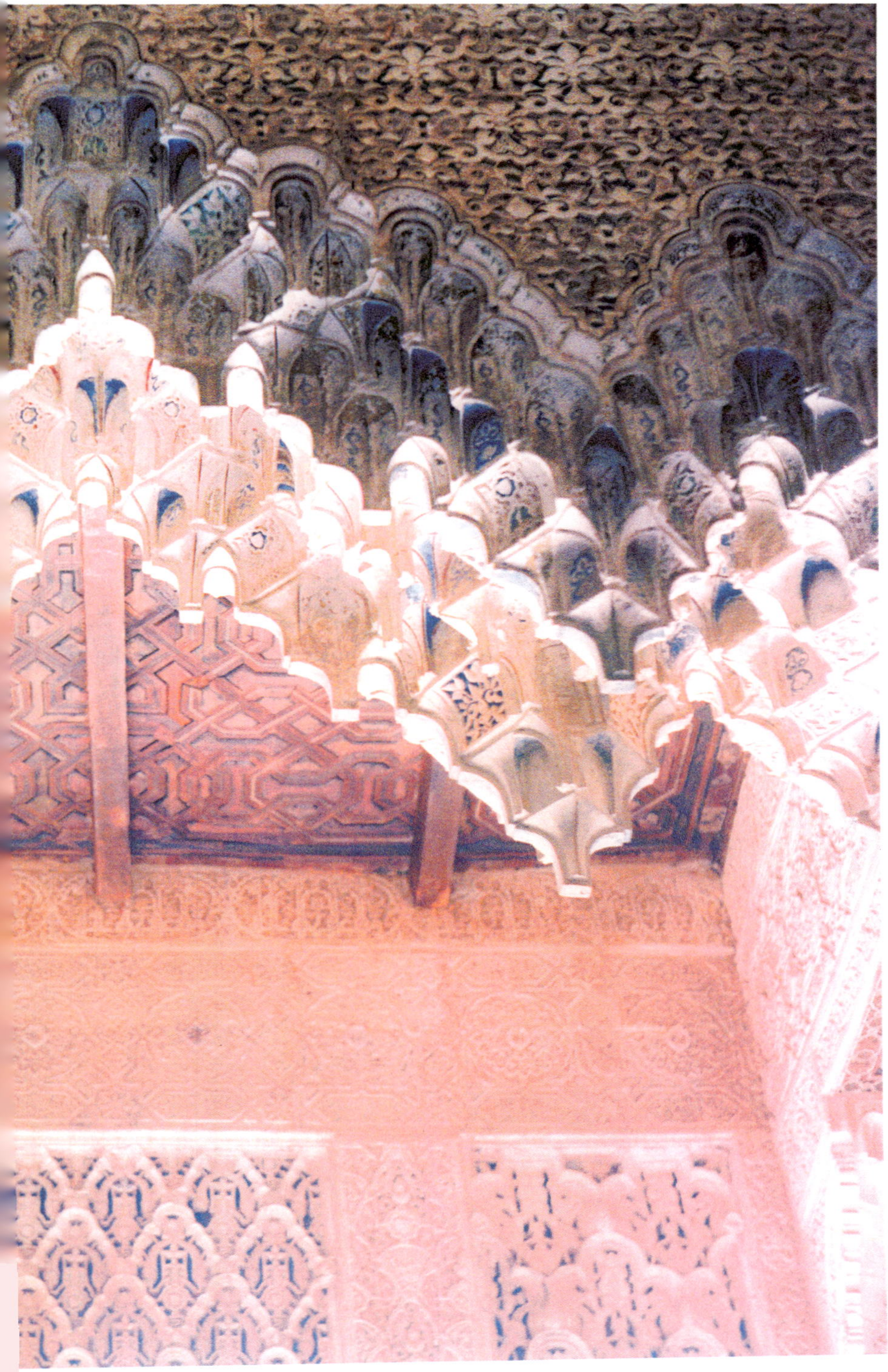

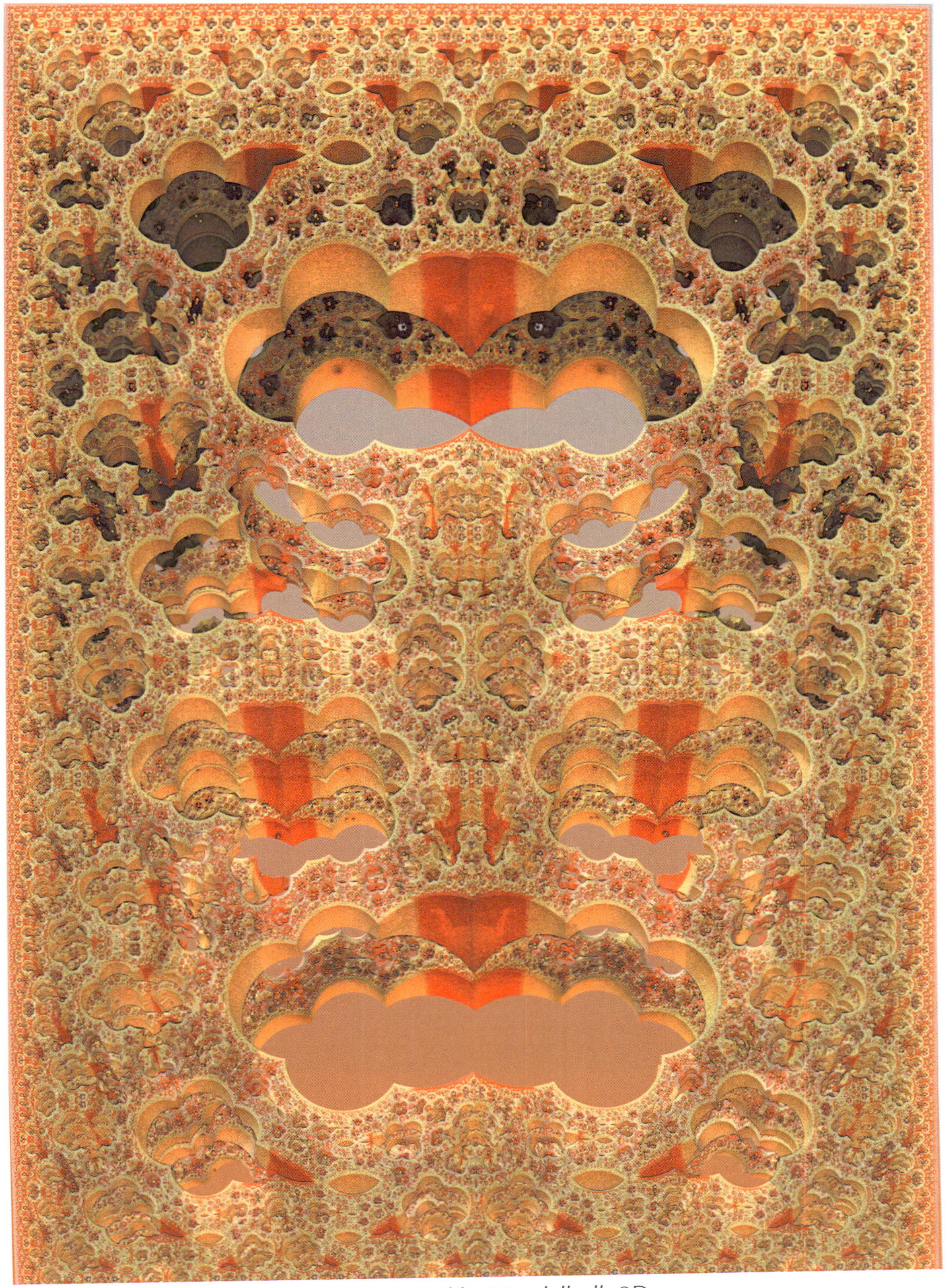

Image created by Mandelbulb 3D

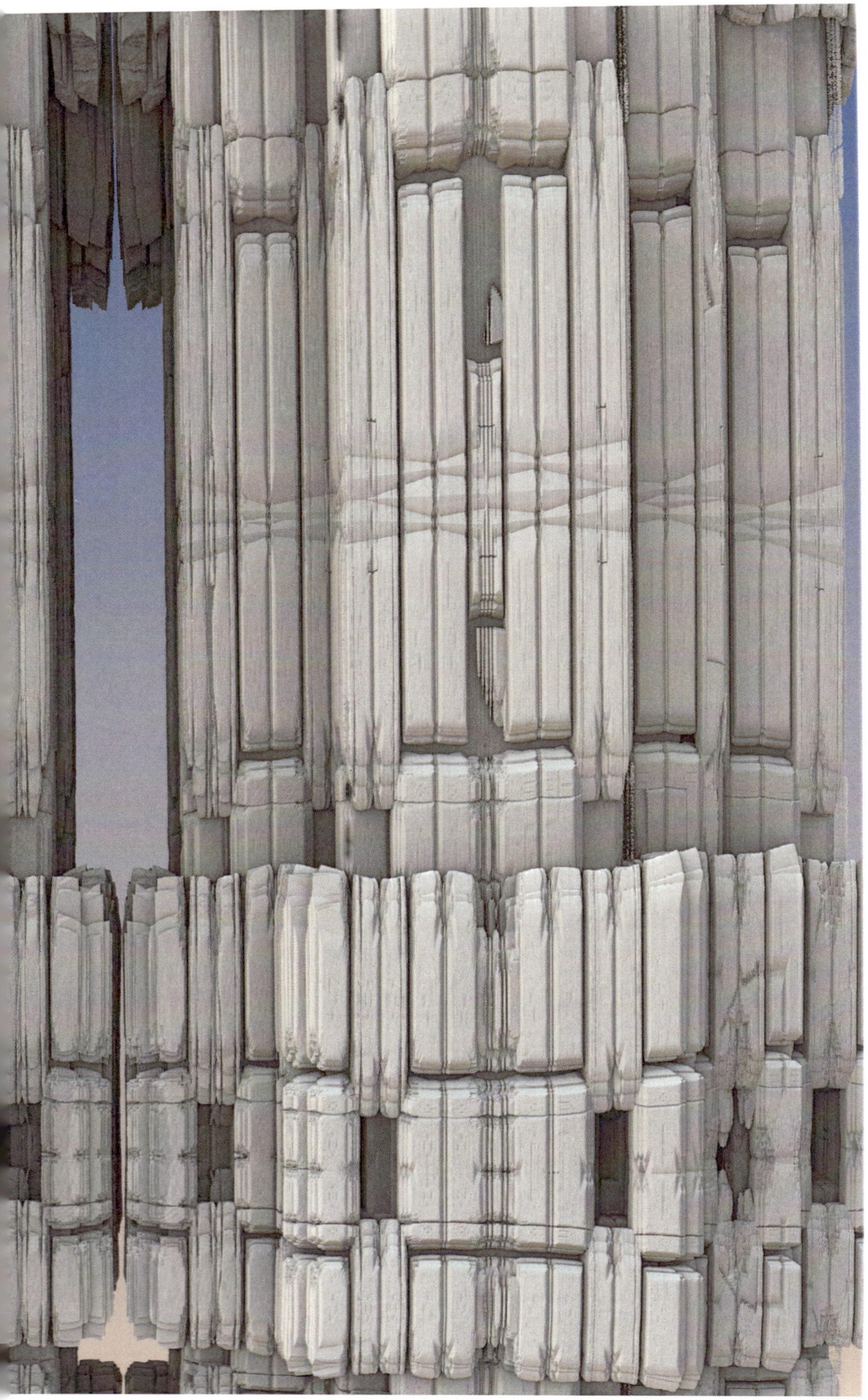

"High-rise" (created in Mandelbulb 3D)

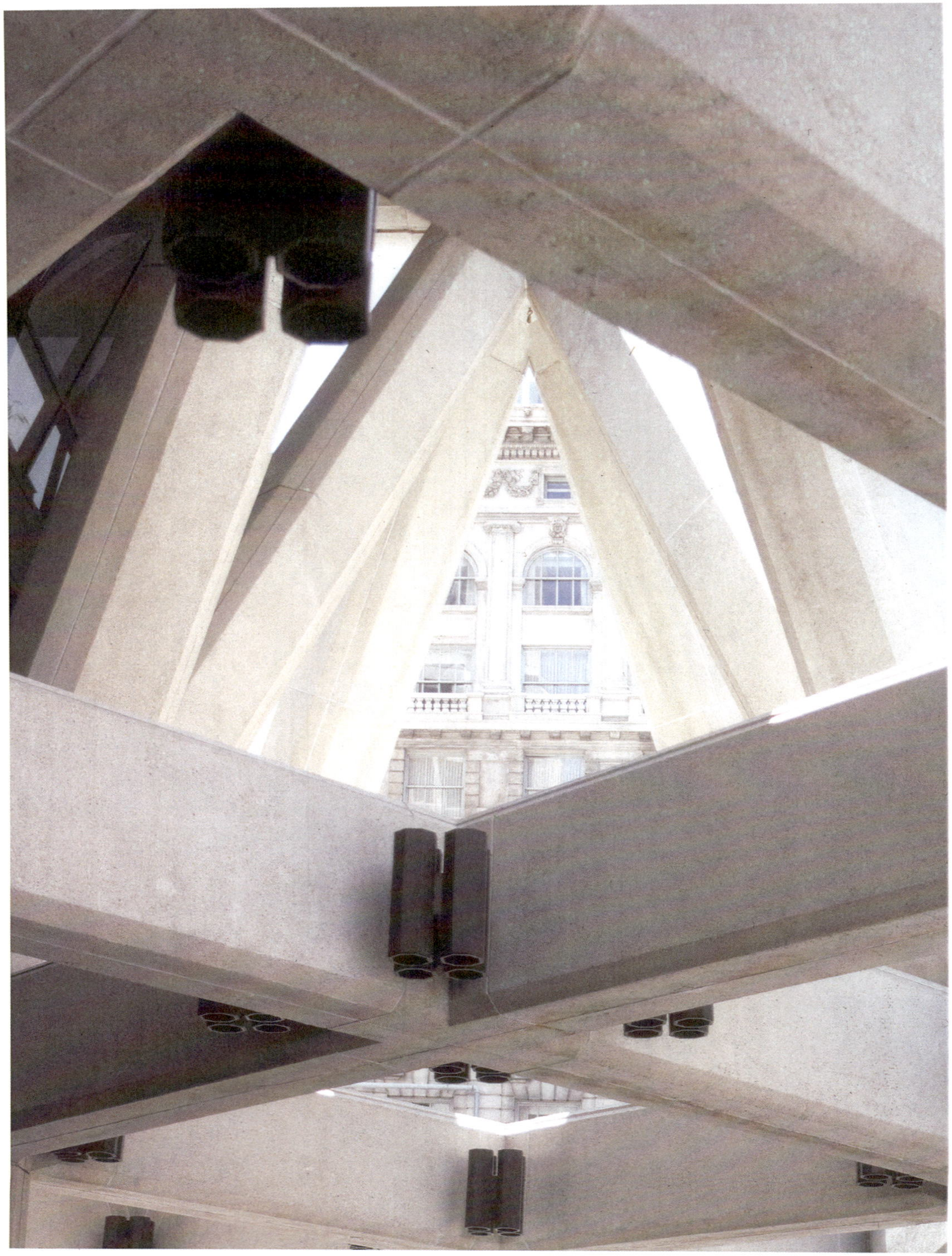

San Francisco, California (Kodachrome 35 mm transparency)

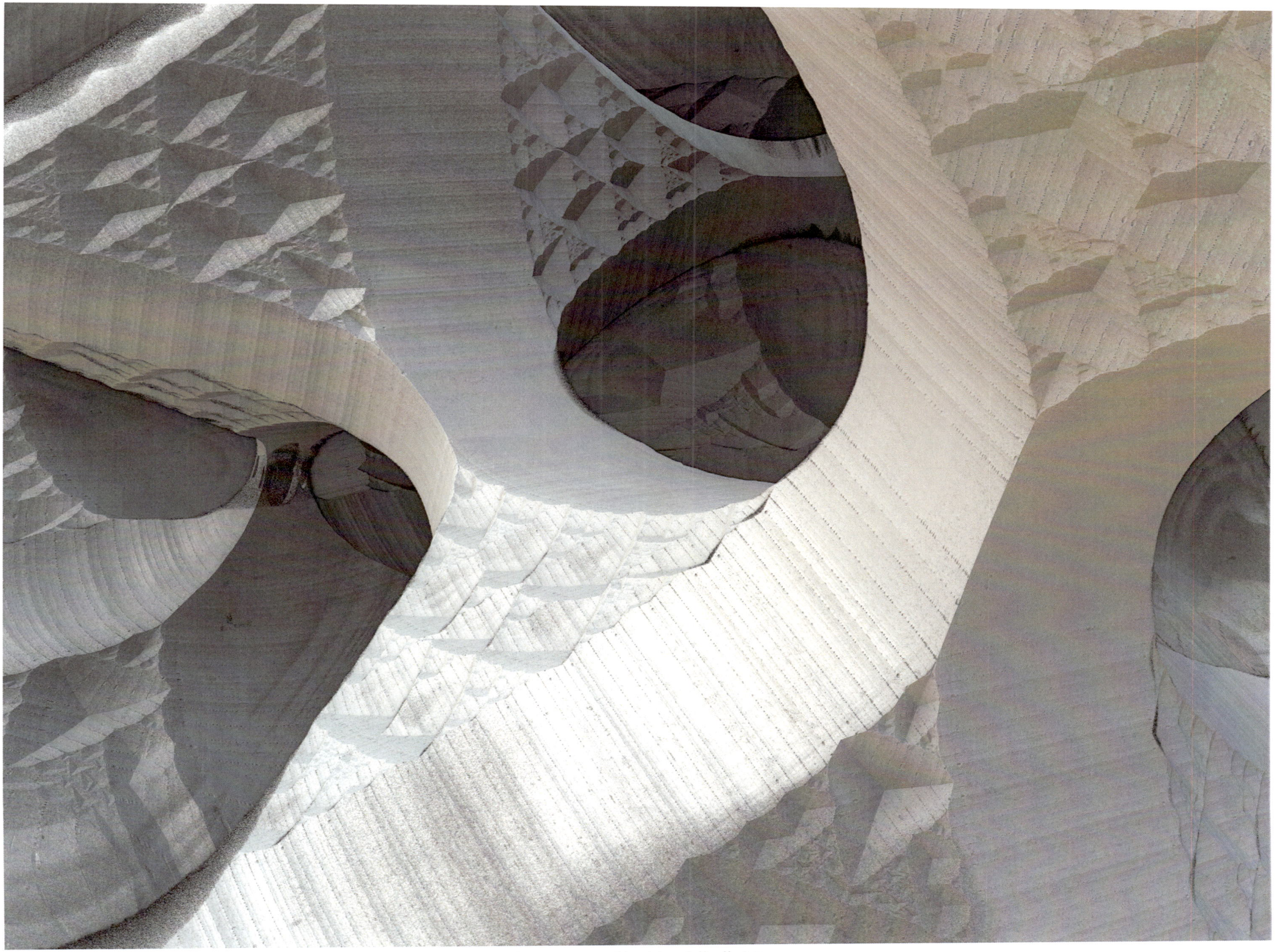

Image created by Mandelbulb 3D

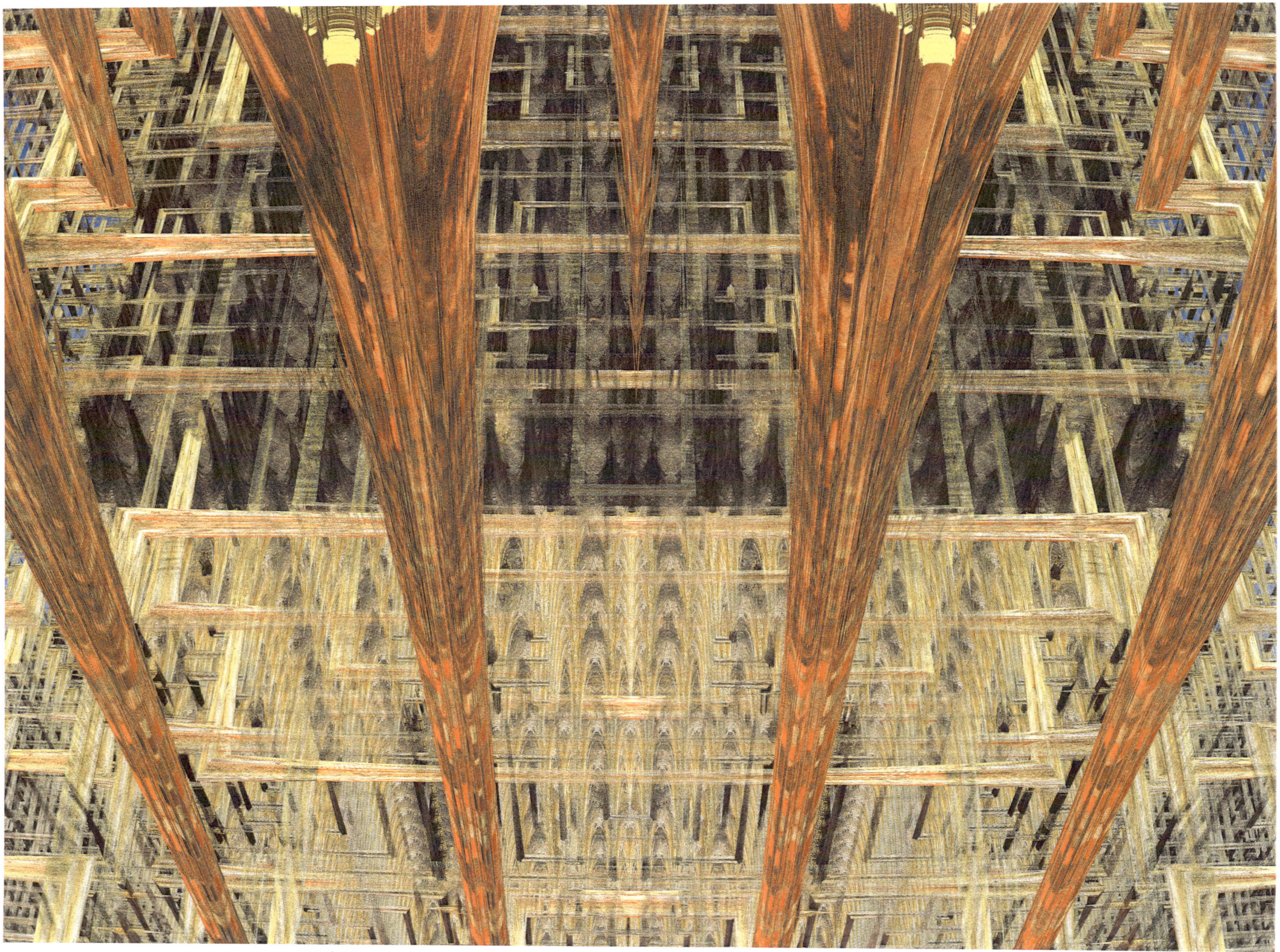

"High-Rise Under Construction, Core Support Structure" (image created by Mandelbulb 3D)

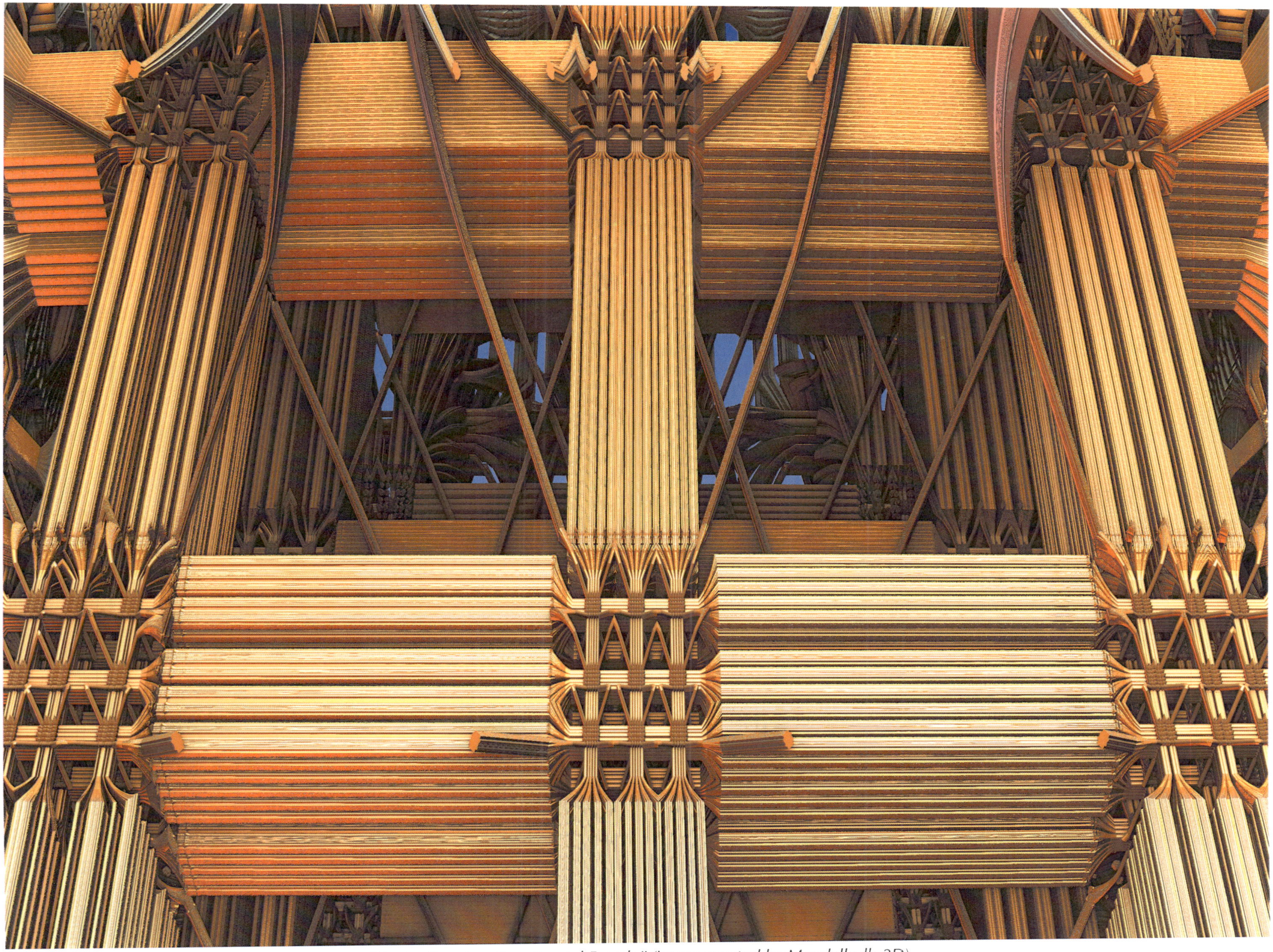

"Under Construction, Frontal Facade" (image created by Mandelbulb 3D)

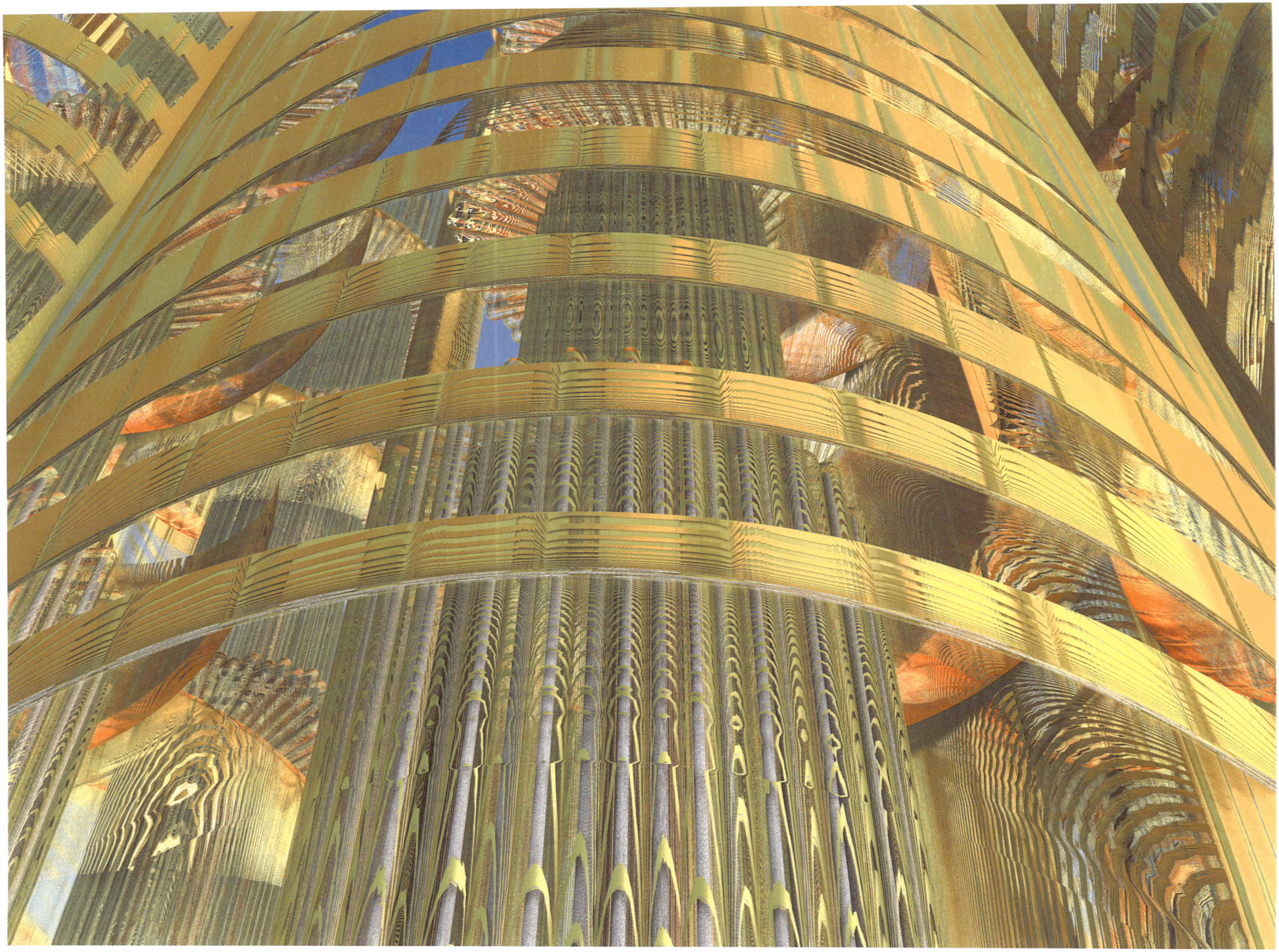

***Above,** tower-like structure; **opposite page,** "Interior Spaces" (all images rendered in Mandelbulb 3D)*

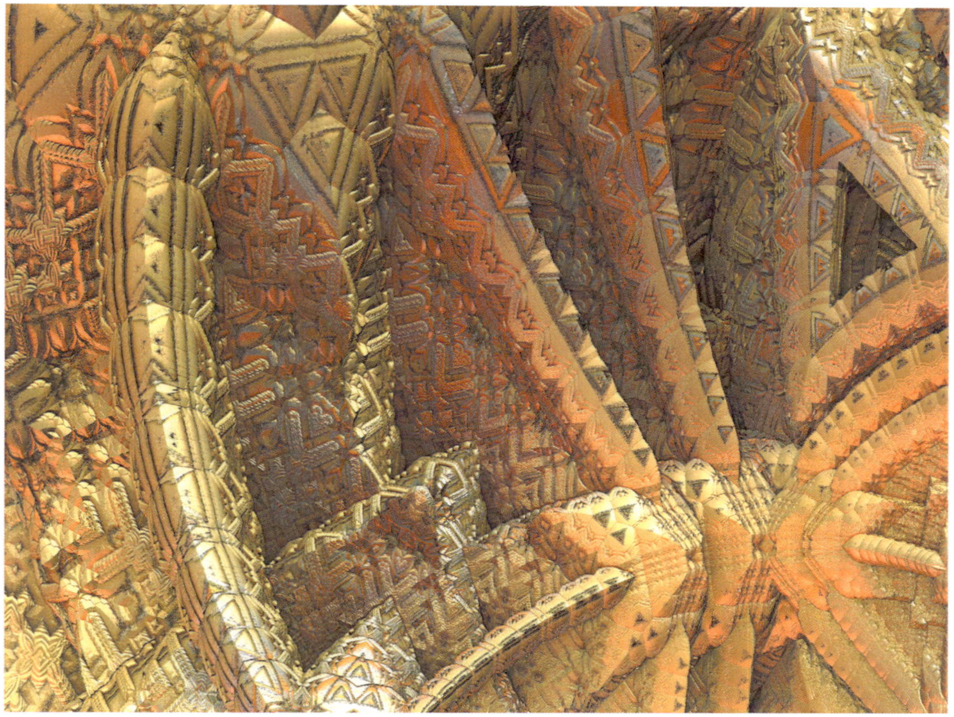
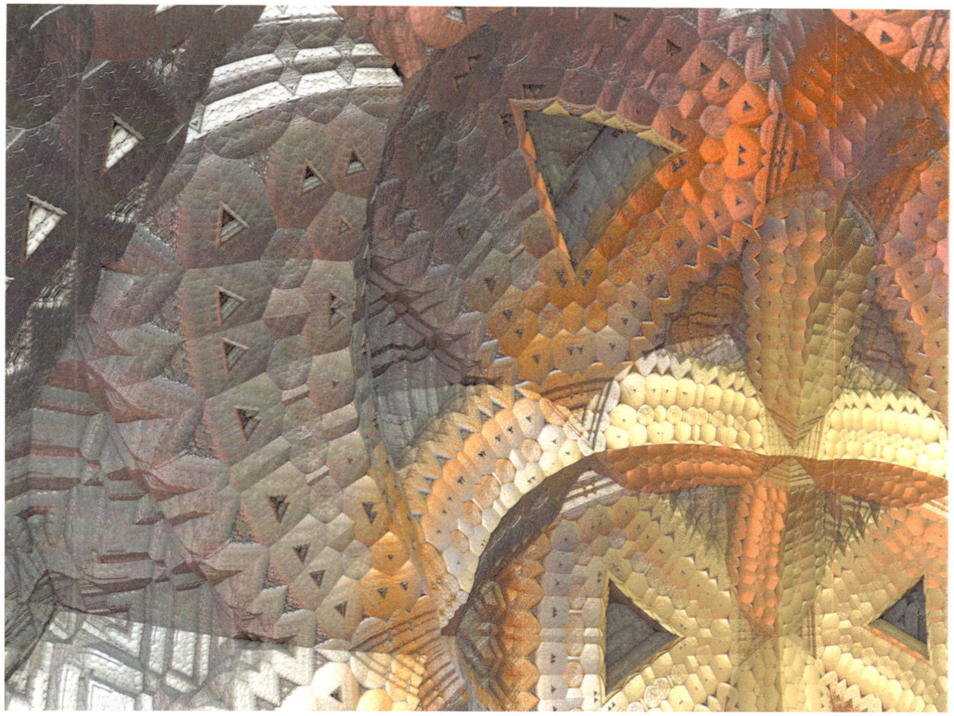
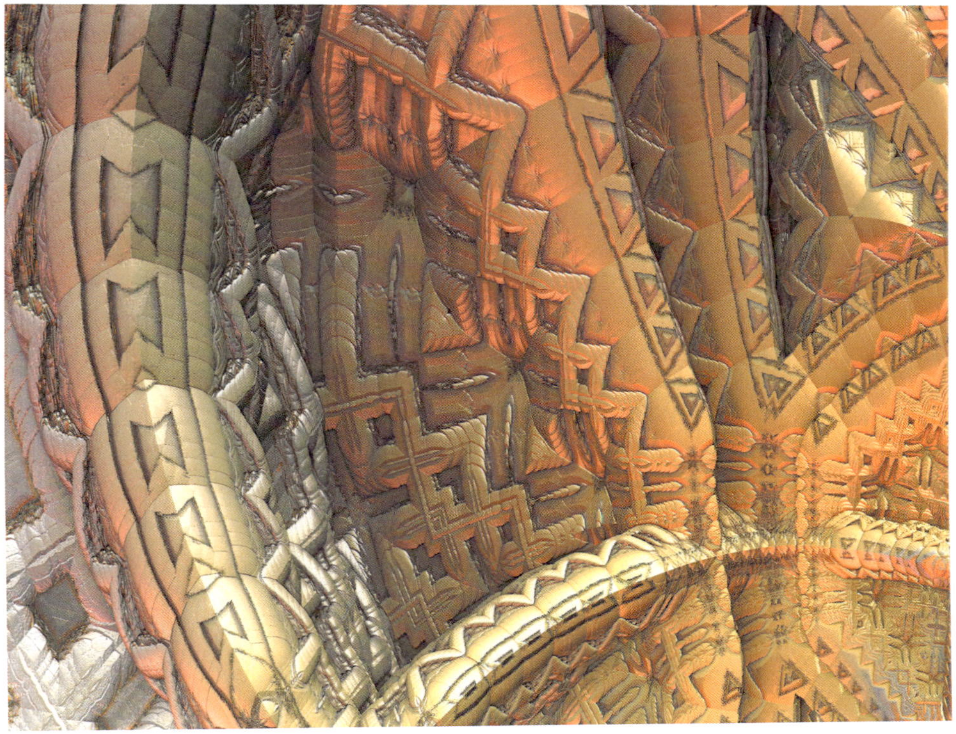
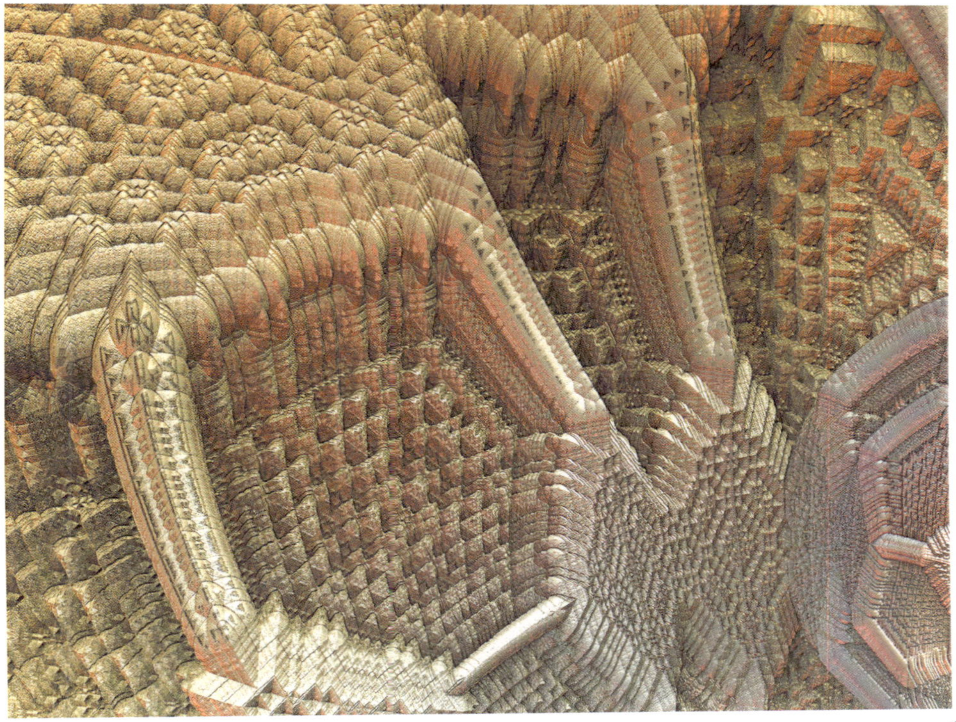

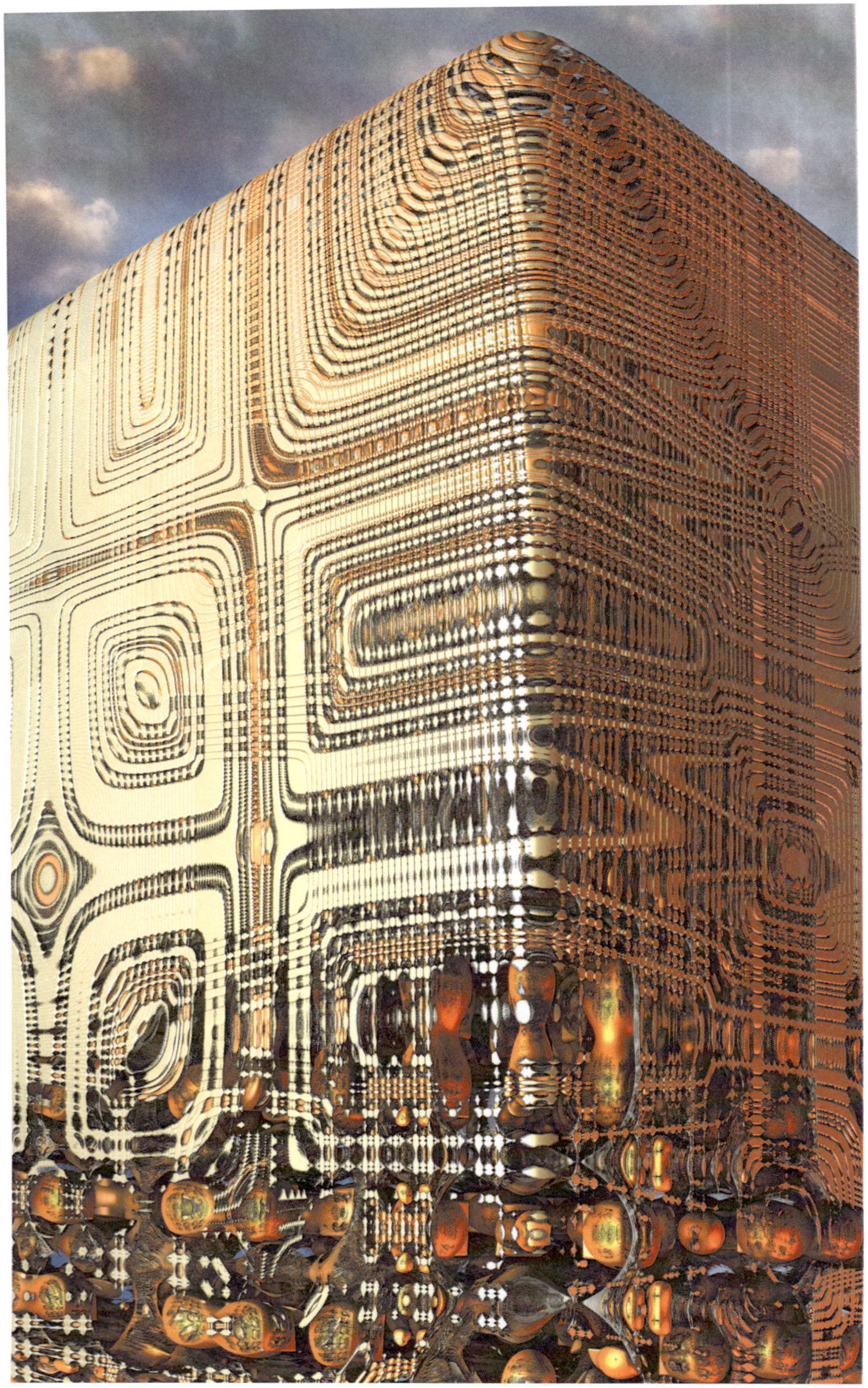

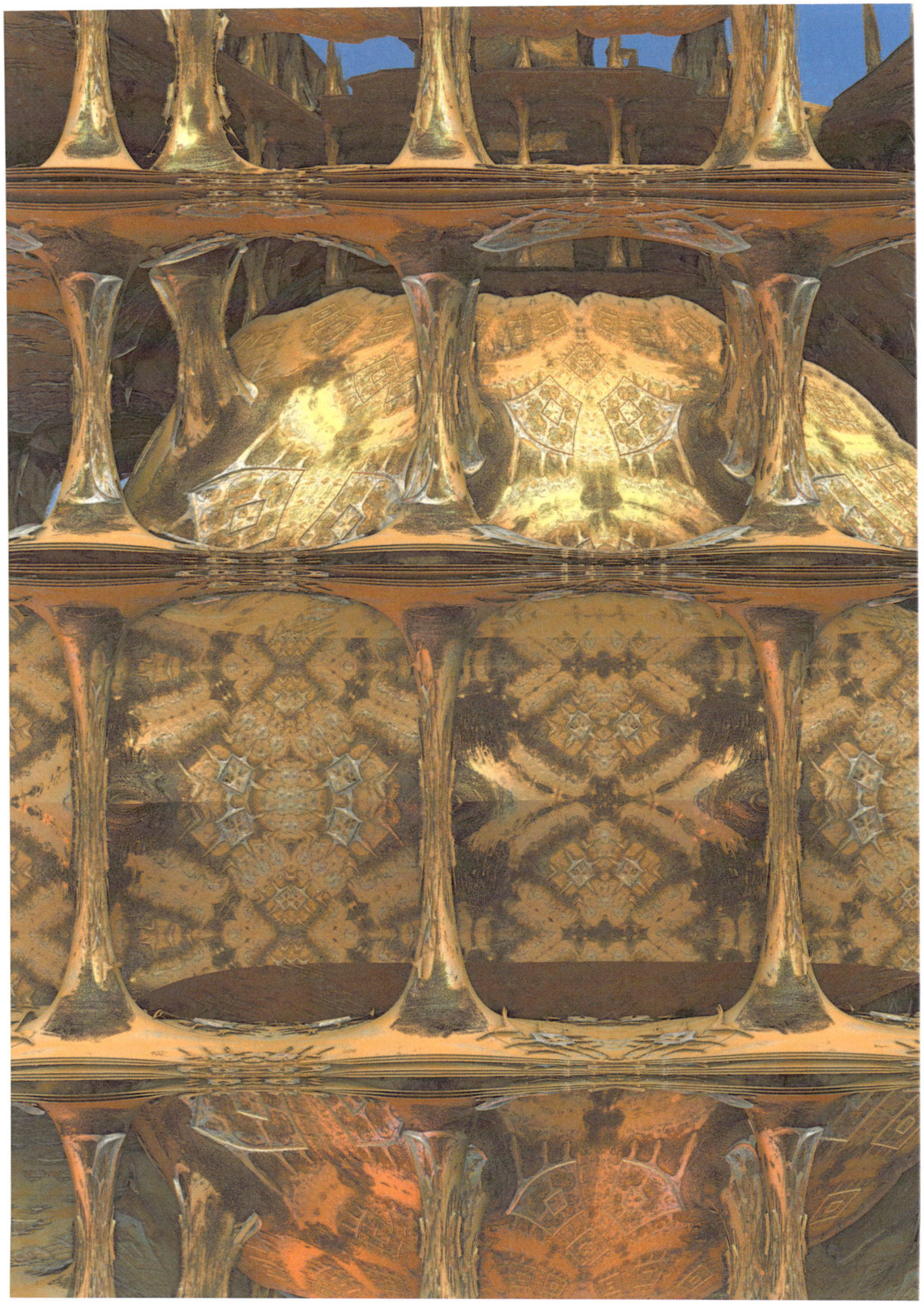

"Manufacturing Facilities," images by Mandelbulb 3D

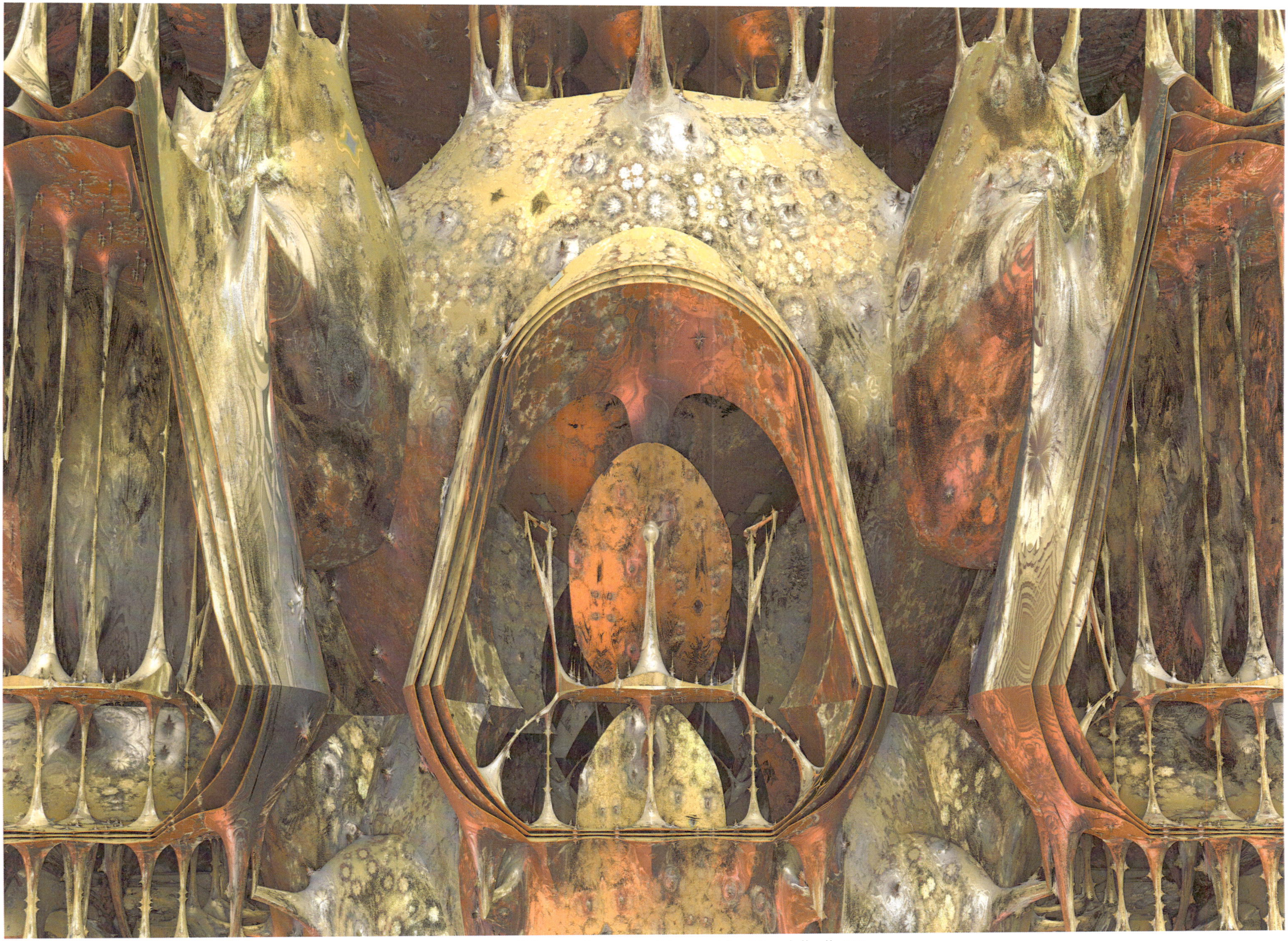

"Mystery Structure," imaged by Mandelbulb 3D

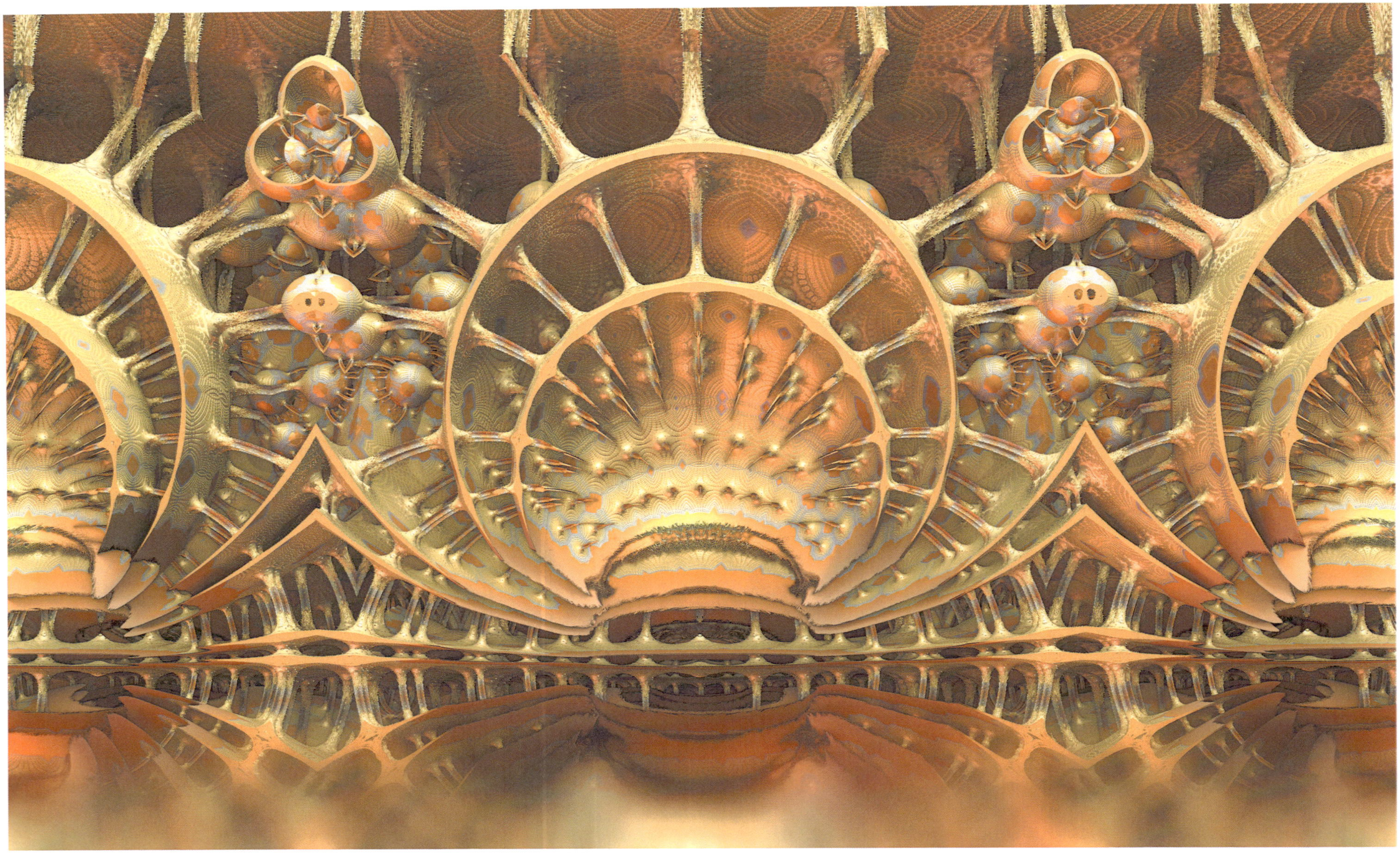

"Facility on Another Planet," image created by Mandelbulb 3D

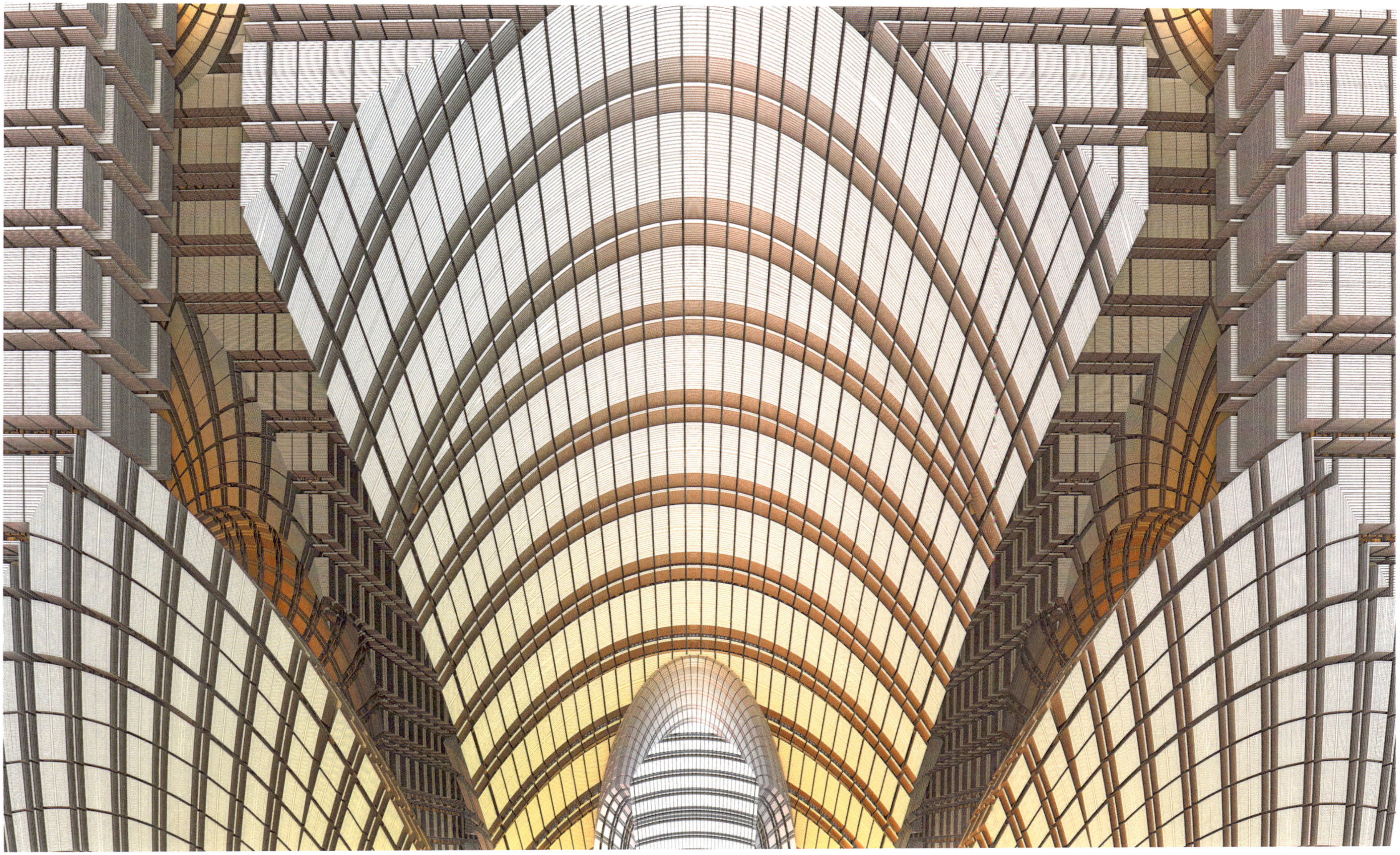

Image created by Mandelbulb 3D resembles an above-ground passageway between two hotels in the suburban Chicago area.

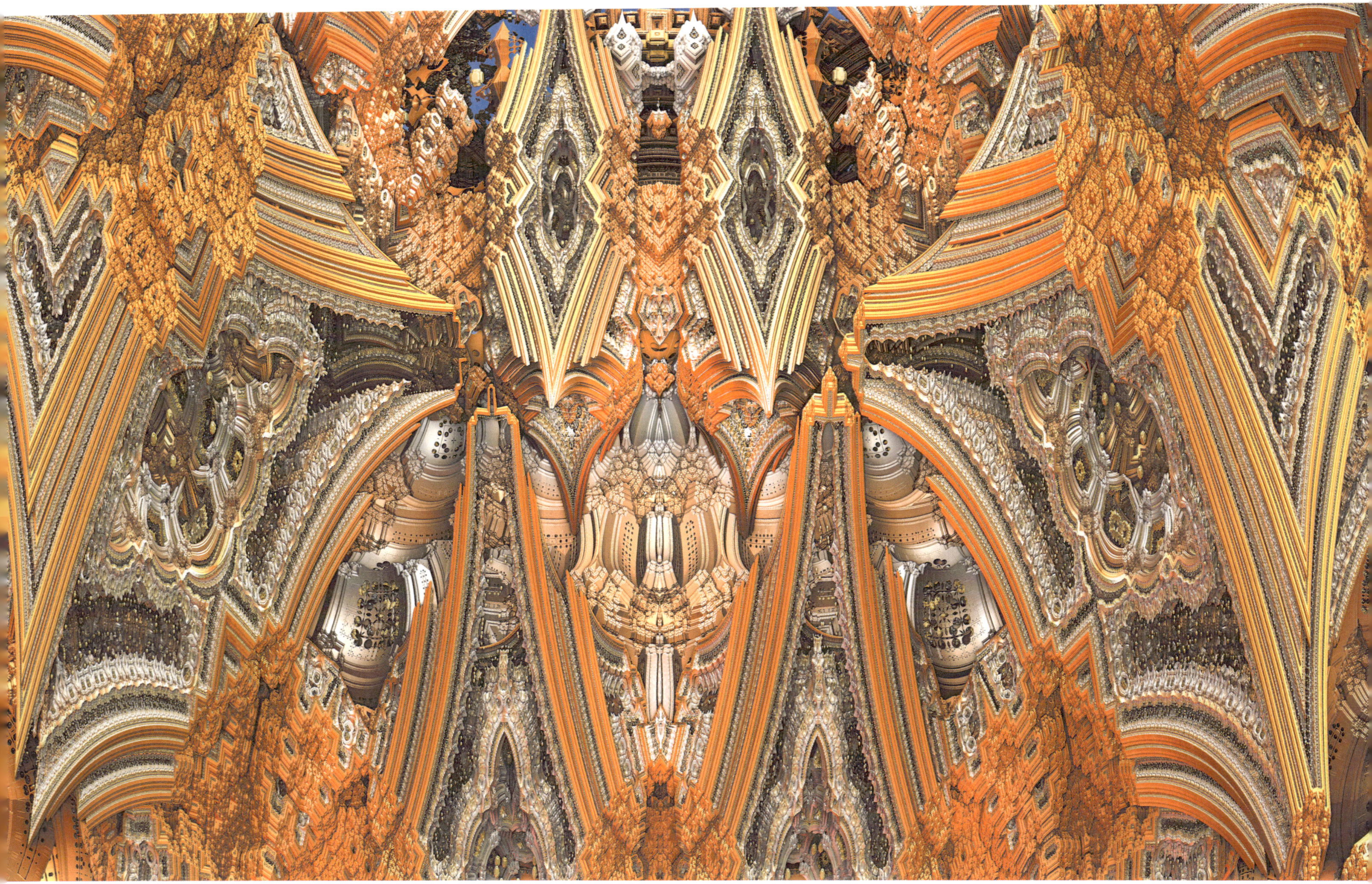

"Interior Sanctuary Space," image created by Mandelbulb 3D

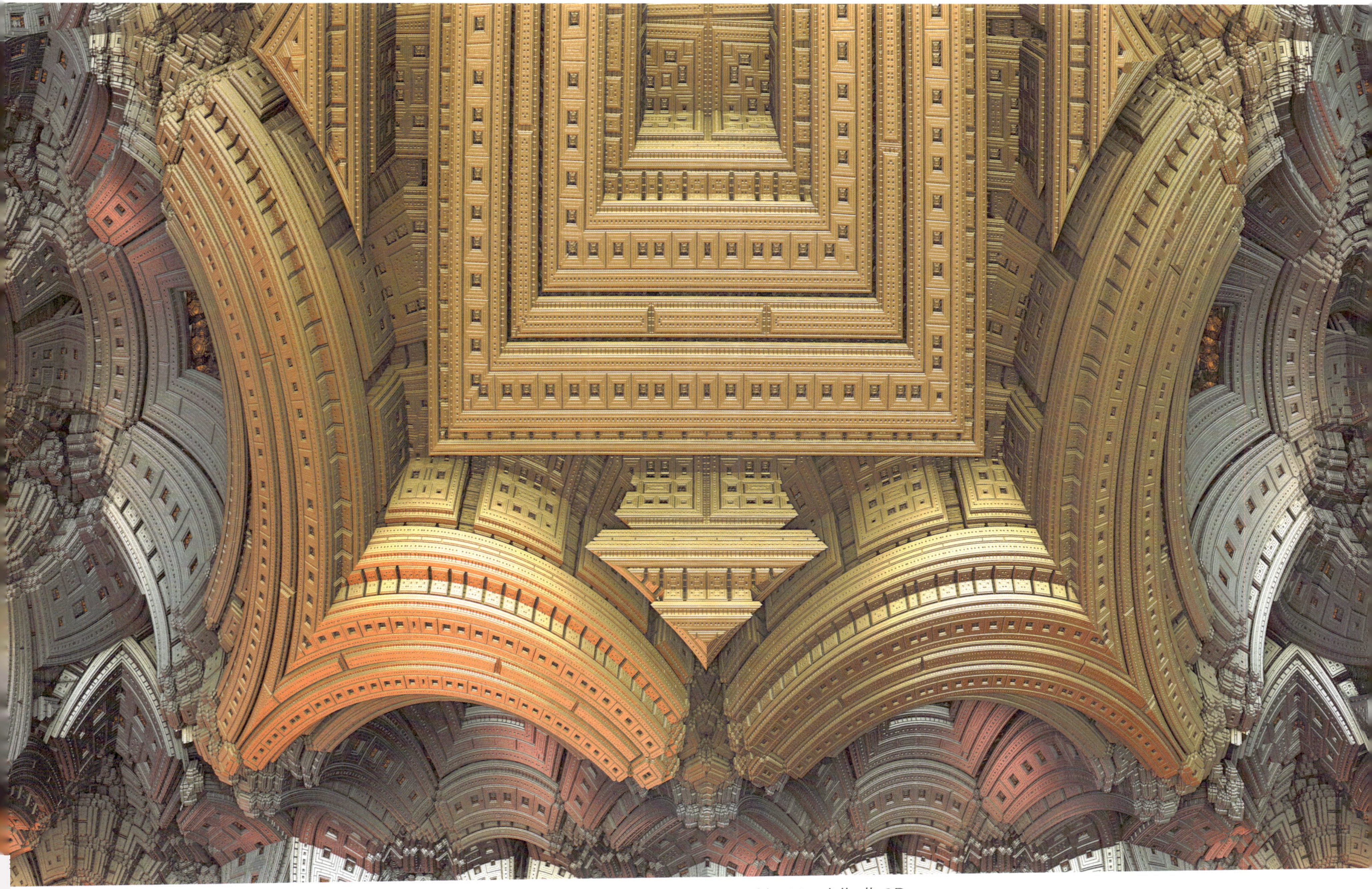

"Vaulted Interior Space," image created by Mandelbulb 3D

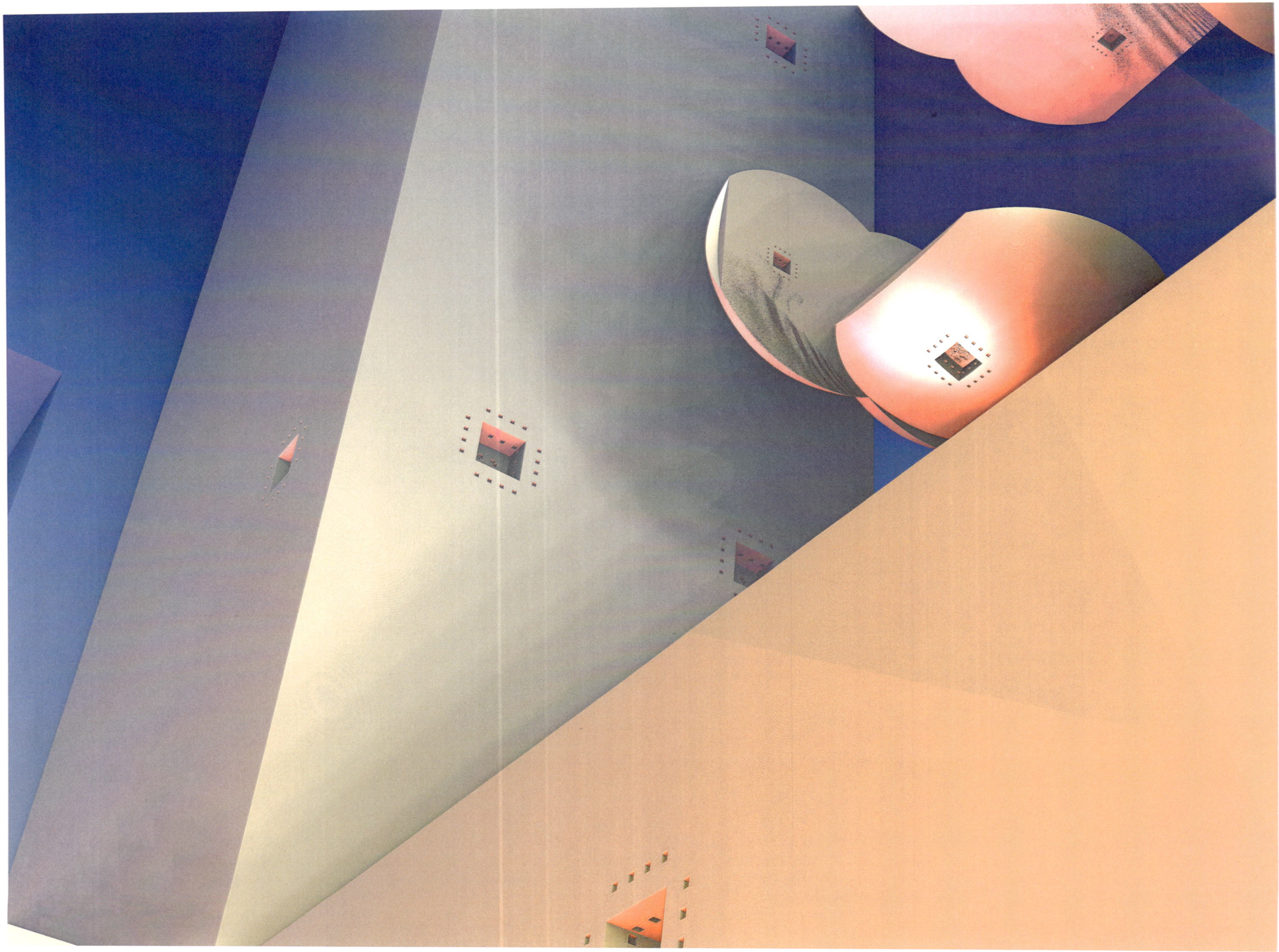

"Building with Microwave Dishes," image created by Mandelbulb 3D

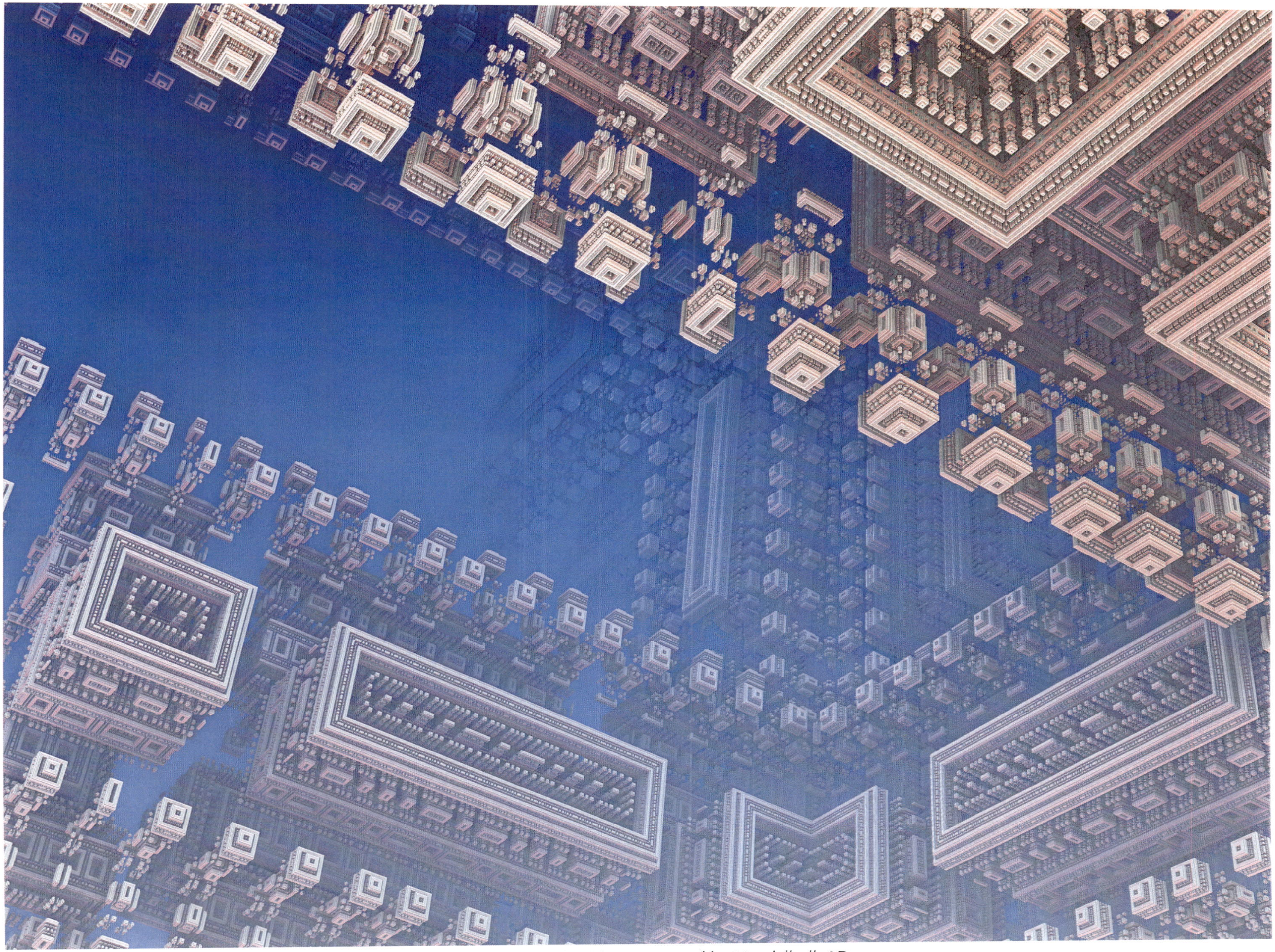

"Building Perspective," image created by Mandelbulb 3D

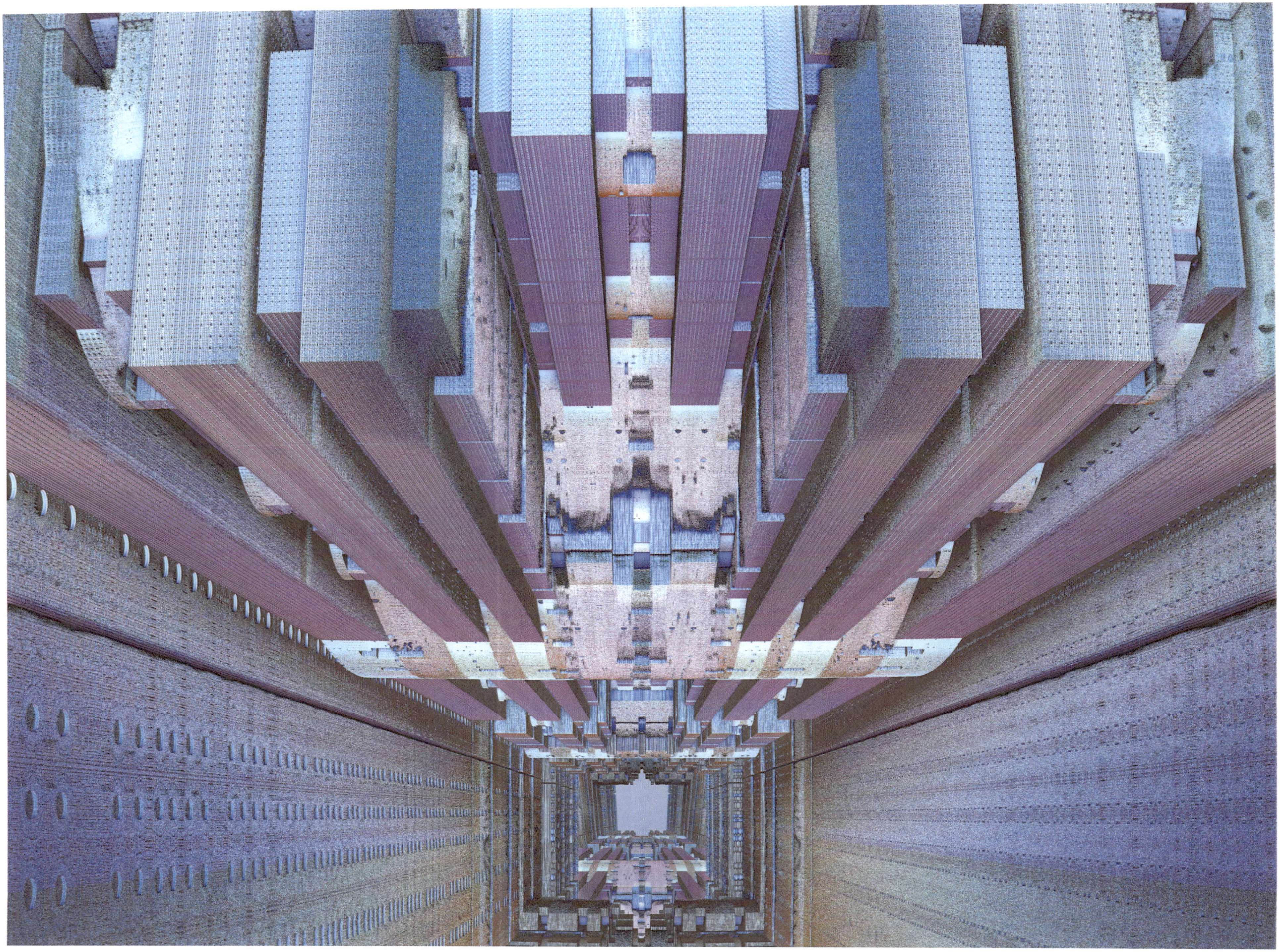

"Loading Port," image created in Mandelbulb 3D

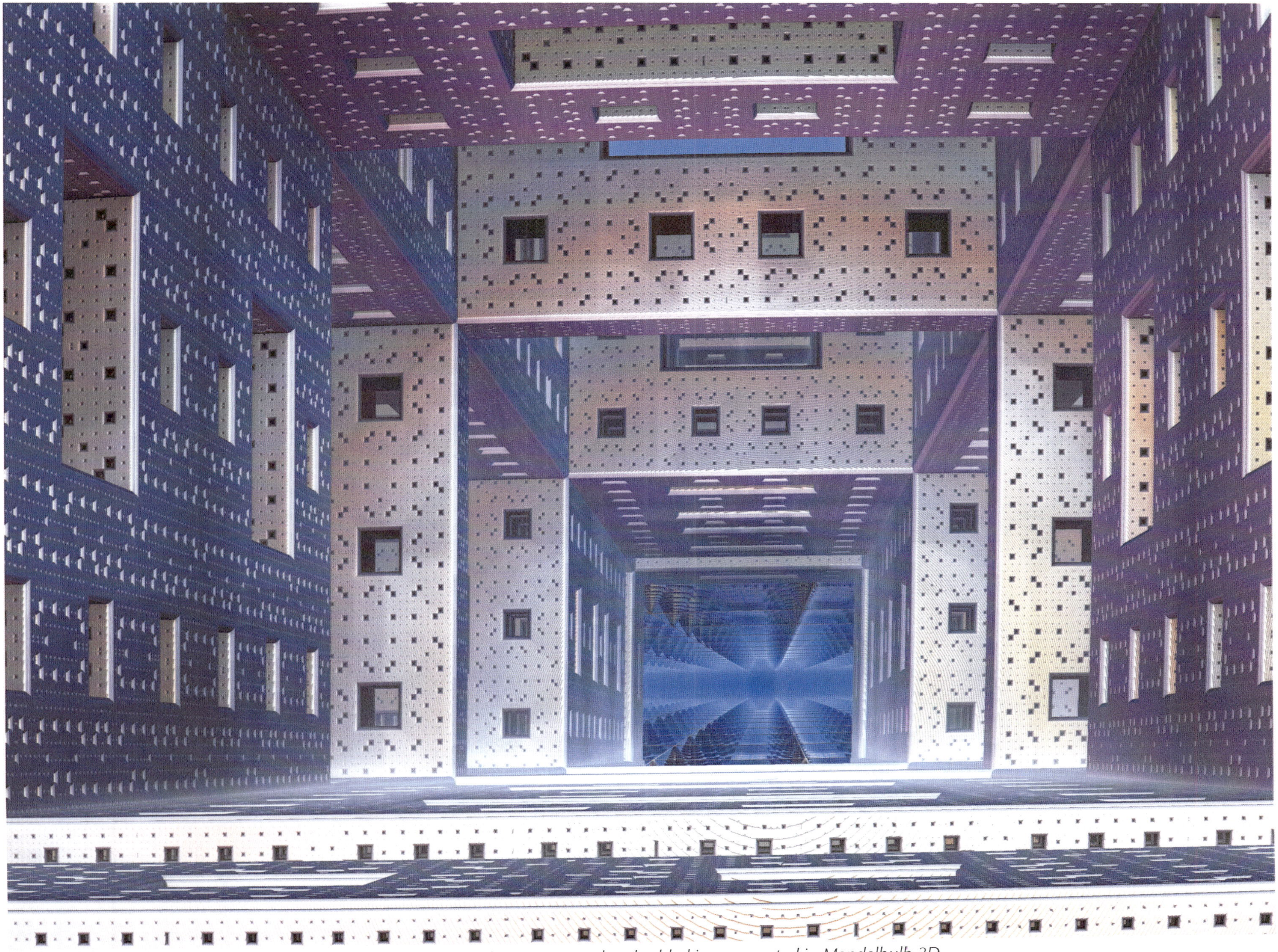

"Stainless Steel Facility," image and embedded image created in Mandelbulb 3D

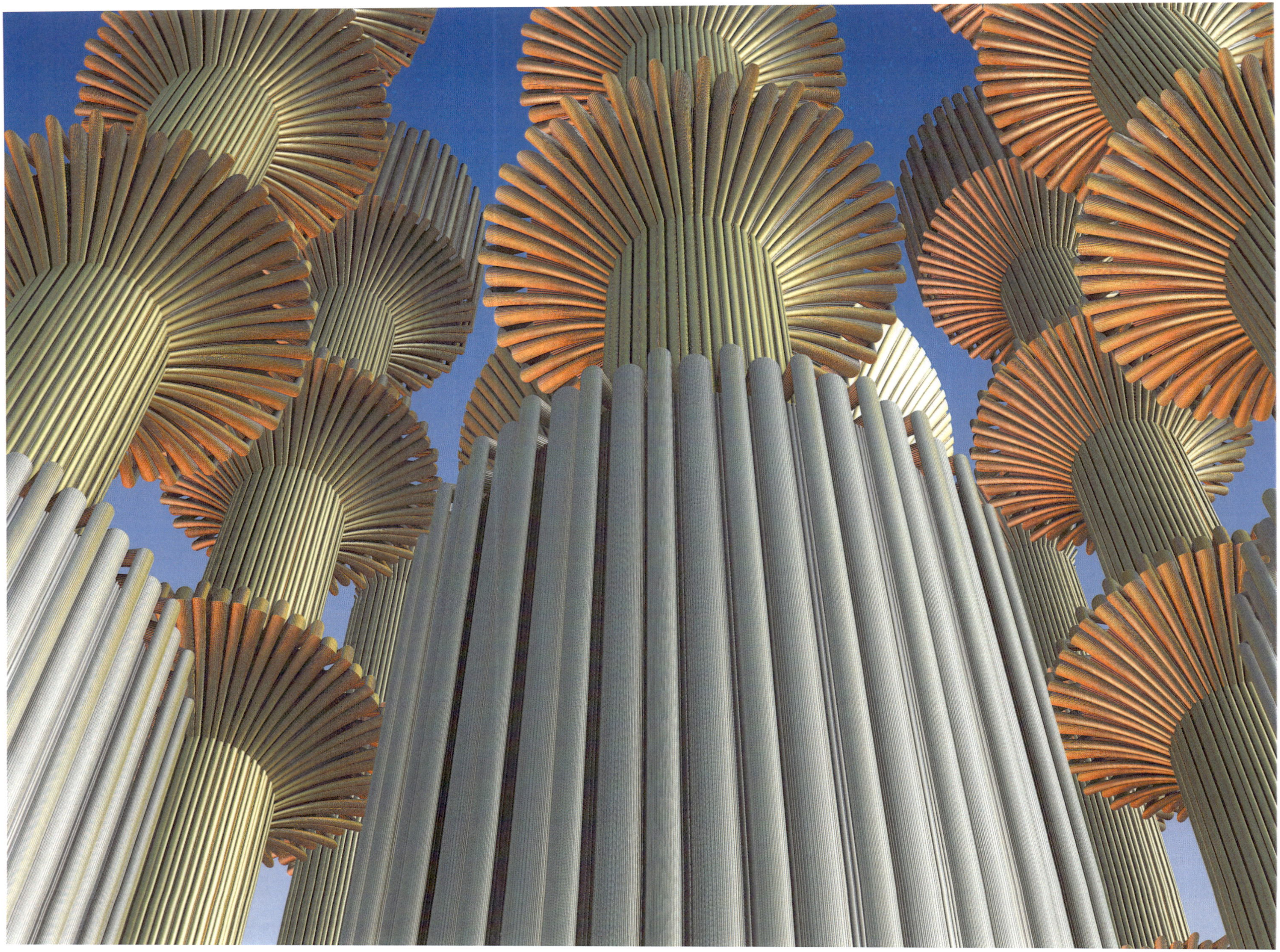

Tower-like structures (image from Mandelbulb 3D)

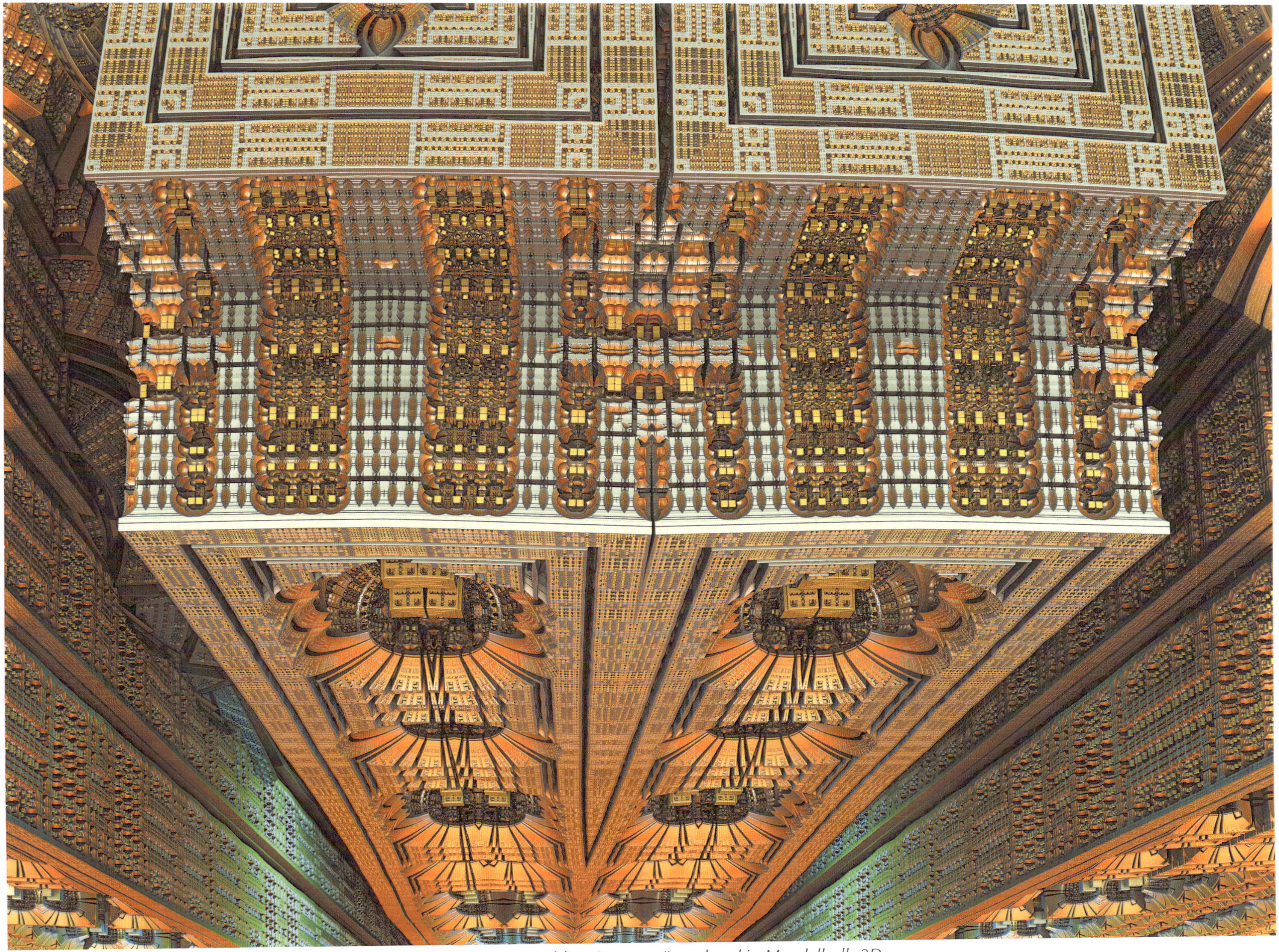

"Interior Building Structure" rendered in Mandelbulb 3D

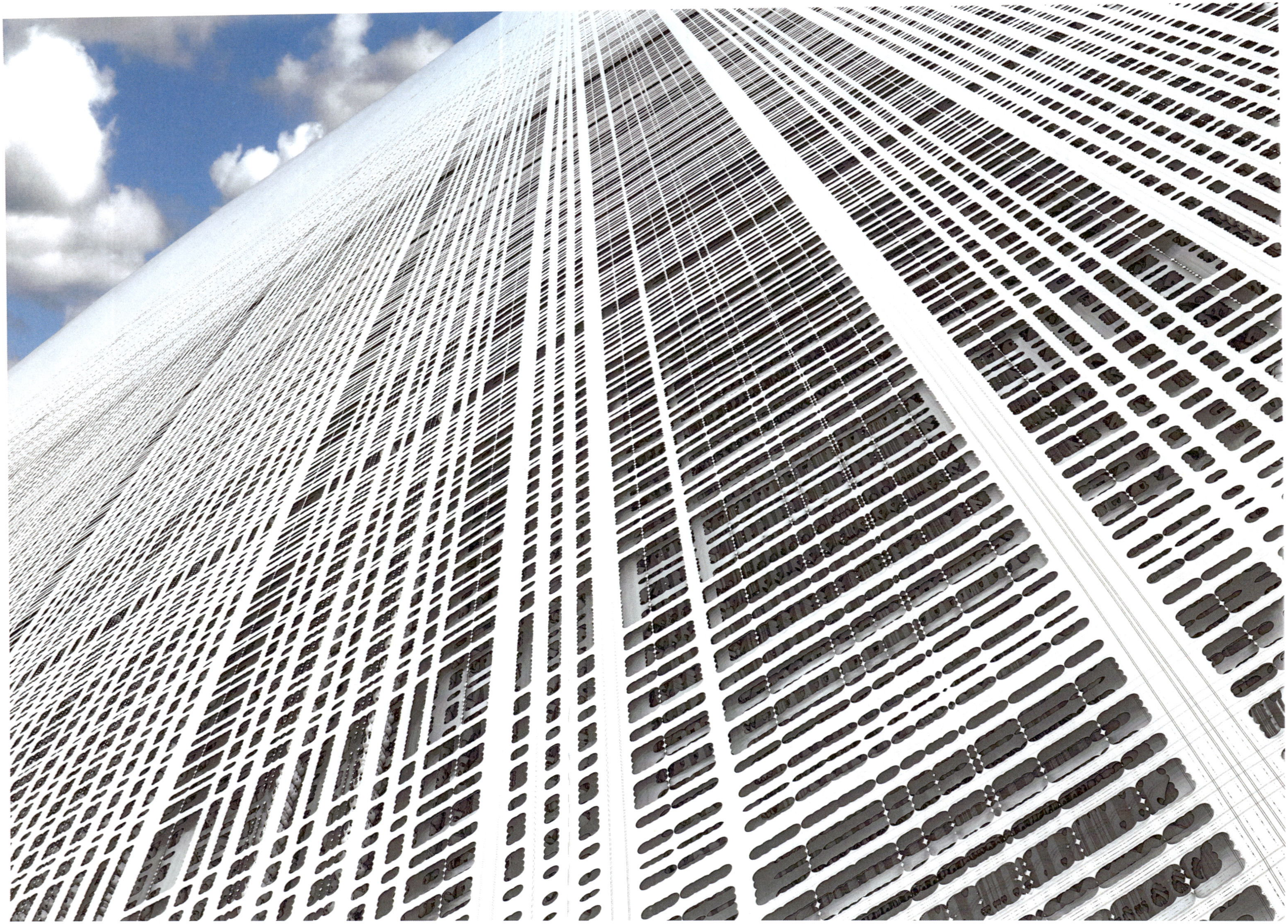

***Above,** "Office Building Facade;" **opposite page,** "Interior Space" (both images created in Mandelbulb 3D)*

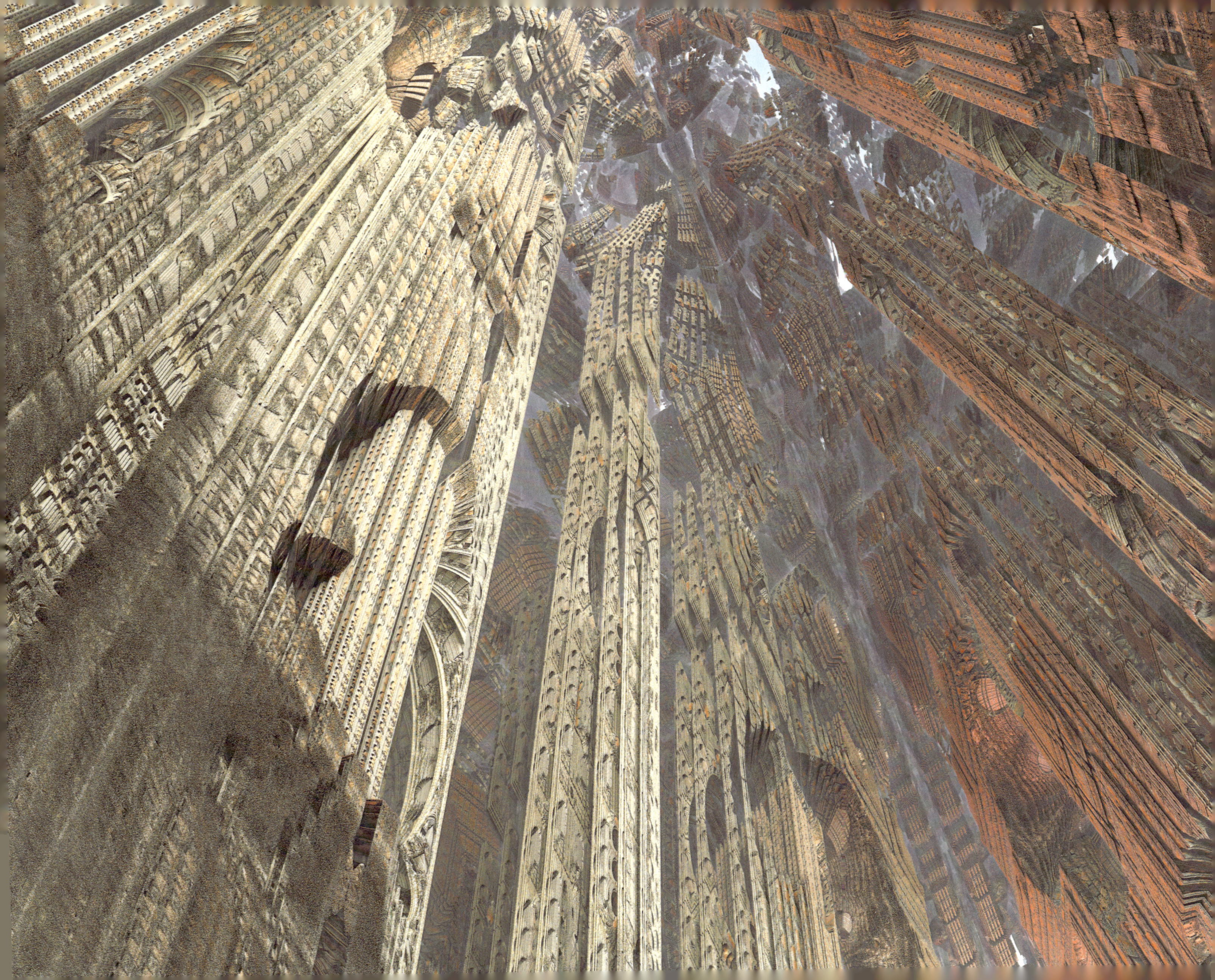

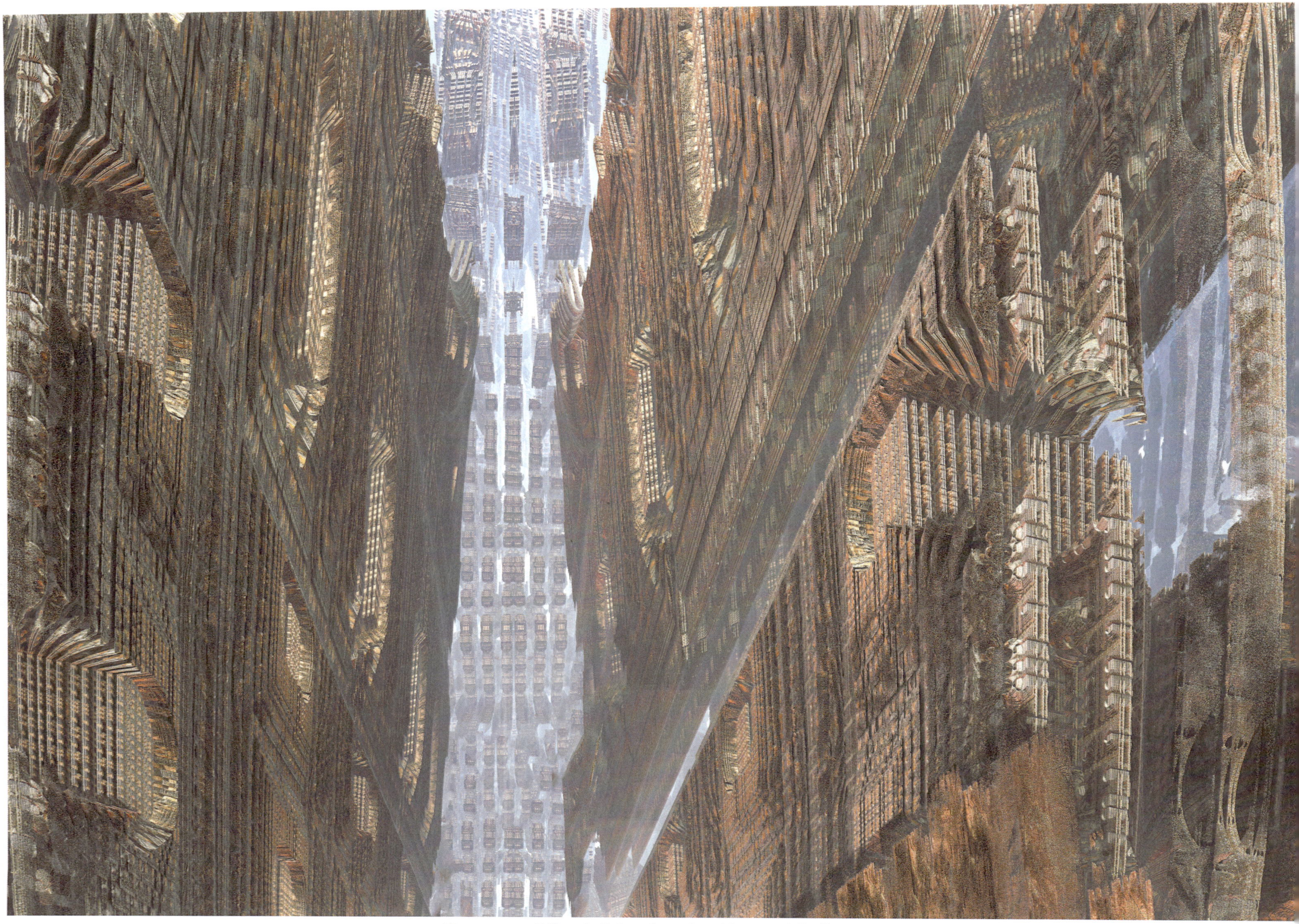

"Downtown Office Buildings" rendered in Mandelbulb 3D

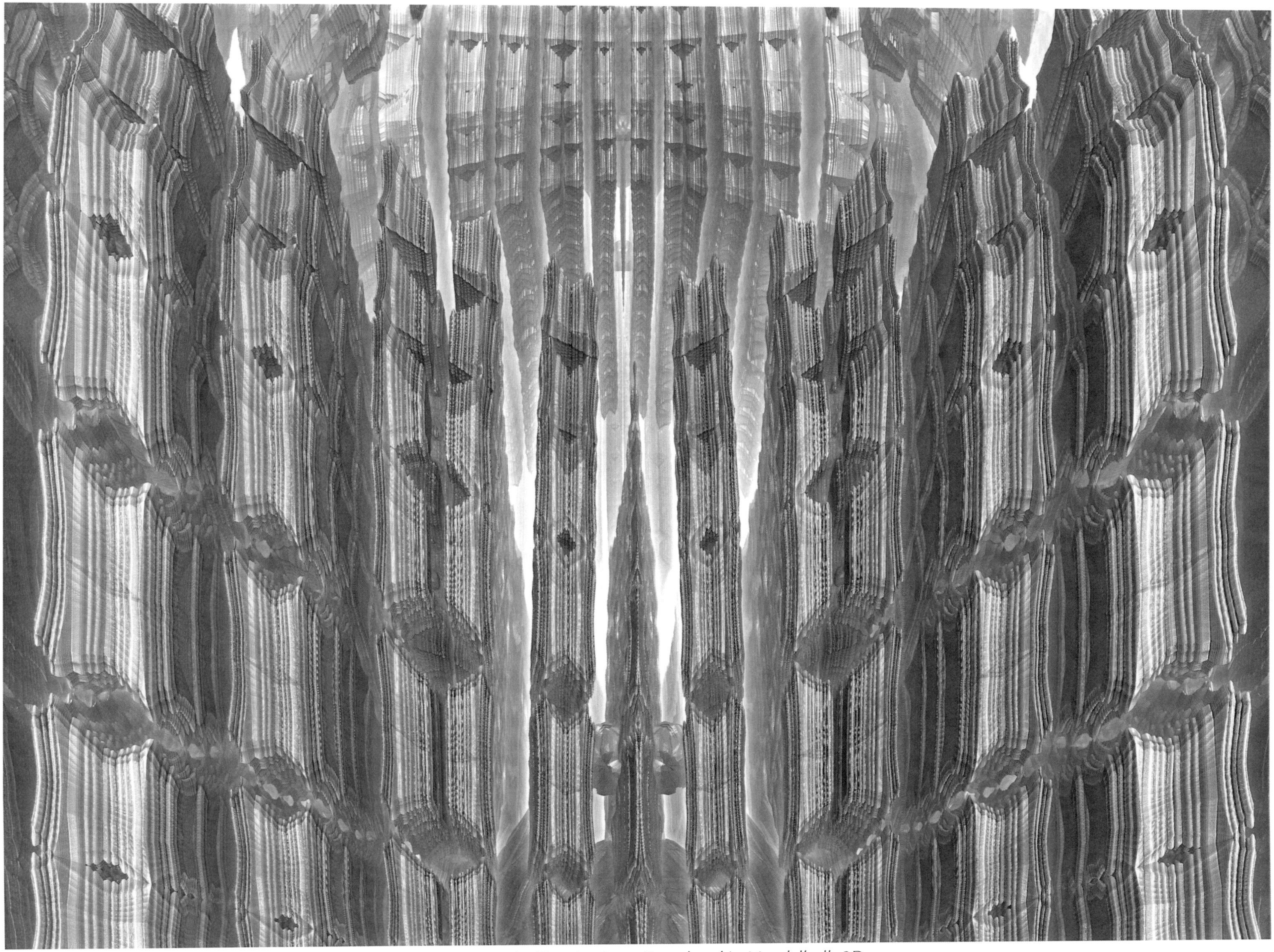

"Interior/Exterior Space" rendered in Mandelbulb 3D

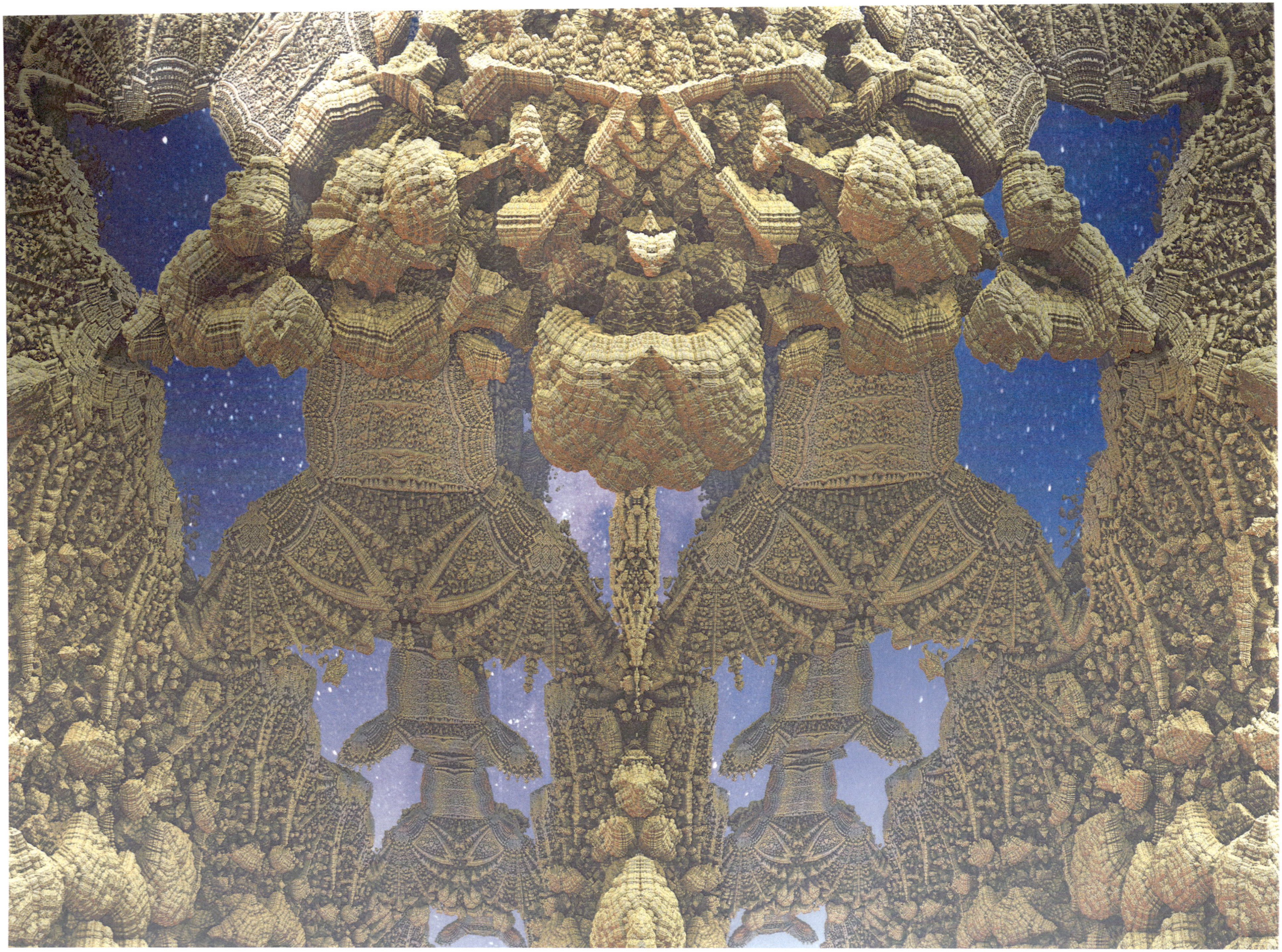

"Structure in the American Southwest at Night;" **opposite page,** *"Mayan Temple." (Both images rendered in Mandelbulb 3D)*

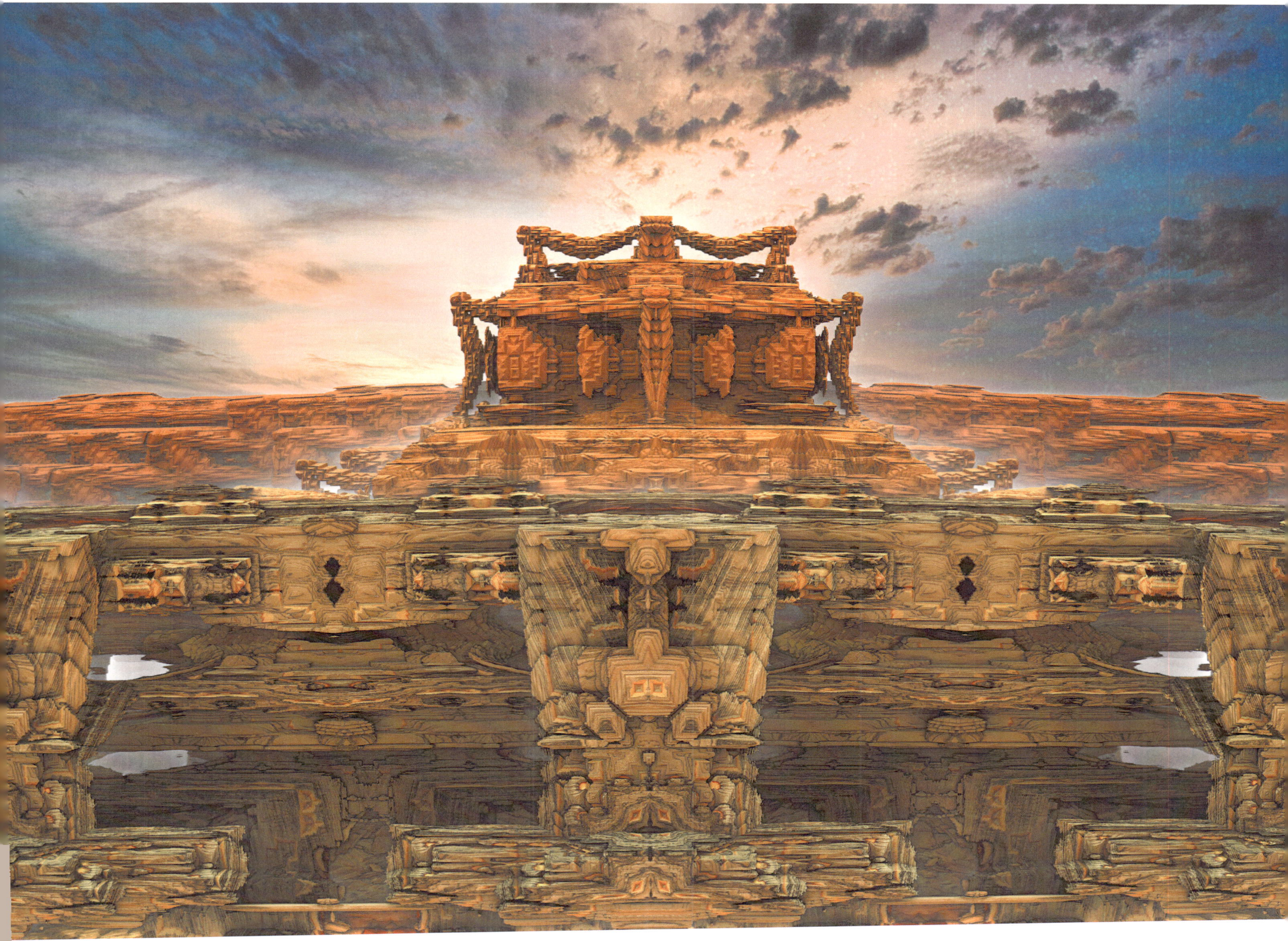

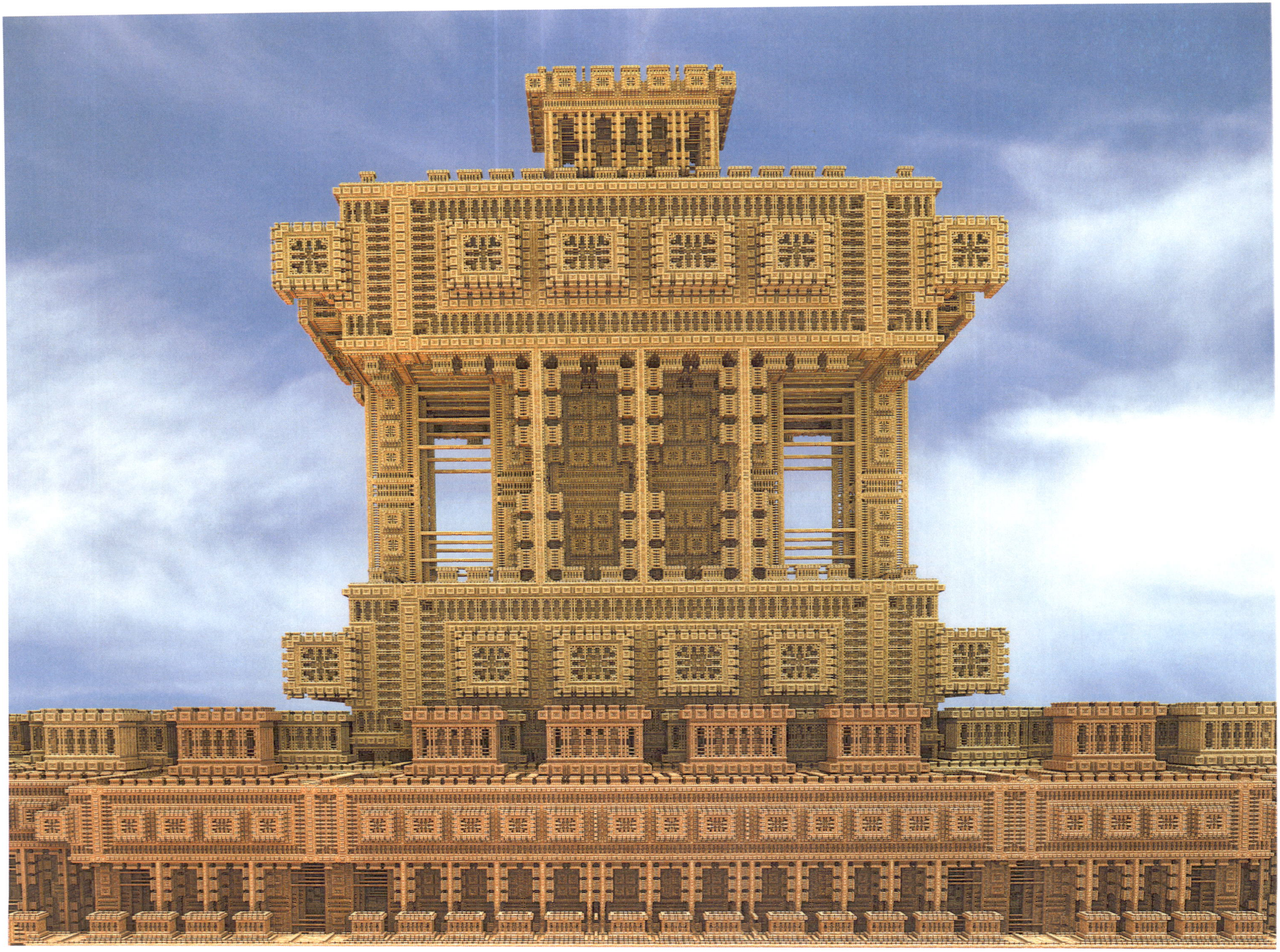

"Southwestern Style," image created by Mandelbulb 3D

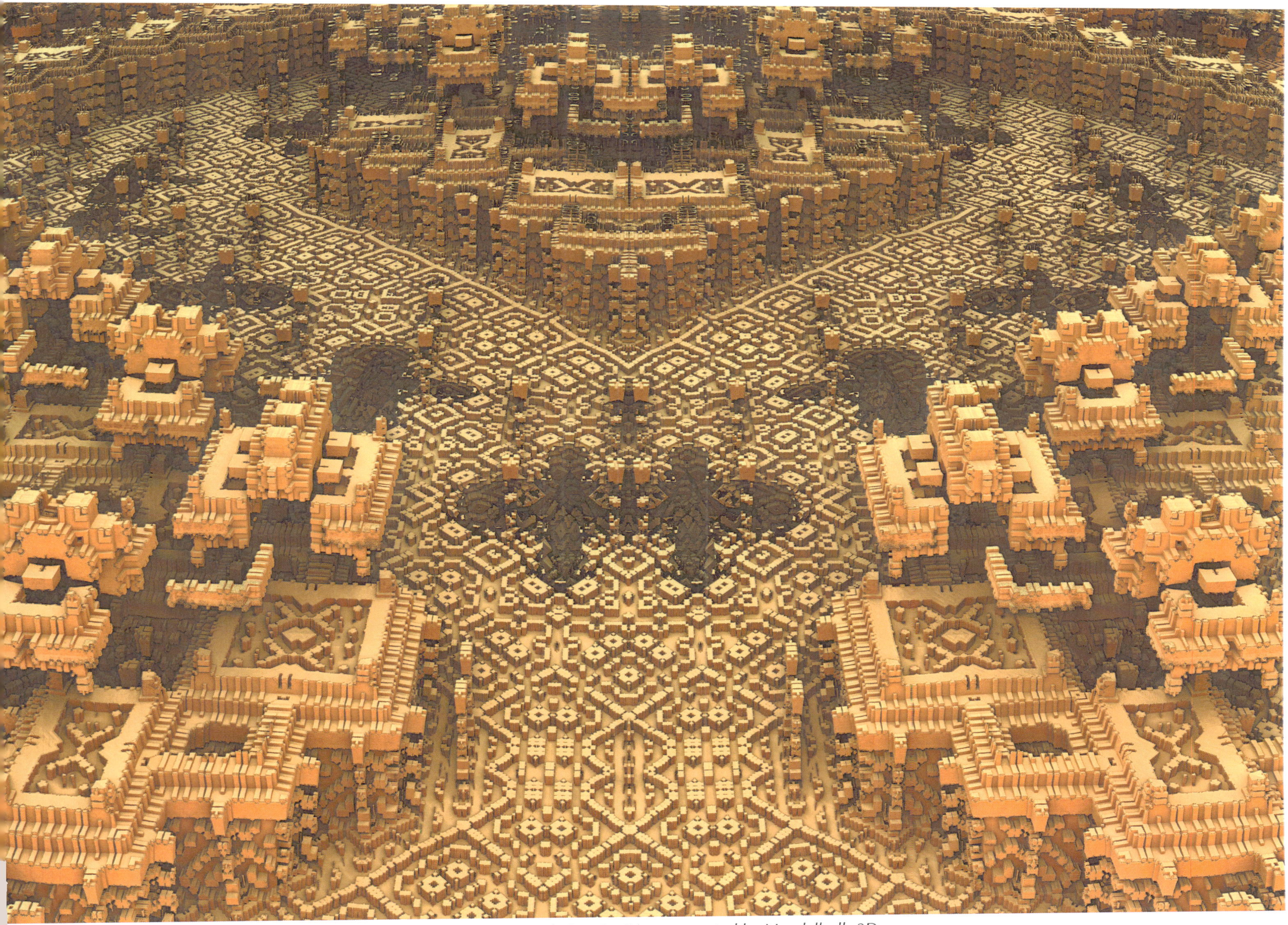

"Mayan Temple Interior," image created by Mandelbulb 3D

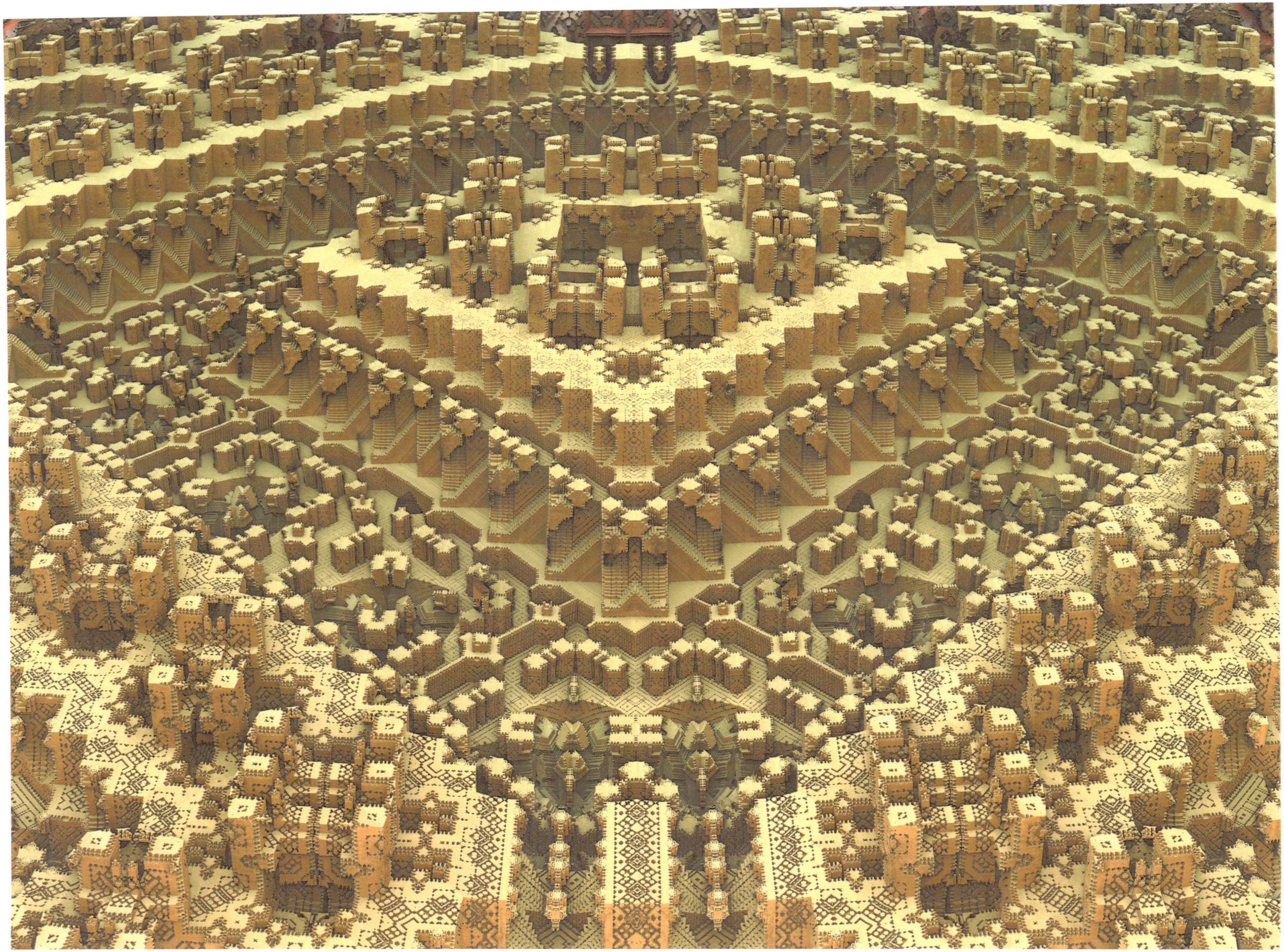

"Diamond-Shaped Courtyard Structure," image created by Mandelbulb 3D

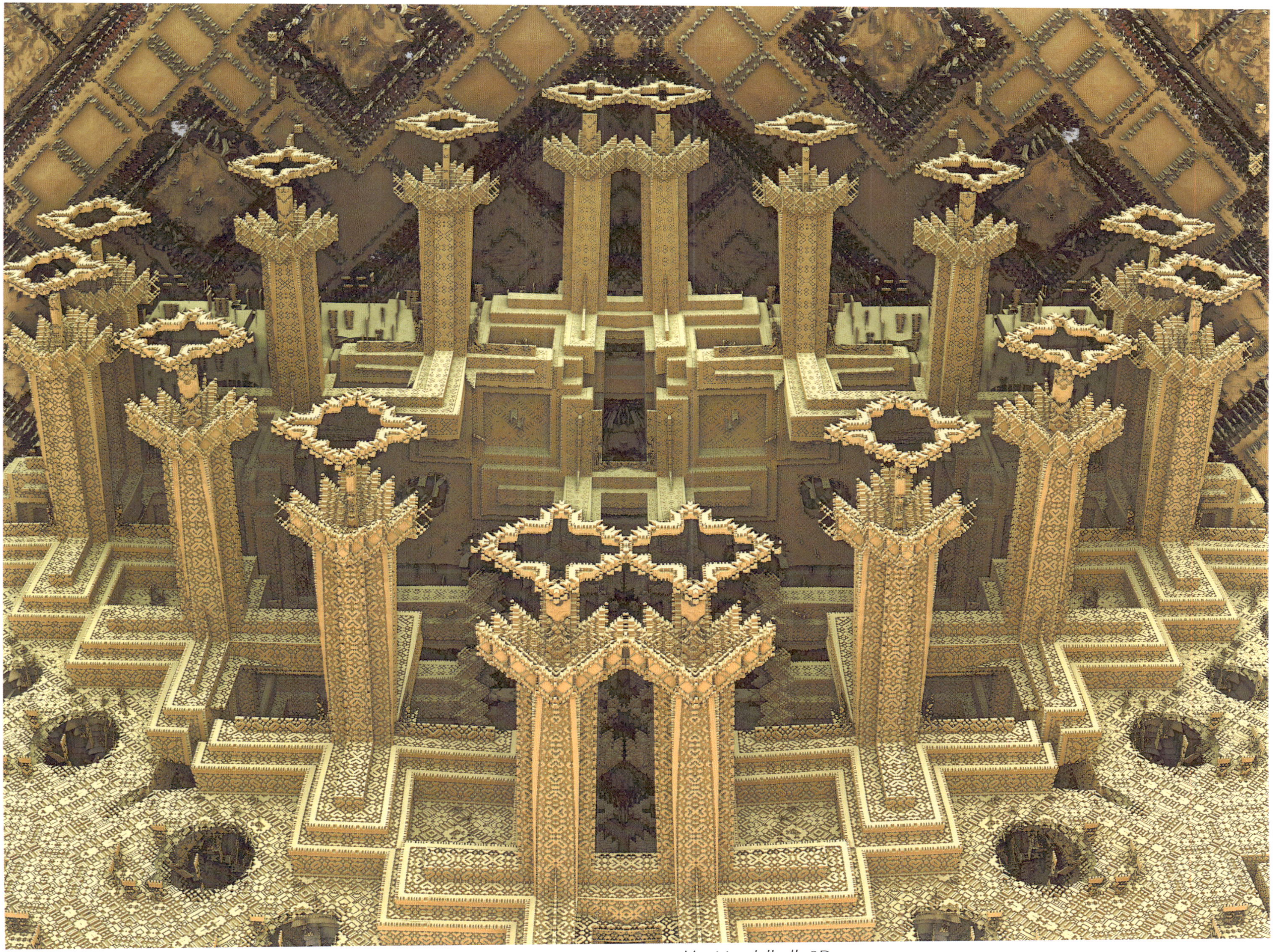

"Temple Interior," image created by Mandelbulb 3D

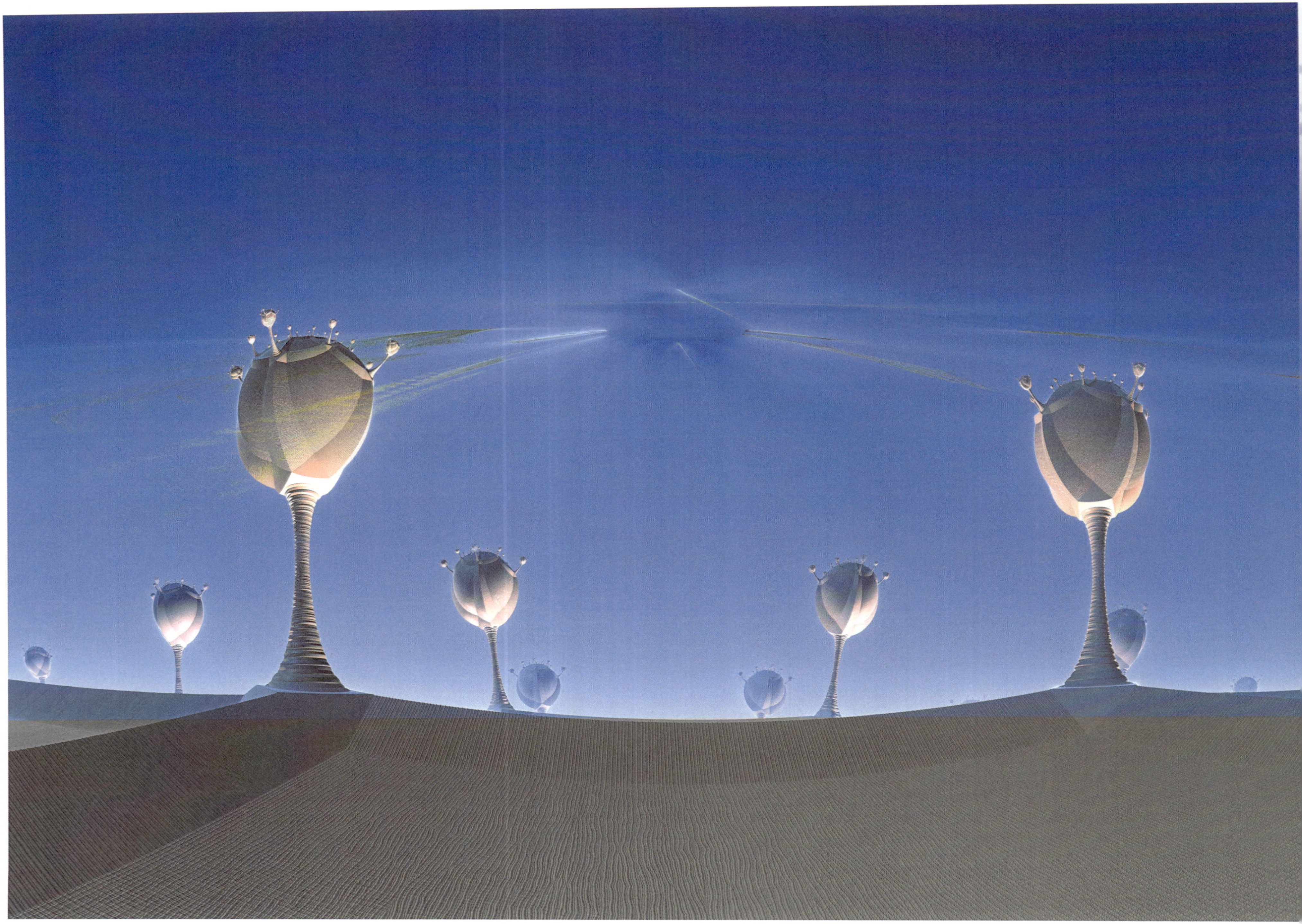

"Another World," image created by Mandelbulb 3D

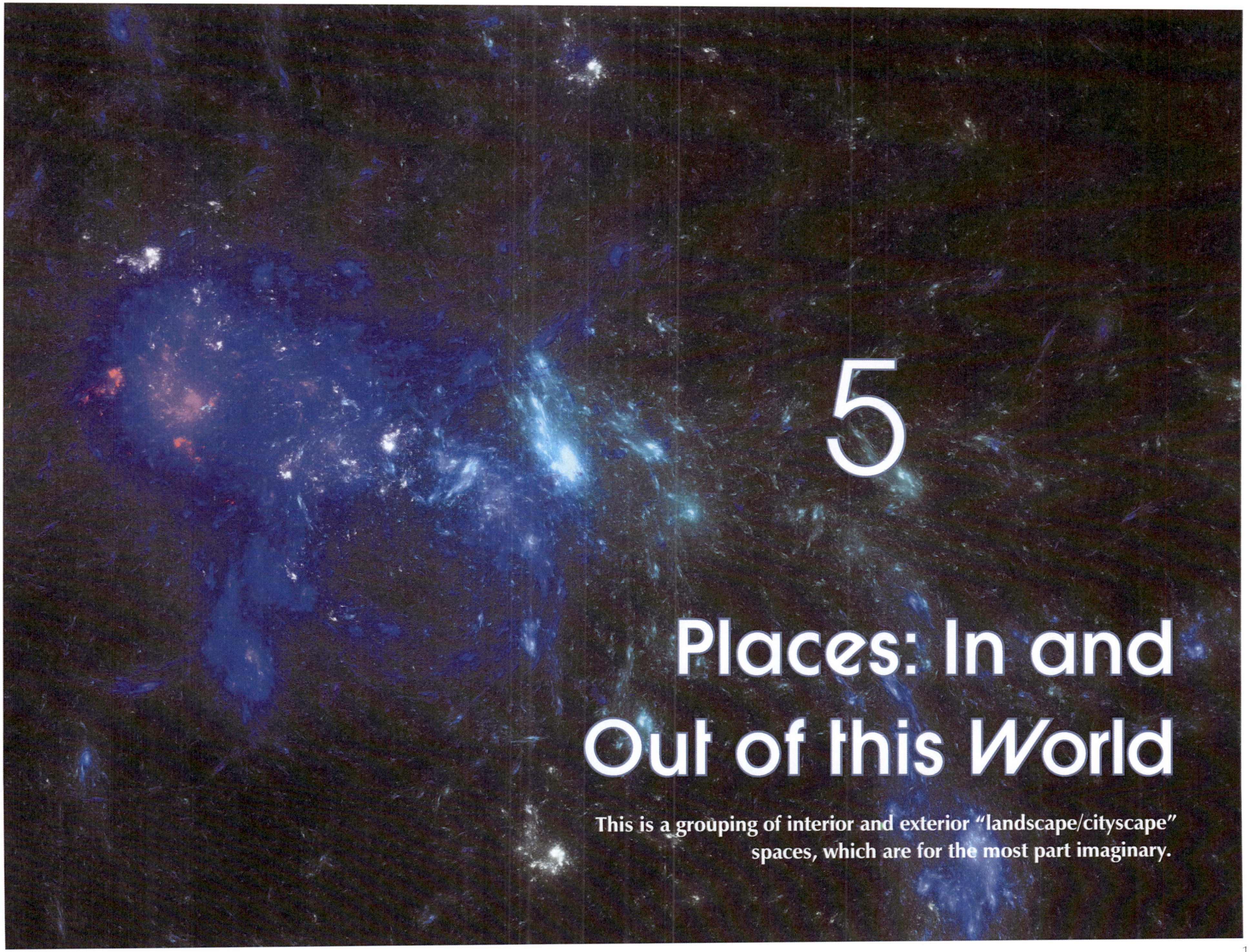

5

Places: In and Out of this *World*

This is a grouping of interior and exterior "landscape/cityscape" spaces, which are for the most part imaginary.

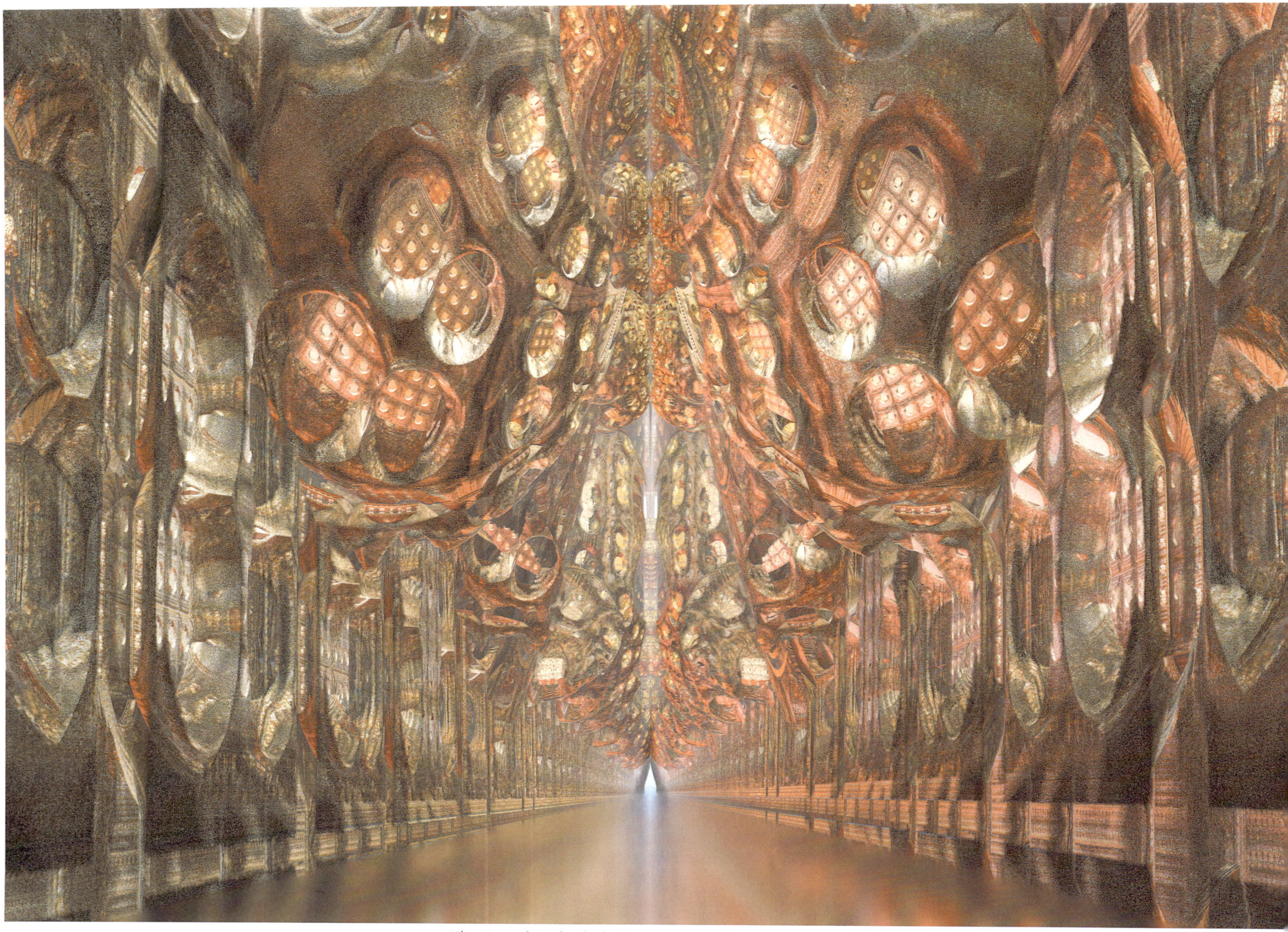

"The Fractal Cathedral" (image created by Mandelbulb 3D)

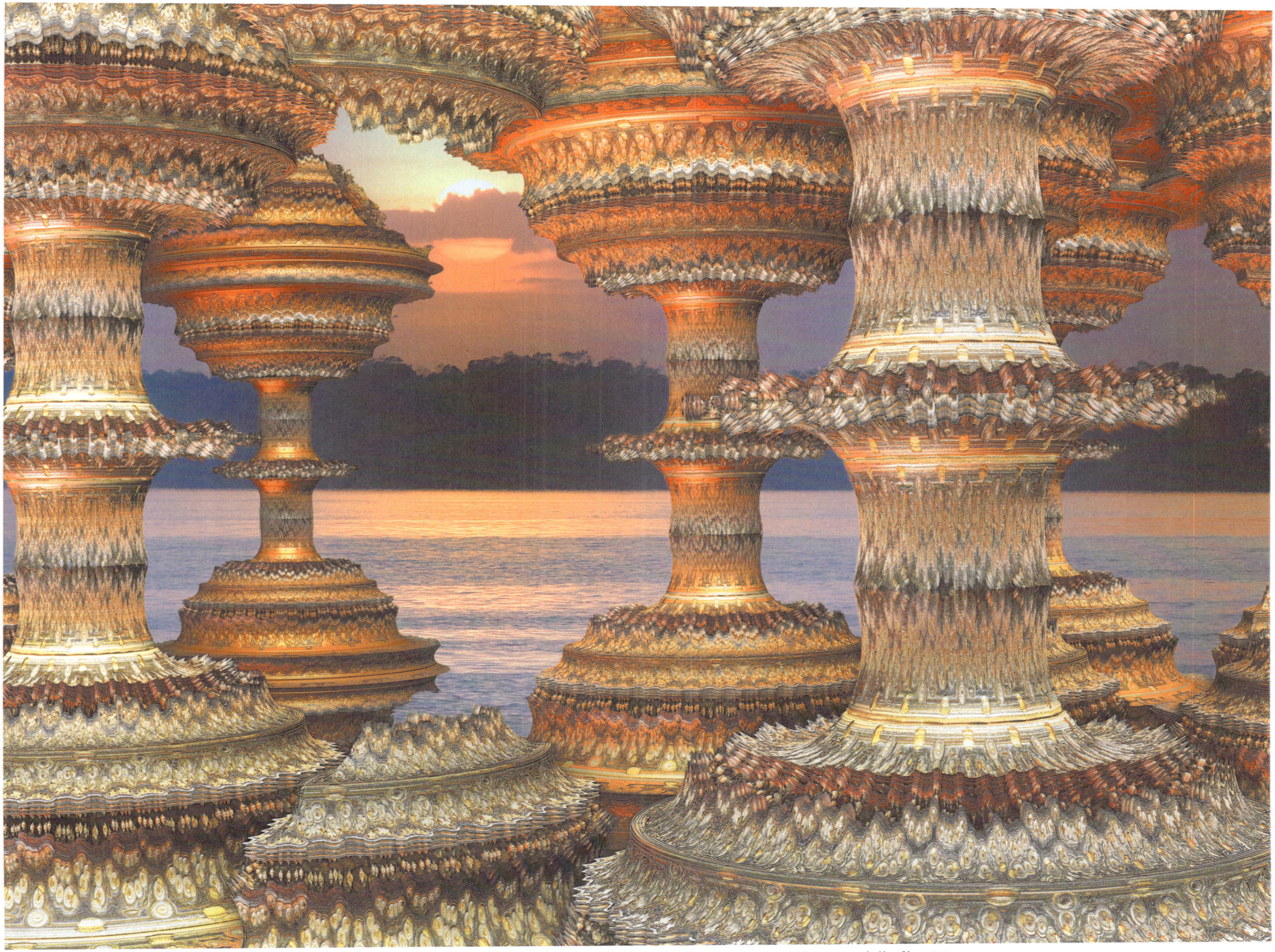

"Sunset at the Beach" (collage: digital photo and image created by Mandelbu'b 3D)

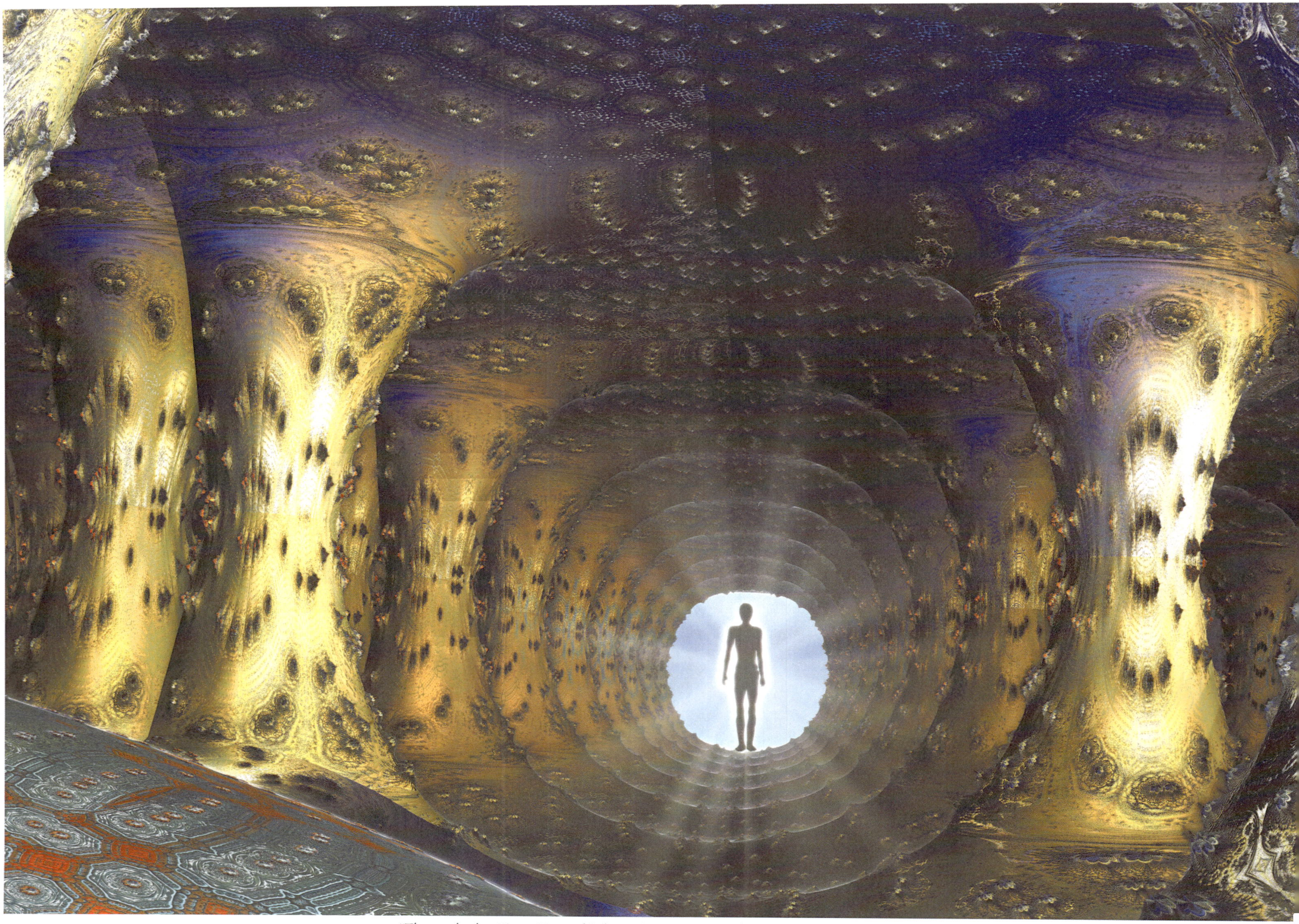

"Through the Time Tunnel" (base image created in Mandelbulb 3D)

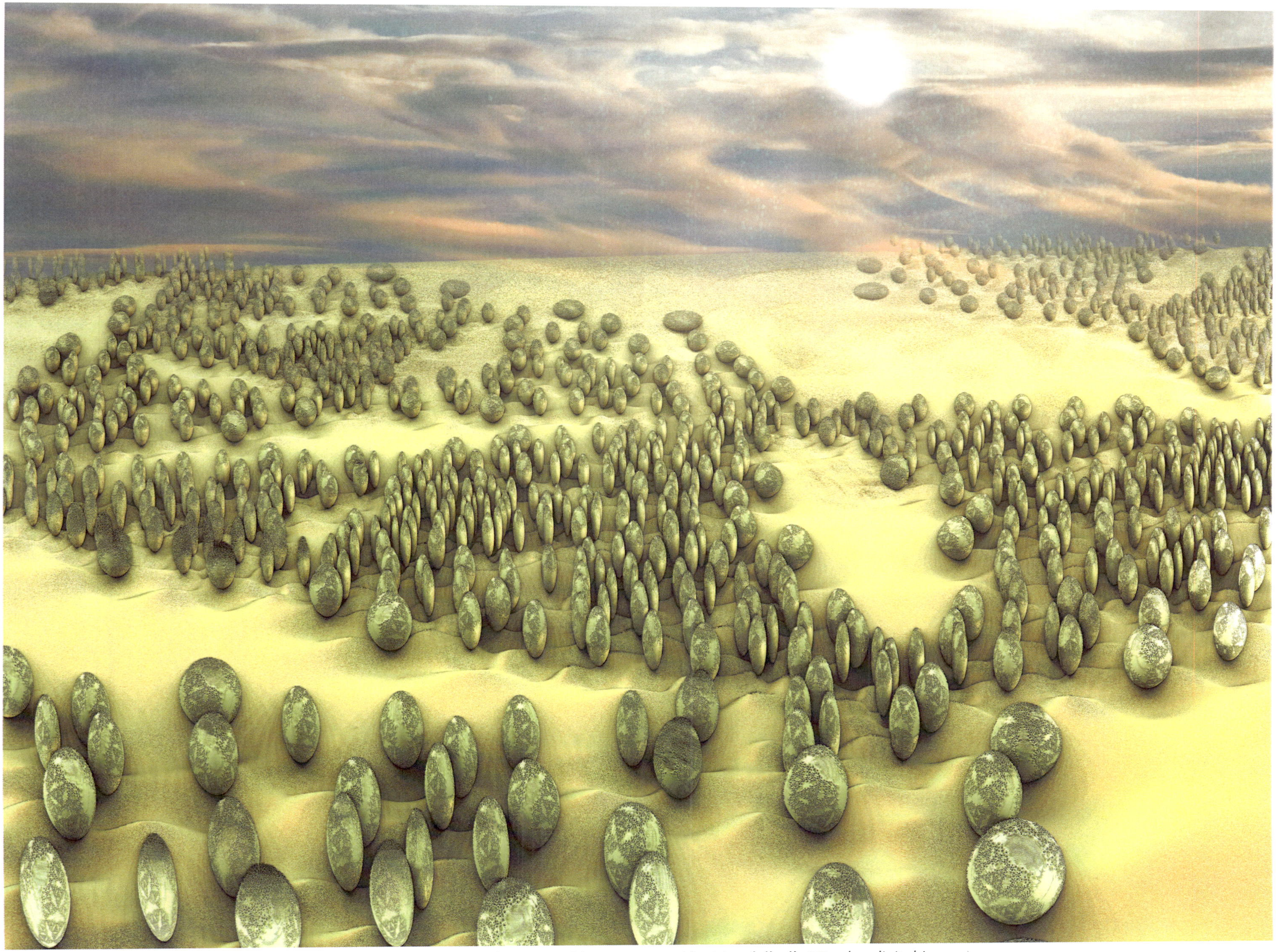

"As Far As You Can See" (foreground image created by Mandelbulb 3D; sky, digital image)

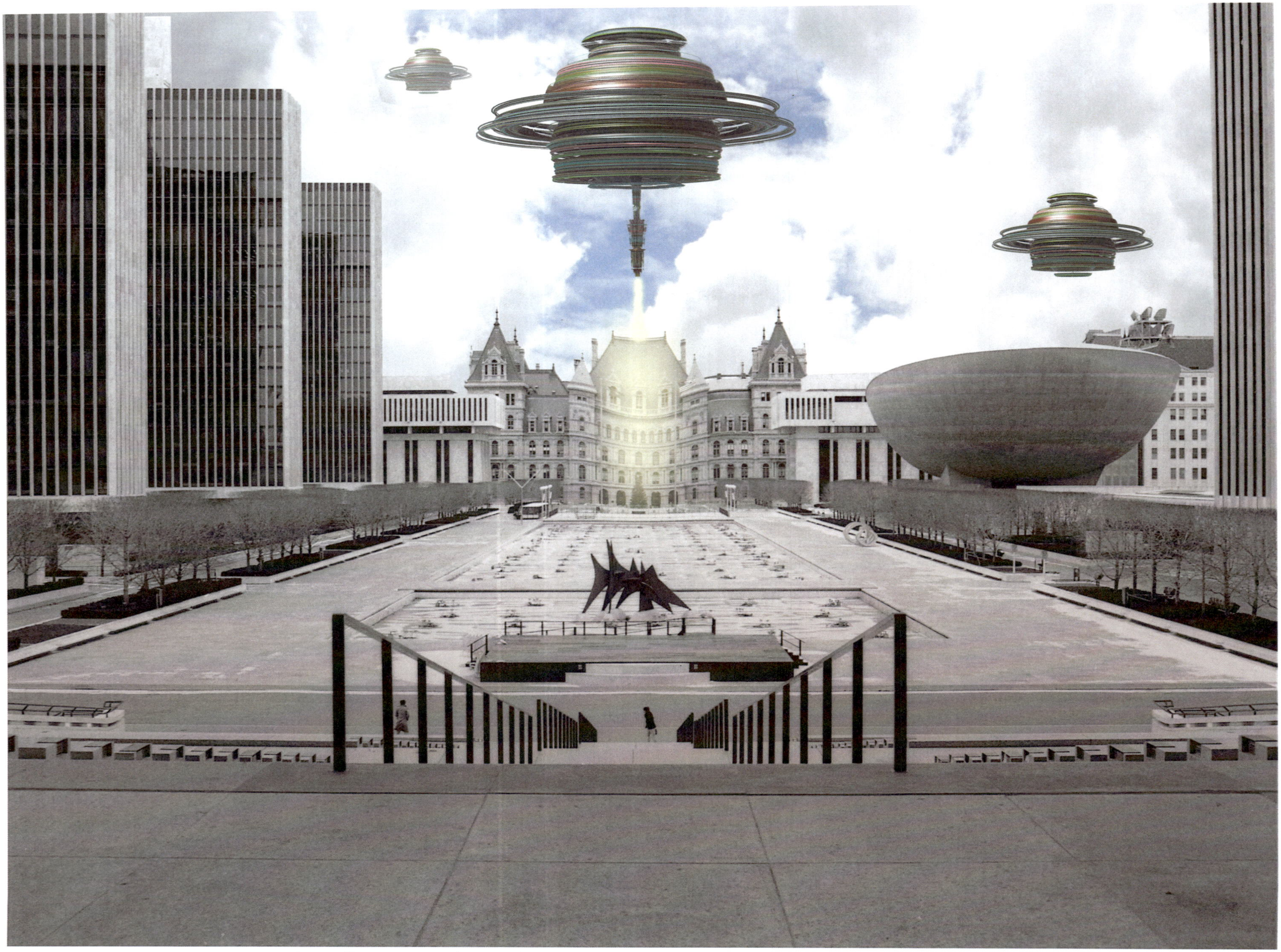

"Attack on Albany, New York Capitol Complex" (photo, 35 mm B&W; saucers created in Mandelbulb 3D)

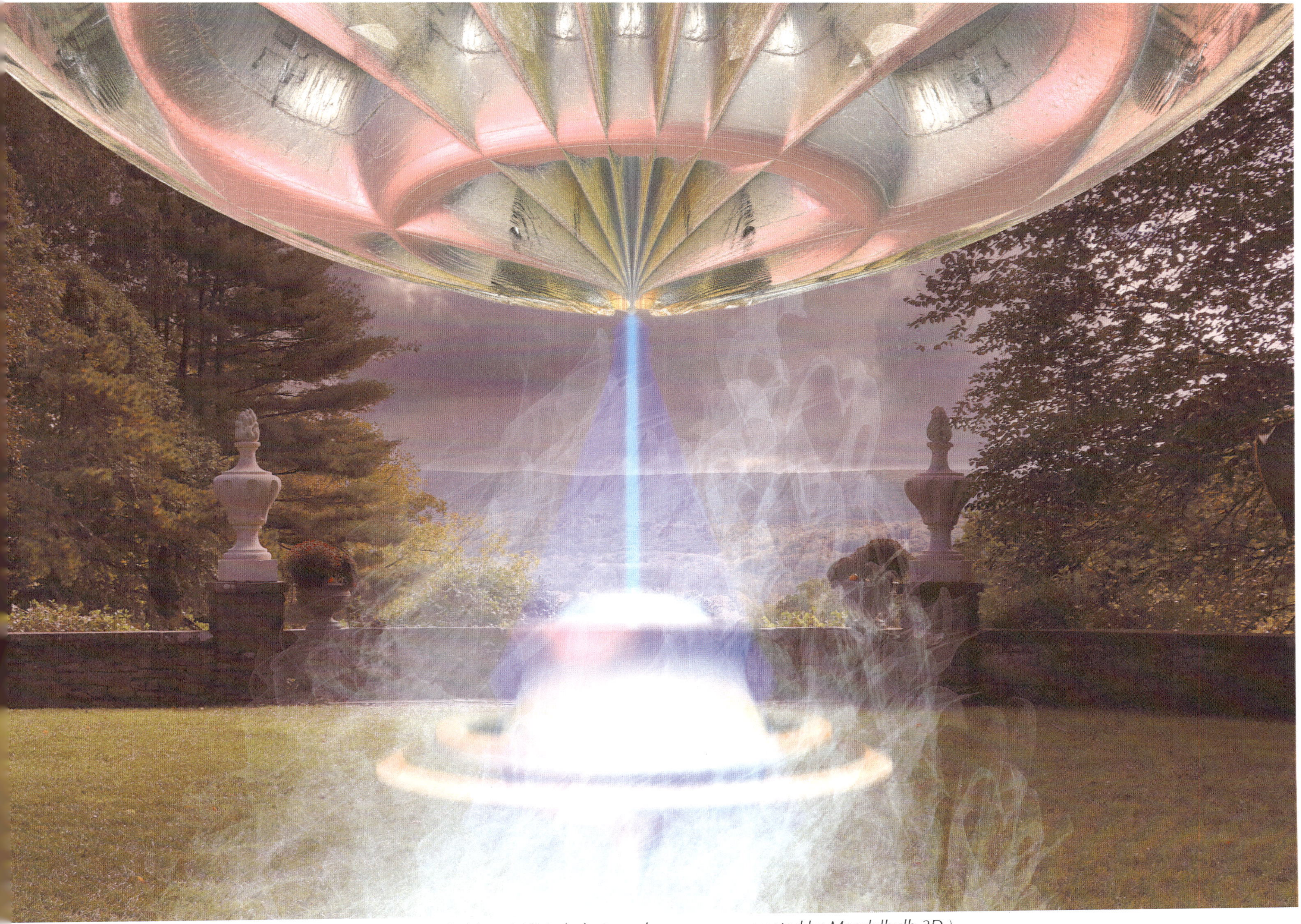

"Courtyard Visitors" (digital photo and saucers were created by Mandelbulb 3D.)

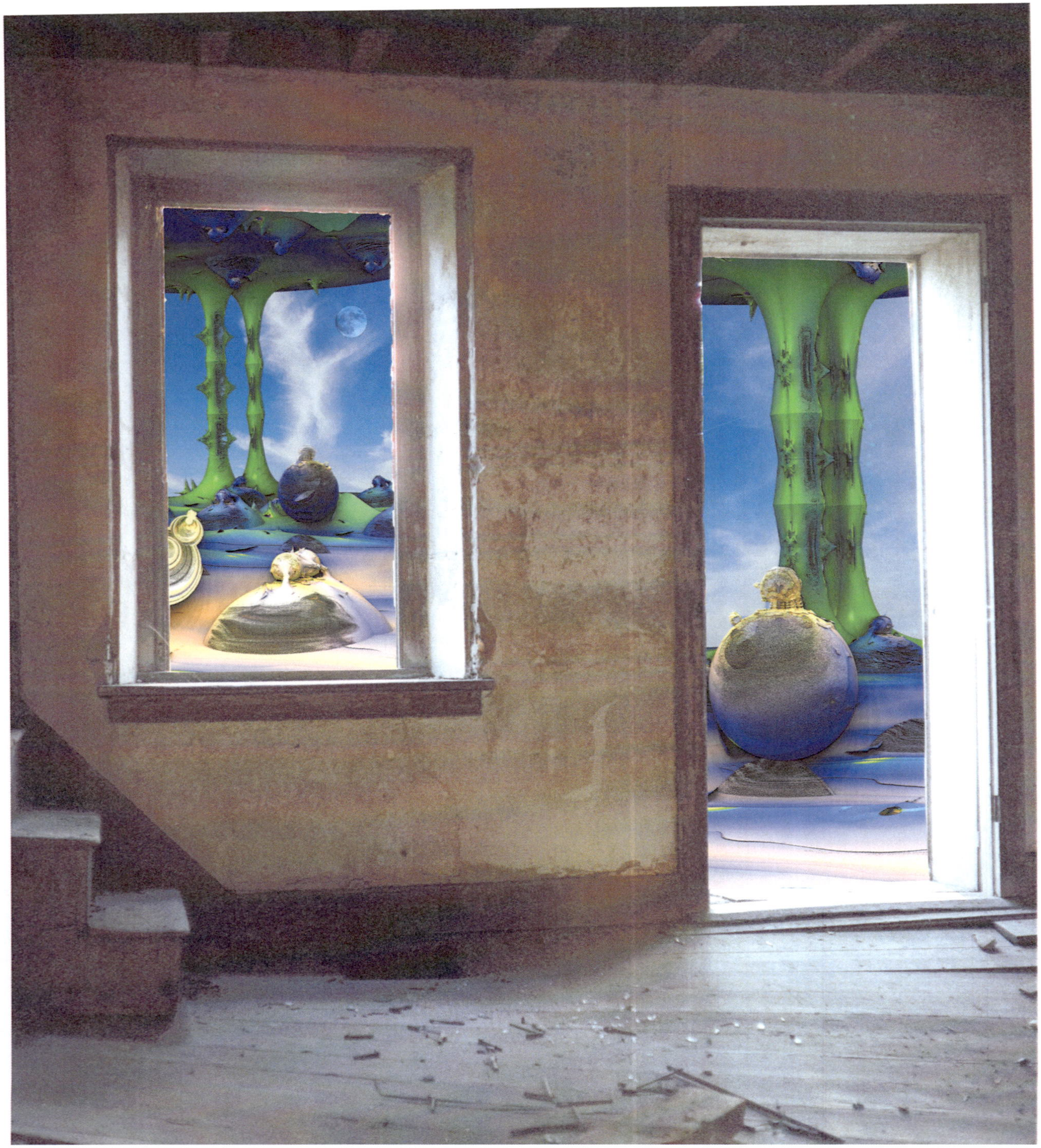

"House Ruins with a View to Another World" (photo, 6x6 cm color negative; exterior from Mandelbulb 3D)

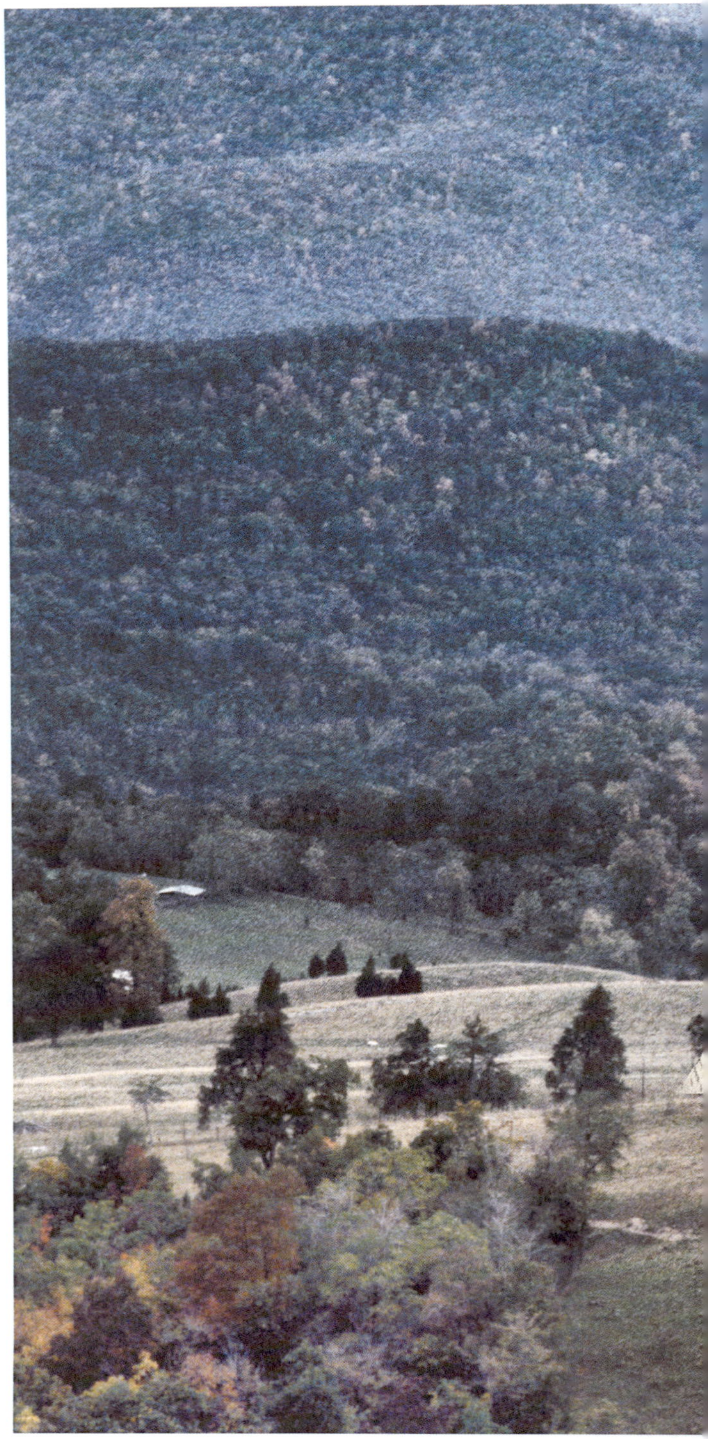

"New York Mountains with Extraterrestrial Pyramid"

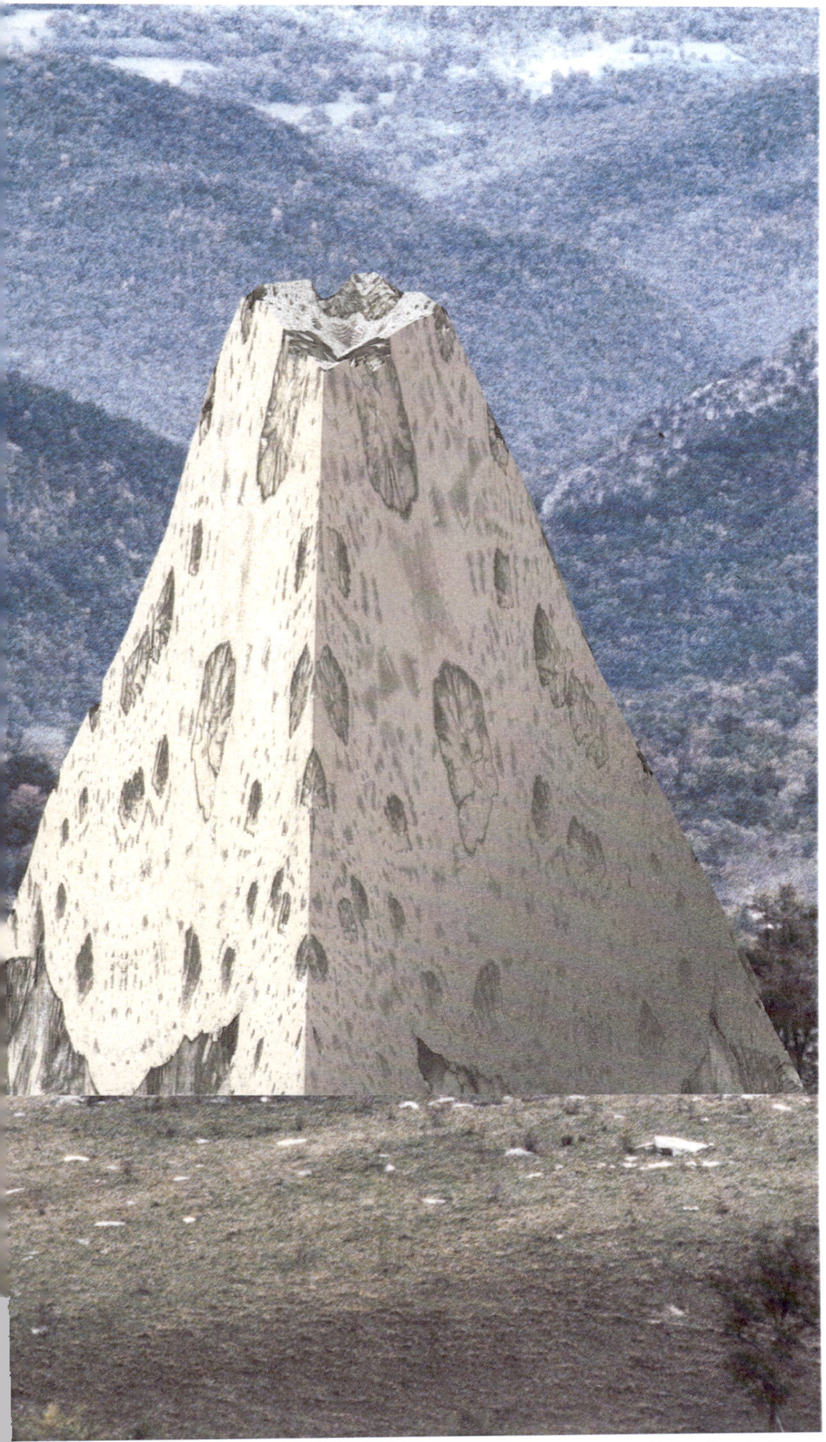
(Photo, 6×6 cm color negative; pyramid from Mandelbulb 3D)

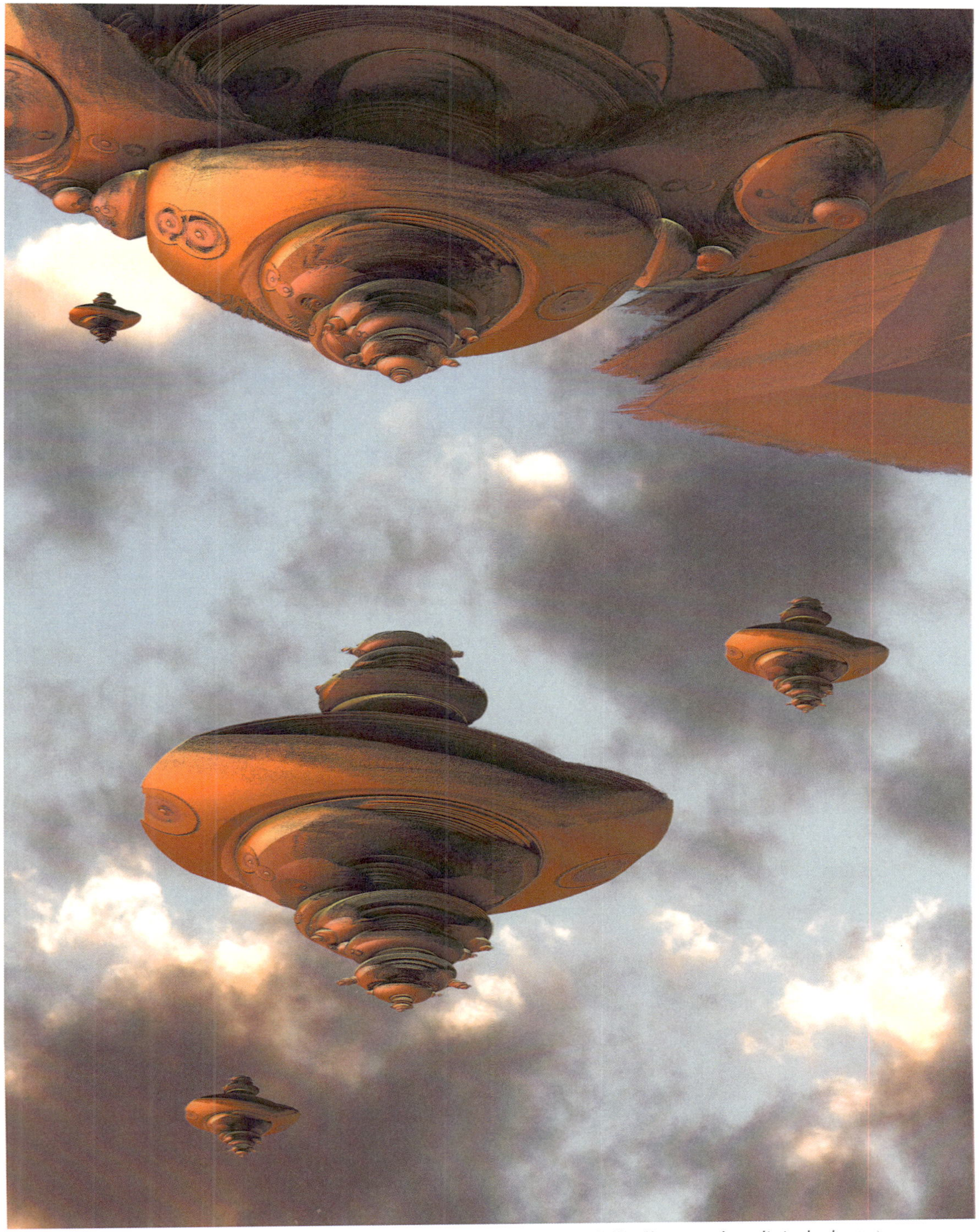
"UFOs over Bucks County, Pa." (saucers from Mandelbulb 3D; sky, digital photo)

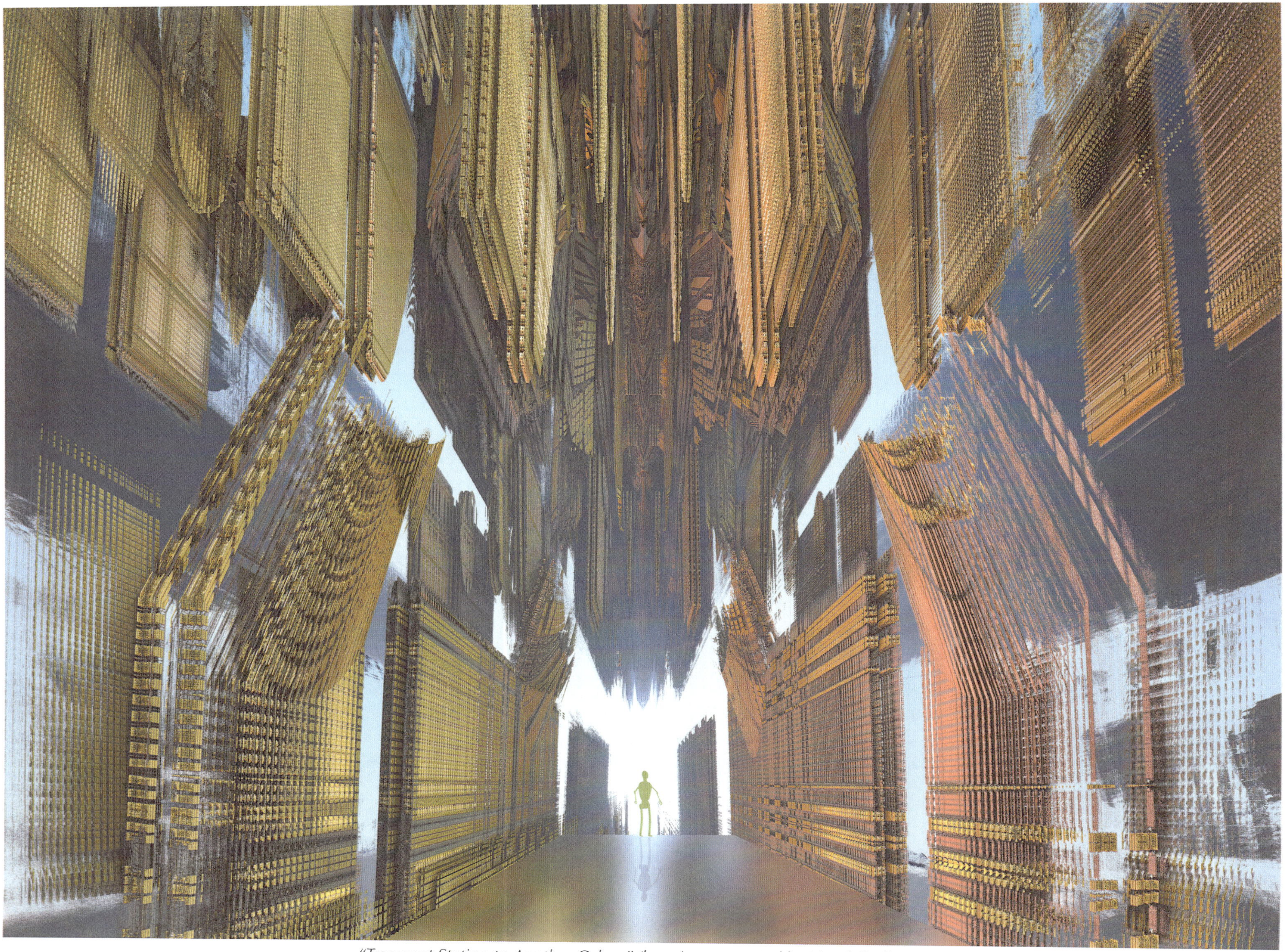

"Transport Station to Another Galaxy" (base image created by Mandelbulb 3D)

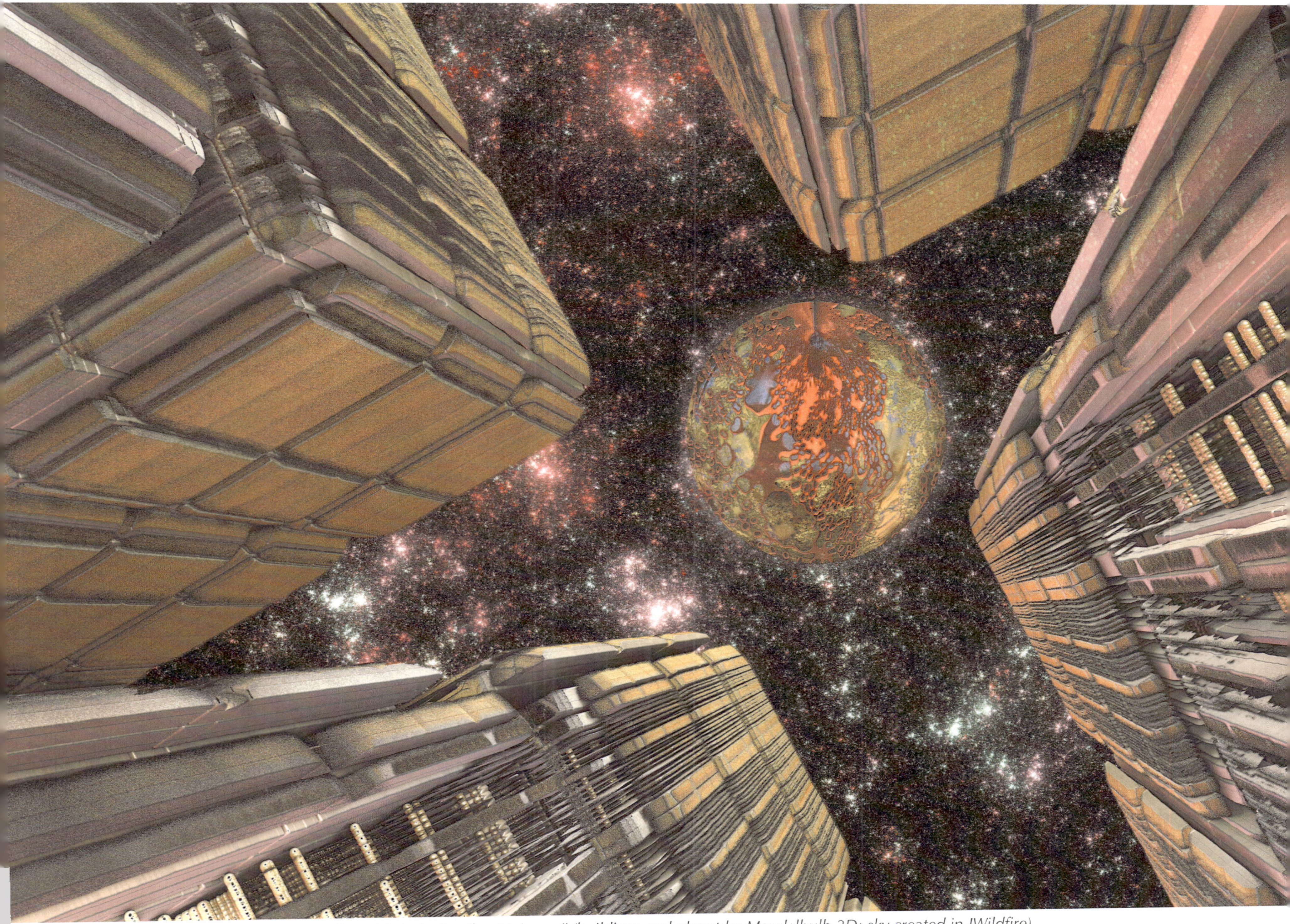

"The City Sky at Night in Another Universe" (buildings and planet by Mandelbulb 3D; sky created in JWildfire)

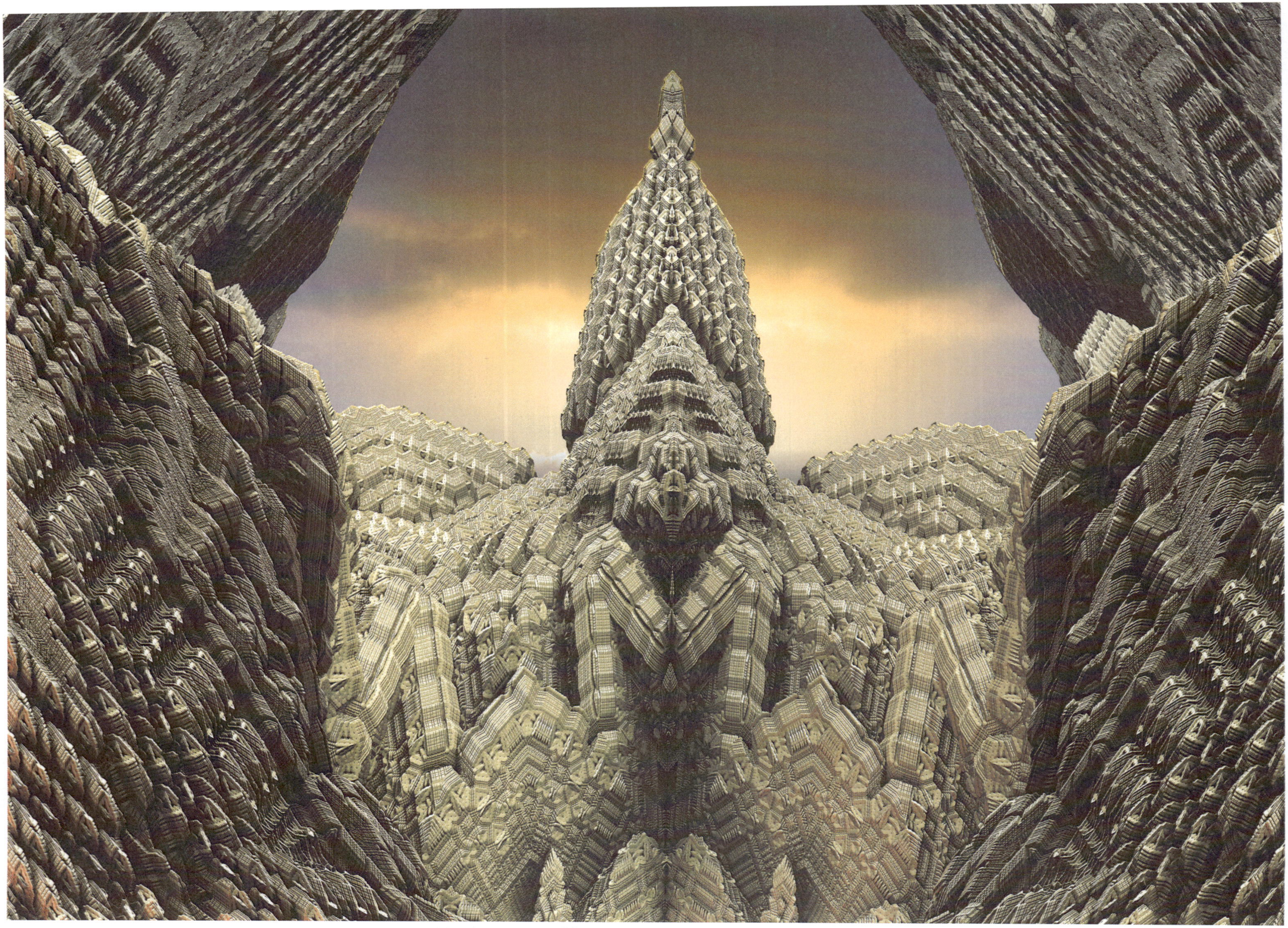

"Headquarters Building" (image created by Mandelbulb 3D)

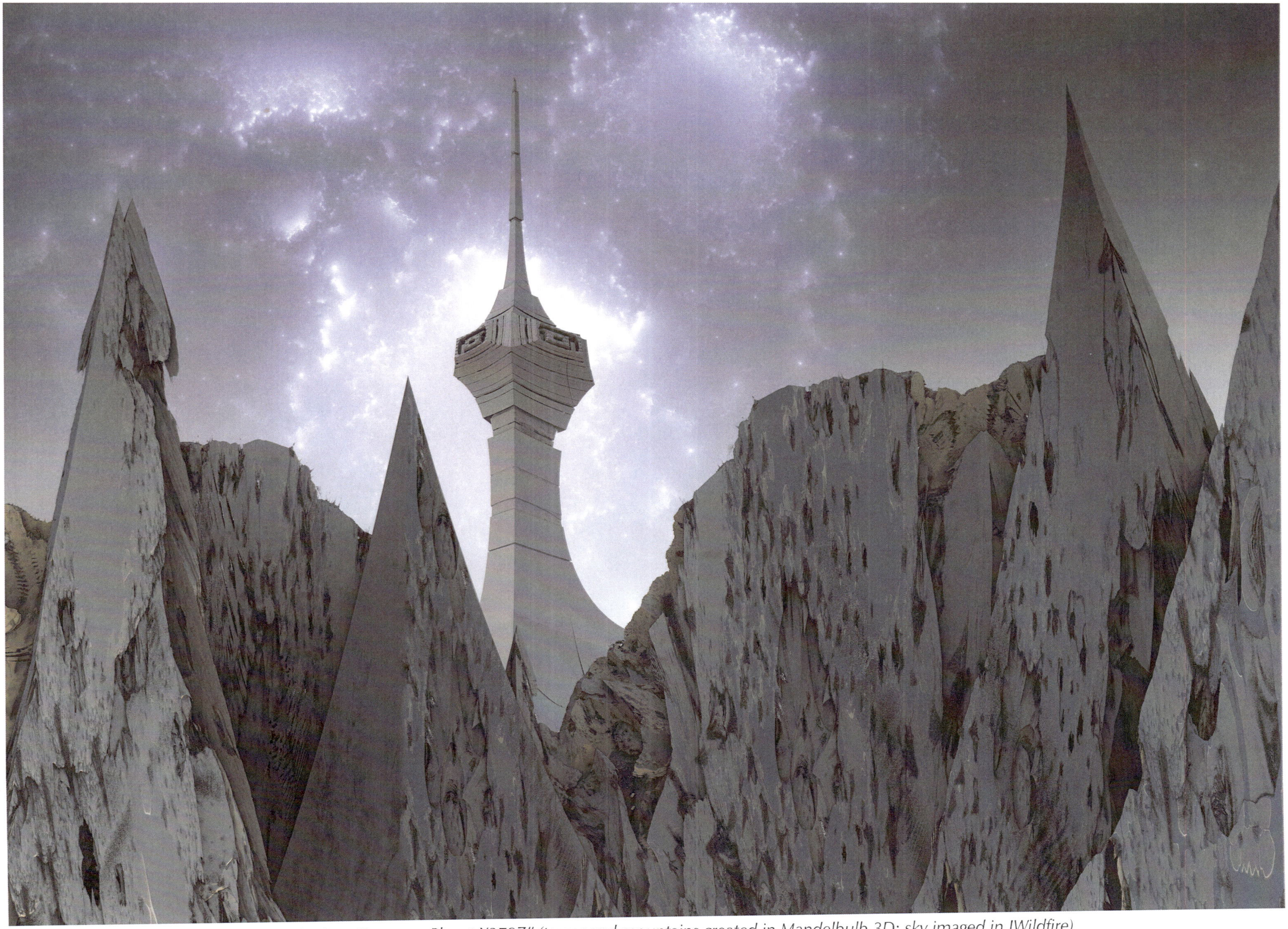

"Communications Tower on Planet X279Z" (tower and mountains created in Mandelbulb 3D; sky imaged in JWildfire)

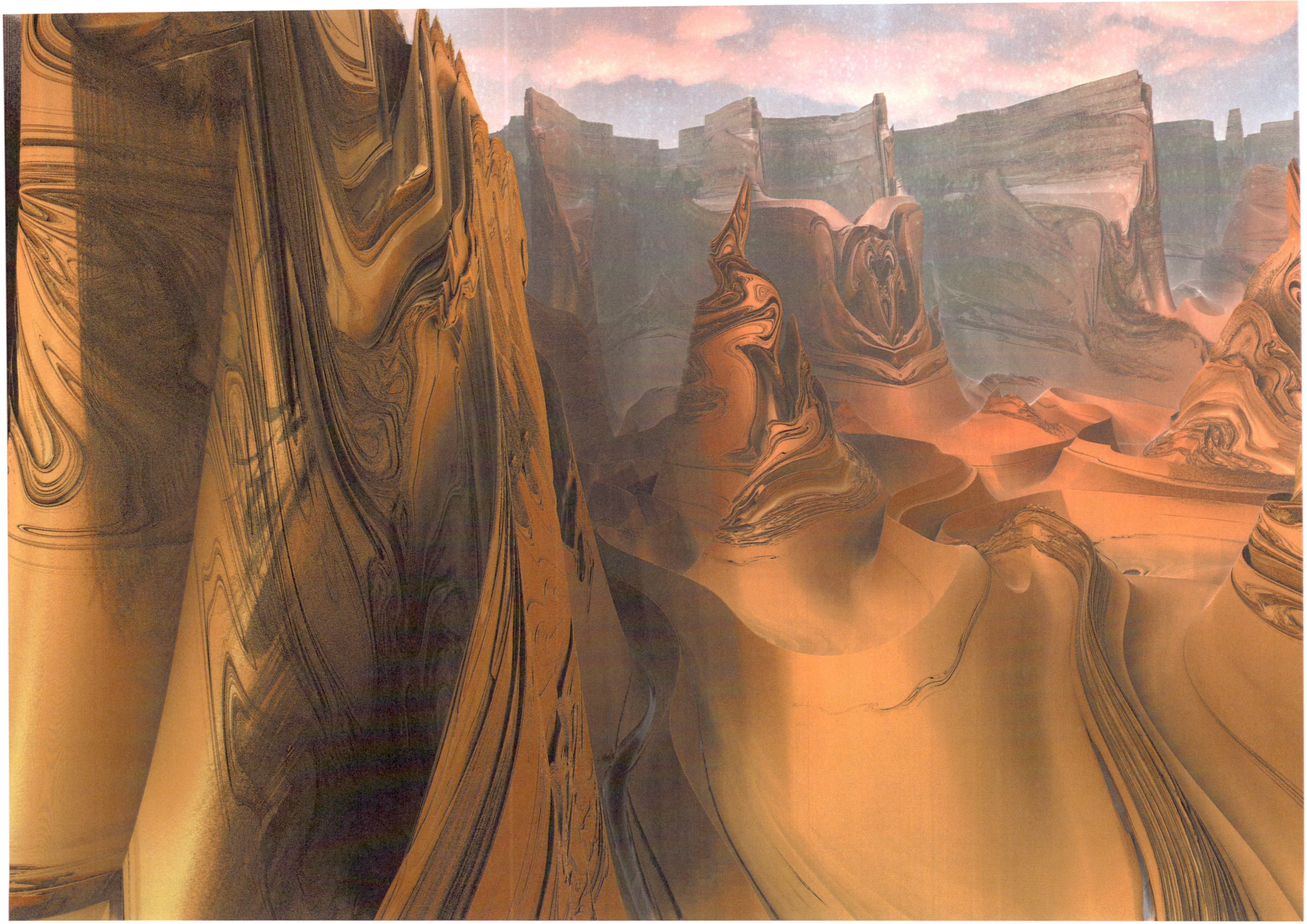

"Yellow Mountains" (image created by Mandelbulb 3D)

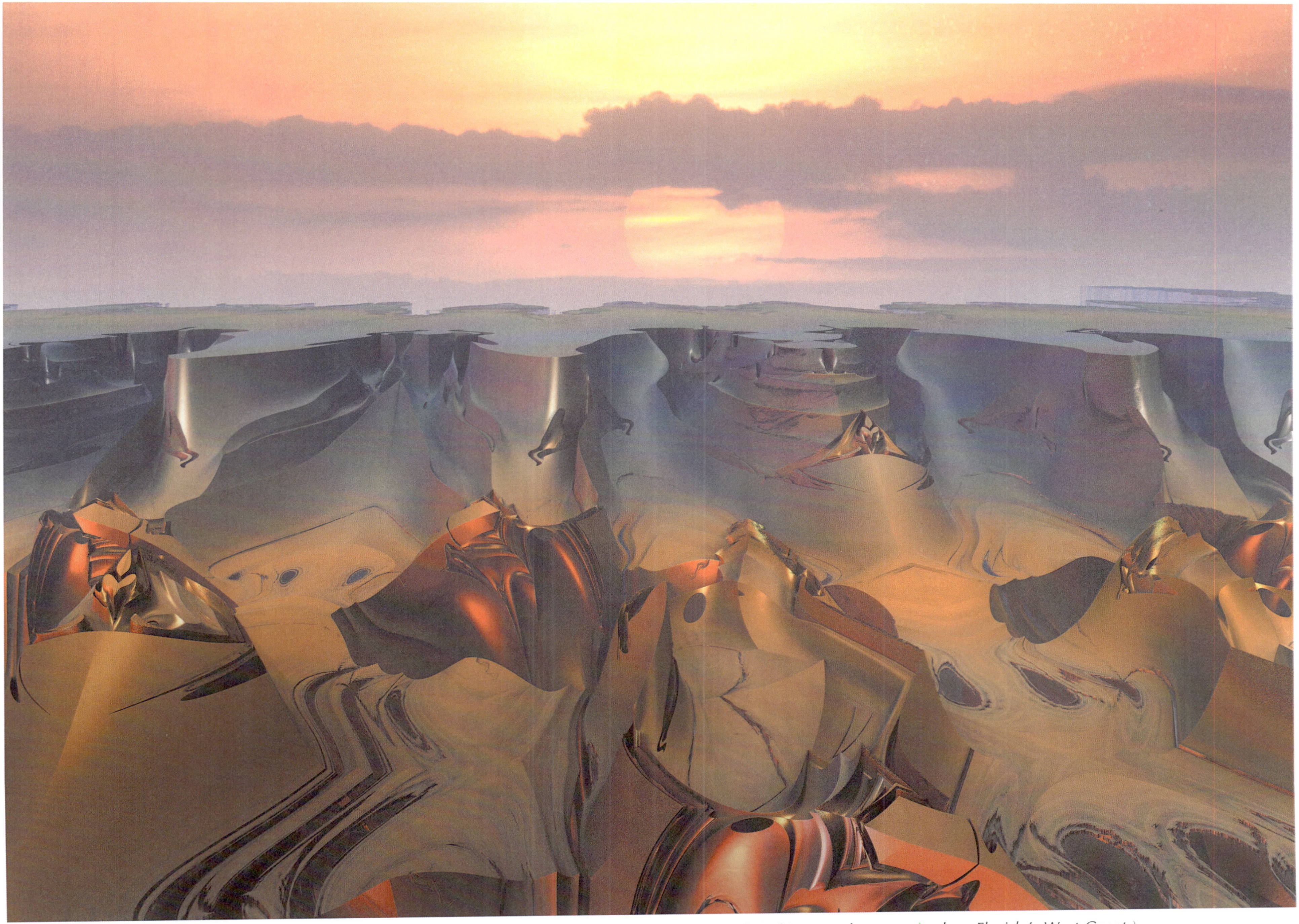

"Sunset over Metal Canyon" (image created by Mandelbulb 3D; sunset is a digital image photographed on Florida's West Coast.)

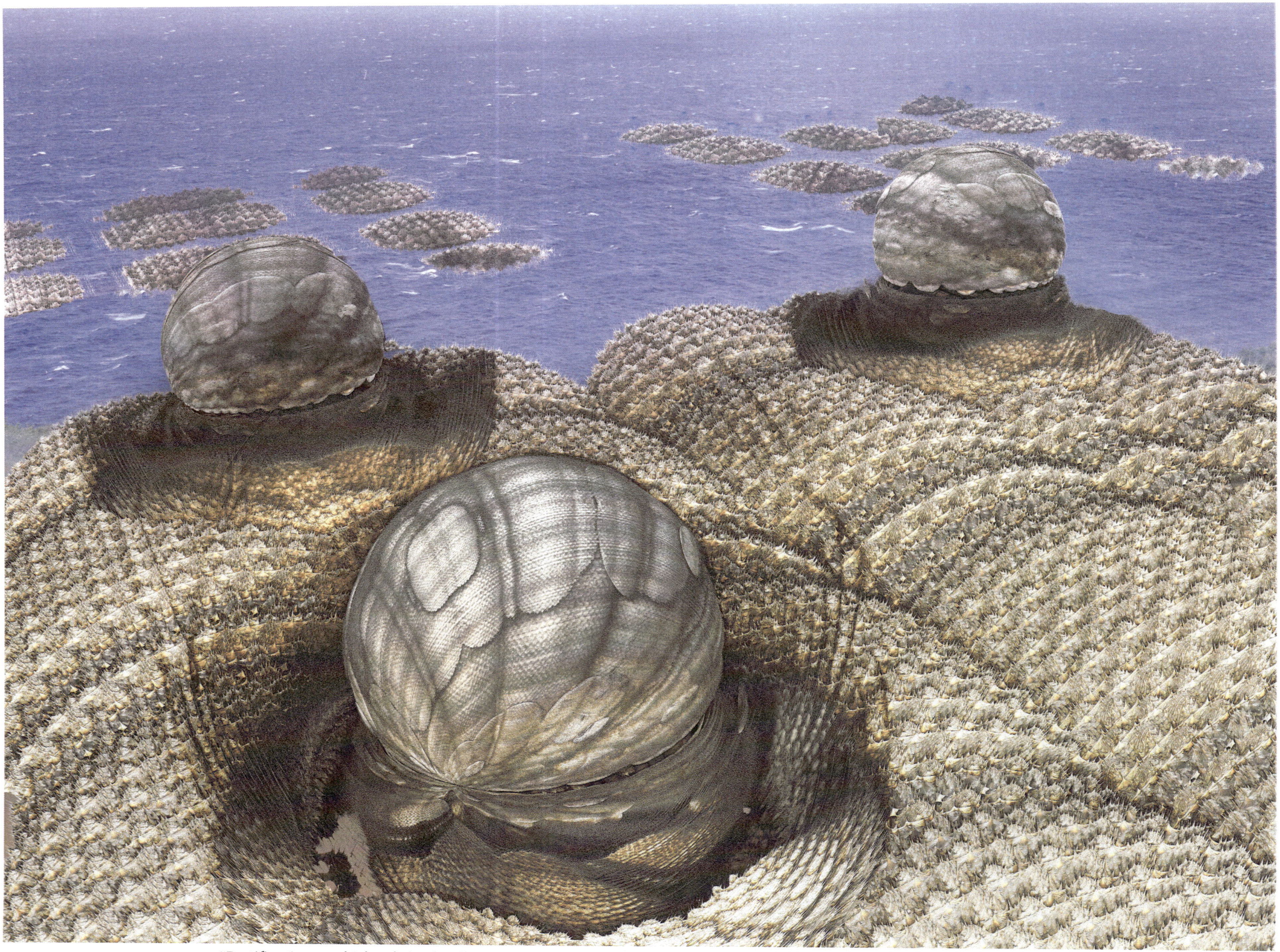

"Fortification and Islands in the Ocean" (image created by Mandelbulb 3D and a 6x6 cm GAF color transparency)

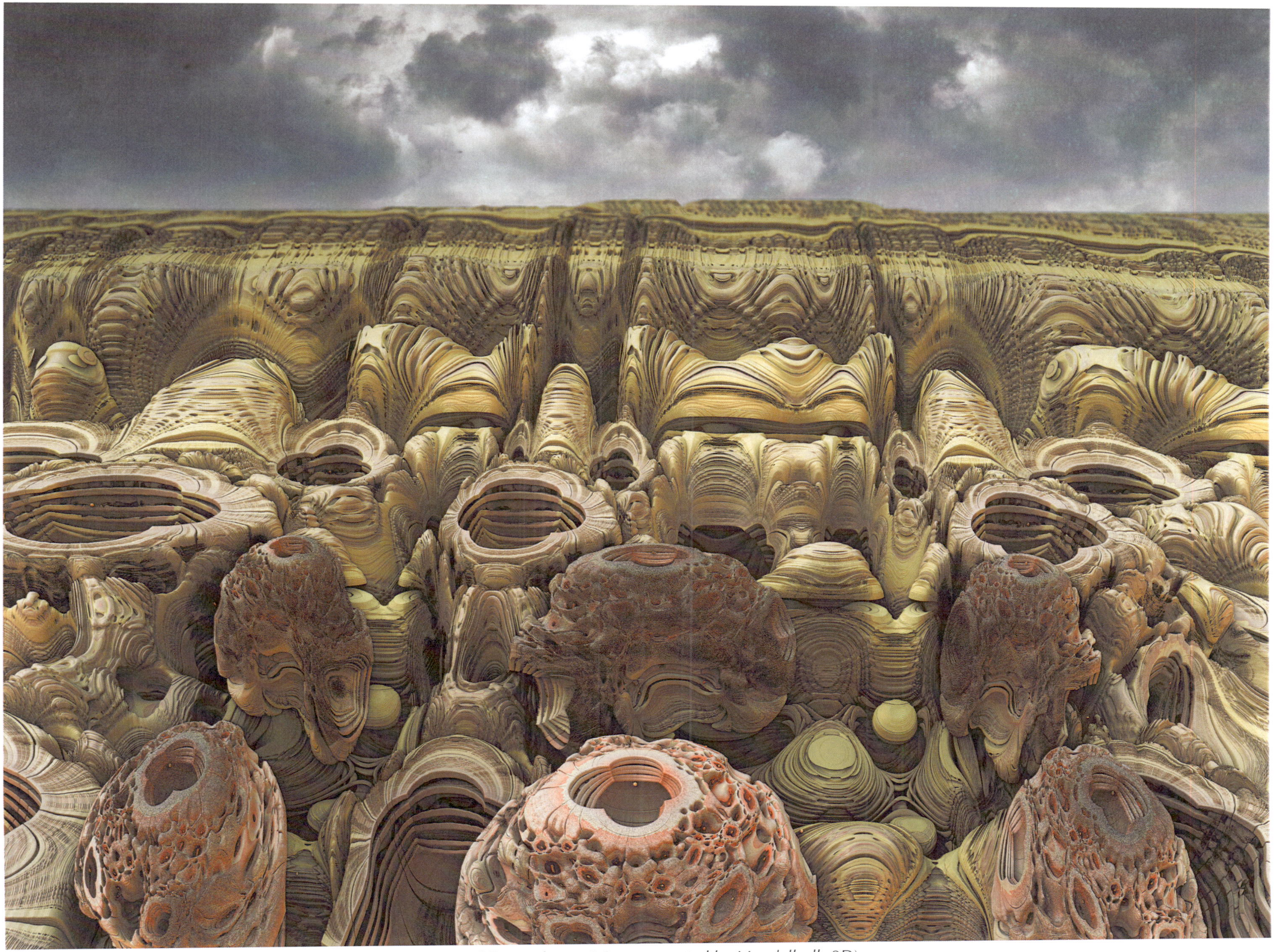

"Unworldly Landscape" (image created by Mandelbulb 3D)

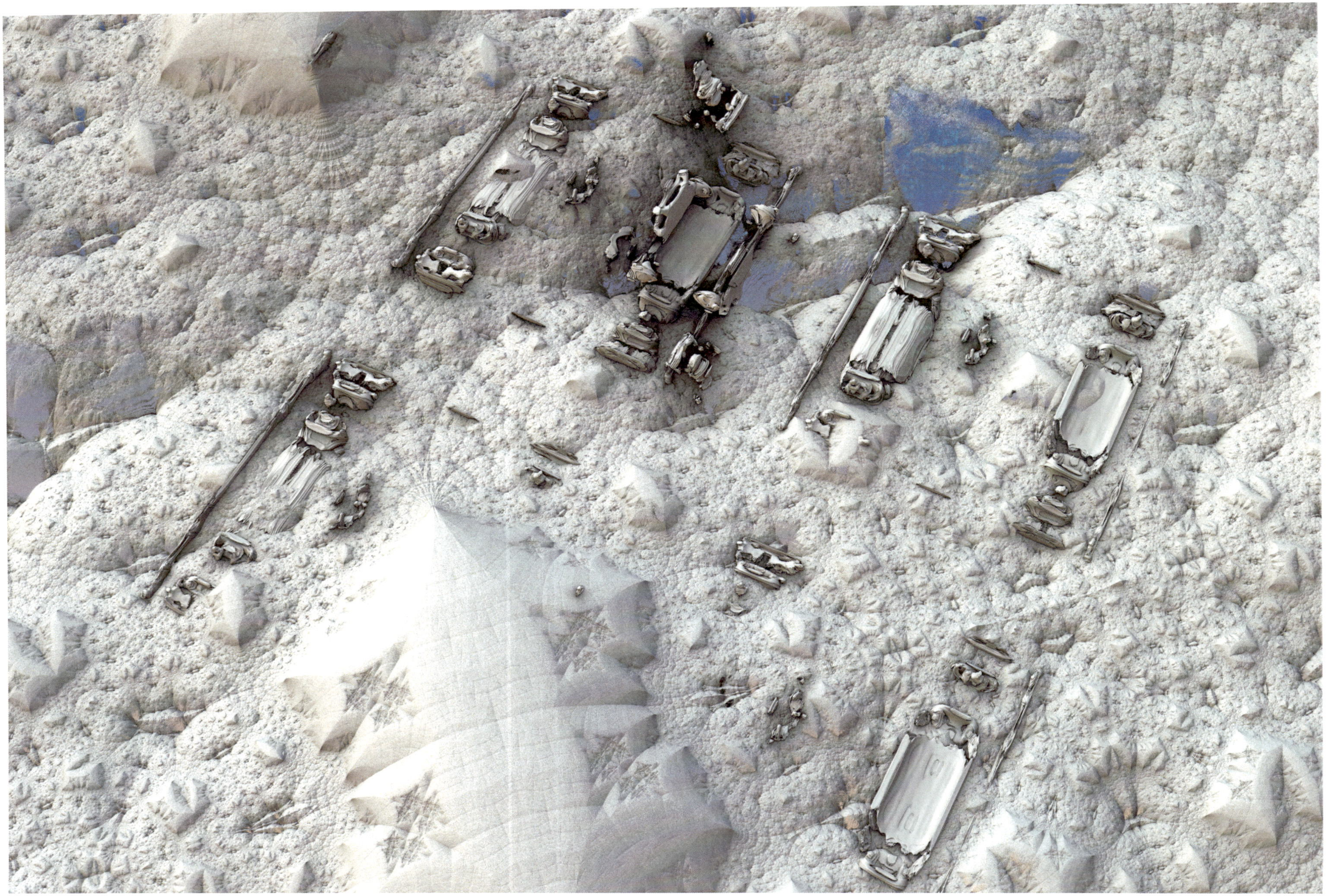

"Ruins of an Ancient City" viewed from above (image created by Mandelbulb 3D)

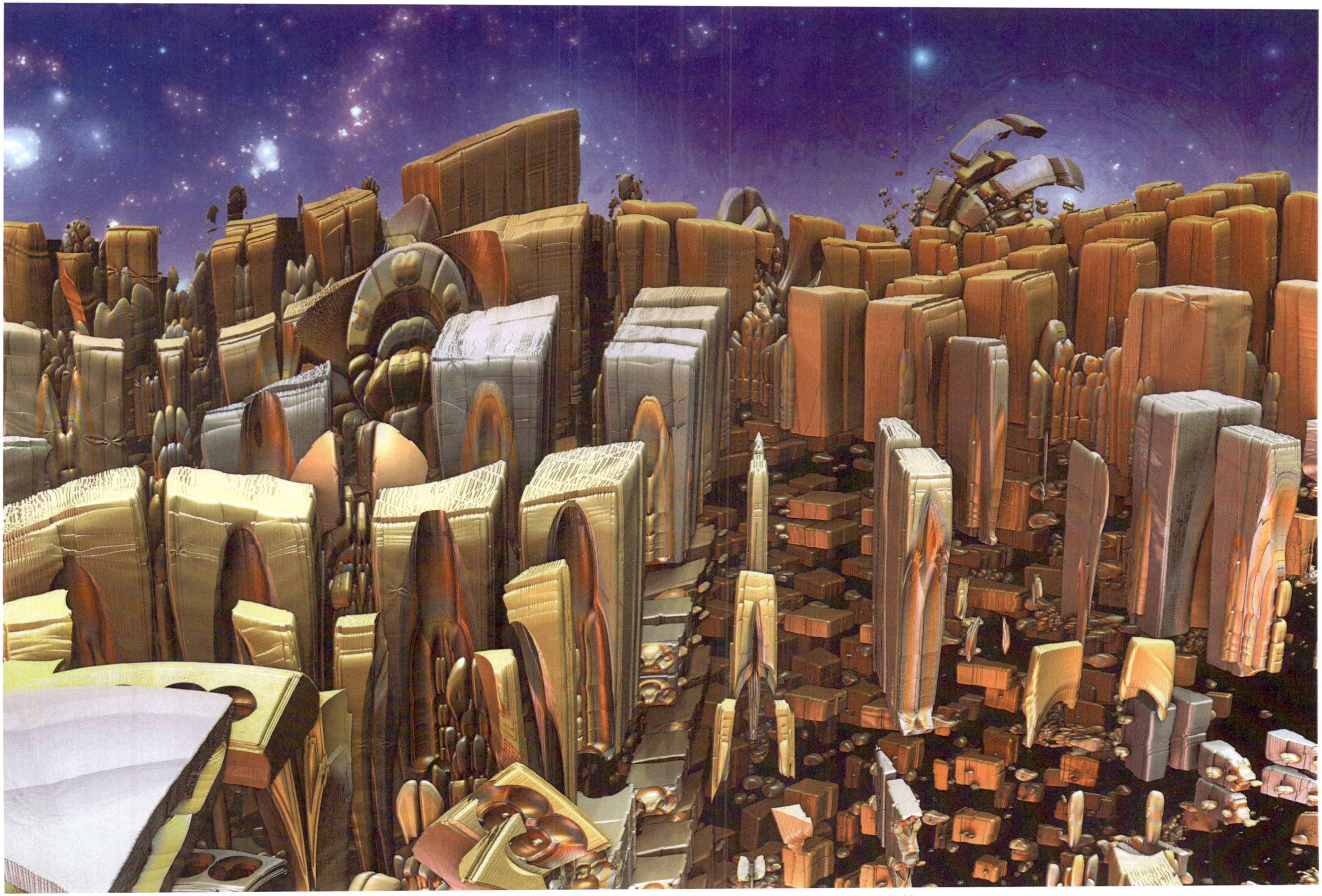

"City on Another Planet" (imaged in Mandelbulb 3D; sky in JWildfire)

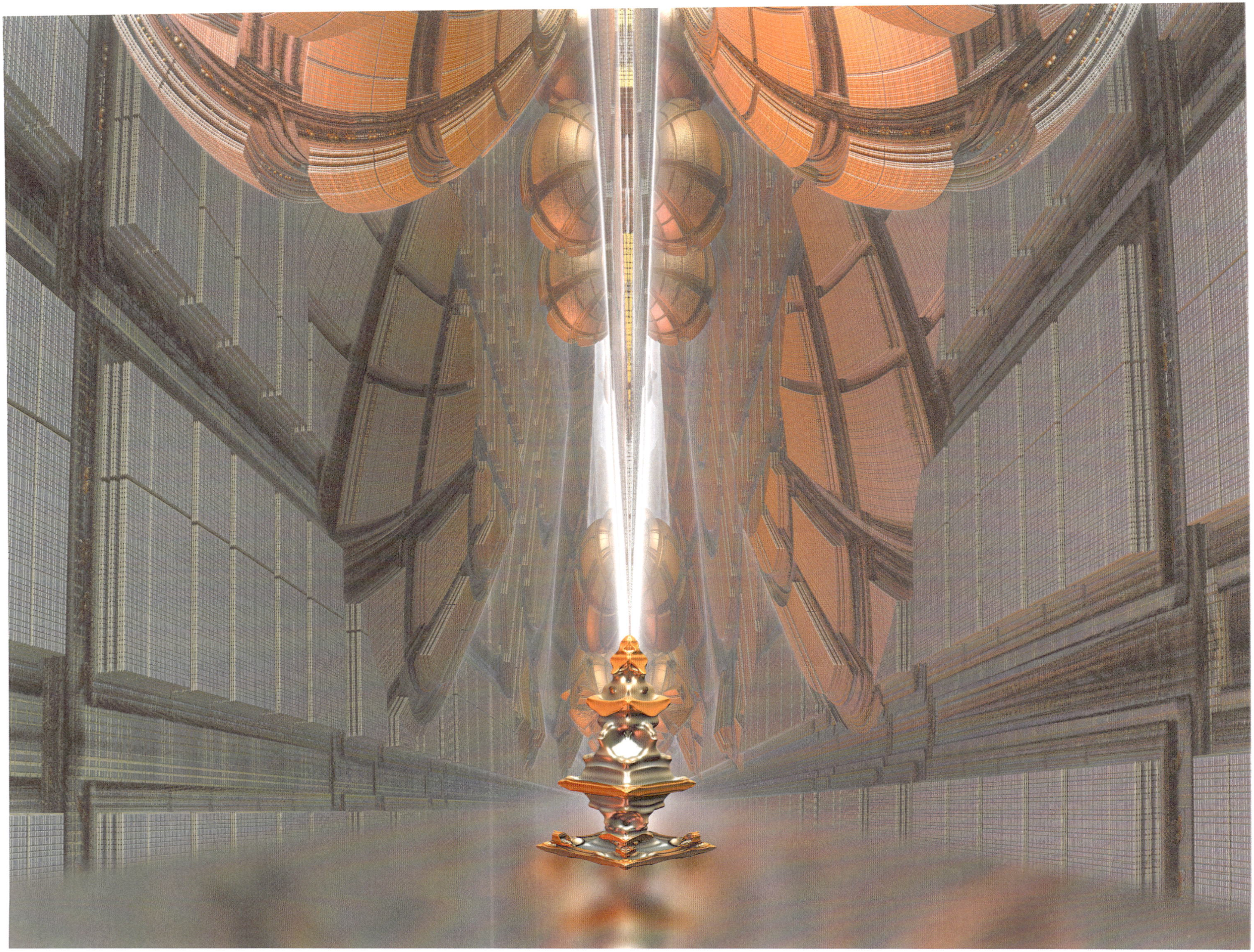

"Grand Hall and Beam" (image created by Mandelbulb 3D)

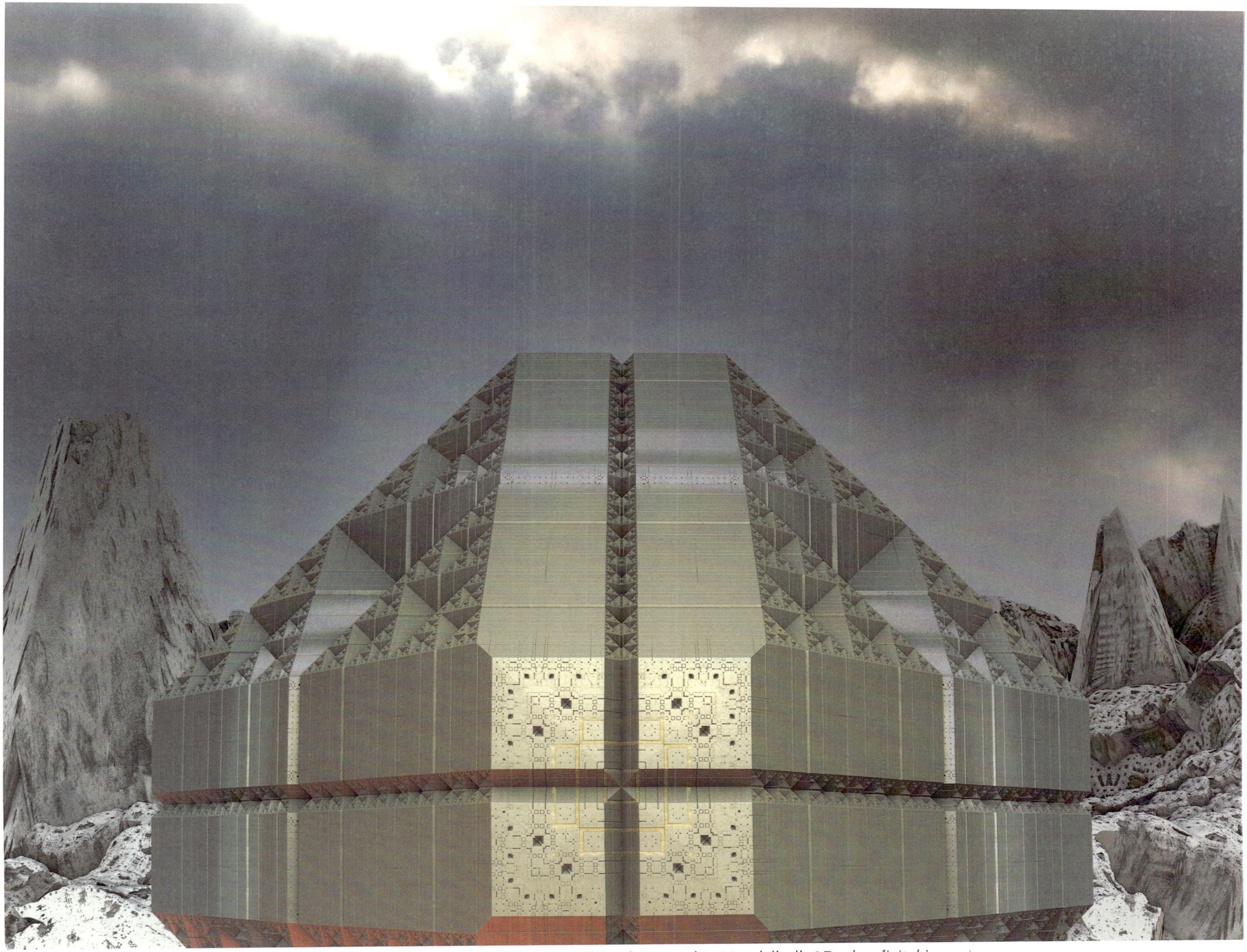

"Exploratory Vehicle on a Faraway Planet" (fractals created in Mandelbulb 3D; sky, digital image)

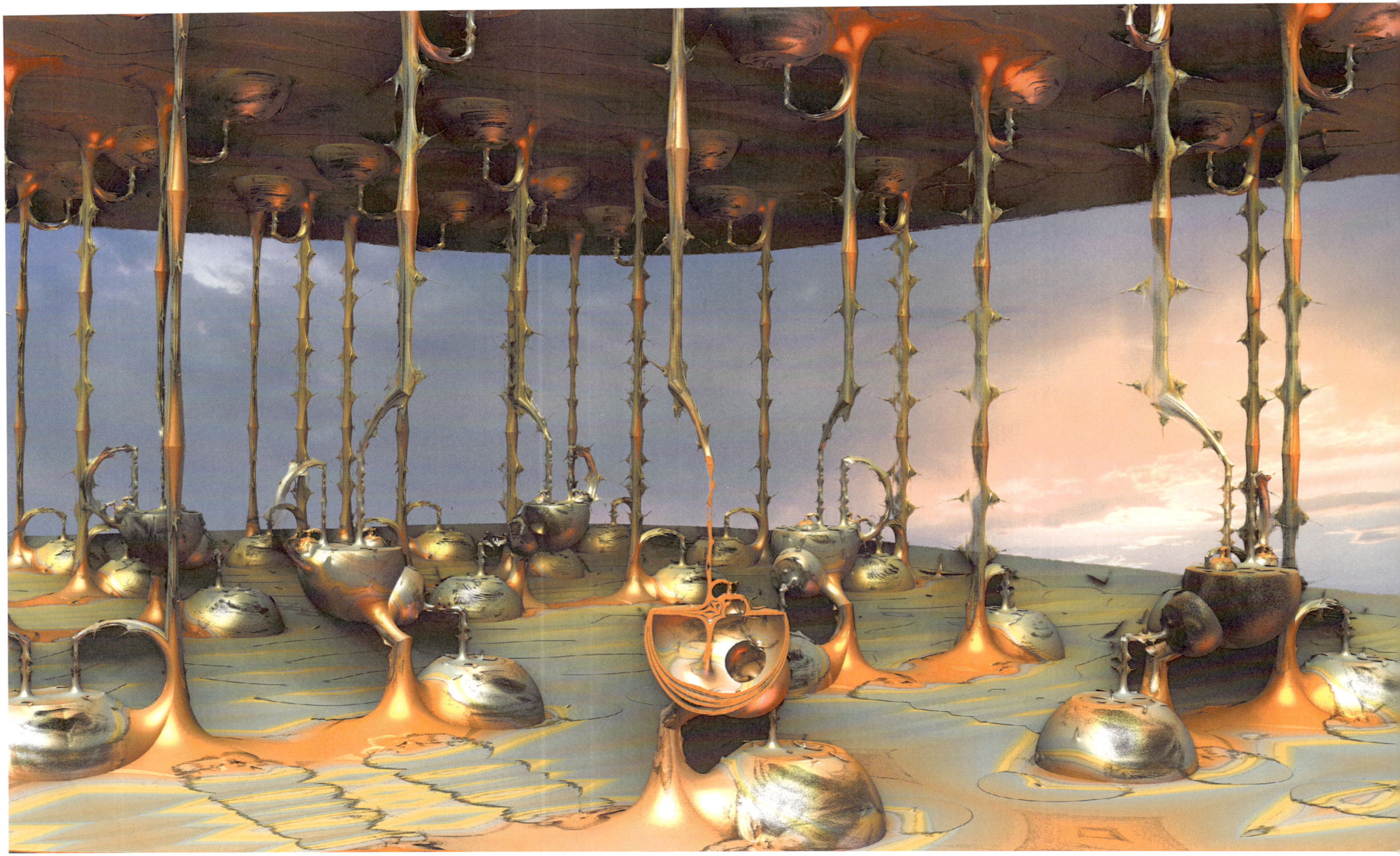

"Space Platform" (image created by Mandelbulb 3D)

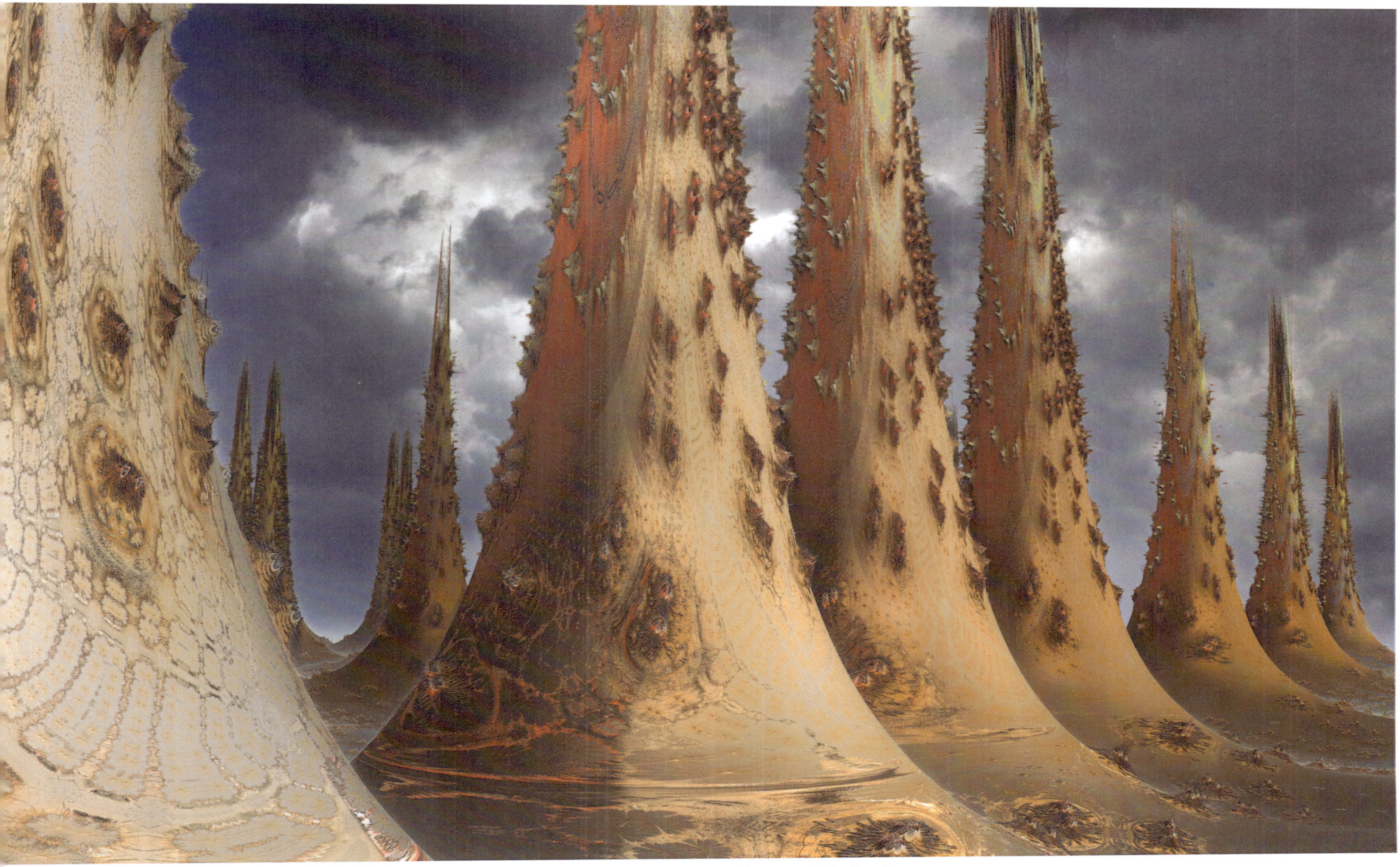

"Petrified Forest" (image created by Mandelbulb 3D)

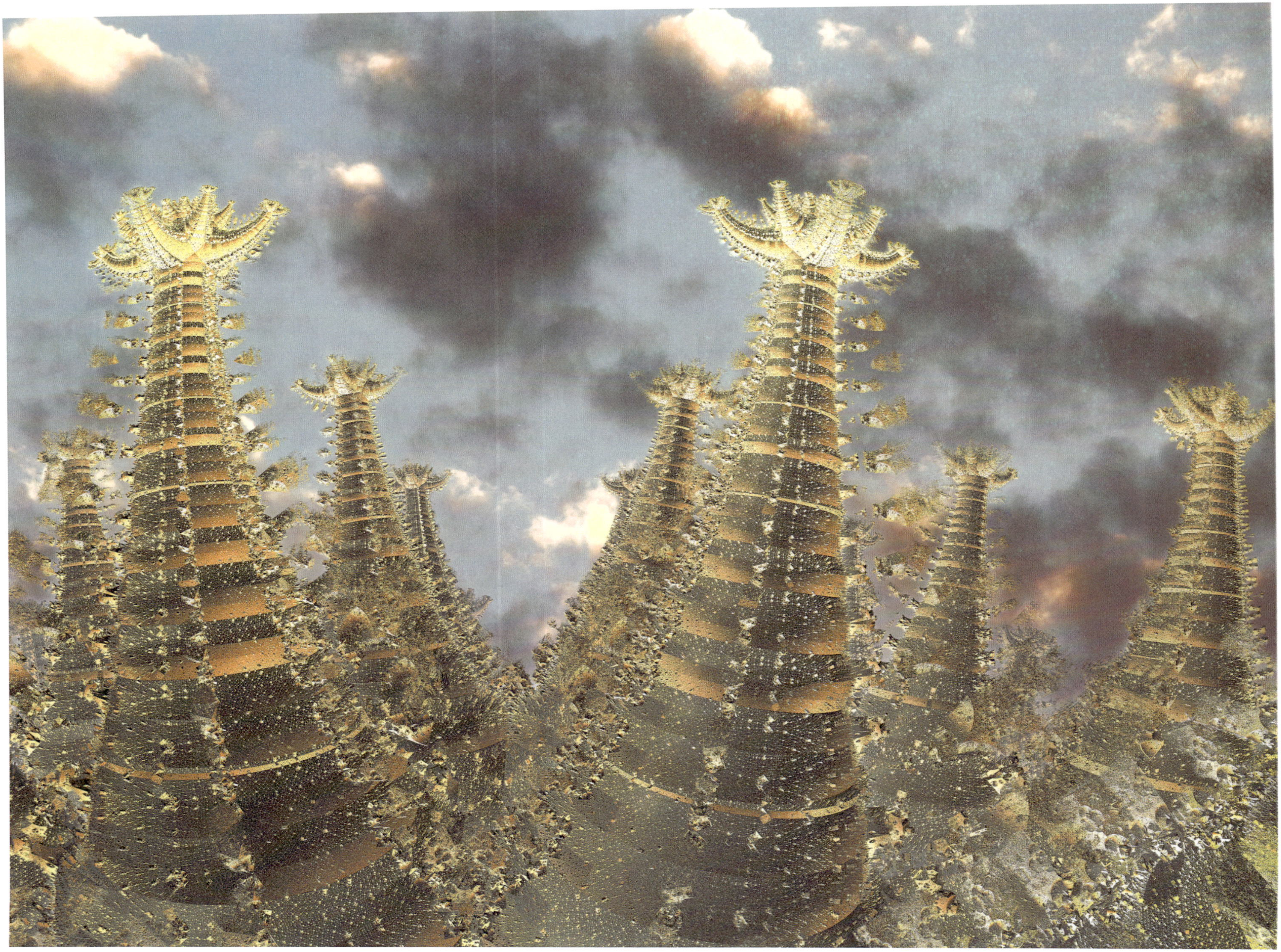

Plant or animal? (image created in Mandelbulb 3D)

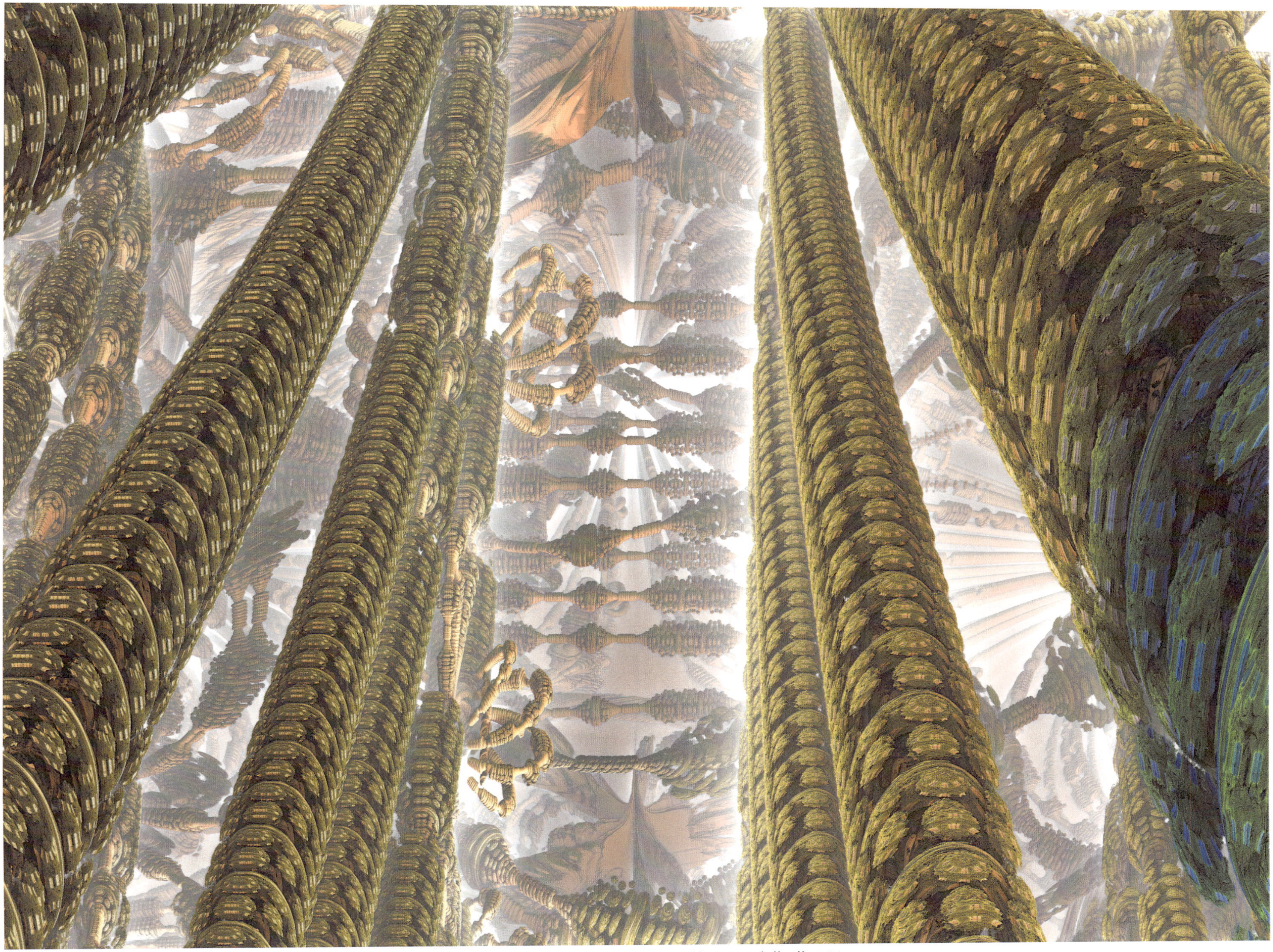

"Interior Space #1" (image created by Mandelbulb 3D)

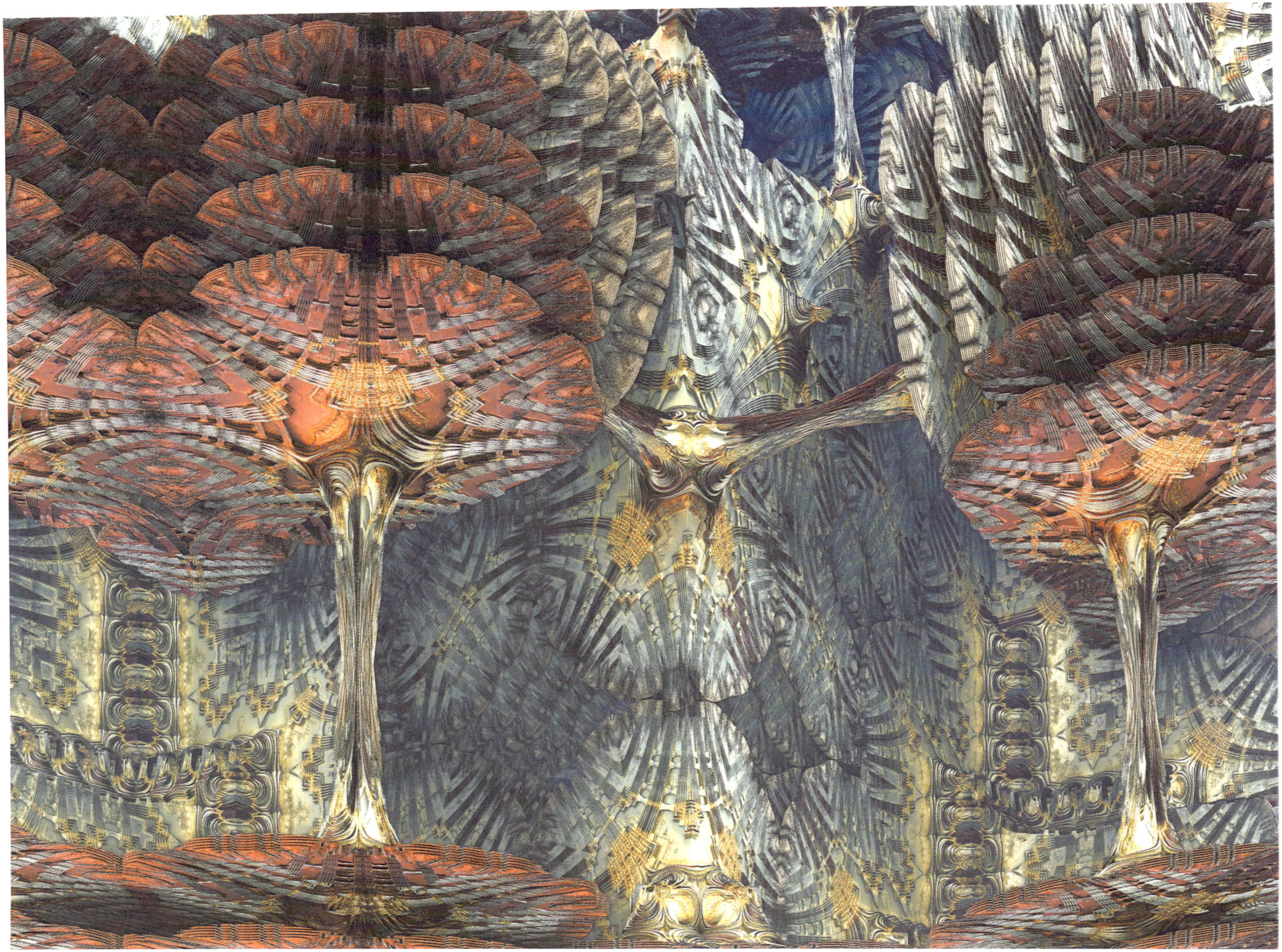

"Interior Space #2" (image created in Mandelbulb 3D)

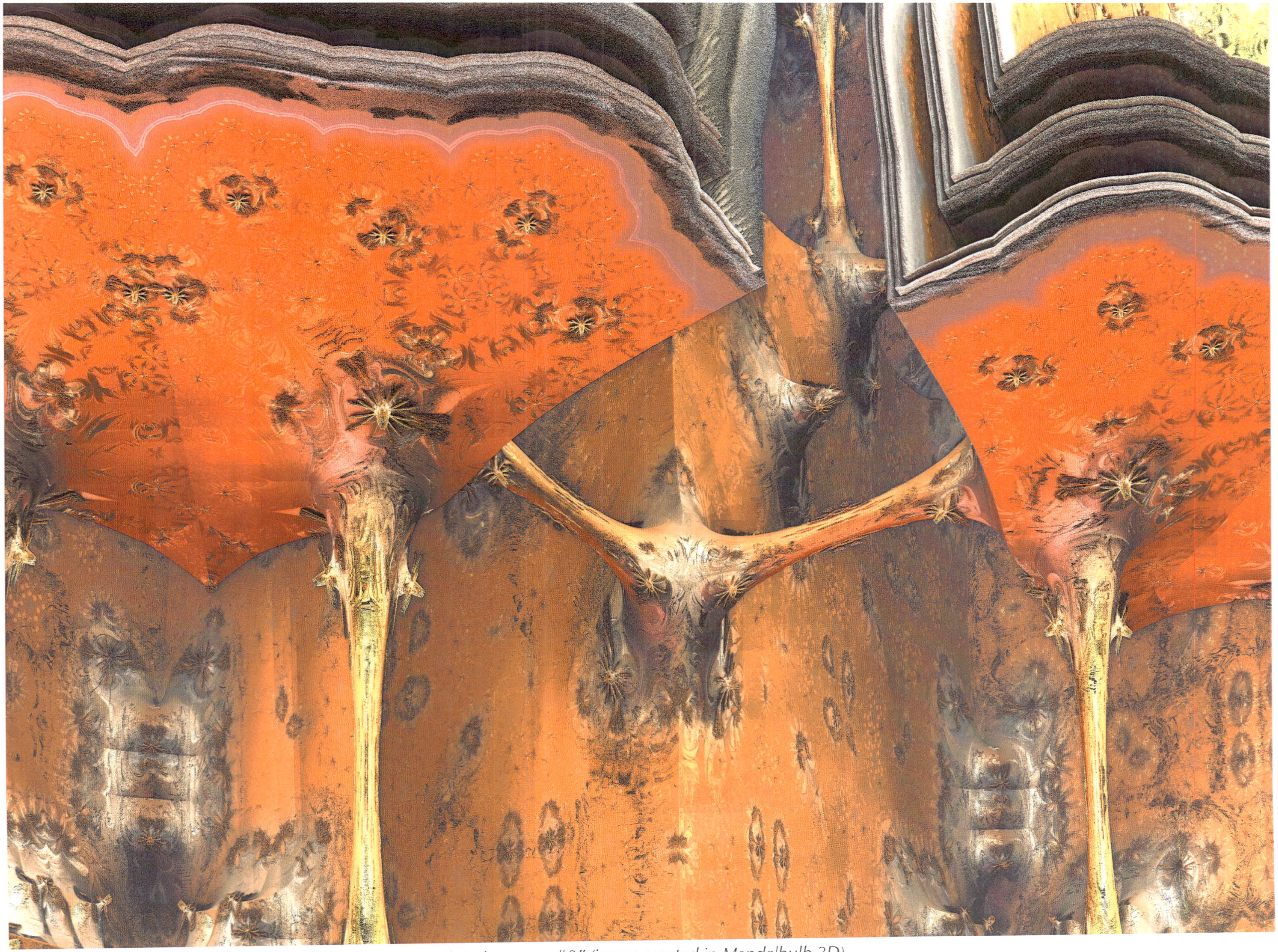

"Interior space #3" (image created in Mandelbulb 3D)

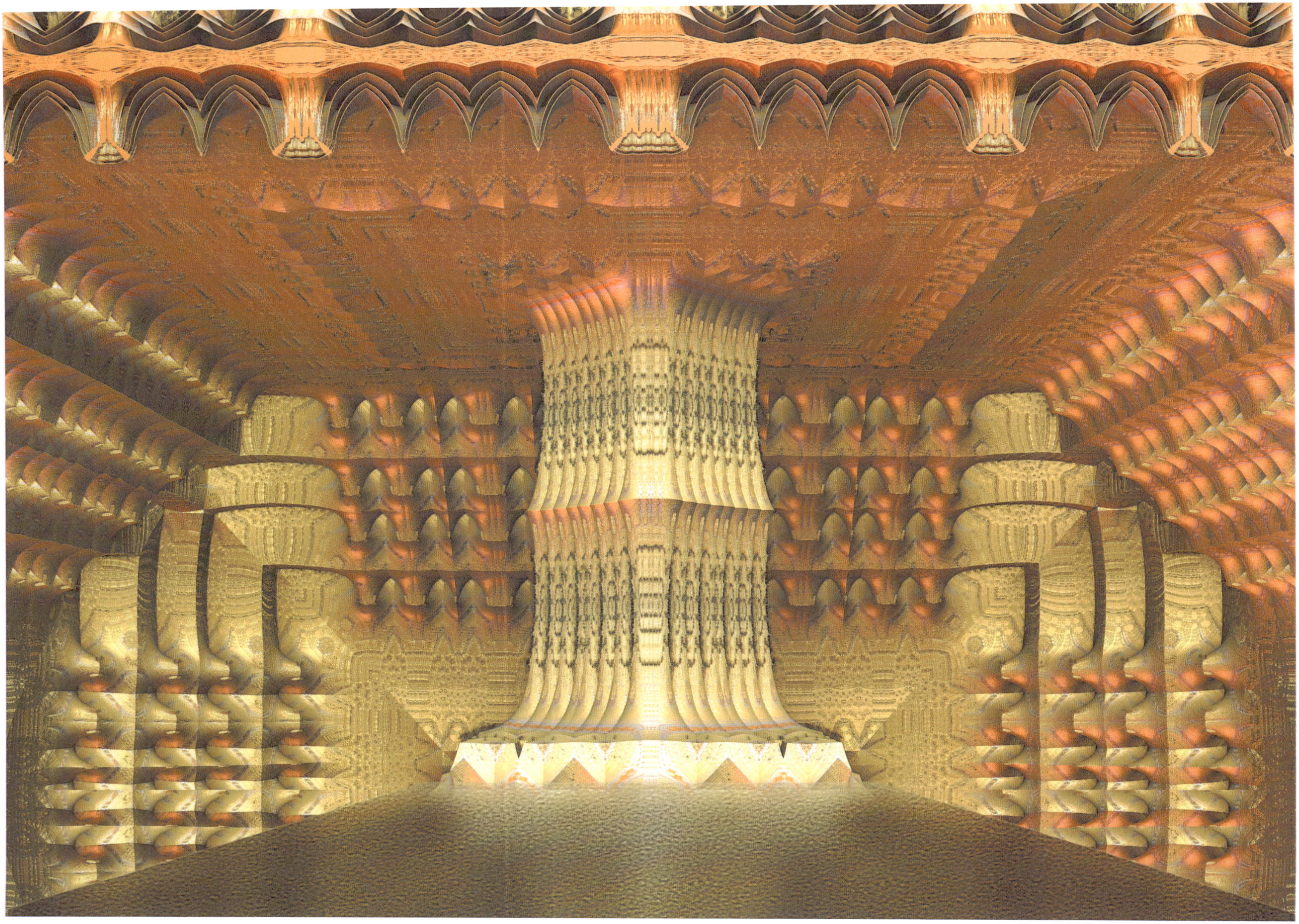

"Front and Center Stage" (image created in Mandelbulb 3D)

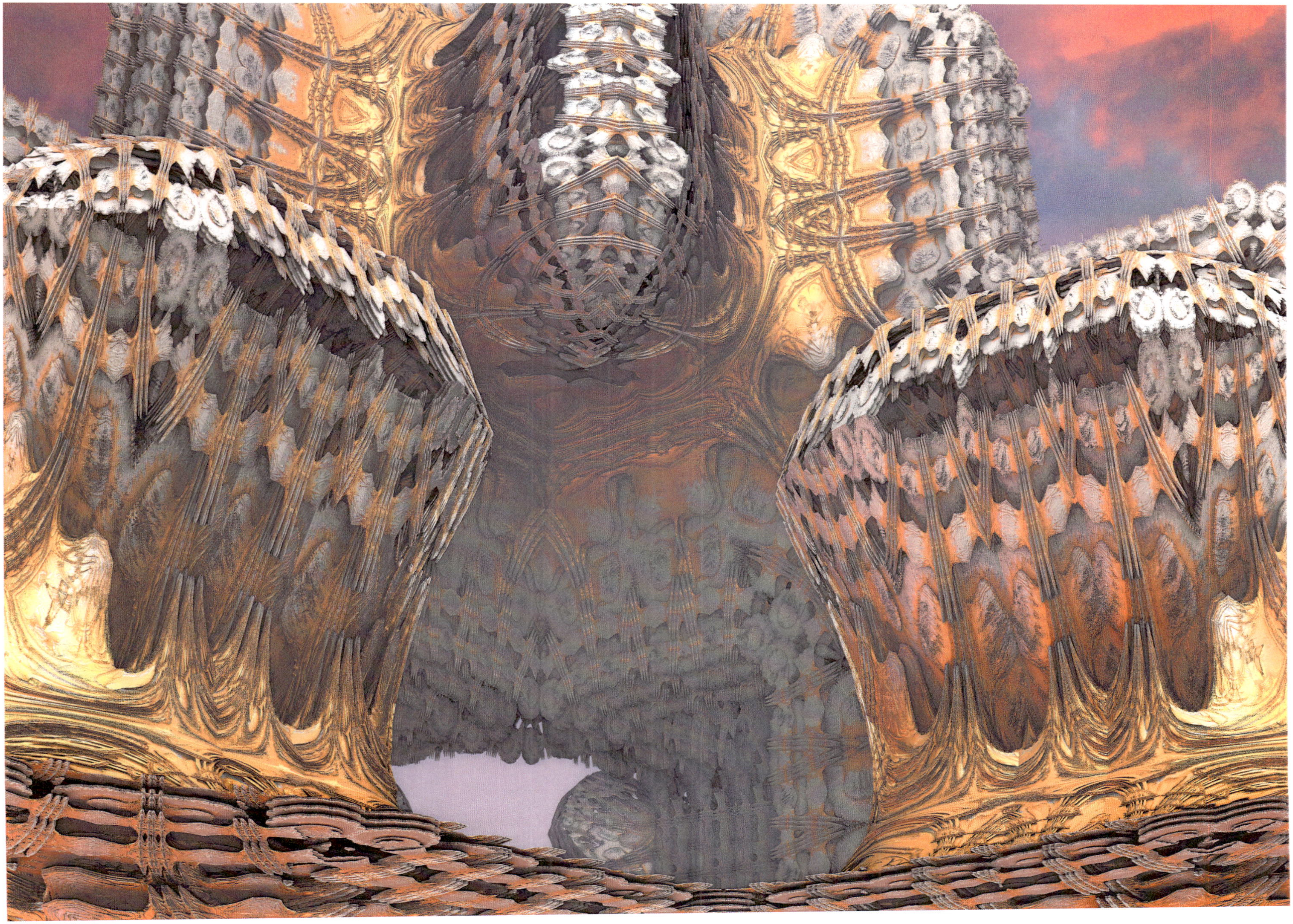

"Exterior Decorative Columns" (image created in Mandelbulb 3D)

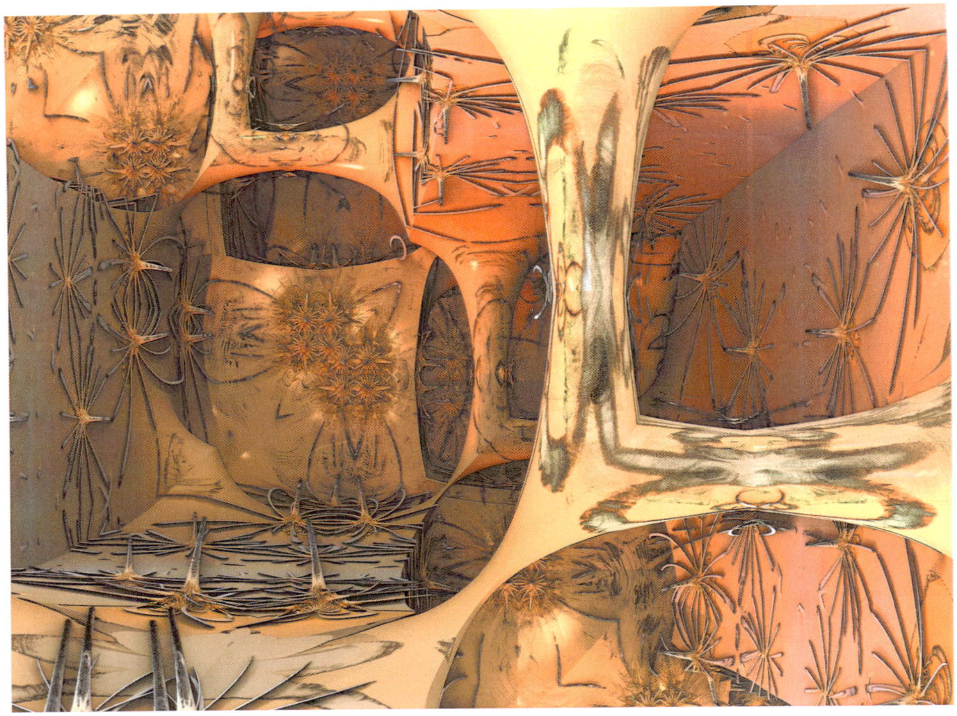
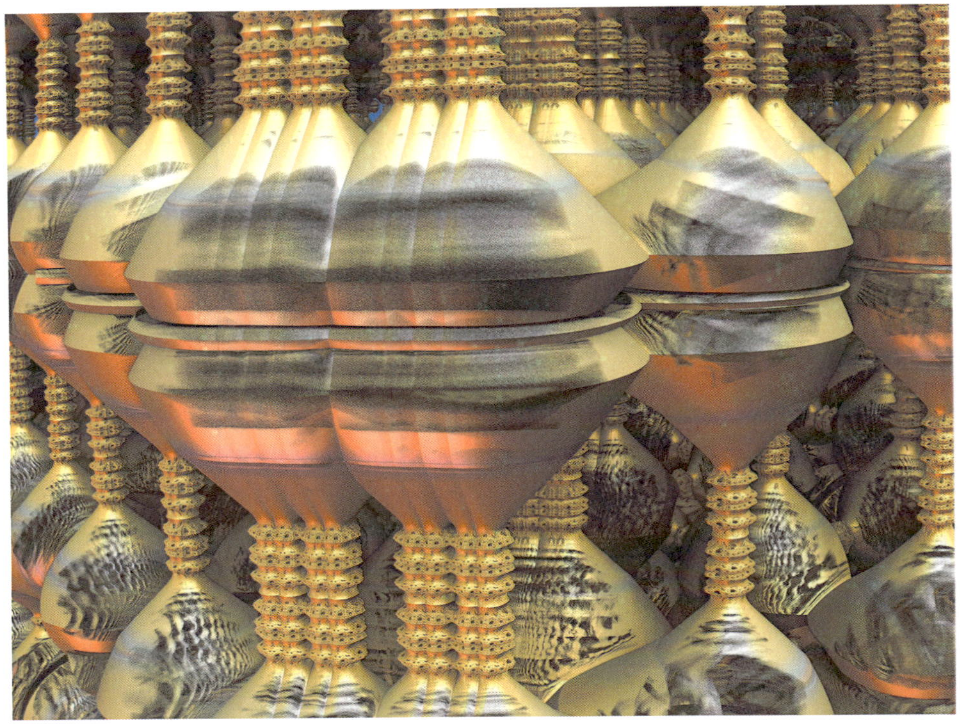
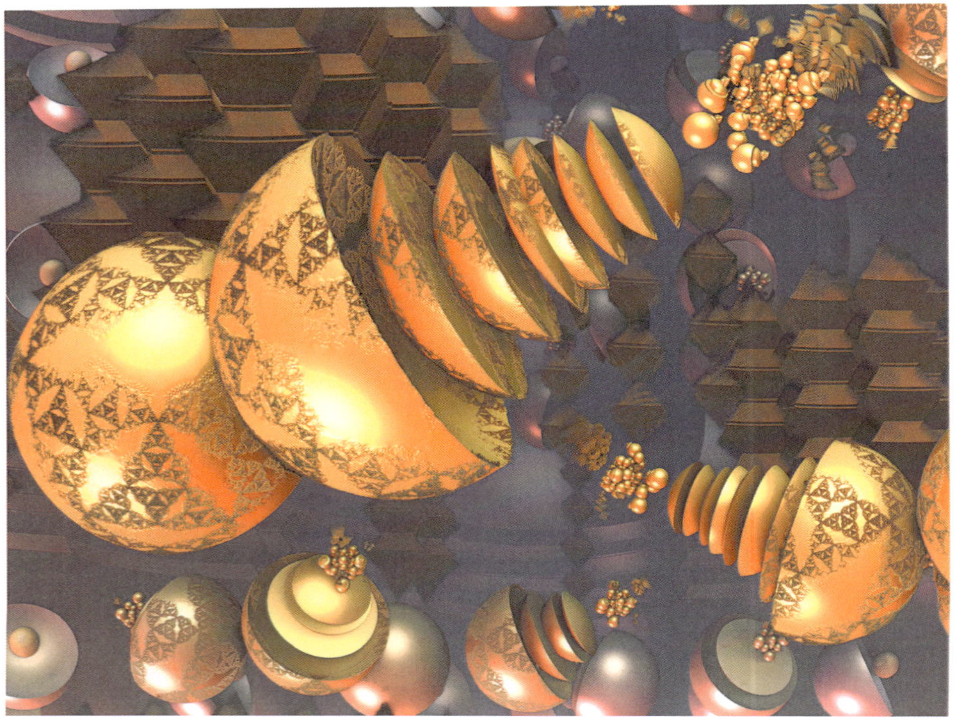
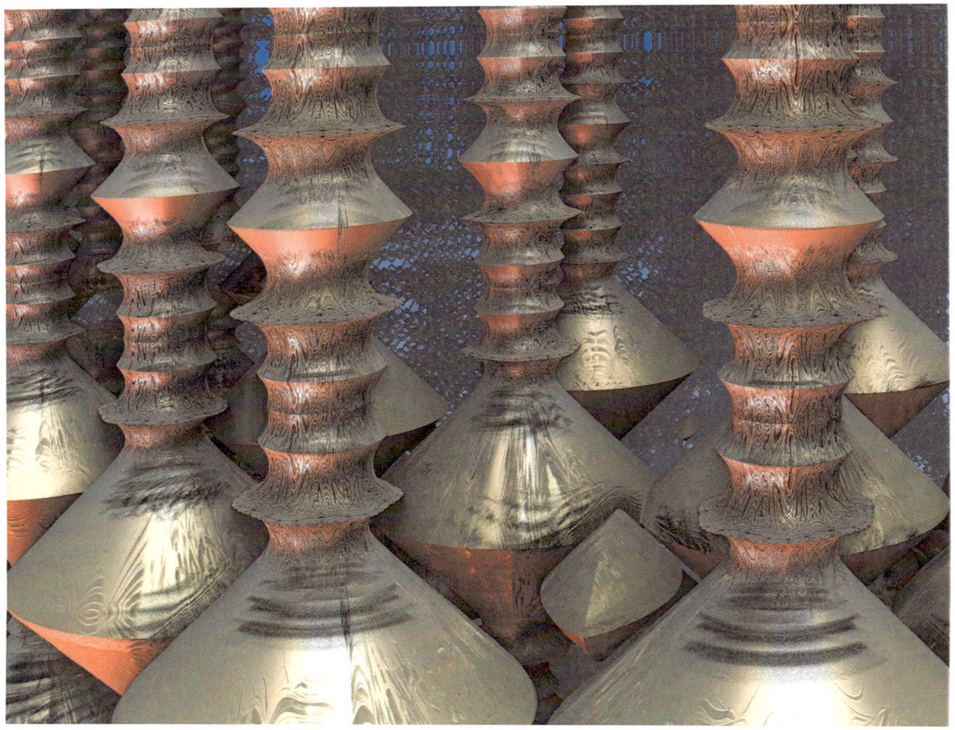

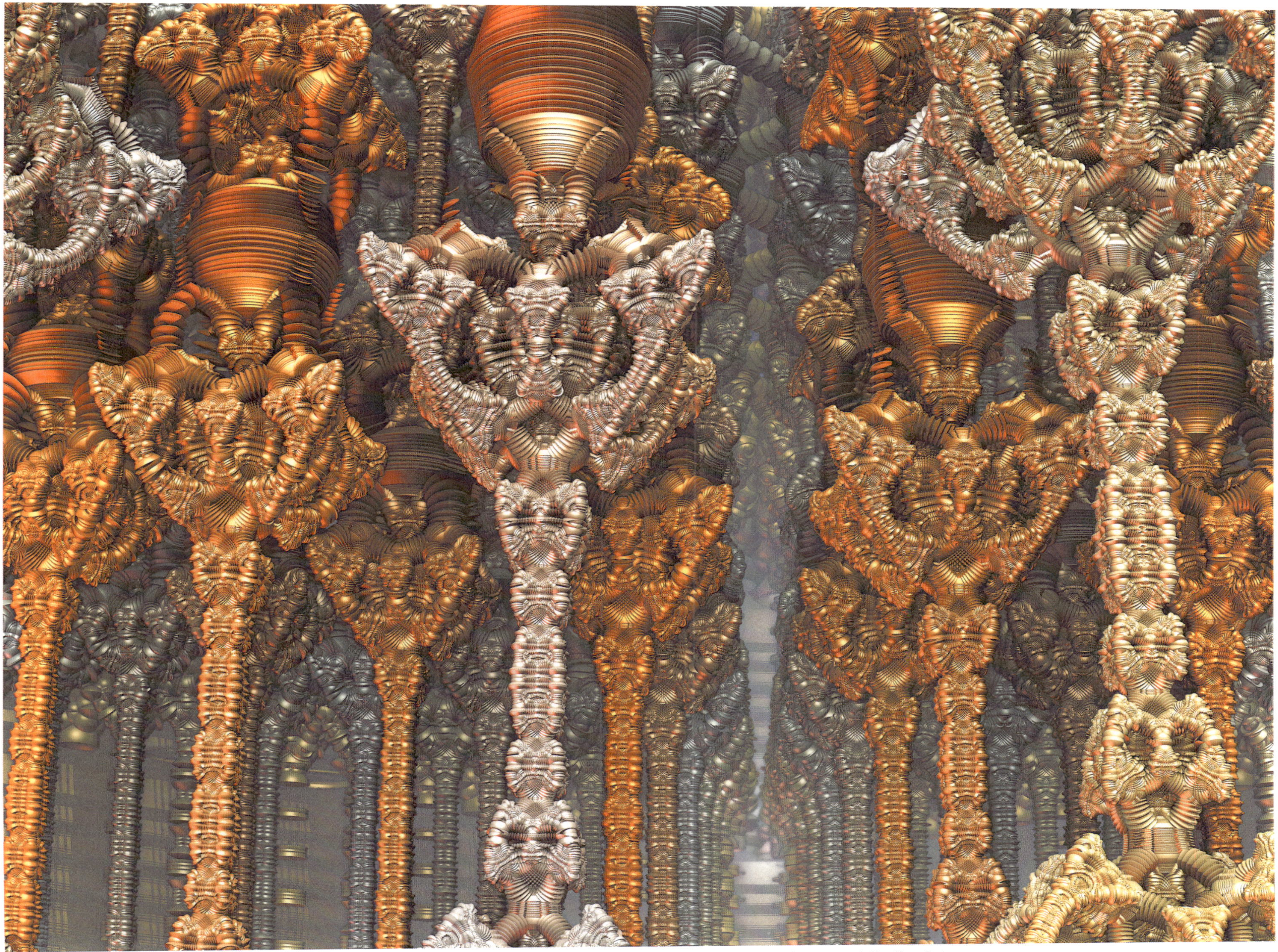

"Tight Interior Spaces" (All images in this spread were created in Mandelbulb 3D.)

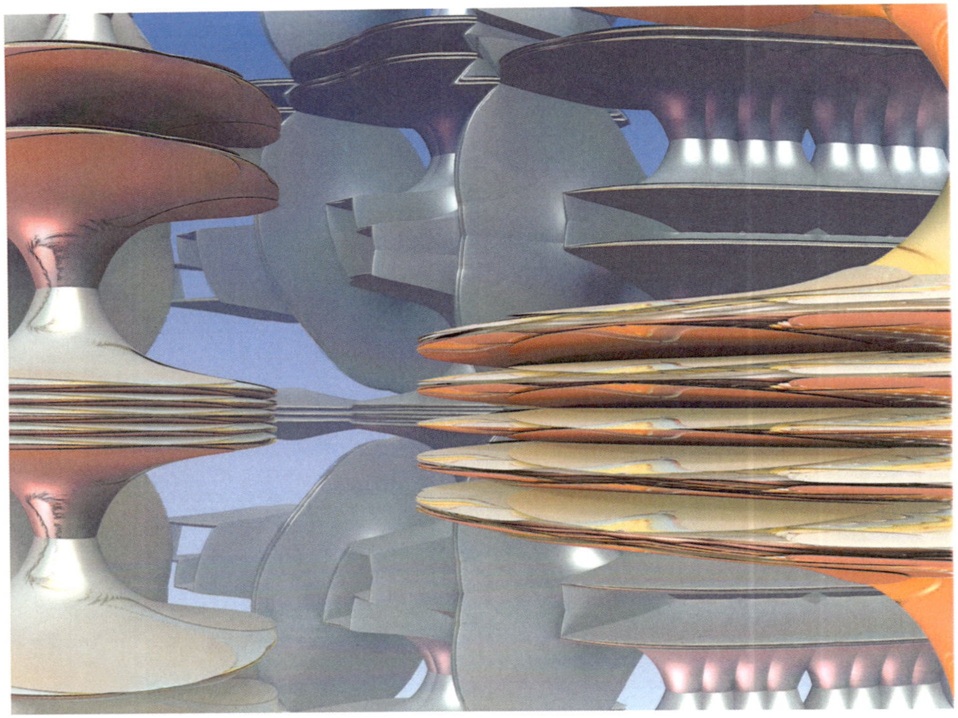
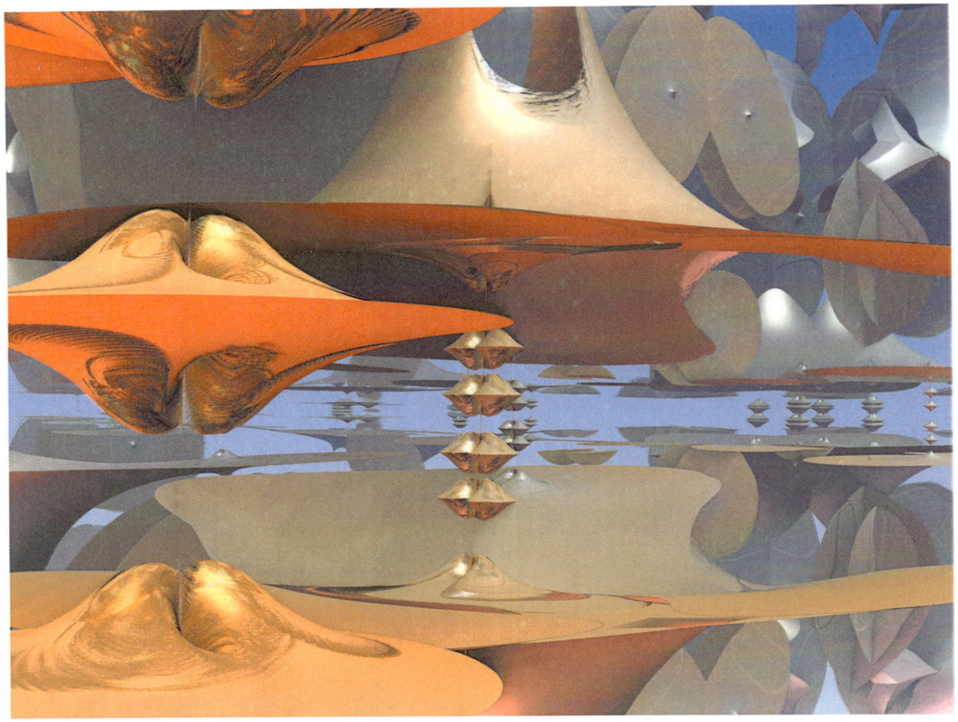
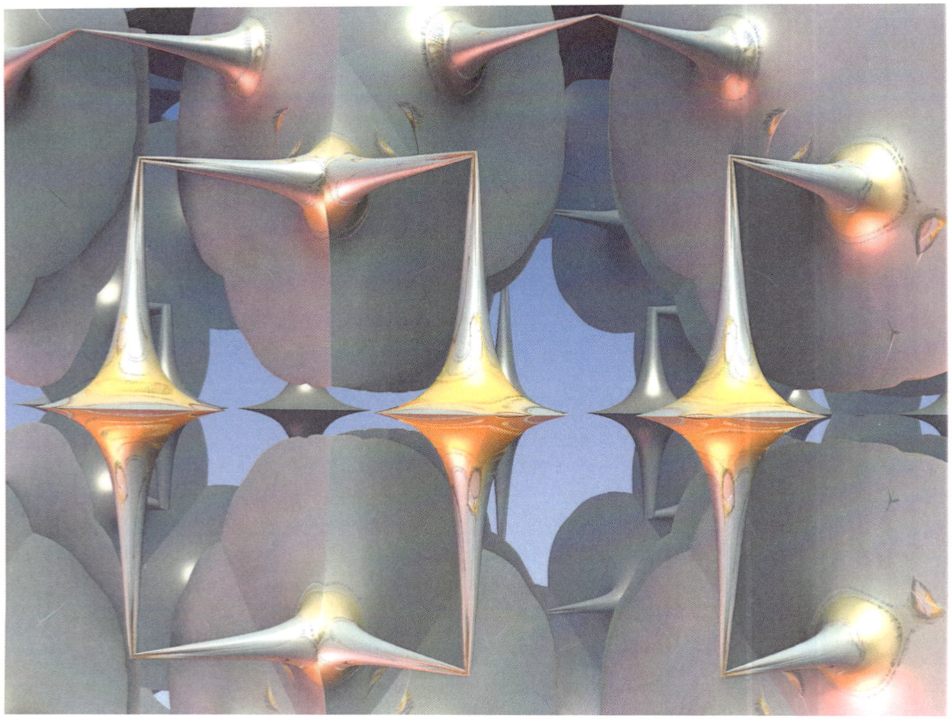
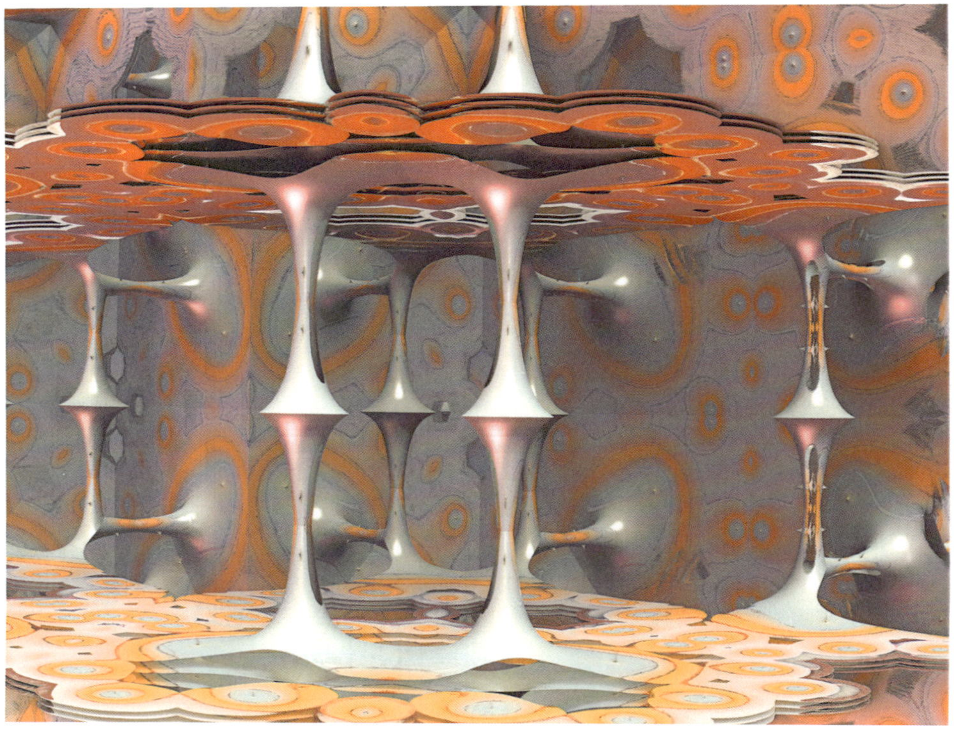

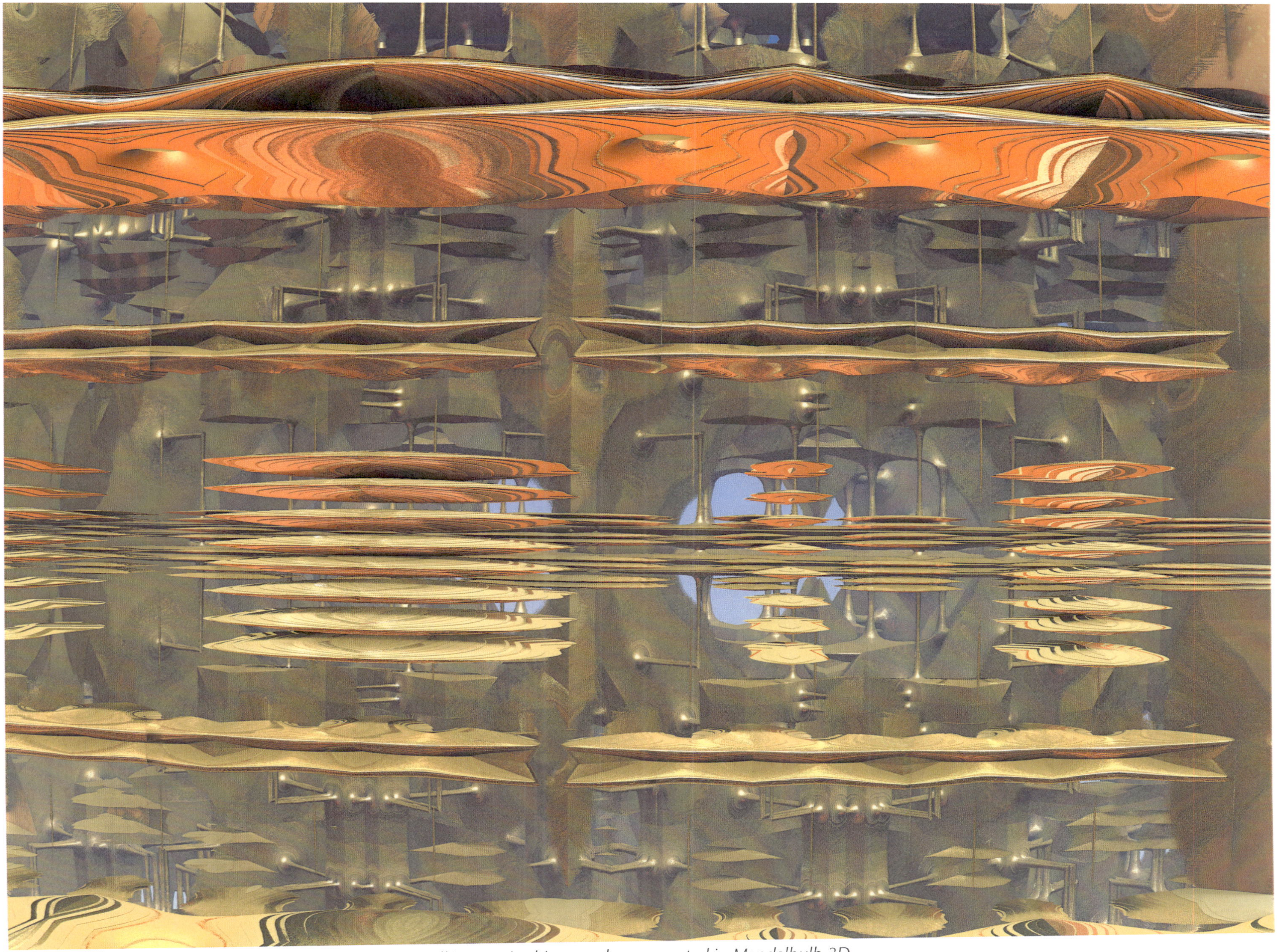

All images in this spread were created in Mandelbulb 3D.

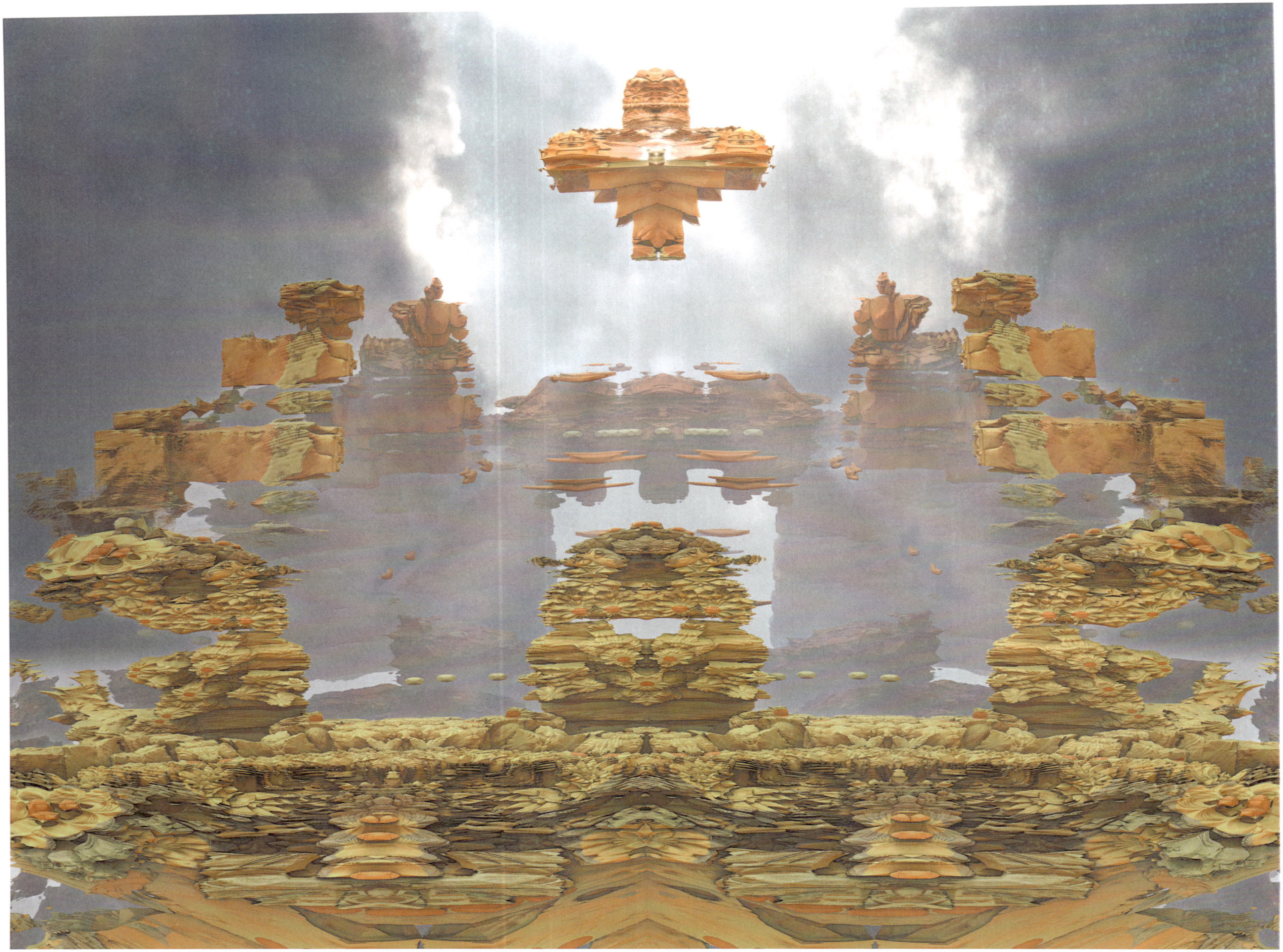

"Camo Space Ship Taking Off" (image created in Mandelbulb 3D; clouds, digital photo)

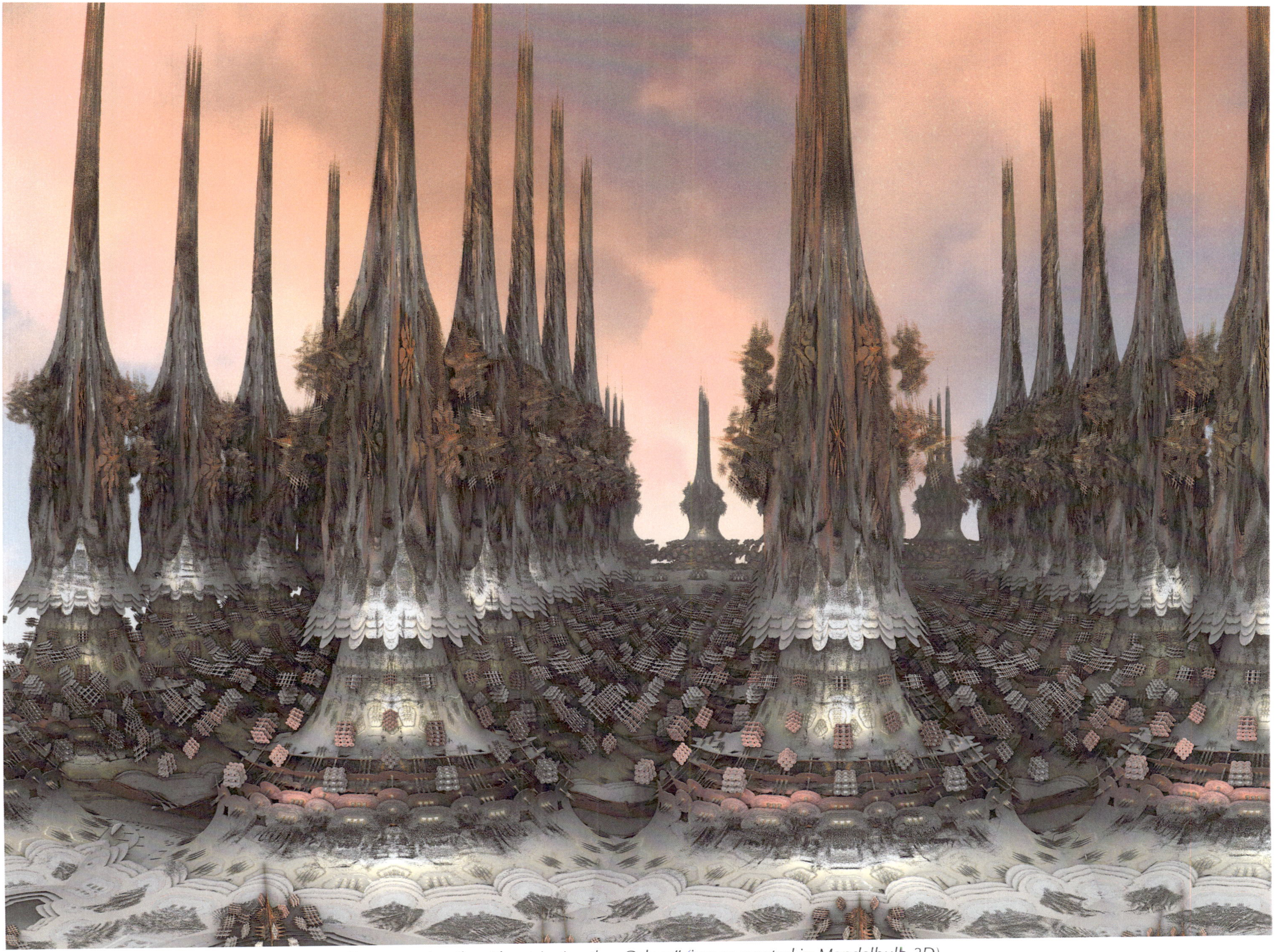

"Desert on Another Planet in Another Galaxy" (image created in Mandelbulb 3D)

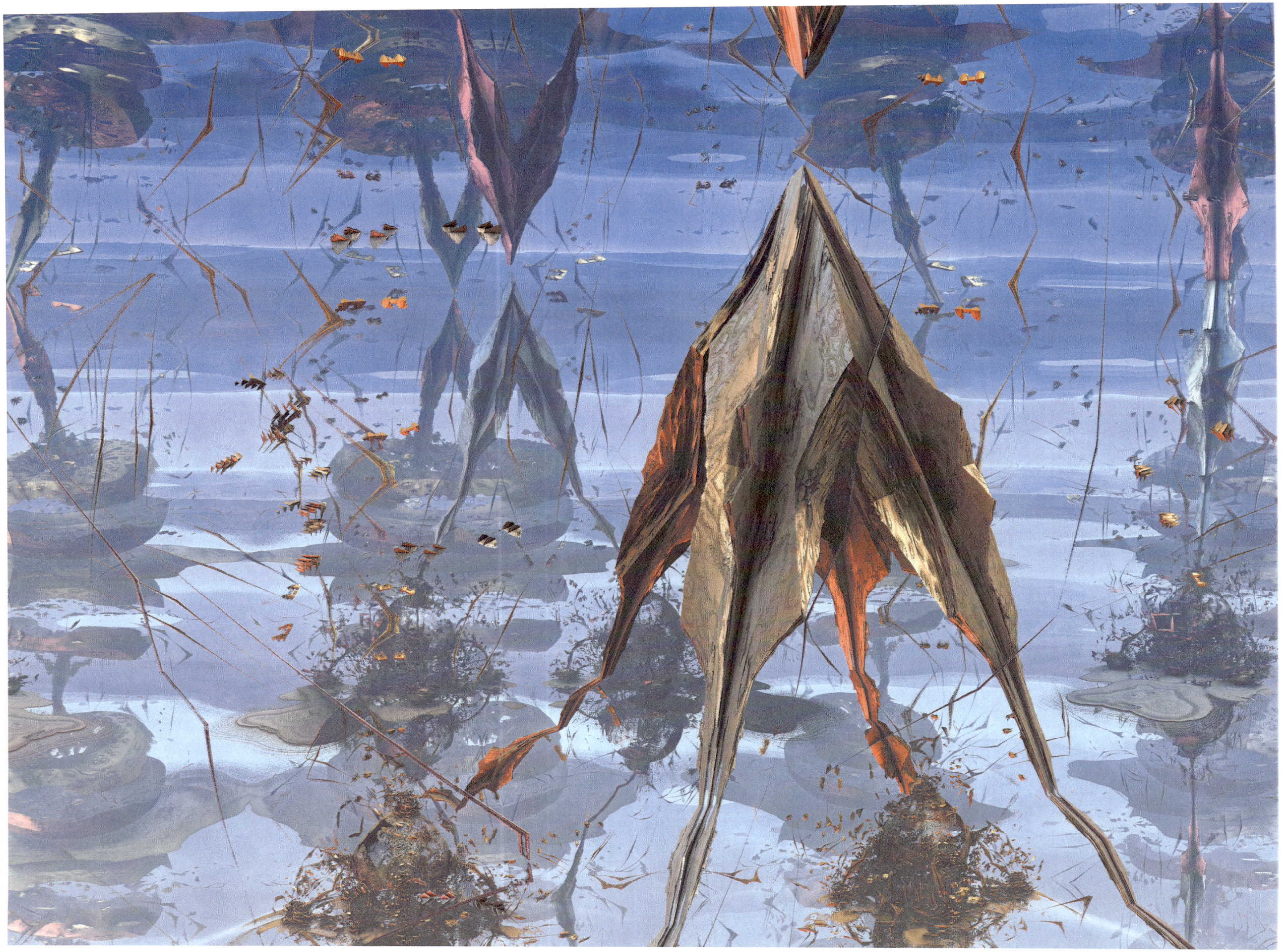

Image created in Mandelbulb 3D

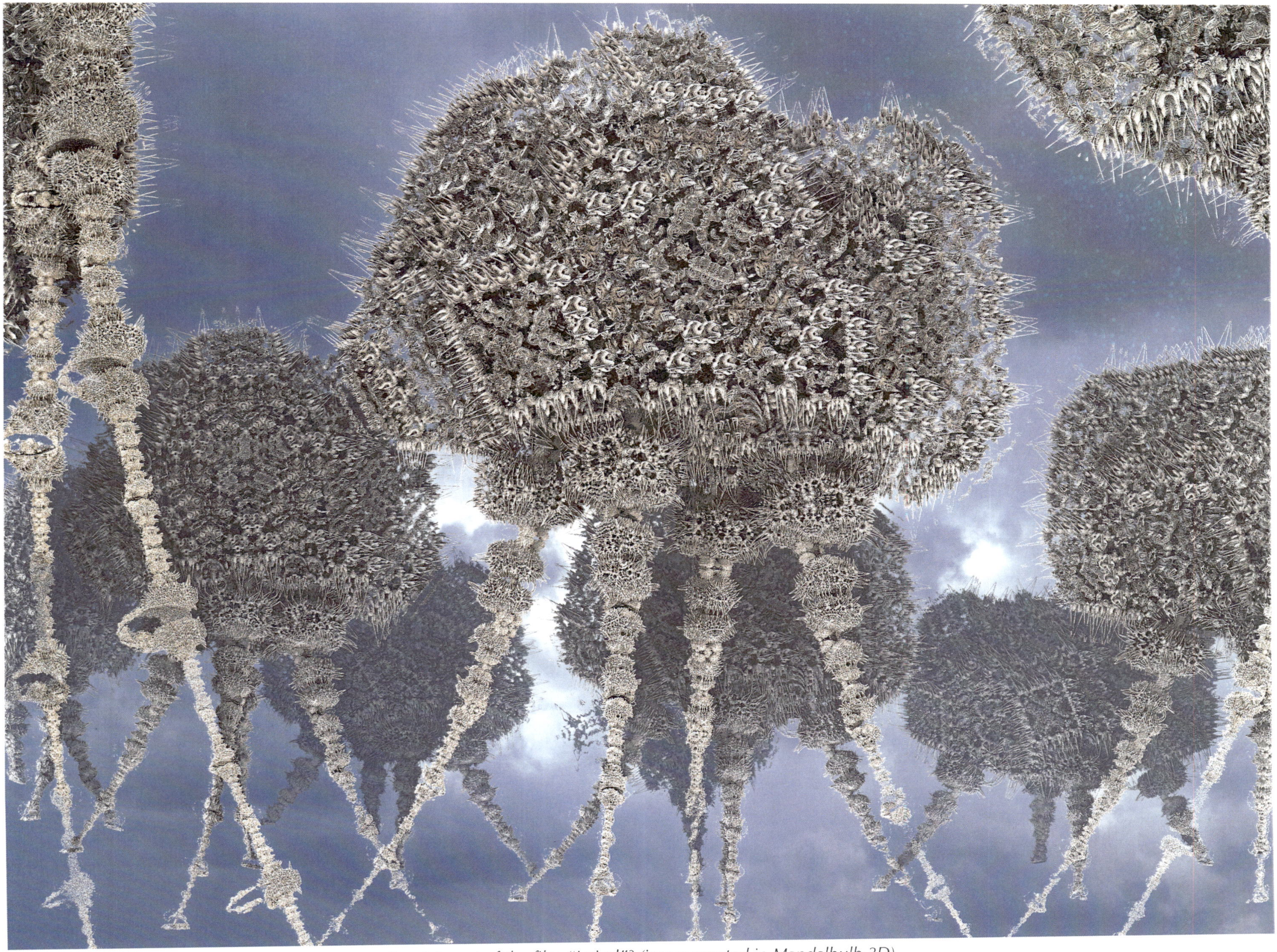

Reminiscent of the film "Arrival"? (image created in Mandelbulb 3D)

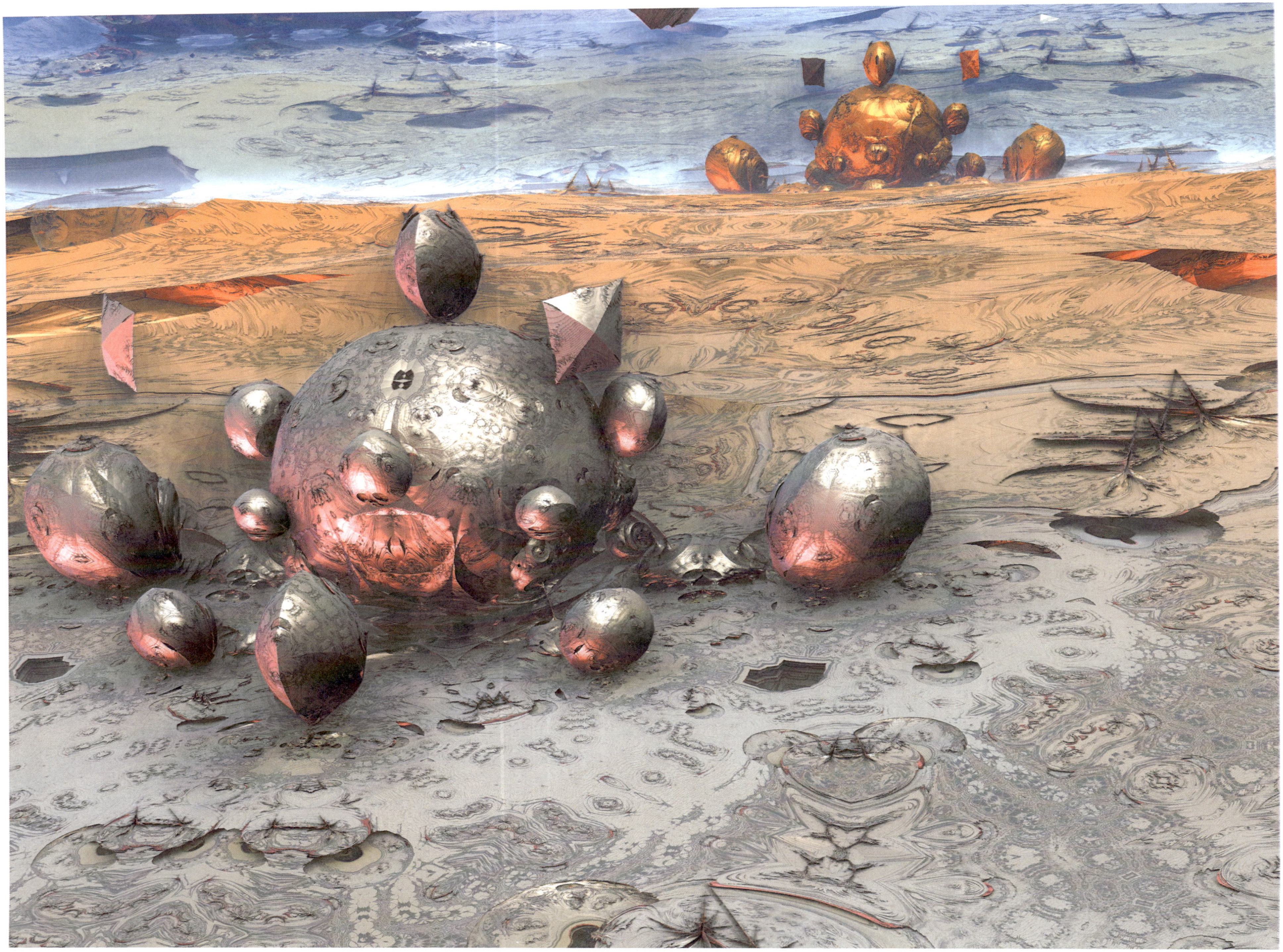

"Space Junk on the Beach," image created in Mandelbulb 3D

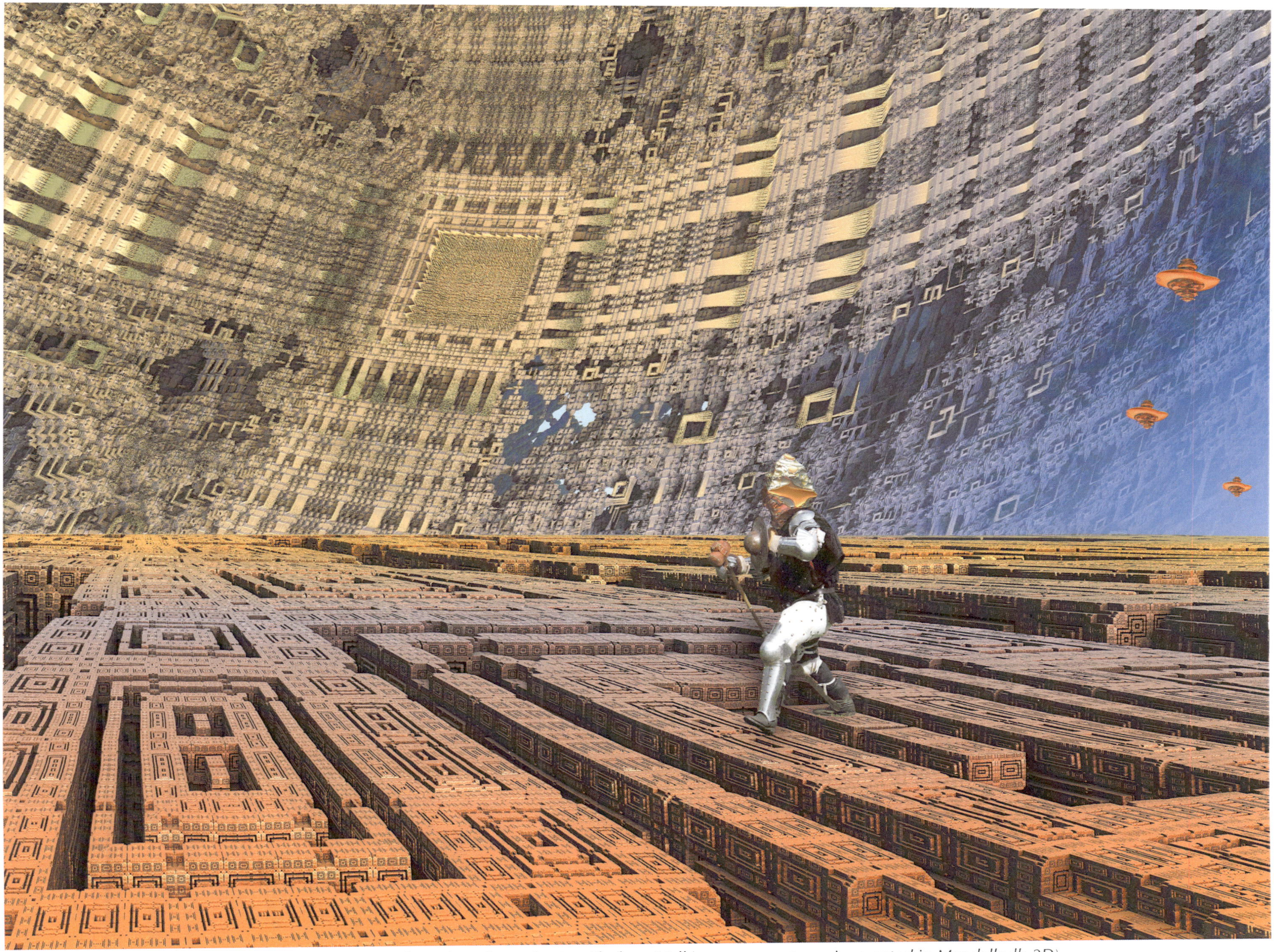

"Lost-in-Time Warrior Trudges Along Space Station Platform" (all images except warrior created in Mandelbulb 3D).

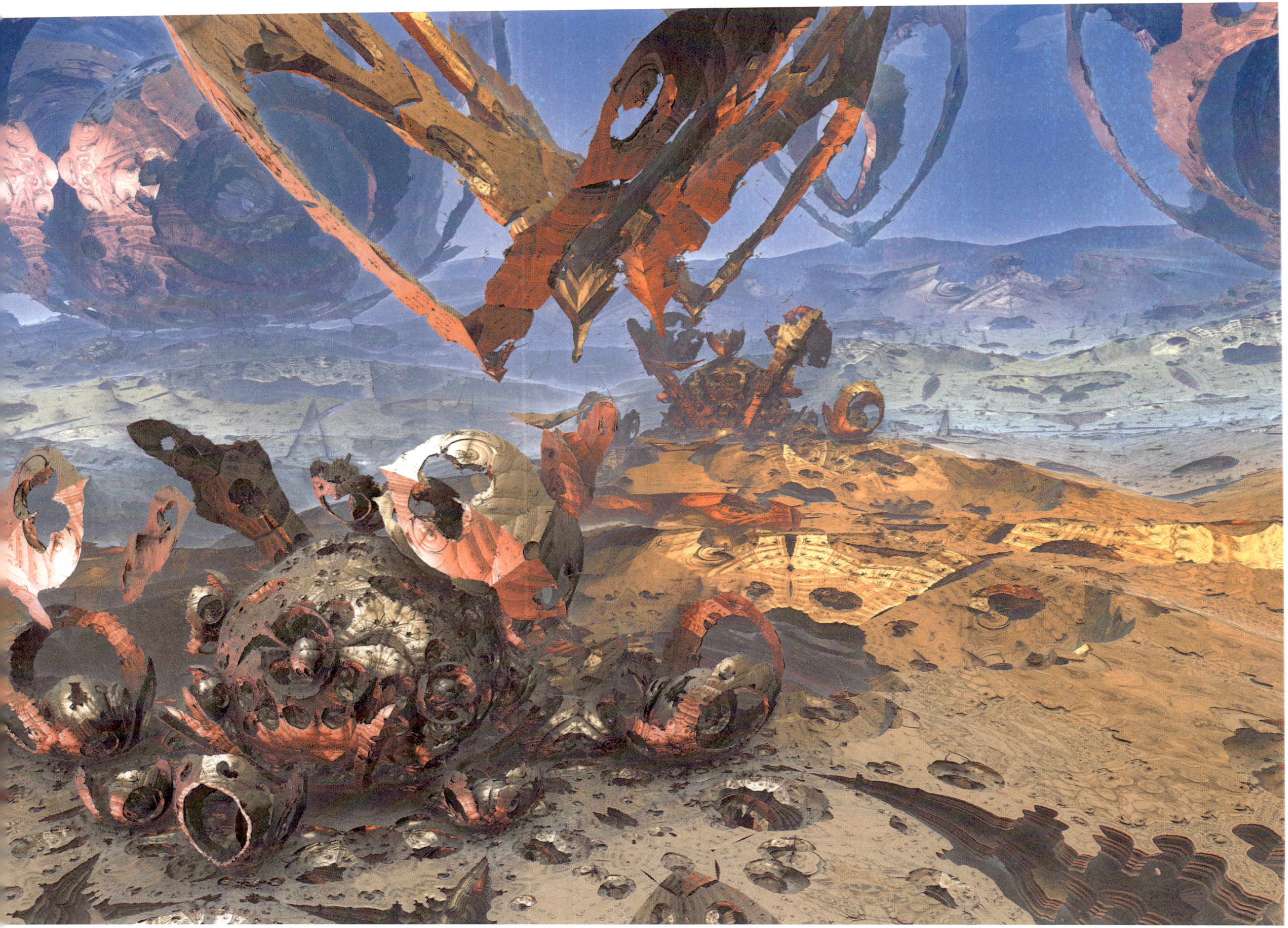

"More Space Junk," image created in Mandelbulb 3D

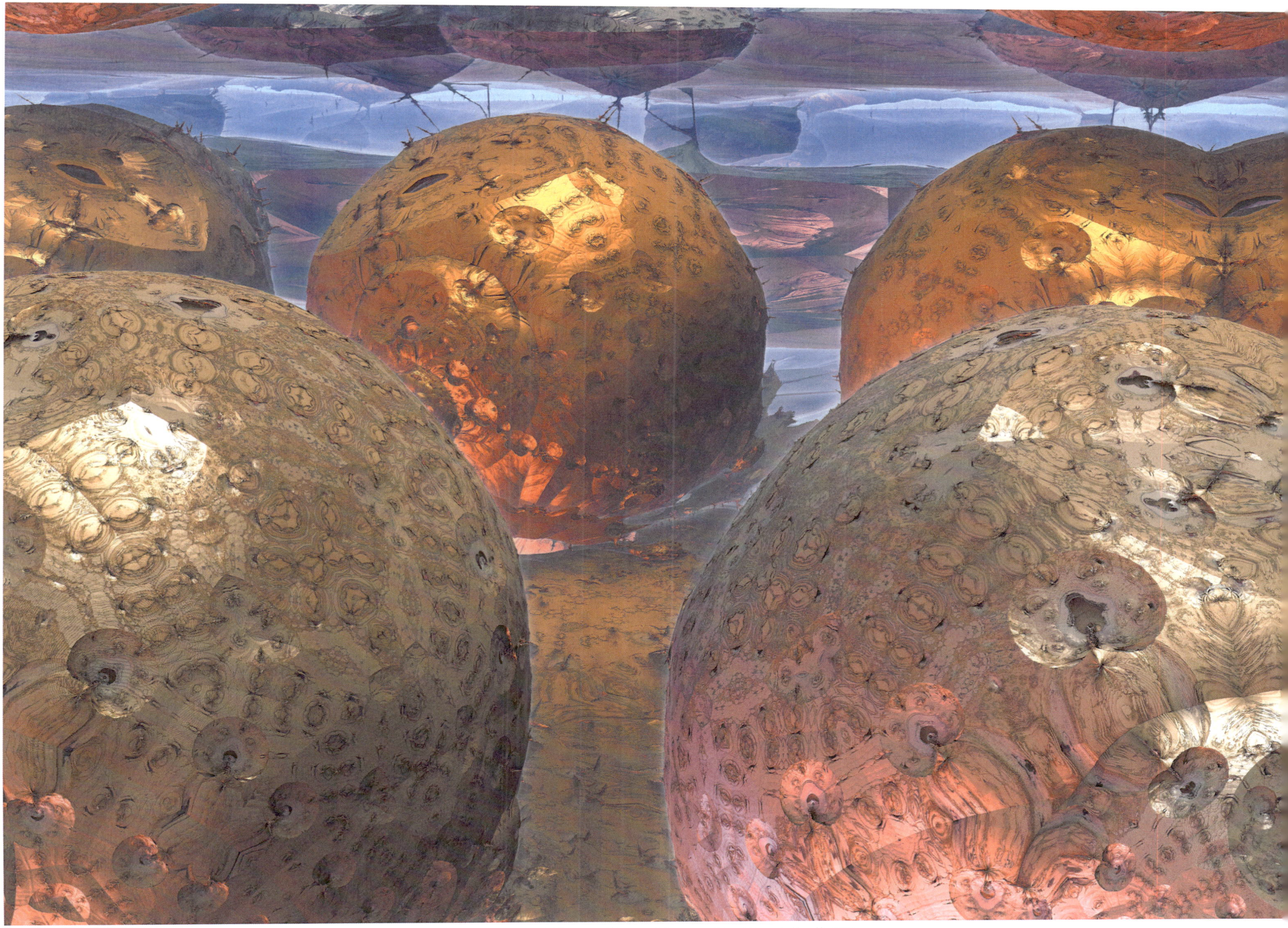

"Living Quarters on a Distant Planet," imaged in Mandelbulb 3D

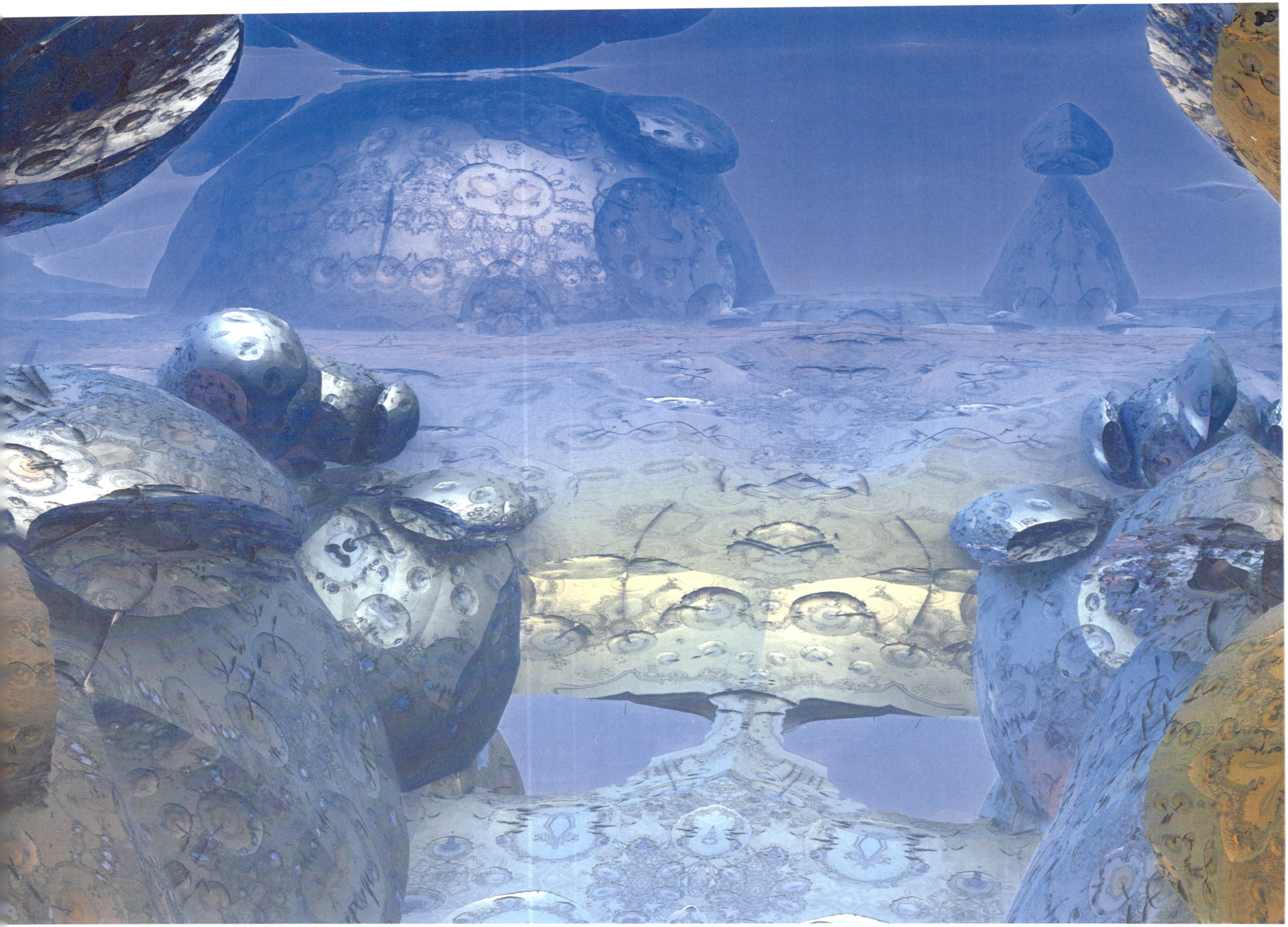

"Operations Center on a Far and Distant Planet," imaged in Mandelbulb 3D

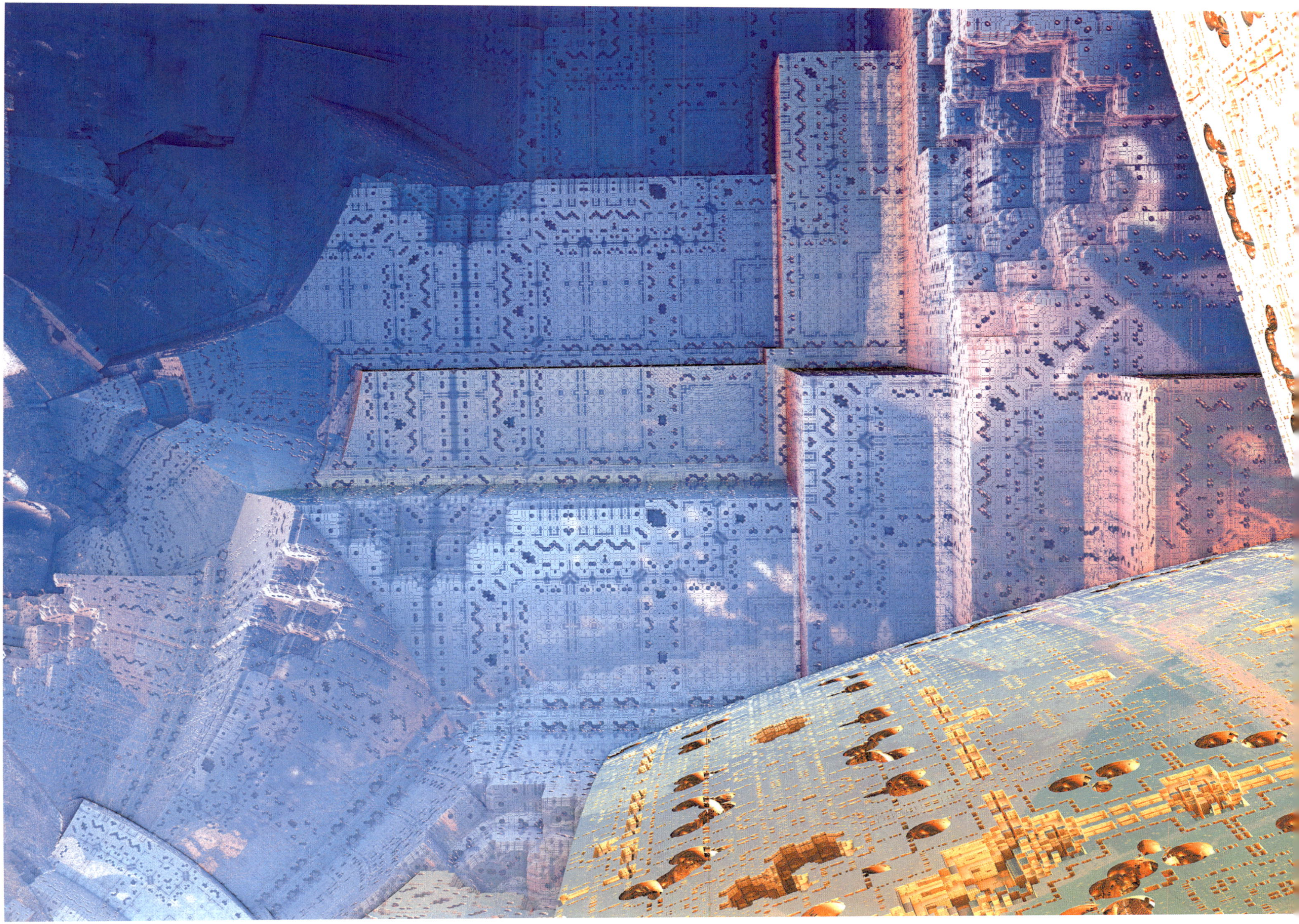

"Structures," imaged in Mandelbulb 3D

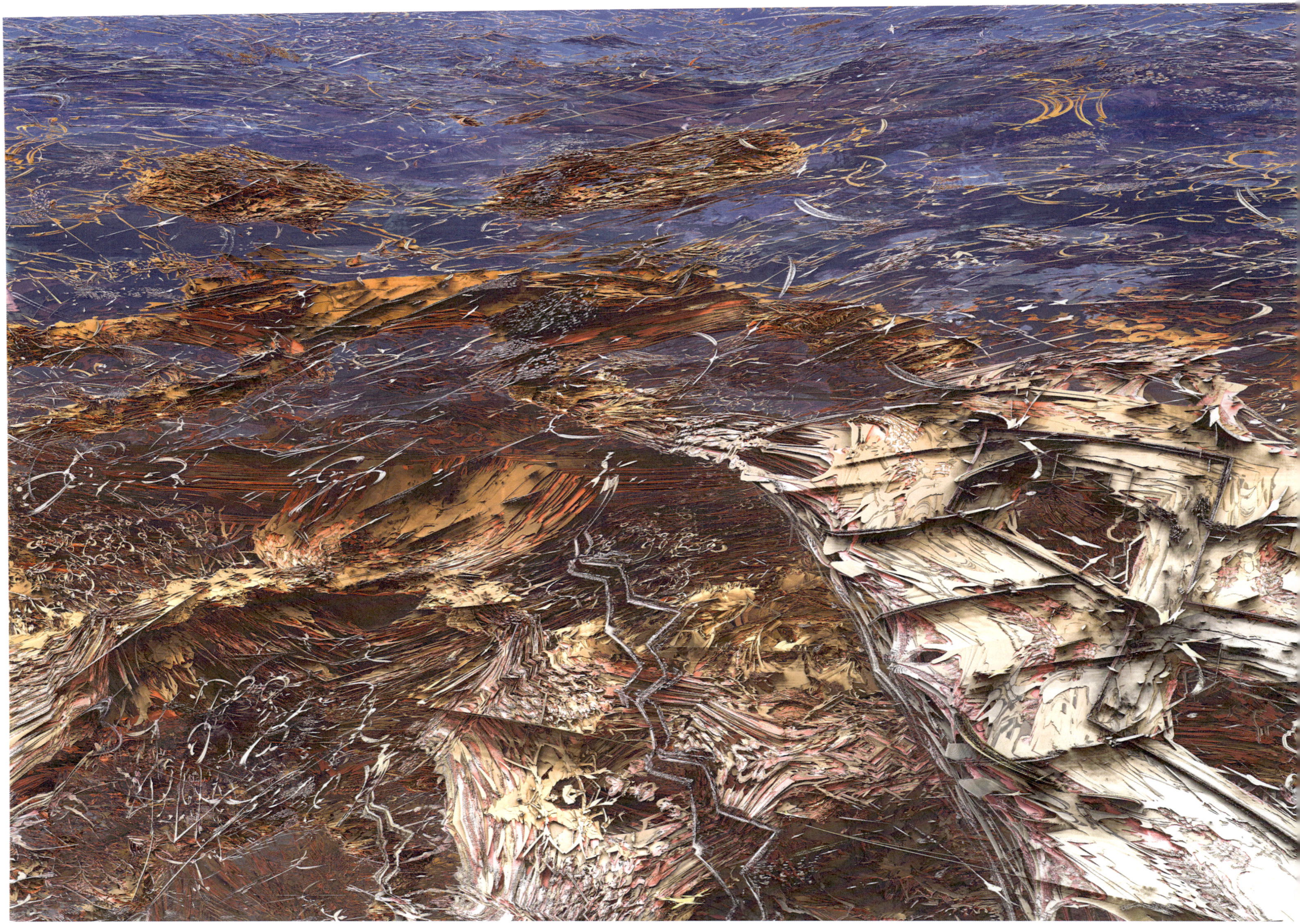

"An Ocean of Scraps and Trash," imaged in Mandelbulb 3D

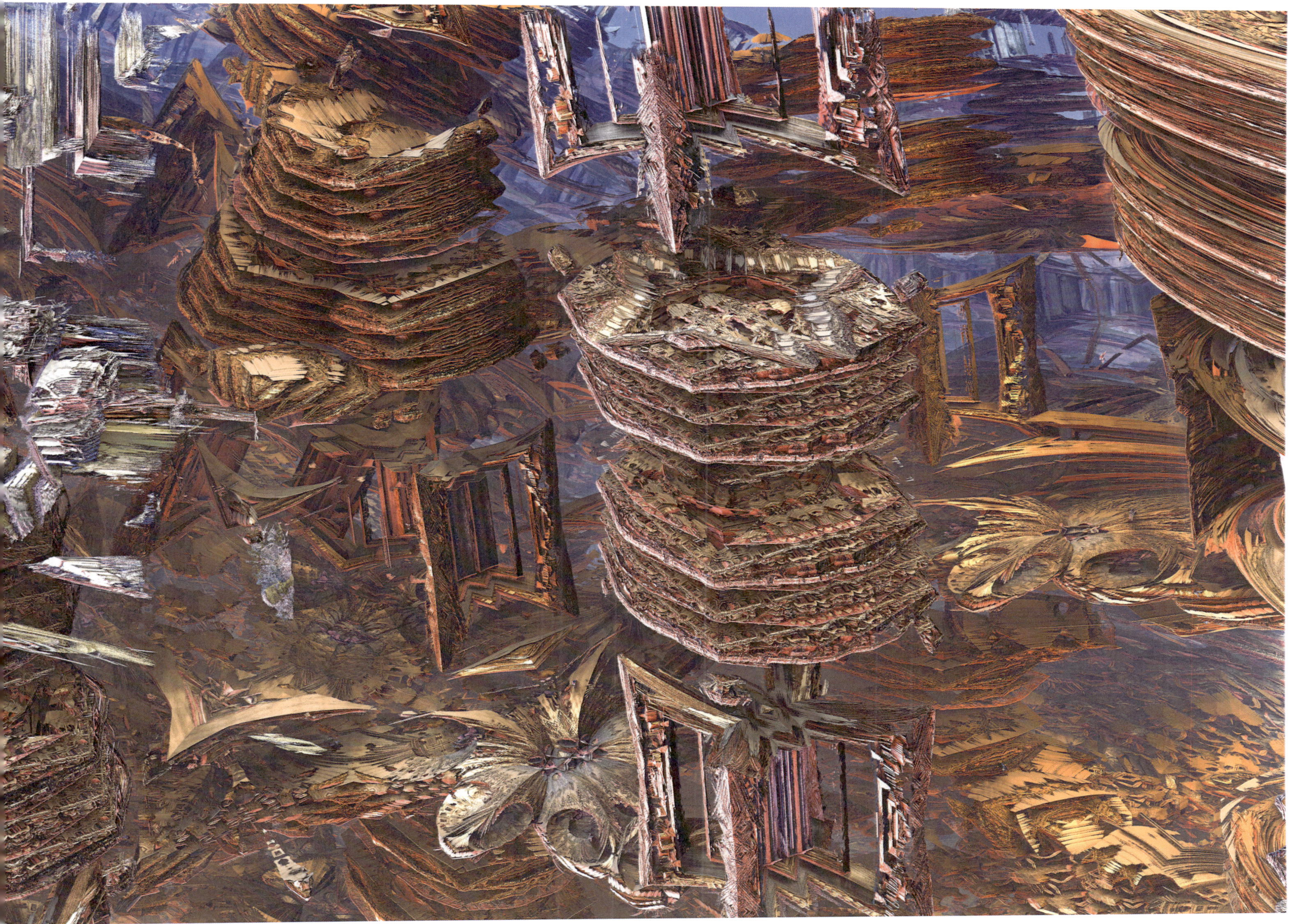

"Damaged Cityscape," imaged in Mandelbulb 3D

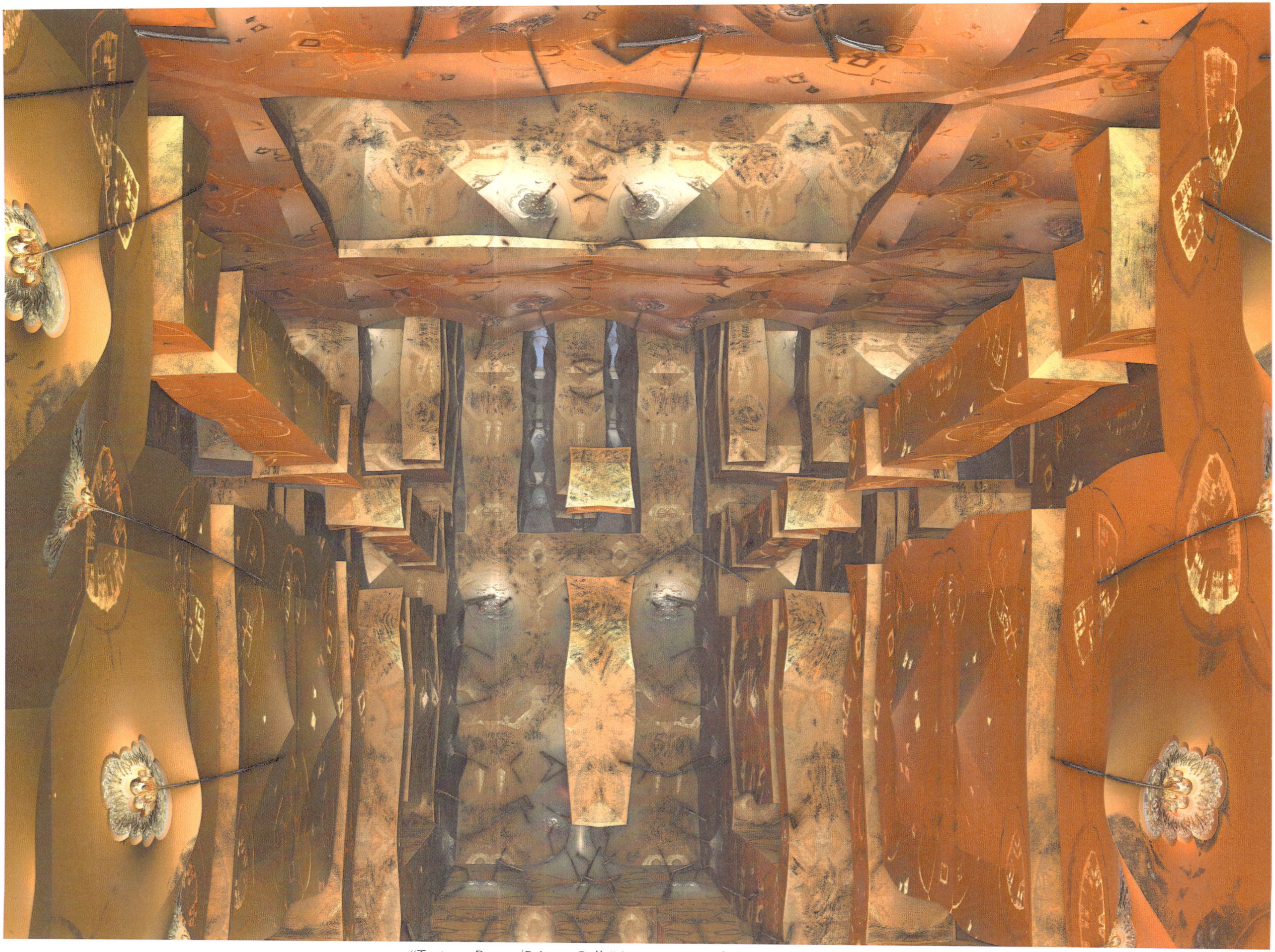

"Torture Room/Prison Cell," image created in Mandelbulb 3D

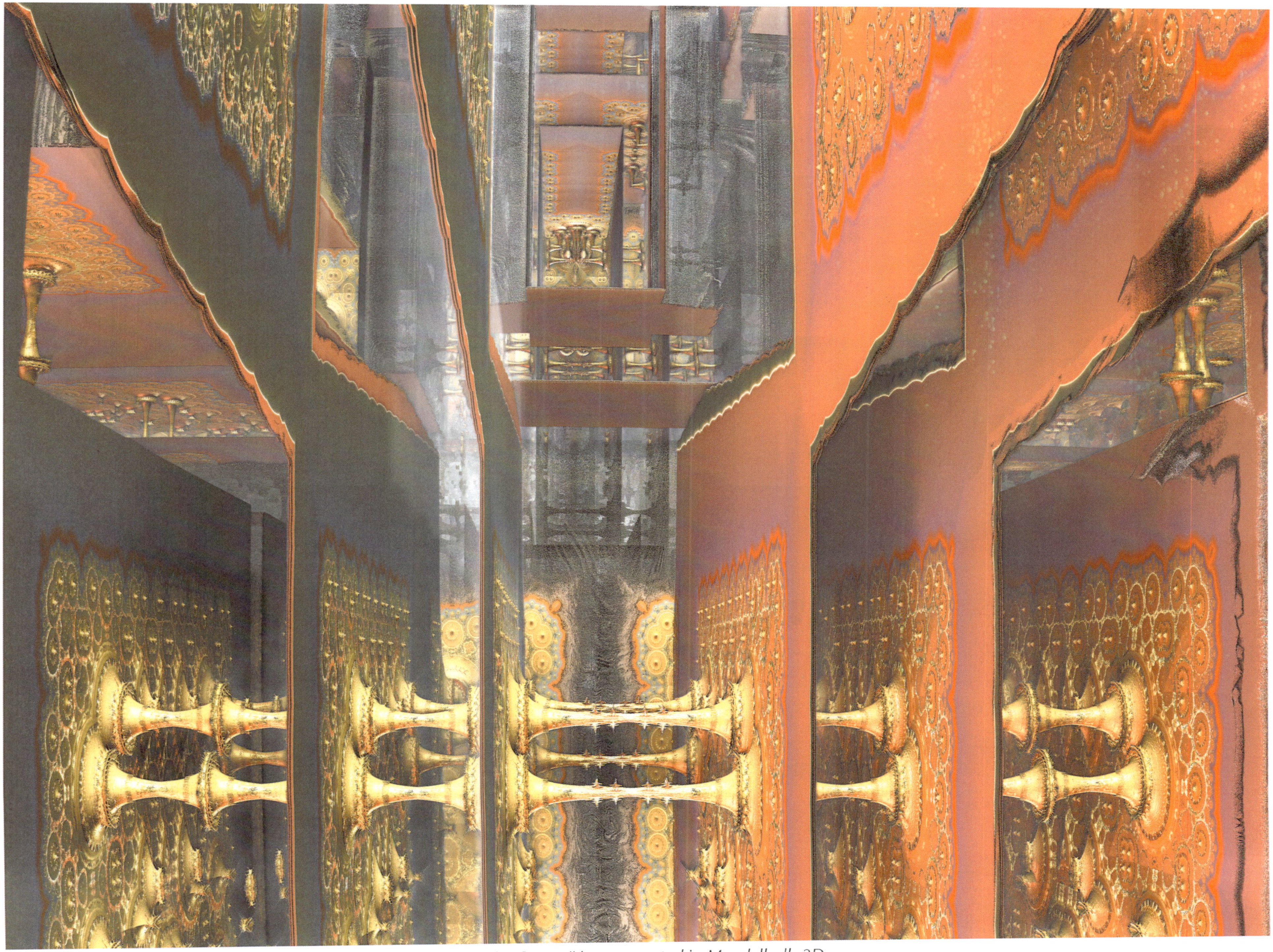

"Interior Space," image created in Mandelbulb 3D

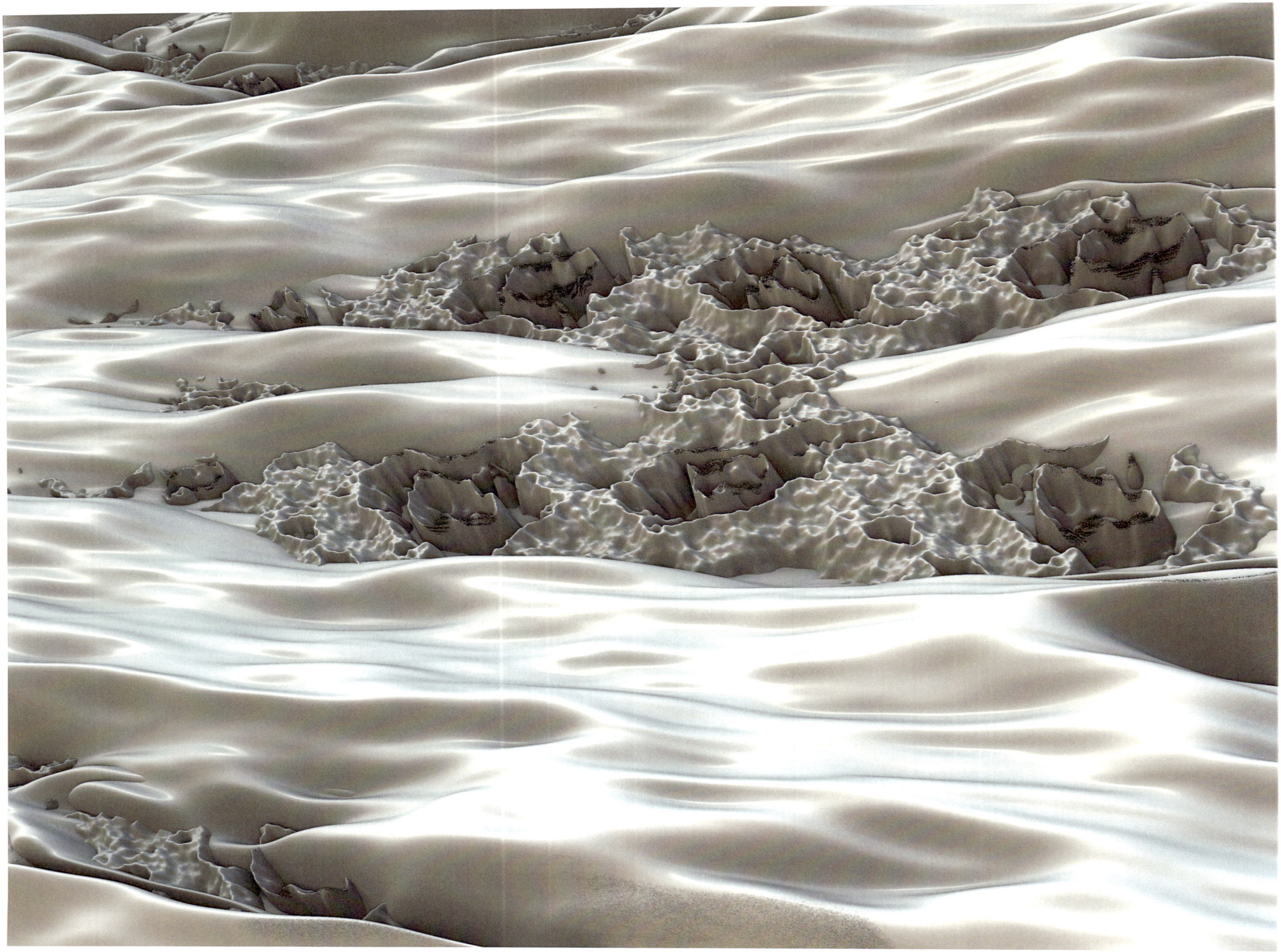

"Plastic-Like Landscape on a Distant Planet," imaged in Mandelbulb 3D

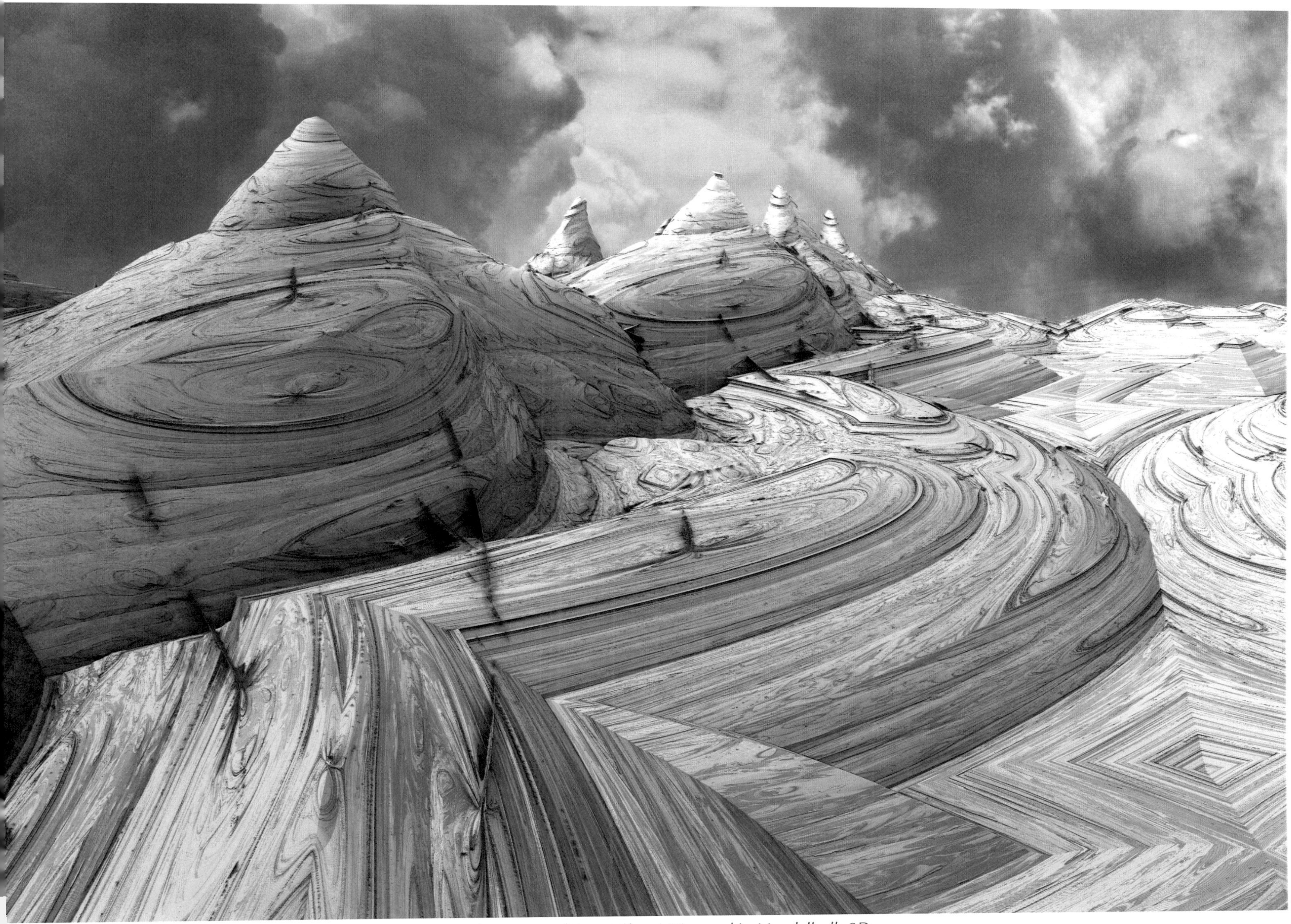

"Landscape on a Distant Planet," imaged in Mandelbulb 3D

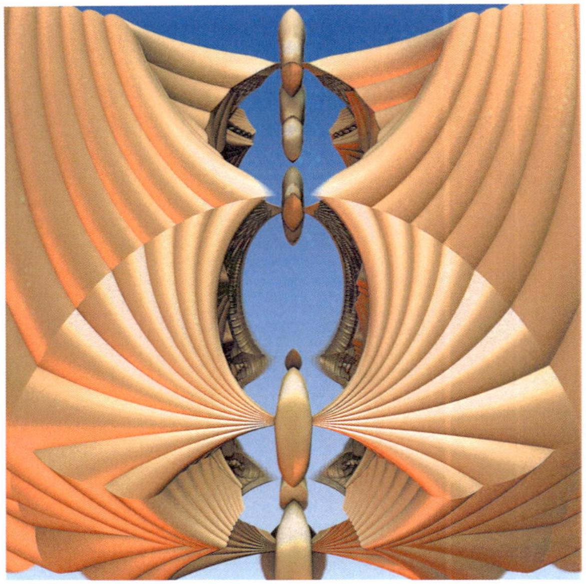
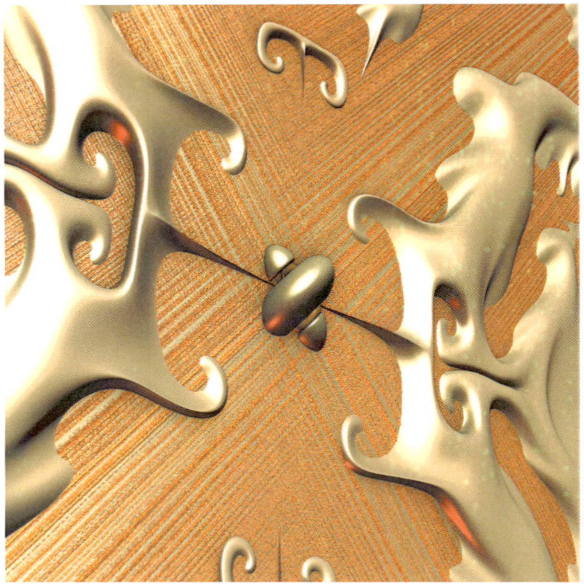
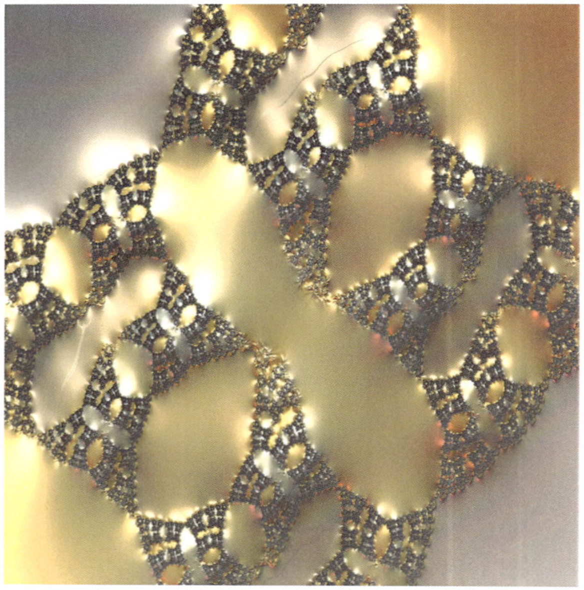
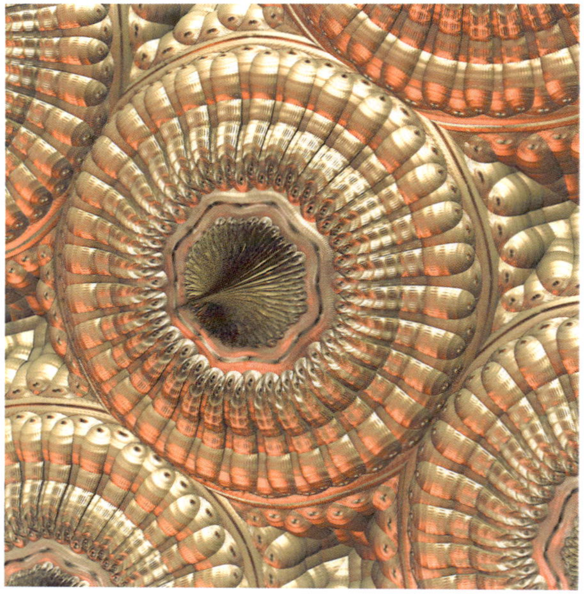

All images created by Mandelbulb 3D

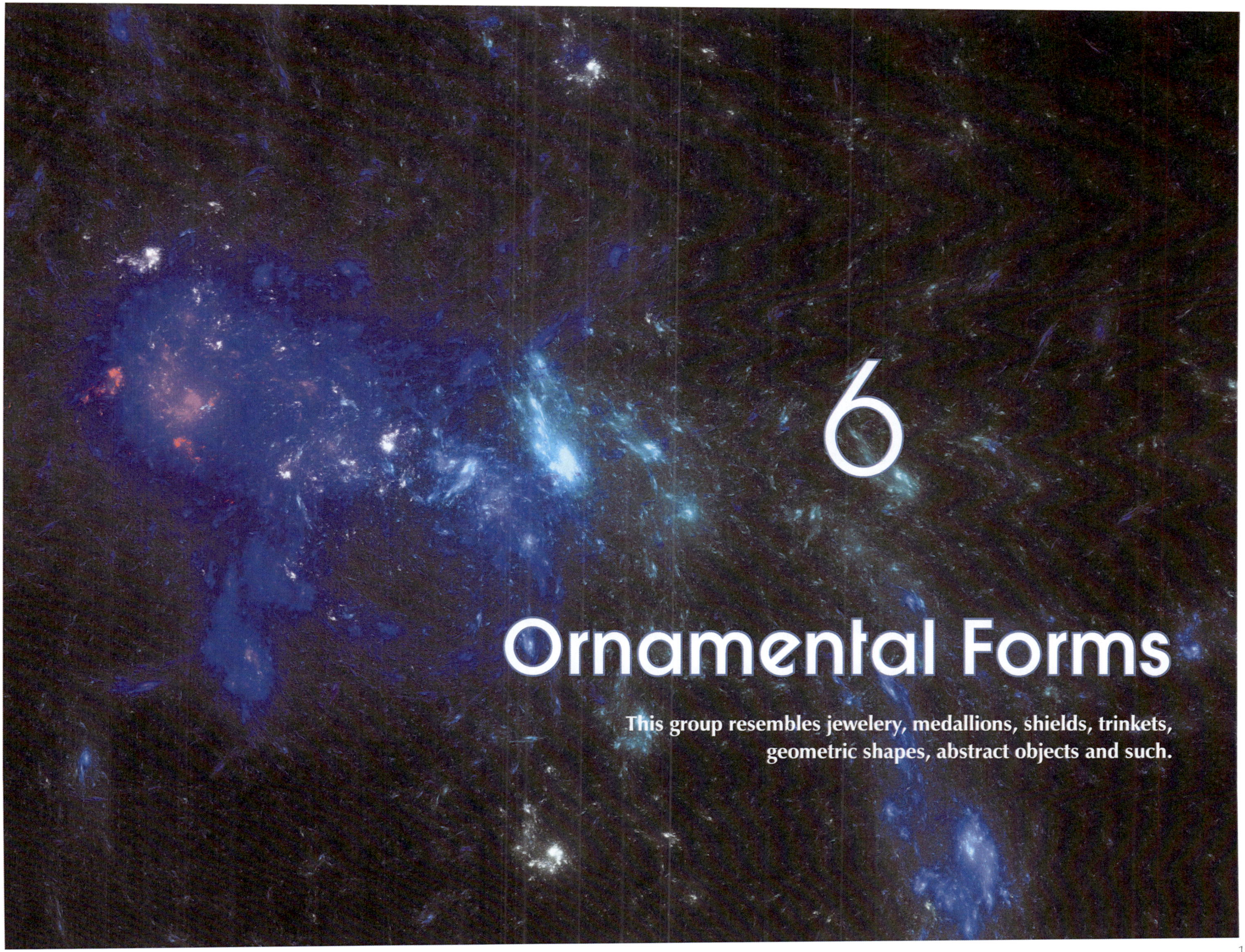

6

Ornamental Forms

This group resembles jewelery, medallions, shields, trinkets, geometric shapes, abstract objects and such.

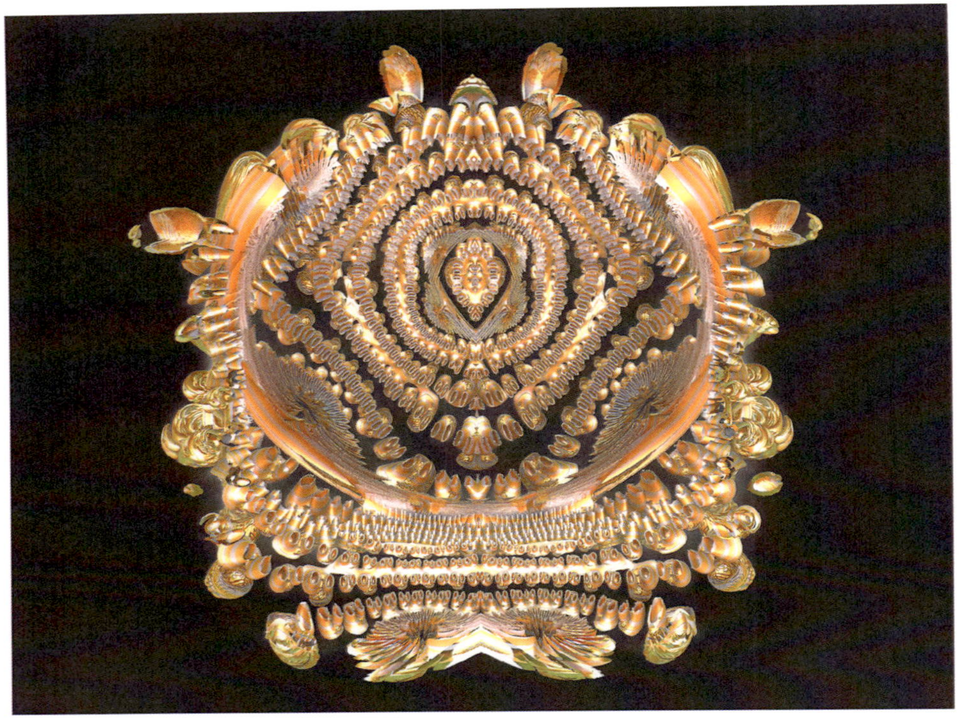

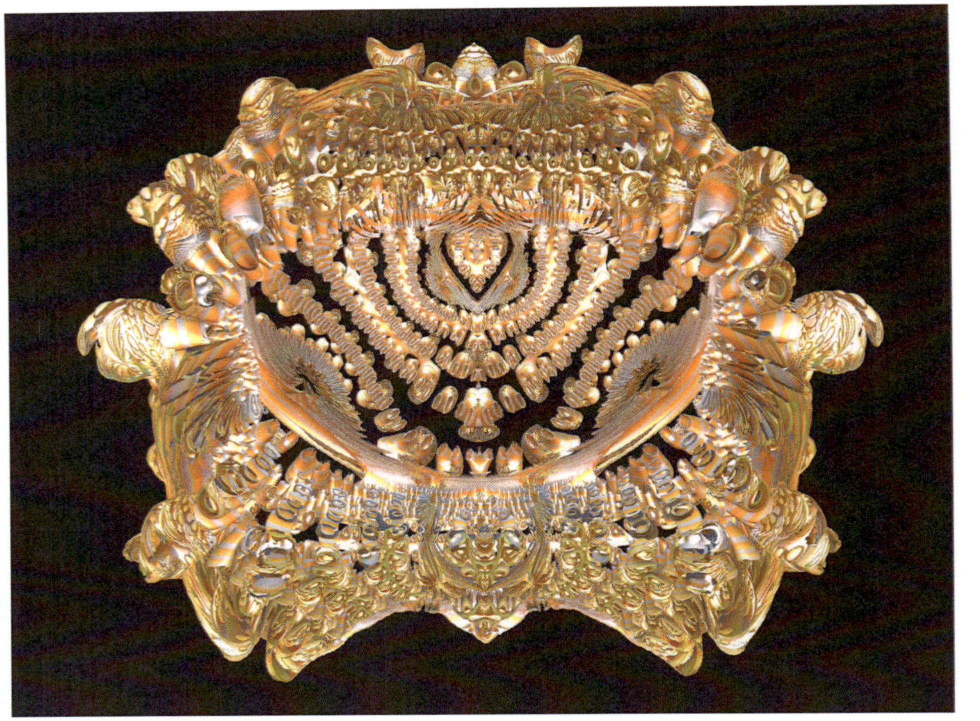

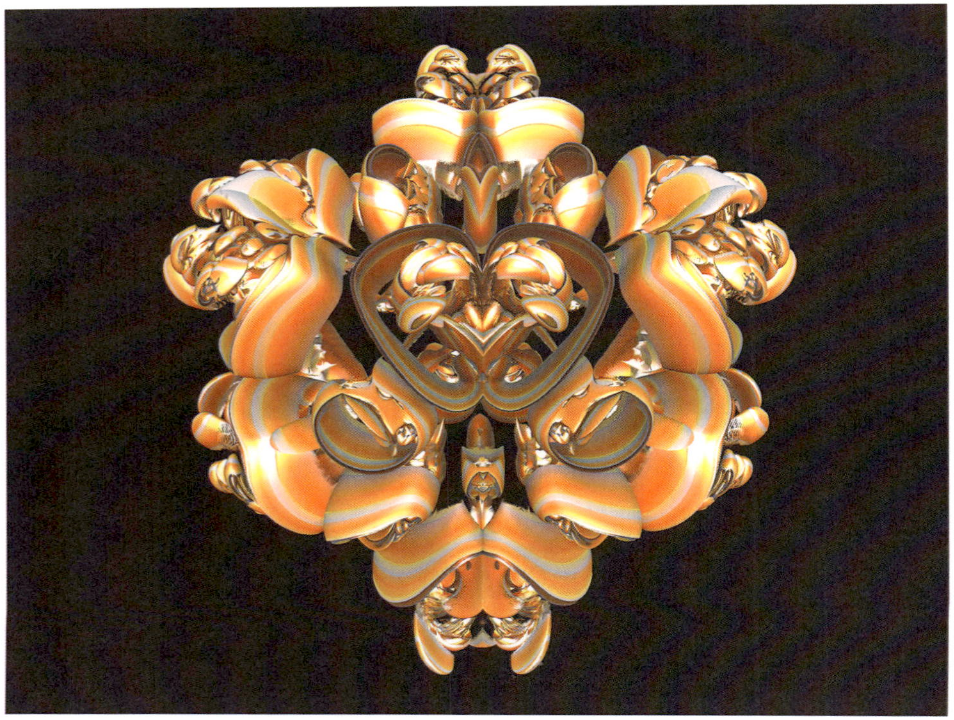

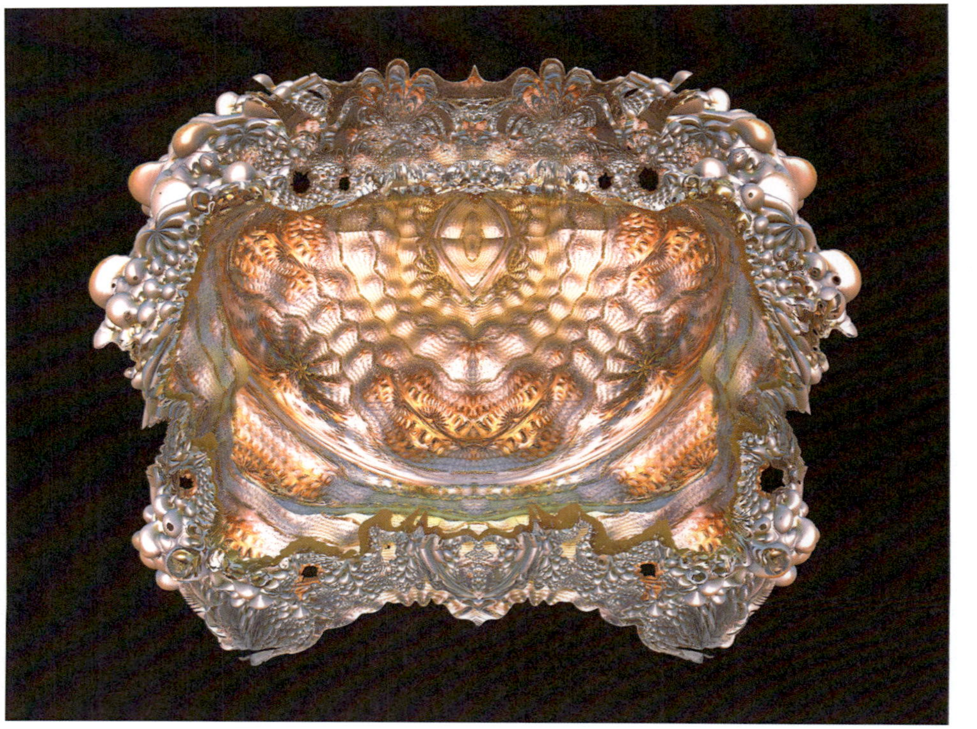

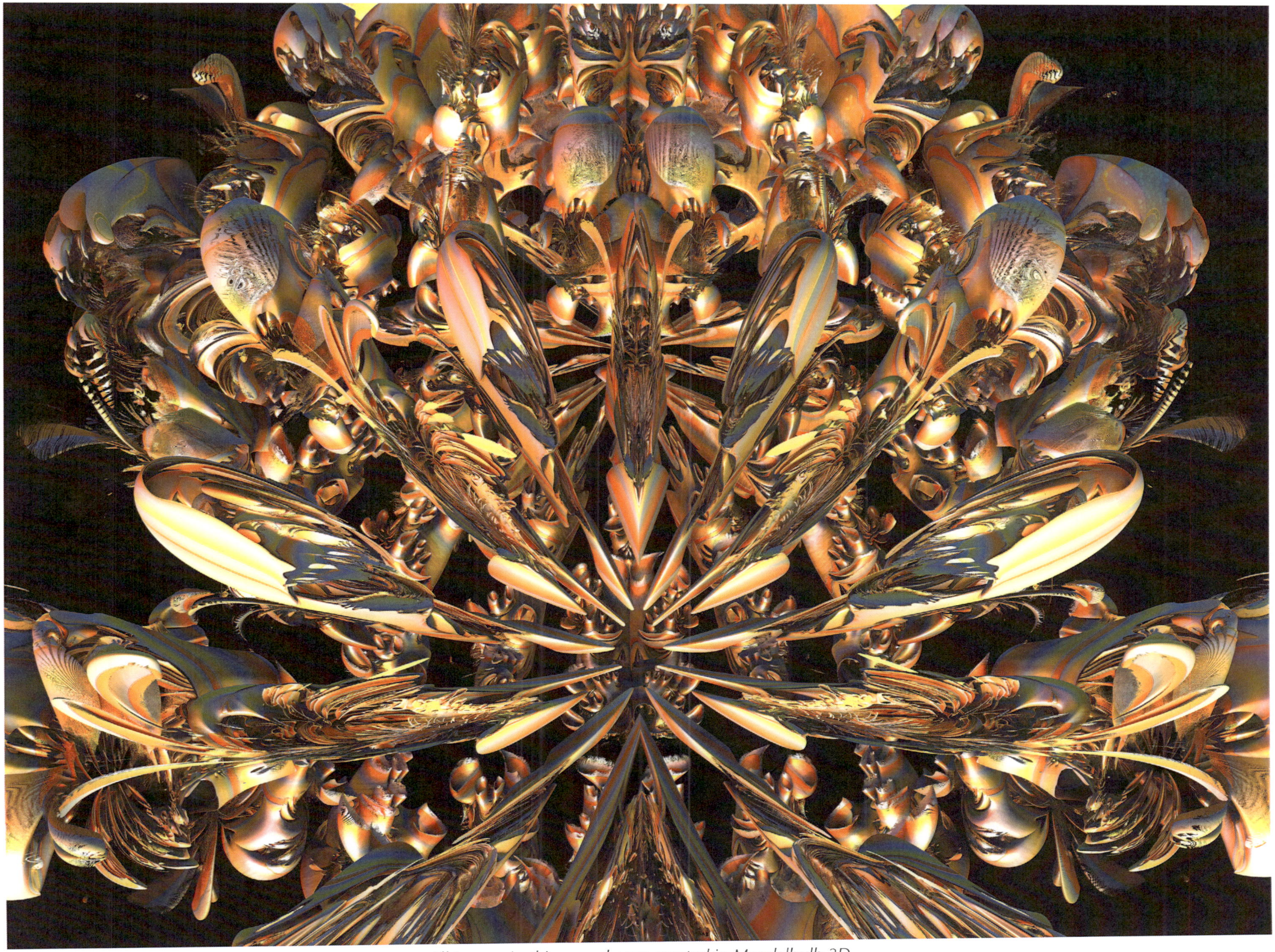

All images in this spread were created in Mandelbulb 3D.

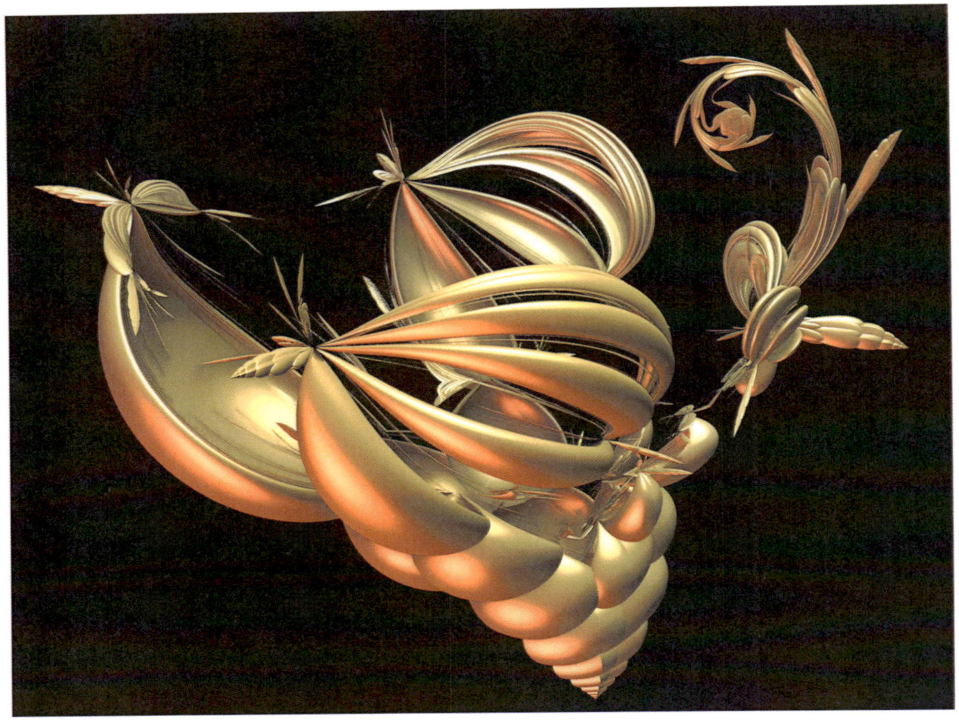
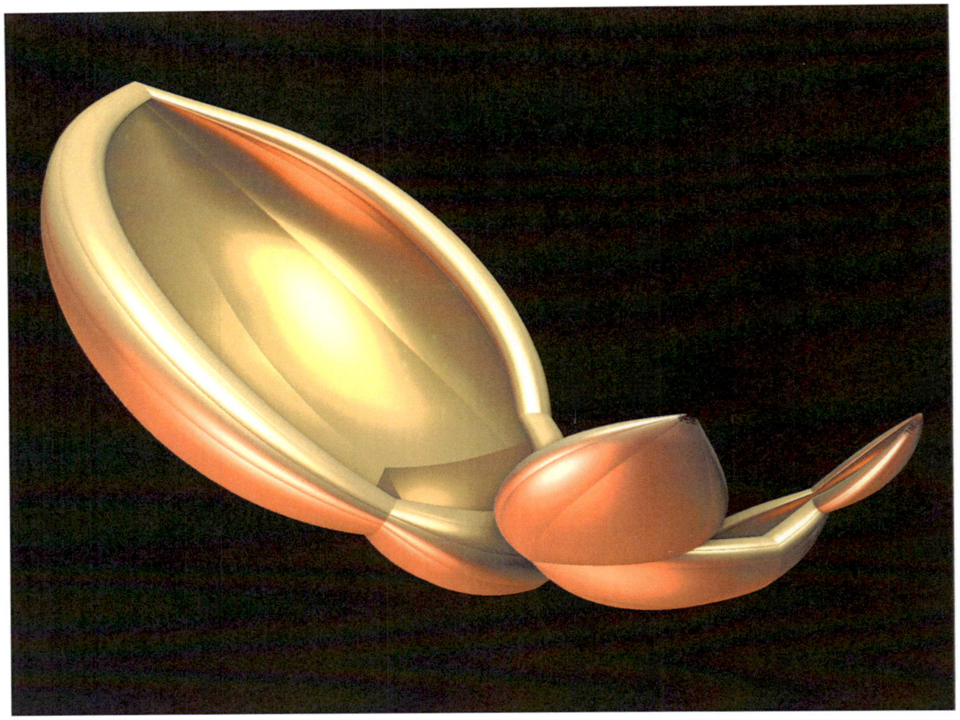
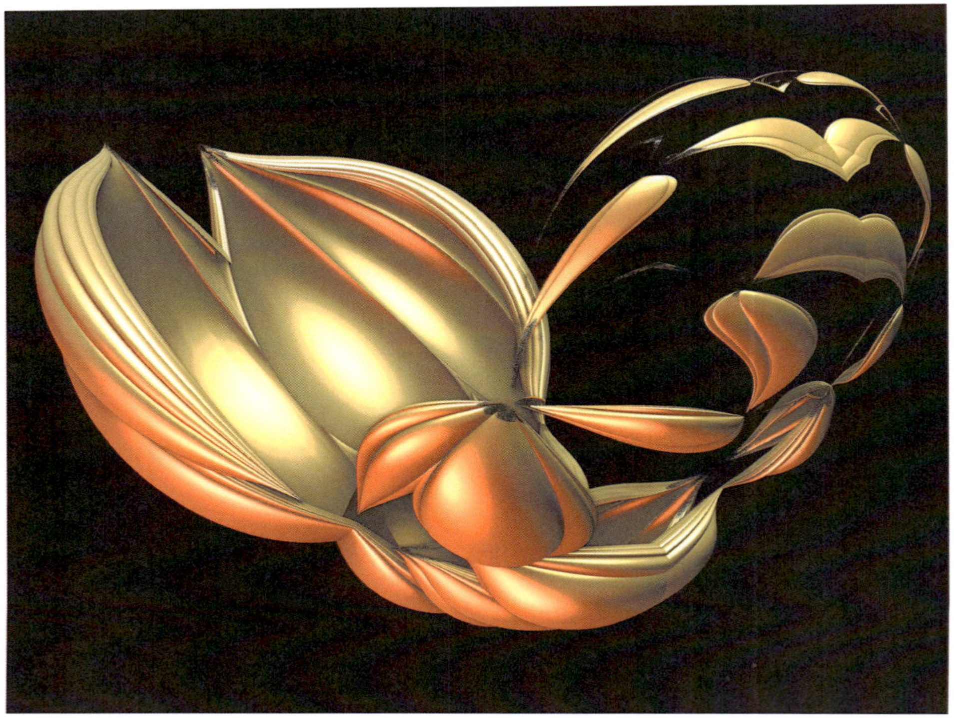
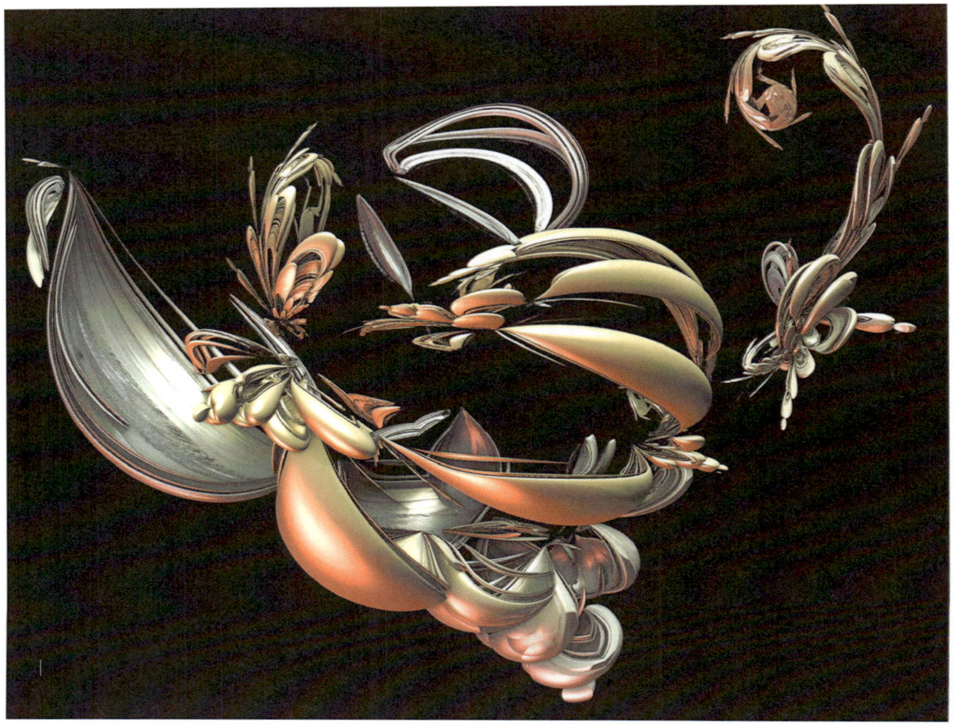

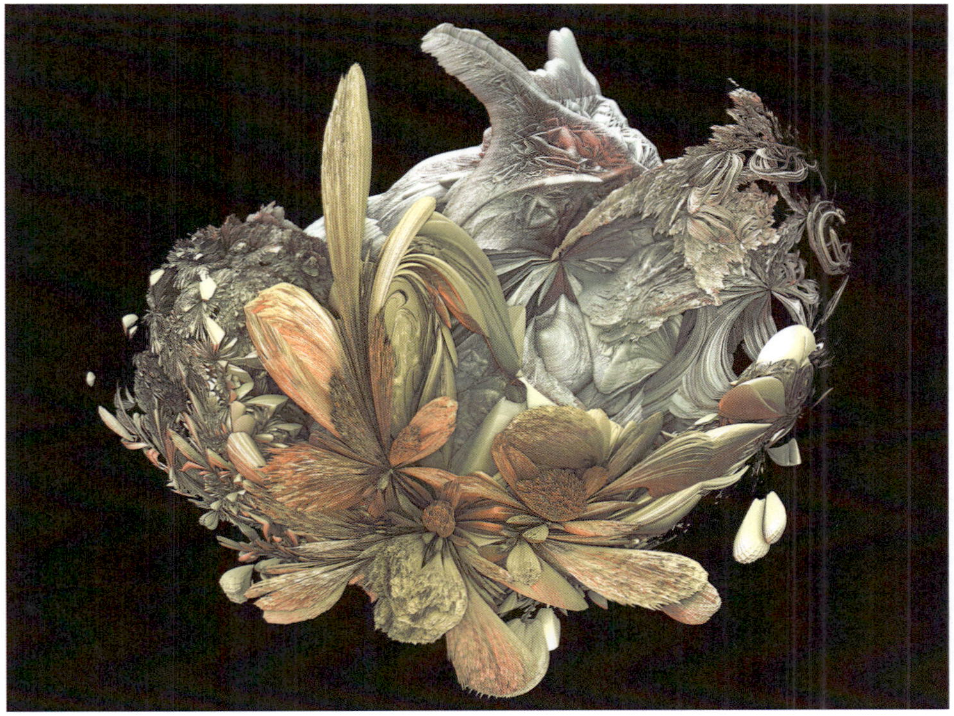

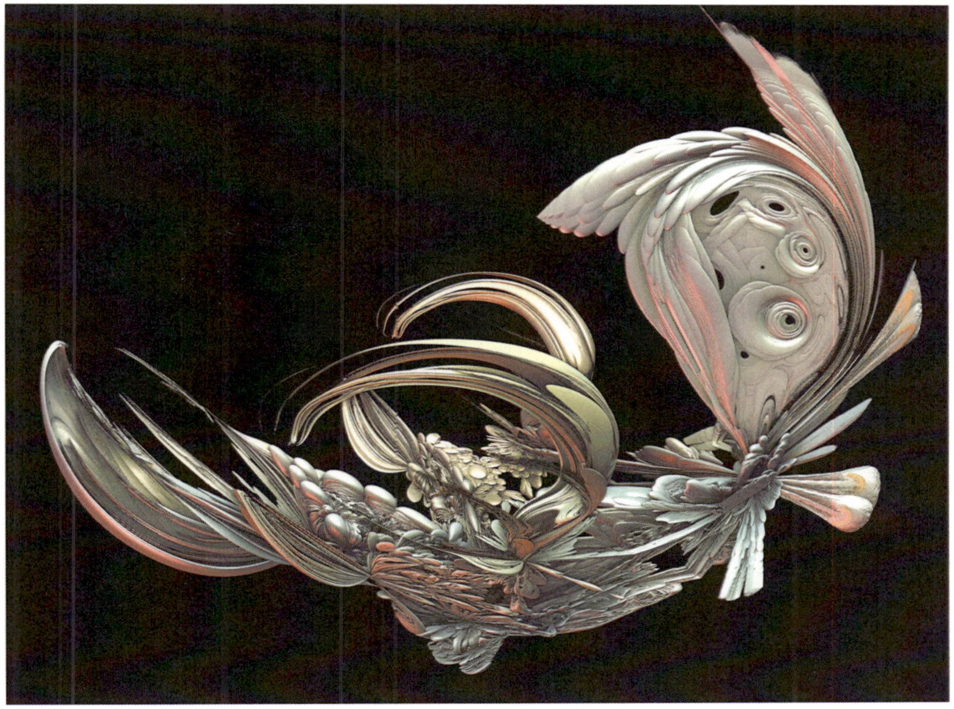

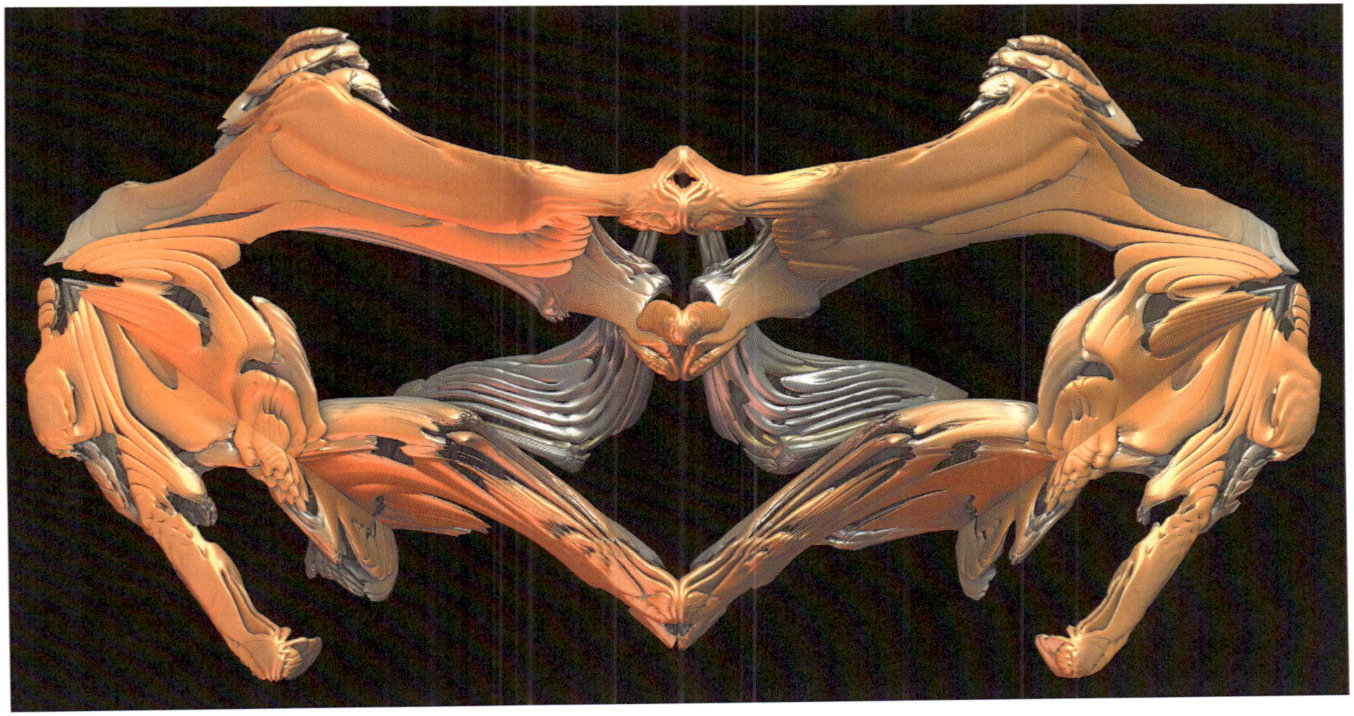

All the images on these two pages were created in Mandelbulb 3D using the "Interpolate mode," except for the image to the ***immediate left,*** *which was extracted from a larger fractal.*

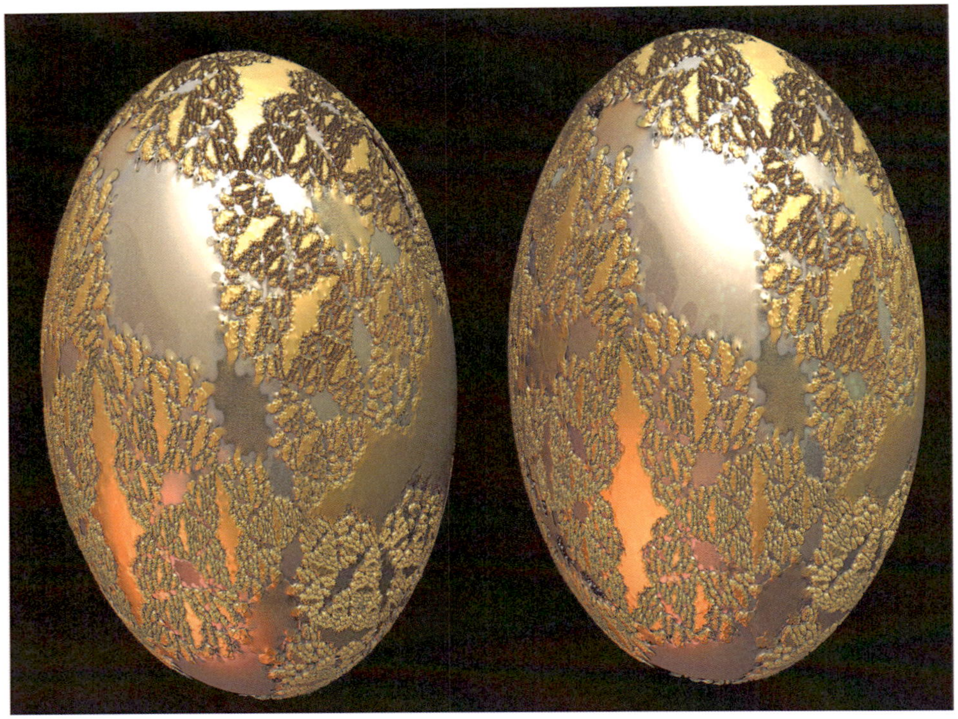

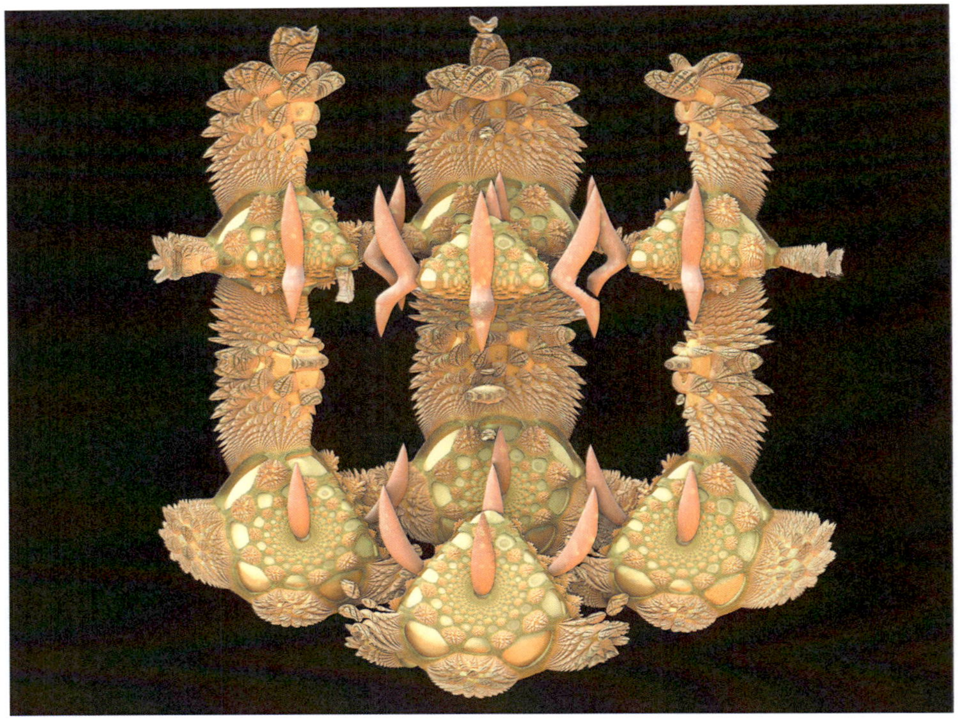

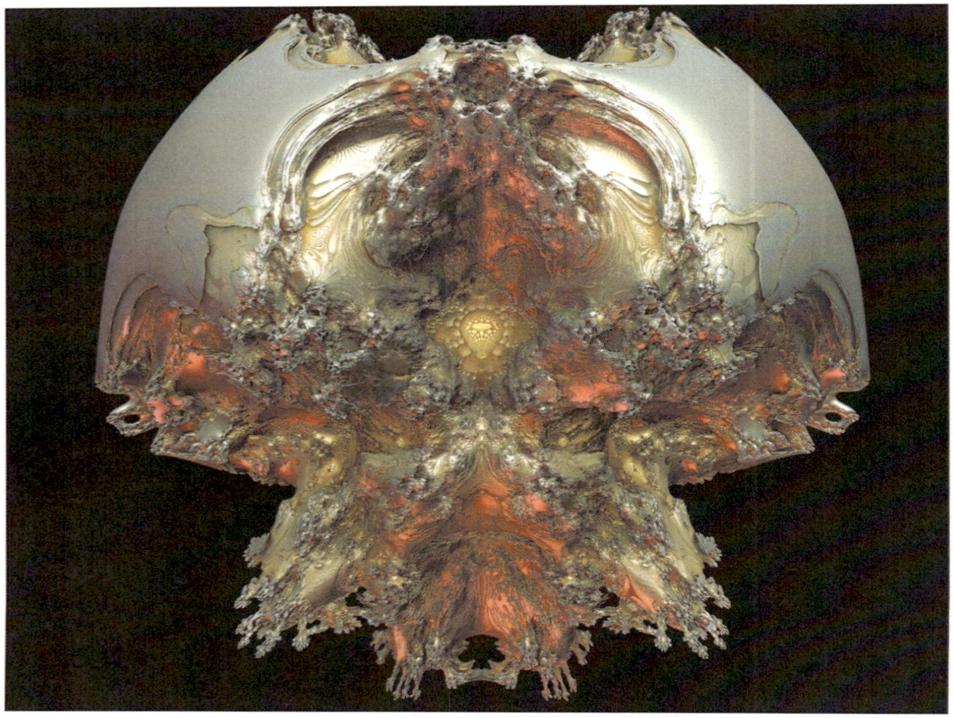

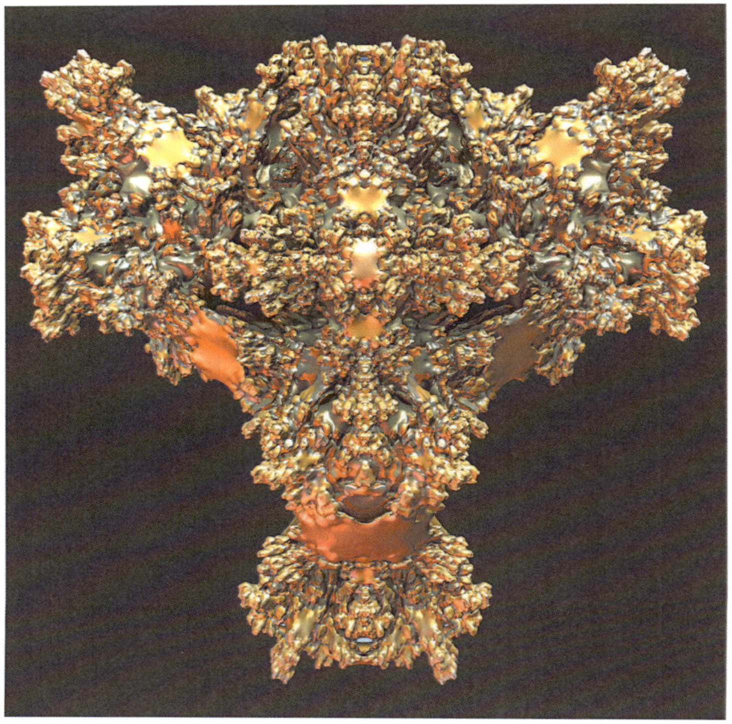

All of the images on these two pages and the following pages were created in Mandelbulb 3D.

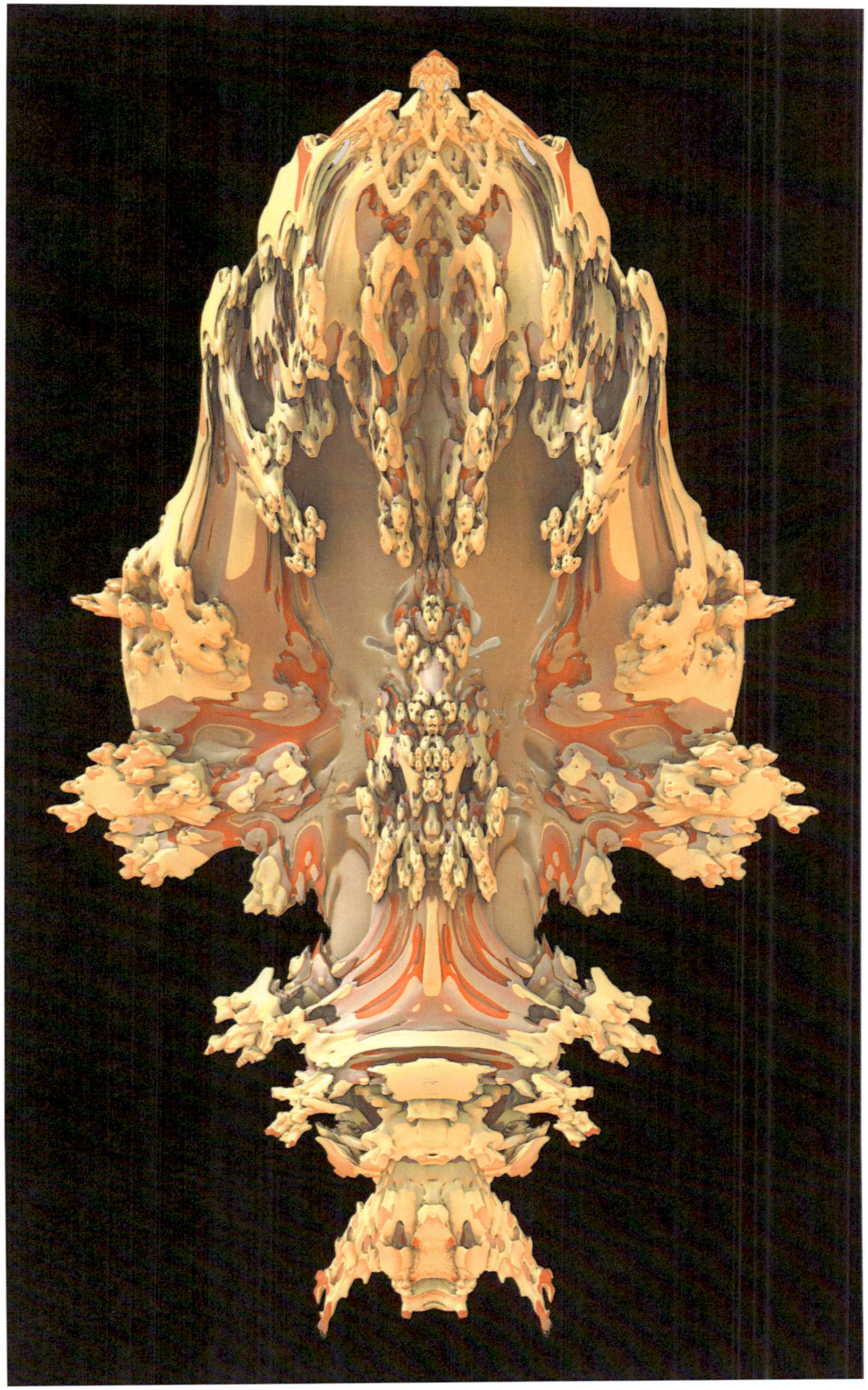

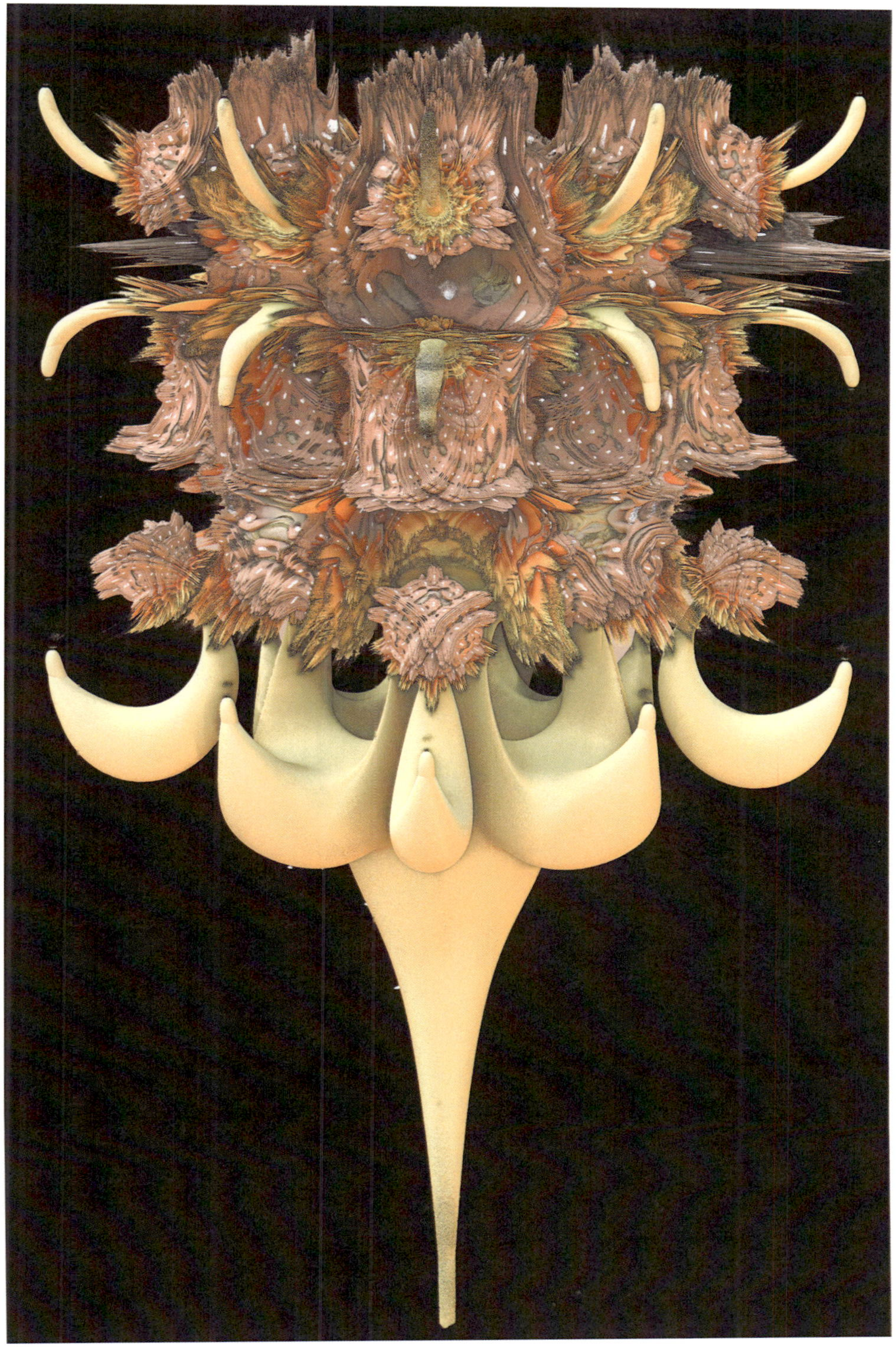

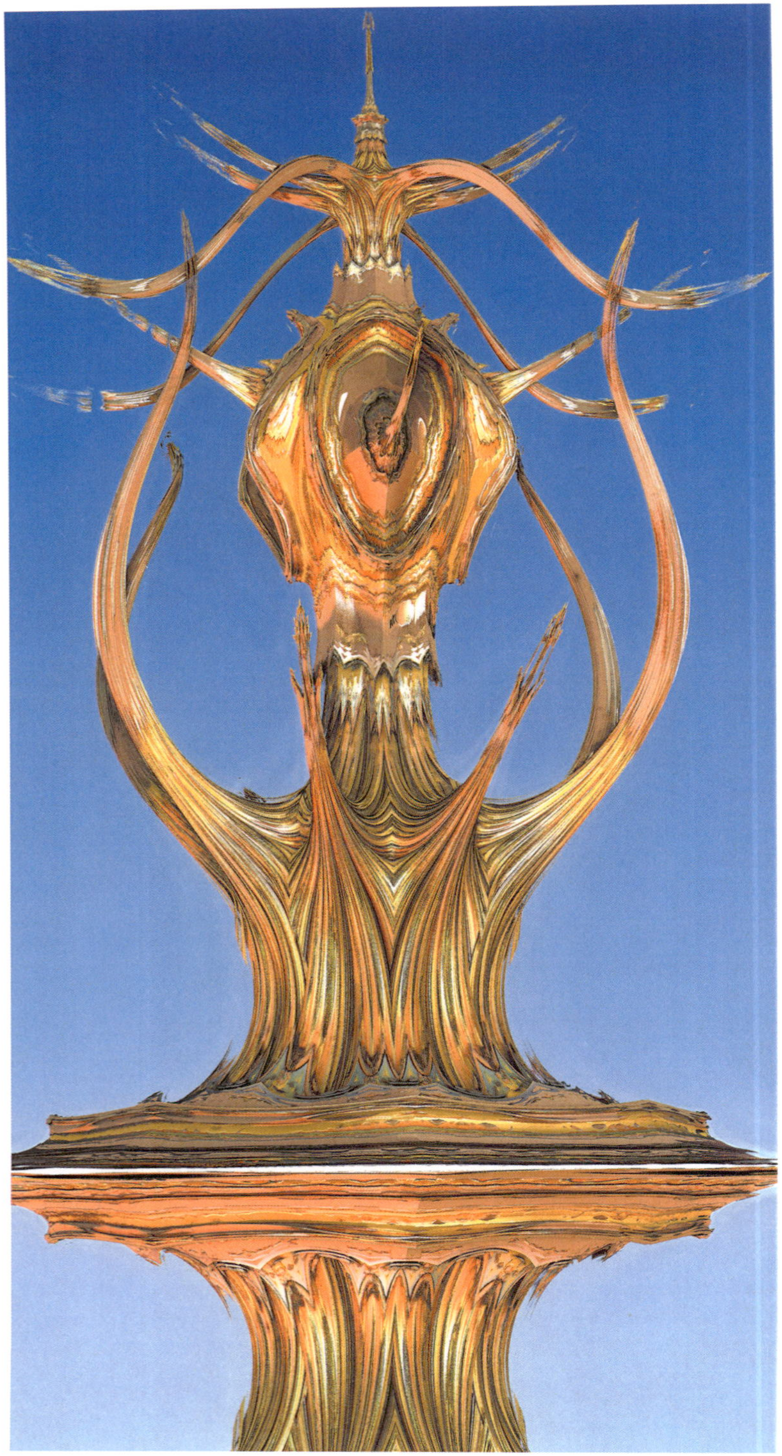

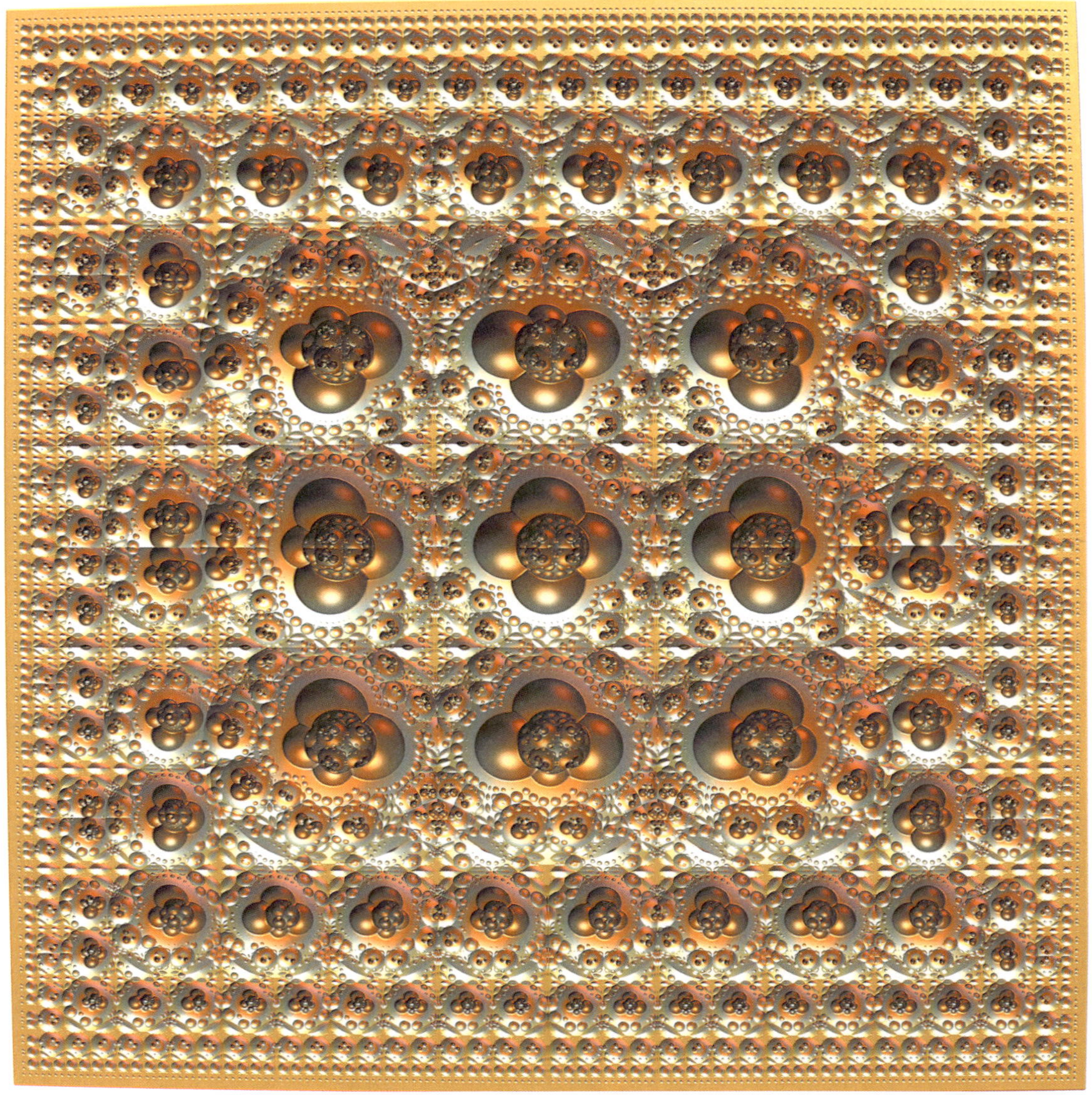

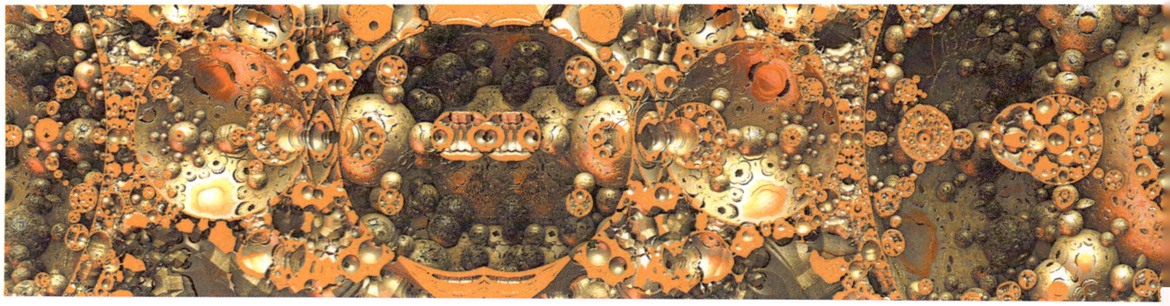

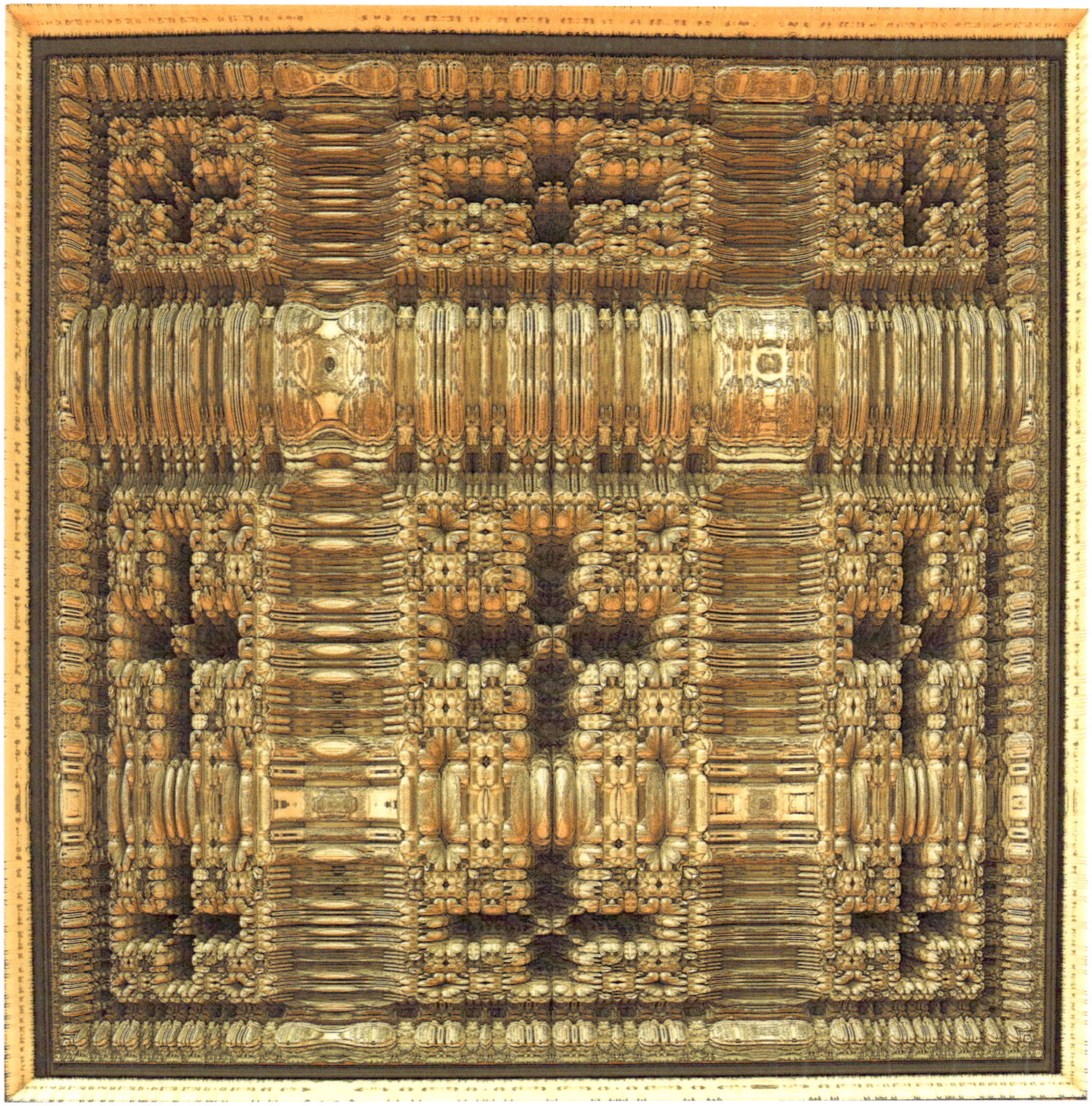

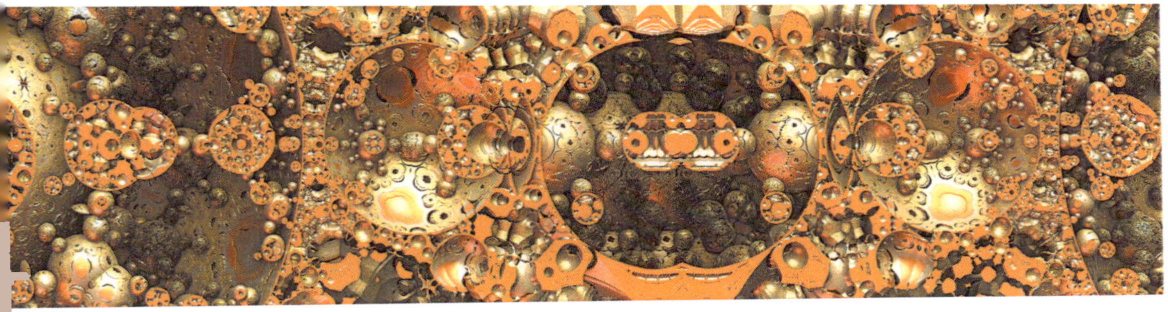

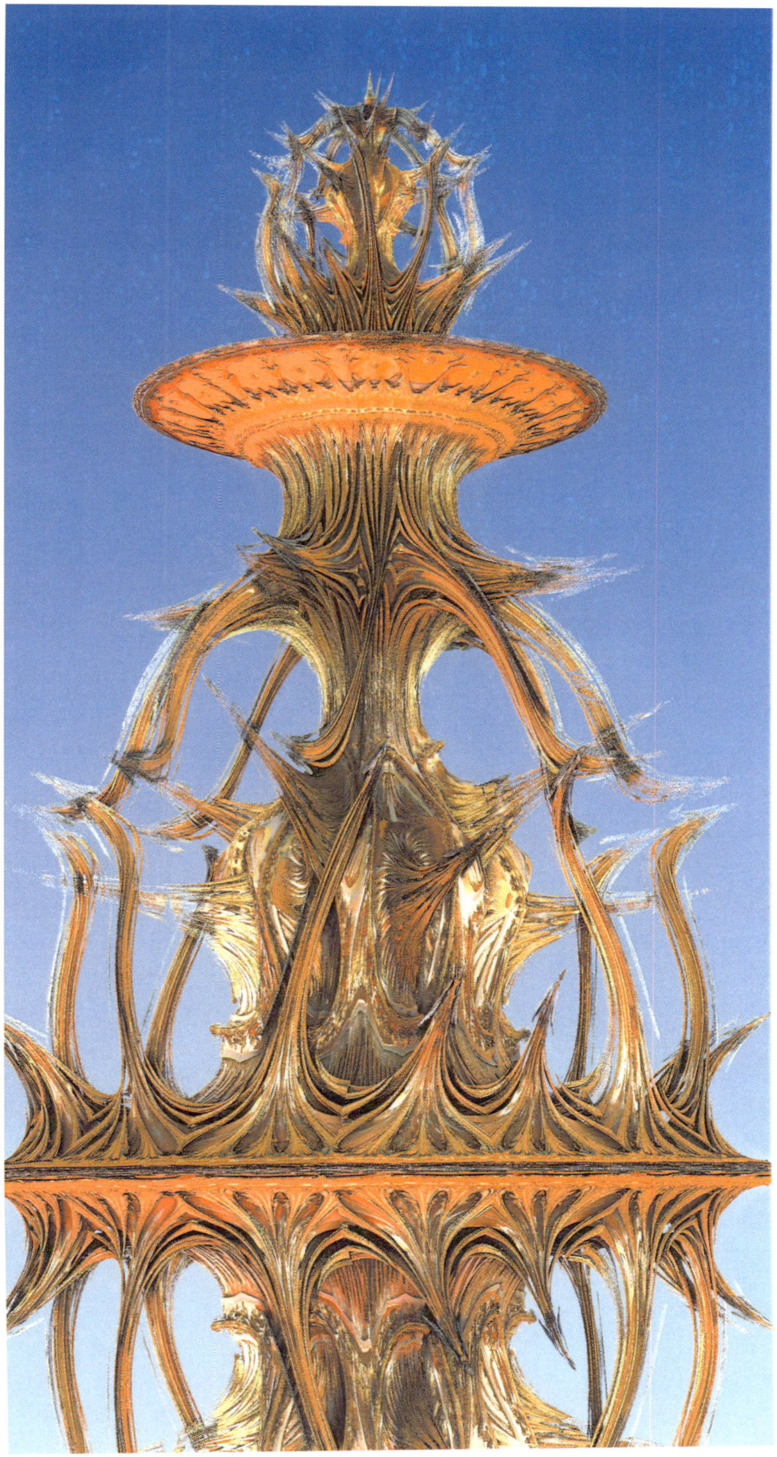

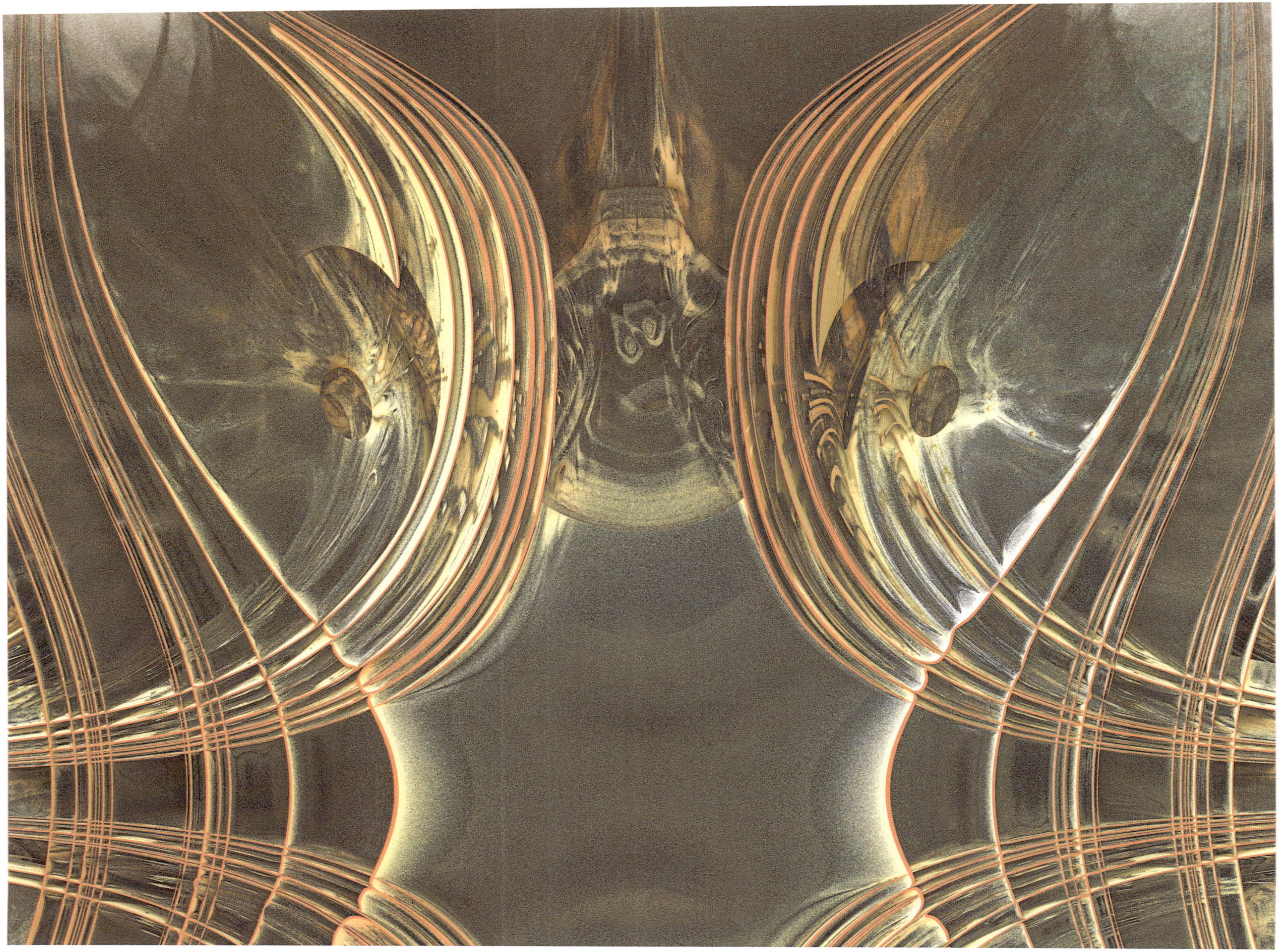

This fractal image was generated by Mandelbulb 3D.

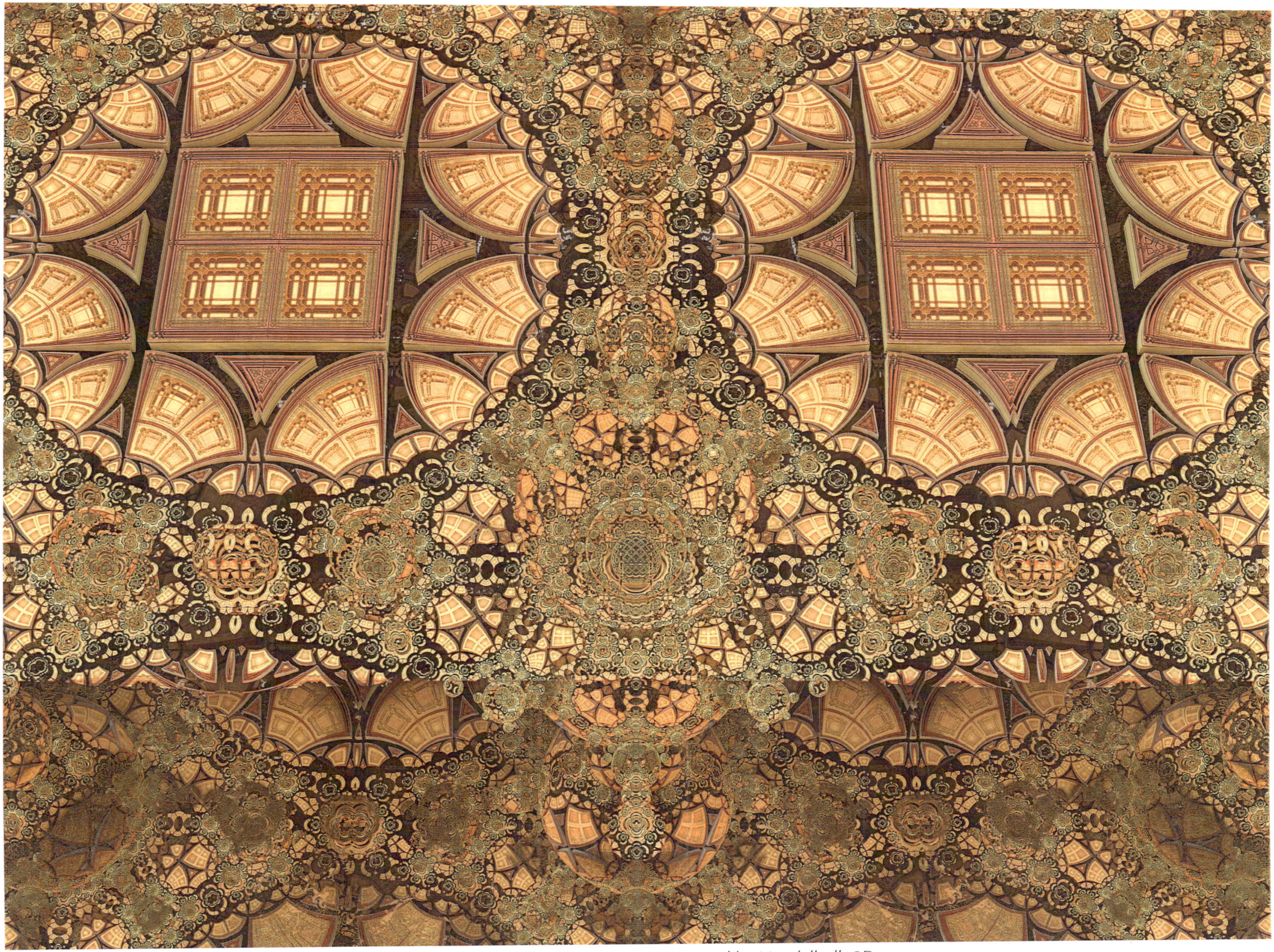

This geometrical fractal image was generated by Mandelbulb 3D.

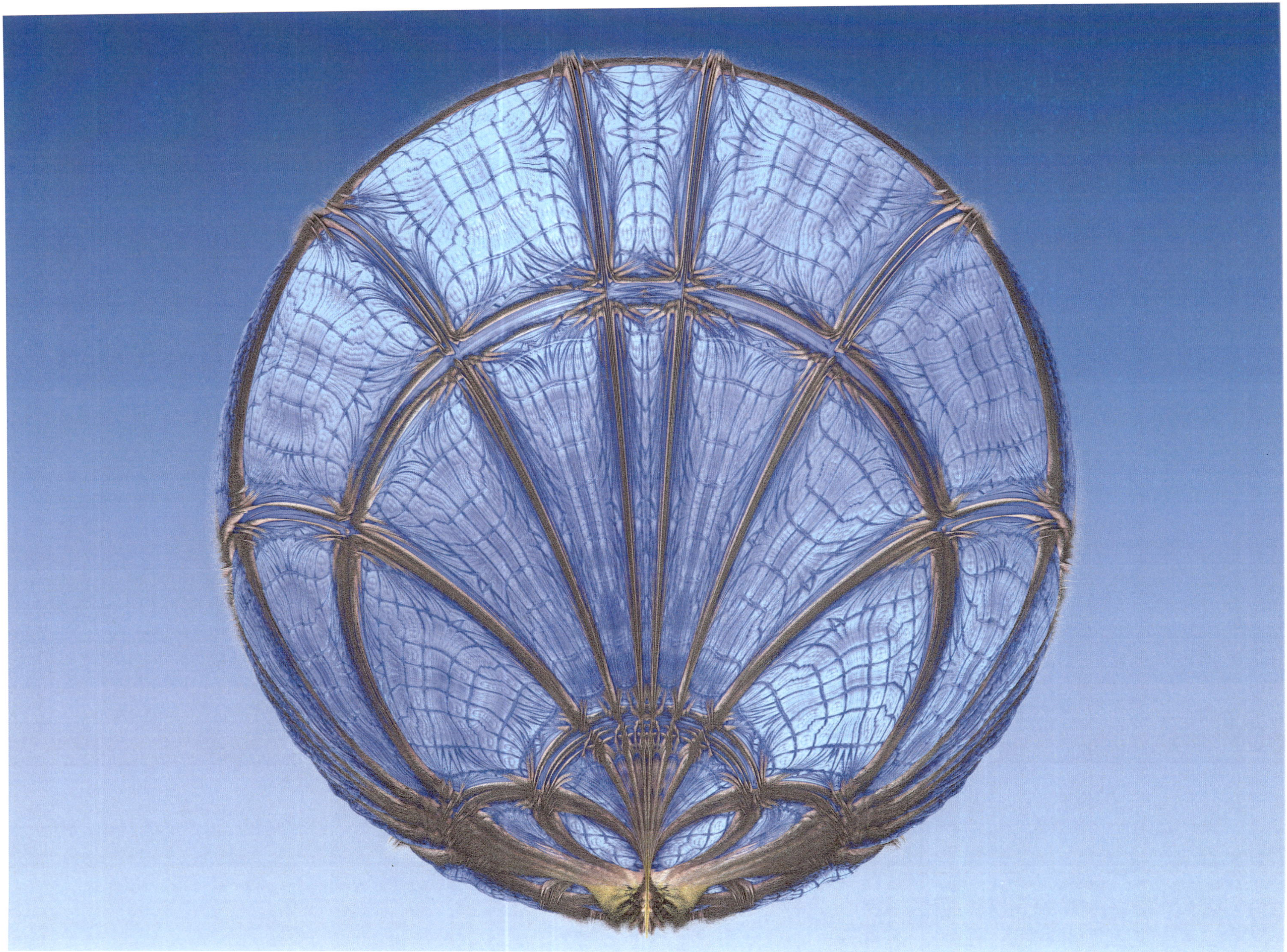

This shell-like fractal image was generated by Mandelbulb 3D.

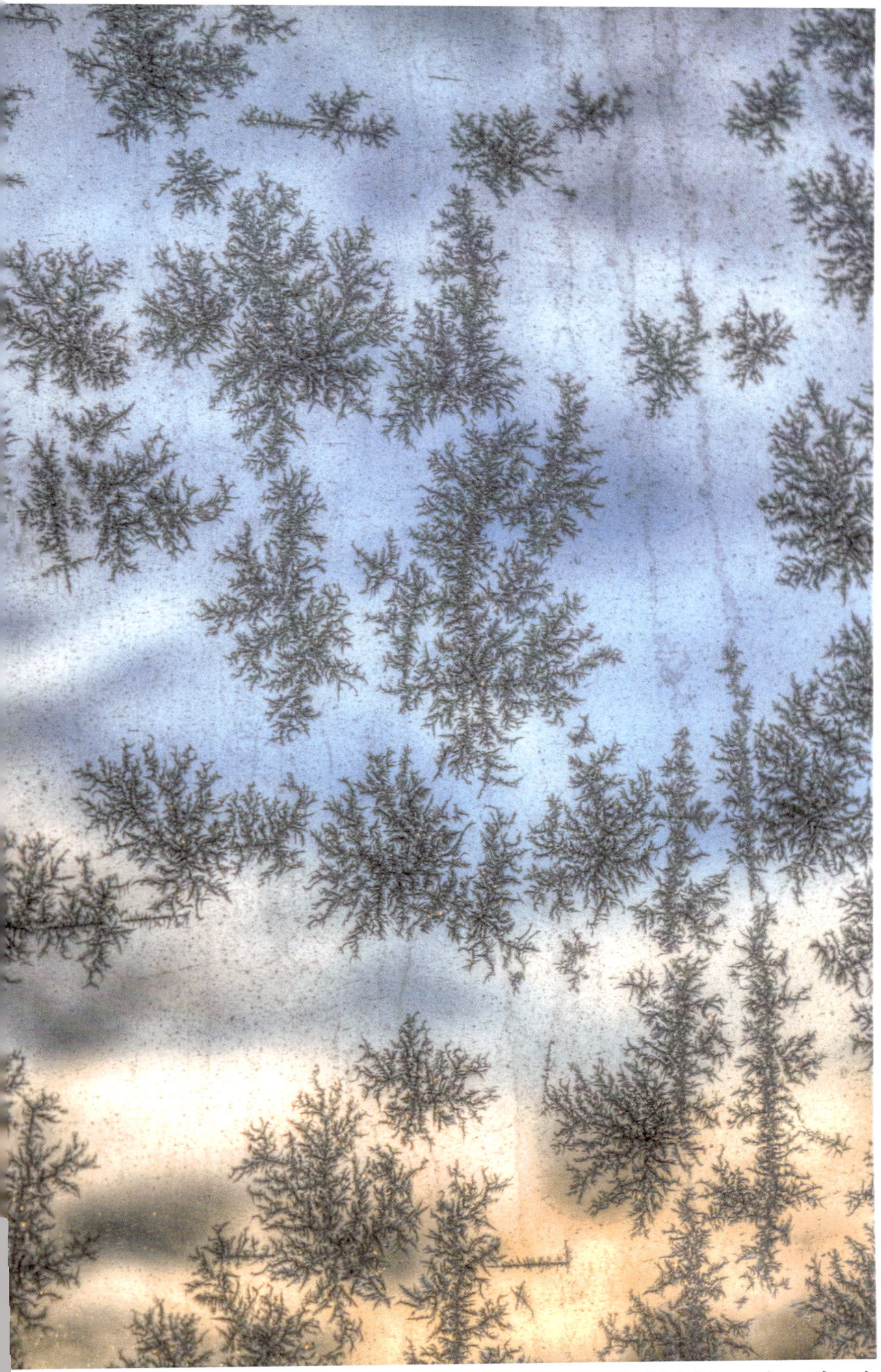

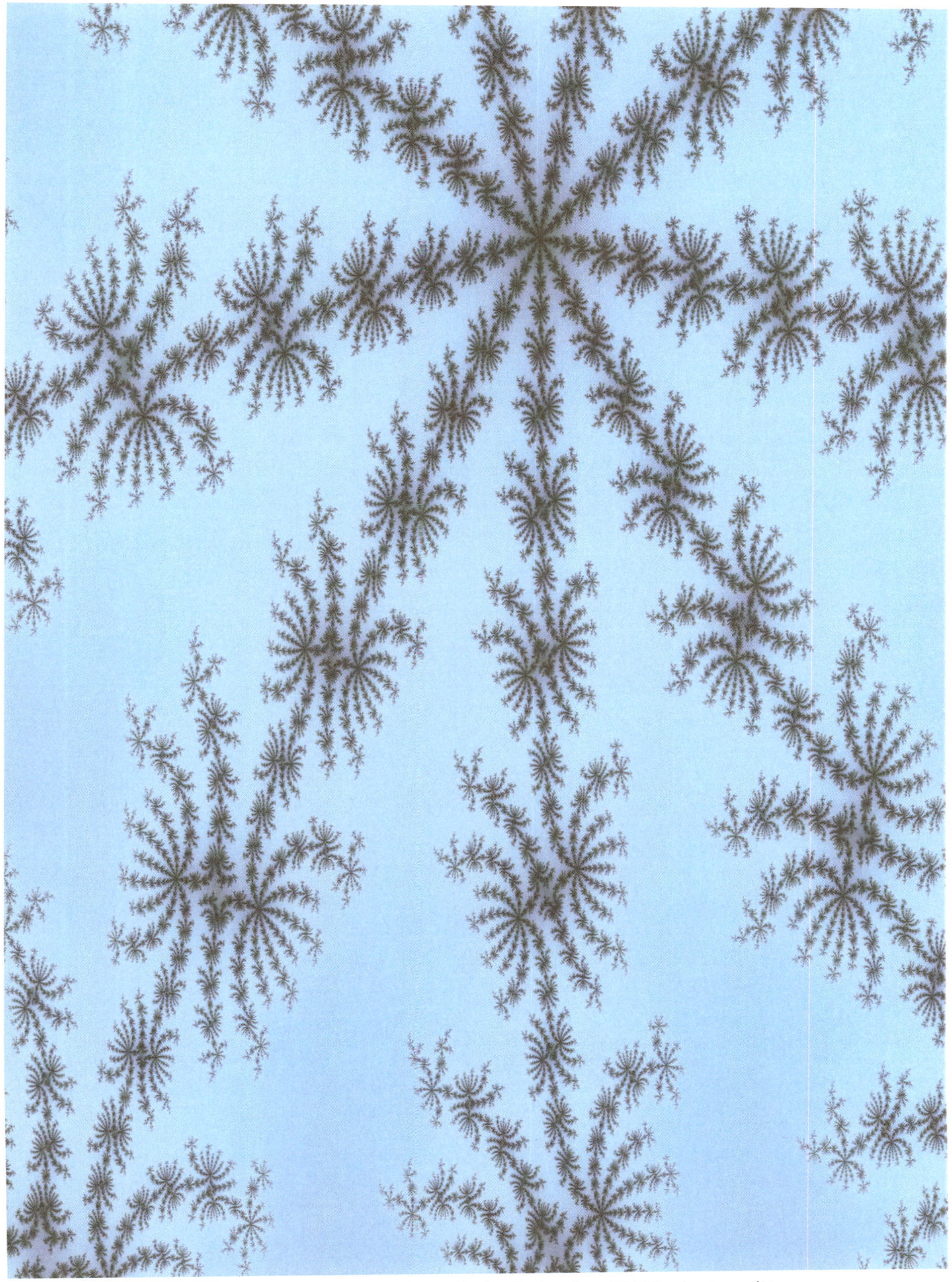

On the left, *digital photo of frost on a windshield; and* ***on the right*** *is the "snowflake" fractal rendered in a fractal plugin in the GiMP photo editor.*

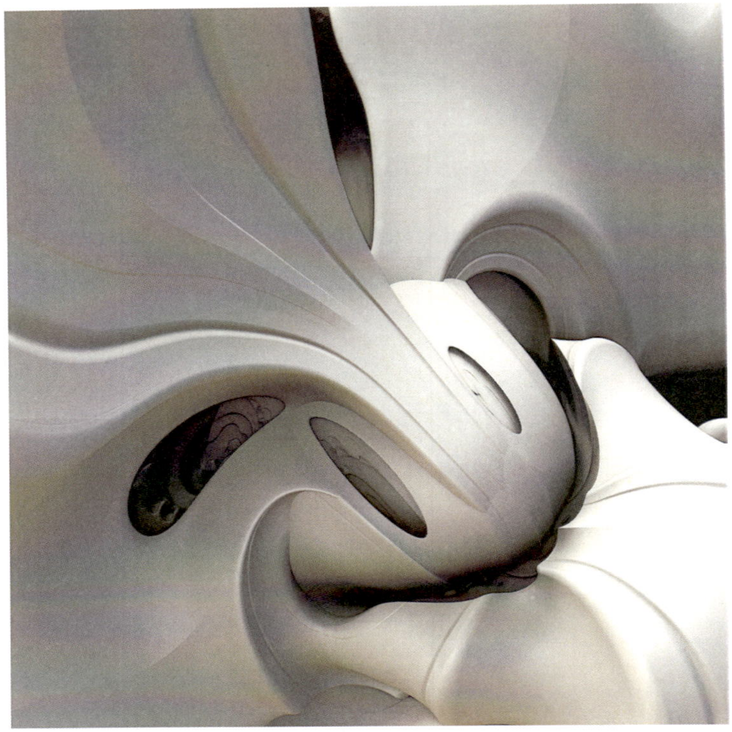

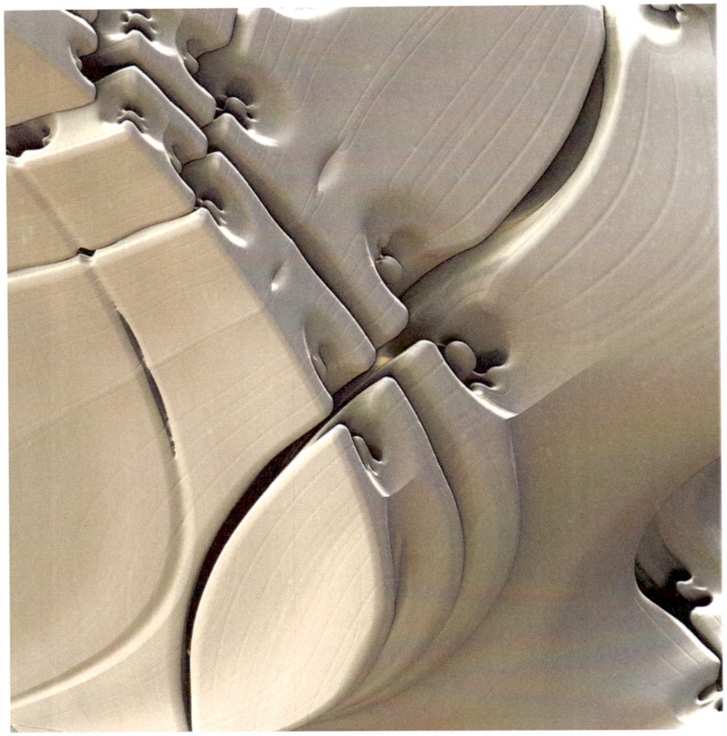

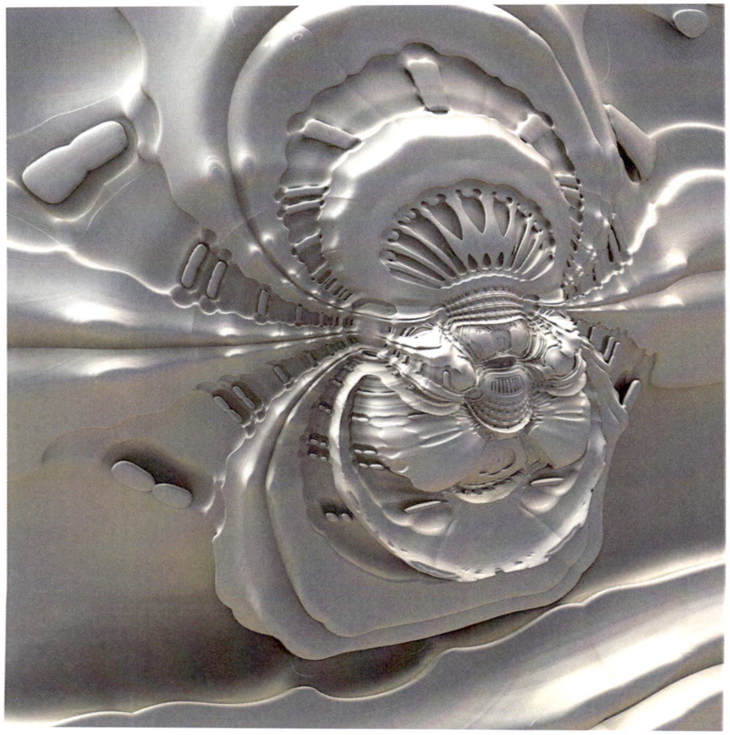

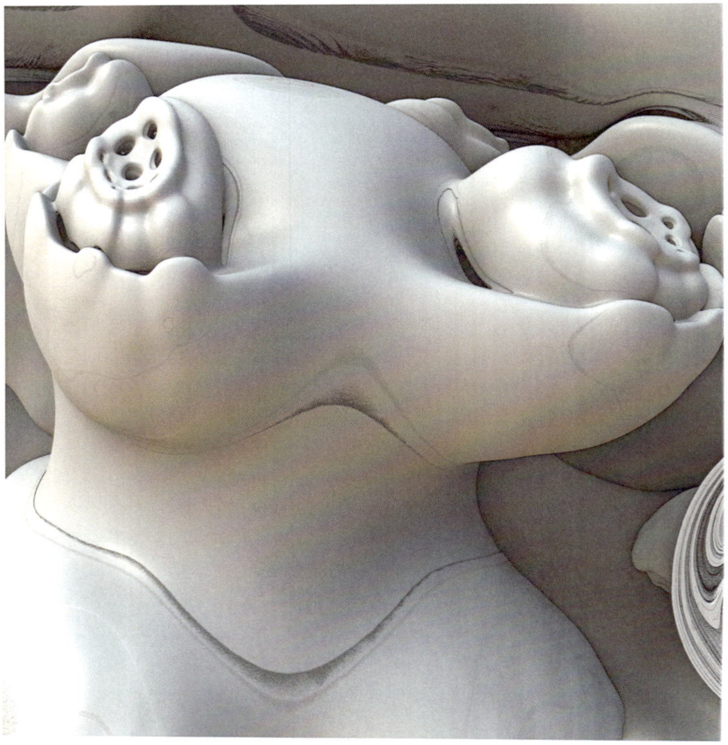

Both pages in this spread: *"Series of abstract shapes" rendered in Mandelbulb 3D. More abstract images follow on the next two pages.*

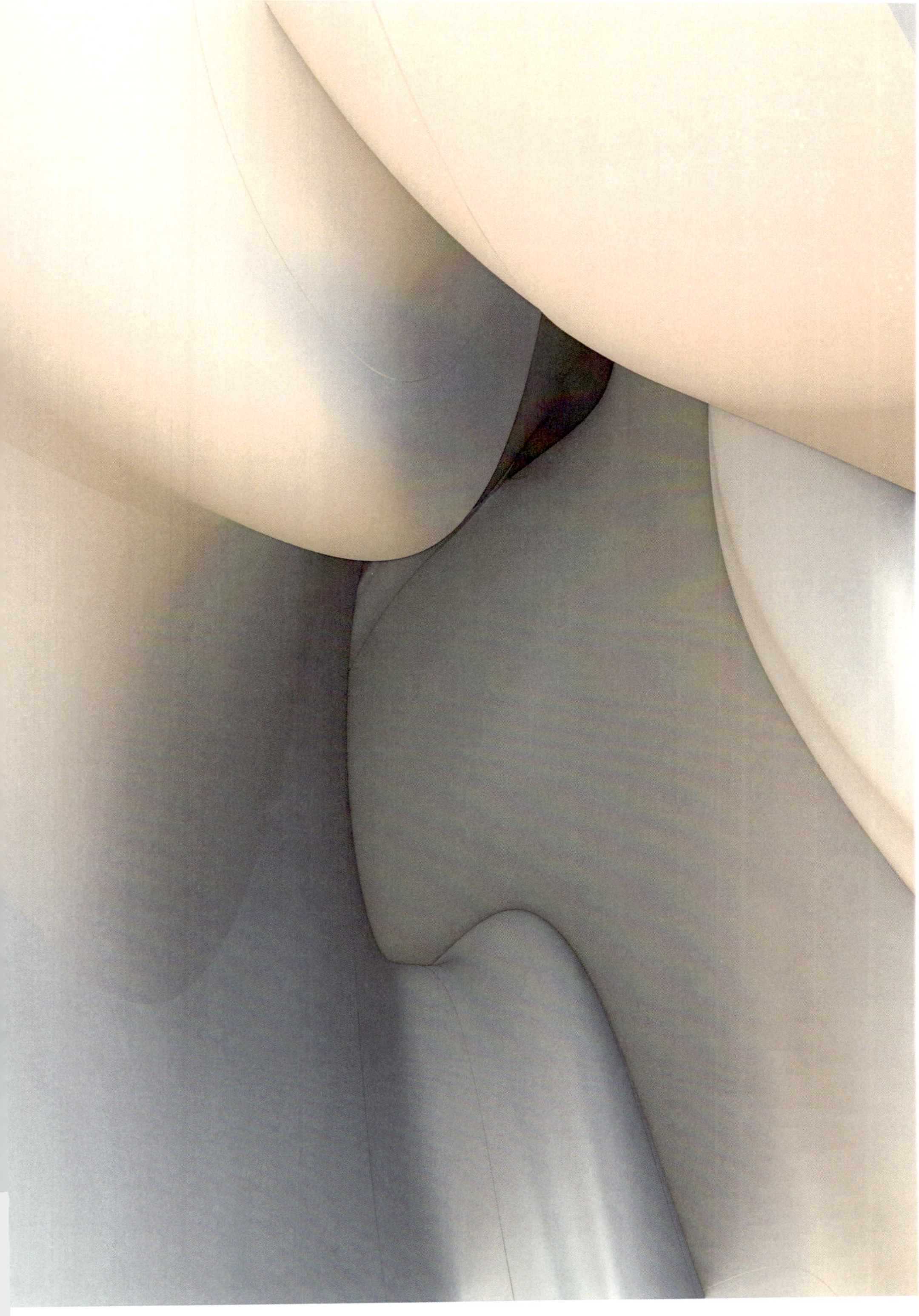

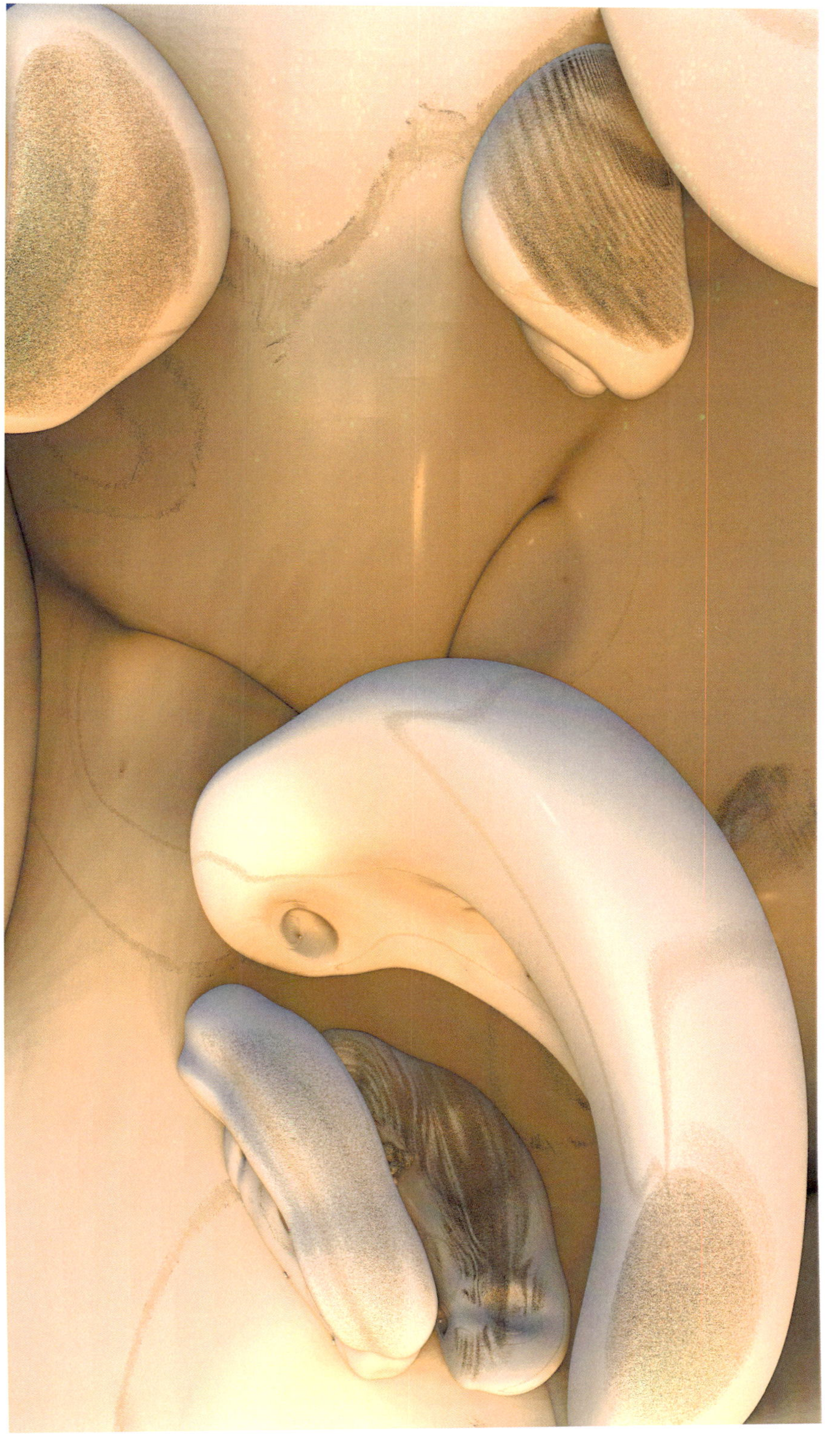

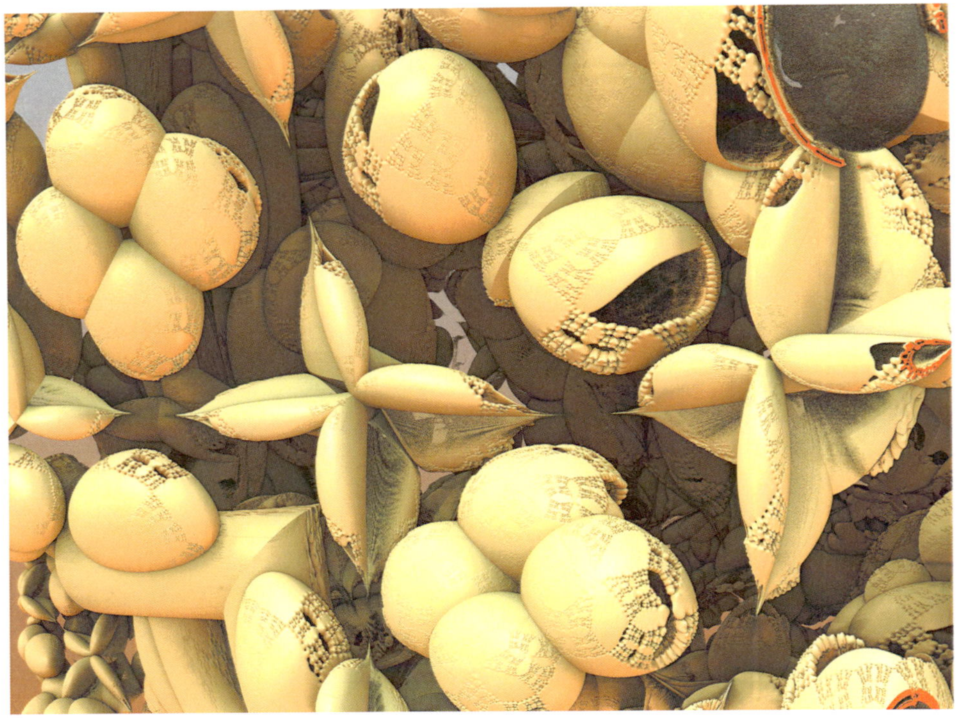
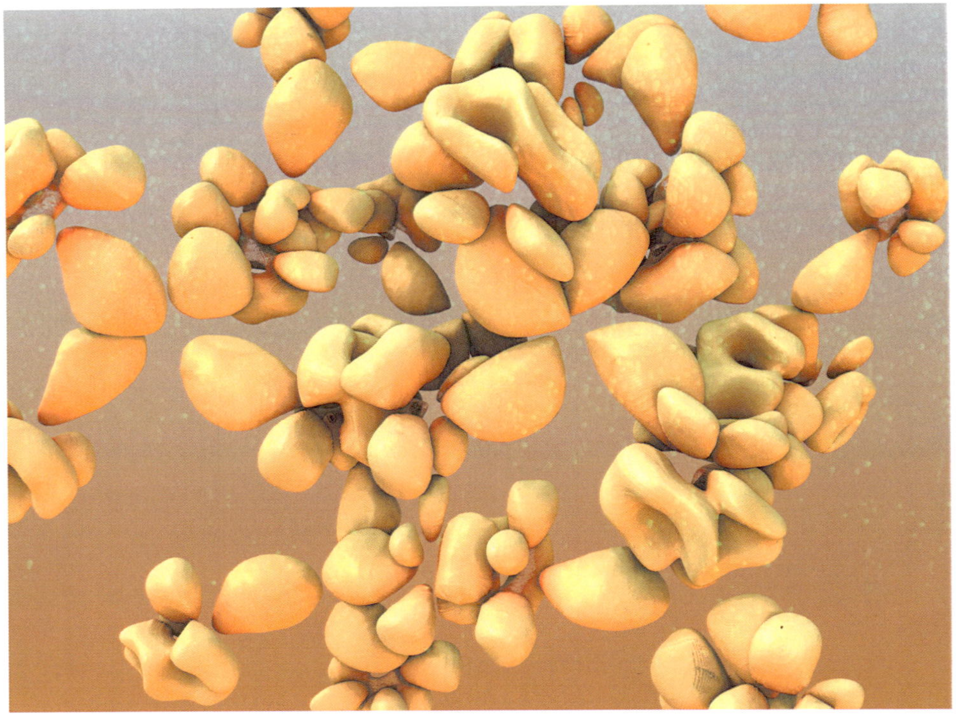
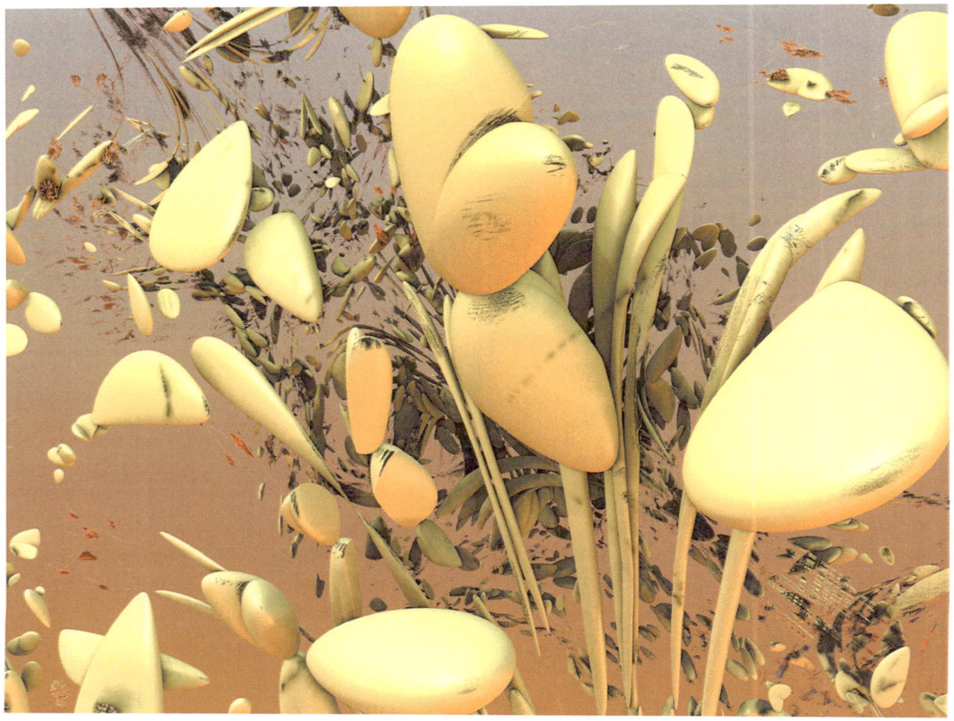
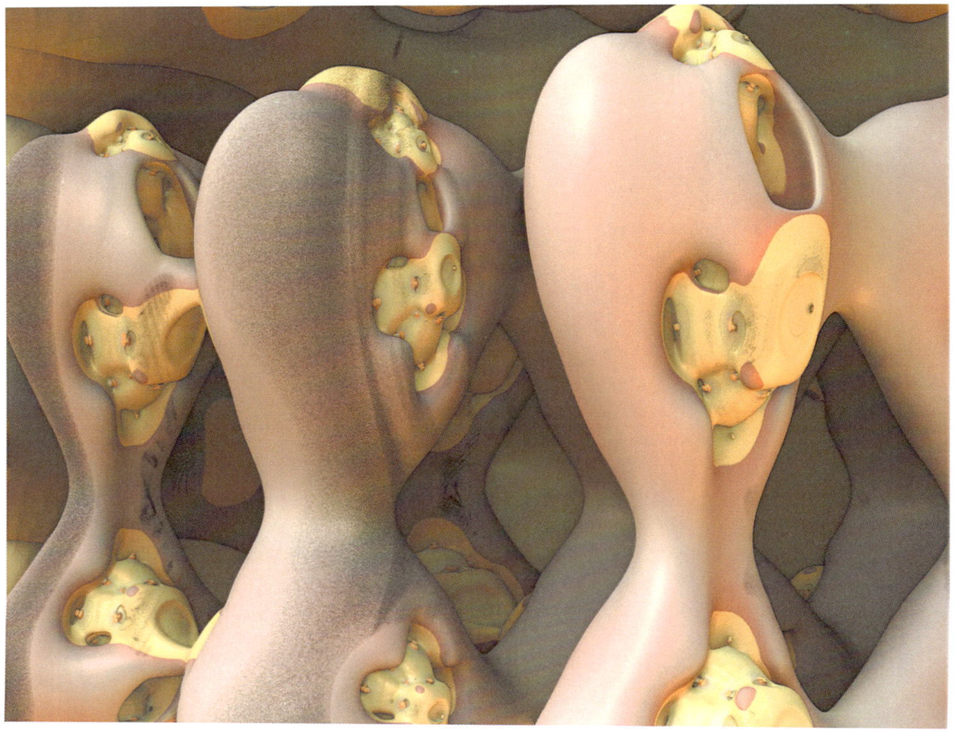

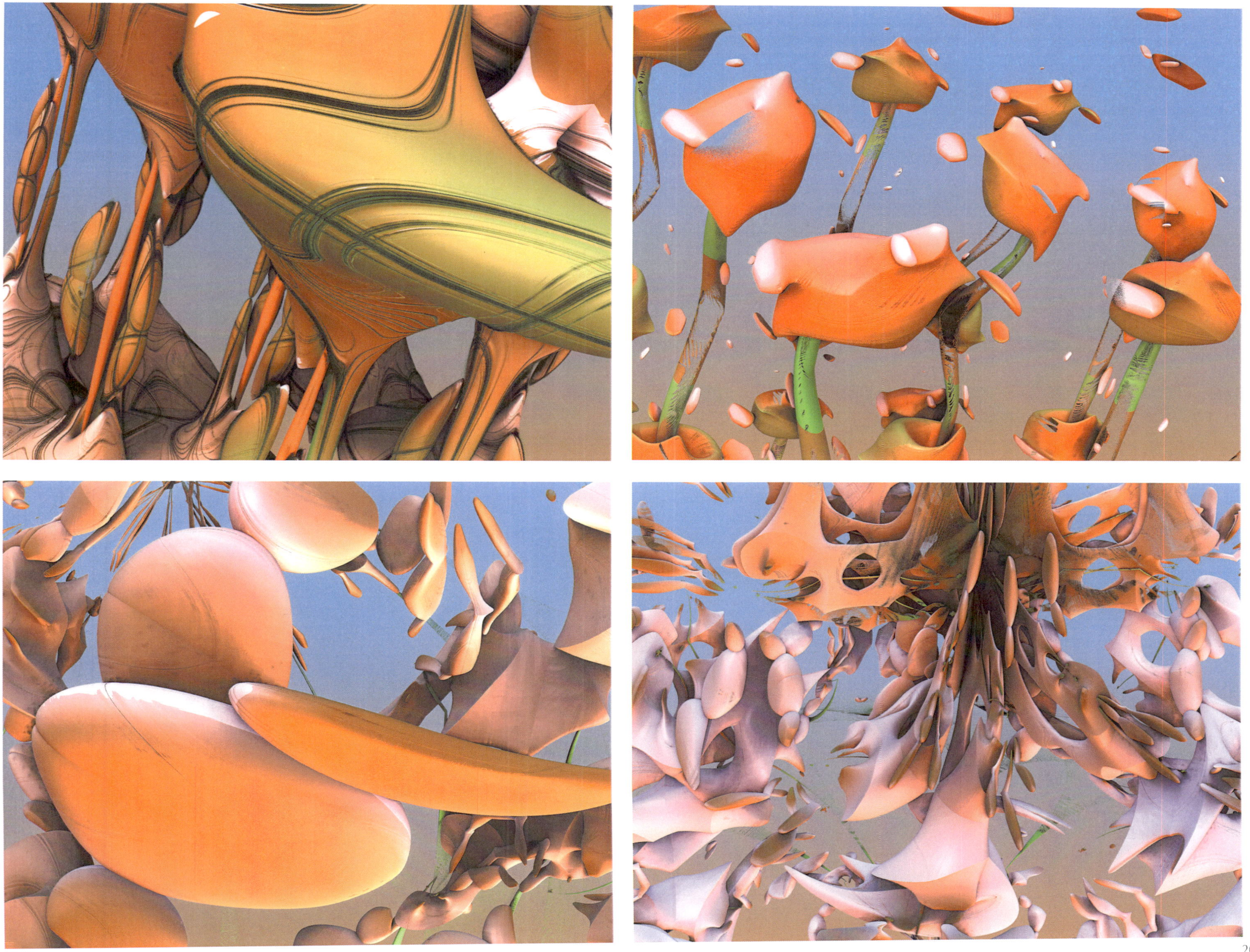

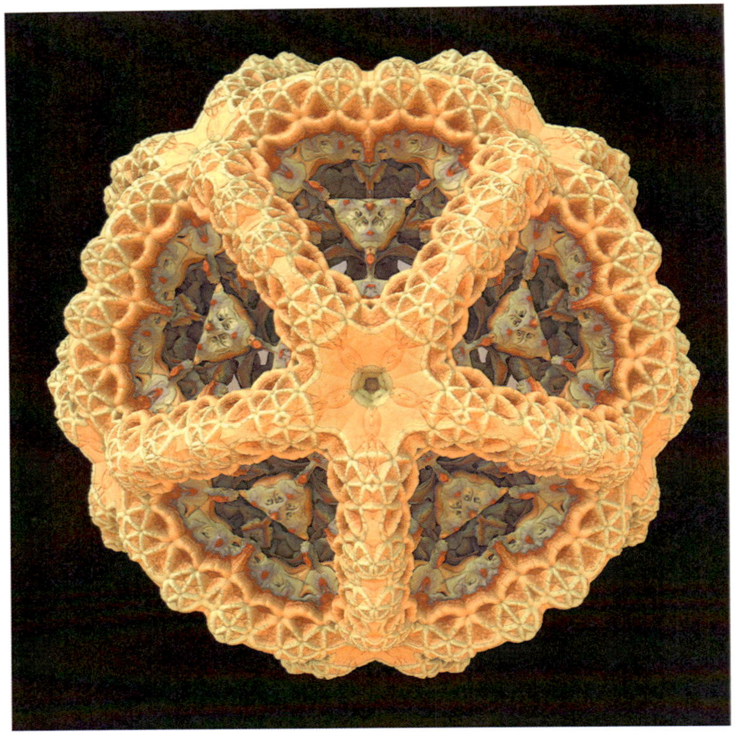

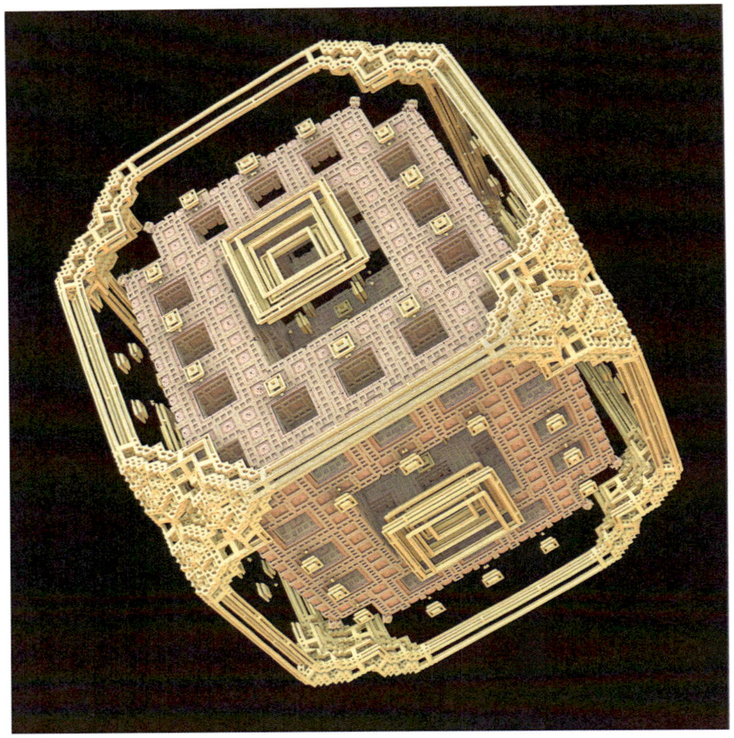

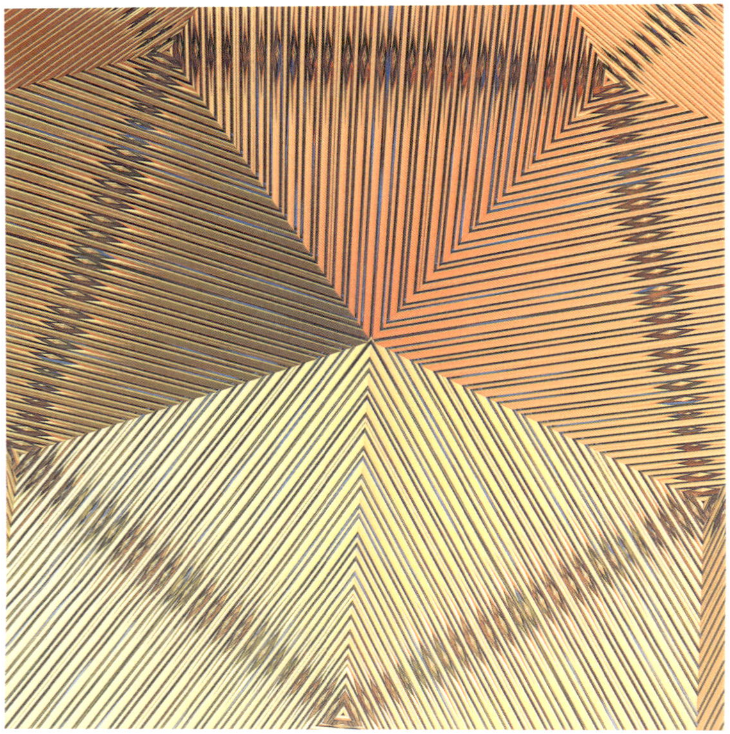

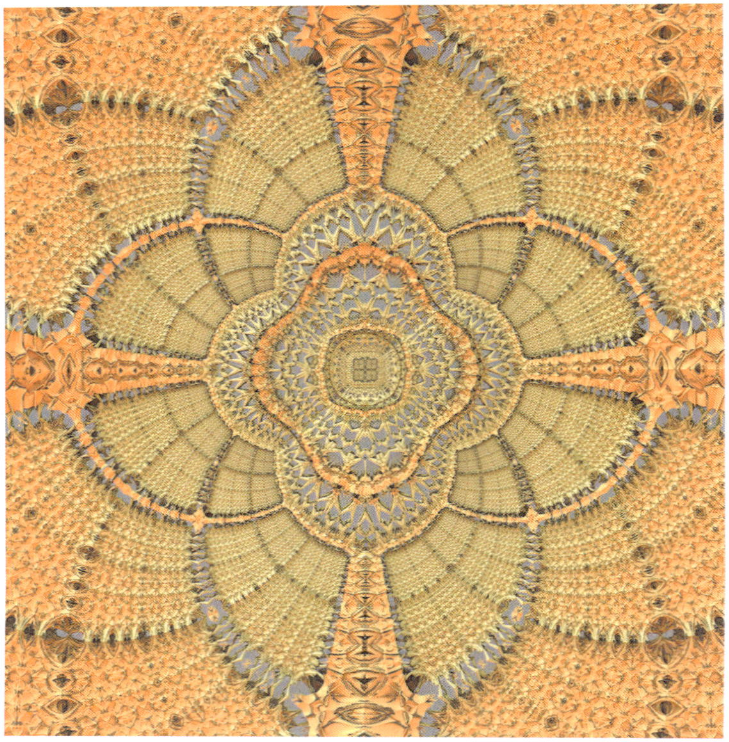

Prior two pages, *ab-stract images;* ***and both of these pages,*** *series of abstract geometrical shapes rendered in Mandelbulb 3D*

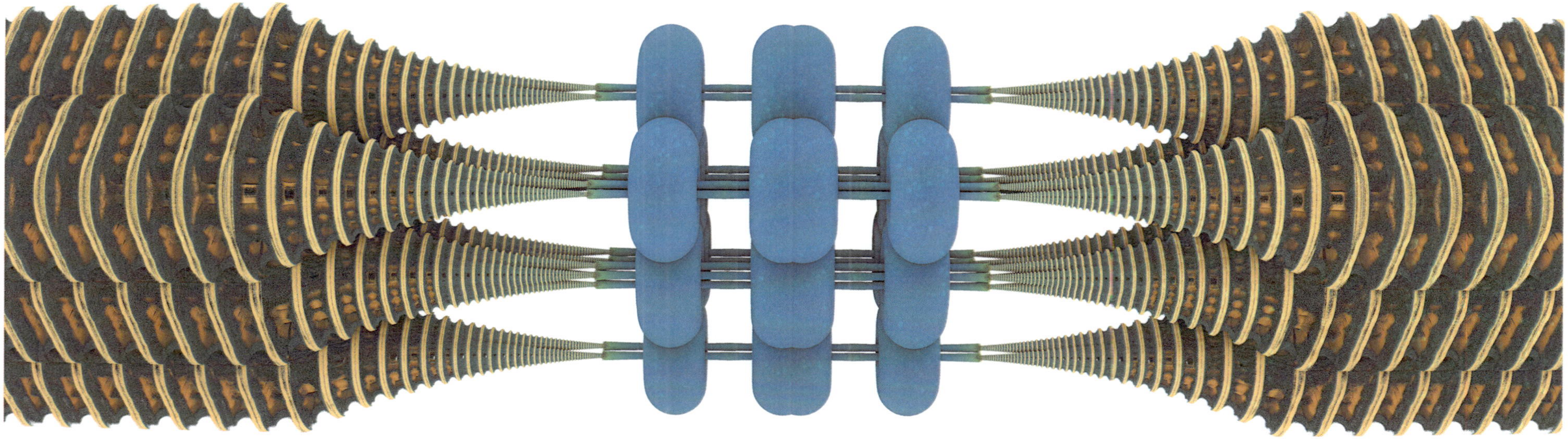

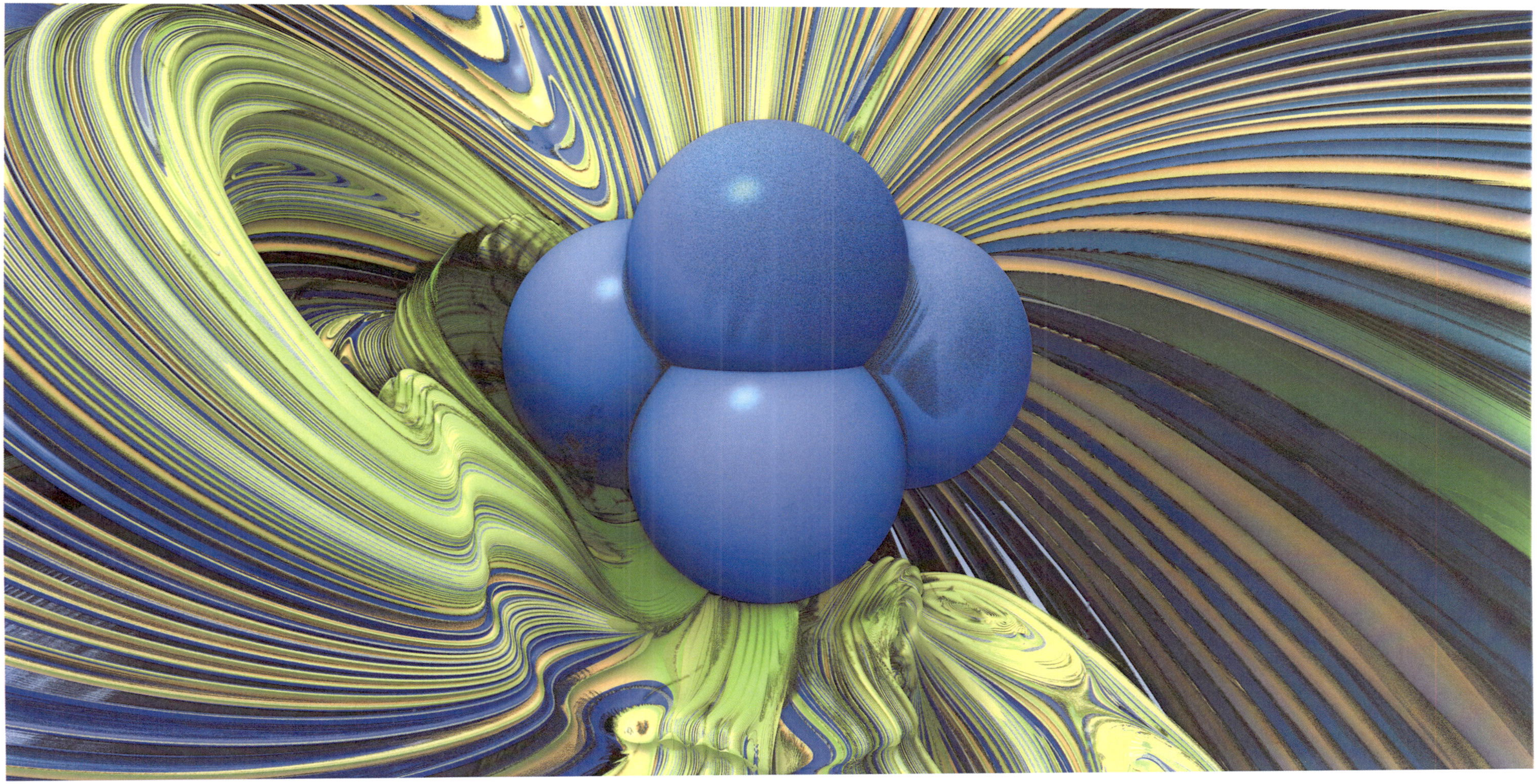

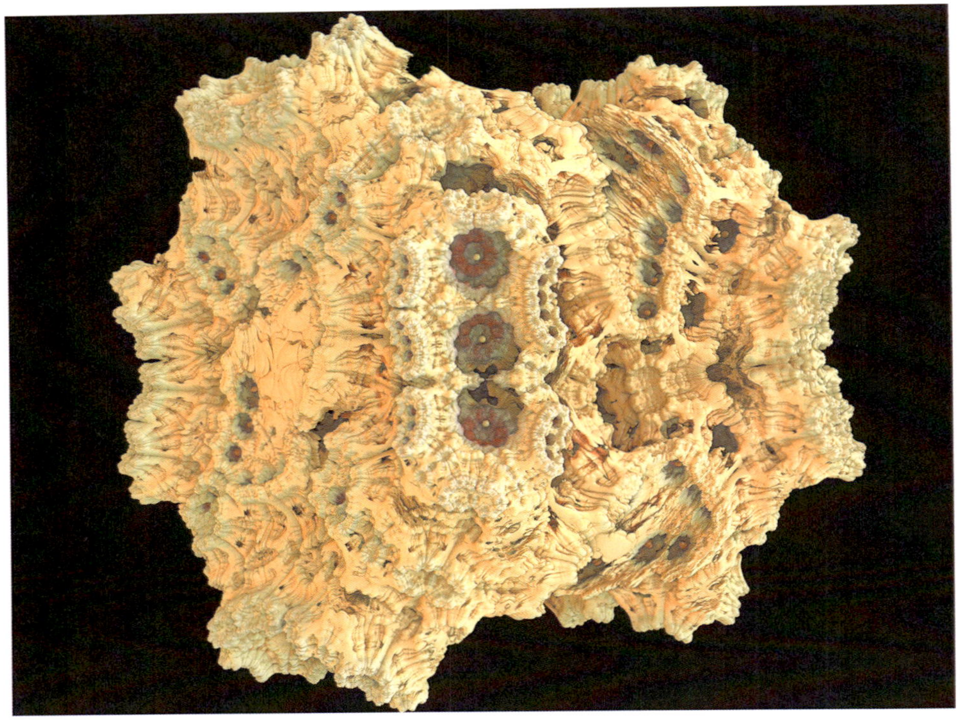

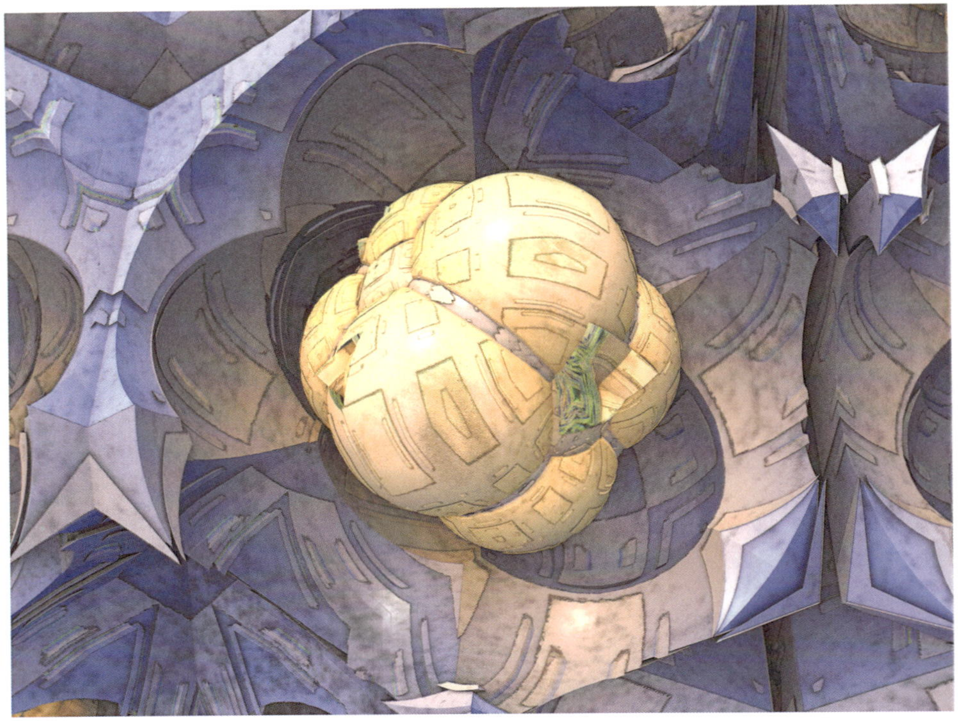

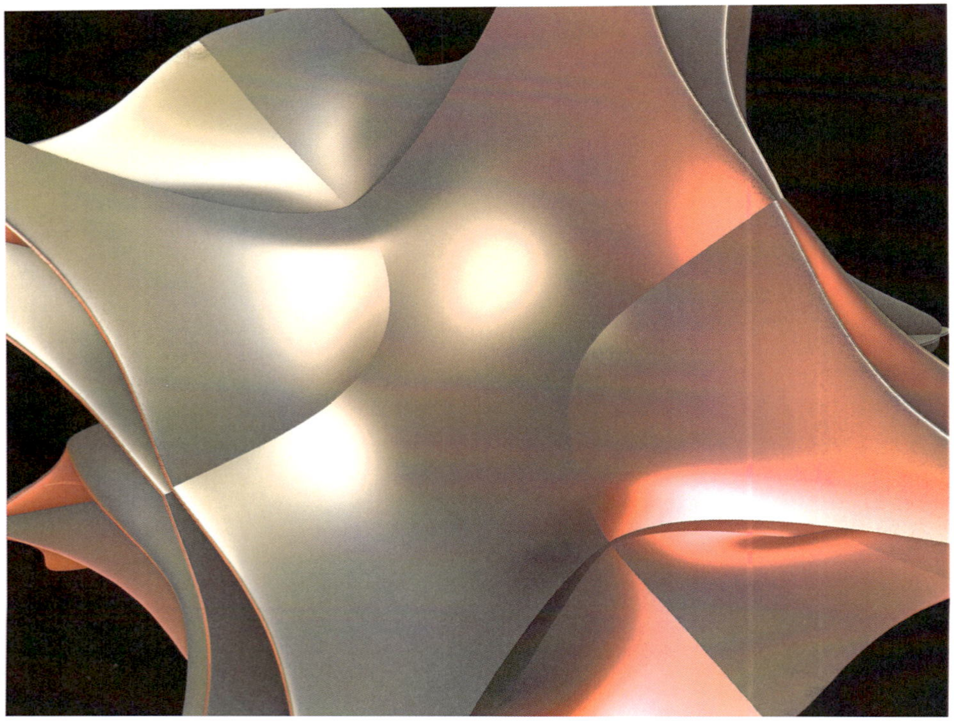

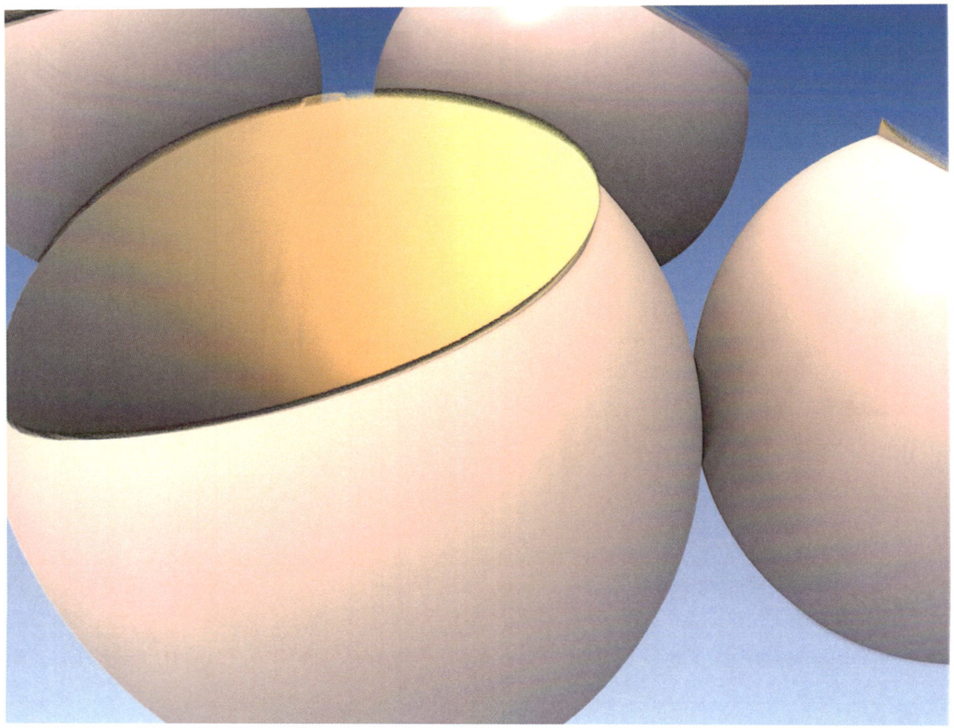

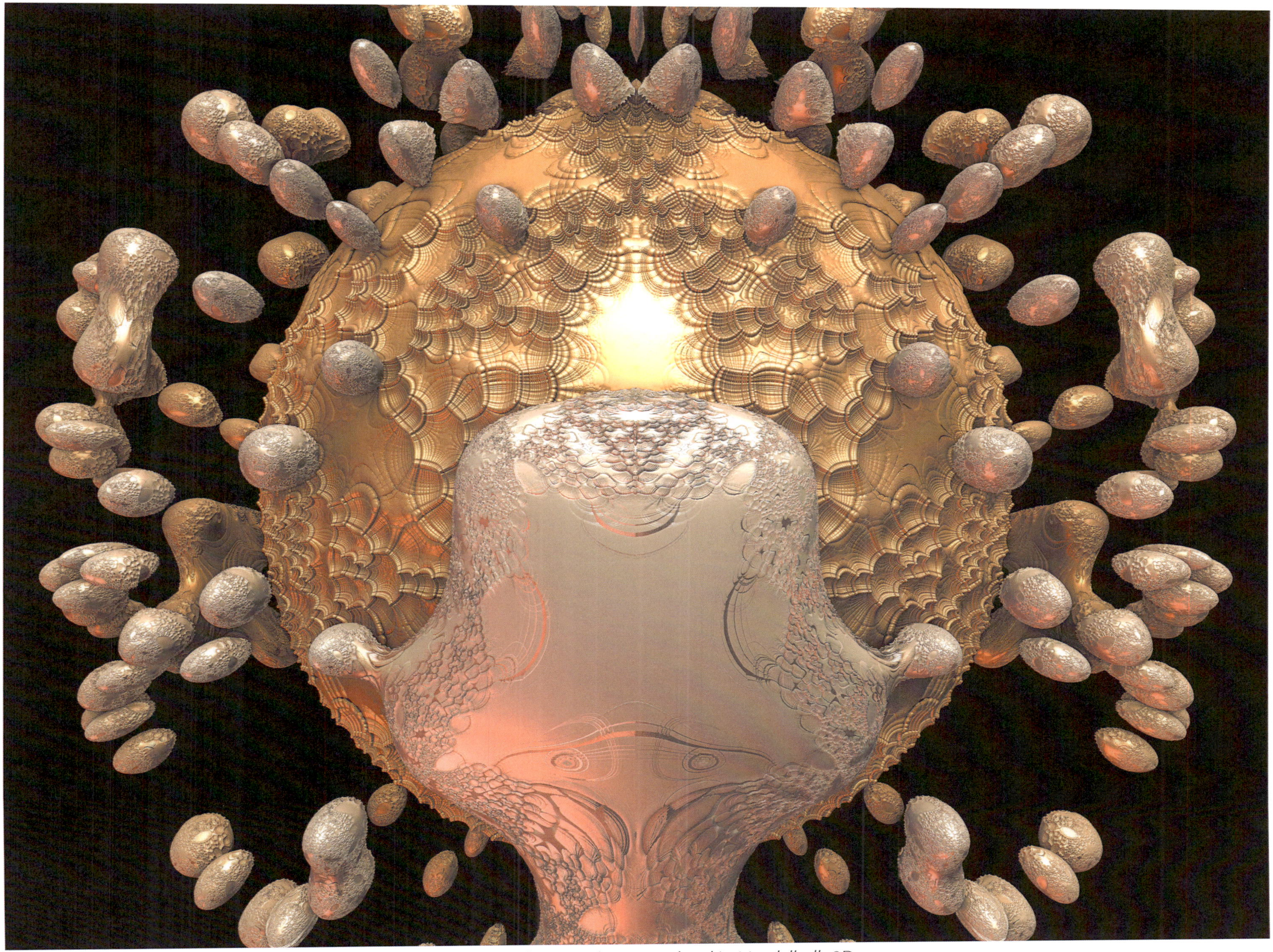

All images on this spread were rendered in Mandelbulb 3D.

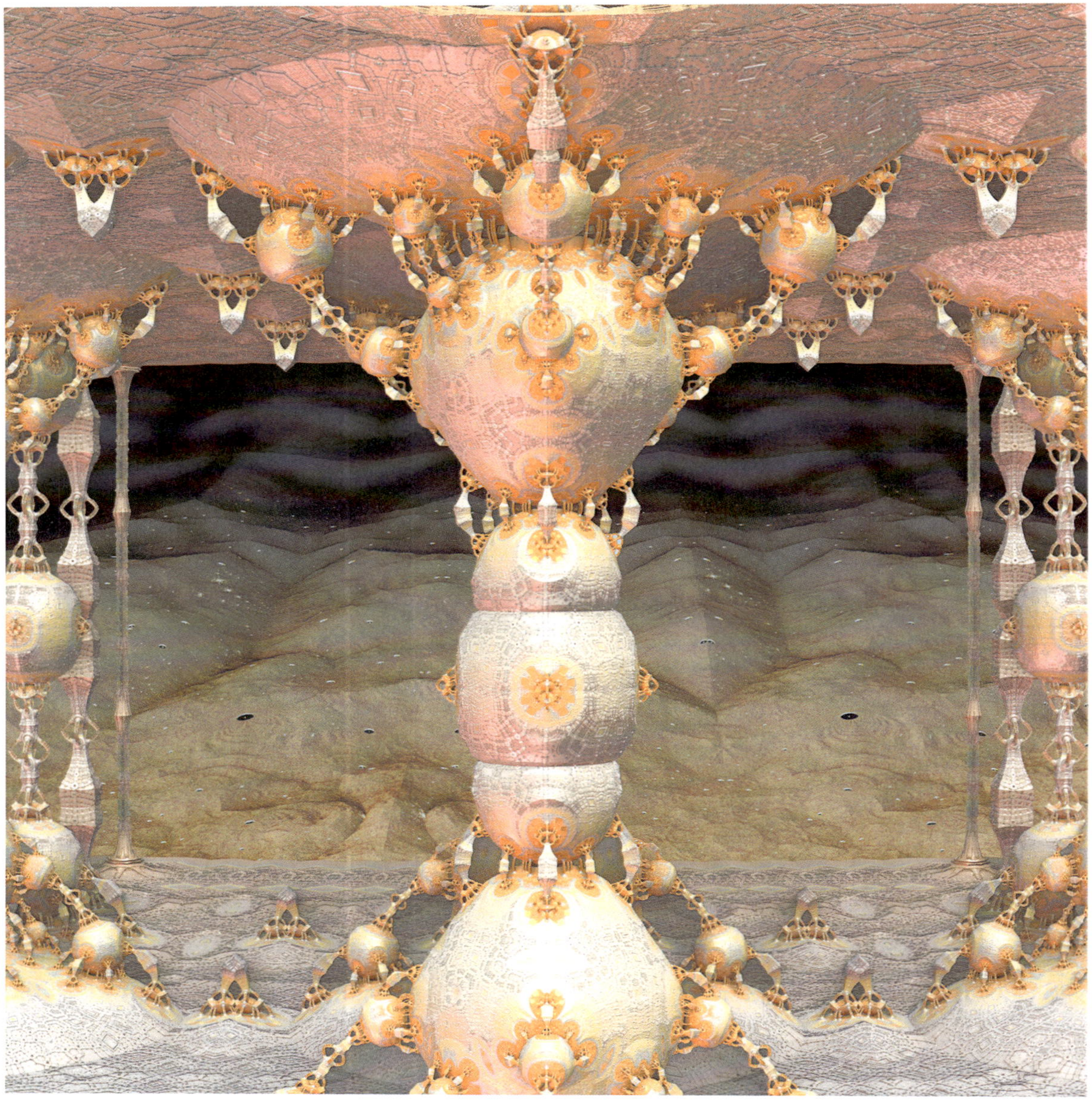

"Venture Beyond This Column?" Image was created in Mandelbulb 3D.

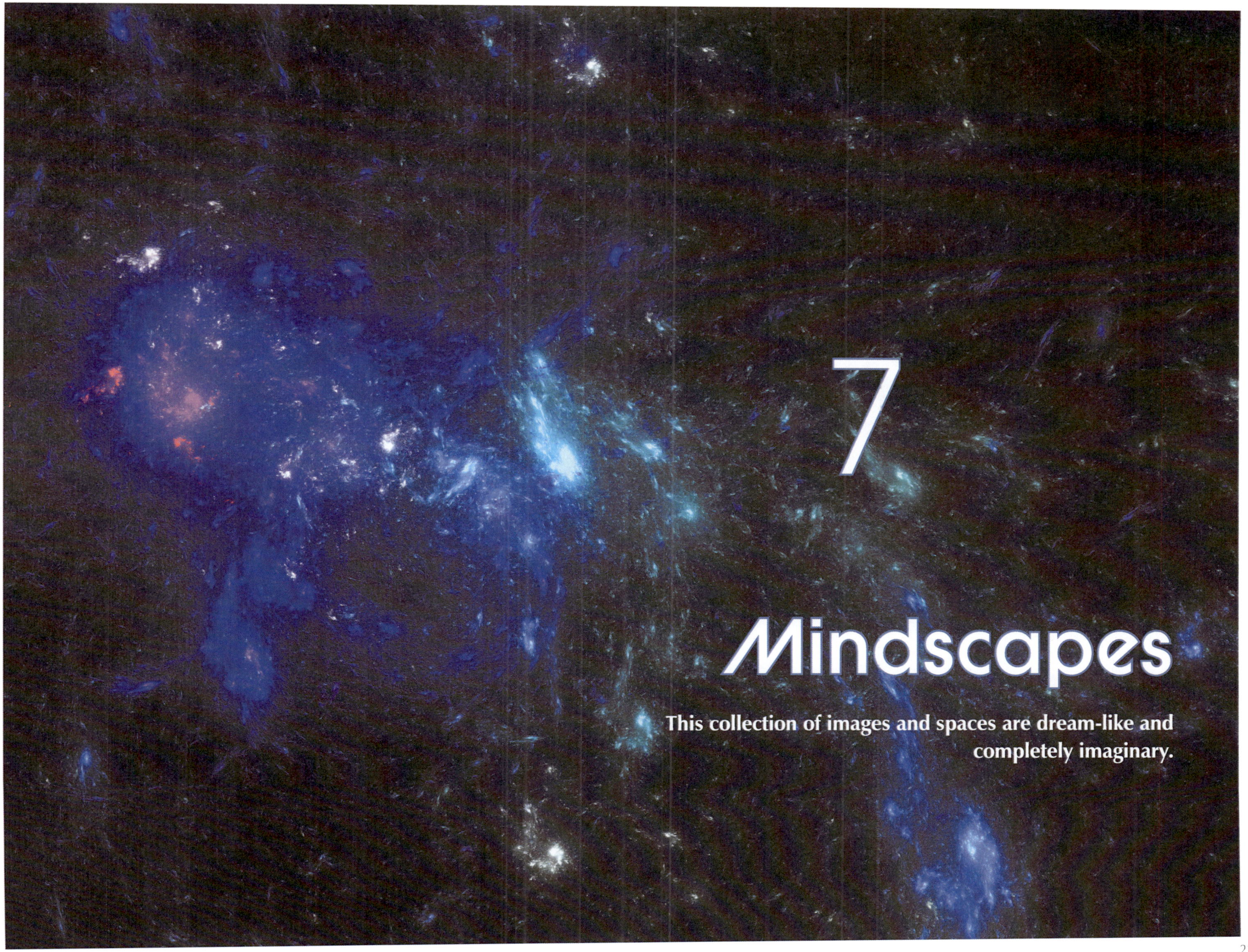

7

Mindscapes

This collection of images and spaces are dream-like and completely imaginary.

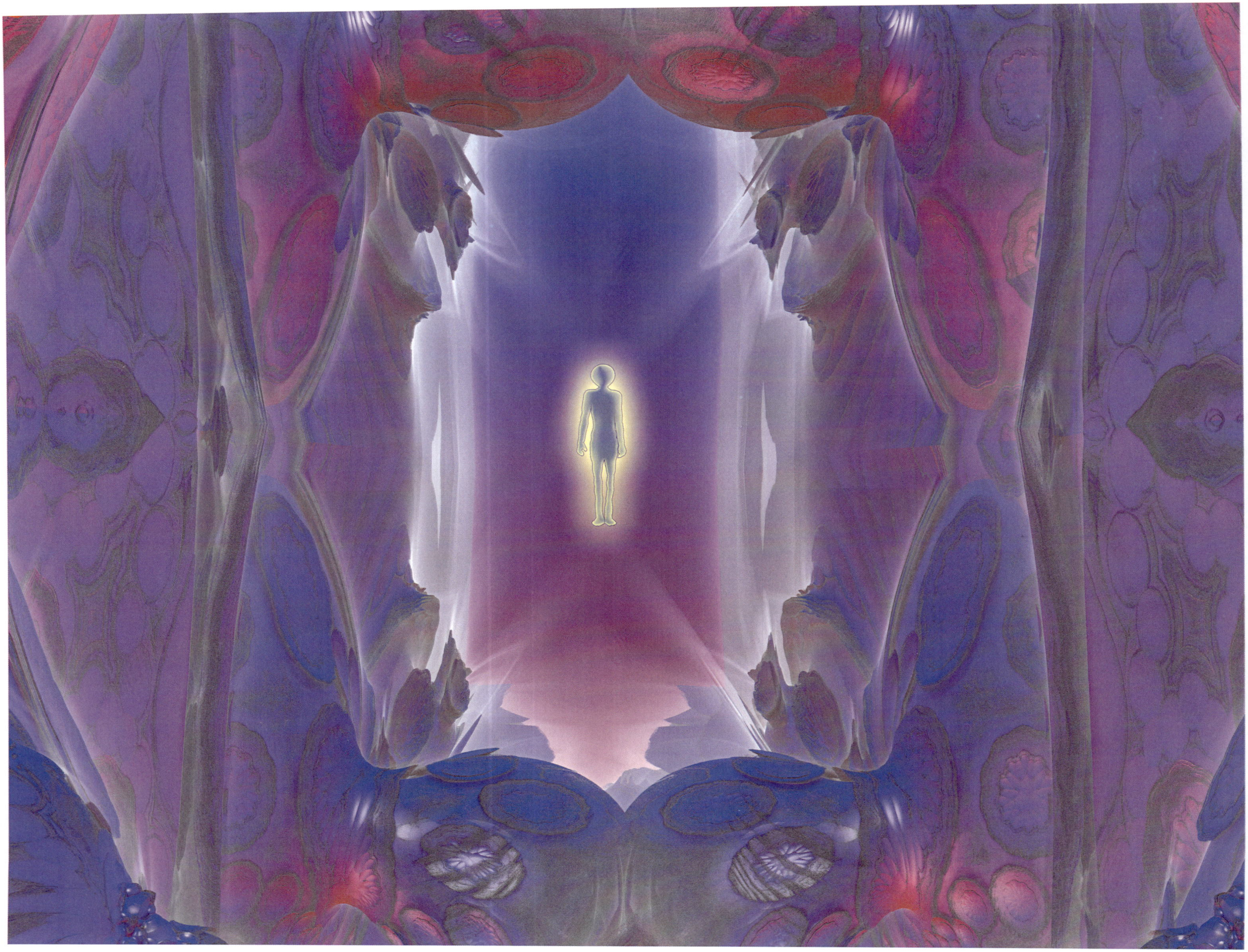

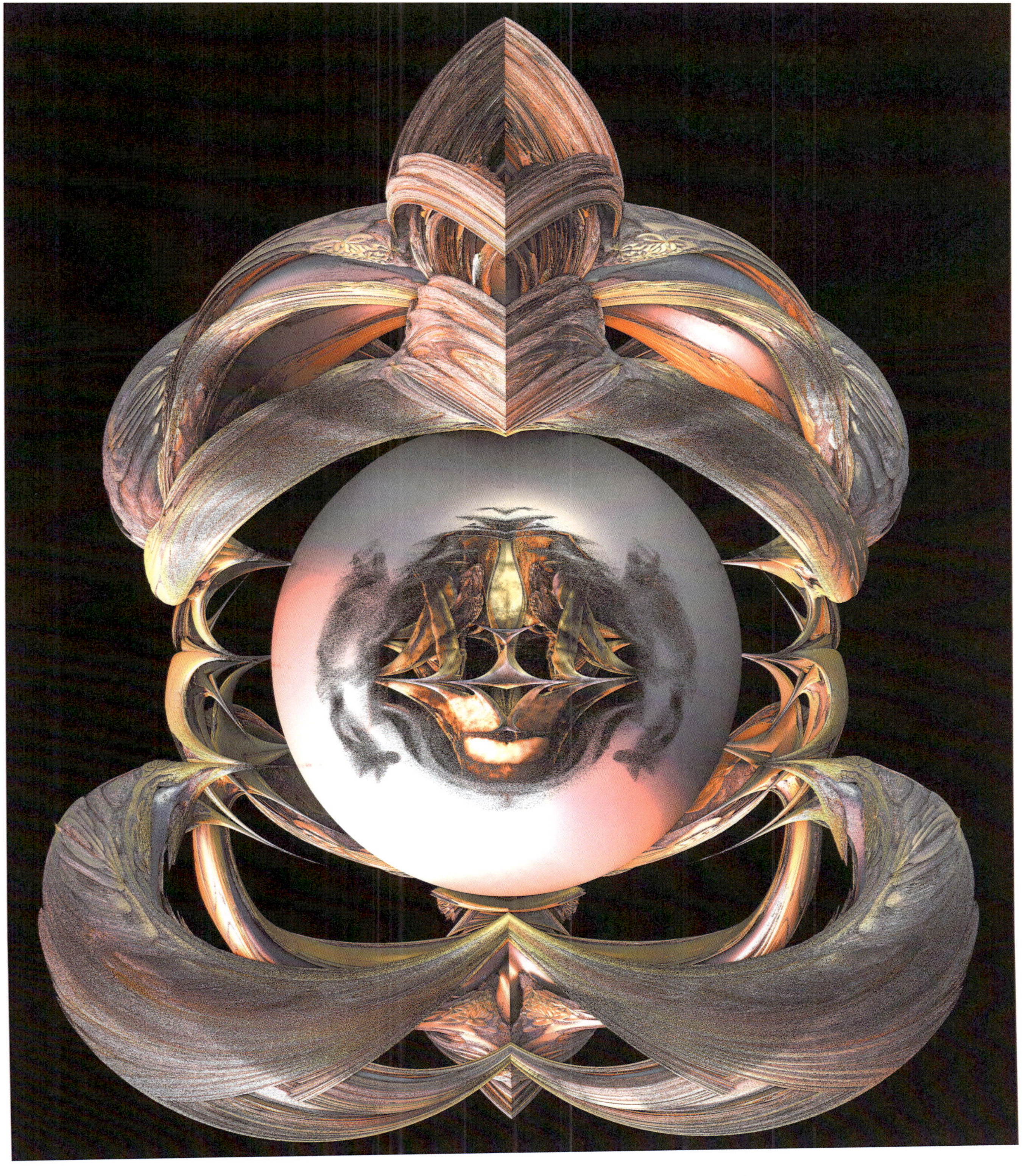

Opposite page, *"Star Gate/Time Tunnel;"* **right,** *"Face in a Coat-of-Arms;" both images rendered in Mandelbulb 3D*

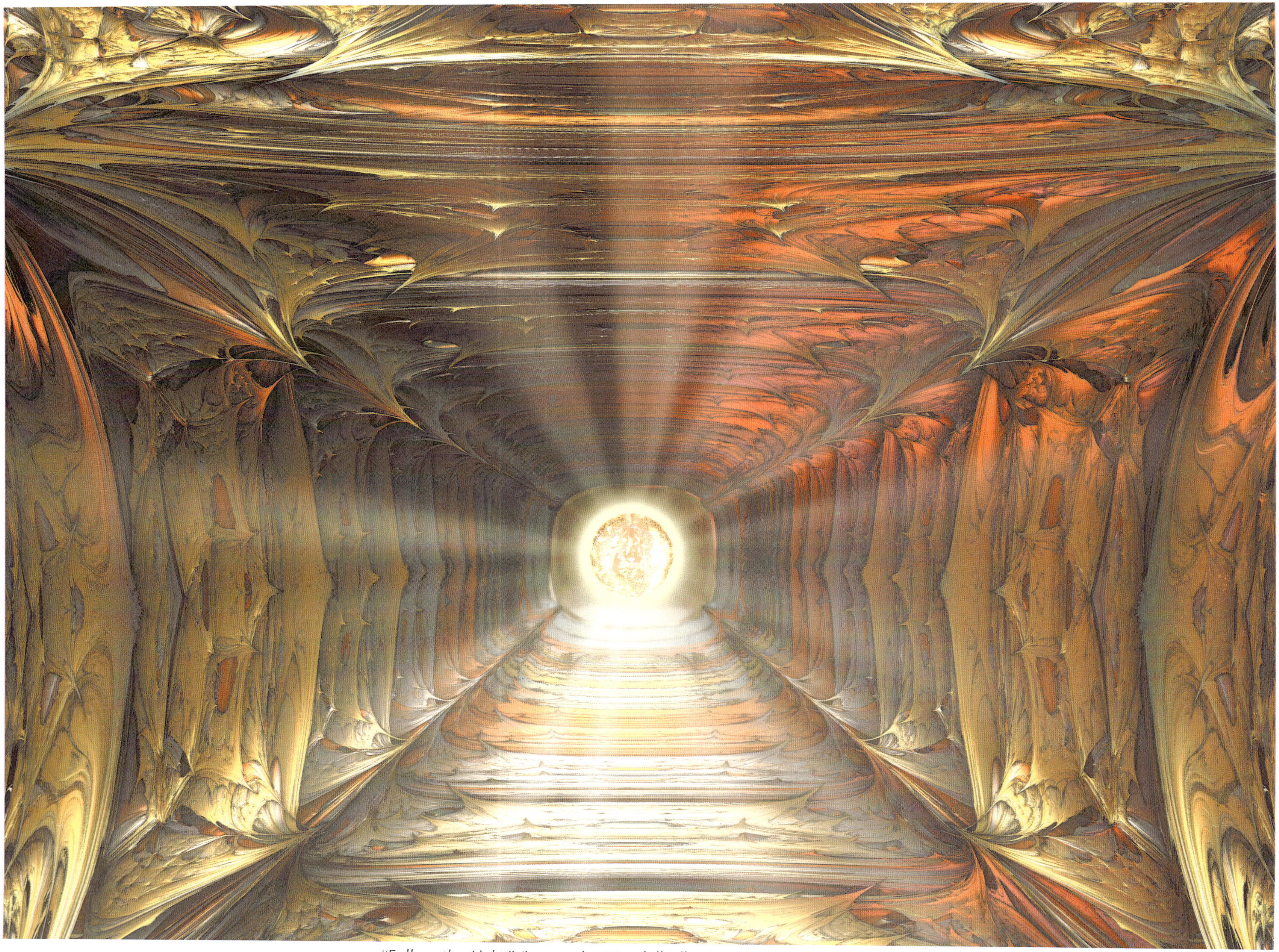

"Follow the Light" (images by Mandelbulb 3D, effect in Luminar Neo)

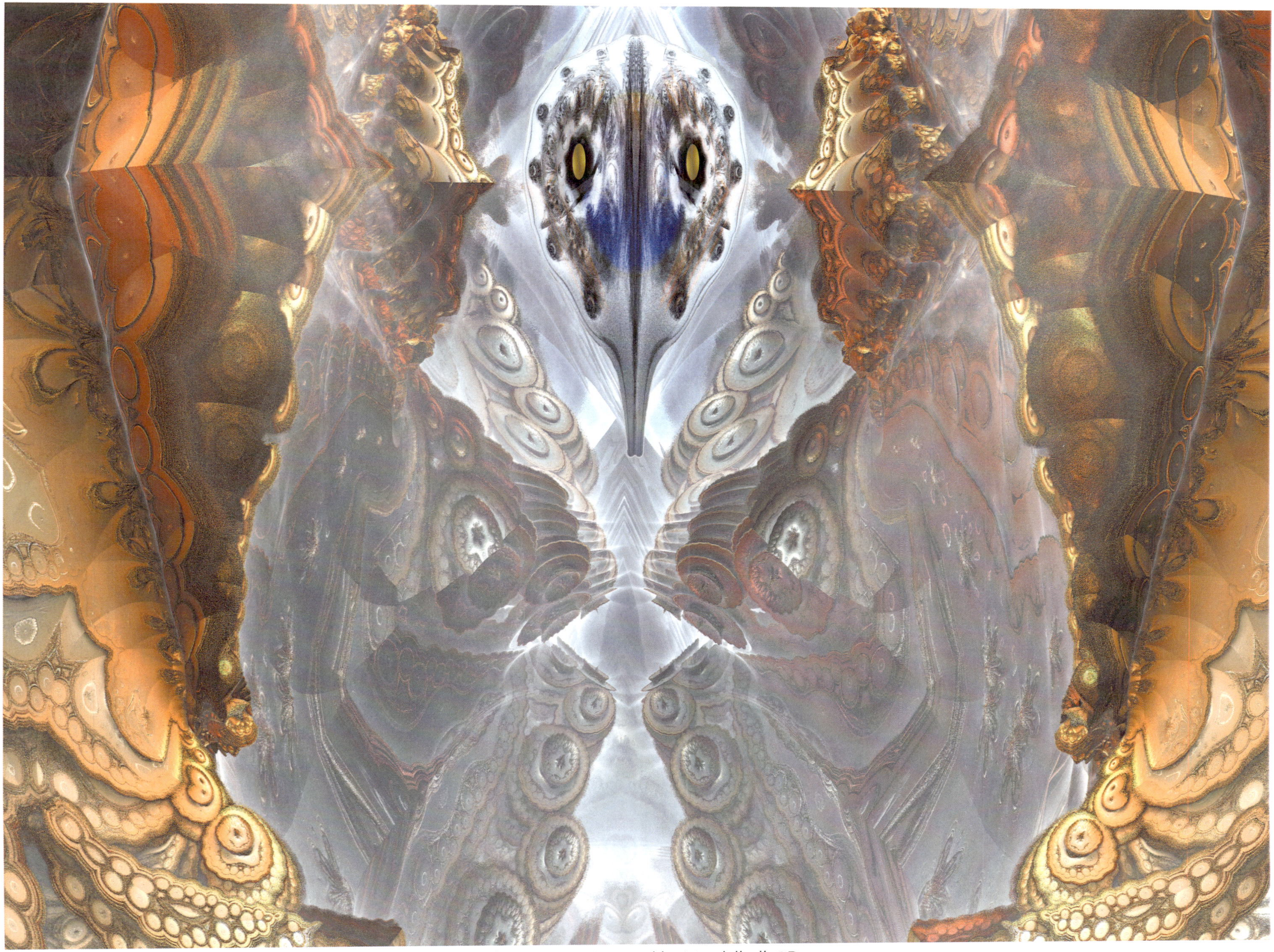

"Alien Monster" created by Mandelbulb 3D

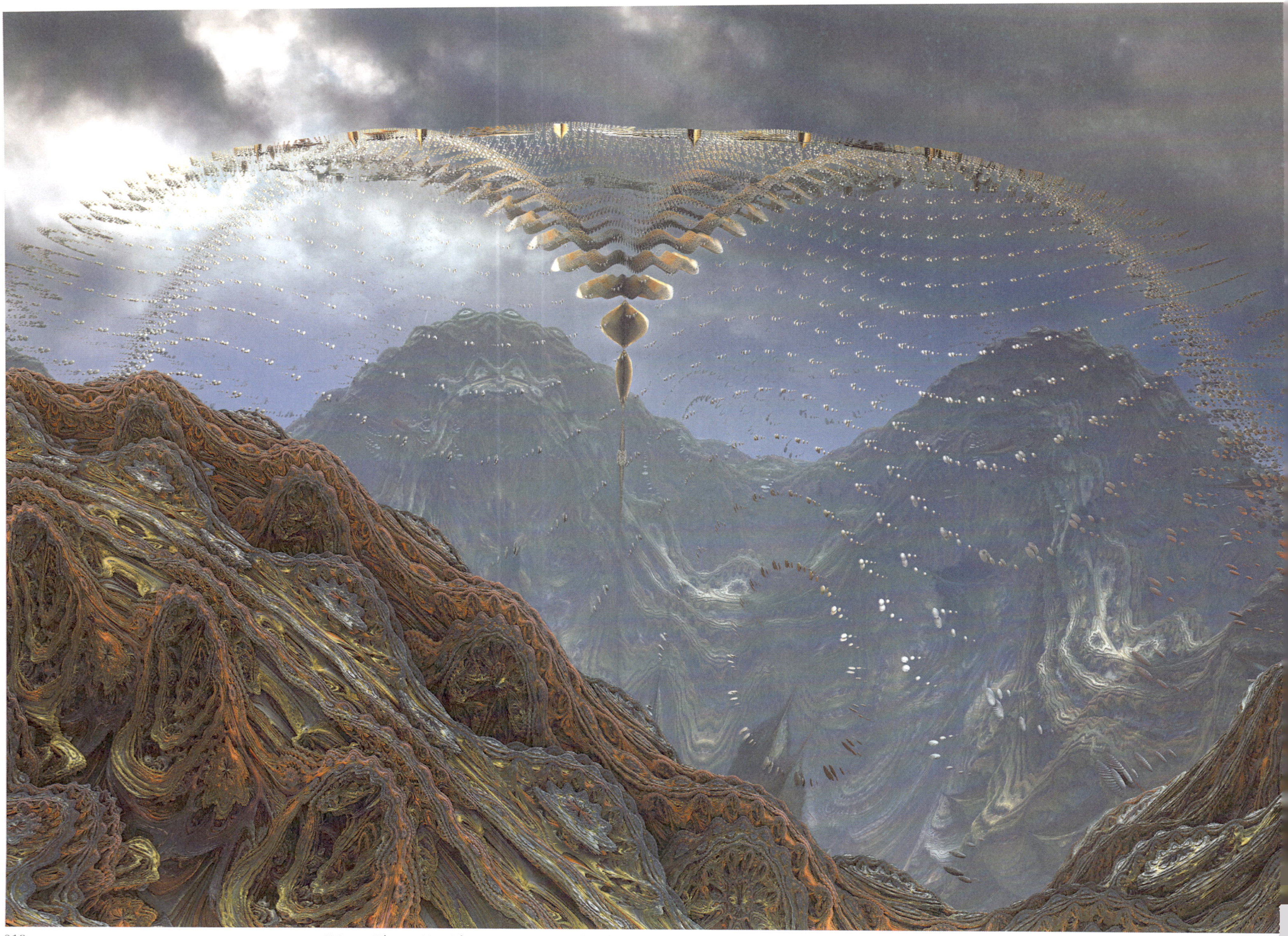

"Not a Planet You'd Want to Visit;" this fractal image was generated by Mandelbulb 3D.

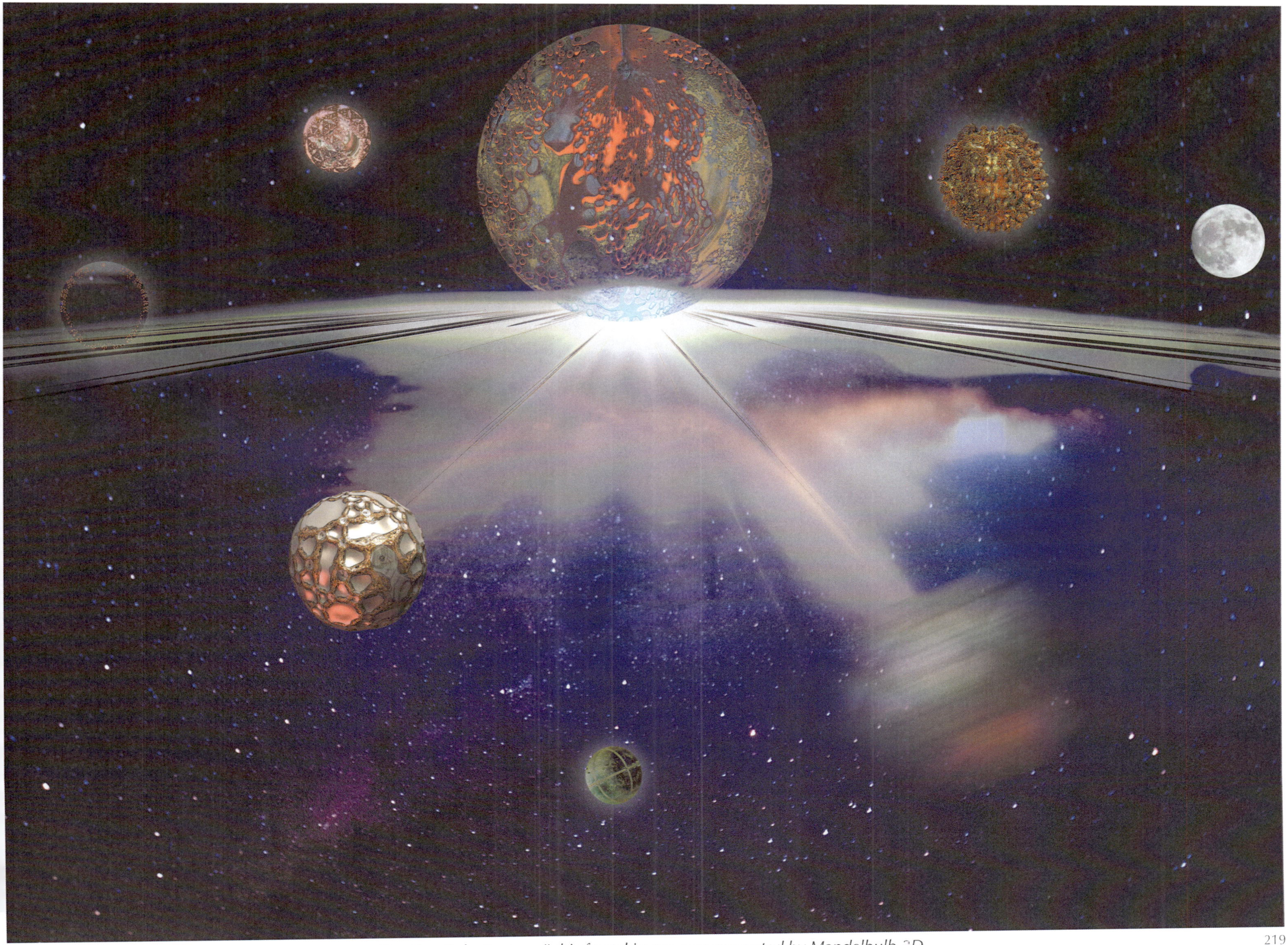

"Another Solar System;" this fractal image was generated by Mandelbulb 3D.

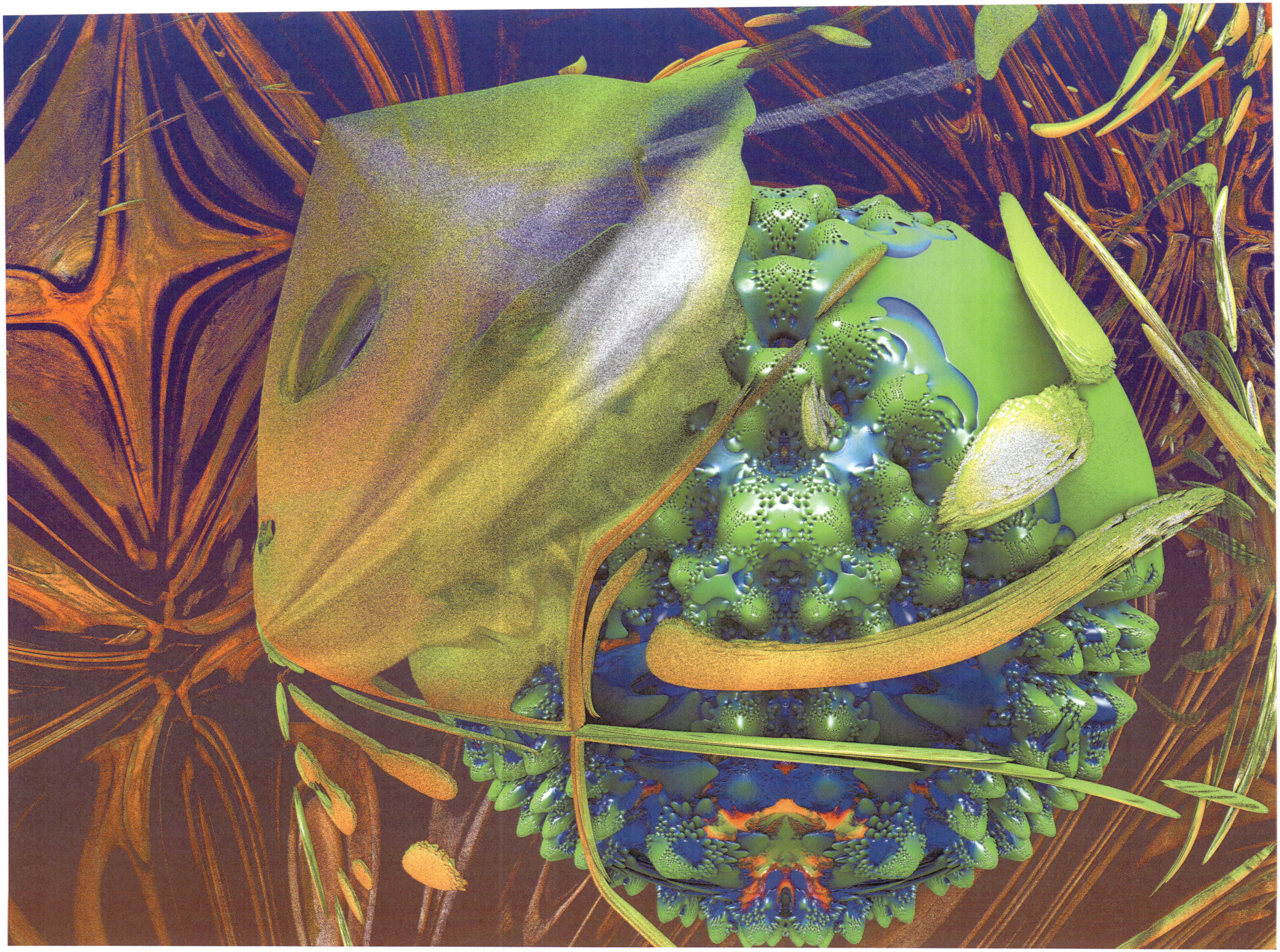

Is it biological or something else? (imaged in Mandelbulb 3D)

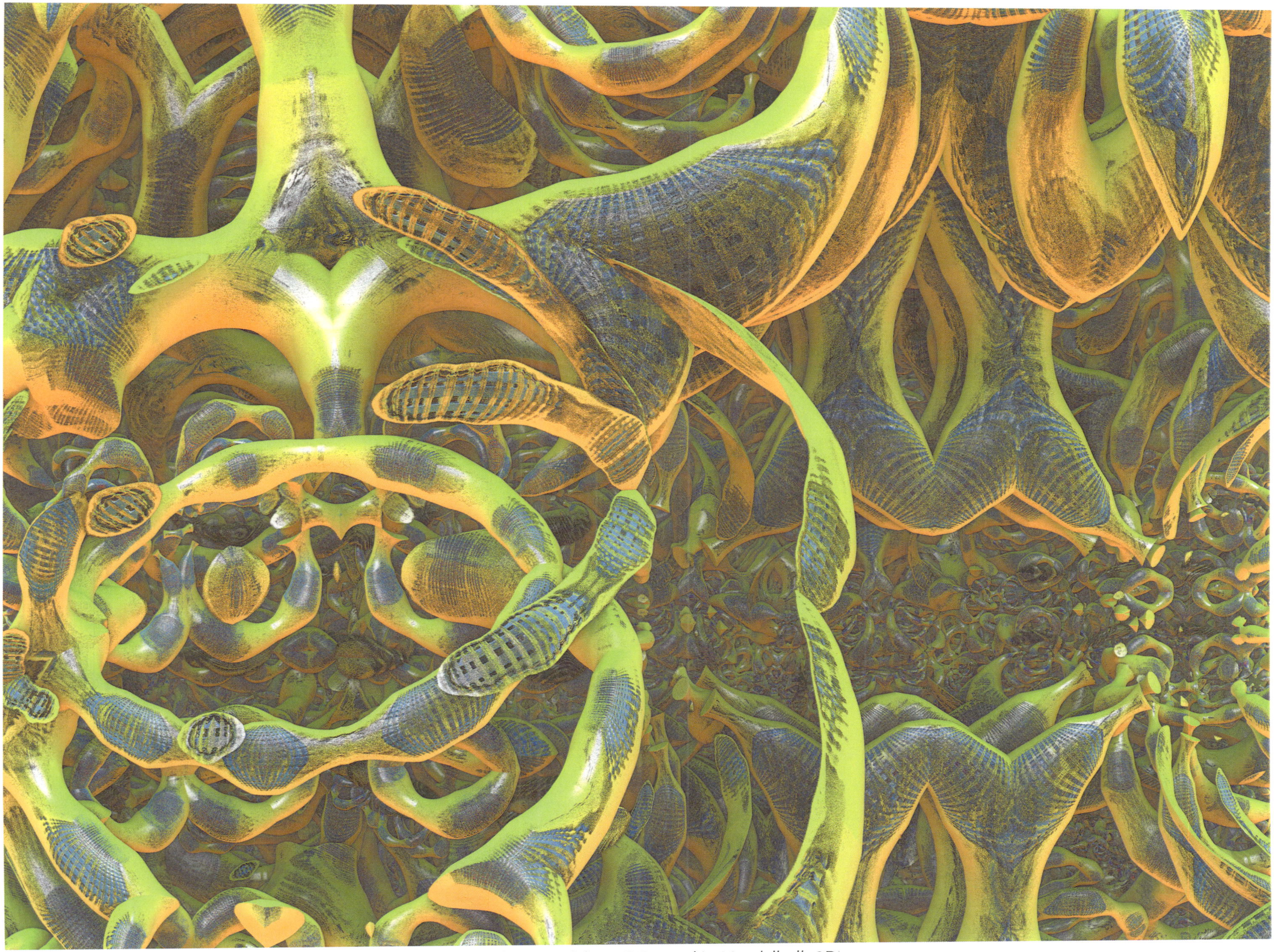

"Under-the-Sea Lifeforms" (imaged in Mandelbulb 3D)

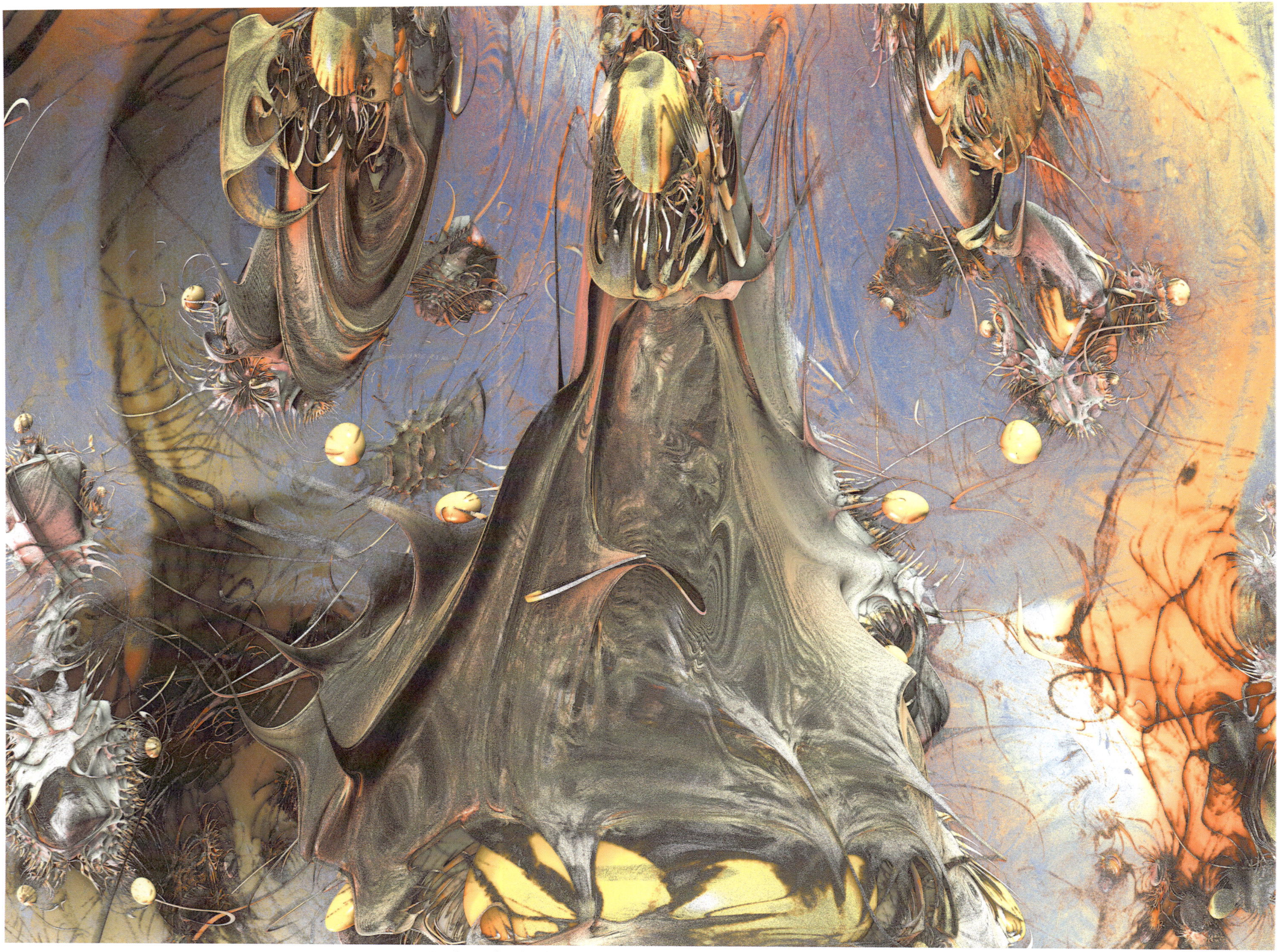

Is it alive, dead, plant or animal? (imaged in Mandelbulb 3D)

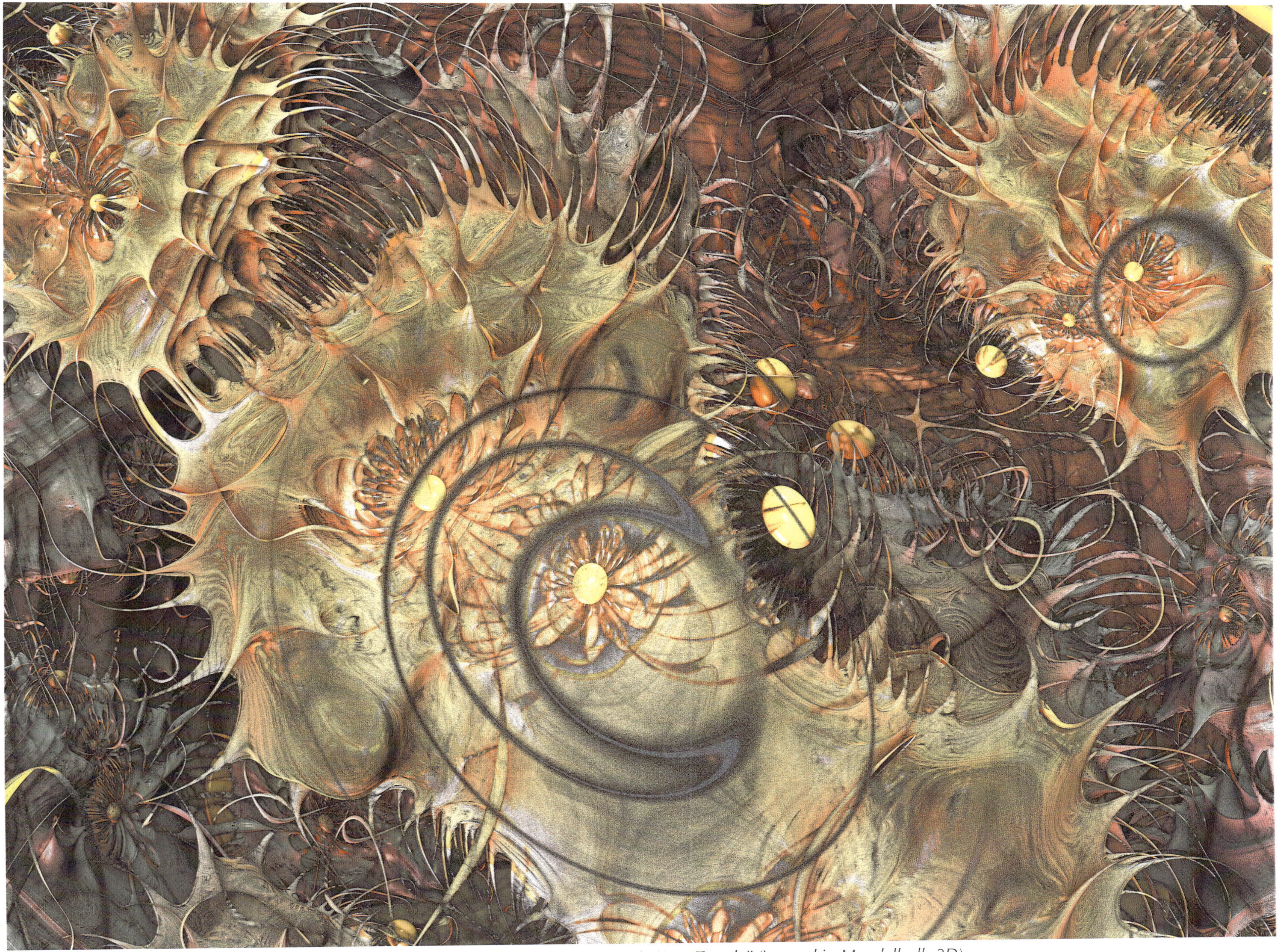

"Not Something You'd Want to Encounter in Your Travels" (imaged in Mandelbulb 3D)

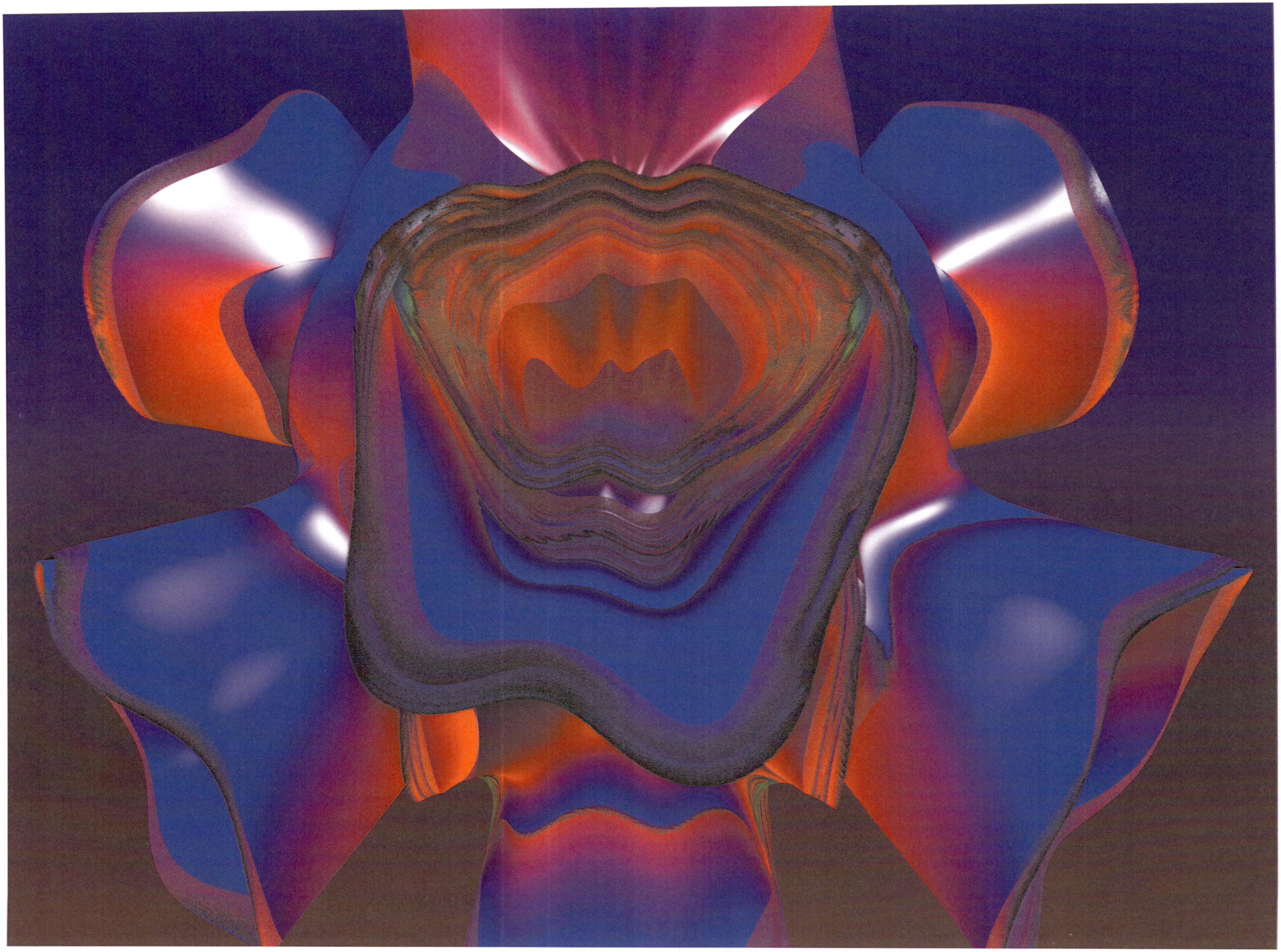

"Six-Way Ion Combiner for Propulsion System," image created in Mandelbulb 3D

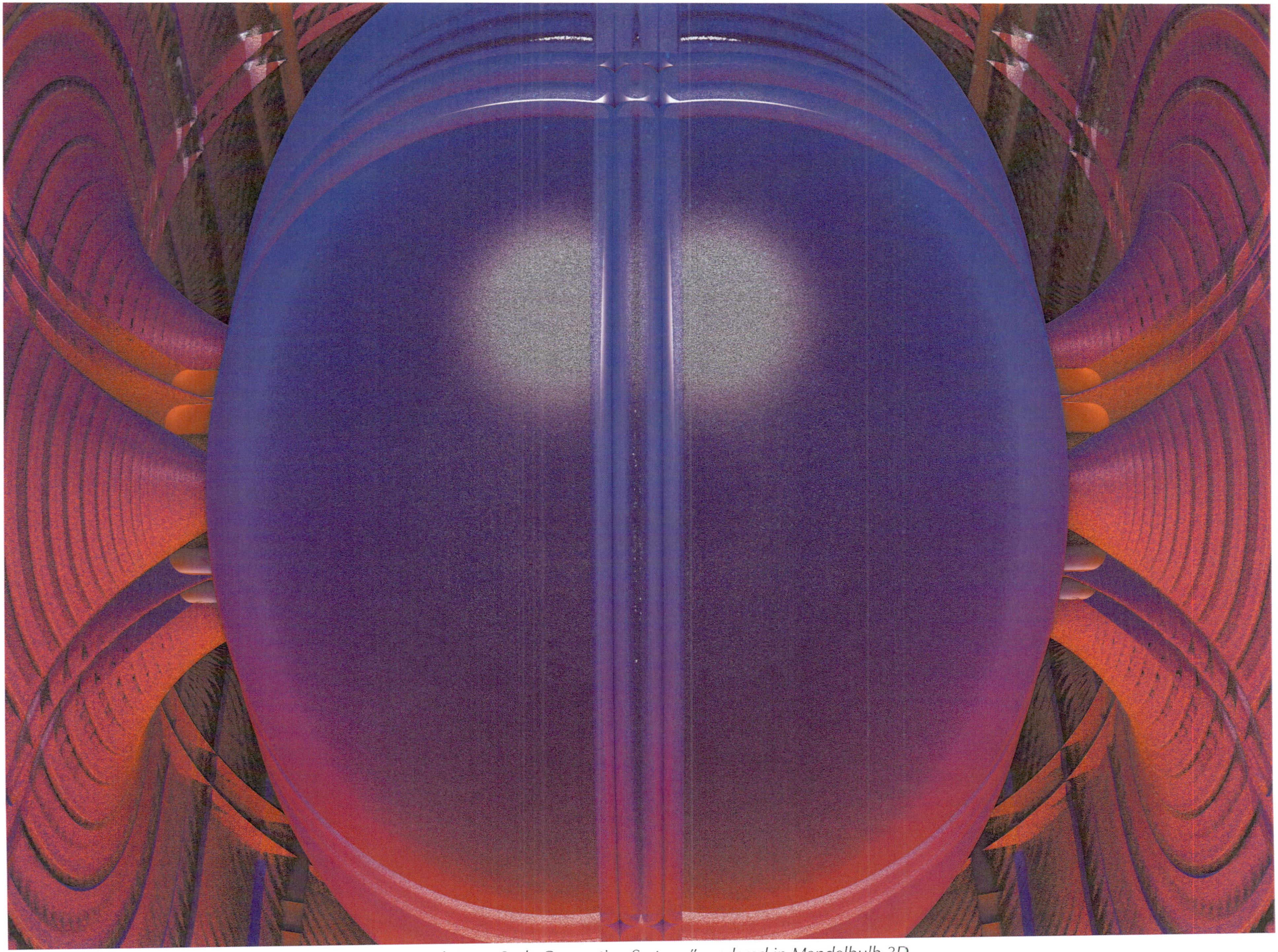

"AI-Based, Large-Scale Computing System," rendered in Mandelbulb 3D

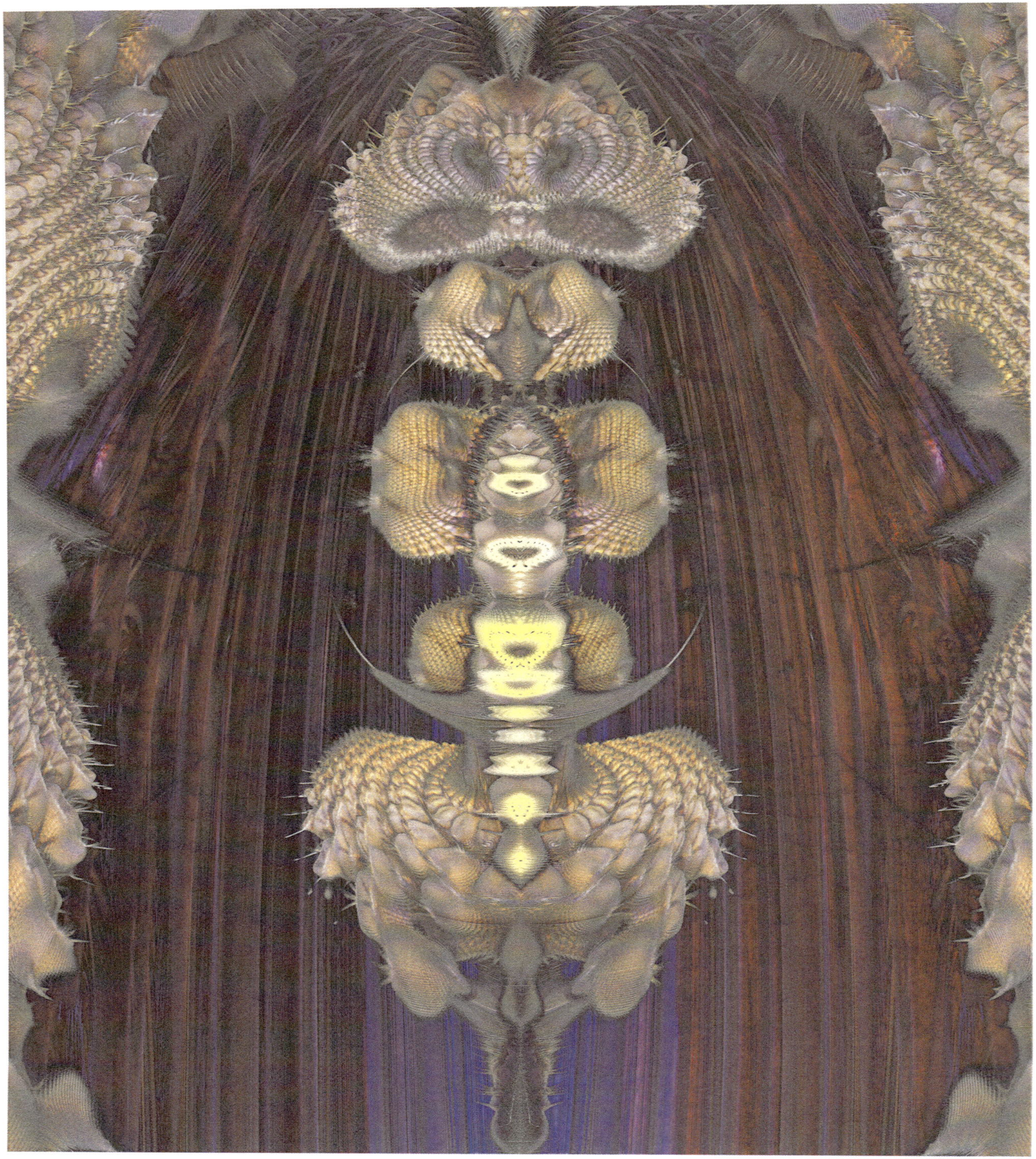

Left, " Exoskeleton" as imaged in Mandelbulb 3D. **Opposite page,** "Series of Skulls and Mask" rendered in Mandelbulb 3D.

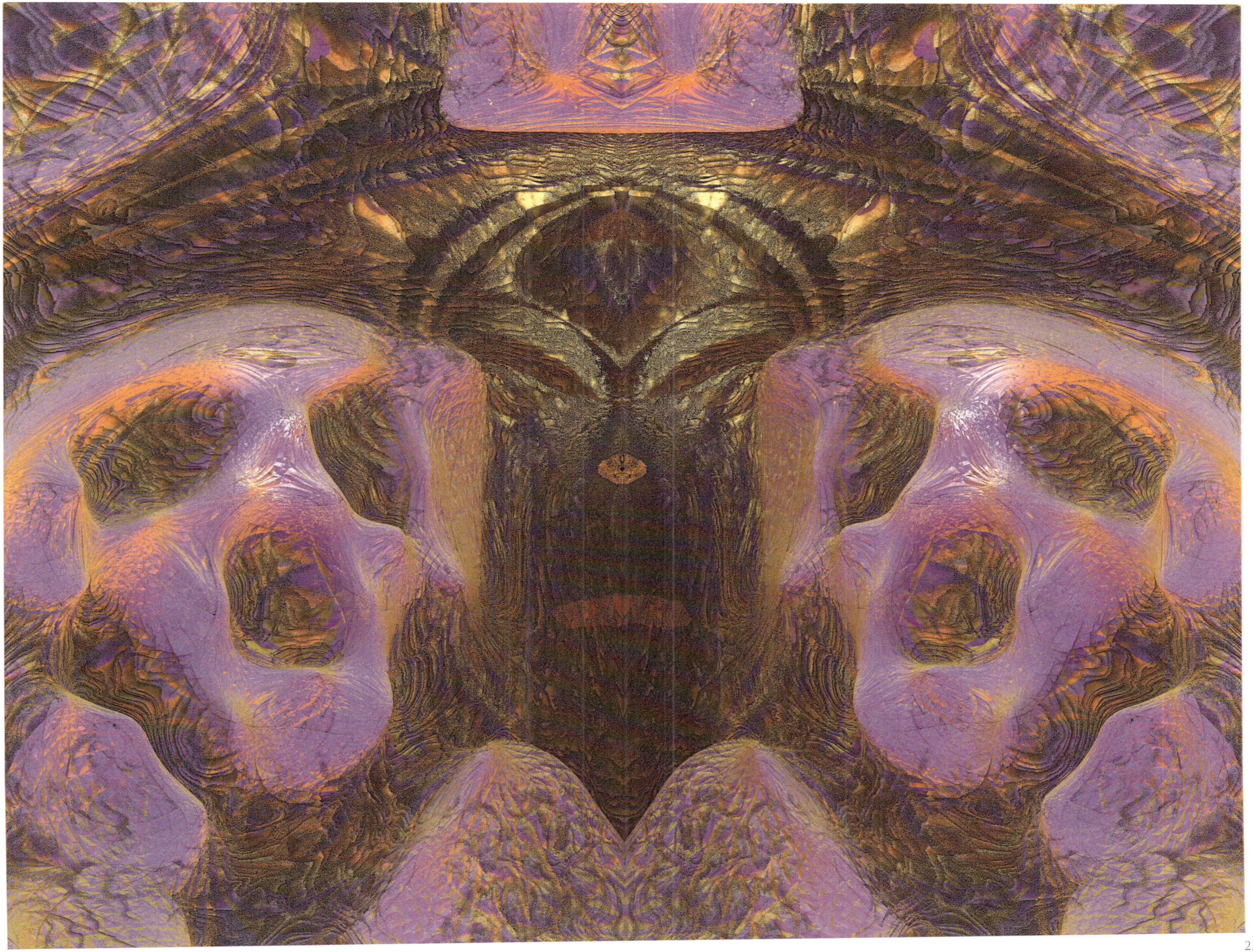

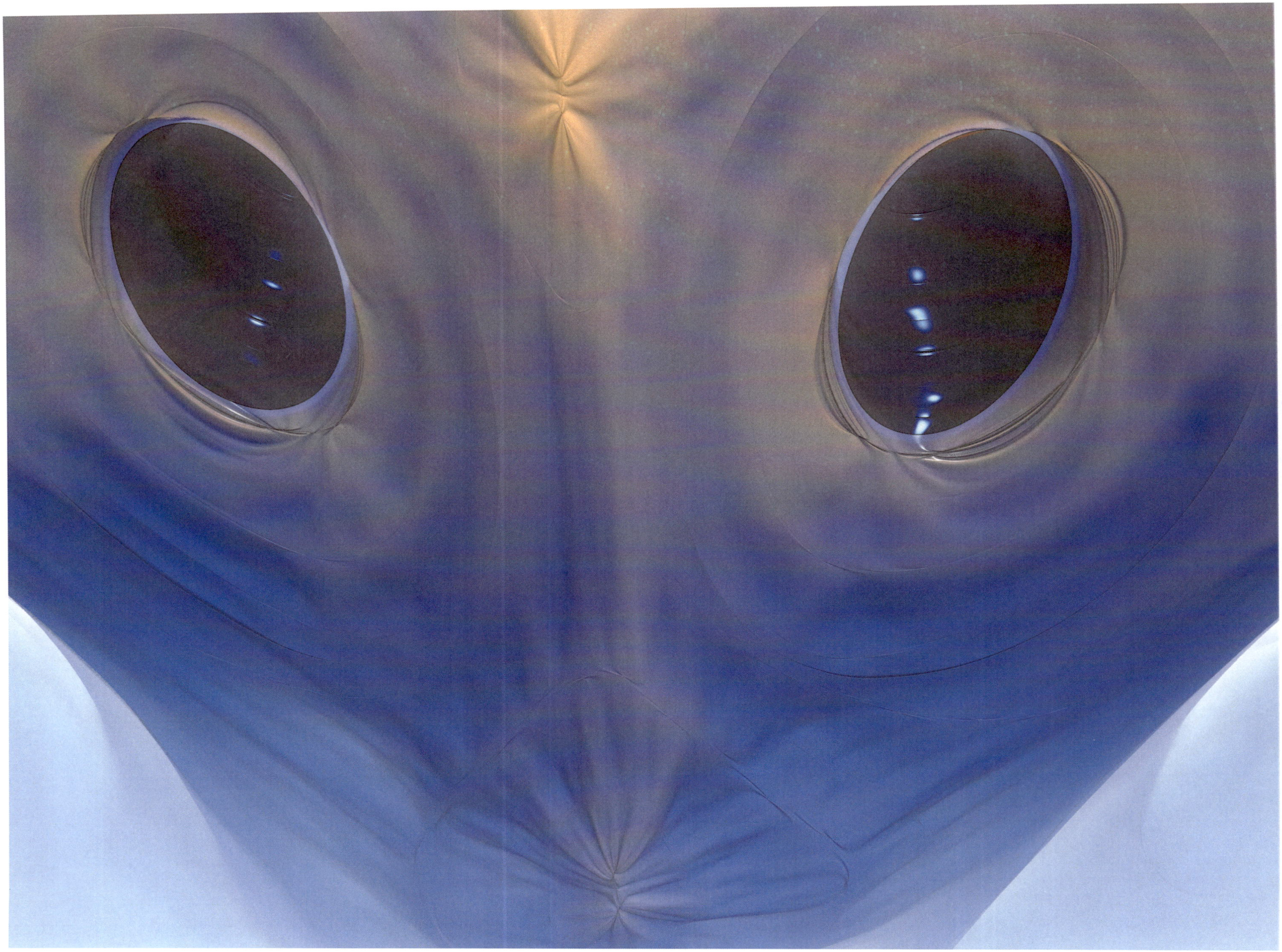

"Your Worst Nightmare, or is it? A 'Gray' Appears in Your Dreams;" image was generated by Mandelbulb 3D.

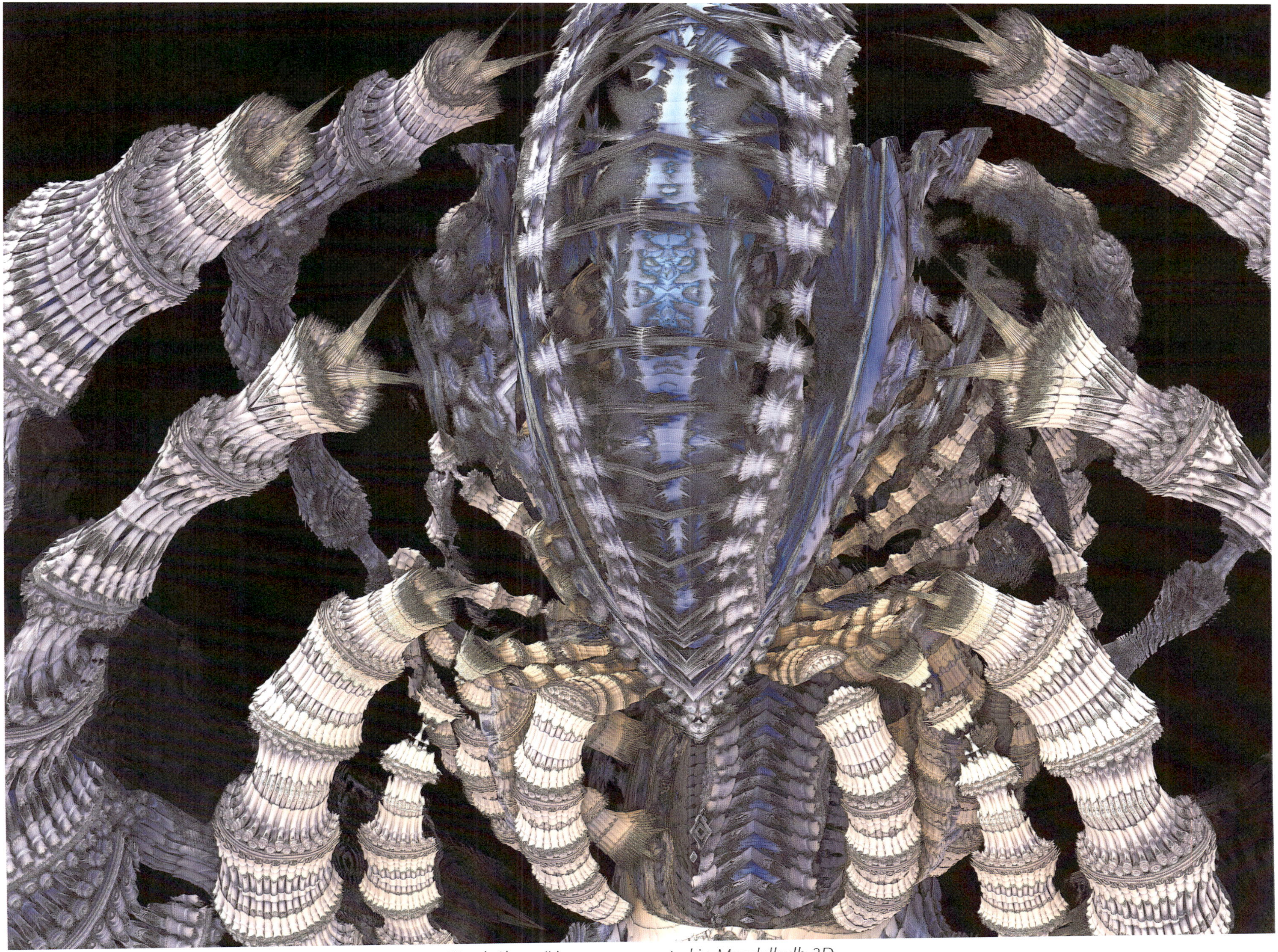

"Freak Show;" image was created in Mandelbulb 3D.

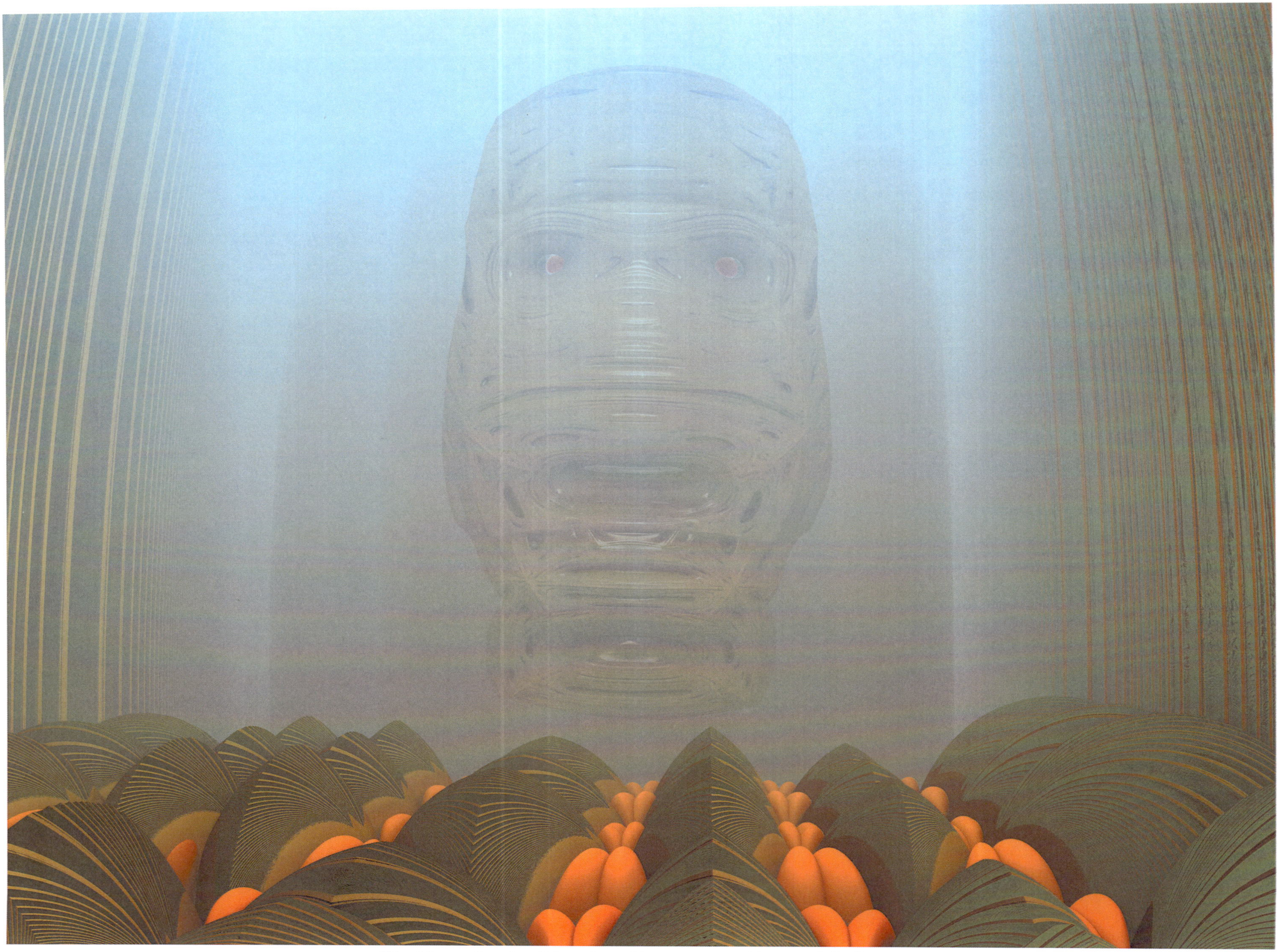

"The Master Speaks..." (two fractal images created by Mandelbulb 3D).

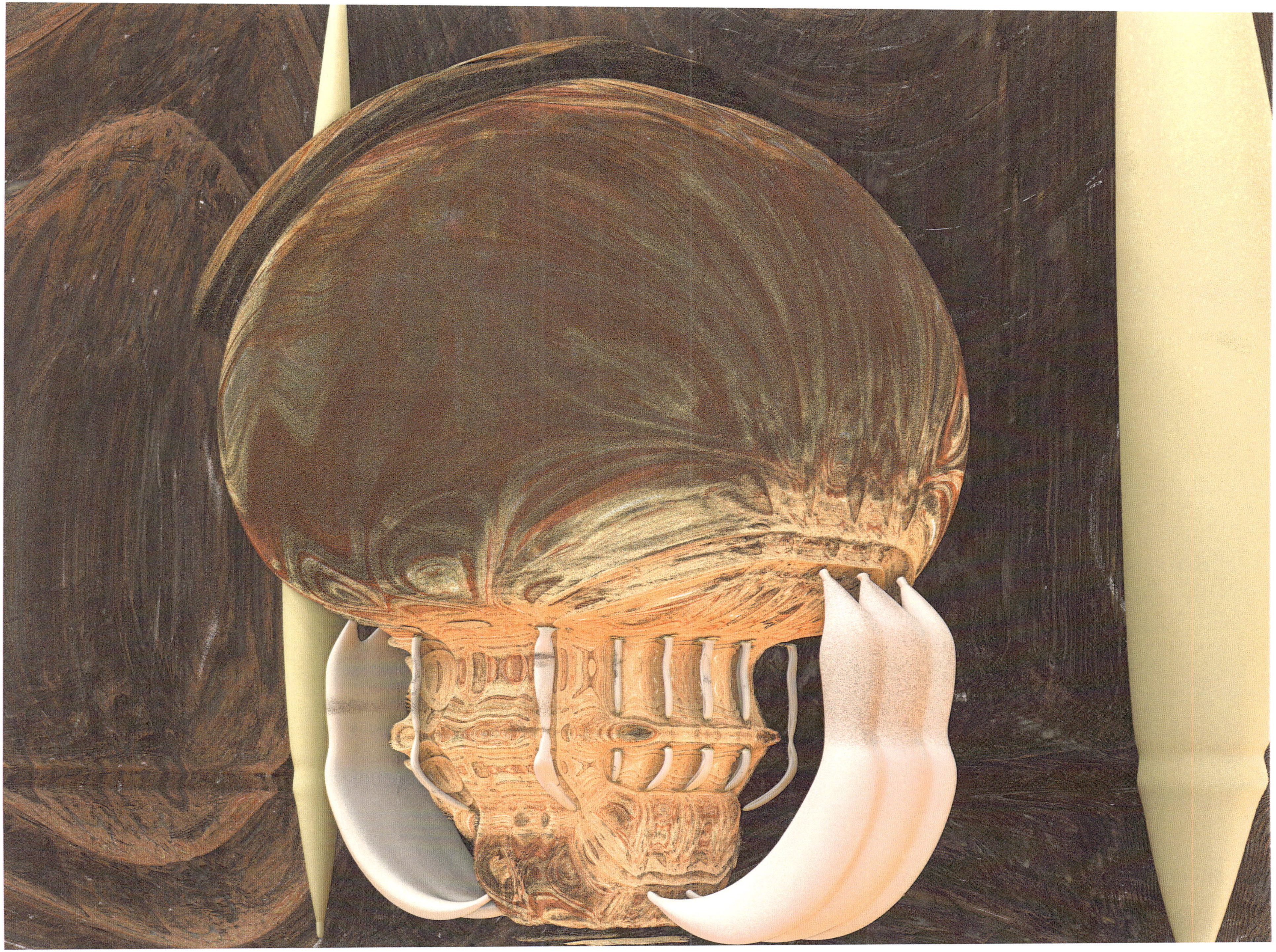

"The Brain" (image, Mandelbulb 3D)

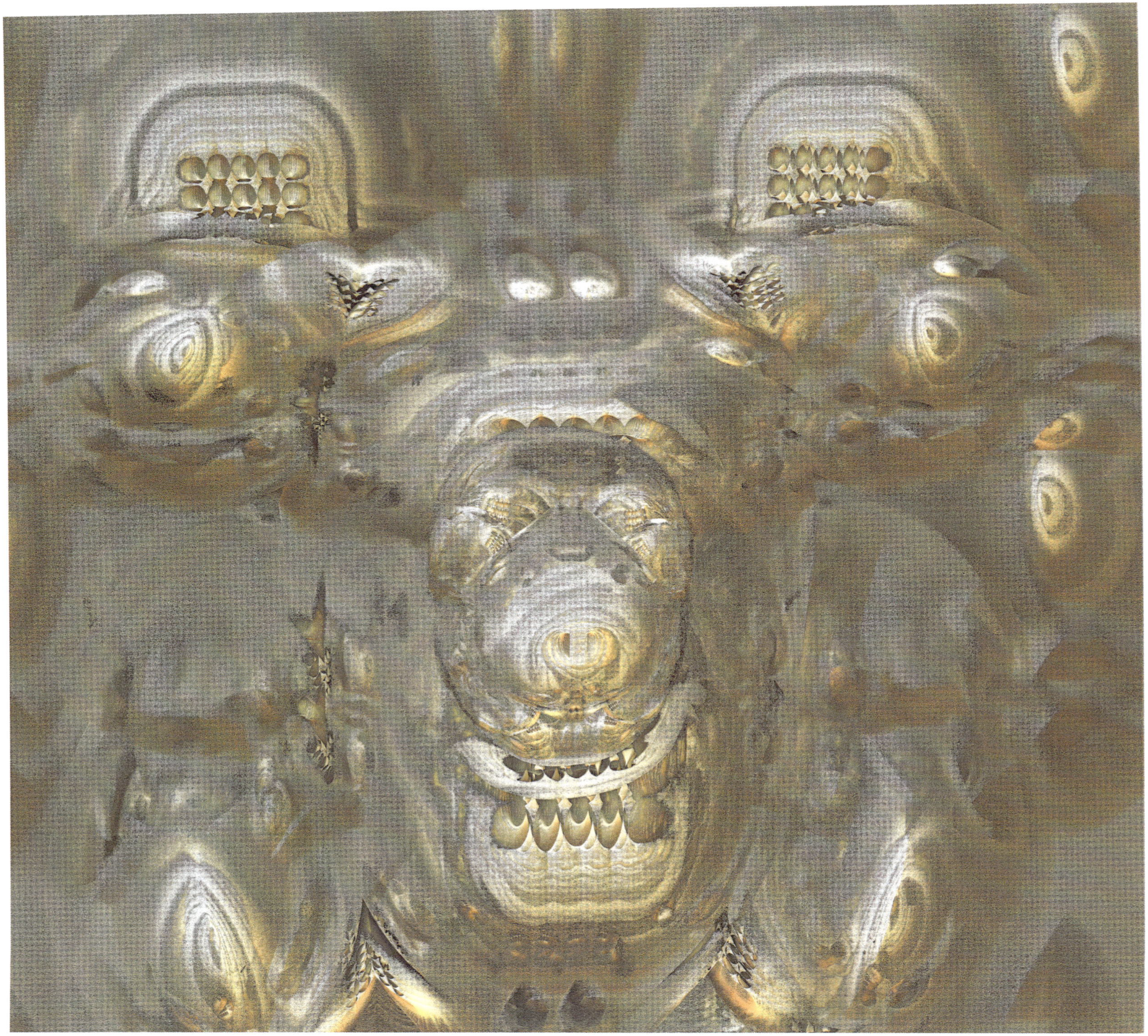

"Bad Dreams!" All the images on these two pages were created in Mandelbulb 3D.

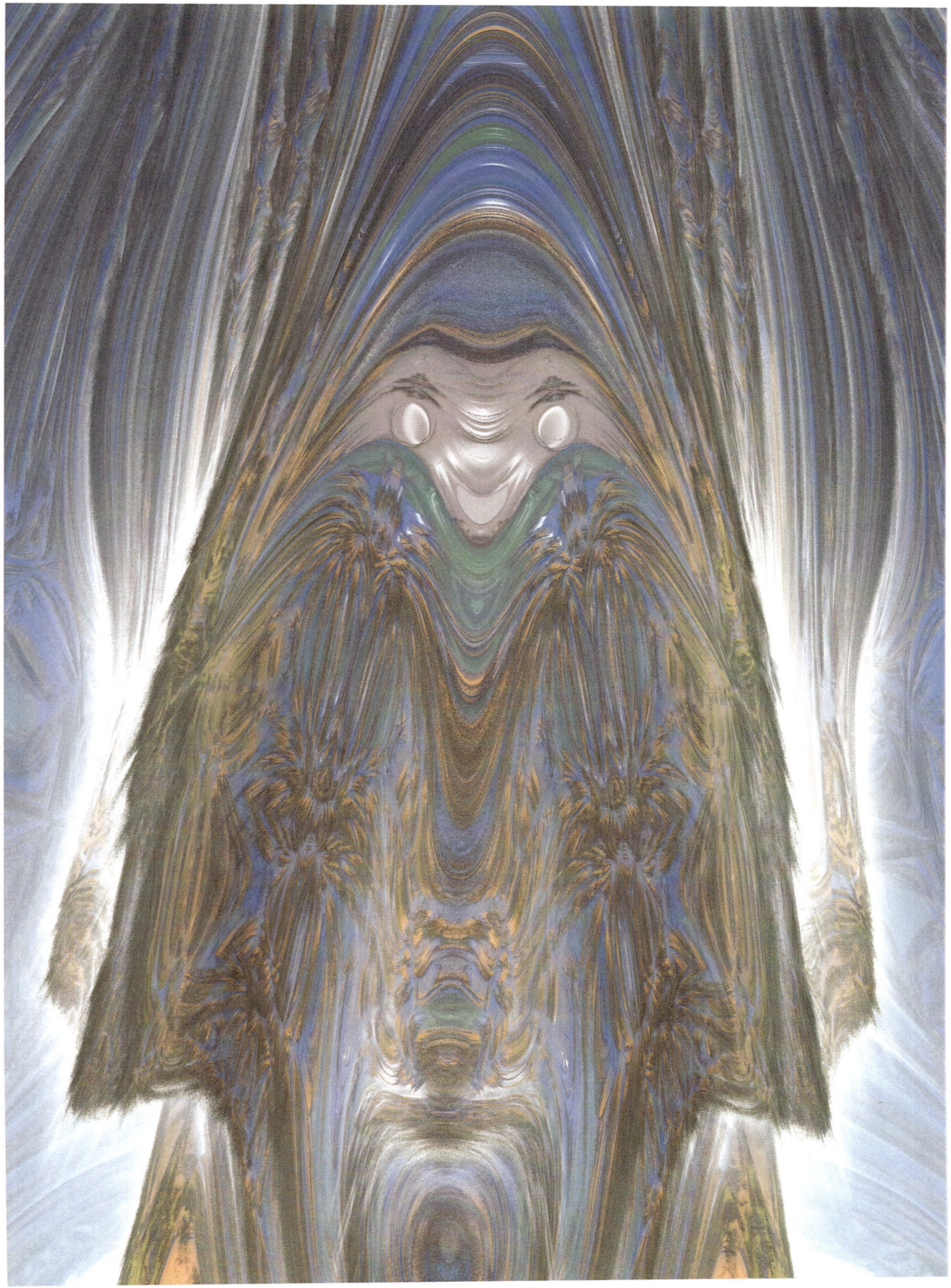

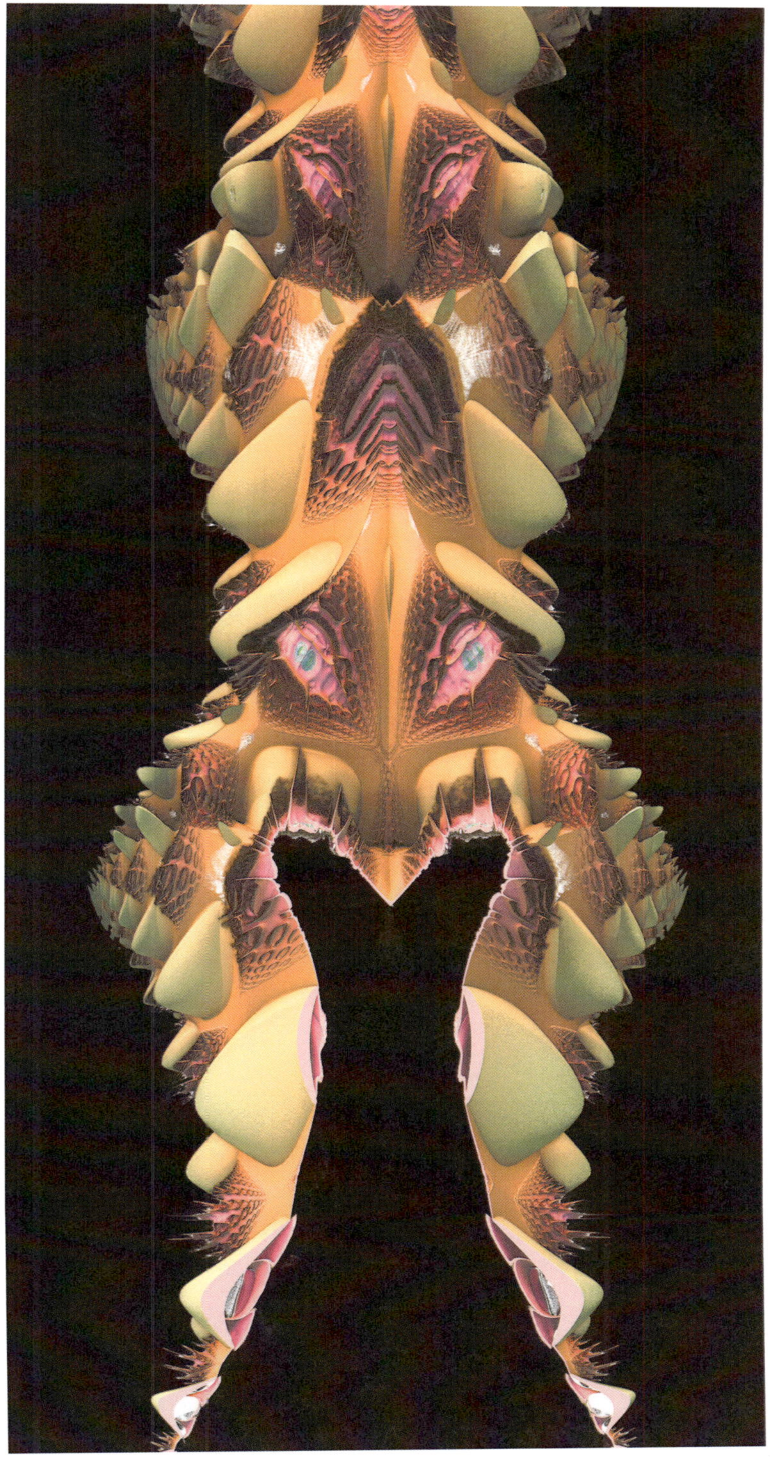

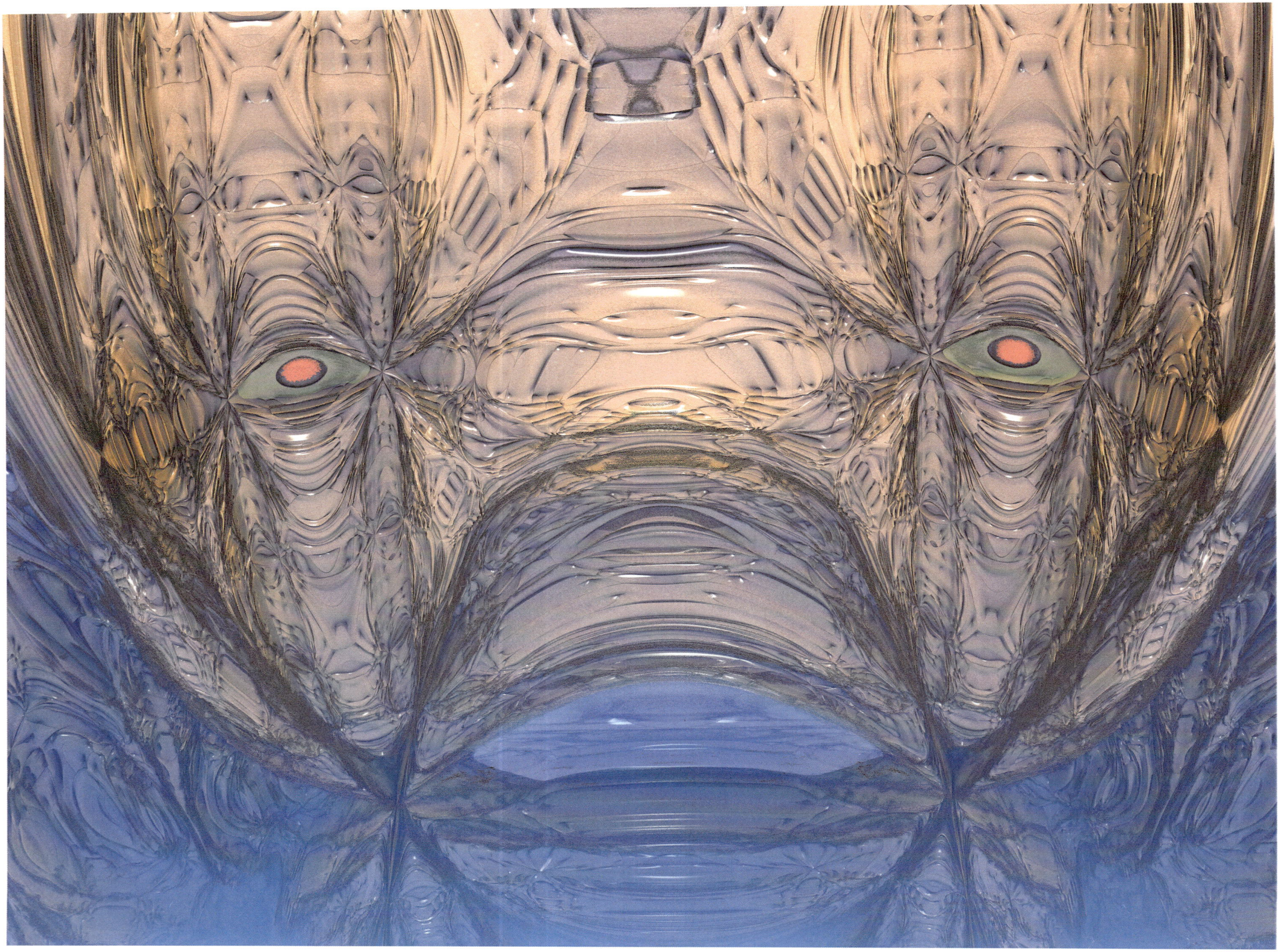

"More Bad Dreams" on this spread—alien faces from Mandelbulb 3D

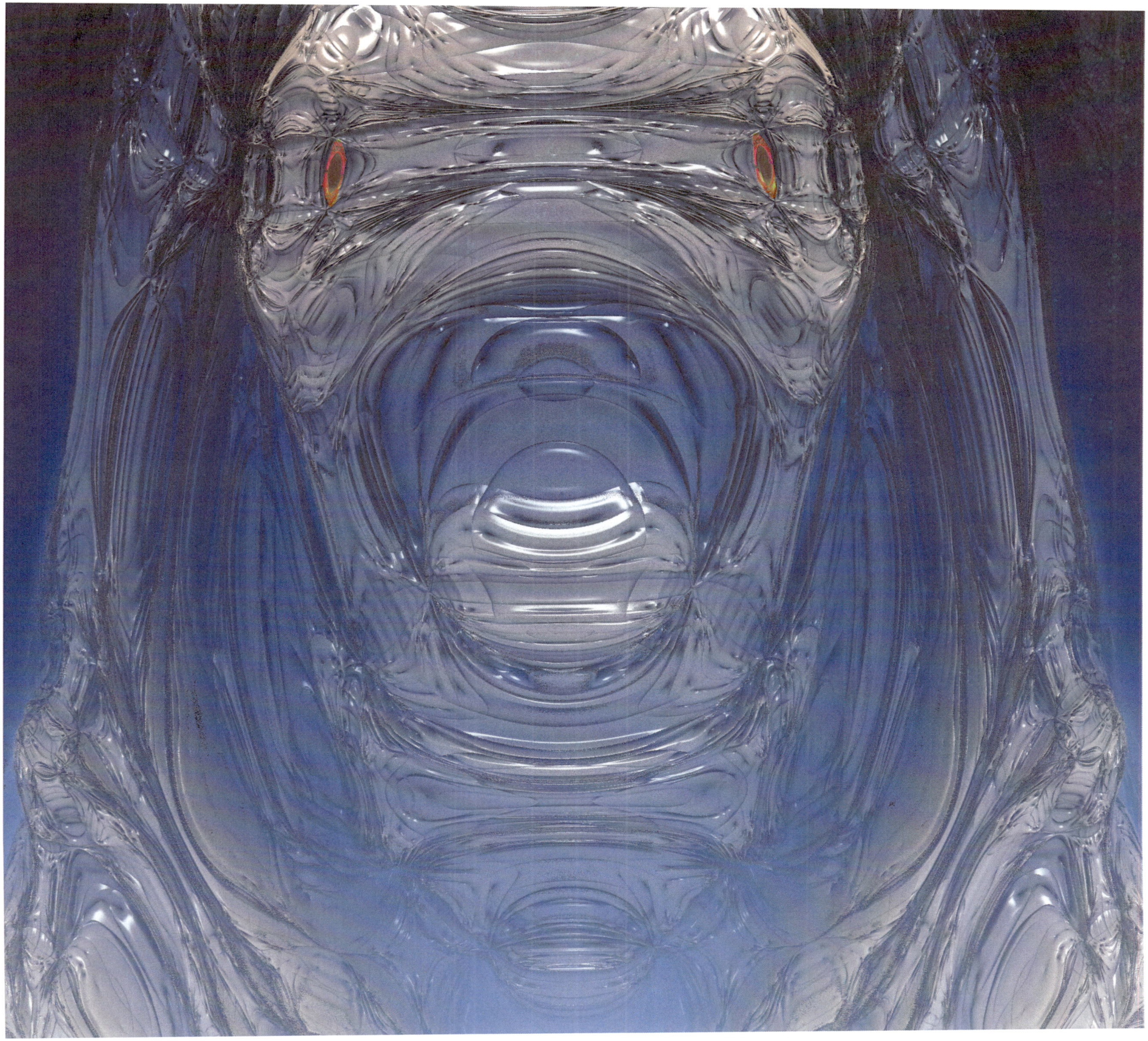

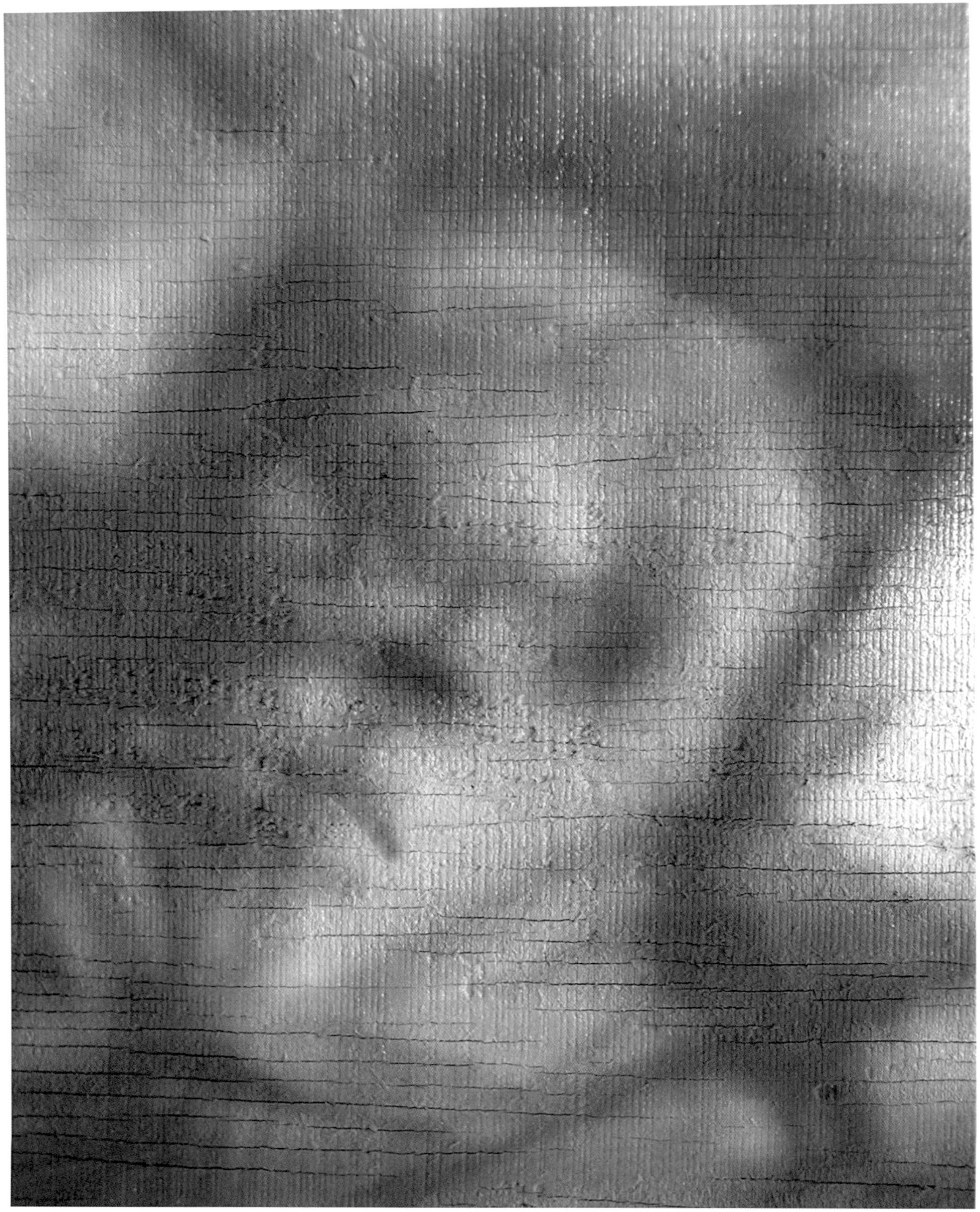

Creepy face? Not a fractal, but a photo of a shadow image cast by tree branches on an exterior wall.

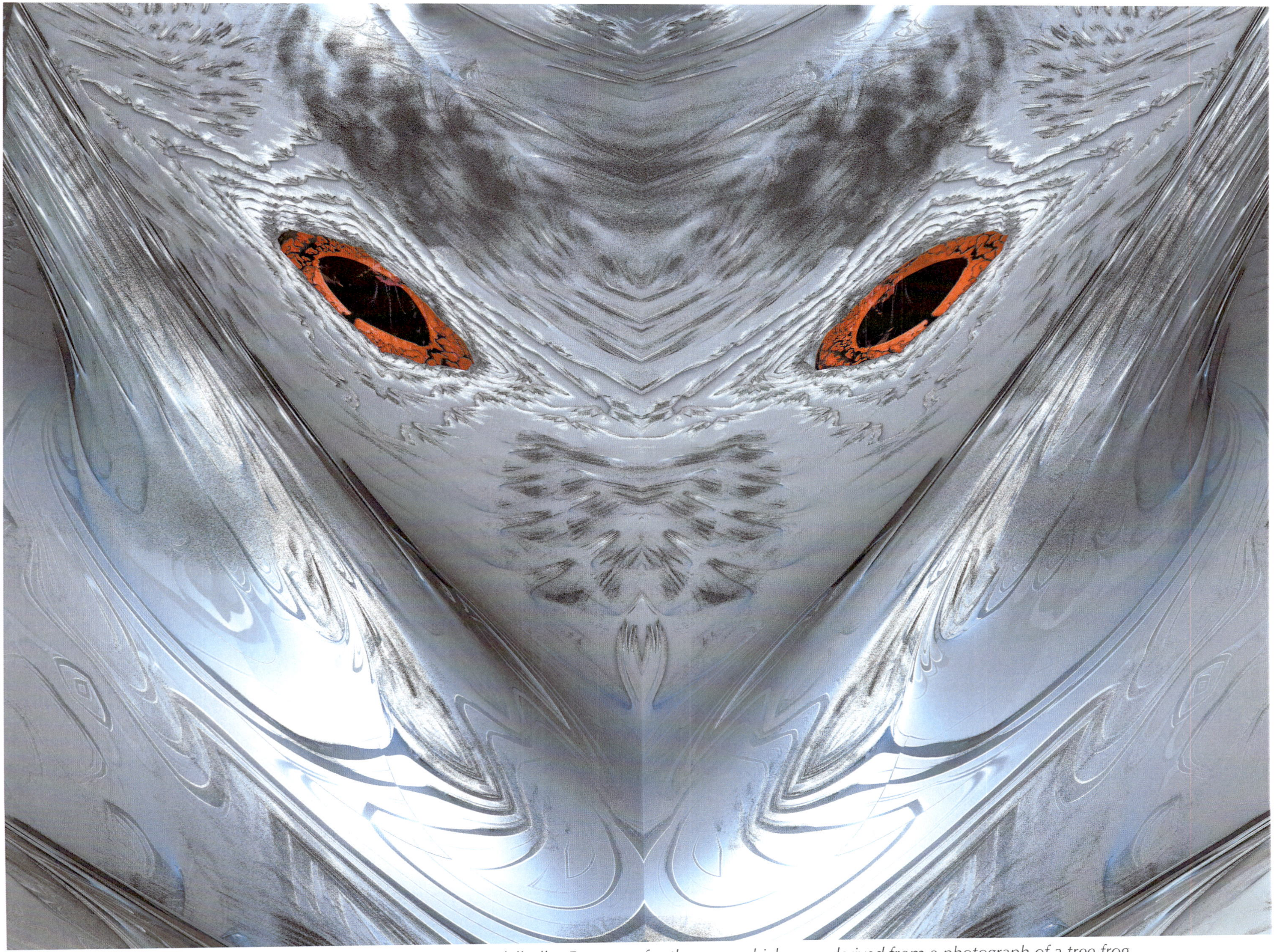

"Alien Face?" This image was generated by Mandelbulb 3D, except for the eyes, which were derived from a photograph of a tree frog.

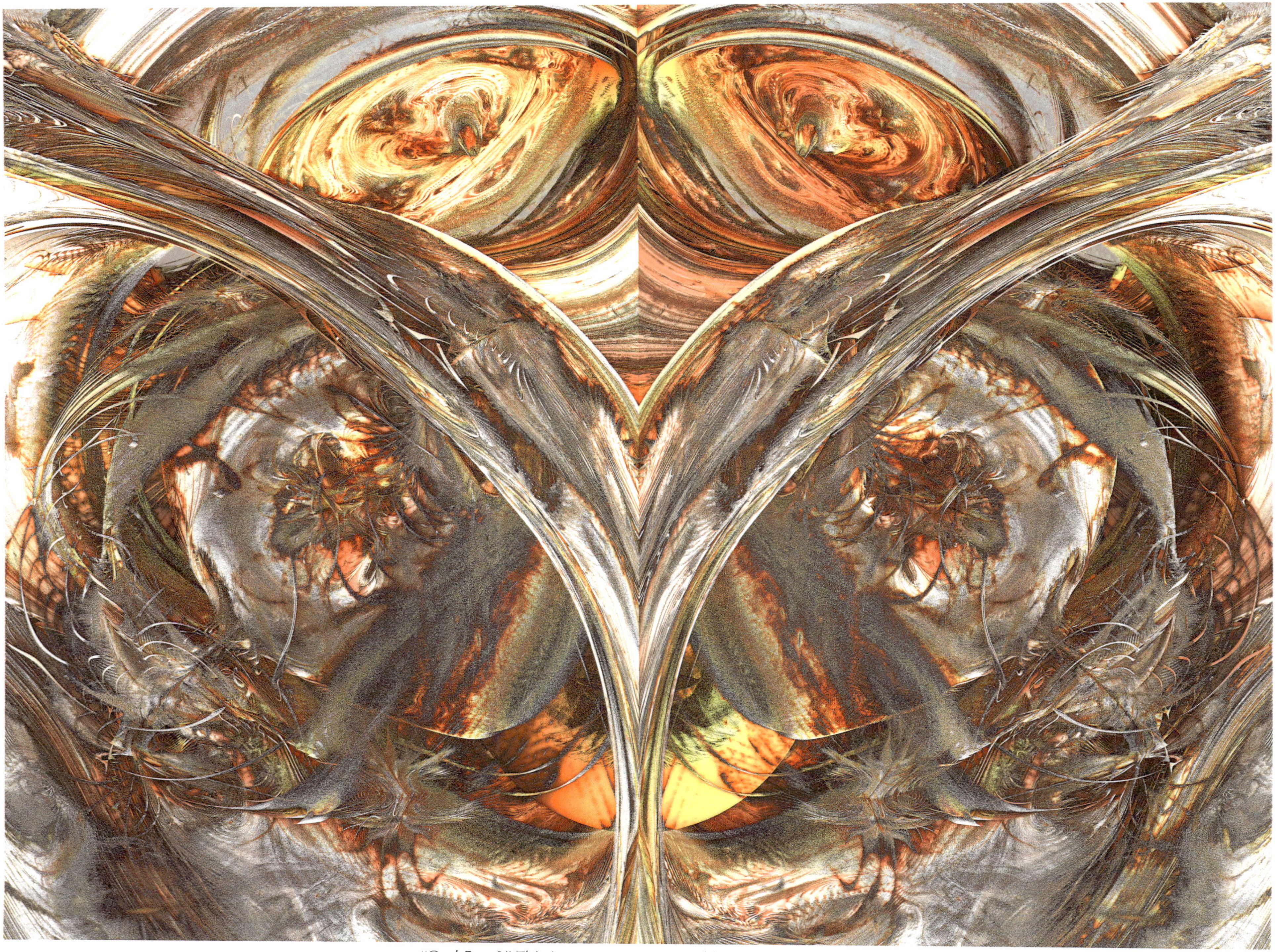

"Owl Face?" This image was generated by Mandelbulb 3D.

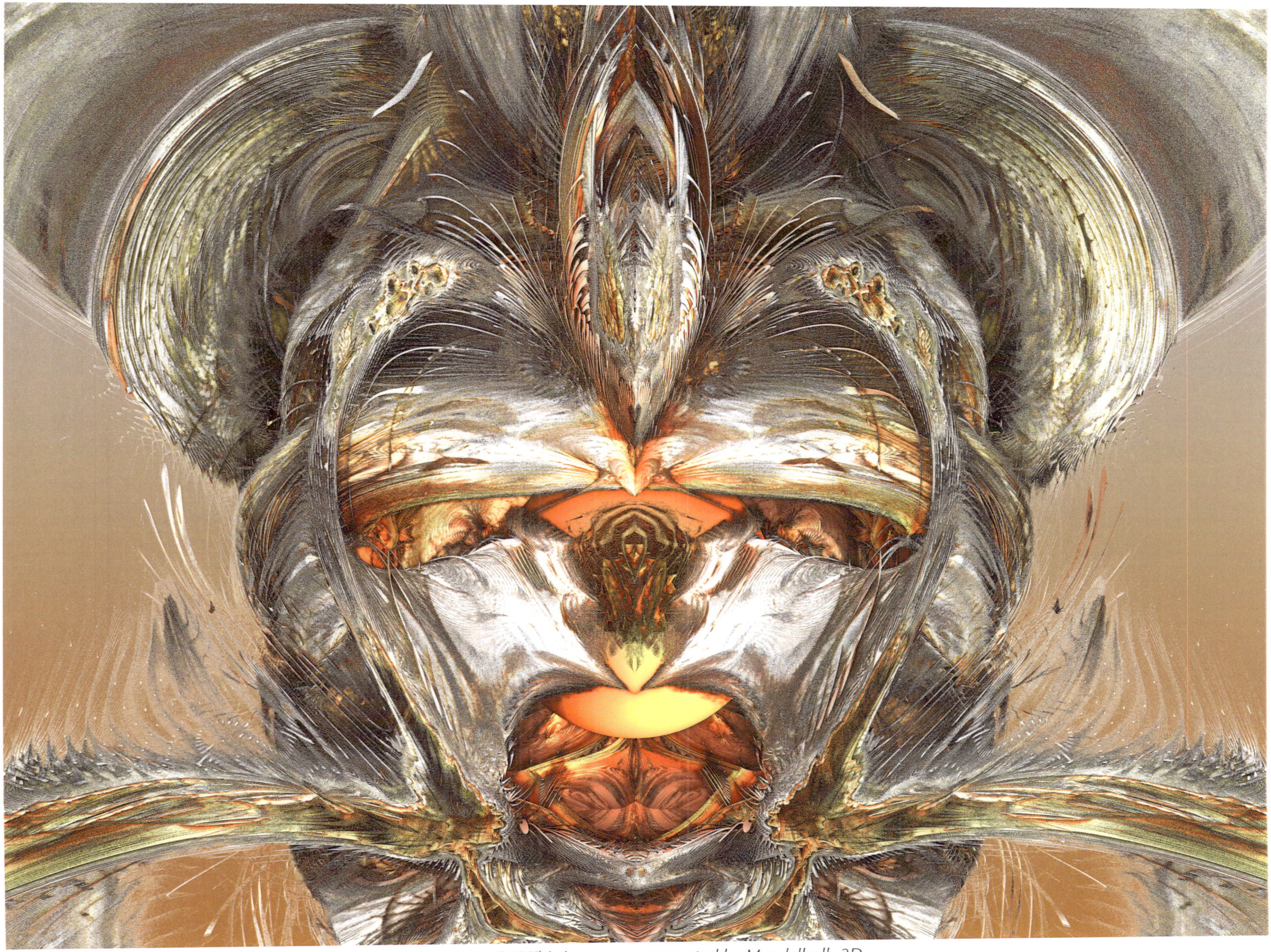

"Alien Face #2" This image was generated by Mandelbulb 3D.

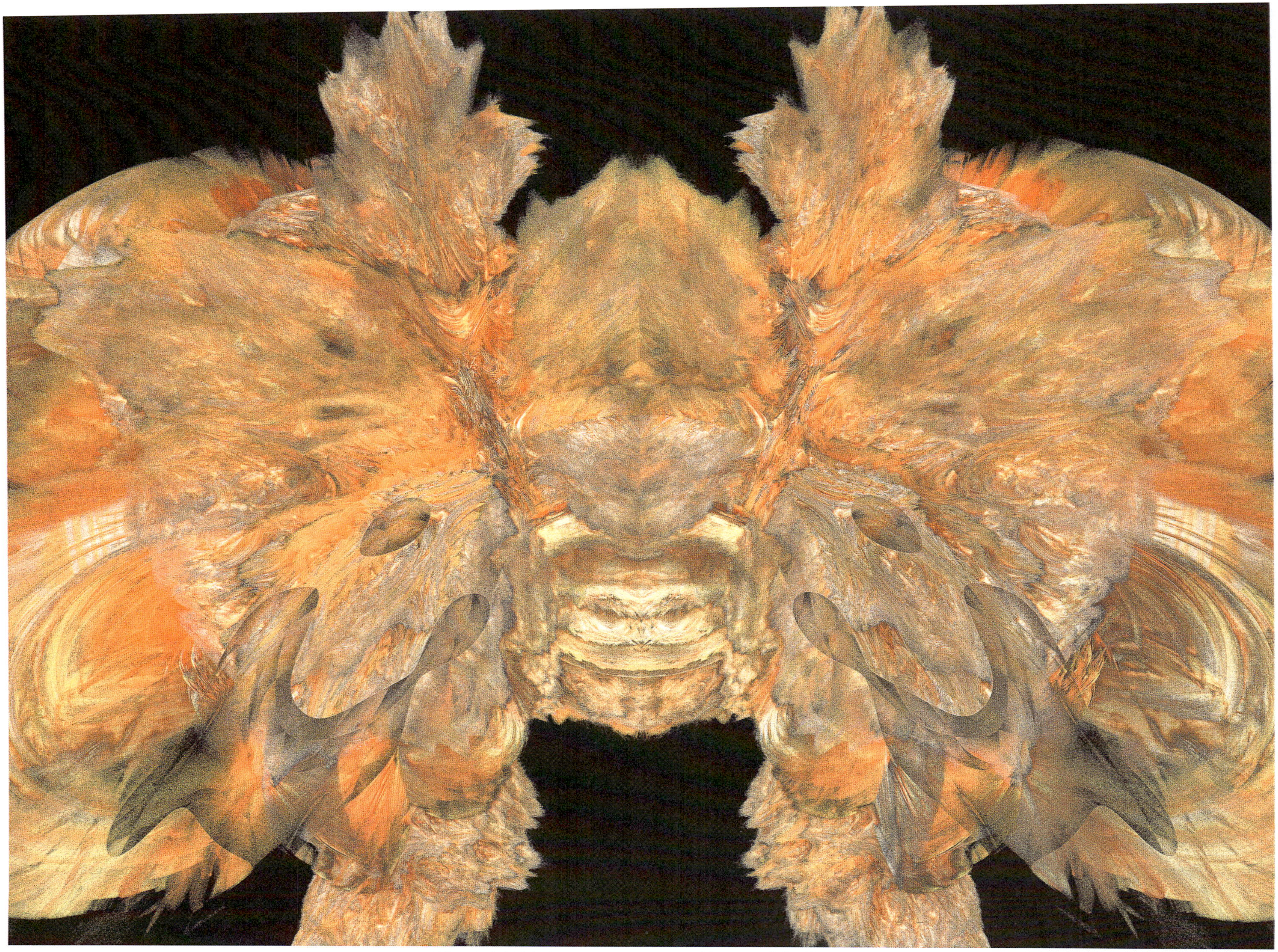

What is it? This image was generated by Mandelbulb 3D.

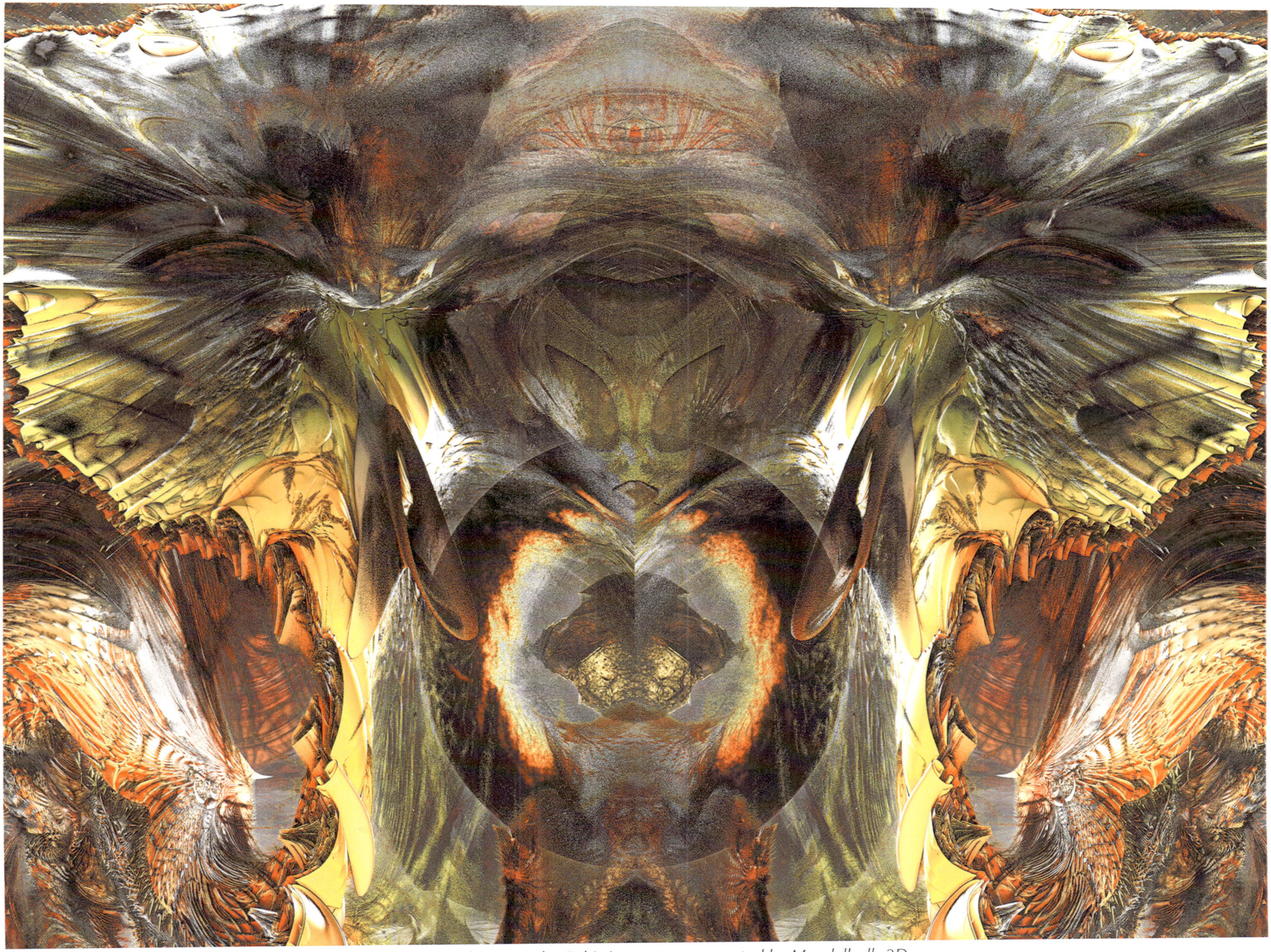

"Evil Being with an Amulet;" this image was generated by Mandelbulb 3D.

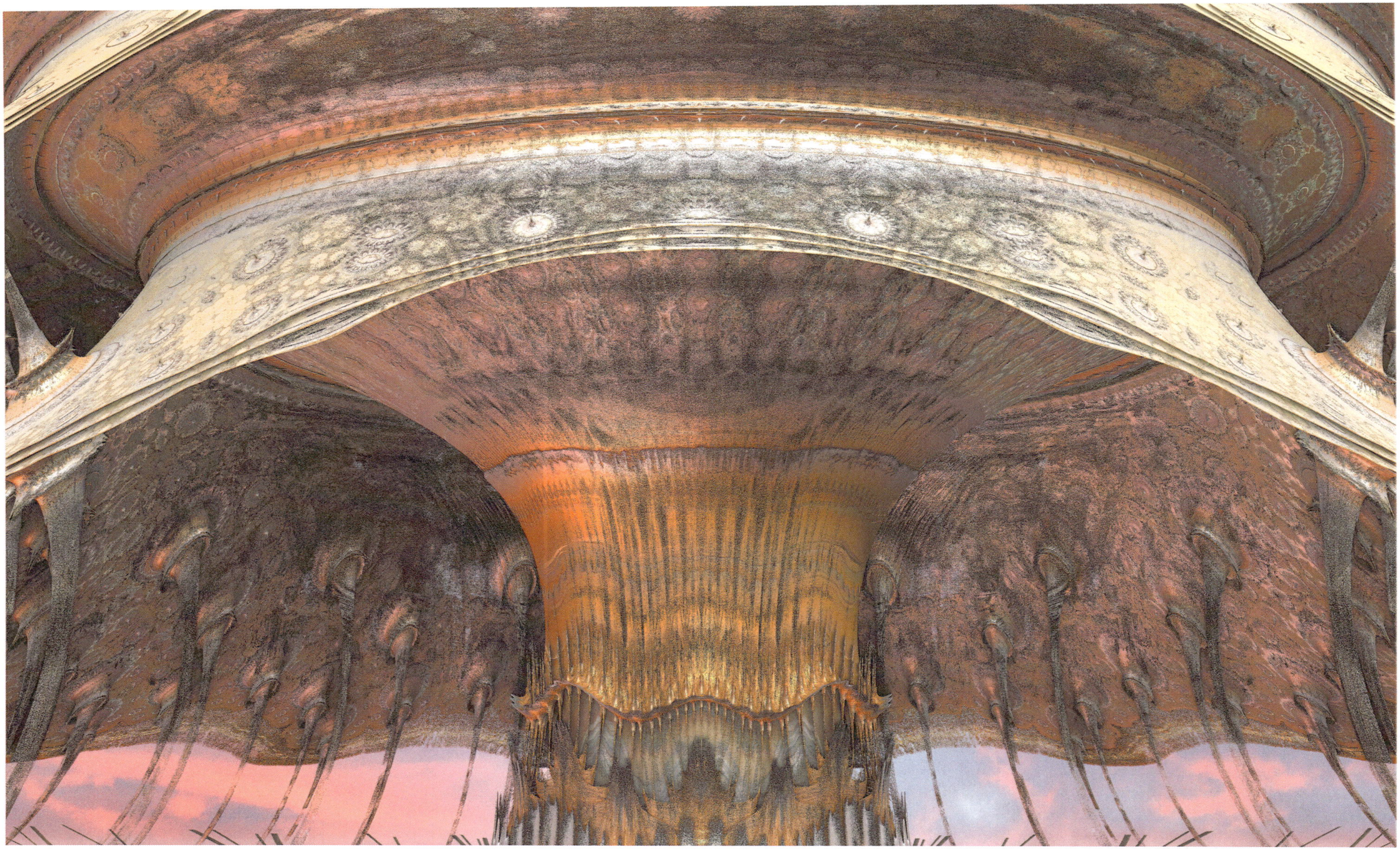

"Giant Alien Mushroom Ship;" image was generated by Mandelbulb 3D.

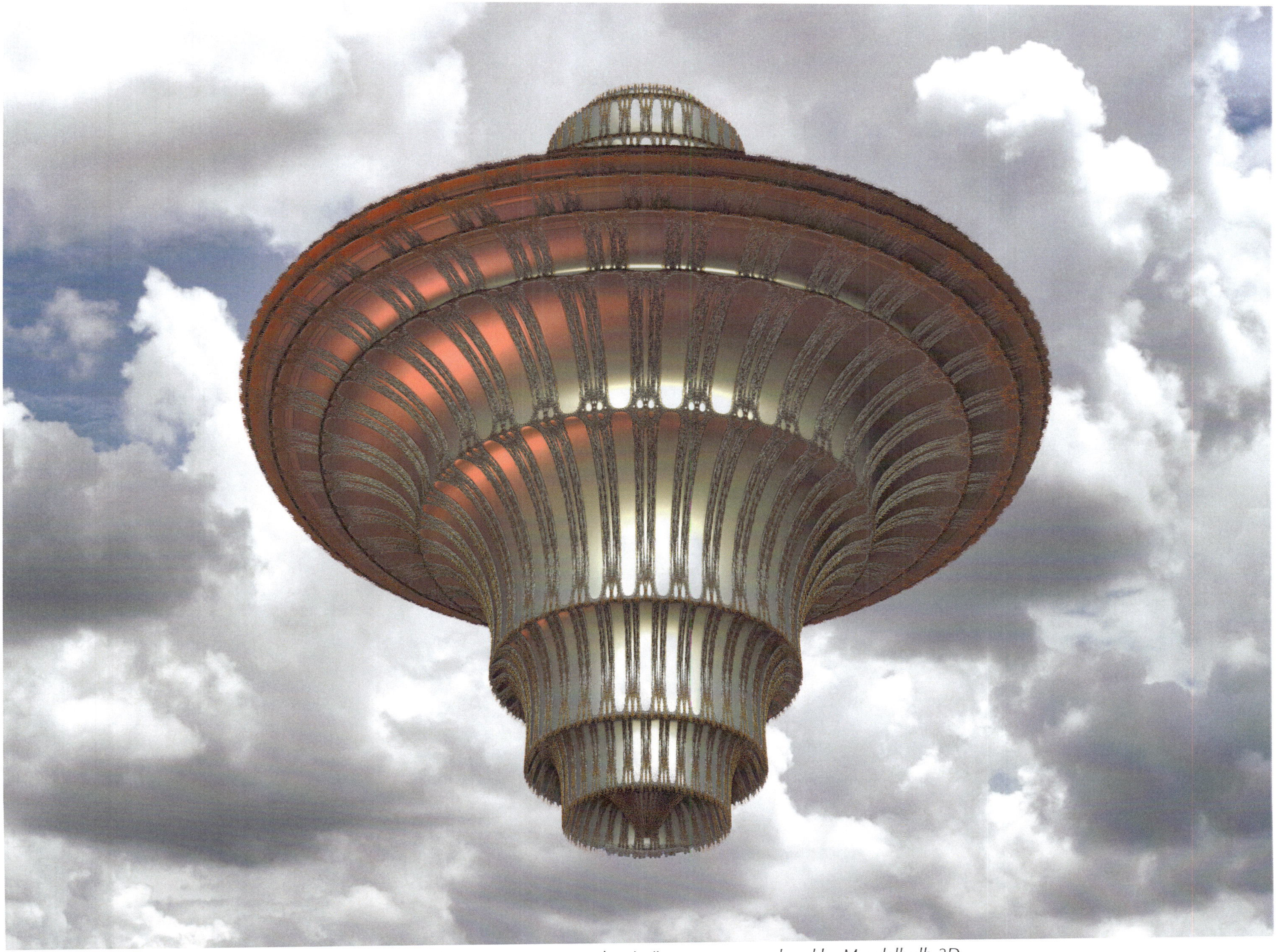

"Mother Ship in Bucks County, Pennsylvania;" saucer was rendered by Mandelbulb 3D.

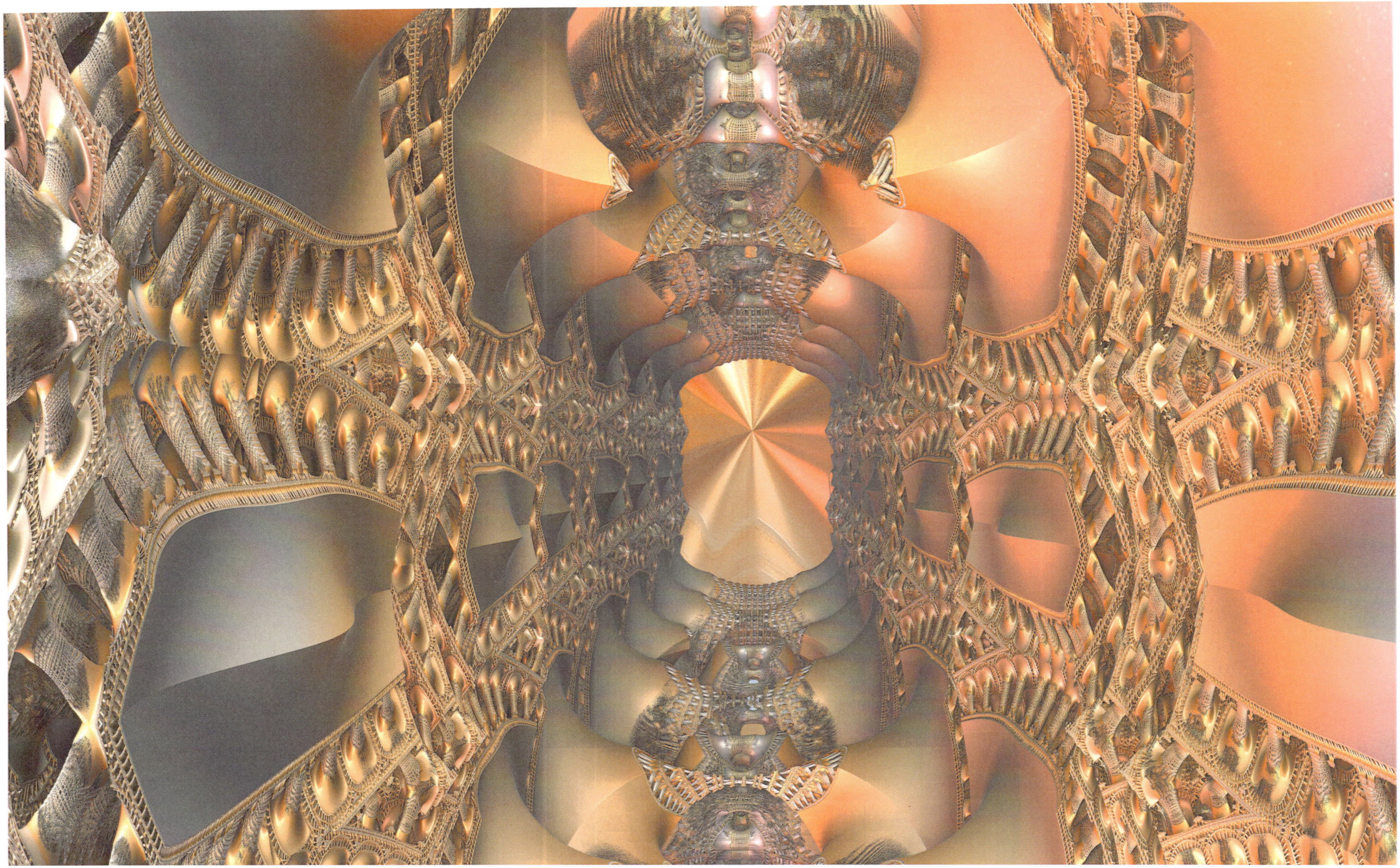

"Space-Time Portal to Another Universe;" this image was rendered by Mandelbulb 3D.

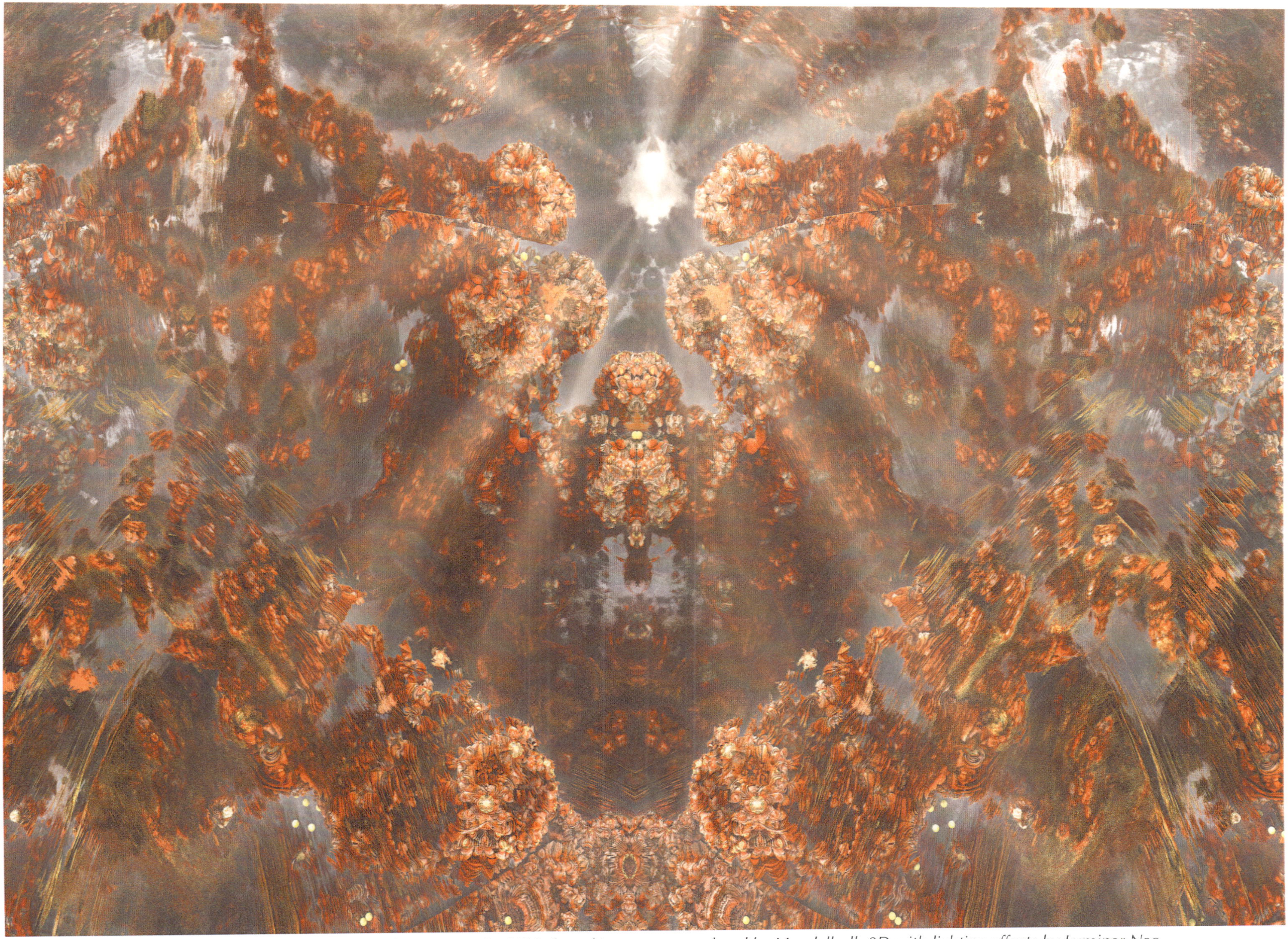

"Primordial Beginning—And Then There Was Light." This fractal image was rendered by Mandelbulb 3D with lighting effects by Luminar Neo.

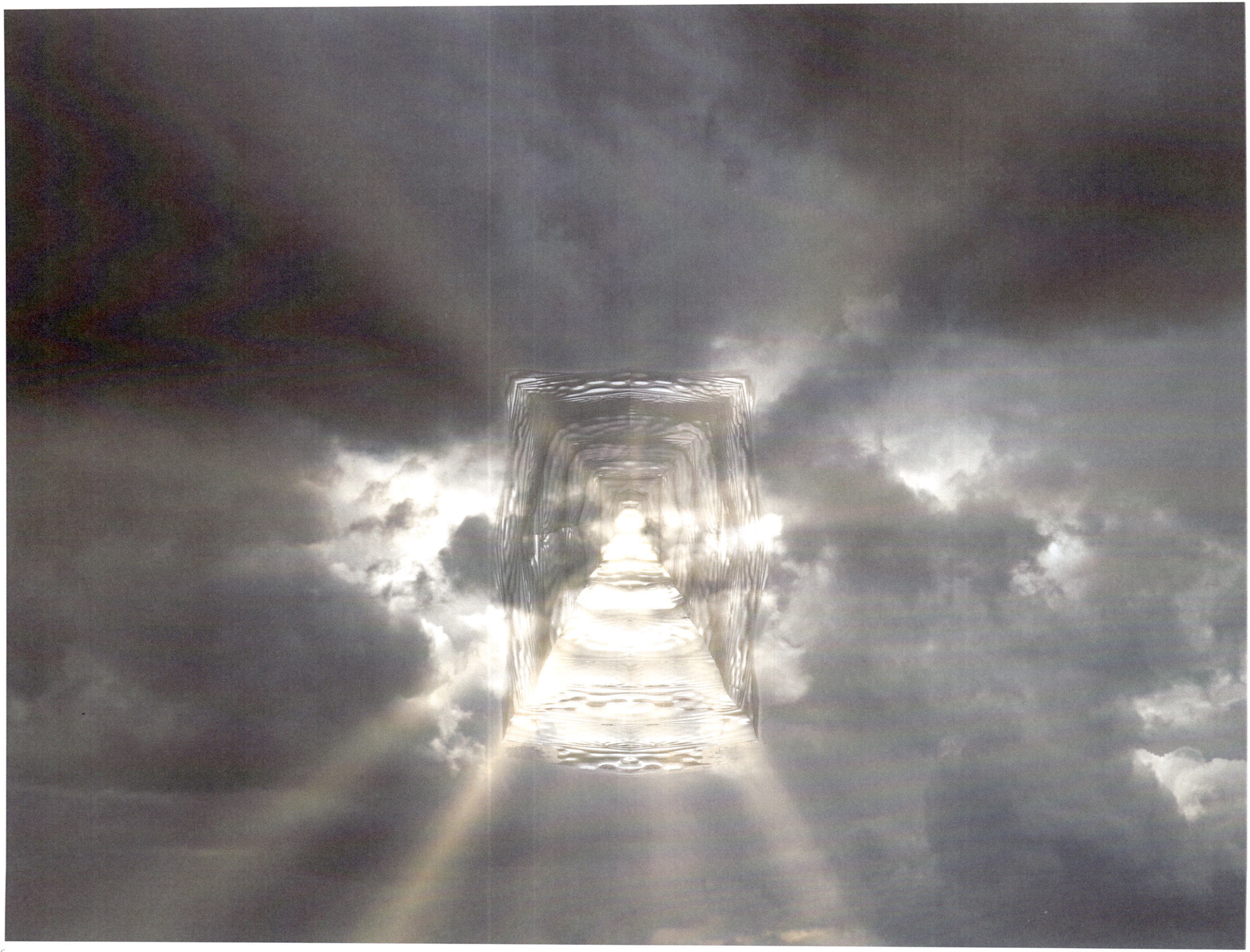

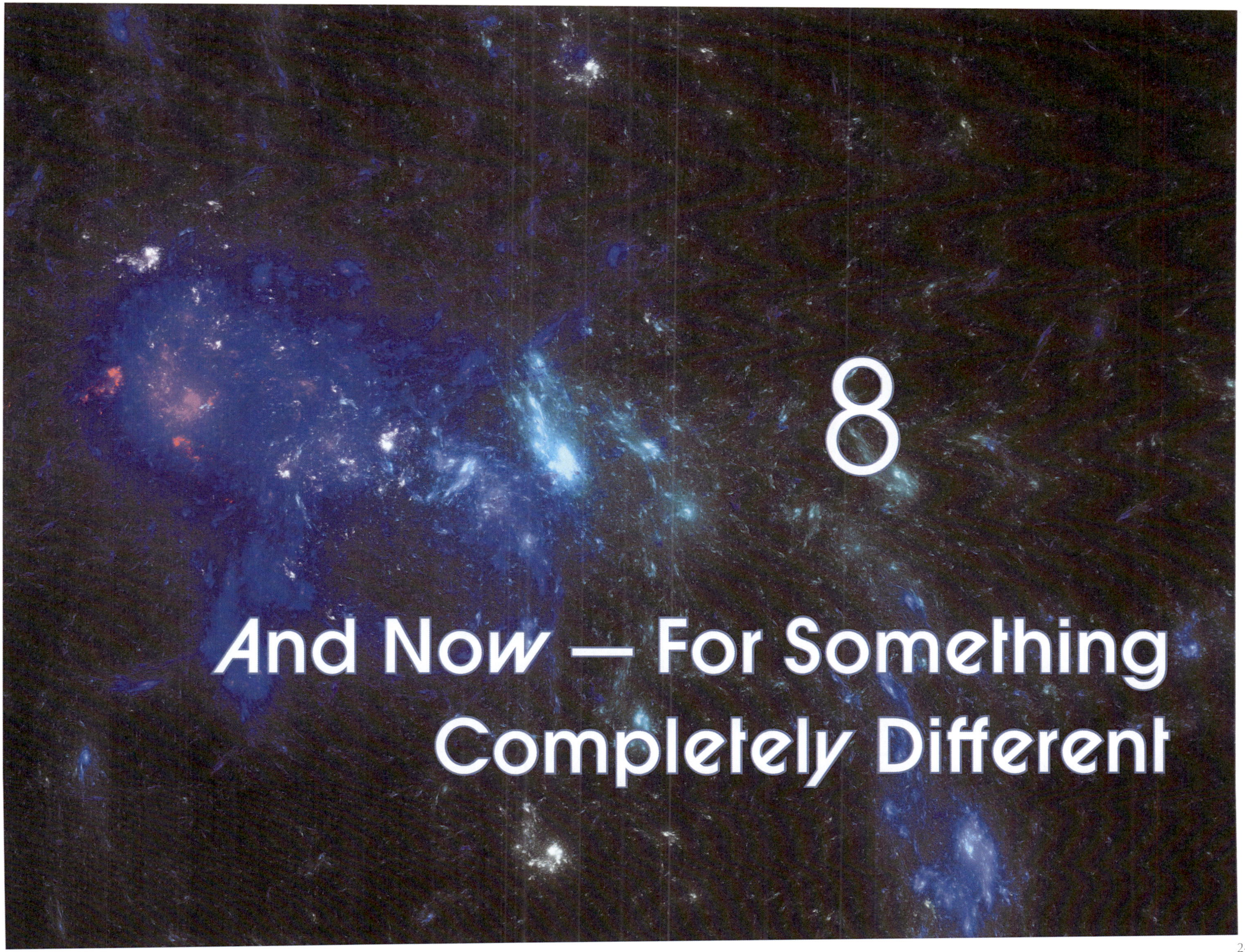

8

And Now — For Something Completely Different

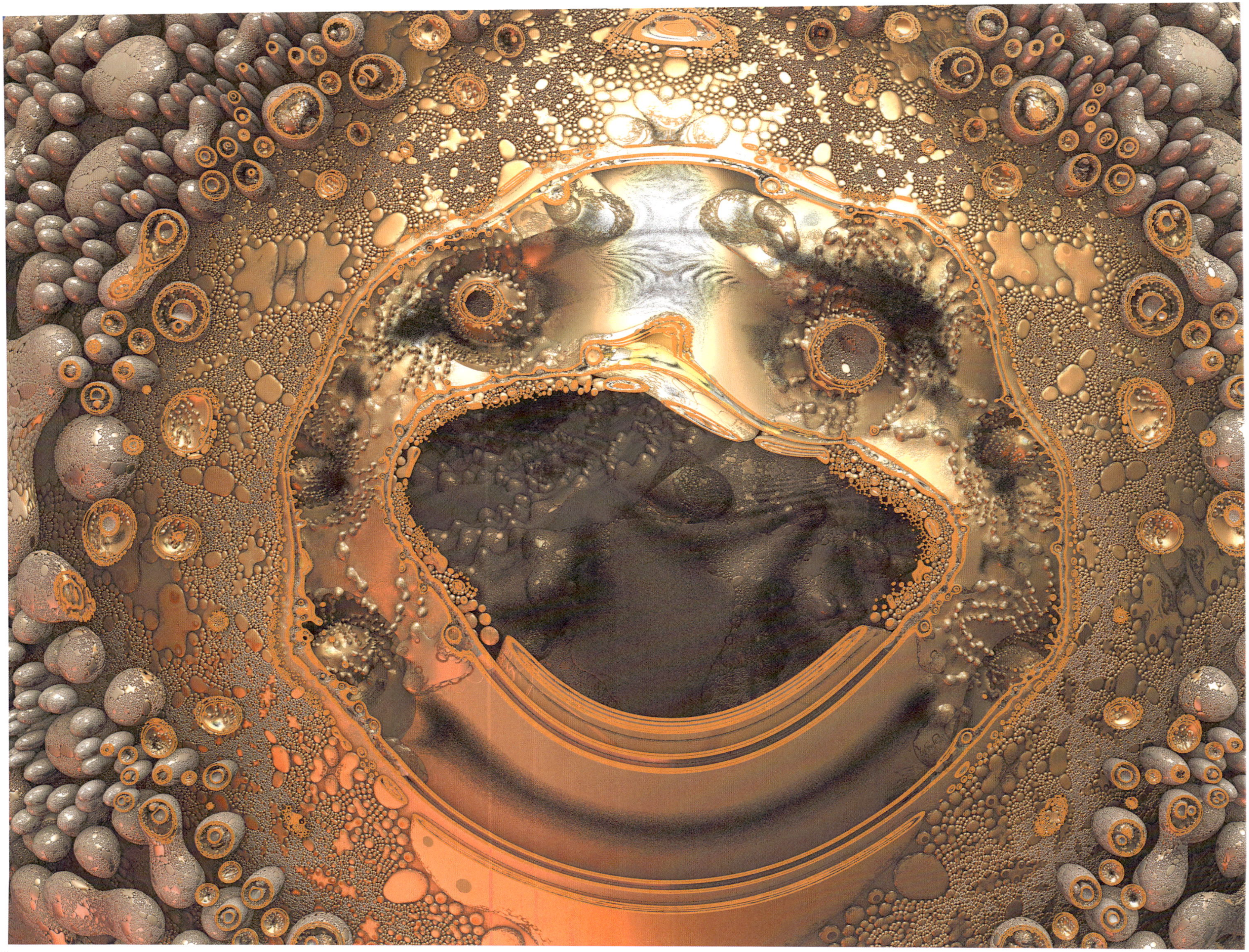

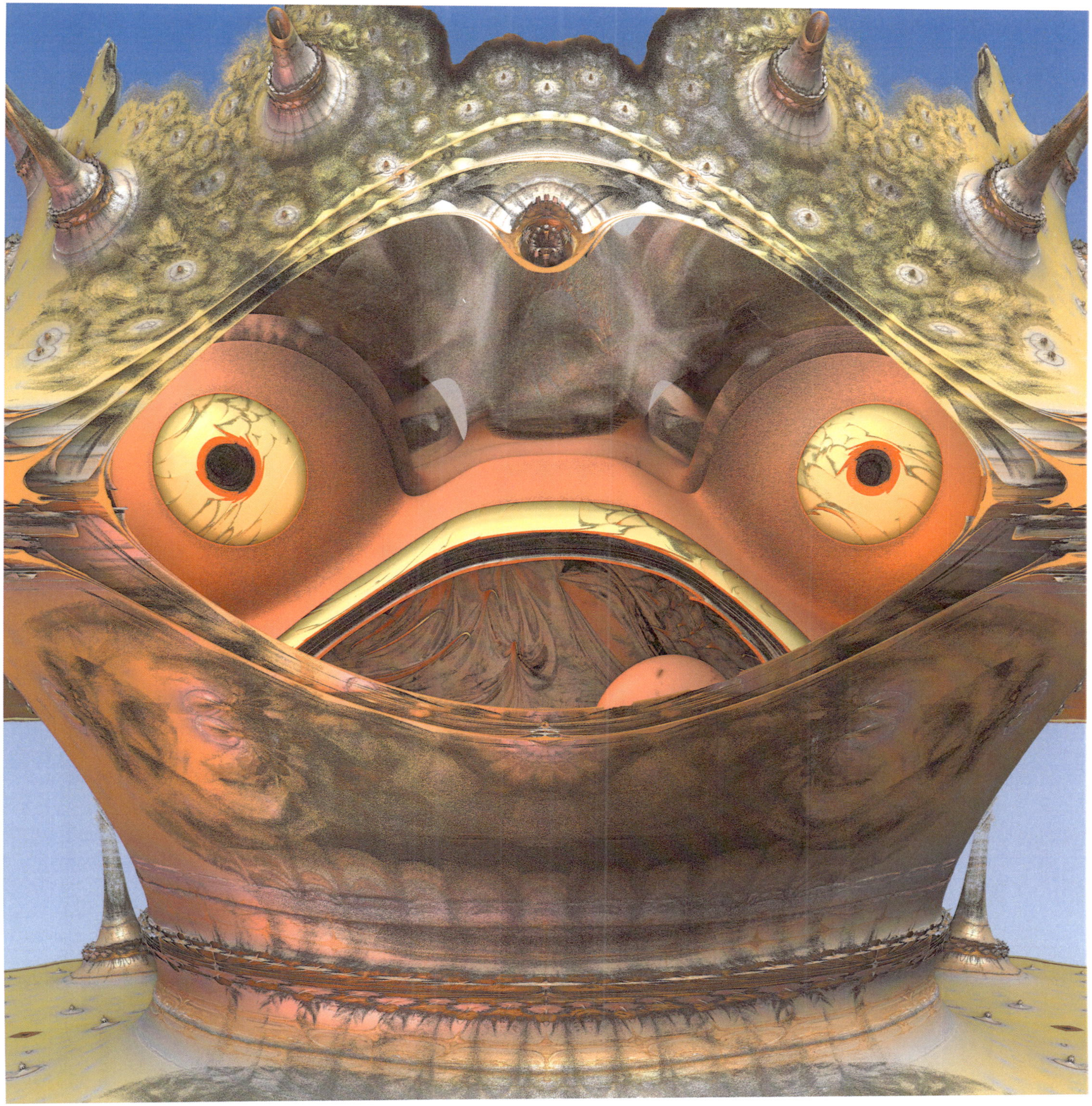

Both images on this spread were generated in Mandelbulb 3D.

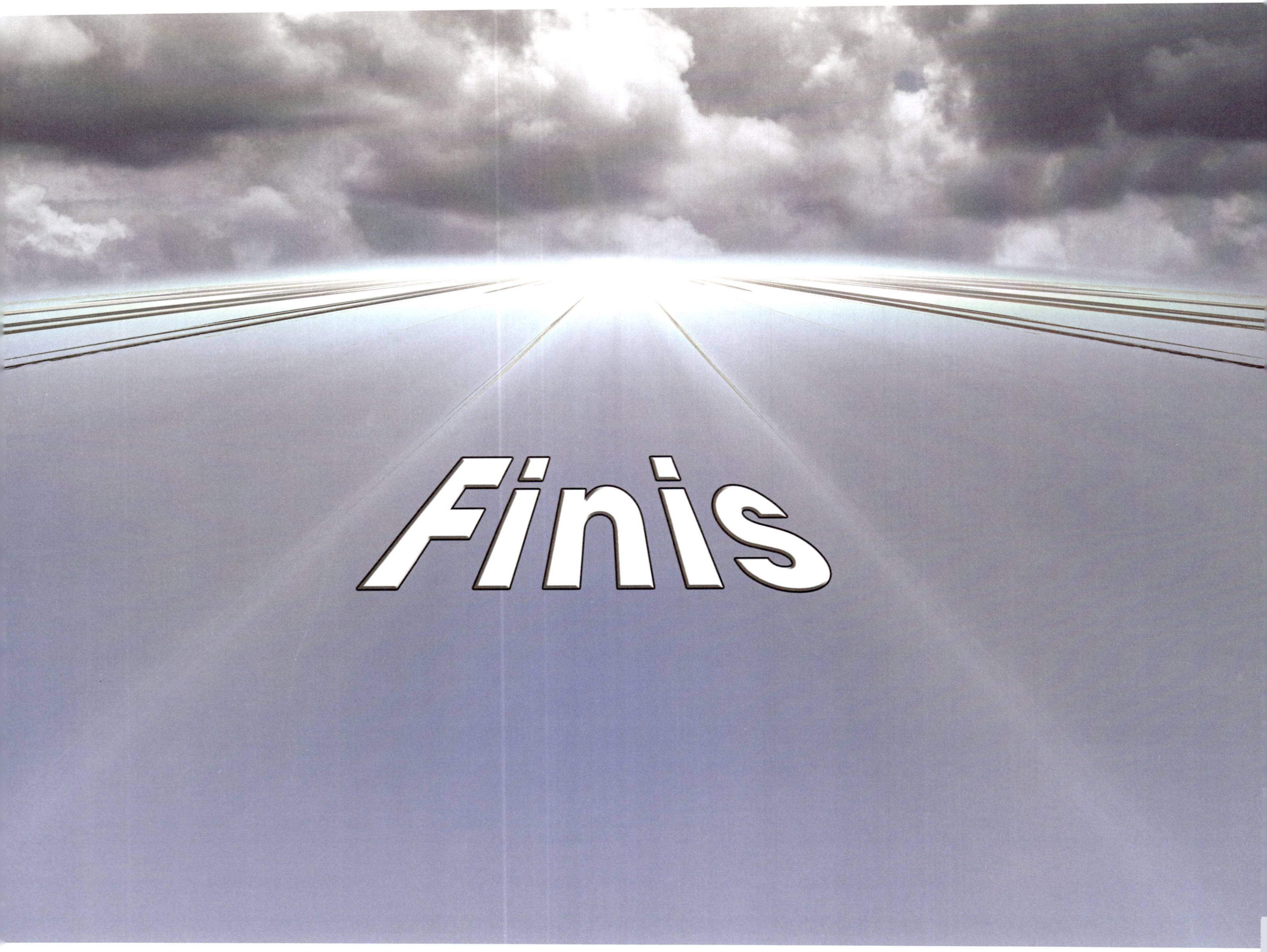
Finis

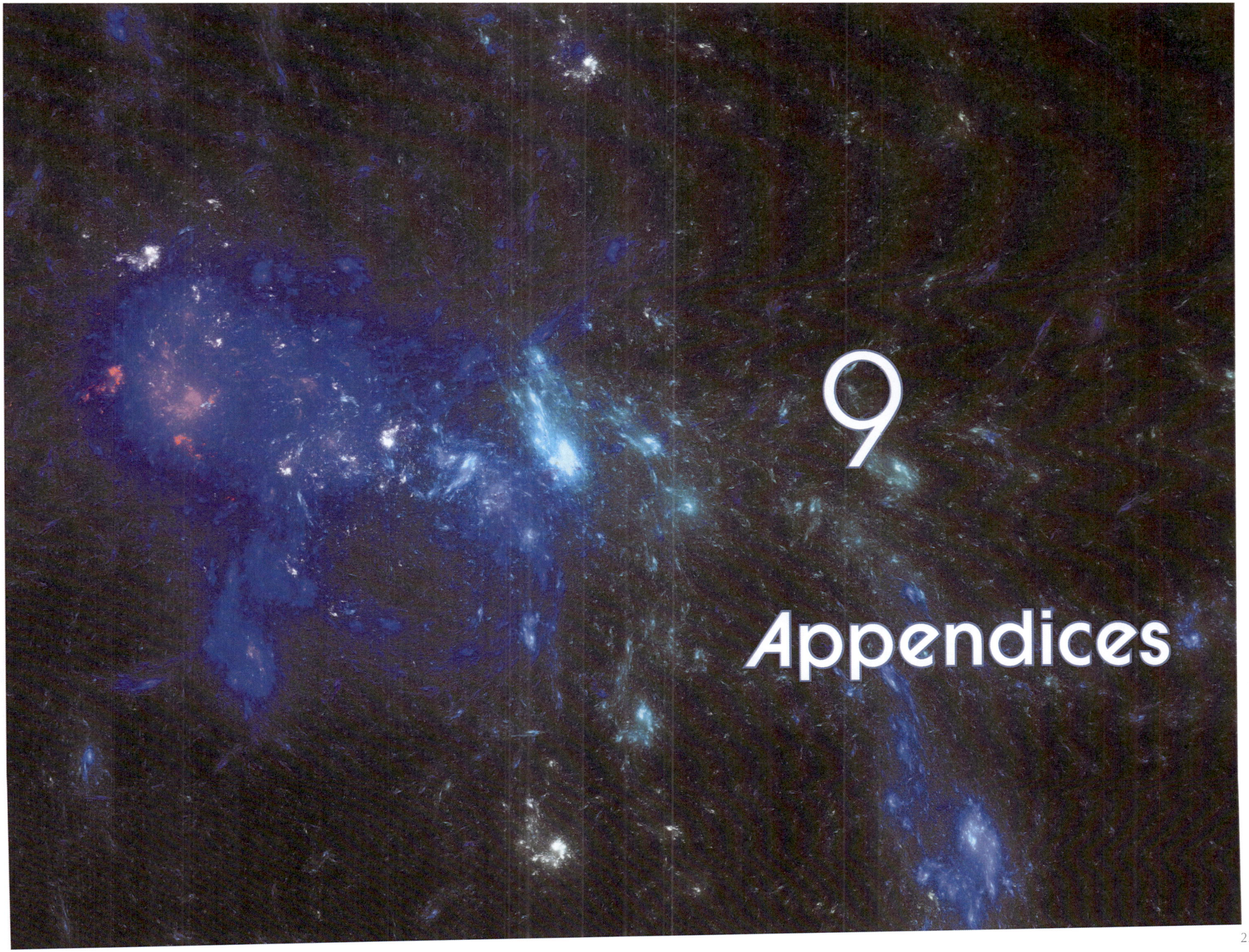

9 Appendices

Appendix A
Notes on production

A brief programming note

Given the scope of this book, to provide all the theory behind fractal image creation would be unnecessarily complex since that's already been done by Mandelbrot himself and other mathematicians in several published books on the subject. The software programs used to generate the images in this book—Mandelbulb 3D and JWildfire—are tools consisting of "building blocks" that allow the user to change coefficients/parameters to fractal types and combine them to create additional interesting images.

The code that the software generates is basically machine language and as such would provide no clarification of the creative process and value to the reader. Instead, the software employs "baked-in formulas" to preclude having to input them, while allowing parameter changes in much the same way that the early mathematicians changed inputs to predict the weather—once they had all the formulas in place.

With these fractal programs, users *can* write their own formulas if desired, but writing them for three and four dimensions—and beyond—would be extraordinarily complex, even for the expert user. For those desiring to download the programs, neither is large in size, and both are easy to get started.

In both programs, one starting image, for example, is plugged in automatically when the program is opened, and one simply hits the "Render" button to create a 3D image. Thus, for the average person who likes to play a little, it's not hard to change two or three allowable parameters for the initial image and to see the new result. And some fractal types will have even more parameters to allow experimentation.

Mandelbulb 3D

Most of the fractal images in this book have been created over the last ten years using Mandelbulb 3D fractal software. Besides static images, Mandelbulb 3D is capable of generating video sequence frames that can be combined in most video editors—much in the same way that cartoons used to be created from a series of hand-drawn images in the days before computers. The software can also generate wireframe still images and exceedingly large still images when needed and is known for creating 3D "bulbs" or objects in space.

Mandelbulb 3D can run on Windows XP through Windows 10, and provides a set of tools for manipulating color and 3D lighting. It also runs in the WINE environment on most Linux distributions. Mandelbulb 3D can be downloaded at https://mb3d.overwhale.com.

The software (as well as the Mandelbulb itself) was initially invented at the online forum known as *fractalforums.com*. Also known as MB3D, it was written by the "user," who goes by the name of Jesse. In writing the code, he used a combination of Delphi (for simplicity and speed of development) and 32-bit assembly language (for speed). Version 1.0 of Mandelbulb 3D was released in 2010. After releasing a lot of updates Jesse retired; his final update was 1.89 to date.

Andreas Maschke, aka *overwhale*, took over the project in 2015 and pushed the source code to GitHub. Maschke remains the current—and only—maintainer of MB3D and has been continuously creating new releases since. The source code of the project is public and currently hosted at GitHub.

I'd like to take a moment to thank those who have written and contributed to this program over the years. Another word of thanks goes out to Hal Tenny who graciously contributed to many of the tutorials for Mandelbulb 3D and provided the base parameters for my modified fractal on page 51.

JWildfire

Some of the backgrounds in this book were created in JWildfire, a free and user-friendly image-processing software, mostly known for its sophisticated flame-fractal-generator and "galaxy" backgrounds. (See the folio headings in this book as well as several non-photographic "sky" images. The program is Java-based, open-source and runs on any major computer platform. There is also a special Android version for mobile devices. The software is completely free and hasn't any locked features, ads or other nagging popups.

Andreas Maschke also maintains the JWildfire program and related website (https://jwildfire.overwhale.com). At the time of this writing, he can be reached via email: thargor6@googlemail.com

Appendix B
The Mandelbrot Set

The Mandelbrot set is defined by the equation:

$$z_n+1 = z_n^2 + c$$

where c and z are complex numbers and n is zero or a positive integer.

Starting with $z_0 = 0$, c is in the Mandelbrot set if the absolute value of z_n never becomes larger than a certain number (that number depends on c), no matter how large n gets.

Stated another way, the set is defined in the complex number plane as the complex numbers c for which the function,

$$f_c(z) = x^2 + c$$

does not diverge to infinity when iterated starting at $z = 0$, that is, for which the sequence $f_c(0)$, $f_c(f_c(0))$, etc. remains bounded in absolute value.

Appendix C:
Additional reading

Books written by Mandelbrot are available on Amazon and at major booksellers and include the following:

Mandelbrot, B. 1983, 2021. *The Fractal Geometry of Nature,* W. H. Freeman & Co Ltd; Echo Point Books & Media, LLC.

Mandelbrot, B. 2020. *Fractals: Form, Chance and Dimension,* Echo Point Books & Media, Reprint.

Mandelbrot, B. and Hudson, Richard L. 2008, 2006. *The Misbehavior of Markets: A Fractal View of Financial Turbulence*, Profile Books, Basic Books.

Mandelbrot, B. 2014. *The Fractalist: Memoir of a Scientific Maverick,* Vintage.

Mandelbrot, B. 2004. *Fractals and Chaos: The Mandelbrot Set and Beyond,* Springer.

Mandelbrot, B. and Damerau, F. J., et al. 2002. *Gaussian Self-Affinity and Fractals: Globality, The Earth, 1/f Noise, and R/S (Selected Works of Benoit B. Mandelbrot,* Springer.

Steven Strogatz, PhD, Cornell University has published the following books:

Strogatz, Stephen. 2015, 2024. *Nonlinear Dynamics and Chaos - Sixth Edition, CRC Press.*

Strogatz, Stephen. 2003. *Sync: The Emerging Science of Spontaneous Order,* Hyperion.

Strogatz, Stephen. 2020. *Infinite Powers: How Calculus Reveals the Secrets of the Universe*, Mariner Books.

Strogatz, Stephen. 2012. *The Joy Of X: A Guided Tour of Math, from One to Infinity*, Houghton Mifflin Harcourt.

Strogatz, Stephen. 2020. *Infinite Powers: The Story of Calculus - The Language of the Universe,* Atlantic Books.

Appendix D:
Tools used in the production of this book:

Mandelbulb 3D (Version 1.99.36)
JWildfire (Version 8.10)
GIMP (GNU Image Manipulation Program) 2.10.30 (Windows)
Quark® XPress® 2022; 2024
Affinity® Photo© (V2.5.x)
Luminar Neo™
Topaz Labs™ AI Sharpen
Canon® Digital Photo Professional (V4)
Microsoft® Windows 10®

Fonts:

Softmaker Software GmbH® (Avignon families)

Bitstream® (Zapf Humanist families)

Also Available... Two eBook Versions

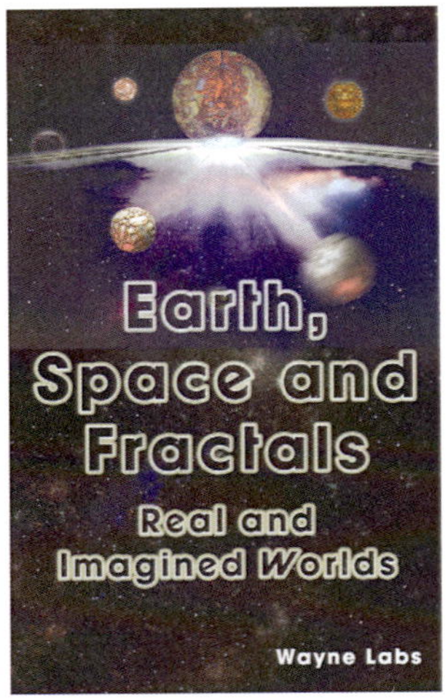

Standard ePUB version

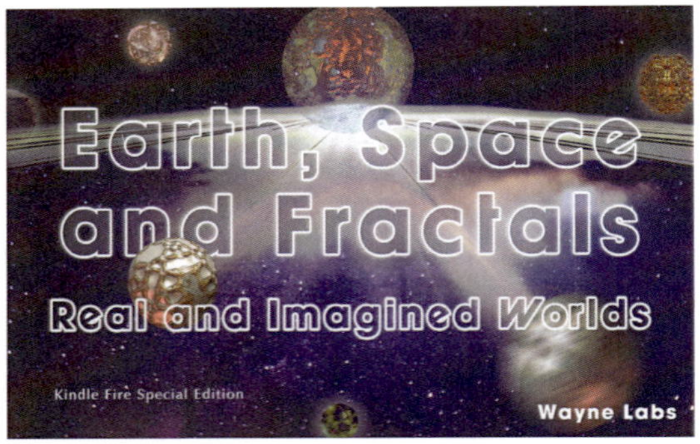

Deluxe Kindle Fire and compatible versions

Why eBooks—since I had only considered print media?
Since fractals are generated on the computer, they're really at their visual best when viewed on the computer—that is, through a backlit screen. In creating these fractals and being able to control the lighting on them, it's possible to get nuances on screen that are really difficult to reproduce on paper—no matter how good the printer is. Why? Prints work with reflected light, and the whitest white you can get is the "base white of the paper," which may have a reflectance of 90 to 95%—give or take a few percentage points—certainly not the white you can get on screen, especially with the new OLED technologies. Paper is already at a disadvantage if it doesn't have a reflectance of 100%.

OLED-based screens can produce pure blacks and pure whites, but conventional LCD screens typically have a contrast ratio of 3000 to 1 or better, which is still better than paper. In camera F-Stops, that's nearly 12 F-Stops or 12 "zones." Renowned Photographer and Master Printer Ansel Adams worked hard in the darkroom to achieve 11 zones on film and paper—with zone 5 being middle gray, zone 0 being pure black, and zone 10 being pure white.

So the challenge in converting on-screen fractals to something of similar display quality on paper is a real challenge. While output on my high-quality pro-printer looks great on glossy art paper, it doesn't guarantee the same results from commercial printers and presses—where the author has little or no control. Could viewing these fractal images even at a lower-resolution on screen justify doing an eBook?

I was skeptical until I got started doing an eBook and viewed it on my tablet in a dark room. Once, I saw the results, I was convinced to generate this book as an eBook in two different formats, which meant two more layouts—one variable and one fixed. Due to file size limit on the ePUB version specified by the distributor, I decided to create a new version for Kindle Fire tablets, which can consume higher resolution images, and file-size limits are not an issue with Amazon. Thus, there are two eBook versions.

Earth, Space and Fractals is available with reflowable text in the standard **EPUB** format. This version features the same photos and fractal images contained in the print version. It can be purchased at most eBook outlets at a list price of $8.99 (**ISBN 978-1-944280-05-5**).

The deluxe version of ***Earth, Space and Fractals*** is available as a **Kindle Fire fixed-format edition** (horizontal or "landscape"). It features additional photos and fractal images fine-tuned to the aspect ratio of Kindle Fire devices. List price is $8.99 **(ISBN 978-1-944280-06-2)** on Amazon.com.

About the Author

Author Wayne Labs is an electrical engineer specializing in radio communications; he holds a commercial General (First Class) Radio Telephone license from the FCC. For the last 30-plus years, he has been a technical editor and writer for industrial automation companies and magazines, including *I&CS (Control Solutions), CONTROL, Control Design, Electronic Design* and *Food Engineering,* where he is still a contributing technical editor. Labs has also exhibited photography in community art shows and has served as a part-time commercial photographer. He operated his darkroom before the days of digital photography and has also been involved in prepress operations for magazines and books.

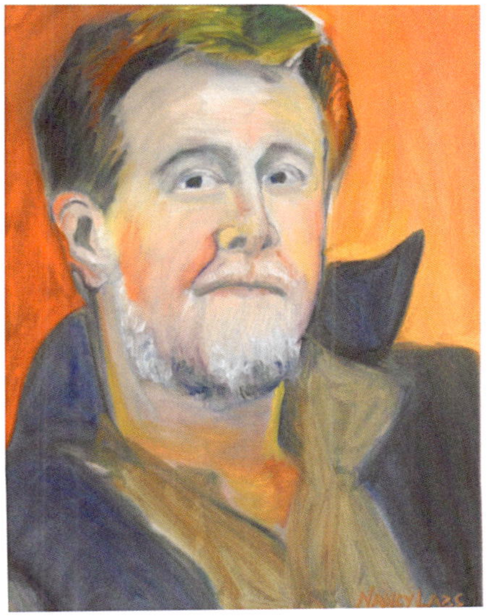

Oil on canvas by Nancy Labs

www.ingramcontent.com/pod-product-compliance
Lightning Source LLC
LaVergne TN
LVRC100248220926
848482LV00033B/355

* 9 7 8 1 9 4 4 2 8 0 0 4 8 *